The Power of Critical Thinking

THE POWER OF
Critical Thinking

SIXTH EDITION

Effective Reasoning About Ordinary and Extraordinary Claims

LEWIS VAUGHN

NEW YORK | OXFORD
OXFORD UNIVERSITY PRESS

Oxford University Press is a department of the University of Oxford. It furthers the University's objective of excellence in research, scholarship, and education by publishing worldwide. Oxford is a registered trade mark of Oxford University Press in the UK and certain other countries.

Published in the United States of America by Oxford University Press
198 Madison Avenue, New York, NY 10016, United States of America.

Library of Congress Cataloging-in-Publication Data

Names: Vaughn, Lewis, author.
Title: The power of critical thinking : effective reasoning about ordinary and extraordinary claims / Lewis Vaughn.
Description: SIXTH EDITION. | New York : Oxford University Press, 2018.
Identifiers: LCCN 2018021275 | ISBN 9780190852719 (pbk.)
Subjects: LCSH: Critical thinking.
Classification: LCC BC177 .V38 2018 | DDC 160–dc23 LC record available at
   https://lccn.loc.gov/2018021275

9 8 7 6 5 4 3 2 1

Printed by LSC Communications, United States of America

To Kathy, for more than I can say

BRIEF CONTENTS

PREFACE   xv

Part One   BASICS
CHAPTER 1   The Power of Critical Thinking   3
CHAPTER 2   Obstacles to Critical Thinking   30
CHAPTER 3   Making Sense of Arguments   58

Part Two   REASONS
CHAPTER 4   Reasons for Belief and Doubt   109
CHAPTER 5   Fallacies and Persuaders   151

Part Three   ARGUMENTS
CHAPTER 6   Deductive Reasoning: Propositional Logic   189
CHAPTER 7   Deductive Reasoning: Categorical Logic   226
CHAPTER 8   Inductive Reasoning   260

Part Four   EXPLANATIONS
CHAPTER 9   Inference to the Best Explanation   315
CHAPTER 10   Judging Scientific Theories   362
CHAPTER 11   Critical Thinking in Morality and the Law   417

APPENDIX A   The Truth About Philosophy Majors   451
APPENDIX B   Essays for Evaluation   457
APPENDIX C   Answers to Exercises   509
APPENDIX D   Answers to Self-Assessment Quizzes   529
APPENDIX E   Critical Thinking and Writing   543

NOTES   559
GLOSSARY   563
CREDITS   568
INDEX   570

CONTENTS

PREFACE   xv

Part One   BASICS

1 The Power of Critical Thinking   3

WHY IT MATTERS   5

HOW IT WORKS   8

    Claims and Reasons   9

    Reasons and Arguments   10

    Arguments in the Rough   16

KEY WORDS   18

SUMMARY   18

EXERCISES   20

FIELD PROBLEMS   26

SELF-ASSESSMENT QUIZ   26

WRITING ASSIGNMENTS   28

2 Obstacles to Critical Thinking   30

PSYCHOLOGICAL OBSTACLES   31

    The Almighty Self   32

    The Power of the Group   38

PHILOSOPHICAL OBSTACLES   43

    Subjective Relativism   43

    Social Relativism   45

    Skepticism   45

KEY WORDS   46

SUMMARY   46

EXERCISES   48

FIELD PROBLEMS   53

SELF-ASSESSMENT QUIZ   53

INTEGRATIVE EXERCISES   55

WRITING ASSIGNMENTS   57

3 Making Sense of Arguments   58

ARGUMENT BASICS   59

JUDGING ARGUMENTS   65

FINDING MISSING PARTS   73

ARGUMENT PATTERNS   79

DIAGRAMMING ARGUMENTS   86

ASSESSING LONG ARGUMENTS   95

KEY WORDS   101

SUMMARY   101

FIELD PROBLEMS   102

SELF-ASSESSMENT QUIZ   102

INTEGRATIVE EXERCISES   104

WRITING ASSIGNMENTS   106

Part Two   REASONS

4 Reasons for Belief and Doubt   109

WHEN CLAIMS CONFLICT   110

EXPERTS AND EVIDENCE   115

PERSONAL EXPERIENCE   121

   Impairment   121

   Expectation   124

   Innumeracy and Probability   126

FOOLING OURSELVES   128

   Resisting Contrary Evidence   128

   Looking for Confirming Evidence   130

   Preferring Available Evidence   132

EVALUATING SOURCES: THE INTERNET AND BEYOND   134

FAKE NEWS   135

ADVERTISING AND PERSUASION   138

　Identification   140

　Slogans   140

　Misleading Comparisons   140

　Weasel Words   141

KEY WORDS   141

SUMMARY   142

EXERCISES   143

FIELD PROBLEMS   146

SELF-ASSESSMENT QUIZ   147

INTEGRATIVE EXERCISES   149

WRITING ASSIGNMENTS   150

5 Fallacies and Persuaders   151

FALLACIES: IRRELEVANT PREMISES   152

　Genetic Fallacy   152

　Composition   153

　Division   154

　Appeal to the Person   155

　Equivocation   156

　Appeal to Popularity   157

　Appeal to Tradition   158

　Appeal to Ignorance   158

　Appeal to Emotion   161

　Red Herring   163

　Straw Man   163

　Two Wrongs Make a Right   166

FALLACIES: UNACCEPTABLE PREMISES   166

　Begging the Question   166

　False Dilemma   167

　Decision-Point Fallacy   169

　Slippery Slope   170

　Hasty Generalization   173

　Faulty Analogy   173

PERSUADERS: RHETORICAL MOVES   174

　Innuendo   174

　Euphemisms and Dysphemisms   174

　Stereotyping   175

　Ridicule   176

　Rhetorical Definitions   176

KEY WORDS 177

SUMMARY 177

EXERCISES 178

FIELD PROBLEMS 182

SELF-ASSESSMENT QUIZ 183

INTEGRATIVE EXERCISES 184

WRITING ASSIGNMENTS 186

Part Three ARGUMENTS

6 Deductive Reasoning: Propositional Logic 189

CONNECTIVES AND TRUTH VALUES 191

    Conjunction 192

    Disjunction 194

    Negation 196

    Conditional 197

CHECKING FOR VALIDITY 201

    Simple Arguments 201

    Tricky Arguments 205

    Streamlined Evaluation 208

PROOF OF VALIDITY 214

    Rules of Inference 215

    Rules of Replacement 217

KEY WORDS 220

SUMMARY 220

FIELD PROBLEMS 221

SELF-ASSESSMENT QUIZ 221

INTEGRATIVE EXERCISES 223

WRITING ASSIGNMENTS 225

7 Deductive Reasoning: Categorical Logic 226

STATEMENTS AND CLASSES 227

TRANSLATIONS AND STANDARD FORM 230

    Terms 232

    Quantifiers 236

DIAGRAMMING CATEGORICAL STATEMENTS 238

SIZING UP CATEGORICAL SYLLOGISMS   243

THE SQUARE OF OPPOSITION   250

CATEGORICAL EQUIVALENCE   252

KEY WORDS   254

SUMMARY   255

FIELD PROBLEMS   256

SELF-ASSESSMENT QUIZ   256

INTEGRATIVE EXERCISES   257

WRITING ASSIGNMENTS   259

8 Inductive Reasoning   260

ENUMERATIVE INDUCTION   261

Sample Size   264

Representativeness   265

Opinion Polls   266

ANALOGICAL INDUCTION   277

CAUSAL ARGUMENTS   285

Testing for Causes   287

Causal Confusions   292

Necessary and Sufficient Conditions   298

KEY WORDS   305

SUMMARY   305

FIELD PROBLEMS   306

SELF-ASSESSMENT QUIZ   307

INTEGRATIVE EXERCISES   309

WRITING ASSIGNMENTS   311

Part Four   EXPLANATIONS

9 Inference to the Best Explanation   315

EXPLANATIONS AND INFERENCE   317

THEORIES AND CONSISTENCY   327

THEORIES AND CRITERIA   328

Testability   331

Fruitfulness   332

Scope   335

Simplicity   338

Conservatism   339

TELLING GOOD THEORIES FROM BAD 345

A Doomed Flight 348

An Amazing Cure 351

KEY WORDS 356

SUMMARY 356

FIELD PROBLEMS 357

SELF-ASSESSMENT QUIZ 357

INTEGRATIVE EXERCISES 359

WRITING ASSIGNMENTS 361

10 Judging Scientific Theories 362

SCIENCE AND NOT SCIENCE 363

THE SCIENTIFIC METHOD 366

TESTING SCIENTIFIC THEORIES 370

JUDGING SCIENTIFIC THEORIES 372

Copernicus Versus Ptolemy 373

Evolution Versus Creationism 375

SCIENCE AND WEIRD THEORIES 388

MAKING WEIRD MISTAKES 389

Leaping to the Weirdest Theory 389

Mixing What Seems with What Is 390

Misunderstanding the Possibilities 391

JUDGING WEIRD THEORIES 392

Crop Circles 393

Talking with the Dead 401

SUMMARY 411

FIELD PROBLEMS 412

SELF-ASSESSMENT QUIZ 412

INTEGRATIVE EXERCISES 414

WRITING ASSIGNMENTS 416

11 Critical Thinking in Morality and the Law 417

MORAL ARGUMENTS 418

MORAL PREMISES 423

MORAL THEORIES 425

Evaluating Moral Theories 426

Two Important Theories 430

LEGAL REASONING 438

A COHERENT WORLDVIEW 439

KEY WORDS   441
SUMMARY   441
EXERCISES   443
FIELD PROBLEMS   447
SELF-ASSESSMENT QUIZ   447
INTEGRATIVE EXERCISES   449
WRITING ASSIGNMENTS   450

APPENDIX A   The Truth About Philosophy Majors   451
APPENDIX B   Essays for Evaluation   457
   Essay   1   Death Penalty Discriminates Against Black Crime Victims   458
   Essay   2   Marine Parks   459
   Essay   3   A Feminist Defense of Pornography   461
   Essay   4   A Defense of Homosexuality   466
   Essay   5   More Innocents Die When We Don't Have Capital Punishment   479
   Essay   6   What's Wrong with Adultery?   480
   Essay   7   A Pat-Down Is Better Than a Blow-Up   484
   Essay   8   The Cohabitation Epidemic   486
   Essay   9   Not Being Vaccinated Is Not Acceptable   488
   Essay 10   Women and the Afghanistan Peace Process   490
   Essay 11   A Deviance from God's Norm   493
   Essay 12   Marriage Still Evolving, as Ever   494
   Essay 13   Slouching Toward Chimeras   495
   Essay 14   Fighting Islamic Extremists Who Stifle Free Speech   497
   Essay 15   Is Sluttishness a Feminist Statement?   499
   Essay 16   Torture: Time for Congress to End the Debate   501
   Essay 17   Torture: Severe Interrogations Work   502
   Essay 18   Freedom of Expression: Protect Student Speech—Even "Unwise"
              Bong Banner   503
   Essay 19   Freedom of Expression: Policy Reflects Common Sense   504
   Essay 20   It's Irresponsible to Spread Fear of Vaccine   505
   Essay 21   Flag Amendment: Flag Needs Protection   507
APPENDIX C   Answers to Exercises   509
APPENDIX D   Answers to Self-Assessment Quizzes   529
APPENDIX E   Critical Thinking and Writing   543

NOTES   559
GLOSSARY   563
CREDITS   568
INDEX   570

LIKE ALL PREVIOUS VERSIONS OF THIS TEXT, THE SIXTH EDITION HAS THREE AIMS: Keep what works, add more of the same where needed, and drop what doesn't. In this case, "what works" means consistency with the insights and needs of teachers of critical thinking. You will find that this new edition of *The Power of Critical Thinking* tries hard to do all these jobs, and a few others as well. The book's original goals still guide its content and presentation: to provide comprehensive coverage of basic critical thinking skills, to include important features and topics often ignored by other texts, and to present all this in a plain-spoken, lively style that encourages students to think, reason, and learn.

Each school year brings another set of students who seem more in need of critical thinking than the last. They confront a media-driven, fallacy-packed, "fake news," information-loaded, spin-doctored, nonsense-rich world. This broad spectrum of challenges to clear thinking seems more than ever to require a broad-spectrum response. So this text focuses on a wide range of critical thinking skills applicable to many kinds of claims, evidence, and arguments, aiming to provide these basic necessities in the clearest, most straightforward way possible.

The heavy coverage of argument and inference is still here, and so is the comprehensive introduction to claims and arguments (Chapter 3); the solid coverage of propositional and categorical logic (Chapters 6 and 7); the substantial attention given to science, the scientific method, and the evaluation of scientific theories (Chapters 9 and 10); and the full treatment of the fundamentals of inductive reasoning, including Mill's methods, enumerative and analogical induction, causal arguments, and opinion polls (Chapter 8).

Uncommon Features

The distinguishing features of this book that are missing in some other texts still fill these pages. They include the following:

- **Comprehensive Coverage of Inference to the Best Explanation.** This text devotes two chapters to inference to the best explanation because (1) it is probably the type of inference that students use most, (2) it can be especially fertile ground for diverse cases and examples that students are likely to find intriguing, and (3) it implies a framework for thinking about claims and theories as well as a method for assessing their worth. Step-by-step instructions and plentiful examples show students how to use this kind of inference to assess theories and claims in science, pseudoscience, ethics, medicine, the media, and popular culture.
- **Extensive Treatment of Scientific Reasoning.** The book offers a chapter each on inductive reasoning and causal arguments (Chapter 8), scientific theories and inference (Chapter 9), and scientific method and theory evaluation (Chapter 10). Extended examples show how scientific reasoning applies to an array of questions in many scientific fields, in everyday life, and even in the realm of extraordinary phenomena.
- **Emphasis on Evaluation of Evidence, Authority, and Credibility.** Throughout this text (and especially in Chapter 4), considerable ink is expended to show students how to assess the evidence and claims proffered by scientists and other experts, the news media, advertisements, and everyday experience. In each case, the relevant principles or procedures are explained and illustrated. Photographs accompanied by thought-provoking captions also prompt students to evaluate evidence—the visual evidence contained in images.
- **Large and Diverse Collections of Exercises.** The exercises number in the hundreds, drawn from a wide range of sources and configured in a variety of forms, with selected answers in Appendix C. For the most part, within each chapter, exercises are presented progressively, from simple to complex and from elementary to more advanced. The exercise types vary widely. Some of the more ambitious ones are as follows:
  - **Field Problems**—exercises that ask students to apply their new skills to claims, arguments, and essays found outside the classroom: on the Internet and in newspapers, magazines, books, and other sources
  - **Integrative Exercises**—exercise sets that overlap with material in previous chapters, reinforcing not only the current lessons but earlier ones as well
  - **Writing Exercises**—writing assignments that ask students to write argumentative essays on selected topics or on arguments presented in the short essays found in Appendix B (Essays for Evaluation)
  - **Self-Assessment Quizzes**—end-of-chapter tests (with answers in Appendix D) that allow students to gauge their understanding of the material
- **A Chapter on Obstacles to Critical Thinking.** Chapter 2 reviews many of the factors that may impede critical thinking—bias, habit, tradition, emotion, skewed perceptions, rationalizations, and certain philosophical

outlooks. Along with explanations of how these factors affect thinking are suggestions on how to avoid or minimize them.
- **A Few Less Noticeable but Useful Features:**
  - Guidelines for evaluating news reports and Web sources (Chapter 4)
  - A discussion of how critical reasoning can be used in the formation of worldviews (Chapter 11)
  - A chapter on moral reasoning that covers moral arguments and the evaluation of moral theories (Chapter 11)
  - Guidelines for evaluating claims about occult, paranormal, or supernatural occurrences (Chapter 10)
  - Critiques of subjective relativism, social relativism, and skepticism (Chapter 11)
  - In each chapter: chapter objectives, summaries, and a list of key terms
  - An end-of-book glossary

New Material and Features

Once again the reviewers of this text—veteran teachers of critical thinking—said the book would be more useful if we changed or added a few things. And they were right, and so we did, as follows:

- **New Guide to Thinking Critically about the Media**: Includes "Evaluating Sources: The Internet and Beyond," "Fake News," and "When You Don't Trust the Mainstream Media."
- **New Material on Important Topics:** "Critical Thinking and Racism," "Moral Dilemmas," and "The Divine Command Theory."
- **Many Revised Text Boxes:** "Critiquing Moral Theories," "The Deadly Post Hoc Fallacy," "Political Straw," "Whose Pants Are on Fire?" "Fallacious Appeals to (Questionable) Authority," and "The Best Explanation for Hurricanes Katrina and Harvey."
- **Updated Material.** Exercises, boxes, and photos have been revised or added to reflect current events, new interests, and social changes.
- **Career Appendix.** A guide to the practical benefits and career opportunities found in studying philosophy.

Ancillary Materials

- Password-protected Ancillary Resource Center (ARC): Includes a Computerized Test Bank, PowerPoint slides, and an Instructor's Manual that contains chapter summaries, answers to exercises, and multiple choice, true/false, and short answer/short essay questions. Visit http://oup-arc.com/vaughn-power-critical-thinking-5e/ to register.
- Dashboard (www.oup.com/us/dashboard): Dashboard delivers quality content, tools and assessments to track student progress in an intuitive, web-based learning environment. *The Power of Critical Thinking* Dashboard site includes interactive flashcards of key terms, as well as 25 multiple-choice and 20 true/false questions per chapter, linked to subject-focused chapter

learning objectives so instructors can analyze students' subject-specific strengths and opportunities for improvement. A built-in color-coded gradebook allows instructors to track student progress.

- A Companion Website (www.oup.com/us/vaughn) contains the following study resources for each chapter: Study questions; flashcards of key terms; chapter summaries; web links to further resources; and self-assessment quizzes with 12 multiple-choice and 10 true/false questions per chapter, automated to reveal the answers as students work through the questions.
- Cartridges for major course management systems are also available, containing all the instructor and student resources from the ARC and Companion Website. For more information, please contact your Oxford University Press representative or call 1-800-280-0280.

Acknowledgments

For this edition, I have even more people to thank for the text's good qualities—and still no one but me to blame for any shortcomings. At the top of the list are my extraordinary editors at Oxford University Press: Robert Miller, Keith Faivre, and Sydney Keen. Without reviewers, this new edition would be far less thorough and useful than it is. They include:

Keith Abney, *California Polytechnic State University*
Janet Amirtharaj, *Rowan-Cabarrus Community College*
Dr. Clinton D. Corcoran, *High Point University*
Tobyn DeMarco, *Bergen Community College*
Jeffrey M. Freelin, *Lincoln University of Missouri*
Ken Hochstetter, *College of Southern Nevada*
Theresa Mayper, *Lamar University*
James A. Stieb, *Philadelphia University, Drexel University, Independence University*
Alban W. Urbanas, *Wesley College*
June Yang, *Grossmont College*

Thanks also to reviewers of previous editions, for their lasting contributions:

Scott Aiken, *Vanderbilt University*

Jami Anderson, *University of Michigan–Flint*

Mark Paul Balok, *Yavapai College*

James Butler, *Berea College*

David E. Campbell, *Humboldt State University*

Jennifer Caseldine-Bracht, *Indiana University-Purdue University–Fort Wayne*

Evgenia Cherkasova, *Suffolk University*

Carlos Colombetti, *Skyline College*

Sharon Crasnow, *Riverside Community College–Norco*

Norman B. Cubbage, *University of Louisville*

Michelle Darnell, *Fayetteville State University and Florida State University*

B. Deckard, *California State University, Long Beach*

S. L. Dwyer, *Georgia State University*

Daniel Engster, *University of Texas at San Antonio*

Jason Ford, *University of Minnesota–Duluth*

Doug Fraleigh, *California State University, Fresno*

Jake Gibbs, *Bluegrass Community & Technical College*

John Gibson, *University of Louisville*

Rex Gilliland, *Southern Connecticut State University*

Ann Glauser, *University of Georgia*

Cynthia Gobatie, *Riverside City College*

Jeffrey C. Goodman, *James Madison University*

Geoffrey Gorham, *St. Olaf College*

Richard A. S. Hall, *Fayetteville State University*

Ken Heiges, *Allan Hancock College*

Paul Herrick, *Shoreline Community College*

Lawrence D. Hultgren, *Virginia Wesleyan College*

David Hunter, *Buffalo State College, SUNY*

Joseph Jebwab, *Kutztown University of Pennsylvania*

Andrew Jones-Cathcart, *College of the Canyons*

Donald K. Kazee, *Northern Kentucky University*

Joanne Kingman-Sanchez, *Pima Community College*

Michael C. LaBossiere, *Florida A&M University*

Sandra Larochelle, *Lakes Region Community College*

Ann Lewald, *Tennessee Technological University*

Stephen Ma, *California State University, Los Angeles*

James Martin, *California State University, San Marcos*

Joshua May, *Cuesta College*

John McClellan, *Carson-Newman University*

Carol McGury, *DePaul University*

Carl Miller, *Fort Hays State University*

Joseph Monast, *Modesto Junior College*

Marsila Moschella, *University of Nevada–Las Vegas*

Keith O'Neill, *Dutchess Community College*

Evaline Otieno, *Oakwood University*

Maria Paleologou, *California State University, Bakersfield*

Lawrence Pasternack, *Oklahoma State University*

Sheela Pawar, *California State University–Dominguez Hills*

Hans Pederson, *Indiana University of Pennsylvania*

Jamie Phillips, *Clarion University of Pennsylvania*

Ed Pluth, *California State University–Chico*

Gretchen Reevy, *Lecturer at California State University–East Bay*

Gregory Rich, *Fayetteville State University*

Victor Rios, Jr., *College of the Desert*

Frank X. Ryan, *Kent State University*

Gregory B. Sadler, *Fayetteville State University*

Michael Sanders, *Cazenovia College*

Ryan Showler, *Yavapai College*

Nicholas K. Simmons, *University of Kansas*

Aeon J. Skoble, *Bridgewater State College*

Marin Smillov, *Santa Fe Community College*

Taggart Smith, *Purdue University*

Glen M. Stanford, *Sam Houston State University*

Ted Stryk, *Roane State Community College*

Ana Torres-Bower, *Cerritos College*

Jill Thomas-Jorgenson, *Lewis & Clark State College*

Gaye Walton-Price, *Contra Costa College*

Jared Welsh, *Georgia State University*

Karen Williams, *San Jose State University*

Helen E. Woodman, *Ferris State University*

Julie Yoo, *California State University, Northridge*

Marie G. Zaccaria, *Georgia Perimeter College, Dunwoody Campus*

Kevin Zanelotti, *Radford University*

Ted Zenzinger, *Regis College*

PART ONE

BASICS

The Power of Critical Thinking

CHAPTER OBJECTIVES

- Understand the definition of *critical thinking* and the importance of the definition terms "systematic," "evaluation," "formulation," and "rational standards."
- Understand how critical thinking relates to logic, the truth or falsity of statements, knowledge, and personal empowerment.

WHY IT MATTERS

- Appreciate why critical thinking is better than the passive acceptance of beliefs.
- Appreciate the relevance of the claim "The unexamined life is not worth living" to critical thinking.
- Understand why the following claims are dubious: "Critical thinking makes people too critical or cynical," "Critical thinking makes people cold and unemotional," and "Critical thinking is the enemy of creativity."
- Appreciate the pervasive use of critical thinking in all human endeavors.
- Understand how critical thinking empowers people.

HOW IT WORKS

- Distinguish between statements and nonstatements.
- Understand the basic concepts of reasons, argument, inference, premises, and conclusion.
- Know how to use indicator words to help pinpoint premises and conclusions.
- Be able to distinguish between passages that do and do not contain an argument.
- Be able to identify arguments in various contexts and distinguish between arguments and superfluous material, arguments and explanations, and premises and conclusions.

Y OU CAME INTO THIS WORLD WITHOUT OPINIONS OR JUDGMENTS OR values or viewpoints—and now your head is brimming with them. If you tried to write them all down, you would be busy for the rest of your life (and would probably win an award for being the world's biggest bore). They help you make your way through the world. They guide you to both failure and success, ignorance and understanding, good and bad, paralysis and empowerment. Some of your beliefs truly inform you, and some blind you. Some are true; some are not. But the question is, which ones are which? This kind of question—a question about the quality of your beliefs—is the fundamental concern of **critical thinking**.

Determining the quality or value of your beliefs is a function of thinking, and the kind of thinking that does this job best is critical thinking—a skill that higher education seeks to foster. This means that critical thinking is not about *what* you think, but *how* you think.

Notice also that the question about the quality of beliefs is not about what factors *caused* you to have the beliefs that you do. A sociologist might tell you how society has influenced some of your moral choices. A psychologist might describe how your emotions cause you to cling to certain opinions. Your best friend might allege that you have unconsciously absorbed most of your beliefs directly from your parents. But none of these speculations have much to do with the central task of critical thinking.

Critical thinking focuses not on what *causes* a belief, but on *whether it is worth believing*. A belief is worth believing, or accepting, if we have *good reasons* to accept it. The better the reasons for acceptance, the more likely the belief is to be true. Critical thinking offers us a set of standards embodied in techniques, attitudes, and principles that we can use to assess beliefs and determine if they are supported by good reasons. After all, we want our beliefs to be true, to be good guides for dealing with the world—and critical thinking is the best tool we have for achieving this goal.

Here's one way to wrap up these points in a concise definition:

CRITICAL THINKING: The systematic evaluation or formulation of beliefs, or statements, by rational standards.

Critical thinking is *systematic* because it involves distinct procedures and methods. It entails *evaluation* and *formulation* because it's used to both assess existing beliefs (yours or someone else's) and devise new ones. And it operates according to *rational standards* in that beliefs are judged by how well they are supported by reasons.

Critical thinking, of course, involves **logic.** Logic is the study of good reasoning, or inference, and the rules that govern it. Critical thinking is broader than logic because it involves not only logic but also the truth or falsity of statements, the evaluation of arguments and evidence, the use of analysis and investigation, and the application of many other skills that help us decide what to believe or do.

Ultimately, what critical thinking leads you to is knowledge, understanding, and—if you put these to work—empowerment. In addition, as you're guided by your instructor through this text, you will come to appreciate some other benefits that cannot be fully explored now: Critical thinking enables problem-solving, active learning, and intelligent self-improvement.

In Chapters 2 and 3 (the rest of Part 1) you'll get a more thorough grounding in critical thinking and logical argument plus plenty of opportunities to practice your new skills. Consider this chapter an introduction to those important lessons.

Why It Matters

In large measure, our lives are defined by our actions and choices, and our actions and choices are guided by our thinking—so our thinking had better be good. Almost every day we are hit by a blizzard of assertions, opinions, arguments, and pronouncements from all directions. They all implore us to believe, to agree, to accept, to follow, to submit. If we care whether our choices are right and our beliefs true, if we want to rise above blind acceptance and arbitrary choices, we must use the tools provided by critical thinking.

We, of course, always have the option of taking the easy way out. We can simply glom onto whatever beliefs or statements come blowing by in the wind, adopting viewpoints because they are favored by others or because they make us feel good. But then we forfeit control over our lives and let the wind take us wherever it will, as if we had no more say in the outcome than a leaf in a storm.

A consequence then of going with the wind is a loss of personal freedom. If you passively accept beliefs that have been handed to you by your parents, your culture, or your teachers, then those beliefs are *not really yours*. You just happened to be in a certain place and time when they were handed out. If they are not really yours, and you let them guide your choices and actions, then they—not you—are in charge of your life. Your beliefs are yours only if you critically examine them for yourself to see if they are supported by good reasons.

> "Are you not ashamed of caring so much for the making of money and for fame and prestige, when you neither think nor care about wisdom and truth and the improvement of your soul?"
> —Socrates

To examine your beliefs in this way is to examine your life, for your beliefs in large measure define your life. To forgo such scrutiny is to abandon your chance of making your life deliberately and authentically meaningful. The great philosopher Socrates says it best: "The unexamined life is not worth living."

Thus, in the most profound sense, critical thinking is not only enlightening, but empowering. This empowerment can take several forms:

Skills for learning and exploring. Some species of critical thinking is essential in every intellectual endeavor, every profession, and every college course. Economics, literature, philosophy, ethics, science, medicine, law—these and many other fields require you to understand and use argument, evaluation, analysis, logic, and evidence. Critical thinking is the common language of many worlds, and practicing it will help you make your way in them.

Defense against error, manipulation, and prejudice. For lack of good critical thinking, many intelligent people have been taken in by clever marketers, dubious "experts," self-serving politicians, charming demagogues, skillful propagandists, misinformed bloggers, woolly conspiracy theorists, misguided gurus, reckless alarmists, knee-jerk partisans, and smooth-talking xenophobes. For want of a little logic and careful reflection, you can easily choose the wrong career, wrong friends, wrong spouse, wrong investments, wrong religion, and wrong leaders. Without some skill in moral reasoning (critical thinking applied to ethics), you risk making bad decisions about right and wrong, about good and bad. Critical thinking is no guarantee against any of these errors, but it does provide your best possible defense.

Tools for self-discovery. A central goal of higher education is to enable students to think critically and carefully for themselves, to confront issues and problems and then devise their own warranted, defensible answers. This means you must be able not only to critically examine the arguments and assertions of others but also to apply these critical powers to your own ideas. To discover what to believe—that is, to find out which claims are worthy of belief—you must weigh them in the balance of critical reasoning. A central question of a mature intellect is, "What should I believe?" This is the fundamental query at the heart of all your conscious life choices. Only you can answer it, and ultimately only critical thinking can guide you to justified answers.

Critical thinking applies not just to some of your individual beliefs, but to all of them together. It applies to your worldview, the vast web of fundamental ideas that help you make sense of the world, what some people call a philosophy of life. We all have a worldview, and most of us want the beliefs that constitute it to be true and coherent (to fit together without internal contradictions). As you will see in Chapter 11, devising a coherent worldview is the work of a lifetime—and can only be done with the help of critical thinking.

Our choice whether to apply critical thinking skills is not an all-or-nothing decision. Each of us uses critical thinking to some degree in our lives. We often evaluate reasons for (and against) believing that someone has committed a crime, that an earnest celebrity is deluded, that one candidate in an election is better than another, that gun control laws should be strengthened or weakened, that we should buy a car, that the legendary Bigfoot does not exist, that a friend is trustworthy, that one university is superior to another, that the bill being considered in Congress would be bad for the environment, that Elvis is living the good life in a witness-protection program. But the more urgent consideration is not just whether we sometimes use critical thinking, but how well we use it.

Many people, however, will have none of this—and perhaps you are one of them. They believe that critical thinking—or what they take to be critical thinking—makes one excessively critical or cynical, emotionally cold, and creatively constrained.

For example, there are some who view anything that smacks of logic and rationality as a negative enterprise designed to attack someone else's thinking and score points by putting people in their place. A few of these take the word *critical* here to mean "faultfinding" or "carping."

Now, no doubt some people try to use critical thinking primarily for offensive purposes, but this approach goes against critical thinking principles. The *critical* in critical thinking is used in the sense of "exercising or involving careful judgment or judicious evaluation." Critical thinking is about determining what we are justified in believing, and that involves an openness to other points of view, a tolerance for opposing perspectives, a focus on the issue at hand, and fair assessments of arguments and evidence. To paraphrase a bumper-sticker slogan: Good critical thinking does not make cynics—people make cynics.

Some people fear that if they apply critical thinking to their lives, they will become cold and unemotional—just like a computer abuzz with logic and rote functions. But this is a confused notion. Critical thinking and feelings actually complement one another. Certainly part of thinking critically is ensuring that we don't let our emotions distort our judgments. But critical thinking can also help us clarify our feelings and deal with them more effectively. Our emotions often need the guidance of reason. Likewise, our reasoning needs our emotions. It is our feelings that motivate us to action, and without motivation our reasoning would never get off the ground.

Then there's this dubious assumption: Critical thinking is the enemy of creativity. To some people, critical thinking is a sterile and rigid mode of thought that constrains the imagination, hobbles artistic vision, and prevents "thinking outside the box." But critical thinking and creative thinking are not opposed to one another. Good critical thinkers can let their imaginations run free just like anyone else. They can create and enjoy poetry, music, art, literature, and plain old fun in the same way and to the same degree as the rest of the world. Critical thinking can complement creative thinking because it is needed to assess and enhance the creation. Scientists, for example, often dream up some very fanciful theories (which are an important part of doing science). These theories pop into their heads in the same sort of ways that the ideas for a great work of art appear in the mind of its creator. But then scientists use all of their critical thinking skills to evaluate what they have produced (as artists sometimes do)—and this critical examination enables them to select the most promising theories and to weed out those that are unworkable. Critical thinking perfects the creation.

"Never, ever, think outside the box."

Why Critical Thinking Matters

- Our thinking guides our actions, so it should be of high quality.
- If you have never critically examined your beliefs, they are not truly yours.
- To examine your beliefs is to examine your life. Socrates: "The unexamined life is not worth living."
- Critical thinking involves determining what we're justified in believing, being open to new perspectives, and fairly assessing the views of others and ourselves.
- Critical thinking provides skills for learning and exploring; defense against error, manipulation, and prejudice; and tools for self-discovery.
- Critical thinking complements both our emotions and our creativity.
- Critical thinking is thinking outside the box.

In a very important sense, critical thinking is thinking outside the box. When we passively absorb the ideas we encounter, when we refuse to consider any alternative explanations or theories, when we conform our ideas to the wishes of the group, when we let our thinking be controlled by bias and stereotypes and superstition and wishful thinking—we are deep, deep in the box. But we rise above all that when we have the courage to think critically. When we are willing to let our beliefs be tried in the court of critical reason, we open ourselves to new possibilities, the dormant seeds of creativity.

Critical thinking covers a lot of territory. It's used across the board in all disciplines, all areas of public life, all the sciences, all sectors of business, and all vocations. It has played a major role in all the great endeavors of humankind—scientific discoveries, technological innovations, philosophical insights, social and political movements, literary creation and criticism, judicial and legal reasoning, democratic nation building, and more. The *lack* of critical thinking has also left its mark. The great tragedies of history—the wars, massacres, holocausts, tyrannies, bigotries, epidemics, and witch hunts—grew out of famines of the mind where clear, careful thinking was much too scarce.

How It Works

As you can see, critical thinking has extremely broad application. Principles and procedures used to evaluate beliefs in one discipline or issue can be used to assess beliefs in many other arenas. Good critical thinking is the same everywhere. Here are the common threads that make it universal.

Claims and Reasons

Critical thinking is a rational, systematic process that we apply to beliefs of all kinds. As we use the term here, *belief* is just another word for statement, or claim. A **statement** is an assertion that something is or is not the case. The following are statements:

- A triangle has three sides.
- I am cold.
- You are a liar.
- You are not a liar.
- I see blue spots before my eyes.
- 7 + 5 = 12
- You should never hit your mother with a shovel.
- The best explanation for his behavior is that he was in a trance.
- Rap music is better than punk rock.
- There are black holes in space.

© 2002 by Randy Glasbergen.
www.glasbergen.com

"What some people fail to grasp, Larry, is the difference between 'thinking outside of the box' and just being a weirdo."

© 2002 by Randy Glasbergen

So statements, or claims, are the kinds of things that are either true or false. They assert that some state of affairs is or is not actual. You may know that a specific statement is true, or you may not. There may be no way to find out at the time if the statement is true or false. There may be no one who believes the statement. But it would be a statement nonetheless.

Some sentences, though, do *not* express statements:

- Does a triangle have three sides?
- Is God all-powerful?
- Turn that music off.
- Stop telling lies.
- Hey, dude.
- Great balls of fire!

The first two sentences are questions. The second two are commands or requests. The fifth sentence is a greeting. The sixth one is an exclamation. None asserts that something is or is not the case.

When you're engaged in critical thinking, you're mostly either evaluating statements or formulating them. In both cases your primary task is to figure out how strongly to believe them. The strength of your belief should depend on the quality of the reasons in favor of the statements. Statements backed by good reasons are worthy of strong acceptance. Statements that fall short of this standard deserve weaker acceptance.

Sometimes you may not be able to assign any substantial weight at all to the reasons for or against a statement. There simply may not be enough evidence to rationally decide. Generally when that happens, good critical thinkers don't arbitrarily choose to accept or reject a statement. They suspend judgment until there is enough evidence to make an intelligent decision.

Reasons and Arguments

Reasons provide support for a statement. That is, they provide us with grounds for believing that a statement is true. Reasons are themselves expressed as statements. So a statement expressing a reason or reasons is used to show that another statement is true or likely to be true. This combination of statements—a statement (or statements) supposedly providing reasons for accepting another statement—is known as an **argument.** Arguments are the main focus of critical thinking. They are the most important tool we have for evaluating the truth of statements (our own and those of others) and for formulating statements that are worthy of acceptance. Arguments are therefore essential for the advancement of knowledge in all fields.

Often people use the word *argument* to indicate a quarrel or heated exchange. In critical thinking, however, *argument* refers to the assertion of reasons in support of a statement.

The statements (reasons) given in support of another statement are called the **premises.** The statement that the premises are intended to support is called the **conclusion.** We can define an argument, then, like this:

ARGUMENT: A group of statements in which some of them (the premises) are intended to support another of them (the conclusion).

The following are some simple arguments:

1. Because banning assault rifles violates a constitutional right, the U.S. government should not ban assault rifles.
2. The *Wall Street Journal* says that people should invest heavily in stocks. Therefore, investing in stocks is a smart move.
3. When Judy drives her car, she's always late. Since she's driving her car now, she will be late.
4. Listen, any movie with clowns in it cannot be a good movie. Last night's movie had at least a dozen clowns in it. Consequently it was awful.
5. The war on terrorism must include a massive military strike on nation X because without this intervention, terrorists cannot be defeated. They will always be able to find safe haven and support in the X regime. Even if terrorists are scattered around the world, support from nation X will increase their chances of surviving and launching new attacks.
6. No one should buy a beer brewed in Canada. Old Guzzler beer is brewed in Canada, so no one should buy it.

Here are the same arguments where the parts are easily identified:

1. [Premise] Because banning assault rifles violates a constitutional right, [Conclusion] the U.S. government should not ban assault rifles.
2. [Premise] The *Wall Street Journal* says that people should invest heavily in stocks. [Conclusion] Therefore, investing in stocks is a smart move.

3. [Premise] When Judy drives her car, she's always late. [Premise] Since she's driving her car now, [Conclusion] she will be late.

4. [Premise] Any movie with clowns in it cannot be a good movie. [Premise] Last night's movie had at least a dozen clowns in it. [Conclusion] Consequently it was awful.

5. [Premise] Without a military intervention in nation X, terrorists cannot be defeated. [Premise] They will always be able to find safe haven and support in the X regime. [Premise] Even if terrorists are scattered around the world, support from nation X will increase their chances of surviving and launching new attacks. [Conclusion] The war on terrorism must include a massive military strike on nation X.

6. [Premise] No one should buy a beer brewed in Canada. [Premise] Old Guzzler beer is brewed in Canada. [Conclusion] So no one should buy it.

"What danger can ever come from ingenious reasoning and inquiry? The worst speculative skeptic ever I knew was a much better man than the best superstitious devotee and bigot."
—David Hume

What all of these arguments have in common is that reasons (the premises) are offered to support or prove a claim (the conclusion). This logical link between premises and conclusion is what distinguishes arguments from all other kinds of discourse. This process of reasoning from a premise or premises to a conclusion based on those premises is called **inference.** Being able to identify arguments, to pick them out of a block of nonargumentative prose if need be, is an important skill on which many other critical thinking skills are based.

Now consider this passage:

The cost of the new XJ fighter plane is $650 million. The cost of three AR21 fighter bombers is $1.2 billion. The administration intends to fund such projects.

Is there an argument here? No. This passage consists of several claims, but no reasons are presented to support any particular claim (conclusion), including the last sentence. This passage can be turned into an argument, though, with some minor editing:

The GAO says that any weapon that costs more than $50 million apiece will actually impair our military readiness. The cost of the new XJ fighter plane is $650 million dollars. The cost of three AR21 fighter bombers is $1.2 billion. We should never impair our readiness. Therefore, the administration should cancel both these projects.

Now we have an argument because reasons are given for accepting a conclusion.

Here's another passage:

Allisha went to the bank to get a more recent bank statement of her checking account. The teller told her that the balance was $1725. Allisha was stunned that it was so low. She called her brother to see if he had been playing one of his twisted pranks. He wasn't. Finally, she concluded that she had been a victim of bank fraud.

Where is the conclusion? Where are the reasons? There are none. This is a little narrative hung on some descriptive claims. But it's not an argument. It could be turned into an argument if, say, some of the claims were restated as reasons for the conclusion that bank fraud had been committed.

Being able to distinguish between passages that do and do not contain arguments is a very basic skill—and an extremely important one. Many people think that if they have clearly stated their beliefs on a subject, they have presented an argument. But a mere declaration of beliefs is not an argument. Often such assertions of opinion are just a jumble of unsupported claims. Search high and low and you will not find an argument anywhere. A writer or speaker of these claims gives the readers or listeners no grounds for believing the claims. In writing courses, the absence of supporting premises is sometimes called "a lack of development."

Here are three more examples of verbiage sans argument:

> Attributing alcohol abuse by children too young to buy a drink to lack of parental discipline, intense pressure to succeed, and affluence incorrectly draws attention to proximate causes while ignoring the ultimate cause: a culture that tolerates overt and covert marketing of alcohol, tobacco and sex to these easily manipulated, voracious consumers. [Letter to the editor, *New York Times*]

> [A recent column in this newspaper] deals with the living quarters of Bishop William Murphy of the Diocese of Rockville Centre. I am so disgusted with the higher-ups in the church that at times I am embarrassed to say I am Catholic. To know that my parents' hard-earned money went to lawyers and payoffs made me sick. Now I see it has also paid for a high-end kitchen. I am enraged. I will never make a donation again. [Letter to the editor, *Newsday*]

> I don't understand what is happening to this country. The citizens of this country are trying to destroy the beliefs of our forefathers with their liberal views. This country was founded on Christian beliefs. This has been and I believe still is the greatest country in the world. But the issue that we cannot have prayer in public places and on public property because there has to be separation of church and state is a farce. [Letter to the editor, *Douglas County Sentinel*]

The passage on alcohol abuse in children is not an argument but an unsupported assertion about the causes of the problem. The passage from the disappointed Catholic is an expression of outrage (which may or may not be justified), but no conclusion is put forth, and no reasons supporting a conclusion are offered. Note the contentious tone in the third passage. This passage smells like an argument. But, alas, there is no argument. Each sentence is a claim presented without support.

"He who knows only his own side of the case, knows little of that. His reasons may be good, and no one may have been able to refute them. But if he is equally unable to refute the reasons on the opposite side; if he does not so much as know what they are, he has no ground for preferring either opinion."

—John Stuart Mill

Sometimes people also confuse **explanations** with arguments. An argument gives us reasons for believing *that something is the case*—that a claim is true or probably true. An explanation, though, tells us *why or how something is the case*. Arguments have something to prove; explanations do not. Ponder this pair of statements:

1. Adam obviously stole the money, for three people saw him do it.
2. Adam stole the money because he needed it to buy food.

Statement 1 is an argument. Statement 2 is an explanation. Statement 1 tries to show that something is the case—that Adam stole the money. And the reason offered in support of this statement is that three people saw him do it. Statement 2 does not try to prove that something is the case (that Adam stole the money). Instead, it attempts to explain why something is the case (why Adam stole the money). Statement 2 takes for granted that Adam stole the money and then tries to explain why he did it. (Note: Explanations can be used as integral *parts* of arguments. As such they are powerful intellectual and scientific tools that help us understand the world, which is why this text has several chapters [Part 4] devoted to explanations used in this way.)

It's not always easy to recognize an argument, to locate both premises and conclusion, but there are a few tricks that can make the job more manageable. For one, there are **indicator words** that frequently accompany arguments and signal that a premise or conclusion is present. For example, in argument 1, cited earlier in this chapter, the indicator word *because* tips us off to the presence of the premise "Because banning assault rifles violates a Constitutional right." In argument 2, *therefore* points to the conclusion "Therefore, investing in stocks is a smart move."

Here are some common premise indicators:

because	due to the fact that	inasmuch as
in view of the fact	being that	as indicated by
given that	since	for
seeing that	assuming that	the reason being
as	for the reason that	

And here are some common conclusion indicators:

therefore	it follows that	it must be that
thus	we can conclude that	as a result
which implies that	so	which means that
consequently	hence	ergo

Using indicator words to spot premises and conclusions, however, is not foolproof. They're just good clues. You will find that some of the words just listed are used when no argument is present. For example,

- I am here *because* you asked me to come.
- I haven't seen you *since* Woodstock.
- He was *so* sleepy he fell off his chair.

> "Why should you mind being wrong if someone can show you that you are?"
>
> —A. J. Ayer

NEWSMAKERS

Political Straw

Political discourse bristles with bad arguments, logical fallacies, rhetorical manipulations, and flat-out lies—the very things that critical thinking can help us defend against. Consider these examples of one of the politician's favorite ploys—the fallacy of the straw man, the distorting, weakening, or oversimplifying of someone's position so it can be more easily attacked or refuted (discussed in detail in Chapter 5).

DONALD TRUMP

"My opponent [Hillary Clinton] wants to essentially abolish the Second Amendment."

DONALD TRUMP

"President Obama and Hillary Clinton have engaged in gross dereliction of duty by surrendering the safety of the American people to open borders, and you know it better than anybody right here in Arizona. You know it."

HILLARY CLINTON

"Back in the Great Recession, when millions of jobs across America hung in the balance, Donald Trump said rescuing the auto industry didn't really matter very much. He said, and I quote again, 'Let it go.'"

HILLARY CLINTON

The Republicans "still want to privatize (Social Security). In fact, their whole idea is to turn over the Social Security trust fund to Wall Street."

RUDY GIULIANI

"Hillary Clinton is for open borders."

BARACK OBAMA

"Secularists are wrong when they ask believers to leave their religion at the door before entering into the public square."

RICK SANTORUM

"Republicans are sick and tired of the political correctness that we can't talk about this," he said. "You can't say the word 'Muslim.'"

Can you tell how each position is being distorted? How common is the straw-man fallacy? Do you think it is effective as a tool of persuasion? Would you fall for this tactic?

Note also that arguments can be put forth without the use of *any* indicator words:

We must take steps to protect ourselves from criminals. We can't rely on the government—law enforcement is already stretched thin. The police can't be everywhere at once, and they usually get involved only after a crime has been committed.

As you may have noticed from these examples, the basic structure of arguments can have several simple variations. For one thing, arguments can have any number of premises. Arguments 1 and 2 have one premise. Arguments 3, 4, and 6, two premises; argument 5, three premises. In extended arguments that often appear in essays, editorials, reports, and other works, there can be many more premises. Also, the conclusion of an argument may not always appear after the premises. As in argument 5, the conclusion may be presented first.

Occasionally the conclusion of an argument can be disguised as a question—even though we would usually expect a question not to be a claim at all. (For purposes of examining such arguments, we may need to paraphrase the conclusion; in some arguments, we may also need to paraphrase premises.) Much of the time readers have little difficulty discerning what the implicit conclusion is. See for yourself:

Do you think for one minute that liberal Democrats in Congress will support a bill that makes gun control legislation impossible? They have never voted that way. They have already declared that they will not allow such a bill. And their leadership has given them their marching orders: Don't support this bill.

Probably the best advice for anyone trying to uncover or dissect arguments is this: *Find the conclusion first*. Once you know what claim someone is trying to prove, isolating the premises becomes much easier. Ask yourself, "What claim is this writer or speaker trying to persuade me to believe?" If the writer or speaker is not trying to convince you of anything, there is no argument to examine.

Arguments in the Rough

As you've probably guessed by now, in the real world, arguments almost never appear neatly labeled as they are here. As suggested earlier, they usually come imbedded in a thicket of other sentences that serve many other functions besides articulating an argument. They may be long and hard to follow. And sometimes a passage that sounds like an argument is not. Your main challenge is to identify the conclusion and premises without getting lost in all the "background noise."

Ponder this passage:

[1] A. L. Jones used flawed reasoning in his letter yesterday praising this newspaper's decision to publish announcements of same-sex unions. [2] Mr. Jones asserts that same-sex unions are a fact of life and therefore should be acknowledged by the news media as a legitimate variation on social partnerships. [3] But the news media are not in the business of endorsing or validating lifestyles. [4] They're supposed to report on lifestyles, not bless them. [5] In addition, by validating same-sex unions or any other lifestyle, the media abandon their objectivity and become political partisans—which would destroy whatever respect people have for news outlets. [6] All of this shows that the news media—including this newspaper—should never (explicitly or implicitly) endorse lifestyles by announcing those lifestyles to the world.

There's an argument here, but it's surrounded by extraneous material. The conclusion is sentence 6—"All of this shows that the news media—including this newspaper—should never (explicitly or implicitly) endorse lifestyles by announcing those lifestyles to the world." Since we know what

> "Ignorance is an evil weed, which dictators may cultivate among their dupes, but which no democracy can afford among its citizens."
> —William Henry Beveridge

> "I respect faith, but doubt is what gets you an education."
> —Wilson Mizner

REVIEW NOTES

Claims, Reasons, and Arguments

- **Statement (claim):** An assertion that something is or is not the case
- **Premise:** A statement given in support of another statement
- **Conclusion:** A statement that premises are used to support
- **Argument:** A group of statements in which some of them (the premises) are intended to support another of them (the conclusion)
- **Explanation:** A statement or statements asserting why or how something is the case
- **Indicator words:** Words that frequently accompany arguments and signal that a premise or conclusion is present

the conclusion is, we can identify the premises and separate them from other information. Sentences 1 and 2 are not premises; they're background information about the nature of the dispute. Sentence 3 presents the first premise, and sentence 4 is essentially a restatement of that premise. Sentence 5 is the second premise.

Stripped clean of nonargumentative material, the argument looks like this:

[Premise] But the news media are not in the business of endorsing or validating lifestyles. [Premise] In addition, by validating same-sex unions or any other lifestyle, the media abandon their objectivity and become political partisans—which would destroy whatever respect people have for news outlets. [Conclusion] All of this shows that the news media—including this newspaper—should never (explicitly or implicitly) endorse lifestyles by announcing those lifestyles to the world.

Now see if you can spot the conclusion and premises in this one:

[1] You have already said that you love me and that you can't imagine spending the rest of your life without me. [2] Once, you even tried to propose to me. [3] And now you claim that you need time to think about whether we should be married. [4] Well, everything that you've told me regarding our relationship has been a lie. [5] In some of your letters to a friend you admitted that you were misleading me. [6] You've been telling everyone that we are just friends, not lovers. [7] And worst of all, you've been secretly dating someone else. [8] Why are you doing this? [9] It's all been a farce, and I'm outta here.

And you thought that romantic love had nothing to do with critical thinking! In this passionate paragraph, an argument is alive and well. The conclusion is in sentence 4: "Well, everything that you've told me . . . has been a lie." Sentence 9, the concluding remark, is essentially a repetition of the conclusion. Sentences 1, 2, and 3 are background information on the current conflict. Sentences 5, 6, and 7 are the premises, the reasons that support the conclusion. And sentence 8 is an exasperated query that's not part of the argument.

You will discover that in most extended argumentative passages, premises and conclusions make up only a small portion of the total wordage. A good part of the text is background information and restatements of the premises or conclusion. Most of the rest consists of explanations, digressions, examples or illustrations, and descriptive passages.

Of all these nonargumentative elements, explanations are probably most easily confused with arguments. As we've seen, arguments try to prove or demonstrate that a statement is true. They try to show *that* something is the case. Explanations, however, do not try to prove that a statement is true. They try to show *why* or *how* something is the way it is. Consider these two statements:

- People have a respect for life because they adhere to certain ethical standards.
- People should have a respect for life because their own ethical standards endorse it.

The first statement is an explanation. It's not trying to prove anything, and no statement is in dispute. It's trying to clarify why or how people have respect for life. The second statement, though, is an argument. It's trying to prove, or provide support for, the idea that people should have a respect for life.

We discuss the basics of explanations in Chapter 9, and we deal with the other nonargumentative elements in Chapters 4 and 5. In the meantime, you should be able to locate the conclusion and premises of an argument—even when there is a lot of nonargumentative material nearby.

Finally, as you can see, learning the principles of critical thinking or logic requires at least some prior knowledge and ability. But, you may wonder (especially if this is your first course in critical or logical reasoning), Where does this prior knowledge and ability come from—and do you have these prerequisites? Fortunately, the answer is yes. Since you are, as Aristotle says, a rational animal, you already have the necessary equipment, namely, a logical sense that helps you reason in everyday life and enables you to begin honing your critical reasoning.

KEY WORDS

argument	explanation	logic
conclusion	indicator words	premise
critical thinking	inference	statement

Summary

- Critical thinking is the systematic evaluation or formulation of beliefs, or statements, by rational standards. Critical thinking is *systematic* because it involves distinct procedures and methods. It entails *evaluation* and *formulation* because it's used to both assess existing beliefs (yours or someone else's) and devise new ones. And it operates according to *reasonable standards* in that beliefs are judged according to the reasons and reasoning that support them.

Why It Matters

- Critical thinking matters because our lives are defined by our actions and choices, and our actions and choices are guided by our thinking. Critical thinking helps guide us toward beliefs that are worthy of acceptance, that can us help be successful in life, however we define success.

- A consequence of not thinking critically is a loss of personal freedom. If you passively accept beliefs that have been handed to you by your family and your culture, then those beliefs are not really yours. If they are not really yours, and you let them guide your choices and actions, then they—not you—are in charge of your life. Your beliefs are yours only if you critically examine them for yourself to see if they are supported by good reasons.

- Critical thinking does not necessarily lead to cynicism. It can complement our feelings by helping us sort them out. And it doesn't limit creativity—it helps perfect it.

How It Works

- Critical thinking is a rational, systematic process that we apply to beliefs of all kinds. *Belief* is another word for statement, or claim. A *statement* is an assertion that something is or is not the case. When you're engaged in critical thinking, you are mostly either evaluating a statement or trying to formulate one. In both cases your primary task is to figure out how strongly to believe the statement (based on how likely it is to be true). The strength of your belief will depend on the strength of the reasons in favor of the statement.

- In critical thinking an argument is not a feud but a set of statements—statements supposedly providing reasons for accepting another statement. The statements given in support of another statement are called the *premises*. The statement that the premises are used to support is called the *conclusion*. An argument then is a group of statements in which some of them (the premises) are intended to support another of them (the conclusion).

- Being able to identify arguments is an important skill on which many other critical thinking skills are based. The task is made easier by indicator words that frequently accompany arguments and signal that a premise or conclusion is present. Premise indicators include *for, since,* and *because.* Conclusion indicators include *so, therefore,* and *thus.*

- Arguments almost never appear neatly labeled for identification. They usually come imbedded in a lot of statements that are not part of the arguments. Arguments can be complex and lengthy. Your main challenge is to identify the conclusion and premises without getting lost in all the other verbiage.

EXERCISES

Exercises marked with * have answers in "Answers to Exercises" (Appendix C). Integrative exercises and writing assignments are not supplied with answers.

Exercise 1.1

REVIEW QUESTIONS

* 1. What is critical thinking?

   2. Is critical thinking primarily concerned with *what* you think or *how* you think?

   3. Why is critical thinking systematic?

* 4. According to the text, what does it mean to say that critical thinking is done according to rational standards?

   5. According to the text, how does a lack of critical thinking cause a loss of personal freedom?

* 6. What does the term *critical* refer to in critical thinking?

   7. How does logic differ from critical thinking?

* 8. What is a statement?

   9. What is an explanation?

  10. According to the text, by what standard should we always proportion our acceptance of a statement?

* 11. What is an argument?

  12. Give an example of an argument with two premises.

  13. What is the function of a premise?

* 14. What is a conclusion?

  15. Why can't a mere assertion or statement of beliefs constitute an argument?

  16. True or false: All disagreements contain an argument.

* 17. Does the following passage contain an argument? *Sample passage:* I couldn't disagree more with Olivia. She says that video games provoke young men to violence and other insensitive acts. But that's just not true.

  18. Does the following passage contain an argument? *Sample passage:* Alonzo asserts that the government should be able to arrest and imprison anyone if they are suspected of terrorist acts. But that's ridiculous. Doing that would be a violation of basic civil liberties guaranteed in the Bill of Rights.

* 19. What are indicator words?

  20. List three conclusion indicator words.

  21. List three premise indicator words.

  22. Give an example of a short argument that uses one or more indicator words.

* 23. What is probably the best strategy for trying to find an argument in a complex passage?

24. True or false: You can almost always find an argument in narrative writing.

Exercise 1.2

For each of the following sentences, indicate whether it is or is not a statement.

* 1. Now that you're mayor of the city, do you still believe that the city government is a waste of time?

2. Do not allow your emotions to distort your thinking.

3. If someone wants to burn the American flag, they should be able to do it without interference from the police.

* 4. Do you think that I'm guilty?

5. Should our religious beliefs be guided by reason, emotion, or faith?

6. Stop driving on the left side of the road!

* 7. The Vietnam War was a terrible mistake.

8. The Vietnam War was not a terrible mistake.

9. I shall do my best to do my duty to God and my country.

* 10. Are you doing your best for God and country?

Exercise 1.3

For each of the following passages indicate whether it constitutes an argument. For each argument specify what the conclusion is.

* 1. René hates Julia, and she always upsets him, so he should avoid her.

2. Do you think the upcoming election will change anything?

3. I pledge allegiance to the flag of the United States of America and to the republic for which it stands, one nation under God, indivisible, with liberty and justice for all.

* 4. Why do you think you have the right to park your car anywhere you please?

5. Wait just a minute. Where do you think you're going?

6. If you smoke that cigarette in here, I will leave the room.

* 7. The *Titanic* sank, and no one came to save it.

8. Jesus loves me, for the Bible tells me so.

9. Spiderman is a better superhero than Superman because kryptonite can't hurt him, and he doesn't have a Lois Lane around to mess things up.

10. "Whether our argument concerns public affairs or some other subject we must know some, if not all, of the facts about the subject on which we are to speak and argue. Otherwise, we can have no materials out of which to construct arguments." [Aristotle, *Rhetoric*]

* 11. If guns are outlawed, then only outlaws will have guns. Don't outlaw guns.

12. If someone says something that offends me, I should have the right to stop that kind of speech. After all, words can assault people just as weapons can.

13. "Citizens who so value their 'independence' that they will not enroll in a political party are really forfeiting independence, because they abandon a share in decision-making at the primary level: the choice of the candidate." [Bruce L. Felknor, *Dirty Politics*]

14. If someone says something that offends me, I cannot and should not try to stop them from speaking. After all, in America, speech—even offensive speech—is protected.

* 15. "Piercing car alarms have disturbed my walks, café meals or my sleep at least once during every day I have lived in the city; roughly 3,650 car alarms. Once, only once, was the wail a response to theft. . . . Silent car alarms connect immediately to a security company, while the noisy ones are a problem, not a solution. They should be banned, finally." [Letter to the editor, *New York Times*]

16. "If history is a gauge, the U.S. government cannot be trusted when it comes to sending our children to war. It seems that many years after Congress sends our children to war, we find out that the basic premise for the war was an intentional lie." [Letter to the editor, *L.A. Daily News*]

Exercise 1.4

For each of the following passages indicate whether it constitutes an argument. For each argument specify both the conclusion and the premises.

* 1. Faster-than-light travel is not possible. It would violate a law of nature.

2. You have neglected your duty on several occasions, and you have been absent from work too many times. Therefore, you are not fit to serve in your current capacity.

3. Racial profiling is not an issue for white people, but it is an issue for African Americans.

* 4. The flu epidemic on the East Coast is real. Government health officials say so. And I personally have read at least a dozen news stories that characterize the situation as a "flu epidemic."

5. The terrorist group ISIS in Syria and Iraq has killed thousands of innocent citizens. They are nothing more than fanatic murderers.

6. "Current-day Christians use violence to spread their right-to-life message. These Christians, often referred to as the religious right, are well known for violent demonstrations against Planned Parenthood and other abortion clinics. Doctors and other personnel are threatened with death, clinics have been bombed, there have even been cases of doctors being murdered." [Letter to the editor, *Arizona Daily Wildcat*]

* 7. "I am writing about the cost of concert tickets. I am outraged at how much ticket prices are increasing every year. A few years ago, one could attend a popular concert for a decent price. Now some musicians are asking as much as $200 to $300." [Letter to the editor, *Buffalo News*]

8. "Homeland security is a cruel charade for unborn children. Some 4,000 per day are killed in their mother's womb by abortion. This American holocaust was legalized by the Supreme Court in an exercise of raw judicial power." [Letter to the editor, *Buffalo News*]

9. Witches are real. They are mentioned in the Bible. There are many people today who claim to be witches. And historical records reveal that there were witches in Salem.

* 10. Stretched upon the dark silk night, bracelets of city lights glisten brightly.

11. Vaughn's car is old. It is beat up. It is unsafe to drive. Therefore, Vaughn's car is ready for the junkyard.

Exercise 1.5

For each of the following conclusions, write at least two premises that can support it. Your proposed premises can be entirely imaginary. To concoct the premises, think of what kind of statement (if true) would convince you to believe the conclusion.

EXAMPLE

Conclusion: Pet psychics can diagnose a dog's heartburn 100 percent of the time.
Premise 1: In the past fifty years, in hundreds of scientific tests, pet psychics were able to correctly diagnose heartburn in dogs 100 percent of the time.
Premise 2: Scientists have confirmed the existence of energy waves that can carry information about the health of animals.

1. What this country needs is more family values.

2. All animals—rodents, dogs, apes, whatever—have moral rights, just as people do.

* 3. Every woman has the right to abort her fetus if she so chooses.

4. When I looked into your eyes, time stood still.

5. Repent! The end is near.

* 6. When it comes to animals, Vaughn doesn't know what he's talking about.

7. Suspicion has arisen regarding the financial dealings of Governor Spendthrift.

8. The Internet is the most dangerous tool that terrorists have in their arsenal.

* 9. The Internet is the best tool that law enforcement officials have against terrorists.

10. Pornography is good for society because it educates people about sexuality.

11. Pornography is bad for society because it misleads people about sexuality.

* 12. *The Sopranos* is the greatest series in the history of TV.

13. It is the duty of every student to prevent this arbitrary tuition increase.

14. Jill cannot hold her liquor.

Exercise 1.6

For each of the following sets of premises, write a conclusion that would be supported by the premises (your conclusion should depend on both premises). Neither the conclusion nor the premises need to be statements that are true. To formulate an appropriate conclusion, try to think of a statement (conclusion) that could reasonably be supported by the premises.

EXAMPLE

Premise 1: The price of your shares in the stock market will continue to decline for at least a year.
Premise 2: Anyone with shares whose price will continue to decline for at least a year should sell now.
Conclusion: You should sell now.

1. Premise 1: You are afraid of heights.
   Premise 2: Anyone who is afraid of heights will fall if he or she climbs a tree.

* 2. Premise 1: School vouchers are being used in thirteen states and the Distric of Columbia.
   Premise 2: School vouchers have decreased the quality of education in every state where they've been used.

3. Premise 1: School vouchers are being used in thirteen states and the Distric of Columbia.
   Premise 2: School vouchers have improved the quality of education in every state where they've been used.

* 4. Premise 1: All married people are happier than unmarried people.
   Premise 2: You are married.

5. Premise 1: If stem-cell research is banned, Edgar will be very happy.
   Premise 2: Stem-cell research is banned.

6. Premise 1: If there is no God, then there is no morality.
   Premise 2: There is no God.

7. Premise 1: There is a God.
   Premise 2: If there is a God, then life has meaning.

* 8. Premise 1: There is a great deal of pornography of all kinds on the Internet.
   Premise 2: The government has essentially established a hands-off policy toward pornography on the Internet.
   Premise 3: Kids everywhere have access to pornography of all kinds on the Internet.

9. Premise 1: People in favor of capital punishment have a complete disregard for human life.

Premise 2: Anyone who has a complete disregard for human life cannot be trusted.

Premise 3: Nancy favors capital punishment.

Exercise 1.7

For each of the following passages, determine if there is an argument present. If so, identify the premises and the conclusion.

* 1. "[T]he Religious Right is *not* 'pro-family.' . . . Concerned parents realize that children are curious about how their bodies work and need accurate, age-appropriate information about the human reproductive system. Yet, thanks to Religious Right pressure, many public schools have replaced sex education with fear-based 'abstinence only' programs that insult young people's intelligence and give them virtually no useful information." [Rob Boston, *Free Inquiry Magazine*]

2. "[Francis Bacon] is the father of experimental philosophy. . . . In a word, there was not a man who had any idea of experimental philosophy before Chancellor Bacon; and of an infinity of experiments which have been made since his time, there is hardly a single one which has not been pointed out in his book. He had even made a good number of them himself." [Voltaire, *On Bacon and Newton*]

* 3. "Is there archaeological evidence for the [Biblical] Flood? If a universal Flood occurred between five and six thousand years ago, killing all humans except the eight on board the Ark, it would be abundantly clear in the archaeological record. Human history would be marked by an absolute break. We would see the devastation wrought by the catastrophe in terms of the destroyed physical remains of pre-Flood human settlements. . . . Unfortunately for the Flood enthusiasts, the destruction of all but eight of the world's people left no mark on the archaeology of human cultural evolution." [Kenneth L. Feder, *Frauds, Myths, and Mysteries*]

4. "Subjectivism claims that what makes an action [morally] right is that a person approves of it or believes that it's right. Although subjectivism may seem admirably egalitarian in that it takes everyone's moral judgments to be as good as everyone else's, it has some rather bizarre consequences. For one thing, it implies that each of us is morally infallible. As long as we approve of or believe in what we are doing, we can do no wrong. But this cannot be right. Suppose that Hitler believed that it was right to exterminate the Jews. Then it was right for Hitler to exterminate the Jews. . . . But what . . . Hitler did was wrong, even if [he] believed otherwise." [Theodore Schick, Jr., *Free Inquiry Magazine*]

Field Problems

1. Obtain the "Letters to the Editor" section of any newspaper (including student newspapers and online newspapers). Select a letter that contains at least one argument. Locate the conclusion and each premise.

   Next go through the letters again to find one that contains no argument at all. Rewrite the letter so that it contains at least one argument. Try to preserve as much of the original letter as possible. Stay on the same topic.

2. Go to www.townhall.com or www.usatoday.com and select an opinion essay on any issue. Identify its premises and conclusion, and decide whether you think the argument is a good one, providing reasons for your judgment.

 Self-Assessment Quiz

Answers appear in "Answers to Self-Assessment Quizzes" (Appendix D).

1. What is an argument?
2. Name at least three premise indicators and three conclusion indicators.
3. Select the sentence that is *not* a statement:

   a. When I met you, you didn't know anything about logic.
   b. Read the story and write a complete review of it.
   c. Four score and seven years ago our fathers brought forth on this continent a new nation.
   d. The best pizza in town can be had at Luigi's.

4. From the following list, select the conclusion that is supported by the premises in the following argument:

   > When conservative Pat Buchanan last spoke on this campus, he was shouted down by several people in the audience who do not approve of his politics. He tried to continue but finally had to give up and walk away. That was unfortunate, but he's not the only one. This kind of treatment has also happened to other unpopular guest speakers. How easily the students at this university forget that free speech is guaranteed by the Bill of Rights. University regulations also support free speech for all students, faculty, and visitors and strictly forbid the harassment of speakers. And this country was founded on the idea that citizens have the right to freely express their views—even when those views are unpopular.

   a. Pat Buchanan is a fascist.
   b. We should never have guest speakers on campus.
   c. Campus speakers should be allowed to speak freely without being shouted down.

d. Some guest speakers deserve to have the right of free speech and some don't.

5. Indicate whether the following passage contains an argument. If it does, specify the conclusion.

> We live in an incredibly over-reactionary society where the mindless forces of victim demagoguery have unfortunately joined with the child-worship industry. It is obviously tragic that a few twisted kids perpetuated such carnage there in Columbine. [Letter to the editor, Salon.com]

6. Indicate whether the following passage contains an argument. If it does, specify the conclusion.

> "War doesn't solve problems; it creates them," said an Oct. 8 letter about Iraq. World War II solved problems called Nazi Germany and militaristic Japan and created alliances with the nations we crushed. . . . The Persian Gulf war solved the problem of the Iraqi invasion of Kuwait. The Civil War solved the problem of slavery. These wars created a better world. War, or the threat of it is the only way to defeat evil enemies who are a threat to us. There is no reasoning with them. There can be no peace with them . . . so it's either us or them. What creates true peace is victory. [Letter to the editor, *New York Times*]

7. Indicate whether the following passage contains an argument. If so, specify the conclusion.

> Paul Krugman will always reach the same answer, namely that President Bush is wrong about everything. This time, he asserts that the federal government is "slashing domestic spending." Really? The president's budget request for 2003 would raise domestic spending 6 percent. Even setting aside spending that is related to homeland security, the president's request was for more than 2 percent growth, or nearly $7 billion in new dollars. In total, over the last five years, domestic spending will have skyrocketed by more than 40 percent. [Letter to the editor, *New York Times*]

For questions 8–12, indicate which sentences or sentence fragments are likely to be conclusions and which are likely to be premises.

8. Therefore, the Everglades will be destroyed within three years.
9. Assuming that you will never reach Boston
10. This implies that you are not driving as safely as you should.
11. Given all the hoopla surrounding the football team
12. It follows that sexual harassment should be a crime.

For questions 13–15, write at least two premises for each of the numbered conclusions. You can make up the premises, but you must ensure that they support the conclusion.

13. DNA evidence should be disallowed in cases of capital murder.

14. Computers will never be able to converse with a human being well enough to be indistinguishable from humans.

15. The great prophet Nostradamus (1503–1566) predicted the September 11 terrorist attacks.

Read the following argument. Then in questions 16–20, supply the information requested. Each question asks you to identify by number all the sentences in the argument that fulfill a particular role—conclusion, premise, background information, example or illustration, or reiteration of a premise or the conclusion. Just write down the appropriate sentence numbers.

[1] Is global warming a real threat? [2] Or is it hype propagated by tree-hugging, daft environmentalists? [3] The president apparently thinks that the idea of global climate change is bunk. [4] But recently his own administration gave the lie to his bunk theory. [5] His own administration issued a report on global warming called the *U.S. Climate Action Report 2002*. [6] It gave no support to the idea that global warming doesn't happen and we should all go back to sleep. [7] Instead, it asserted that global warming was definitely real and that it could have catastrophic consequences if ignored. [8] For example, global climate change could cause heat waves, extreme weather, and water shortages right here in the United States. [9] The report is also backed by many other reports, including a very influential one from the United Nations. [10] Yes, George, global warming is real. [11] It is as real as typhoons and ice storms.

16. Conclusion.
17. Premise or premises.
18. Background information.
19. Example or illustration.
20. Repetition of conclusion or premise.

 ## Writing Assignments

1. Select an issue from the following list and write a three-page paper defending a claim pertaining to the issue.

   • Should there be a constitutional amendment banning the desecration of the American flag?
   • Should a representation of the Ten Commandments be allowed to be displayed in a federal courtroom?
   • Should the legal drinking age be lowered?
   • Should the private ownership of fully automatic machine guns be outlawed?

2. Read Essay 1 ("Death Penalty Discriminates Against Black Crime Victims") in Appendix B, specify the conclusion and premises presented in it, and outline the argument in detail.

3. Write a two-page essay in which you defend a conclusion that contradicts the one in Essay 1. Pretend that all the evidence cited in Essay 1 actually supports your argument. You may alter the description of the evidence accordingly.

4. Study the argument presented in Essay 2 ("Marine Parks"). Identify the conclusion and the premises and objections considered. Then write a two-page rebuttal to the essay. That is, show that the essay's argument is faulty. You may cite imaginary—but reasonable—evidence.

Obstacles to Critical Thinking

CHAPTER OBJECTIVES

- Appreciate that there are ways to (1) detect errors in our thinking, (2) restrain the attitudes and feelings that can distort our reasoning, and (3) achieve a level of objectivity that makes critical thinking possible.
- Understand that the most common impediments to critical thinking can be sorted into two categories: (1) those hindrances that arise because of *how* we think and (2) those that occur because of *what* we think.

PSYCHOLOGICAL OBSTACLES

- Learn how to detect and overcome self-interested thinking by (1) watching out for instances when your deliberations get personal, (2) being alert to ways that critical thinking can be undermined, and (3) ensuring that no relevant evidence or ideas have been left out.
- Appreciate how group thinking can distort critical thinking.
- Understand the meaning and be able to cite examples of *peer pressure*, *appeal to popularity*, *appeal to common practice*, and *stereotyping*.

PHILOSOPHICAL OBSTACLES

- Know what a worldview is and how certain pivotal ideas in a worldview can undermine critical thinking.
- Be able to critique the doctrine of subjective relativism.
- Be able to critique the doctrine of social relativism.
- Know the definition of philosophical skepticism and how the view relates to critical thinking.

CRITICAL THINKING DOES NOT HAPPEN IN A VACUUM BUT IN AN "ENVIRONMENT" that's often hostile to it. It takes place in the real world in the minds of real people who almost always have thoughts and feelings and experiences that, given half a chance, would sabotage critical reasoning at every turn. The sparkling palace of our mind is grand—except for the demons chained in the basement.

Recall our definition of critical thinking: *The systematic evaluation or formulation of beliefs, or statements, by rational standards.* This means, of course, that several factors must be present for the process of critical thinking to be fully realized. If the process fails to be systematic, or falls short of being a true evaluation or formulation, or ignores rational standards, critical thinking can't happen. Because we are fallible, there are a thousand ways that this failure of reason could come about. And there is no cure for our fallibility.

We should expect then that thinking critically will often be difficult and even unpleasant (as painful truths sometimes are), and indeed it is. But there are ways to (1) detect errors in our thinking (even subtle ones), (2) restrain the attitudes and feelings that can distort our reasoning, and (3) achieve a level of objectivity that makes critical thinking possible.

Doing all this—and doing it consistently—requires *awareness, practice,* and *motivation.* If we are to think critically, we must be *aware* of not only what good critical thinking involves but also what sloppy thinking entails. Then we must *practice* avoiding the pitfalls and using the skills and techniques that critical thinking requires. And we must be *motivated* to do all of this, for it is unlikely that we will use critical thinking very much if we can't appreciate its value and therefore have little motivation to make the extra effort.

We can sort the most common impediments to critical thinking into two main categories: (1) those hindrances that arise because of *how* we think and (2) those that occur because of *what* we think. There is some overlap in these categories; how people think is often a result of what they think and vice versa. But in general, category 1 obstacles are those that come into play because of psychological factors (our fears, attitudes, motivations, and desires), and category 2 impediments are those that arise because of certain philosophical ideas we have (our beliefs about beliefs). For example, a category 1 hindrance is the tendency to conform our opinions to those of our peers. This conformism often grows out of some psychological need that is part of our personality. A common category 2 problem is the belief that objectivity in thinking is impossible or that we really don't know anything or that we don't know what we think we know.

In this chapter we review the most common category 1 and 2 barriers to critical thinking and practice uncovering and neutralizing them. The motivation to learn these lessons well is up to you.

Psychological Obstacles

No one is immune to category 1 obstacles. We are all heir to psychological tendencies and habits that affect our behavior and channel our thinking. They tend to persist or recur, haunting our minds until we have the awareness and the will to break free of them.

Francis Bacon on Critical Thinking

Francis Bacon (1561–1626), the godfather of modern science, articulated basic principles and methods of science and advocated their use in the careful pursuit of reliable knowledge. He also warned about common mistakes in thinking that can doom the scientific enterprise and lead to biased perceptions and serious error. Bacon asserted that preventing these mistakes is possible through scientific, down-to-earth thinking—approximately what we would call *critical thinking,* a necessary and powerful tool in the search for truth. He termed the mistakes "the idols of the mind" because he thought that people not only commit the errors but revere them as one would revere a false god.

Bacon focused on four kinds of idols that he considered especially prevalent and destructive. The first type is "The Idols of the Tribe"—the problems in thinking that arise from human nature generally. This is the fallacy of presuming that our biased perceptions are automatically a true reflection of the objective world, that knowledge is to be found inside us without any reference to the real world.

The second group consists of "The Idols of the Cave"—the biases that are unique to each individual. These develop from each person's personality, education, and experiences. Bacon claimed that we each live in our own cave, "which refracts and discolors the light of nature."

Then there are "The Idols of the Marketplace"—the impediments to clear thinking that develop from our imprecise and careless use of language. As Bacon said, "the ill and unfit choice of words wonderfully obstructs the understanding."[1]

Finally are "The Idols of the Theater"—the ideologies or systems of thought that are "but so many stage-plays, representing worlds of their own creation after an unreal and scenic fashion."[2] These barriers to good critical thinking have little or nothing to do with the real world but are nevertheless thought to be accurate and profound.

The Almighty Self

As humans we spend a great deal of time protecting, maintaining, and comforting our own mental life, our own *selves*—a perfectly natural urge that does no harm until we push our self-serving efforts too far. How far is too far? From the standpoint of critical thinking, we have taken things too far when we accept claims for no good reason—when our thinking is no longer systematic and rational. In the service of our almighty selves, we distort our judgment and raise our risk of error, which is ironically a risk to ourselves.

Self-interested thinking takes several forms. We may decide to accept a claim *solely on the grounds that it advances, or coincides with, our interests.* Self-interest can manifest itself as wishful thinking, cherry-picking information, slanting feelings, adopting an overly optimistic perspective, and maintaining an illusion of control. You may think, "I believe the city should lower the sales tax for convenience stores because I own a convenience store," or, "I am against all forms of gun control because I am a hunter," or, "This university should not raise tuition because I am a student, and I don't want to pay more tuition." There is nothing inherently wrong with accepting a claim that furthers your own interests. The problem arises when you accept a claim *solely because* it furthers your interests. Self-interest alone simply cannot establish the truth of a claim. To base your beliefs on self-interest alone is to abandon critical thinking.

Here's a classic example of self-interested thinking depicted in the film *Twelve Angry Men*:

Twelve jurors sit in a room deliberating over whether to find the defendant guilty of murder. The accused is a teenage boy who has grown up in the rough and impoverished streets of the inner city. At first, all but one juror (the jury foreman) vote guilty. The foreman convinces the other jurors to examine the evidence once again. Their deliberations go on for hours, and as they do, the prosecution's case slowly falls apart. Damning evidence that had seemed so strong earlier was now shown to be full of holes. They take another vote, but this time eleven jurors, including the foreman, vote not guilty, while one man (juror number 3) insists that the other jurors are deluded and that the boy is undoubtedly guilty. The jurors ask him to explain his reasons. He angrily insists again that the boy is guilty, but he can't provide any evidence or reasons that suggest the boy's guilt. He just rants at the other jurors. Finally the other jurors think they understand what's behind the seemingly irrational stance of juror number 3: He wants to convict the boy for personal reasons—perhaps because of a troubled relationship with his own son or because of some other bias that has nothing to do with the guilt or innocence of the defendant.

In this example, the other members of the jury eventually realize that the judgments of juror

Often what we think we see in vague stimuli turns out to be something that our minds have made up. We see bunnies, bearded men, and Elvis in formless clouds and smoke. We hear words and animal noises in garbled audio (like records played backward). This phenomenon is known as *pareidolia*. A good example is this stunning photo taken by NASA's Hubble Space Telescope showing the Cone Nebula, a massive pillar of gas and dust, the breeding ground for stars. Some Christians say they perceive something else in the picture: the head of Jesus Christ crowned with a ring of stars. The "Jesus Nebula" they call it. What image do you think would be picked out by Hindus or Muslims? What do you see?

number 3 are self-serving, linked to his own emotional needs. What gave him away? An obvious clue is his emotional protestations. But an even more telling clue is his rejection of all relevant evidence. The reasons for acquitting are perfectly clear to the other jurors, but he won't (or can't) consider them. In everyday life, these two clues often signal the presence of powerful self-interest at work.

The influence of self on your thinking can take another form. You may be tempted to accept claims *for no other reason than that they help you save face.* We all like to think of ourselves as excelling in various ways. We may believe that we are above average in intelligence, integrity, talent, compassion, physical beauty, sexual prowess, athletic ability, and much more. But we not only like to think such things about ourselves, we want others to think the same about us. The rub comes, however, when we accept or defend claims just to cover up the cracks in our image. You make a mistake, and so you blame it on someone or something else. You behave badly, and you try to justify your behavior. You make a judgment or observation that turns out to be wrong, and you're too embarrassed or proud to admit it. You rationalize, make excuses, play up the positive, play down the negative. (In Chapter 4 we'll learn that sometimes self-interested thinking can even alter our perceptions.)

The consequences of self-centered thinking can be, well, self-destructive. In the realm of critical thinking, this devotion to yourself can prevent careful evaluation of claims, limit critical inquiry, blind you to the facts, provoke self-deception, engender rationalizations, lead you to suppress or ignore evidence, and beget wishful thinking. And these mistakes can decrease your chances of success (however you define success) and hamper your personal growth, maturity, and self-awareness. Such egocentricism can also leave you wide open to propaganda and manipulation by people who appeal to your personal desires and prejudices. How easy would it be for people to control your choices and thoughts if they told you exactly what you wanted to hear? (There are in-depth discussions of these lapses in critical thinking in Chapters 4 and 5.)

> "To be conscious that you are ignorant is a great step to knowledge."
> —Benjamin Disraeli

Other people (especially those who know you fairly well) may be amused or puzzled by your stubborn adherence to claims that obviously conflict with the evidence. Or they may think it odd that you cling to ideas or behaviors that you loudly condemn in others.

DILBERT: © Scott Adams/Dist. By United Feature Syndicate, Inc.

FURTHER THOUGHT

When We Construct the Facts Ourselves

Psychologists have long known that a great deal of what we experience is *fabricated by ourselves.* That is, our own desires and expectations help form an impressive proportion of our perceptions, memories, and beliefs. Here are two examples documented by scientific research:

- There are probably hundreds of stories about ghosts and aliens showing up in people's bedrooms. Whatever is going on here, it certainly doesn't need to be supernatural. Researchers have shown that when people are in that drowsy state just before sleep, they often have weird hallucinations known as *hypnagogic imagery.* These images come on suddenly, are not under the sleeper's control, and can seem as realistic as physical objects in the room. Images range from faces in the dark to ghostly shapes and colored geometric shapes.
- Research has shown that our memories aren't exact copies of past events. The recall of eyewitnesses, for instance, is notoriously iffy. In the act of recall, they try to reconstruct a memory—but the reconstruction is frequently inexact, resulting in distortions and missing details. Stress can exaggerate these problems. Our memories can be drastically changed if we later come across new information—even if the information is brief and wrong. Most amazing of all, our expectations about the way things should be can insert or delete elements of a memory. If we expect to see a gun in the hand of a bank robber, we may remember exactly that even though no gun was involved.

Part of the job of critical thinking, of course, is to counteract all these tendencies—or help you recognize them when they happen.

When examining a claim or making a choice, how can you overcome the excessive influence of your own needs? Sometimes you can do it only with great effort, and sometimes the task is much easier, especially if you remember these three guidelines:

- Watch out when things get very personal.
- Be alert to ways that critical thinking can be undermined.
- Ensure that nothing has been left out.

Watch Out When Things Get Very Personal

You are most likely to let your self-interest get in the way of clear thinking when you have a big personal stake in the conclusions you reach. You may be deeply committed to a particular view or belief, or you may want desperately for a particular claim to be false or unjustified, or you may be devoted not to particular claims but to *any* claims that contradict those of someone you dislike. Such zeal can wreck any attempt at careful, fair evaluation of a claim.

The twentieth-century philosopher Bertrand Russell asserts that the passionate holding of an opinion is a sure sign of a lack of reasons to support the opinion:

> When there are rational grounds for an opinion, people are content to set them forth and wait for them to operate. In such cases, people do not hold their opinions with passion; they hold them calmly, and set forth their reasons quietly. The opinions that are held with passion are always those for which no good ground exists; indeed the passion is the measure of the holder's lack of rational conviction.[3]

The dead giveaway that you are skewing your thinking is a surge of strong emotions (like the one that gripped juror number 3). If your evaluation or defense of a position evokes anger, passion, or fear, your thinking could be prejudiced or clouded. It is possible, of course, to be emotionally engaged in an issue and still think critically and carefully. But most of the time, getting worked up over a claim or conclusion is reason enough to suspect that your thinking is not as clear as it should be.

The rule of thumb is: If you sense a rush of emotions when you deal with a particular issue, stop. Think about what's happening and why. Then continue at a slower pace and with greater attention to the basics of critical reasoning, double-checking to ensure that you are not ignoring or suppressing evidence or getting sloppy in your evaluations.

 FURTHER THOUGHT

Is It Wrong to Believe Without Good Reasons?

Some philosophers have asserted that it is morally wrong to believe a proposition without justification or evidence. One of these is the famous biologist Thomas Henry Huxley. Another is mathematician W. K. Clifford (1845–1879). This is how Clifford states his view:

> It is wrong always, everywhere, and for anyone, to believe anything upon insufficient evidence. If a man, holding a belief which he was taught in childhood or persuaded of afterwards, keeps down and pushes away any doubts which arise about it in his mind . . . and regards as impious those questions which cannot easily be asked without disturbing it—the life of that man is one long sin against mankind.[4]

Clifford thinks that belief without evidence is immoral because our actions are guided by our beliefs, and if our beliefs are unfounded, our actions (including morally relevant actions) are likely to be imprudent.

Be Alert to Ways That Critical Thinking Can Be Undermined

If you understand the techniques and principles of critical thinking, and you have practiced applying them in a variety of situations, you are more likely than not to detect your own one-sided self-centered thinking when it occurs. An alarm should go off in your head: "Warning—faulty reasoning."

When your alarm sounds, double-check your thinking, look for lapses in arguments and claims, and weed them out.

Ensure That Nothing Has Been Left Out

A common flaw in reasoning is the failure to consider evidence or arguments that *do not support* preferred claims or positions. For example, you may secretly want a particular claim to be true, so you knowingly or unknowingly look for evidence in its favor but ignore evidence against it. The chances of making this mistake increase markedly when you are reasoning for the sake of self.

This kind of preferential treatment for some statements and not others is part of a common phenomenon called *selective attention* (see Chapters 4 and 5). In selective attention, we notice certain things and ignore others—usually without even being aware that we're doing it. We may ignore facts that contradict our beliefs and search out facts that support them. Scientific research has repeatedly confirmed this behavior. In a typical study, researchers showed subjects both *evidence for* and *evidence against* the reality of extrasensory perception (ESP). Subjects who already doubted the existence of ESP accurately recalled both kinds of evidence. But subjects who already believed in ESP remembered both kinds of evidence as *proving* ESP. They somehow recalled even the disconfirming evidence as supporting their belief in ESP!

The remedy for this problem is to *make a conscious effort to look for opposing evidence.* Don't consider your evaluation of a statement or argument finished until you've carefully considered *all the relevant reasons.* Ask yourself, "What is the evidence or reasons against this statement?"

> "The fact that an opinion has been widely held is no evidence whatever that it is not absurd; indeed in view of the silliness of the majority of mankind, a widespread belief is more likely to be foolish than sensible."
>
> —Bertrand Russell

REVIEW NOTES

Avoiding Self-Interested Thinking

- Watch out when things get personal and you become emotionally vested in an issue.
- Beware of the urge to distort your thinking to save face.
- Be alert to ways that critical thinking can be undermined.
- Ensure that nothing has been left out of consideration.
- Avoid selective attention.
- Make a conscious effort to look for opposing evidence.

Are You a Conformist? Take This Test and Find Out

To some extent we all conform our ideas and behavior to group influences, but some people go overboard. Take the following test to find out if you're one of them. Check off each statement that applies to you, then add up the numbers of each checked statement to get your score. The lower your score, the more conformist you are.

+100   You usually change your beliefs for good reasons.
+1   You change your beliefs for good reasons only when money is involved.
−10   You usually change your beliefs for no reason whatsoever.
−15   You automatically change your beliefs when your friends ridicule them.
−30   You automatically change your beliefs when total strangers ridicule them.
−40   You change your beliefs whenever you see a TV ad.
−42   You change your beliefs to be accepted into a group.
−50   You change your clothes to be accepted into a group.
−50   You would change your car to be accepted into a group.
−100   You would change your beliefs *and* your physical features to be accepted into a group.

If your score is below zero, *do not* drop your course in critical thinking. If it's *way, way* below zero, you need more than a course in critical thinking. Is this a bogus test? Yes, totally. If you figured that out by the second statement, give yourself 1000 points.

This approach is at the heart of science. A basic principle of scientific work is not to accept a favored theory until competing (alternative) theories are thoroughly examined. (More on this in Chapter 10.)

The Power of the Group

In the television series *Star Trek: The Next Generation,* the crew of the starship *Enterprise* encounters an unusual threat: the Borg. The Borg is a collective of individual minds that have been stripped of individuality and merged into a single group-mind with evil intentions. Much of the Borg storyline (which spans several episodes) is about the dignity and importance of individualism as opposed to the conformism of the Borg hive. The thought of losing one's self in the monolithic Borg is presented as a profound tragedy—a theme that strikes a chord with humans. Individualism, independence, and freedom of thought are what we want, what we must have.

Or so we say. Despite our apparent longings, we humans spend a great deal of our time trying to conform to, or be part of, groups. We want to belong, we want the safety and comfort of numbers, we want the approval of our beloved tribe. All of which is perfectly normal. We are, after all, social creatures. Conformist tendencies are a fact of life. But trouble appears when our conformism hampers—or obliterates—critical thinking.

We all belong to multiple groups—family, employees, gender, church, club, professional society, political party, advocacy group, you name it—and we can be susceptible to pressure from all of them. Much of the time, there is intense pressure to fit into groups and to adopt ideas, attitudes, and goals endorsed by them. Sometimes the influence of the group is subtle but strong and can occur in

www.CartoonStock.com

the most casual, "unofficial" gatherings. The claims and positions adopted by the group can be implicit, never spoken, but well understood. The political chat group online, the group of Christians or Muslims or Jews who happen to meet on the bus, the collection of peers who support the same political cause—all these can exert a noticeable influence on our beliefs.

Group pressure to accept a statement or act in a certain way has several overlapping subtypes (some of which we'll cover in more detail in later chapters). When the pressure to conform comes from your peers, it's called—surprise—**peer pressure.** When the pressure comes from the mere popularity of a belief, it's known as—believe it or not—an **appeal to popularity** (also known as an appeal to the masses). When the pressure comes from what groups of people do or how they behave, it's called an **appeal to common practice.** In all cases, the lapse in critical thinking comes from the use of group pressure *alone* to try to support a claim (see Chapter 5).

Group pressure can happen quickly. For example, if you're listening to a speech by a member of your own political party, you may immediately find yourself positively disposed toward the speaker—not because you agree with him but because he's a member of your group.

Group pressure can also take a while. Consider:

Lillian has just become a new member of the Democratic Club on campus, an association of Democrats and political liberals. She has been trying to join the club ever since her freshman year. She likes being in a group that shares most of her beliefs, and she feels that just being a member of the club—whose members include many of the brightest students on campus—boosts her up a notch or two socially. She soon finds out that she agrees with club members on every political and social issue—except one. Everyone else in the group is adamantly opposed to capital punishment. Lillian favors it because she researched all the arguments for and against it and concluded that the pro side was stronger. But she doesn't

> "Believe nothing, no matter where you read it, or who said it, no matter if I said it, unless it agrees with your own reason and your own common sense."
> —The Buddha

want to jeopardize her membership because of her stand on this one issue. So she never mentions it. Whenever she hears arguments against the death penalty, she believes them to be faulty. But after a few months, she learns to ignore the arguments. In fact, she tries not to think about the subject at all. Over time, her views on the subject change, until finally she finds herself being wholeheartedly against the death penalty.

Here, the need to belong slowly usurps critical reasoning in a specific subject area (capital punishment). On other topics, Lillian may be an astute critical thinker.

There's another kind of group influence that we have all fallen prey to: the pressure that comes from presuming that our own group is the best, the right one, the chosen one, and all other groups are, well, not as good. You can see this kind of ethnocentrism in religions, political parties, generations, social classes,

> "A great many people think they are thinking when they are really rearranging their prejudices."
> —William James

💡 **FURTHER THOUGHT**

Prejudice, Bias, and Racism

Group pressure often leads to prejudice, bias, and racism. (To a lesser extent, so does self-interest.) But what do these terms mean?

Prejudice in its broadest sense is a judgment or opinion—whether positive or negative—based on insufficient reasons. But usually the term is used in a more narrow way to mean a negative, or adverse, belief (most often about people) without suf-

Critical thinking against racism. In 1957 during efforts to integrate schools in Little Rock, Arkansas, a black student is jeered as she attempts to attend classes at an all-white high school. (Will Counts Collection: Indiana University Archives)

ficient reasons. At the heart of prejudice, then, is a failure of critical thinking. And the use of critical thinking is an important part of eradicating prejudiced views.

Bias is another word for prejudice, both in the general and the narrow sense. Sometimes the word is also used to mean an inclination of temperament or outlook—as in "My bias is in favor of tougher laws."

Racism is a lack of respect for the value and rights of people of different races or geographical origins. Usually this attitude is based on prejudice—specifically an unjustified belief that one group of people is somehow superior to another.

REVIEW NOTES

Avoiding Group Pressure on Your Thinking

- Group pressure can come in the form of peer pressure, appeals to popularity, and appeals to common practice.
- Group-centered thinking can degenerate into narrow-mindedness, resistance to change, and stereotyping.
- The best way to defend yourself against group thinking is to always proportion your acceptance of a claim according to the strength of reasons.

 NEWSMAKERS

Left-Wing/Right-Wing Bias

Is there a left-wing bias in the news media? A right-wing bias? Some swear the *New York Times* and PBS slant the news to the left; others say *Fox News* tilts it to the right. The charge that the news is politically slanted—left or right—regularly starts arguments (the nasty, pointless kind) and usually lacks supporting evidence. Whether the allegation is true is not an issue we can settle here, and fortunately we need not settle it to apply critical thinking to the news media.

As detailed in Chapter 4, many factors can render news reports unreliable, incomplete, or misleading—even when no political bias is at work. Critical thinking requires that we not assume without good reason that a report gives us an entirely accurate picture. The best way to ensure that we get the whole story is to read a variety of newspapers, newsmagazines, opinion journals, and websites.

The worst approach is to rely only on news sources that reinforce our existing political views. People have a natural tendency to seek out only evidence that supports their treasured beliefs and to resist evidence that contradicts them. They want to watch, hear, and read only what is psychologically comforting—and to avoid what disturbs their worldview. But this strategy undermines serious inquiry and reflection, stunts our understanding, and blights independent thinking.

Do you ever read magazines, newspapers, or websites that run counter to your political beliefs? Do you associate only with people who share your political views? Do you ever seriously consider plausible objections to your positions? Do you think the availability of other points of view online helps open up the debate beyond older media biases? Or does it just reinforce what readers of each blog already think they know?

and many other groups. The assumption that your group is better than others is at the heart of prejudice.

This we-are-better pressure is probably the most powerful of all. We all have certain beliefs not because we have thought critically about them but because our parents raised us to believe them or because the conceptual push and pull of our social group has instilled them in us. That is, we may believe what we believe—and assume that our beliefs are better than anyone else's—because we were born into a family or society that maintains such views. We may be a Catholic or a Democrat or a racist primarily because we were born into a Catholic or Democratic or racist family or society. Like the influence of the self, this endemic pressure can lead to wishful thinking, rationalization, and self-deception. Group thinking can also easily generate narrow-mindedness, resistance to change, and **stereotyping** (drawing conclusions about people without sufficient reasons). (Again, more on these problems in Chapters 4 and 5.)

But as comfortable as our inherited beliefs are, when we accept them without good reason, we risk error, failure, and delusion. And as we discussed in Chapter 1, if we have certain beliefs solely because they were given to us, they are not really our beliefs. The sign of a maturing intellect is having the will and the courage to gradually prune beliefs that are groundless.

For critical thinkers, the best way to deal with the power of the group is to proportion your belief to the strength of reasons.

After thinking critically about claims favored by groups, you may find that the claims are actually on solid ground, and you really do have good reason to accept them. Or you may find that there is no good reason for believing them, and so you don't accept them. Either way, critical thinking will give you a clearer view of the group and yourself.

Critical thinking then is independent thinking. And in the West and many other parts of the world, those who achieve independent thinking—the Aristotles, the Einsteins, the Shakespeares, the Michaelangelos—are revered.

Philosophical Obstacles

A **worldview** is a philosophy of life, a set of fundamental ideas that helps us make sense of a wide range of important issues in life. The ideas are fundamental because they help guide us in the evaluation or acceptance of many other less basic ideas. They are answers to the "big questions" of life, such as, What do I know? Is knowledge possible? What is real and what is not? How do I know which actions are morally right?

The interesting thing about worldviews is that we all have one, for we all have adopted (or inherited) certain fundamental ideas about the world. You may have unknowingly absorbed the ideas from your family or society, and you may not have thought much about them, but you have a worldview nonetheless. Even the rejection of all worldviews is a worldview.

In Chapter 11 we discuss how critical thinking can help you construct a worldview that is founded on good reasons. For now, we need to investigate how some elements of a worldview—certain fundamental but problematic ideas—may undermine critical thinking. These notions can give rise to category 2 obstacles to critical reason, for they may affect our thinking through the content of our beliefs.

Subjective Relativism

Like science, critical thinking may be underpinned by a number of propositions that few people would think to question. Science, for example, is based on the proposition that the world is publicly understandable—that it has a certain structure (independent of what anyone thinks), that we can know the structure, and that this knowledge can be acquired by anyone. Critical thinking is based on similar ideas. Among the most basic is the notion that the truth of a claim does not depend on what a person thinks. That is, your believing that something is true *does not make it true.*

The idea that truth depends on what someone believes is called **subjective relativism,** and if you accept this notion or use it to try to support a claim, you're said to commit the **subjectivist fallacy.** This view says that truth depends not on the way things are but solely on what someone believes. Truth, in other words, is relative to persons. Truth is a matter of what a person believes—not a matter of how the world is. This means that a proposition can be true for one person, but not for another. If you believe that dogs can fly, then it is true (for you) that dogs can fly. If someone else believes that dogs cannot fly, then it is true (for him) that dogs cannot fly.

You've probably encountered subjective relativism more often than you realize. You may have heard someone (maybe even yourself!) say, "This is *my* truth, and that's *your* truth," or, "This statement is true *for me.*"

Many critics of subjective relativism maintain that it can undermine critical thinking in a fundamental way. In large part, critical thinking is about determining whether statements are true or false. But if we can make a statement true just by believing it to be true, then critical thinking would seem to be unnecessary. The subjectivist fallacy, they say, may be an excuse to forgo the tough job of critical inquiry.

Most philosophers see the situation this way: We use critical thinking to find out whether a statement is true or false—*objectively* true or false. Objective truth is about the world, about the way the world is regardless of what we may believe about it. To put it differently, there is a way the world is, and our beliefs do not make it. The world is the way it is, regardless of how we feel about it.

These same philosophers would probably be quick to point out that some objective truths *are* about our subjective states or processes. It might be true, for example, that you're feeling pain right now. But if so, the claim that you are feeling pain right now is an objective truth about your subjective state.

Also, they would readily admit that there are some things about ourselves that obviously *are* relative because they are one way for us and another way for someone else. You may like ice cream, but someone else may not. Your liking ice cream is then relative to you. But the truth about these states of affairs is not relative.

Subjective relativism (as well as other forms of relativism) is controversial, and we needn't spend much time on it here. But you should know at least that many philosophers have (through the use of critical thinking!) uncovered some odd implications that seem to render the view implausible. First, they point out that if we could make a statement true just by believing it to be true, we would be infallible. We could not possibly be in

> "Man is a credulous animal, and must believe *something*; in the absence of good grounds for belief, he will be satisfied with bad ones."
> —Bertrand Russell

Social relativism implies that societies are infallible—even about such horrors as the Nazis' imprisonment and murder of millions of people in World War II.

error about anything that we sincerely believed. We could never be mistaken about where we parked the car or what we said about jelly beans or what some general said about carpet bombing. Personal infallibility is, of course, absurd, and this possibility seems to weigh heavily against subjective relativism.

Many critics think that subjective relativism's biggest problem is that it's self-defeating. It defeats itself because its truth implies its falsity. The relativist says, "All truth is relative." If this statement is objectively true, then it refutes itself because if it is objectively true that "All truth is relative," then the statement itself is an example of an objective truth. So if "All truth is relative" is objectively true, it is objectively false.

Social Relativism

To escape the difficulties of subjective relativism, some people posit **social relativism,** the view that truth is relative to societies. The claim is that truth depends not on an individual's beliefs, but on society's beliefs. So a claim can be true for the Chinese but false for Americans, true for college students but false for public officials, true for Baptists but false for atheists. To many, this kind of relativism, like the subjective kind, also seems to render critical thinking superfluous.

Social relativism is attractive to many because it seems to imply an admirable egalitarianism—the notion that the beliefs of different societies are all equal. But a lot of philosophers maintain that it has most of the same defects that subjective relativism has. For example, according to social relativism, individuals aren't infallible, but societies are. The beliefs of whole societies cannot be mistaken. But this notion of societal infallibility is no more plausible than the idea of individual infallibility. Is it plausible that no society has ever been wrong about anything—never been wrong about the causes of disease, the best form of government, the number of planets in our solar system, the burning of witches, the Nazi policy of killing six million Jews?

Critics like to point out that just as subjective relativism is self-defeating, so is social relativism. The claim that "All truth is relative to societies" is self-defeating because if it is objectively true, then it is an example of an objective truth—and that means that the claim is objectively false.

If you accept relativism, you may be tempted to care very little about critical thinking, and that would be your loss. Fortunately, there is no good reason why you should neglect critical thinking in the name of relativism.[5]

> "What we need is not the will to believe, but the will to find out."
> —Bertrand Russell

Skepticism

If knowledge were impossible, critical thinking—as a way of coming to know the truth or falsity of claims—would seem to be out of a job. Most of us, though, believe that we *can* acquire knowledge. We think that we know a great many things—that we are alive, that our shoes are a certain color, that there is a tree on the lawn, that the Earth is not flat, that rabbits cannot fly, that $2 + 2 = 4$. But not everyone would agree. There are some who believe that we know much less than we think we do or nothing at all. This view is known as **philosophical skepticism,** and thinkers who raise doubts about how much we know are known as **philosophical skeptics.**

This is no place to dive into a debate on skepticism, but we can take a quick look at the most important type of philosophical skepticism and see what, if anything, it has to do with critical thinking. This form of skepticism says that knowledge requires certainty—if we are to know anything, we must be certain of it. This means that our knowledge isn't knowledge unless it is beyond any *possibility* of doubt. If knowledge requires certainty, however, there is very little that we know because there are always considerations that can undermine our certainty.

But it seems that our knowledge *does not* require certainty. All of us can cite many situations in which we do seem to have knowledge—even though we do not have absolutely conclusive reasons. We usually would claim to know, for example, that it is raining, that our dog has spots, that we were born, that the moon is not made of green cheese—even though we are not absolutely certain of any of these. These situations suggest that we do know many things. We know them not because they are beyond all *possible* doubt, but because they are beyond all *reasonable* doubt. Doubt is always possible, but it is not always reasonable. Rejecting a reasonable claim to knowledge just because of the bare possibility that you may be wrong is neither reasonable nor necessary.

Critical thinking does have a job to do in our efforts to acquire knowledge. Its task, however, is not to help us find claims that we cannot possibly doubt but to help us evaluate claims that vary in degrees of reasonable doubt—that is, from weak reasons (or no reasons) to very strong reasons. Critical thinking, then, promotes *reasonable skepticism* and tries to avoid the trap of philosophical skepticism.

🔑 KEY WORDS

appeal to common practice	**philosophical skepticism**	**stereotyping**
appeal to popularity (or to the masses)	**philosophical skeptics**	**subjective relativism**
peer pressure	**social relativism**	**subjectivist fallacy**
		worldview

Summary

- Critical thinking takes place in a mental environment consisting of our experiences, thoughts, and feelings. Some elements in this inner environment can sabotage our efforts to think critically or at least make critical thinking more difficult. Fortunately, we can exert some control over these elements.

With practice, we can detect errors in our thinking, restrain attitudes and feelings that can disrupt our reasoning, and achieve enough objectivity to make critical thinking possible.

- The most common of these hindrances to critical thinking fall into two main categories: (1) those obstacles that crop up because of *how* we think and (2) those that occur because of *what* we think. The first category is comprised of psychological factors such as our fears, attitudes, motivations, and desires. The second category is made up of certain philosophical beliefs.

Psychological Obstacles

- None of us is immune to the psychological obstacles. Among them are the products of egocentric thinking. We may accept a claim solely because it advances our interests or just because it helps us save face. To overcome these pressures, we must (1) be aware of strong emotions that can warp our thinking, (2) be alert to ways that critical thinking can be undermined, and (3) ensure that we take into account *all* relevant factors when we evaluate a claim.
- The first category of hindrances also includes those that arise because of group pressure. These obstacles include conformist pressures from groups that we belong to and ethnocentric urges to think that our group is superior to others. The best defense against group pressure is to proportion our beliefs according to the strength of reasons.

Philosophical Obstacles

- We may also have certain core beliefs that can undermine critical thinking (the second category of hindrances). Subjective relativism is the view that truth depends solely on what someone believes—a notion that may make critical thinking look superfluous. But subjective relativism leads to some strange consequences. For example, if the doctrine were true, each of us would be infallible. Also, subjective relativism has a logical problem—it's self-defeating. Its truth implies its falsity. There are no good reasons to accept this form of relativism.
- Social relativism is the view that truth is relative to societies—a claim that would also seem to make critical thinking unnecessary. But this notion is undermined by the same kinds of problems that plague subjective relativism.
- Philosophical skepticism is the doctrine that we know much less than we think we do. One form of philosophical skepticism says that we cannot know anything unless the belief is beyond all possible doubt. But this is not a plausible criterion for knowledge. To be knowledge, claims need not be beyond all possible doubt, but beyond all *reasonable* doubt.

EXERCISES

Exercises marked with * have answers in "Answers to Exercises" (Appendix C). Quizzes, integrative exercises, and writing assignments are not supplied with answers.

Exercise 2.1

REVIEW QUESTIONS

* 1. According to the text's definition of critical thinking, what factors must be present for critical thinking to be realized?

2. What are the two main categories of common obstacles to critical thinking?

3. What did W. K. Clifford say about the morality of believing claims?

4. What is stereotyping?

* 5. From the standpoint of critical thinking, what event signals that we have allowed our bias in favor of our selves go too far?

6. According to the text, what effect can our urge to save face have on our thinking?

* 7. When are you most likely to let your self-interest get in the way of clear thinking?

8. How does subjective relativism imply infallibility?

9. How are subjective and social relativism sefl-defeating?

10. According to the text, how might selective attention affect your thinking when you are examining evidence for or against a claim?

* 11. How might the influence of a group that you belong to affect your attempts to think critically?

12. According to the text, what is the most powerful group pressure of all?

13. What is the appeal to popularity?

* 14. What is a worldview?

15. In order to know something, must it be beyond all possible doubt? Why or why not?

16. According to the text, how could subjective relativism make critical thinking unnecessary?

* 17. Is critical thinking concerned with the *objective* or the *subjective* truth of claims?

18. What is social relativism?

19. What is philosophical skepticism?

20. Does our knowledge require certainty?

* 21. What kind of doubt is involved in the acquisition of knowledge?

Exercise 2.2

For each of the following passages, indicate whether it contains examples of self-interested thinking, face-saving, or group pressure. Some of these are really tough.

* 1. Mary: Animals have the same rights as humans.
  Jenna: What makes you think that?
  Mary: I love animals, and there are so many that are treated horribly all over the world. It's heartbreaking.

2. Jonathan: My essay is better than Julio's.
  Betty: Why do you think that yours is better than all the others? Do you agree that the content and writing of all the essays are similar?
  Jonathan: Well, yes.
  Betty: Do you agree that all the other benchmarks of quality are nearly identical?
  Jonathan: Yes, but mine is still better.

3. Dear friends, as your state senator I will continue my tireless work on your behalf. I will continue to use my considerable talents to make this district even better. I will continue to let my integrity be the guide for all my actions.

* 4. We cannot allow those people to move into this neighborhood. They're not like us.

5. I oppose women becoming members of this club. If I endorsed their claims, every friend I've got in the club would turn his back on me.

6. His statements about the West Bank are all false, of course. He's an Israeli.

* 7. Christianity is superior to all other religions. I was raised Christian, and all my relatives are Christians. This is the only religion I've known, and the only one I need.

8. I'm due for tenure next year, so I am in favor of continuing the tradition of tenure at this university.

9. The United States is the greatest nation on the face of the earth. I don't know anything about other countries, and I don't want to know.

* 10. If Joan is appointed to the committee, I am guaranteed to have a job for the rest of my life. I wholeheartedly favor Joan's appointment.

11. Free speech should not extend to pornographers. Right now they are allowed to espouse their smut on the Internet and many other places. That's just not how I was raised.

Exercise 2.3

Read each of the following claims. Then select from the list any statements that, if true, would constitute good reasons for accepting the claim. Be careful: In some questions, none of the choices is correct.

* 1. John: The newspaper account of the charges of pedophilia lodged against Father J. Miller, a Catholic priest in our town, should never have been printed.

    a. The charges are false.
    b. John is a Catholic.
    c. Important evidence that would exonerate Father Miller was not mentioned in the newspaper account.
    d. The town is predominantly Catholic.

2. Alice: The speed limit on I-95 should be 70 mph.

    a. Raising the speed limit to 70 mph would result in faster and safer traffic.
    b. The state commission on highways did a study showing that I-95 should have a limit of 70 mph.
    c. Alice travels I-95 every day and needs to drive 70 mph to get to work on time.
    d. Alice drives I-95 every day.

* 3. Janette: Women are less violent and less emotional than men.

    a. A study from Harvard shows that women are less violent and less emotional than men.
    b. Janette is a woman.
    c. Janette is a member of a group of women who are fighting for the rights of women.
    d. Janette and all her friends are women.

4. Brie: People should buy stock in IBM, an action that will push the price per share higher.

    a. Brie owns a large proportion of IBM stock.
    b. Brie is chair of the board at IBM.
    c. The stock market is weak.
    d. Brie has a large family to support.

5. Colonel Stockton: The United States should attack the terrorists in Iran, even at the risk of a full-scale war with Arab states.

    a. The terrorists have humiliated Colonel Stockton's forces.
    b. The terrorists have humiliated the United States.
    c. Colonel Stockton is loyal to his troops, all of whom want to attack the terrorists in Iran.
    d. Attacking the terrorists in Iran would cause no casualties and would result in world peace.

* 6. Morgan: Capital punishment is always wrong.

    a. All of Morgan's friends agree that capital punishment is wrong.
    b. If Morgan favored capital punishment, her friends would abandon her.

c. Morgan is president of the Anti–Capital Punishment League.

d. Morgan has already made her views known and cannot change her mind without seeming to be inconsistent.

7. Angelo: Marijuana should be legalized.

a. All of Angelo's friends smoke marijuana.

b. Legalizing marijuana would reduce the consumption of marijuana and save lives, money, and resources.

c. Angelo has already said on television that marijuana should be legalized.

d. Angelo likes to smoke marijuana.

Exercise 2.4

Read each of the following passages. Indicate whether it contains examples of the kind of group pressure that encourages people to conform (peer pressure or appeal to popularity) or the type that urges people to think that one's own group is better than others. For each example of group pressure, specify the possible negative consequences. A couple of these are very difficult to classify.

* 1. Ortega is deeply religious, attending church regularly and trying to abide by church law and the Scriptures. He has never considered any other path. He believes that laws should be passed that forbid people to shop on Sunday and that designate Easter as a national holiday.

2. John goes to a prestigious college where many students use illegal drugs. Nearly everyone in John's frat house uses them. So far, he hasn't tried any, but his frat brothers frequently ask if he wants some. And he has noticed that he is rarely invited to any frat parties.

* 3. A northeast college has invited a famous writer to be a guest speaker in the campuswide distinguished speaker series. She is an accomplished poet and essayist. She is also a Marxist and favors more socialism in the United States. During her speech she is shouted down by a small group of conservative students and faculty.

4. Yang Lei is a conservative columnist for one of the best conservative journals in the country. But she yearns for greener pastures—namely, a regular column for a weekly news magazine. She gets her dream job, though the magazine does have liberal leanings. The first few columns she writes for the magazine are a shock to her friends. Politically they are middle-of-the-road or even suspiciously liberal.

5. Alex is a fourth-grade teacher at a suburban elementary school in Tennessee. He is liked by students and teachers alike, and he has superior teaching skills. He is also a homosexual. When a group of fundamentalist Christians learn that Alex is gay, they pressure the school board to fire him.

6. Sylvia writes a column for the university newspaper. In her last install-ment, she argues that in a time of national crisis, the U.S. justice depart-ment should have the power to arrest and detain literally anyone suspected of terrorism. Her arguments are well supported and pres-ented with a tone of tolerance for those who disagree with her. And most students do disagree—vehemently. Hundreds of letters to the editor arrive at the newspaper, each one denouncing Sylvia and calling her a fascist and a few names that could not be published. In Sylvia's next column, she apologizes for her statements, says that she made serious errors, and declares that her statements should be viewed as hypothetical.

* 7. Advertisement: When you make the best car in the world, everyone wants it. Audi XK2. A car in demand.

Exercise 2.5

Read each of the following scenarios. Indicate whether it contains examples of self-interested thinking or face-saving and, for each instance, specify the possible negative consequences.

* 1. Barbara thinks that she is a superior student with excellent writing and math skills. She frequently says so to her friends and sometimes ridicules other people's grades and test scores. She predicts that her SAT scores will be in the 2100s. When she finally takes the test, she's calm, alert, and eager to get a fantastic score. Afterwards she says that she feels great. Her scores come back in the 1200s. She explains that the test doesn't count be-cause it's obviously scored wrong and, besides, she's not a good test taker.

* 2. City assemblyman Jackson is in a position to cast the deciding vote on two proposals for the development of a new city park. Proposal 1 offers a parcel of land near the assemblyman's house, which affords him a beauti-ful view. Its drawbacks are that it costs twice as much as proposal 2 and cannot be easily accessed by most of the public. Proposal 2 suggests a parcel of land near the center of town. It is convenient to the public, has a more beautiful setting, and will raise property values in the area. Assemblyman Jackson says that the obvious best choice is proposal 1.

3. Antonio is a college student who responds predictably to his scores on tests. If the score is high, he remarks that he hardly studied at all and that his score ranks among the highest in the class. If the scores are low, he says that the instructor grades unfairly, that the test was flawed, and that he intends to protest his grade to the grade-review committee.

4. Sheila is a bright medical scientist. For years she has been working on a series of clinical studies that could establish her favorite medical hypothesis—that high doses of vitamin E can cure skin cancer. Each study in the series has added more evidence suggesting that the hypothesis is probably true. The last study in the series is crucial. It is a much larger

study than the others, and it will confirm or invalidate the usefulness of vitamin E for skin cancer. When the study is completed, she examines the data. Instead of confirming her hypothesis, the study suggests not only that her pet idea is unfounded but also that the doses of vitamin E used are toxic, causing terrible side effects in patients. She concludes, though, that the study results do not disconfirm her hypothesis but are merely inconclusive.

5. David and Max are in a heated debate about the theory of biological evolution. David rejects the theory in favor of creationism, which says that life on earth was created or facilitated by a supreme intelligence. Max rejects creationism in favor of evolution. David marshals an abundance of facts that seem to prove his case. In addition, he alleges that evolution is false because there are huge gaps in the fossil record suggesting that there has never been a smooth, tidy progression of species from earlier forms to later forms. Max has no answer for this fossil-record gap argument and looks exasperated. David is about to declare victory when Max suddenly begins to quote the research findings of reputable biologists showing that there really are no gaps. After the debate some of Max's friends quietly congratulate him for being clever enough to quote research findings that are fictitious.

 Field Problems

1. Recall a situation in your past in which your beliefs were skewed by self-interest, face-saving, or group pressure. Think about (1) how one or more of these three factors affected your beliefs, (2) what consequences (negative or positive) resulted from the event, and (3) what beliefs you might have acquired if you had used critical thinking. Take notes to help you remember the facts and be prepared to present your story in class.

2. Recall a situation in which the beliefs of someone you know were skewed by self-interest, face-saving, or group pressure to conform. Identify the three factors mentioned in the preceding question.

 Self-Assessment Quiz

Answers appear in "Answers to Self-Assessment Quizzes" (Appendix D).

1. According to the definition of critical thinking given in the text, what factors must be present for critical thinking to be realized?

2. From the standpoint of critical thinking, what event signals that we have allowed our bias in favor of our selves to go too far?

3. According to the text, how might selective attention affect our thinking when we are examining evidence for or against a claim?

4. According to the text, what is probably the most powerful group pressure of all?

5. According to the text, what is a worldview?

6. What kind of doubt is involved in the acquisition of knowledge?

7. According to the text, why is it important to look for opposing evidence when evaluating claims?

Read each of the following scenarios. Indicate whether it contains examples of self-interested thinking, face-saving, or both.

8. Edgar predicts that Horace Windblower will win the 2016 presidential election. In fact, he bets money on it and brags that he always predicts the winners. Windblower loses by the widest margin in U.S. history. At first, Edgar refuses to pay the bet but finally relents. He claims that the election was rigged from the very beginning.

9. Lois strongly believes in UFO abductions—people being kidnapped by space aliens. She says that she has absolute proof: a small piece of metal that she says is "not of this earth" and a cut on her shin that she says came from alien probes. However, several metallurgists in the area say that the piece of metal is ordinary aluminum. And her daughter reminds her that she got the cut on her shin when she ran into a desk drawer. Lois doesn't say anything else about her "evidence," and she asserts that the real proof is in the skies in the form of alien spacecraft.

10. One day Julie and Jill hear their instructor read a list of arguments for and against abortion. Half the arguments are pro, and half con. Julie is in on the pro side, Jill on the con side. Later when they discuss the abortion arguments, they recall the facts differently. Julie remembers that most of the arguments were for abortion rights. Jill remembers only the arguments against abortion and can't recall any pro arguments.

Specify whether the following passages are examples of face-saving, self-serving, or group-pressure thinking, or a combination of these.

11. The world would be better off if everything were run by Republicans.

12. Everyone believes in affirmative action. That fact alone ought to convince you to do the same.

13. Look, every student I know cheats on exams once in a while. So why not you? Why do you have to be such a Boy Scout?

14. People should do whatever makes them happy.

15. Congressman Hornblower: Anyone who doesn't believe in God shouldn't have a say in how this nation is run. I don't think that atheists should even be citizens.

16. Yes, I smoked marijuana in college, but I didn't inhale.

17. In the United States about 90 percent of the population has some kind of religious belief or denominational affiliation. In light of this, how can you say you're an unbeliever? If you're an unbeliever, you're un-American.

Read each of the following passages and indicate whether it is an example of the subjectivist fallacy or social relativism.

18. This may not be your truth, but it's my truth.

19. It's true for me that killing innocent civilians is morally wrong. It may not be true for you.

20. Chinese diplomat: My country cannot be judged by some universal standard. It must be judged by its own unique criteria and norms.

 ## Integrative Exercises

These exercises pertain to material in Chapters 1 and 2.

1. What is an argument?

2. What is a statement, or claim? (Give an example of a statement and an example of a sentence that is not a statement.)

3. In what ways can a group that you belong to affect your evaluation of a claim?

4. According to the text, what critical thinking principle should you invoke when you're trying to think clearly under group pressure?

For each of the following passages, indicate whether it contains an argument. For each argument, specify what the conclusion is and whether the passage contains an appeal to popularity or peer pressure.

5. You can never escape your past because your memory will always remind you of it.

6. Cloning any biological entity (including humans) is not worth the risk involved. Scientists have already reported some unexpected, dangerous side effects in the cloning of plants, and the clone of the famous Dolly the sheep has exhibited some cellular abnormalities.

7. Cloning is perfectly safe. It's only religious nuts and conservative politicians who are making a big fuss about it.

8. It will be a great day when the Pentagon has to have a bake sale to raise money for bombs and guns and education gets billions of dollars.

9. Capitalism is an immoral, oppressive system. That's just the way I was raised.

10. If you burn the American flag, you are guilty of treason. The flag is our country, and harming our flag is harming our country. Harming our country is treason.

11. Most Canadians believe that the prime minister is doing a great job. You can't argue with the people. Therefore, he is doing a great job.

12. All your friends think your views on abortion are ridiculous. That should be proof enough that you're wrong.

Read each of the following claims. Then select from the list any statements that, if true, would constitute good reasons for accepting the claim. Some statements may have no good reasons listed.

13. Corporation executives who cook the books should be imprisoned.

    a. Everyone in the business world believes that cooking the books should be punished by imprisonment.
    b. Polls show that most Americans are in favor of imprisoning executives who cook the books.
    c. In Russia it is common practice to imprison executives who cook the books.
    d. Imprisoning executives who cook the books is the only way to save American business from disaster and the only morally correct course of action.

14. Psychic predictions in tabloid newspapers are almost always accurate.

    a. This claim is true for me, even if it isn't true for you.
    b. It is impossible to know anything, so there is no way that anyone can legitimately claim that tabloid psychics are almost always right.
    c. Massive amounts of research into psychic phenomena prove that tabloid psychics are usually correct in their predictions.
    d. Believing that psychics cannot predict anything accurately is close-minded and petty. I refuse to be that way.

15. There is an afterlife. After you die, your essence lives on.

    a. I have to believe in an afterlife. The alternative is too terrible to contemplate.
    b. Over 80 percent of Americans believe in an afterlife.
    c. This society believes that there is an afterlife.
    d. On the radio I told two million people that there is an afterlife. So I have to believe in it. Otherwise, I'll look like a fool.

For each of the following passages, determine whether an argument is present and whether peer pressure or an appeal to popularity is being used. Some passages may not contain arguments, and some may not contain examples of group pressure.

16. "Barbara Ehrenreich wrote tongue-in-cheek in her June column, 'First, challenge anyone to find in the Bible . . . a single phrase or sentence forbidding the fondling or sodomizing of altar boys.' . . . In fact, the Bible does have at least a single phrase or sentence forbidding just such a thing. In 1 Corinthians 6:9 (New International Version), Paul has a list of those who will not inherit the Kingdom. Although far from settled, one of the words in the list suggests that men in a mentoring relationship with young boys are 'wicked' if they engage in sexual acts with the boys." [Letter to the editor, *The Progressive*, July 2002]

17. "[A] political scientist at the Massachusetts Institute of Technology says, 'I expect robust Internet voting by 2010.' He may be right, but would this be a good thing? Remote voting by way of the Internet would privatize one of our few remaining civic rituals. Balloting technology is not politically neutral. The history of elections administration in this country shows that different ways of voting allocate political values differently." [Letter to the editor, *New York Times*]

18. You must reject the proposition that violence in this country proves we need stronger gun-control laws. First, there is no documented connection between violence and the availability of guns. Second, if you accept the proposition, you will be the laughingstock of all of your fellow conservatives.

19. To teens, getting fake IDs to sneak into clubs and taverns may seem like a good idea, but it's not. I think every teenager who tries it should be arrested.

20. Every thinking person in this country would disagree with you.

 Writing Assignments

1. Read Essay 3 ("A Feminist Defense of Pornography") in Appendix B and write a summary of the essay in 75 to 100 words, specifying the premises, conclusion, and supporting evidence.

2. Study the argument presented in Essay 4 ("A Defense of Homosexuality"). Write a three-page assessment of the argument, touching on the truth of the premises and conclusion and the logic of the argument as a whole.

3. Select an issue from the following list and write a three-page paper defending a statement pertaining to the issue. Follow the procedure discussed in Appendix E for identifying a thesis and an appropriate argument to defend it.

   - Are the media biased?
   - Should a single corporation be allowed to own as many media outlets (newspapers, radio and TV stations, publishers, etc.) as it wants?
   - Should the U.S. government be allowed to arrest and indefinitely imprison without trial any American citizen who is suspected of terrorism?
   - Should racial profiling be used to do security screening of airline passengers?

Making Sense of
Arguments

ARGUMENT BASICS

- Distinguish between deductive and inductive arguments.
- Understand the terms *valid*, *invalid*, and *sound*.
- Understand the terms *strong*, *weak*, and *cogent*.

JUDGING ARGUMENTS

- Be able to follow the four-step procedure for determining whether an argument is deductive or inductive, good or bad.
- Be familiar with indicator words that suggest that an argument is deductive or inductive.

FINDING MISSING PARTS

- Know how to use the three-step procedure for uncovering implicit premises.

ARGUMENT PATTERNS

- Memorize and be able to recognize the argument patterns known as *modus ponens*, *modus tollens*, *hypothetical syllogism*, *denying the antecedent*, *affirming the consequent*, and *disjunctive syllogism*.
- Be able to use the counterexample method for determining if a deductive argument is valid or invalid.

DIAGRAMMING ARGUMENTS

- Understand the definition of *dependent* and *independent premises*.
- Be able to follow the five-step procedure to diagram arguments, both simple and complex ones, including those embedded in extraneous material.

ASSESSING LONG ARGUMENTS

- Understand the challenges involved in assessing long arguments.
- Be able to follow the four-step procedure for diagramming long arguments.

I N THIS CHAPTER WE RESUME OUR DISCUSSION OF ARGUMENTS BEGUN IN CHAPTER 1, delve deeper into the dynamics and structure of different argument types, and get a lot more practice in identifying and critiquing simple (and not so simple) arguments in their "natural habitat."

Remember, in Chapter 1 we defined an argument as a group of statements in which some of them (the premises) are intended to support another of them (the conclusion). An essential skill is the ability to identify arguments in real-life contexts and to distinguish them from nonarguments. To recognize an argument, you must be able to identify the premises and the conclusion. Indicator words such as *because* and *since* often signal the presence of premises, and words such as *therefore* and *thus* can point to a conclusion.

Argument Basics

The point of *devising* an argument is to try to show that a statement, or claim, is worthy of acceptance. The point of *evaluating* an argument is to see whether this task has been successful—whether the argument shows that the statement (the conclusion) really is worthy of acceptance. When the argument shows that the statement is worthy of acceptance, we say that the argument is *good*. When the argument fails to show that the statement is worthy of acceptance, we say that the argument is *bad*. There are different ways, however, that an argument can be good or bad. There are different ways because there are different types of arguments.

Arguments come in two forms—**deductive** and **inductive.** A deductive argument is intended to provide logically *conclusive* support for its conclusion. An inductive argument is intended to provide *probable*—not conclusive—support for its conclusion.

A deductive argument that succeeds in providing such decisive logical support is said to be **valid;** a deductive argument that fails to provide such support is said to be **invalid.** A deductively valid argument is such that if its premises are true, its conclusion *must* be true. That is, if the premises are true, there is *no way* that the conclusion can be false. In logic, *valid* is not a synonym for true. A deductively valid argument simply has the kind of logical structure that *guarantees* the truth of the conclusion *if* the premises are true. "Logical structure" refers not to the content of an argument but to its construction, the way the premises and conclusion fit together. Because of the guarantee of truth in the conclusion, deductively valid arguments are said to be **truth-preserving.**

Here's a simple deductively valid argument:

All dogs have fleas.
Bowser is a dog.
So Bowser has fleas.

And here's a golden oldie.

All men are mortal.
Socrates is a man.
Therefore, Socrates is mortal.

FURTHER THOUGHT

Persuading or Reasoning?

A fundamental distinction in critical thinking is this: Persuading someone to agree with you is not the same thing as presenting them with a good argument. You can influence people's opinions by using words to appeal to their ego, gullibility, bigotry, greed, anger, prejudice, and more. You just have to use emotional language, psychological ploys, semantic or syntactic tricks, and outright lies. But having done so, you would not have demonstrated that *any* belief is true or warranted. You would not have shown that a claim is *worthy of acceptance*. This latter task is a matter of logic and argument. The machinations of raw persuasion are not.

Certainly the presentation of a good argument (in the critical thinking sense) can

Great persuaders aren't necessarily great critical thinkers.

sometimes be psychologically compelling. And there are times when persuasion through psychological or emotional appeals is appropriate, even necessary. You just have to keep these two functions straight in your mind.

And one in regular paragraph form:

> [Premise] If abortion is the taking of a human life, then it's murder.
> [Premise] It is the taking of a human life. [Conclusion] So it necessarily follows that abortion is murder.

In each of these arguments, if the premises are true, the conclusion must be absolutely, positively true. It is impossible for the premises to be true and the conclusions false. The conclusion *logically follows* from the premises. And the order of the premises makes no difference.

A deductively *invalid* version of these arguments might look like this:

> All dogs are mammals.
> All cows are mammals.
> Therefore, all dogs are cows.

> If Socrates has horns, he is mortal.
> Socrates is mortal.
> Therefore, Socrates has horns.

"In the midst of chaos, Larry is the clear voice of reason. Get him the hell out of here."

In each of these, the conclusion does *not* logically follow from the premises. Each is an attempt at a deductively valid argument, but the attempt fails. And, again, this would be the case regardless of the order of the premises.

An inductive argument that succeeds in providing probable—but not conclusive—logical support for its conclusion is said to be **strong.** An inductive argument that fails to provide such support is said to be **weak.** An inductively strong argument is such that if its premises are true, its conclusion is *probably* or *likely* to be true. The structure of an inductively strong argument cannot guarantee that the conclusion is true if the premises are true—but the conclusion can be rendered probable and worthy of acceptance. (Here again, the structure and content of an argument are distinct elements.) Because the truth of the conclusion cannot be guaranteed by the truth of the premises, inductive arguments are not truth-preserving.

Let's turn our first two deductively valid arguments into inductively strong arguments:

Most dogs have fleas.
Therefore, Bowser, my dog, probably has fleas.

Ninety-eight percent of
    humans are mortal.
Socrates is human.
Therefore, Socrates is likely to be mortal.

"The most perfidious way of harming a cause consists of defending it deliberately with faulty arguments."

—Friedrich Nietzsche

Notice that in the first argument, it's entirely possible for the premise to be true and the conclusion false. After all, if only *most* dogs have fleas, there is no guarantee that Bowser has fleas. Yet the premise, if true, makes the conclusion probably true. Likewise, in the second argument it is possible that even if 98 percent of humans are mortal and Socrates is human, the conclusion that Socrates is mortal could be false. But the premises, if true, make it likely that the conclusion is true.

Here are three more inductive arguments about some everyday concerns:

Almost every computer I've purchased at an online store has been a dud.
Therefore, the next computer I purchase at the same online store will likely be a dud.

Maria's car broke down yesterday.
When it broke down, it made the same noise and spewed the same stinky exhaust that it always does when it breaks down.
Maria's car breaks down a lot.
Her mechanic, who does excellent work, always says the same thing: The problem is the carburetor.
Therefore, Maria's car trouble yesterday was probably due to a carburetor problem.

Nine toddlers out of the thirty-two at the day care center have a cold. Therefore, probably every child there has a cold.

Logical validity or logical strength is an essential characteristic of good arguments. But there is more to good arguments than having the proper structure. Good arguments also have *true premises*. A good argument is one that has the proper structure—*and* true premises. Take a look at this argument:

All pigs can fly.
Vaughn is a pig.
Therefore, Vaughn can fly.

The premises of this argument are false—but the conclusion follows logically from those premises. It's a deductively valid argument with all the parts in the right place—even though the premises are false. But it is not a good argument. A good argument must have true premises, and this argument doesn't. A deductively valid argument that has true premises is said to be **sound.** A sound argument is a good argument, which gives you good reasons for accepting its conclusion.

Note, however, that deductively valid arguments can have true or false premises and true or false conclusions. Specifically, deductively valid arguments can have false premises and a false conclusion, false premises and a true conclusion, and true premises and a true conclusion. A valid argument, though, cannot have true premises and a false conclusion—that's impossible. See for yourself:

False Premises, False Conclusion
All dogs have flippers.
All cats are dogs.
Therefore, all cats have flippers.

False Premises, True Conclusion
Bowser is a cat.

All cats are mammals.
Therefore, Bowser is a mammal.

True Premises, True Conclusion
Bowser is a dog.
All dogs are mammals.
Therefore, Bowser is a mammal.

 FURTHER THOUGHT

Arguments About Necessary and Sufficient Conditions

Another useful kind of argument is built on the concepts of *necessary* and *sufficient conditions*. In Chapter 8 we discuss these ideas in connection with causal arguments (inductive arguments whose conclusions contain claims about the causes of things). But here we just need to understand that the concepts can be important in an even broader range of contexts.

We sometimes speak of the conditions (or features) that a thing *must* have in order to be that thing. These are called necessary conditions. For example, being a bird is a necessary condition for being an eagle; the presence of oxygen is a necessary condition for combustion to occur; and being male is a necessary condition for being an uncle. An eagle is an eagle only if it is a bird; combustion can occur only if oxygen is present; and someone can be an uncle only if he is male. A thing often has more than one necessary condition. The necessary conditions for combustion to occur are oxygen, heat, and fuel. If even one of these conditions is absent, combustion will not occur.

Often we are also interested in the conditions that *guarantee* that something exists or is a certain kind of thing. These are known as sufficient conditions. Being a human male with a niece or nephew is a sufficient condition for being an uncle. The sufficient condition for combustion is the combination of all the necessary conditions.

Conditions can also be *both* necessary and sufficient. Fuel being heated to a certain temperature in the presence of oxygen is both a necessary and sufficient condition for combustion.

Now suppose someone argues for the conclusion that no one ever becomes a criminal unless he or she is raised in a single-parent home. That is, she asserts that the necessary and sufficient condition for becoming a criminal is to have been raised in a household headed by just one parent. To refute this claim, all you have to do is show that this condition is *not* necessary and sufficient for becoming a criminal. You just have to produce one example of someone who is a criminal but did not come from a household headed by just one parent. And, of course, such examples abound and can be incorporated into your counterargument.

A good inductive argument must also have true premises. For example:

Scientific studies show that 99 percent of dogs have three eyes.
So it's likely that the next dog I see will have three eyes.

This is an inductively strong argument, but it's not a good argument because its premise is false. When inductively strong arguments have true premises, they are said to be **cogent**. Good inductive arguments are cogent. Bad inductive arguments are not cogent.

You may have noticed another important difference between deductive and inductive arguments. The kind of support that a deductive argument can give a conclusion is *absolute*. Either the conclusion is shown to be true, or it is not. There is no sliding scale of truth or falsity. The support that an inductive argument can provide a conclusion, however, can vary from weak to extremely strong.

Both deductive and inductive arguments can be manipulated in various ways to yield new insights. For example, let's say that you have formulated a valid deductive argument, and you know that the conclusion is false. From these facts you can infer that at least one of the premises is false. Using this tack, you can demonstrate that a premise is false because in a valid argument it leads to an absurd conclusion. Or let's say that you've fashioned a valid argument, and you know that your premises are true. Then you can infer that the conclusion must be true—even if it's contrary to your expectations. Or maybe you put forth a strong inductive argument, and you know that the premises are questionable. Then you know that the conclusion also can't be trusted.

If you don't already have a sense of the wide-ranging usefulness of deductive and inductive arguments, the coming pages will make the point clear. You will find abundant evidence that the utility of both types of arguments is

---

 REVIEW NOTES

Deductive and Inductive Arguments

- A deductive argument is intended to provide conclusive support for its conclusion.
- A deductive argument that succeeds in providing conclusive support for its conclusion is said to be valid. A valid argument is such that if its premises are true, its conclusion must be true.
- A deductively valid argument with true premises is said to be sound.
- An inductive argument is intended to provide probable support for its conclusion.
- An inductive argument that succeeds in providing probable support for its conclusion is said to be strong. A strong argument is such that if its premises are true, its conclusion is probably true.
- An inductively strong argument with true premises is said to be cogent.

universal. They apply everywhere, work everywhere, and instruct everywhere—in everyday and professional life (Chapters 4–8), in scientific and extraordinary realms (Chapters 9–10), and in moral and philosophical explorations (Chapter 11).

 EXERCISE

Exercise 3.1

1. What is a deductive argument?
2. What is an inductive argument?
3. Are inductive arguments truth-preserving? Why or why not?
* 4. The terms *valid* and *invalid* apply to what types of arguments?
5. What kind of guarantee does a deductive argument provide when it is valid?
6. Can an inductive argument guarantee the truth of the conclusion if the premises are true? Why or why not?
7. What is the difference between an inductively strong argument and an inductively weak one?
* 8. What is the term for valid arguments that have true premises?
9. What is the term for strong arguments that have true premises?
10. Can a valid argument have false premises and a false conclusion? False premises and a true conclusion?
11. What logical conclusion can you draw about an argument that is valid but has a false conclusion?
* 12. Is it possible for a valid argument to have true premises and a false conclusion?
13. In what way are conclusions of deductive arguments absolute?

Judging Arguments

When it comes to deductive and inductive arguments, the most important skills you can acquire are being able to identify them and determining whether they are good or bad. Much of the rest of this text is devoted to helping you become proficient in these skills. This chapter will serve as your first lesson and give you a chance to practice what you learn.

So the obvious questions here are: When you come face to face with an argument to evaluate, (1) how can you tell whether it's deductive or inductive, and (2) how can you determine whether it gives you good reasons for accepting the conclusion (whether it's sound or cogent)? The following is a suggested four-step procedure for answering these questions. We will elaborate on it here and in later chapters.

Step 1. Find the argument's conclusion and then its premises. Use the techniques you learned in Chapter 1. You'll have plenty of chances to hone this skill in upcoming chapters.

DILBERT: © Scott Adams/Dist. By United Feature Syndicate, Inc.

Step 2. Ask: Is it the case that if the premises are true the conclusion *must* be true? If the answer is yes, treat the argument as *deductive,* for it is very likely meant to offer conclusive support for its conclusion. The argument, then, is deductively valid, and you should check to see if it's sound. If the answer is no, proceed to the next step.

Step 3. Ask: Is it the case that if the premises are true, its conclusion is *probably* true? If the answer is yes, treat the argument as *inductive,* for it is very likely meant to offer probable support for its conclusion. The argument, then, is inductively strong, and you should check to see if it's cogent. If the answer is no, proceed to the next step.

Step 4. Ask: Is the argument intended to offer conclusive or probable support for its conclusion but *fails* to do so? If you reach this step, you will have already eliminated two possibilities: a valid argument and a strong one. The remaining options are an invalid argument or a weak one. So here you must discover what type of (failed) argument is intended. These two guidelines can help you do that:

> GUIDELINE 1: Generally if an argument looks deductive or inductive because of its form, assume that it is intended to be so.

Bad arguments may sometimes look like good arguments because the arrangement of their premises and conclusion—their form—is similar to that found in reliable arguments. (You saw some of these reliable argument forms in the argument examples presented earlier in this chapter.) Such argument forms are an indication of what kind of argument is intended, and that fact gives you some guidance on determining argument type.

> GUIDELINE 2: Generally if an argument looks deductive or inductive because of indicator words (and its form yields no clues), assume that it is intended to be so.

"He who strikes the first blow admits he's lost the argument."
—Chinese Proverb

Arguments are often accompanied by words or phrases that identify them as deductive or inductive. Terms that signal a deductive argument include "It necessarily follows that," "it logically follows that," "absolutely," "necessarily," and

NEWSMAKERS

Inconsistent to a Fault

In case you didn't know already, because of strong bias, public figures often make pronouncements that are logically inconsistent (as well as moronic, offensive, and mystifying). Worse, the rest of the world may swallow the contradictory statements without noticing anything amiss. For example:

- If a TV pundit finds that his favorite politician has been having an extra-marital affair, he declares the episode a "personal matter" that should not be publicly discussed. But if a politician he loathes is guilty of the same indiscretion, he declares it an outrage and can't stop talking about it on the air.
- In support of a vice presidential candidate whose only executive experience is a term as mayor of a small town, a radio talk show host insists that such experience is perfect preparation for being vice president. But she asserts that another vice presidential candidate whom she opposes and who has almost identical credentials is unsuitable for the office—because he doesn't have enough executive experience.
- Commentators criticize a woman televangelist for making sexist remarks about another woman—but they use the same sexist language to deride the televangelist.

Such contradictions abound in the public square and go largely unnoticed by the media. A few astute commentators, though, are happy to point out such addled thinking.

No matter who is guilty of it, this brand of inconsistency shows that bias is hard at work, undercutting clear thinking. And when we inconsistently apply a rule or standard of judgment, the rule or standard itself is called into question.

If we take an extramarital affair or blatant sexism seriously only when it suits our rhetorical aims, do we really believe these issues are important?

How can we detect this problem in ourselves? We can manage it only through careful reflection on the logic of what we say. One trick is what can be called the "turned tables" test. If you criticize someone or something you dislike for violating some standard, ask yourself: Would I judge someone or something I like in the same way for the same reasons? Logic demands that you treat equals equally.

Try this: Think of the strongest criticism you could make about the behavior of the political leader you respect the least. Now suppose your favorite political leader is guilty of the same behavior. Would you be willing to criticize him or her just as strongly?

"certainly." Words signaling an inductive argument include "likely," "probably," "chances are," "odds are," and "it is plausible that." Such indicator words, though, are not foolproof clues to argument type because they are sometimes used in misleading ways. For example, someone might end an inductively strong argument with a conclusion prefaced with "it necessarily follows that," suggesting that the argument is deductively valid. But argument-type indicators may still be useful, especially when the argument form yields no clues (when guideline 1 doesn't apply).

In step 4, once you discover which kind of argument is intended, you will know that it is either invalid or weak (because in steps 2 and 3 we eliminated the possibility of a valid or strong argument). The only remaining task is to determine whether the premises are true.[1]

Let's try out the four-step procedure on a few arguments. Consider this one:

[Premise] Unless we do something about the massive AIDS epidemic in Africa, the whole continent will be decimated within six months. [Premise] Unfortunately we won't do anything about the AIDS epidemic in Africa. [Conclusion] It necessarily follows that the whole of Africa will be decimated within six months.

Step 1 is already done for us; the premises and conclusion are clearly labeled. In step 2, we must ask, "Is it the case that if the premises are true, the conclusion must be true?" The answer is yes: If it's true that the AIDS epidemic in Africa will decimate the population in six months unless "we do something," and it's true that "we won't do anything," then the conclusion that Africa will be decimated in six months *must* be true. So this argument is deductively valid. To determine if it's sound, we would need to check to see if the premises are true. In this case, the first premise is false because, under current conditions, it would take longer than six months for the epidemic to decimate the whole continent. The other premise ("we won't do anything") is at least dubious since we can't predict the future. So what we have here is a deductively valid argument that's unsound—a bad argument.

Now let's analyze this one:

[Premise] This week, under pressure from the American Civil Liberties Union, the school board rescinded its policy of allowing school-sponsored public prayers at football games. [Premise] All the school board members agreed with the policy change. [Premise] And a memo from the board was circulated to all students, teachers, and coaches declaring that there will be no more public prayers at football games. [Conclusion] Let's face it, the days of public prayers at our school football games are over.

From step 2 we can see that even if this argument's three premises are all true, the conclusion can still be false. After all, even if everything described in the premises happens, there still could be a public prayer at a football game (perhaps because of some mistake or an act of protest on the part of school-prayer advocates). So the argument can't be deductively valid. But if we go through step 3, we can see that if all the premises are true, the conclusion is likely to be true, making the argument inductively strong. If the premises *are* true, the argument would be cogent.

See what you think of this one:

[Premise] If you act like Bart Simpson, you will be respected by all your classmates. [Premise] But you don't act like Bart Simpson. [Conclusion] It follows that you will not be respected by all of your classmates.

This argument flunks the tests in steps 2 and 3: It is not deductively valid, and it is not inductively strong. But it does resemble a deductive argument in two ways. First, it displays a pattern of reasoning that can, at first glance, seem deductive. Actually, it uses an argument pattern that is always deductively *invalid* (called denying the antecedent, an argument form we will look at shortly). This alone should be evidence enough that the argument is indeed deductive but invalid. But it also contains an argument indicator phrase ("it follows that") that suggests an attempt at a deductive form.

You'll get a lot more exposure to argument forms and indicator words in the rest of this chapter (and the rest of this text). Ultimately, practice in distinguishing different types of arguments and their relative worth is the only way to gain proficiency (and confidence!) in making these judgments.

 FURTHER THOUGHT

When Reasoning Wrecks . . . Leave the Scene of the Accident

Sometimes arguments go off into a ditch and you don't know why. Here's an example of a wrecked argument from the great American satirical writer Ambrose Bierce (1842–1914?). What's wrong here?

Sixty men can do a piece of work sixty times as quickly as one man.
One man can dig a posthole in sixty seconds.
Therefore, sixty men can dig a posthole in one second.

So far we've spent most of our time assessing the logical structure of arguments—that is, whether they are valid/invalid or strong/weak. We haven't focused as much attention on evaluating the truth of premises because that's a big issue best considered separately—which is what we do in Part 2 of this book.

 EXERCISES

Exercise 3.2

For each of the following arguments, follow the four-step procedure to determine whether it is deductive or inductive, valid or invalid, and strong or weak. Indicate the results of applying each step.

EXAMPLE 1

Colonel Mustard did not commit the murder. Someone who had committed the murder would have dirt on his shoes and blood on his hands. Colonel Mustard has neither.

> Step 1: Conclusion: Colonel Mustard did not commit the murder. Premises: Someone who had committed the murder would have dirt on his shoes and blood on his hands. Colonel Mustard has neither.
>
> Step 2: Deductively valid.
>
> Step 3: Does not apply.
>
> Step 4: Does not apply.

EXAMPLE 2

Most people who smoke pot are irresponsible and forgetful. Looks like you smoke pot all the time. Ergo, you're irresponsible and forgetful. Can you remember that?

> Step 1: Conclusion: Ergo, you're irresponsible and forgetful. Premises: Most people who smoke pot are irresponsible and forgetful. Looks like you smoke pot all the time.
>
> Step 2: Not deductively valid.
>
> Step 3: Inductively strong.
>
> Step 4: Does not apply.

1. Either Jack is lying or he is not. If his ears turn red, he's lying. If they don't turn red, he's telling the truth. His ears are red. Jack is lying.

* 2. Ethel graduated from Yale. If she graduated from Yale, she probably has a superior intellect. She has a superior intellect.

3. If you go to that party, you're completely nuts. You're going to the party. It necessarily follows that you're nuts.

4. "Good sense is of all things in the world the most equally distributed, for everybody thinks himself so abundantly provided with it, that even those most difficult to please in all other matters do not commonly desire more of it than they already possess." [René Descartes, *A Discourse on Method*]

5. All philosophers are absent-minded. All philosophers are teachers. It necessarily follows that all absent-minded people are teachers.

* 6. Every musician has had special training, and everyone with special training has a college degree. Thus, every musician has a college degree.

7. People with high IQs also have psychic abilities. People with high SAT scores—which are comparable to high IQ scores—also probably have psychic abilities.

8. If Elvis Presley's name is spelled wrong on his tombstone, there must be some kind of conspiracy surrounding the death of the King. His name is spelled wrong. Therefore, there's a conspiracy.

* 9. Some actors sing, and some play a musical instrument. So some actors who sing also play a musical instrument.

10. Anyone who is not a bigot will agree that Chris is a good fellow. Some people in this neighborhood think that he's anything but a good fellow. Some people in this neighborhood are bigots.

11. "In the actual living of life there is no logic, for life is superior to logic." [Daisetz Teitaro Suzuki, *Essays in Zen Buddhism*]

12. A vase was found broken on the floor; some money had been taken out of the safe; and there were strange scratches on the wall. It therefore follows that someone obviously burglarized the place.

13. All the evidence in this trial suggests that Lizzy Borden is guilty of murder. Let's face it: She's probably guilty.

14. If everything was all right, there would be no blood on the floor. Of course, there is plenty of blood on the floor. Therefore, everything is not all right.

* 15. If minds are identical to brains—that is, if one's mind is nothing but a brain—androids could never have minds because they wouldn't have brains. Clearly, a mind is nothing but a brain, so it's impossible for androids to have minds.

16. "From infancy, almost, the average girl is told that marriage is her ultimate goal; therefore her training and education must be directed towards that end." [Emma Goldman, "Marriage and Love"]

17. If you have scratches on your body that you can't account for, and you feel that you have been visited by space aliens, then you really have been visited by space aliens. You have such scratches, and you have experienced such feelings. Doubtless you have been visited by space aliens.

18. If bombs are falling on London, war has started. The bombs are falling now. War has begun.

Exercise 3.3

For each of the following arguments, indicate whether it is valid or invalid, strong or weak.

1. Alice says that nothing is sacred. So intolerance toward other religions is okay.

2. Social welfare is by definition a handout to people who have not worked for it. But giving people money that they have not earned through labor is not helping anyone. It follows then that social welfare does not help anyone.

* 3. If CNN reports that war has started in Iraq, then war has started in Iraq. CNN has reported exactly that. War must have started.

4. If $r = 12$, then $s = 8$; $r = 12$; therefore, $s = 8$.

5. Any sitcom that tries to imitate *The Big Bang Theory* is probably a piece of trash. All of this season's sitcoms try to ape *Big Bang*. They've gotta be trash.

6. "Poetry is finer and more philosophical than history; for poetry expresses the universal and history only the particular." [Aristotle, *Poetics*]

7. Either you're lying or you're not telling the whole story. You're obviously not lying, so you're just relating part of the story.

* 8. Either your thinking is logical or it is emotional. It's obviously not logical. It's emotional.

9. My friends say that asteroids are not real. I've never found a single asteroid or a piece of one. People claim to have found some, but I don't believe them. There are no such things as asteroids.

10. A Gallup poll says that 80 percent of Americans believe in the existence of heaven, but only 40 percent say they believe in hell. People are just too willing to engage in wishful thinking.

11. Many young black men have been shot dead by white police officers. Black people have often been harassed by white policemen. From these facts we can conclude that the recent tragic shooting in Chicago of a black teen by a white police officer was a case of first-degree murder.

12. "We say that a person behaves in a given way because he possesses a philosophy, but we infer the philosophy from the behavior and therefore cannot use it in any satisfactory way as an explanation, at least until it is in turn explained." [B. F. Skinner, *Beyond Freedom and Dignity*]

13. You flunked the last three tests. You didn't show up for the last eight classes. And you haven't written any of the essays. Looks like you don't know the material.

* 14. Bachelors are unmarried. George is a bachelor. He has never taken a wife.

15. Bachelors are unmarried, and George acts like he's not married. He's a bachelor for sure.

16. If Alicia is alone on a trip, she will be afraid. She's alone on the latest trip. She is afraid.

17. If the universe had a beginning, then it was caused to begin. We know that the universe did have a beginning in the form of the Big Bang. So it was

caused to come into existence. If it was caused to come into existence, that cause must have been God. God caused the universe to come into existence.

* 18. If the United States is willing to wage war in the Middle East, it can only be because it wants the oil supplies in the region. Obviously the United States is willing to go to war there. The United States wants that oil.

19. "Someone must have been telling lies about Joseph K., for without having done anything wrong he was arrested one fine morning." [Franz Kafka, *The Trial*]

20. Anyone willing to take the lives of innocent people for a cause is a terrorist. Many Christians, Jews, and Muslims have taken innocent lives in the name of their religious cause. Many Christians, Jews, and Muslims have been terrorists.

21. If he comes back, it's probably because he wants money. There he is. He wants money.

22. If you're eighteen, you're eligible to vote. But you're only seventeen. You're not eligible to vote.

* 23. I like geometry. My geometry teacher likes me. Therefore I will pass my geometry course with flying colors.

Finding Missing Parts

Sometimes arguments not only are faulty but also have a few pieces missing. Premises (and sometimes even conclusions)—material needed to make the argument work—are often left unstated. These implicit premises, or assumptions, are essential to the argument. Of course, certain assumptions are frequently left unsaid for good reason: They are obvious and understood by all parties to the argument, and boredom would set in fast if you actually tried to mention them all. If you wish to prove that "Socrates is mortal," you normally wouldn't need to explain what *mortal* means and that the name Socrates does not refer to a type of garden tool. But many arguments do have unstated premises that are not only necessary to the chain of reasoning but also must be made explicit to fully evaluate the arguments.

For instance:

The easy availability of assault rifles in the United States has increased the risk of death and injury for society as a whole. Therefore, assault rifles should be banned.

Notice that there is a kind of disconnect between the premise and the conclusion. The conclusion follows from the premise *only* if we assume an additional premise, perhaps something like this: "Anything that increases the risk of death and injury for society as a whole should be banned." With this additional premise, the argument becomes:

The easy availability of assault rifles in the United States has increased the risk of death and injury for society as a whole. Anything that increases the risk of death and injury for society as a whole should be banned. Therefore, assault rifles should be banned.

FURTHER THOUGHT

Reasoning and the Law

Though arguments and critical thinking are used (and abused) everywhere, their presence is especially obvious in law. Arguments are essential parts of legal reasoning at several levels—in the making of laws, in criminal and civil proceedings,  in judicial rulings, in the weighing of evidence, and in the application of legal precedent.

- **Legislation.** The making of new laws usually involves considerable debate about the wisdom of the legislation, and reasoned argument is the presumed medium of the deliberations. For example:

  Suppose . . . that there is currently no law requiring children to wear bicycle helmets. Assume moreover that the American Medical Association (AMA), acting on the belief that we ought to prevent unnecessary injuries and/or deaths of children, convinces the legislature to hold hearings to consider the merits of adopting such a law. What would be the major content of such hearings? Obviously, *arguments* regarding the pros and cons of bicycle helmet legislation. The AMA might testify, for example, that we can save children from serious injury and even death by implementing such a law; some parents may share the concerns of the AMA, while other parents might argue that this constitutes an illegitimate intrusion by the government into what are private family matters; legal authorities might point out the difficulty they would face in enforcing such a law . . . and some might argue that the policy would place an unfair burden on the poor who cannot afford high-priced helmets.[2]

- **Legal proceedings.** In civil matters, litigation takes the form of opposing parties arguing the merits of their side. The point of the arguments is to show that a litigant did (or did not) legally transgress in some way. In criminal cases, prosecutors argue that the defendant did in fact commit a crime, marshalling evidence and testimony to support that conclusion. Defending attorneys argue against the conclusion, trying to cast doubt on the supporting reasons or showing why the conclusion must be false. The arguments are mainly inductive, often including the inductive pattern known as inference to the best explanation (see Chapter 9). Using this latter kind of argument, the prosecutor contends that the best explanation of the evidence is that the defendant committed the crime; the defense may then maintain that there is a better explanation (that the defendant was framed, was mistaken for someone else, etc.).

- **Judicial rulings.** The thinking involved in judicial decisions is complex, entailing judgments about the meaning and application of statutes, assessments of the relevance and implications of cases, and reasoning of both the deductive and inductive kind. The overarching pattern is that of argument: the conclusion is the final judicial judgment, and the premises (the reasons behind the judgment) generally refer to statutes, previous cases, or other sources of judicial authority. A common argument pattern is *analogical induction*, or argument by analogy (see Chapter 8). A judge first decides that the present case is relevantly similar (analogous) to a previously decided case; then she reasons that since the earlier case was treated in a particular fashion, the present case should be treated in a similar way. In Anglo-American law, decisions in previous cases (legal precedents) carry considerable judicial weight, and arguments by analogy reflect this fact.

For further discussion of legal reasoning, see Chapter 11.

Now that all the premises are spelled out, you can evaluate the *full* argument just as you would any other. Not only that, but you can see that the unstated premise is questionable, which is the case with many implicit premises. Not everyone would agree that anything raising the risk of death or injury should be banned, for if that were the case we would have to outlaw automobiles, airplanes, most prescription drugs, most occupations, and who knows how many kitchen appliances! Many unstated premises are like this one: They're controversial and therefore should not be left unexamined.

Here's another one:

Anyone who craves political power cannot be trusted to serve the public interest. Senator Blowhard can't be trusted to serve the public interest.

As stated, this argument seems like a rush to judgment because the first premise concerns *anyone* who craves power, and suddenly Senator Blowhard is denounced as untrustworthy. Something's missing. What we need is another premise connecting the first premise to the conclusion: "Senator Blowhard craves political power." Now let's plug the implicit premise into the argument:

Anyone who craves political power cannot be trusted to serve the public interest. Senator Blowhard craves political power. He can't be trusted to serve the public interest.

I've never met anyone like you. You're just wrong about everything.

www.CartoonStock.com

"The difficult part in an argument is not to defend one's opinion, but rather to know it."
—André Maurois

So exactly when should we try to ferret out an unstated premise? The obvious answer is that we should do so when there appears to be something essential missing—an implied, logical link between premises and conclusion that is not a commonsense, generally accepted assumption. Such implicit premises should never be taken for granted because, among other things, they are often deliberately hidden or downplayed to make the argument seem stronger.

Be aware, though, that many times the problem with an argument is not unstated premises, but invalid or weak structure. Consider this:

> If Tariq works harder, he will pass his calculus course. But he will not work harder, so he will not pass calculus.

This argument is invalid; the conclusion does not follow from the premises. Like most invalid arguments, it can't be salvaged without altering it beyond what is clearly implied. It's just a bad argument. The same goes for weak arguments. They usually can't be fixed up without adding or changing premises gratuitously. Remember, the point of articulating unstated premises is to make explicit what is already implicit. Your job as a critical thinker is *not* to make bad arguments good; that task falls to the one who puts forth the argument in the first place.

To make sure that your investigation of implicit premises is thorough and reasonable, work through the following three-step process.[3]

Step 1. Search for a credible premise that would make the argument *valid,* one that would furnish the needed link between premise (or premises) and conclusion. Choose the supplied premise that

a. is most plausible

and

b. fits best with the author's intent.

The first stipulation (a) means that you should look for premises that are either true or, at least, not obviously false. The second stipulation (b) means that premises should fit—that is, at least not conflict—with what seems to be the author's point or purpose (which, of course, is often difficult to discern). If the premise you supply is plausible and fitting (with author's intent), use it to fill out the argument. If your supplied premise is either not plausible or not fitting, go to step 2.

Step 2. Search for a credible premise that would make the argument as *strong* as possible. Choose the supplied premise that fulfills stipulations a and b. If the premise you supply is plausible and fitting, use it to fill out the argument. If your supplied premise is either not plausible or not fitting, consider the argument beyond repair and reject it.

Step 3. Evaluate the reconstituted argument. If you're able to identify a credible implicit premise that makes the argument either valid or strong, assess this revised version of the argument, paying particular attention to the plausibility of the other premise or premises.

Now let's apply this procedure to a few arguments:

> If the Fed lowers interest rates one more time, there will be a deep recession. I'm telling you there's going to be a deep recession.

The first step is to see if there's a credible premise that would make the argument valid. We can see right away that one premise will do the trick: "The Fed has lowered interest rates again." Adding it to the argument will supply the needed link between the existing premise and the conclusion. We also can see that our new premise is plausible (the Fed has lowered interest rates again) and seems to fit with the point of the argument (to prove that there will be a recession). Our resulting argument, though, is probably not a good one because the premise about the effect of the Fed's lowering interest rates is dubious.

Now examine this one:

> Security officer Jones lied on her employment application about whether she had a criminal record. Security officer Jones will do a lousy job of screening passengers for weapons.

The sentence "Security officer Jones will do a lousy job of screening passengers for weapons" is the conclusion here. To try to make this argument valid, we would need a premise like "Any security officer at La Guardia airport who has lied on his or her employment application about having a criminal record will do a lousy job of screening passengers for weapons." This premise fits the point of the argument, but it isn't plausible. Surely it cannot be the case that *any* security officer who has lied will do a lousy job of screening. A more plausible premise is "Most security officers at La Guardia airport who have lied on their employment applications about having a criminal record will do a lousy job of screening passengers for weapons." This premise will do, and this is now a good argument—assuming that the other premise is true.

What about this one:

> The use of marijuana should be legal because it's an act that brings pleasure to people's lives.

To make this argument valid, we would need to add this premise (or one like it): "Any act that brings pleasure to people's lives should be legal." But this premise is hard to accept since many heinous acts—such as murder and theft—may bring pleasure to some people, yet few of us would think those acts should be legal. To try to make the argument strong, we might add this premise instead: "Some acts should be legal simply because they bring pleasure to people's lives." This premise is actually controversial in some quarters, but it at least is not obviously false. It also fits with the point of the argument. If we decide that the premise is neither plausible nor fitting, we would declare the argument beyond repair.

 **EXERCISES**

Exercise 3.4

I. For each of the following arguments, identify the implicit premises that will make the argument valid.

EXAMPLE

The engine is sputtering. It must be out of gas.
Implicit premise: Whenever the engine sputters, it's out of gas.

* 1. Any senator who is caught misusing campaign funds should resign his seat. Senator Greed should resign.
 2. Not everyone in this country has health insurance. Therefore, health care is a disaster.
 3. In the first week at the box office, the movie grossed over $30 million. So it's sure to win at least one Oscar.
 4. The FBI doesn't have a very serious focus on stopping terrorism. Another major terrorist attack will happen in this country.
* 5. The author of the book on interventionist wars is either biased or incompetent as a journalist. So she's biased.
 6. The conflict in Indonesia is a genuine war. So it can't possibly be morally justified.
 7. Hillary Clinton has amazing name recognition. So she will go far.
 8. The U.S. government should limit its activities to the Western Hemisphere because it doesn't have the resources to cover the whole world.
* 9. If the engine starts right away, it's because of the tune-up I gave it. Must be because of the tune-up I gave it.
 10. Taslima did not criticize U.S. military action in the Gulf War or in the war in Afghanistan. She must be a hawk.

II. To each of the following arguments, change or add a premise that will make the argument strong.

 1. The Republicans are more articulate about their policies and more realistic about world events than the Democrats are. They will surely win the next election.
 2. Aziz regularly eats at McDonald's, so Aziz is likely to gain a few pounds.
* 3. Six out of ten of my teenage friends love rap music. So 60 percent of all teens love rap music.
 4. Seventy-one percent of the faculty and staff at Goddard Community College are Democrats. So most of the students are probably Democrats.
 5. Miriam was in the library when the books were stolen from the librarian's desk. She was also seen hanging around the desk. So she's probably the one who stole them.

* 6. If Assad's fingerprints are on the vase, then he's probably the one who broke it. He's probably the one who broke it.

7. If the president needs more money to balance the federal budget, he will get it from Social Security. Well, he's almost certainly going to get it from Social Security.

8. Ninety percent of students at Boston College graduate with a B.A. degree. Li Fong will probably graduate from Boston College with a B.A. degree.

* 9. The murder rates in most large American cities on the East Coast are very high. The murder rates in most large cities in the West and Midwest are very high. So the murder rate in New Orleans must be very high.

10. John has a typical American diet. His fat intake is probably excessively high.

Argument Patterns

Earlier we discussed the importance of being familiar with argument patterns, or forms, the structures on which the content is laid. The point was that knowing some common argument forms makes it easier to determine whether an argument is deductive or inductive. But being familiar with argument forms is also helpful in many other aspects of argument evaluation. Let's take a closer look at some of these forms.

Since argument forms are structures distinct from argument content, we can easily signify different forms by using letters to represent statements in the arguments. Each letter represents a different statement in much the same way that letters are used to represent values in a mathematical equation. Consider this argument:

> *If the job is worth doing, then it's worth doing well.*
> *The job is worth doing.*
> *Therefore, it's worth doing well.*

We can represent this argument like this:

> *If* p, *then* q.
> p.
> *Therefore,* q.

Notice that the first line in the argument is a compound statement—it's composed of at least two constituent statements, which are represented in this case by *p* and *q*. So we have three statements in this argument that are arranged into an argument form, one that is both very common and always valid. We can plug any statements we want into this form, and we will still get a valid argument. The premises may be true or false, but the form will be valid.

Some of the more common argument patterns that you encounter are like this pattern—they're deductive, and they contain one or more **conditional**, or if-then, premises. The first statement in a conditional premise (the *if* part) is known as the **antecedent.** The second statement (the *then* part) is known as the **consequent.**

The pattern shown here is called **affirming the antecedent** or, to use the Latin term, ***modus ponens.*** Any argument in the *modus ponens* form is valid—if the premises are true, the conclusion absolutely must be true. This means that if

"If *p*, then *q*" and "*p*" are both true, the conclusion has to be true also. These facts, then, provide a way to quickly size up an argument. If it's in the form of *modus ponens*, it's valid, regardless of the content of the statements.

Another common argument form is called **denying the consequent,** or **modus tollens:**

> *If Austin is happy, then Barb is happy.*
> *Barb is not happy.*
> *Therefore, Austin is not happy.*

The form of *modus tollens* is:

> *If* p, *then* q.
> *Not* q.
> *Therefore, not* p.

Like *modus ponens, modus tollens* is always valid. If the premises are true, the conclusion must be true. So any argument that's in the *modus tollens* pattern is valid.

A third common argument form is called **hypothetical syllogism.** "Hypothetical" is just another term for conditional. A **syllogism** is a deductive argument made up of three statements—two premises and a conclusion. (*Modus ponens* and *modus tollens* are also syllogisms.) In a hypothetical syllogism, all three statements are conditional, and the argument is always valid:

> *If the ball drops, the lever turns to the right.*
> *If the lever turns to the right, the engine will stop.*
> *Therefore, if the ball drops, the engine will stop.*

 REVIEW NOTES

Valid Argument Forms

AFFIRMING THE ANTECEDENT
(*Modus Ponens*)   EXAMPLE

If *p*, then *q*.	If Spot barks, a burglar is in the house.
p.	Spot is barking.
Therefore, *q*.	Therefore, a burglar is in the house.

DENYING THE CONSEQUENT
(*Modus Tollens*)   EXAMPLE

If *p*, then *q*.	If it's raining, the park is closed.
Not *q*.	The park is not closed.
Therefore, not *p*.	Therefore, it's not raining.

Hypothetical Syllogism   EXAMPLE

If *p*, then *q*.	If Ajax steals the money, he will go to jail.
If *q*, then *r*.	If Ajax goes to jail, his family will suffer.
Therefore, if *p*, then *r*.	Therefore, if Ajax steals the money, his family will suffer.

Here's the symbolized version:

> *If* p, *then* q.
> *If* q, *then* r.
> *Therefore, if* p, *then* r.

People often use hypothetical syllogisms to reason about causal chains of events. They try to show that one event will lead inexorably to a sequence of events, finally concluding in a single event that seems far removed from the first. This linkage has prompted some to label hypothetical syllogisms "chain arguments."

There are two common argument forms that are *not* valid, though they strongly resemble valid forms. One is called **denying the antecedent.** For example:

> *If Einstein invented the steam engine, then he's a great scientist.*
> *Einstein did not invent the steam engine.*
> *Therefore, he is not a great scientist.*

Denying the antecedent is represented like this:

> *If* p, *then* q.
> *Not* p.
> *Therefore, not* q.

You can see the problem with this form in the preceding argument. Even if the antecedent is false (if Einstein did not invent the steam engine), that doesn't show that he's not a great scientist because he could be a great scientist on account of some other great achievement. Thus, denying the antecedent is clearly an invalid pattern: It's possible for the premises to be true and the conclusion false.

Here's another example of this form:

> *If science can prove that God is dead, then God is dead.*
> *Science cannot prove that God is dead.*
> *Therefore, God is not dead.*

Even if science cannot prove that God is dead, that in itself does not show that God is not dead. Perhaps God is dead even though science cannot prove it. In other words, it's possible for both premises to be true while the conclusion is false.

There's another common invalid form you should know about: **affirming the consequent.** Here's an instance of this form:

> *If Buffalo is the capital of New York, then Buffalo is in New York.*
> *Buffalo is in New York.*
> *Therefore, Buffalo is the capital of New York.*

We represent this form like this:

> *If* p, *then* q.
> q.
> *Therefore,* p.

"Mistakes are made on two counts: an argument is either based on error or incorrectly developed."
—Thomas Aquinas

Invalid Argument Forms

AFFIRMING THE CONSEQUENT

If *p*, then *q*.

q.

Therefore, *p*.

EXAMPLE

If the cat is on the mat, she is asleep.

She is asleep.

Therefore, she is on the mat.

DENYING THE ANTECEDENT

If *p*, then *q*.

Not *p*.

Therefore, not *q*.

EXAMPLE

If the cat is on the mat, she is asleep.

She is not on the mat.

Therefore, she is not asleep.

Obviously, in this form it's possible for the premises to be true while the conclusion is false, as this example shows. This pattern, therefore, is invalid.

Finally, we come to a common argument form called **disjunctive syllogism.** It's valid and extremely simple:

> *Either Ralph walked the dog, or he stayed home.*
> *He didn't walk the dog.*
> *Therefore, he stayed home.*

The symbolized form:

> *Either* p *or* q.
> *Not* p.
> *Therefore,* q.

Keep in mind that in a disjunctive syllogism, either disjunct can be denied, not just the first one.

These six deductive argument forms (four valid ones and two invalid ones) can help you streamline the process of argument evaluation. If you want to find out quickly if a deductive argument is valid, you can use these patterns to do that. (Remember, a good deductive argument has both a valid form and true premises.) You need only to see if the argument fits one of the forms. If it fits a valid form, it's valid. If it fits an invalid form, it's invalid. If it doesn't fit any of the forms, then you need to find another way to evaluate the argument. The easiest way to regularly apply this form-comparison technique is to memorize all six forms so you can identify them whenever they arise.

Sometimes you can see right away that an argument has a valid or invalid form. At other times, you may need a little help figuring this out, or you may want to use a more explicit test of validity. In either case, the *counterexample method* can help. With this technique you check for validity by simply devising a parallel argument that has the same form as the argument you're

> ## REVIEW NOTES
>
> ## Disjunctive Syllogism
>
> SYMBOLIZED VERSION   EXAMPLE
>
>   Either *p* or *q*.   Either we light the fire or we will freeze.
>
>   Not *p*.   We will not light the fire.
>
>   Therefore, *q*.   Therefore, we will freeze.

evaluating (the test argument) but has obviously *true premises and a false conclusion*. Recall that any argument having true premises and a false conclusion cannot be valid. So if you can invent such an argument that also has the same pattern as the test argument, you've proved that the test argument is invalid.

Let's say that you are confronted with this argument:

If crime is increasing, then our nation has abandoned God.
Our nation has abandoned God.
Therefore, crime is increasing.

And to check this test argument, you come up with this parallel argument:

If George is a dog, then he is warm-blooded.
George is warm-blooded.
Therefore, he is a dog.

This argument has the same pattern as the previous one—but the premises are true, and the conclusion is false. So the test argument is invalid. You may have already guessed that it is an instance of affirming the consequent. The counterexample method, though, works not just for the deductive forms we've discussed but for all deductive forms. (We will discuss other deductive forms in upcoming chapters.)

Consider another counterexample test. The argument in question is:

If Jackson drinks a lot of orange juice, he will get better.
He didn't drink a lot of orange juice.
Therefore, he will not get better.

And the parallel argument is:

If horses could fly, they would be valuable.
But horses cannot fly.
Therefore, horses are not valuable.

The argument to be tested is, of course, an example of denying the antecedent, and the counterexample method shows it to be invalid.

Exercise 3.5

For each of the following arguments, determine whether it is valid or invalid and indicate the argument pattern.

* 1. If the Pilgrims built that wall, there would be archeological evidence of that.
     But there is no such evidence.
     So the Pilgrims did not build that wall.

  2. If the butler didn't kill the master, then the maid did.
     The butler didn't kill him.
     So the maid killed him.

  3. Either John drove home or he stayed late.
     He didn't drive home.
     Therefore, he stayed late.

  4. If the South Africans have nuclear weapons, the South African jungle will be radioactive.
     The South African jungle is radioactive.
     Therefore, the South Africans have nuclear weapons.

  5. If the *New York Times* comes out in favor of the liberal democrats, they will win the election. But the newspaper will not come out in favor of the liberal democrats, so they will not win.

* 6. If CNN News omits important news stories, then it is irresponsible.
     It is not irresponsible.
     So CNN News does not omit important news stories.

  7. If ESP (extrasensory perception) were real, psychic predictions would be completely reliable.
     Psychic predictions are completely reliable.
     Therefore, ESP is real.

  8. If Miley Cyrus keeps playing the role of the twisted tart on stage, she will lose all her fans. Well, she has stopped playing that role, so she will not lose all her fans.

* 9. If ESP (extrasensory perception) were real, psychic predictions would be completely reliable.
     ESP is real.
     Therefore, psychic predictions are completely reliable.

 10. If laws could stop crime, there would be no crime.
     But there is crime.
     Therefore, laws cannot stop crime.

 11. If I perceive what appears to be a red door, then there really is a red door there.
     There really is a red door there.
     Therefore, I perceive what appears to be a red door.

12. If it rains, Alex will get wet.
    If Alex gets wet, he will be upset.
    Therefore, if it rains, Alex will be upset.

Exercise 3.6

For each of the following premises, fill out the rest of the argument to make it valid in two different ways—*modus ponens* and *modus tollens*.

1. If God is in his heaven, then all is right with the world.
* 2. If Lino is telling the truth, he will admit to all charges.
3. If some wars are just, then pacifism is false.
4. If the new vaccine prevents the spread of the virus, the researchers who developed the vaccine should get the Nobel Prize.
* 5. If religious conflict in Nigeria continues, thousands more will die.
6. If p, then q.
7. If the glaciers are melting, global warming has increased.
8. If there is such a thing as moral progress—that is, social changes in which we judge states of affairs to be "better" now than before—then the Enlightenment ideal of moral perfection is possible.
* 9. If solar power can supply six megawatts of power in San Francisco (which is certainly not the sunniest place in the world), then solar power can transform the energy systems in places like Texas and Arizona.
10. If my honorable colleague would stop listening to only his own voice for less than sixty seconds, he would doubtless be astonished that there are other minds in the world with other ideas.

Exercise 3.7

Use the counterexample method to create a parallel argument for each of the invalid arguments in Exercise 3.5. Write out each parallel argument and represent its form using letters as discussed earlier. Answers are provided for 4, 5, 7, 8, and 11.

EXAMPLE

Test Argument:
    If the president cuts taxes again, there will be a long-term recession.
    There will be a long-term recession.
    Therefore, the president will cut taxes.

Parallel Argument:
    If Donald Trump could fly, he would be famous.
    He is famous.
    Therefore, he can fly.

    If a, then b.
    b.
    Therefore, a.

Diagramming Arguments

Most of the arguments we've looked at so far have been relatively simple. When arguments are more complex (in real life they usually are!), you may find it increasingly difficult to sort out premises from conclusions and argument parts from non-argumentative background noise. If you can visualize an argument's structure, though, the job gets much easier. That's where argument diagramming comes in.

Let's begin by diagramming the following argument:

> *There is no question in my mind. I therefore maintain that Colonel Mustard is the murderer. Because if he did it, he would probably have bloodstains on the sleeve of his shirt. The bloodstains are tiny, but they are there. Any observant person could see them. Also the murder weapon was within the colonel's reach for quite a while before the crime was committed. And since of all the people in the house at the time he alone does not have an airtight alibi, he must be the killer.*

The first thing we do is underline (or circle) any premise or conclusion indicator words (e.g., "therefore," "since," and "because"):

> *There is no question in my mind. I <u>therefore</u> maintain that Colonel Mustard is the murderer. <u>Because</u> if he did it, he would probably have bloodstains on the sleeve of his shirt. The bloodstains are tiny, but they are there. Any observant person could see them. Also the murder weapon was within the colonel's reach for quite a while before the crime was committed. And <u>since</u> of all the people in the house at the time he alone does not have an airtight alibi, he must be the killer.*

Next we number all the statements (and *only* the statements) in the passage in sequential order. (For the purposes of diagramming, an if-then statement is considered one statement, and multiple statements in a single compound sentence are to be counted as separate statements. Such statements are usually joined by "and," "or," and "but.") Then we look for the conclusion and draw a <u>wavy line</u> under it. Only after we've zeroed in on the conclusion should we try to locate the premises, which we can indicate by <u>underlining</u> them:

> *(1) There is no question in my mind. (2) <u>I therefore maintain that Colonel Mustard is the murderer.</u> (3) <u>Because if he did it, he would probably have bloodstains on the sleeve of his shirt.</u> (4) <u>The bloodstains are tiny, but they are there. (5) Any observant person could see them. (6) Also the murder weapon was within the colonel's reach for quite a while before the crime was committed. (7) And since of all the people in the house at the time he alone does not have an airtight alibi,</u> he must be the killer.*

And then we cross out all extraneous statements—those that are neither premises nor conclusions, those that are redundant, and those that are nothing more than background information or other logically irrelevant material.

*(1) ~~There is no question in my mind~~. (2) <u>I therefore
maintain that Colonel Mustard is the murderer.
(3) Because if he did it, he would probably have bloodstains on the sleeve of his shirt. (4) The bloodstains
are tiny, but they are there.</u> ~~(5) Any observant person could see them.~~ (6) <u>Also the murder weapon was
within the colonel's reach for quite a while before the
crime was committed. (7) And since of all the people
in the house at the time he alone does not have an air-
tight alibi</u>, ~~he must be the killer~~.*

Allen is far less argumentative since
Angie's introduction to falconry.

By permission of the Jerry Van Amerongen and Creators
Syndicate, Inc.

Finally, we draw the diagram. Place the numbers of
the premises above the number for the conclusion. Then
draw arrows from the premises to the conclusion they
support. Each arrow represents a logical relationship between premise and conclusion, a relationship that we
normally indicate with the word "therefore" or "is a
reason or premise for."

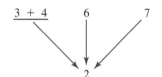

In this diagram you can see that premises 3 and 4 are handled differently
from premises 6 and 7. The reason is that some premises are **independent** and
some are **dependent.**

An independent premise offers support to a conclusion *without the help of any
other premises.* If other premises are omitted or undermined in an argument, the
support supplied by an independent premise does not change. We represent this
fact in the diagram by drawing separate arrows from premises 6 and 7 to the
conclusion. Premise 6 gives independent support to the conclusion, and premise
7 gives independent support to the conclusion. If we delete one of these premises,
the support that the other one gives does not change.

Premises 3 and 4 are dependent premises. They do depend on each other to
jointly provide support to a conclusion. If either premise 3 or 4 is removed, the
support that the remaining premise supplies is undermined or completely canceled out. By itself, premise 3 ("Because if he did it, he would probably have
bloodstains on the sleeve of his shirt") offers no support whatsoever to the conclusion ("Colonel Mustard is the murderer"). And by itself, premise 4 ("The
bloodstains are tiny, but they are there") doesn't lend any support to the conclusion. But together, premises 3 and 4 offer a good reason to accept the conclusion.
We represent dependent premises by joining them with a plus sign ("+") and
underlining them, as in our diagram. Since dependent premises together act as a
single premise, or reason, we draw a single arrow from the combined premises
("3 + 4") to the conclusion. With the diagram complete, we can see clearly that

two independent premises and one set of dependent premises provide support for the conclusion (statement 2).

Now, consider this argument:

> (1) *The famous trial lawyer Clarence Darrow (1857–1938) made a name for himself by using the "determinism defense" to get his clients acquitted of serious crimes. (2) The crux of this approach is the idea that humans are not really responsible for anything they do because they cannot choose freely—they are "determined," predestined, if you will, by nature (or God) to be the way they are. (3) So in a sense, Darrow says, humans are like wind-up toys with no control over any action or decision. (4) They have no free will. (5) Remember that Darrow was a renowned agnostic who was skeptical of all religious claims. (6) But Darrow is wrong about human free will for two reasons. (7) First, in our moral life, our own commonsense experience suggests that sometimes people are free to make moral decisions. (8) We should not abandon what our commonsense experience tells us without good reason—and (9) Darrow has given us no good reason. (10) Second, Darrow's determinism is not confirmed by science, as he claims—but actually conflicts with science. (11) Modern science says that there are many things (at the subatomic level of matter) that are not determined at all: (12) They just happen.*

Indicator words are scarce in this argument, unless you count the words "first" and "second" as signifying premises. After we number the statements consecutively, draw a wavy line under the conclusion, underline the premises, and cross out extraneous statements, the argument looks like this:

> (1) ~~The famous trial lawyer Clarence Darrow (1857–1938) made a name for himself by using the "determinism defense" to get his clients acquitted of serious crimes.~~ (2) ~~The crux of this approach is the idea that humans are not really responsible for anything they do because they cannot choose freely—they are "determined," predestined, if you will, by nature (or God) to be the way they are.~~ (3) ~~So in a sense, Darrow says, humans are like wind-up toys with no control over any action or decision. (4) They have no free will. (5) Remember that Darrow was a renowned agnostic who was skeptical of all religious claims.~~ (6) But Darrow is wrong about human free will for two reasons. (7) First, in our moral life, our own commonsense experience suggests that sometimes people are free to make moral decisions. (8) We should not abandon what our commonsense experience tells us without good reason—and (9) Darrow has given us no good reason. (10) Second, Darrow's determinism is not confirmed by science, as he claims—but actually conflicts with science. (11) Modern science says that there are many things (at the subatomic level of matter) that are not determined at all: (12) ~~They just happen.~~

To simplify things, we can eliminate several statements right away. Statements 1 through 4 are just background information on Darrow's views. Statement 5 is irrelevant to the argument; his agnosticism has no logical connection to the premises or conclusion. Statement 12 is a rewording of statement 11.

> ### REVIEW NOTES
>
> ## Diagramming Arguments: Step by Step
>
> 1. Underline all premise or conclusion indicator words, such as "since," "therefore," and "because." Then number the statements.
> 2. Find the conclusion and draw a wavy line under it.
> 3. Locate the premises and underline them.
> 4. Cross out all extraneous material—redundancies, irrelevant sentences, questions, exclamations.
> 5. Draw the diagram, connecting premises and conclusions with arrows showing logical connections. Include both dependent and independent premises.

After this elimination process, only the following premises and conclusion (statement 6) remain:

(6) But Darrow is wrong about human free will for two reasons.
(7) First, in our moral life, our commonsense experience suggests that sometimes people are free to make moral decisions.
(8) We should not abandon what our commonsense experience tells us without good reason.
(9) Darrow has given us no good reason.
(10) Darrow's determinism is not confirmed by science, as he claims—but actually conflicts with science.
(11) Modern science says that there are many things (mostly at the subatomic level of matter) that are not determined at all.

The question is, how are these premises related to the conclusion? Well, premises 7, 8, and 9 are dependent premises supporting the conclusion. Taken separately, these premises are weak, but together they constitute a plausible reason for accepting statement 6. Premise 10 directly supports the conclusion, and it in turn is supported by premise 11. These logical relationships can be diagrammed like this:

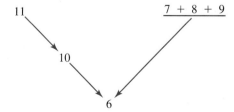

Now read this one:

As the Islamic clerics cling to power in Iran, students there are agitating for greater freedom and less suppression of views that the clerics dislike. Even though ultimate power in Iran rests with the mullahs, it is not at all certain where the nation is headed. Here's a radical suggestion: The Islamic republic in Iran will fall within the next five years. Why do I say this? Because the majority of Iranians are in favor of democratic reforms, and no regime can stand for very long when citizens are demanding access to the political process. Also, Iran today is a mirror image of the Soviet Union before it broke apart—there's widespread dissatisfaction and dissent at a time when the regime seems to be trying to hold the people's loyalty. Every nation that has taken such a path has imploded within five years. Finally, the old Iranian trick of gaining support for the government by fomenting hatred of America will not work anymore because Iran is now trying to be friends with the United States.

When we number the statements and underline the indicators, we get this:

(1) As the Islamic clerics cling to power in Iran, students there are agitating for greater freedom and less suppression of views that the clerics dislike. (2) Even though ultimate power in Iran rests with the mullahs, it is not at all certain where the nation is headed. Here's a radical suggestion: (3) The Islamic republic in Iran will fall within the next five years. Why do I say this? (4) <u>Because</u> the majority of Iranians are in favor of democratic reforms, (5) and no regime can stand for very long when citizens are demanding access to the political process. (6) Also, Iran today is a mirror image of the Soviet Union before it broke apart—there's widespread dissatisfaction and dissent at a time when the regime seems to be trying to hold the people's loyalty. (7) Every nation that has taken such a path has imploded within five years. (8) Finally, the old Iranian trick of gaining support for the government by fomenting hatred of America will not work anymore (9) <u>because</u> Iran is now trying to be friends with the United States.

And here's the passage with the premises and conclusion underlined and the extraneous material crossed out:

(1) ~~As the Islamic clerics cling to power in Iran, students there are agitating for greater freedom and less suppression of views that the clerics dislike. (2) Even though ultimate power in Iran rests with the mullahs, it is not at all certain where the nation is headed. Here's a radical suggestion:~~ (3) <u>The Islamic republic in Iran will fall within the next five years.</u> Why do I say this? (4) <u>Because the majority of Iranians are in favor of democratic reforms,</u> (5) <u>and no regime can stand for very long when citizens are demanding access to the political process.</u> (6) Also, <u>Iran today is a mirror image of the Soviet Union before it broke apart—there's widespread dissatisfaction and dissent at a time when the regime seems to be trying to hold the people's loyalty.</u> (7) <u>Every nation that has taken such a path has imploded within five years.</u> (8) <u>Finally, the old Iranian trick of gaining support for the government by fomenting hatred of America will not work anymore</u> (9) <u>because Iran is now trying to be friends with the United States.</u>

The conclusion is statement 3, and the premises are statements 4 through 9. The first two statements are extraneous. Statements 4 and 5 are dependent premises, and so are statements 6 and 7. Statements 8 and 9 constitute an argument that gives support to the passage's conclusion. Statement 8 is the conclusion;

statement 9, the premise. Notice also that the sentence "Why do I say this?" is not diagrammed at all because it's not a statement. The diagram of this argument is as follows:

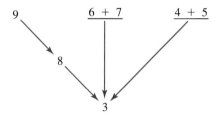

By the time you work through the diagramming exercises in this chapter, you will probably be fairly proficient in diagramming arguments of all kinds. Just as important, you will have a better appreciation of how arguments are built, how they're dissected, and how you can judge their value in a penetrating, systematic way.

 EXERCISES

Exercise 3.8

For each of the following diagrams, devise an argument whose premises and conclusion can be accurately depicted in the diagram. Write out the argument, number each statement, and insert the numbers into the diagram at the appropriate places.

* 1.

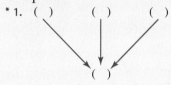

2.

3.

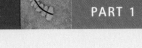

*4.

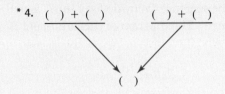

5.

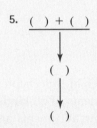

6.

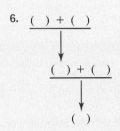

7.

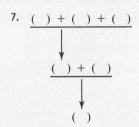

Exercise 3.9

Diagram the following arguments using the procedure discussed in the text.

1. I shouldn't take physics this semester. My course load is already too heavy. There's no room for the course in my schedule. And I don't like physics.

2. The president is soft on the environment. He has weakened clean-air regulations and lifted restrictions on logging in the West.

3. Congressman Porkbarrel is either dishonest or incompetent. He's not incompetent, though, because he's expert at getting self-serving legislation through Congress. I guess he's just dishonest.

4. If an individual in a coma is no longer a person, then giving him a drug to kill him is not murder. Such an individual is in fact not a person. Therefore, giving him the drug is not murder.

5. "The City Council deserves the gratitude of all New Yorkers for introducing a bill to ban the use of cell phones in places of public performance. . . . These rules may be hard to enforce, but so are bans on littering, auto horn honking and other quality-of-life offenses. By changing the law, the city will send a clear message that cell phone abuse is not just an etiquette issue but robs audience members of their right to enjoy the performance they paid for." [Letter to the editor, *New York Times*, November 28, 2002]

* 6. If Marla buys the house in the suburbs, she will be happier and healthier. She is buying the house in the suburbs. So she will be happier and healthier.

7. If you gain too much weight, your blood pressure will increase. If your blood pressure increases, your risk of stroke or heart attack rises. Therefore, gaining too much weight can increase your risk of stroke and heart attack.

8. "Grow accustomed to the belief that death is nothing to us, since every good and evil lie in sensation. However, death is the deprivation of sensation. Therefore . . . death is nothing to us." [Epicurus]

9. "A cause-and-effect relationship is drawn [by those opposed to pornography] between men viewing pornography and men attacking women, especially in the form of rape. But studies and experts disagree as to whether any relationship exists between pornography and violence, between images and behavior. Even the pro-censorship Meese Commission Report admitted that the data connecting pornography to violence was unreliable." [*Free Inquiry*, Fall 1997]

* 10. The existence of planets outside our solar system is a myth. There is no reliable empirical evidence at all showing that planets exist outside our solar system.

11. If Li Yang gets a high score on her test, she will have a perfect grade point average. If she gets a low score, she will drop out of school. She will get a high score on the test, so she will have a perfect grade point average.

12. Most atheists are liberals, and George is an atheist. Therefore, George is probably a liberal. Therefore, George is probably in favor of increased welfare benefits because most liberals are in favor of increased welfare benefits.

13. Bill is a student at Yale. No student at Yale has won the Nobel Prize. Therefore, Bill has not won the Nobel Prize.

14. "An international agreement proscribes the use of gas and so germ warfare must be developed." [Germaine Greer, *The Female Eunuch*]

15. The only valid reasons for dishonorably discharging someone from the Army are health problems and violations of Army regulations. So if Amal says that he was dishonorably discharged for simply being gay, he is lying or is mistaken. He is not lying. So he is mistaken.

16. "It is clear that archaeologists have not yet come to terms with dowsing [the alleged ability to detect underground water or treasure by paranormal means]. Where it has been the subject of tests, the tests have been so poorly designed and executed that any conclusion whatsoever could have been drawn from them. The fact that such tests are usually carried out only by researchers with a prior positive view of dowsing means that the conclusions will likely also be positive. The normal processes of peer review and scholarly discussion have also failed to uncover the lack of properly controlled test conditions in such studies as those of Bailey et al. and Locock, causing a generation of students and general readers in the United Kingdom, at least, to remain under the impression that the reality of archaeological dowsing had been all but confirmed by science." [*Skeptical Inquirer*, March/April 1999]

* 17. There are at least two main views regarding the morality of war. Pacifism is the view that no war is ever justified because it involves the taking of human life. Just-war theory is the view that *some* wars are justified for various reasons—mostly because they help prevent great evils (such as massacres, "ethnic cleansing," or world domination by a madman like Hitler) or because they are a means of self-defense. I think that our own moral sense tells us that sometimes (in the case of World War II, for example) violence is occasionally morally justified. It would be hard for anyone to deny that a war to prevent something like the Holocaust is morally right.

18. Some say that those without strong religious beliefs—nonbelievers in one form or another—cannot be moral. But millions upon millions of people have been nonbelievers or nontheists and yet have produced some of the most noble and most morally principled civilizations in history. Consider the Buddhists of Asia and the Confucianists of China. Consider also the great secular philosophers from the ancient Greeks to the likes of Bertrand Russell and John Searle of the twentieth century.

19. Either Maggie, Jose, or Ling broke the window. Jose couldn't have done it because he was studying in his room and was observed the whole time. Maggie couldn't have done it because she was out of town at the time and has witnesses to prove it. So the perpetrator had to be Ling.

* 20. The picnic will probably be spoiled because there is a 90 percent probability of rain.

21. The Golden Gate Bridge will probably be attacked by terrorists within the next two years. The latest intelligence reports from the Justice Department confirm this prediction. Plus terrorists have already stated publicly that they intend to destroy various symbolic structures or monuments in the United States, including Mount Rushmore and the Golden Gate.

22. We shouldn't pay Edward an allowance because he never does any work around the house, and he will probably just waste the money because he has no conception of the value of anything.

Assessing Long Arguments

The general principles of diagramming can help you when you have to evaluate arguments that are much longer and more complicated than most of those in this chapter. Some arguments are embedded in extended passages, persuasive essays, long reports, even whole books. In such cases, the kind of *detailed* argument diagramming we use to analyze short passages won't help you much. In very lengthy works, our five-step diagramming procedure would be tedious and time-consuming—if not maddening. But the *general approach* used in the procedure is relevant to longer arguments.

When you have to evaluate a very long passage, you're almost always faced with three obstacles:

1. Only a small portion of the prose may contain statements that serve as the premises and conclusion. (The rest is background information, reiterations of ideas, descriptions, examples, illustrations, asides, irrelevancies, and more.)
2. The premises or conclusion may be implicit.
3. Many longer works purporting to be filled with arguments contain very few arguments or none at all. (It's common for many books—even best sellers—to pretend to make a case for something but to be devoid of genuine arguments.)

Fortunately, you can usually overcome these impediments if you're willing to put in some extra effort. The following is a four-step procedure that can help.

Step 1. Study the text until you thoroughly understand it. You can't locate the conclusion or premises until you know what you're looking for—and that requires having a clear idea of what the author is driving at. Don't attempt to find the conclusion or premises until you "get it." This understanding entails having an overview of a great deal of text, a bird's-eye view of the whole work.

Step 2. Find the conclusion. When you evaluate extended arguments, your first task, as in shorter writings, is to find the conclusion. There may be several main conclusions or one primary conclusion with several subconclusions (as depicted in some of the previous argument diagrams). Or the conclusion may be nowhere explicitly stated but embodied in metaphorical language or implied by large tracts of prose. In any case, your job is to come up with a single conclusion statement for each conclusion—even if you have to paraphrase large sections of text to do it.

Step 3. Identify the premises. Like the hunt for a conclusion, unearthing the premises may involve condensing large sections of text into manageable form—namely, single premise statements. To do this, you need to disregard extraneous material and keep your eye on the "big picture." Just as in shorter arguments, premises in longer pieces may be implicit. At this stage you shouldn't try to incorporate the details of evidence into the premises, though you must take them into account to fully understand the argument.

Step 4. Diagram the argument. After you identify the premises and conclusion, diagram them just as you would a much shorter argument.

FURTHER THOUGHT

No Arguments, Just Fluff

Once you get really good at spotting arguments in a variety of passages, you may be shocked to see that a massive amount of persuasive writing contains no arguments at all. Apparently many people—including some very good writers—think that if they clearly express their opinions, then they have given an argument. You could look at this state of affairs as evidence that people are irrational—or you could view it as a time-saver: No need to waste your time on a bunch of unsupported opinions.

Unsupported opinions are everywhere, but they seem to permeate political writing, letters to the editor, and anything that's labeled "spiritual." Sometimes opinions are so weakly supported that they're almost indistinguishable from completely unsupported ones. Here's a taste:

> My family and friends have season tickets for the Buffalo Bandits. The disrespect that is shown to America by this team is appalling, particularly in this time of war. As both the Canadian and American national anthems are sung before each game, members of the team are hopping around, tugging at their uniforms, talking and carrying on amongst themselves. The players can't even wait for the national anthem to finish before they run off to their respective field positions. Whether one is for or against the war is irrelevant. Have some respect for America and what it stands for. [Letter to the editor, *Buffalo News* website]

No argument here, just indignation.

> So after a decade of progress, we have our smog problem back (as if it ever left). Another problem overlooked? Couldn't be because of all the giant behemoths (SUVs) on the road, could it? Nah. Or letting all the trucks from south of the border into our country without safety and smog inspections could it? Nah. It couldn't be because the government needs to have control of all it surveys? Nah. It must be something simpler, you think? Nah. [Letter to the editor, *Daily News* (Los Angeles) website]

No argument here either.

> How little is said of the soul-life and its complete identification with the human being! To most men the soul is something apart from themselves that is only to be talked of and trusted in on special occasions: There is no real companionship, no intimate affiliation, between men's minds and souls in their everyday existence. Now there is in every man a divine power, and when that divinity, which is real self, is acknowledged and understood by the mind, it takes a very active part in man's life—indeed, it could fill at the very least one-half of his thought-life. [Theosophy website]

Nope.

Let's see how this procedure works on the following selection:

The Case for Discrimination

Edgardo Cureg was about to catch a Continental Airlines flight home on New Year's Eve when he ran into a former professor of his. Cureg lent the professor his cell phone and, once on board, went to the professor's seat to retrieve it. Another passenger saw the two "brown-skinned men" (Cureg is of Filipino descent, the professor Sri Lankan) conferring and became alarmed that they, and another man, were "behaving suspiciously." The three men were taken off the plane and forced to get later flights. The incident is now the subject of a lawsuit by the ACLU.

Several features of Cureg's story are worth noting. First, he was treated unfairly, in that he was embarrassed and inconvenienced because he was wrongly suspected of being a terrorist. Second, he was not treated unfairly, because he was not wrongly suspected. A fellow passenger, taking account of his apparent ethnicity, his sex and age, and his behavior, could reasonably come to the conclusion that he was suspicious. Third, passengers' anxieties, and their inclination to take security matters into their own hands, increase when they have good reason to worry that the authorities are not taking all reasonable steps to look into suspicious characters themselves. . . .

Racial profiling of passengers at check-in is not a panacea. John Walker Lindh could have a ticket; a weapon could be planted on an unwitting 73-year-old nun. But profiling is a way of allocating sufficiently the resources devoted to security. A security system has to, yes, discriminate—among levels of threat. [*National Review,* July 1, 2002]

In this example, the author has given us a break by alluding to the conclusion in the title: Discrimination by racial profiling is a justified security measure. Notice that this conclusion is not explicitly stated in the text but is implied by various remarks, including "A security system has to, yes, discriminate." Given this conclusion, we can see that the entire first paragraph is background information—specifically, an example of racial profiling. The first premise is implicit. We glean it from the comments in the second paragraph: Racial profiling is a reasonable response in light of our legitimate concerns about security. The second premise is explicit: Profiling is a way of allocating sufficiently the resources devoted to security.

Laid out in neat order, this argument looks like this:

> (1) Racial profiling is a reasonable response in light of our legitimate concerns about security.
> (2) Profiling is a way of allocating sufficiently the resources devoted to security.
> (3) Therefore, discrimination by racial profiling is a justified security measure.

"Our minds anywhere, when left to themselves, are always thus busily drawing conclusions from false premises."
—Henry David Thoreau

The diagram of this argument looks like this:

A fact that can further complicate the argument structure of a long passage is that complex arguments can sometimes be made up of simpler arguments (sub-arguments). For example, the conclusion of a simple argument can serve as a premise in another simple argument, with the resulting chain of arguments constituting a larger complex argument. Such a chain can be long. The complex argument can also be a mix of both deductive and inductive arguments. Fortunately, all you need to successfully analyze these complex arguments is mastery of the elementary skills discussed earlier.

Let's take a look at another long passage:

Contemporary debates about torture usually concern its use in getting information from suspects (often suspected terrorists) regarding future attacks, the identity of the suspects' associates, the operations of terrorist cells, and the like. How effective torture is for this purpose is in dispute, mostly because of a lack of scientific evidence on the question. We are left with a lot of anecdotal accounts, some of which suggest that torture works, and some that it doesn't. People who are tortured often lie, saying anything that will make the torturers stop. On the other hand, in a few instances torture seems to have gleaned from the tortured some intelligence that helped thwart a terrorist attack.

Is torture sometimes the right thing to do? The answer is yes: in rare situations torture is indeed justified. Sometimes torturing a terrorist is the only way to prevent the deaths of hundreds or thousands of people. Consider: In Washington, D.C., a terrorist has planted a bomb set to detonate soon and kill a half million people. FBI agents capture him and realize that the only way to disarm the bomb in time is for the terrorist to tell them where it is, and the only way to get him to talk is to torture him. Is it morally permissible then to stick needles under his fingernails or waterboard him? The consequences of not torturing the terrorist would be a thousand times worse than torturing him. And according to many plausible moral theories, the action resulting in the best consequences for all concerned is the morally correct action. When we weigh the temporary agony of a terrorist against the deaths of thousands of innocents, the ethical answer seems obvious.

The length of this passage might suggest to you that the argument within it is long and tangled. But that's not the case here. The conclusion is this: In rare situations torture is morally justified. The first paragraph just provides background information; the second contains two premises. A paraphrase of the first premise would go something like this: In a ticking-bomb scenario, the consequences of not torturing a terrorist would be far worse than those of torturing him. The second premise says that the morally right action is the one that results in the best consequences for all concerned. Notice that these premises are dependent ones.

The argument then looks like this:

(1) In a ticking-bomb scenario, the consequences of not torturing a terrorist would be far worse than those of torturing him.

(2) The morally right action is the one that results in the best consequences for all concerned.

(3) Therefore, in rare situations torture is morally justified.

And the diagram looks like this:

The best way to learn how to assess long passages is to practice, which you can do in the following exercises. Be forewarned, however, that this skill depends heavily on your ability to understand the passage in question. If you do grasp the author's purpose, then you can more easily paraphrase the premises and conclusion and uncover implicit statements. You will also be better at telling extraneous stuff from the real meat of the argument. (Also see Appendix E: Critical Thinking and Writing.)

 EXERCISES

Exercise 3.10

For each of the following passages, (1) list the conclusion and premises and (2) diagram the argument.

* 1. "There are those who maintain . . . that even if God is not required as the author of the moral law, he is nevertheless required as the enforcer of it, for without the threat of divine punishment, people will not act morally. But this position is [not plausible]. In the first place, as an empirical hypothesis about the psychology of human beings, it is questionable. There is no unambiguous evidence that theists are more moral than non-theists. Not only have psychological studies failed to find a significant correlation between frequency of religious worship and moral conduct, but convicted criminals are much more likely to be theists than atheists. Second, the threat of divine punishment cannot impose a moral obligation, for might does not make right. Threats extort; they do not create a moral duty." [*Free Inquiry*, Summer 1997]

2. "I love *Reason* [magazine], but [regarding a previous article by Nick Gillespie] I'm wondering if all the illegal drugs that Nick Gillespie used to take are finally getting to him. He has a right to speak out against President Bush, but when he refers to him as "the millionaire president

who waited out the Vietnam War in the Texas Air National Guard," it reminds me of the garbage rhetoric that I might see if I were reading Ted Rall, or Susan Sontag, or one of the other hate-mongering, America-bashing, leftist whiners. That kind of ad hominem attack is not only disrespectful to a man who is doing a damned good job as commander-in-chief (with approval ratings of more than 80 percent); it detracts from the whole point of the article." [Letter to the editor, *Reason*, July 2002]

3. "The fifth way [of proving that God exists] is taken from the governance of the world. We see that things which lack knowledge, such as natural bodies, act for an end, and this is evident from their acting always, or nearly always, in the same way, so as to obtain the best result. Hence it is plain that they achieve their end, not fortuitously, but designedly. Now whatever lacks knowledge cannot move towards an end, unless it be directed by some being endowed with knowledge and intelligence; as the arrow is directed by the archer. Therefore some intelligent being exists by whom all natural things are directed to their end; and this being we call God." [Thomas Aquinas, *Summa Theologica*]

4. "The first thing that must occur to anyone studying moral subjectivism [the view that the rightness or wrongness of an action depends on the beliefs of an individual or group] seriously is that the view allows the possibility that an action can be both right and not right, or wrong and not wrong, etc. This possibility exists because, as we have seen, the subjectivist claims that the moral character of an action is determined by individual subjective states; and these states can vary from person to person, even when directed toward the same action on the same occasion. Hence one and the same action can evidently be determined to have—simultaneously—radically different moral characters. . . . [If] subjectivism . . . does generate such contradictory conclusions, the position is certainly untenable." [Phillip Montague, *Reason and Responsibility*]

5. A Florida judge dismissed a lawsuit that accused the Vatican of hiding instances of sexual abuse by priests. The suit was thrown out because Florida's statute of limitations had run out on the case. I submit that the dismissal was proper and ethical considering the community stature and function of priests and the benefits that accrue to society in the aftermath of the decision. Let's consider community stature first. The community stature of priests must always be taken into account in these abuse cases. A priest is not just anybody; he performs a special role in society—namely, to provide spiritual guidance and to remind people that there is both a moral order and a divine order in the world. The priest's role is special because it helps to underpin and secure society itself. Anything that could undermine this role must be neutralized as soon as possible. Among those things that can weaken the priestly role are publicity, public debate, and legal actions. Abuse cases are better handled in private by those who are keenly aware of the importance of a positive public image of priests. And what of the benefits of

curtailing the legal proceedings? The benefits to society of dismissing the legal case outweigh all the alleged disadvantages of continuing with public hearings. The primary benefit is the continued nurturing of the community's faith, without which the community would cease to function effectively.

KEY WORDS

affirming the
  antecedent

affirming the
  consequent

antecedent

cogent argument

conditional statement

consequent

deductive argument

denying the
  antecedent

denying the
  consequent

dependent premise

disjunctive syllogism

hypothetical syllogism

independent premise

inductive argument

invalid argument

modus ponens

modus tollens

sound argument

strong argument

syllogism

truth-preserving

valid argument

weak argument

Summary
Argument Basics

- Arguments come in two forms: deductive and inductive. A deductive argument is intended to provide logically conclusive support for a conclusion; an inductive one, probable support for a conclusion. Deductive arguments can be valid or invalid; inductive arguments, strong or weak. A valid argument with true premises is said to be sound. A strong argument with true premises is said to be cogent.

Judging Arguments

- Evaluating an argument is the most important skill of critical thinking. It involves finding the conclusion and premises, checking to see if the argument is deductive or inductive, determining its validity or strength, and discovering if the premises are true or false.

Finding Missing Parts

- Sometimes you also have to ferret out implicit, or unstated, premises. Finding implicit premises is a three-step process.

Argument Patterns

- Arguments can come in certain common patterns, or forms. Two valid forms that you will often run into are *modus ponens* (affirming the antecedent) and *modus tollens* (denying the consequent). Two common invalid forms are denying the antecedent and affirming the consequent.
- Using the counterexample method can help you determine whether a deductive argument is valid or invalid.

Diagramming Arguments

- Analyzing the structure of arguments is easier if you diagram them. Argument diagrams can help you visualize the function of premises and conclusions and the relationships among complex arguments with several subarguments.

Assessing Long Arguments

- Assessing very long arguments can be challenging because they may contain lots of verbiage but few or no arguments, and many premises can be implicit. Evaluating long arguments, though, requires the same basic steps as assessing short ones: (1) Ensure that you understand the argument, (2) locate the conclusion, (3) find the premises, and (4) diagram it to clarify logical relationships.

 Field Problems

1. Find a 150- to 200-word passage purporting to present an argument for a particular view but actually being devoid of arguments. Look in magazine or newspaper letters to the editor or advocacy or political websites. Then rewrite the passage and include an argument for the original view.
2. Visit a website intended to support a particular view on a social or political issue. Using the information on the website, write a 100-word passage containing an argument for a view that the website might endorse.
3. Visit www.townhall.com, www.usatoday.com, or www.csmonitor.com. Find an essay arguing for a particular view, and identify the premises and the conclusion. Decide whether you think the argument a good one. Be prepared to explain why.

 Self-Assessment Quiz

Answers appear in "Answers to Self-Assessment Quizzes" (Appendix D).

1. What is a deductive argument? an inductive argument?
2. What is a valid argument? an invalid one? What is a strong inductive argument?
3. What is a sound argument?

Indicate whether the following arguments are deductive or inductive.

4. If you refuse to surrender, then you will be arrested. You refuse to surrender. Prepare yourself: You will be arrested.

5. There's an 80 percent chance that the hurricane will veer northward tomorrow and hit Tampa. So Tampa will probably feel the force of the hurricane tomorrow.

6. Ethel is reckless. She is going to have an accident sooner or later.

7. Whatever Hillary Clinton says is true. She says that the Republicans are weak. So the Republicans are weak.

In each of the following arguments, identify the implicit premise that will make the argument either valid or strong.

8. Jones has never openly criticized any military action against any Middle Eastern nation. He is a warmonger.

9. Maria failed her driving test three times. She's probably not paying attention.

10. If 60 percent of people believe in astrology or tarot cards, the future of the country does not look bright. Grades in college science courses will probably drop dramatically.

For each of the following exercises, provide an example of the argument pattern indicated.

11. *Modus ponens.*

12. *Modus tollens.*

13. Denying the antecedent.

14. Affirming the consequent.

Diagram the following arguments.

15. Cole is up to no good. He's been acting suspiciously for days, and he told Rachel that he was going to steal something valuable.

16. The sitcom *Friends* is becoming really lame. The writing is predictable and plodding. The acting is worse than ever.

17. If dolphins have minds comparable to ours, then these creatures are self-conscious, intelligent, and creative. If they are self-conscious, then they should react appropriately when they see their reflections in a mirror. They do react appropriately. If they're intelligent, they should be able to solve complex problems. They can solve such problems. If they're creative, they should be able to create some form of art. In a rudimentary way, they do create art. They are definitely self-conscious, intelligent, and creative.

18. If the dictum to always tell the truth in all circumstances is a valid moral principle, then it should fit well with our considered moral judgments. But it does not fit well with our considered moral judgments because there are times when lying is actually the right thing to do, as when we lie to save a life. So the dictum to always tell the truth is not a valid moral principle.

19. I don't think that I should vote for any independent candidate in the next election. Independents never win, and I want the person I vote for

to win. Also, independents have a tendency to be a little wacky. And we definitely don't need any more wacky politicians in power.

20. Creationism is an inadequate theory about the origins of life. It conflicts with science, and it is incapable of predicting any new facts.

 Integrative Exercises

These exercises pertain to material in Chapters 1–3.

For each of the following passages, indicate whether it contains an argument. If it does, specify the conclusion and premises, any argument indicator words, whether the argument is deductive or inductive, and whether it contains an example of face-saving or group-pressure thinking. Also identify any implicit premises and diagram the argument.

1. If Anne is in town, then she's staying at the Barbary Hotel. She's in town. Therefore, she's staying at the Barbary Hotel.

2. If the death penalty deterred anyone from crime, then there would be a lower crime rate in countries that have the death penalty than in countries that do not. But crime rates are often higher in countries with the death penalty. So the death penalty is really no crime deterrent.

3. "In the wake of the attacks of September 11th, 2001, the governments of Canada and the United States have passed sweeping anti-terrorism bills that effectively lay the groundwork for the criminalization of ideas. One consequence has been . . . the policing of freedom of expression. In Canada, a post–September 11th exhibit of contemporary Arab-Canadian art at the National Museum in Ottawa was abruptly cancelled by the organizers to allow the curators to 'reconsider' the political works on display: the exhibition did go ahead as scheduled, but only after a determined public campaign challenging the museum's actions." [*Alternative Press Review,* Spring 2002]

4. "[Is] there scientific evidence that prayer really works? . . . The problem with . . . any so-called controlled experiment regarding prayer is that *there can be no such thing as a controlled experiment concerning prayer.* You can never divide people into groups that received prayer and those that did not. The main reason is that there is no way to know that someone did not receive prayer. How would anyone know that some distant relative was not praying for a member of the group . . . identified as having received no prayer?" [*Free Inquiry,* Summer 1997]

5. "Going hand in hand with the fundamental dishonesty of America's news media is the second problem: hypocrisy. The news media claims to disdain capitalism and profit, yet most media outlets are part of huge for-profit corporations that engage in fierce, often cutthroat, competition." [Accuracy in Media, www.aim.org, October 28, 2002]

6. "[C]urrent-day Christians use violence to spread their right-to-life message. These Christians, often referred to as the religious right, are well

known for violent demonstrations against Planned Parenthood and other abortion clinics. Doctors and other personnel are threatened with death, clinics have been bombed, there have even been cases of doctors being murdered." [Letter to the editor, *Daily Wildcat,* September 17, 2002]

7. Everyone knows how beneficial an operating casino can be to a city of this size. But since establishing a casino here is prohibitively expensive, we need to try to institute gambling on a smaller scale—by placing a few slot machines in government buildings.

8. The financial health of the banking industry will improve dramatically in the next few months. This improvement will immediately lead to more lenient loan terms for individuals. So it's better to wait a few months to ask a bank for a loan.

9. We evaluated the accuracy of recent news reports on a wide range of news topics. We focused on reports aired or published by three major media outlets. We found that 40 percent of their news reports were highly inaccurate. So, though it's hard to believe, 40 percent of all the news reports that people are exposed to are questionable.

10. A recent poll shows that 76 percent of Americans believe in life after death. In addition, there are thousands of first-person reports of either contacting dead people or seeing their spirits. Life after death is a reality.

11. These are Canada geese. Canada geese mate for life, so these Canada geese are paired up forever.

12. If sex education in the schools can reduce the teen pregnancy rate or help delay the onset of teen sexual activity, I'm all for it. A recent study of several hundred teens showed that sex education in school lowered the incidence of teen pregnancy. We should have sex ed in all public schools.

13. The worst calamity that will befall the world in the next twenty years will be the use of small nuclear weapons by terrorists or rogue states. The death toll from such a state of affairs is likely to be higher than that of any other kind of human devastation. The United Nations just issued a report that comes to the same conclusion. We should act now to prevent the proliferation of nuclear weapons and nuclear-weapons-grade material from falling into the wrong hands.

14. Many surveys show that most people not only believe in "remote viewing" (the ability to observe distant locations without using the physical senses) but also think that science has already proved its existence. This demonstrates that the majority of people are scientifically illiterate. If they understood the least bit about the methods of science and how it reaches conclusions, they would denounce silly ideas like remote viewing—or at least not accept them blindly.

15. Magazines regularly publish articles on "the sexiest man alive" or "the most beautiful woman in the world." All you have to do to see that these claims of superior attractiveness are bunk is to stroll down any main thoroughfare in any nation's capital. There you will see people—male and female—who make the magazines' favorite personifications of beauty or sexiness look like dogs.

16. The biblical story of Noah and the ark is immediately shown to be a fraud or fantasy by one fact: The volume of dung produced by the ark's animals (one pair of everything!) would fill a hundred arks, and shoveling all that stuff overboard would have taken scores of laborers working round the clock for two years.

17. Peanuts are good for you. A million little monkeys can't be wrong.

18. "There is no justice in the world. Amelia Earhart's plane went down, and despite fifty years of looking, no one has ever been able to find her. But Yasser Arafat's plane goes down, and he's rescued in fifteen minutes." [Jay Leno, *The Tonight Show*]

19. "The following is in response to the letter, 'Let the Middle East fight its own wars.' I can understand the writer's concern about not wanting to start a war with Iraq. However, if Saddam Hussein poses a threat to the whole world—be it with nuclear or germ warfare—shouldn't we Americans take it upon ourselves to help protect the world? Or should we sit back and wait until Saddam is triumphant in developing his nuclear arsenal? Our intervention is considered necessary for all the present turmoil that's been taking place in the Middle East. We are the most intelligent and developed country in the world. We owe it to the lesser-developed counties to be peacekeepers. I ask the writer this: Where would the world be today if the United States had sat back and watched as Adolf Hitler rained terror on Europe?" [Letter to the editor, *Buffalo News,* November 29, 2002]

20. Freedom is a necessary component of the good life. The good life is something that every human being has a right to. Everything that humans have a right to should be acquired by any means necessary. Therefore, any war conducted to secure freedom for any of us is justified.

 Writing Assignments

1. Study the argument presented in Essay 3 ("A Feminist Defense of Pornography") in Appendix B. Identify the conclusion and the premises and objections considered. Then write a two-page critique of the essay's argument.

2. Write a three-page essay arguing for a position that directly contradicts the conclusion defended in Essay 3. You may cite imaginary but reasonable evidence.

3. Select an issue from the following list and write a three-page paper defending a claim pertaining to the issue. Follow the procedures discussed in Appendix E for outlining the essay and identifying a thesis.

   • Should the U.S. government be permitted to kill American citizens overseas who have been identified as terrorists?

   • Should the federal government permit same-sex marriages?

   • Does pornography lead to violence against women?

   • Should the police or other security officers be permitted to use racial profiling to prevent terrorist attacks?

PART TWO

REASONS

Reasons for Belief and Doubt

WHEN CLAIMS CONFLICT

- Understand that when a claim conflicts with other claims we have good reason to accept, we have good grounds for doubting it.
- Recognize that if a claim conflicts with our background information, we have good reason to doubt it.
- Appreciate that when we are confronted with a claim that is neither completely dubious nor fully credible, we should proportion our belief to the evidence.
- Realize that it's not reasonable to believe a claim when there is no good reason for doing so.

EXPERTS AND EVIDENCE

- Understand what makes someone an expert and what does not.
- Understand that if a claim conflicts with expert opinion, we have good reason to doubt it.
- Realize that when the experts disagree about a claim, we have good reason to doubt it.
- Be able to recognize fallacious appeals to authority.
- Be able to distinguish true experts from nonexperts by using the four indicators of expertise.

PERSONAL EXPERIENCE

- Understand that it's reasonable to accept the evidence provided by personal experience only if there's no good reason to doubt it.
- Appreciate the importance of the common factors that can give us good reason to doubt the reliability of personal experience—impairment, expectation, and innumeracy.

FOOLING OURSELVES

- Appreciate why we need to resist the human tendency to resist contrary evidence.
- Become sensitive to the possibility of confirmation bias.
- Be alert to the possibility of the availability error.

L ET'S REMIND OURSELVES ONCE AGAIN WHY WE'VE COME THIS WAY. IF WE CARE whether our beliefs are true or reliable, whether we can safely use them to guide our steps and inform our choices, then we must care about the reasons for accepting those beliefs. The better the reasons for acceptance, the more likely are the beliefs, or statements, to be true. Inadequate reasons, no reasons, or fake reasons (discussed in the next chapter) should lead us not to accept a statement, but to doubt it.

As we saw in earlier chapters, the reasons for accepting a statement are often spelled out in the form of an argument, with the statement being the conclusion. The reasons and conclusion together might compose a deductive argument or an inductive argument. In such cases, the reasons are normally there in plain sight. But in our daily lives statements, or claims, usually confront us alone without any accompanying stated reasons. An unsupported claim may be the premise of an argument (and its truth value may then determine whether the argument is sound or cogent). Or it may simply be a stand-alone assertion of fact. Either way, if we care whether the claim is acceptable, we must try to evaluate the claim as it stands.

> "The whole problem with the world is that fools and fanatics are always so certain of themselves, but wiser people so full of doubts."
> —Bertrand Russell

Of course, it helps to be knowledgeable about the subject matter of a claim. But understanding and applying some critical thinking principles for assessing unsupported claims can be even more useful. Let's take a close look at these.

When Claims Conflict

Suppose you come across this claim in a reputable local newspaper:

[Claim 1] The historic Sullivan Building at the corner of Fifth and Main Streets was demolished yesterday to make way for a parking lot.

But say you have very good reasons to believe this claim:

[Claim 2] The historic Sullivan Building at the corner of Fifth and Main Streets was NOT demolished yesterday to make way for a parking lot.

Favorite Unsupported Claims

In the Information Age, you don't have to look far for unsupported claims. They jump out at you from all directions. Many of them are a joy to behold because they're so imaginative, unusual, or provocative. They don't offer much of a challenge for critical thinkers, but they sure are fun. The following is a little sampling from cyberspace.

- "Become INVISIBLE! This is not a toy, a magic trick or a scam. This is not an illusion, a rip-off or a Ninja technique. **The Secrect of Invisibility** renders you completely invisible. This method is currently used by the CIA and foreign intelligence agencies. Don't Scoff! You can go anywhere, at anytime, without being seen."

- "Is it strange how, when we are in the middle of summer, it can be raining out, and one day it is very 'hot,' the next day it is 15 degrees cooler, and two days later, it is 'hot' again? Does this seem strange? How about earthquakes in parts of the world, that are so devastating, that if they were to happen here, our whole economy could be ruined. Do you think it is 'odd' that people would suggest that the government can and does control the weather? I know it sounds a little paranoid, but if you do the research to investigate, you will undoubtedly arrive at the same conclusions. Our weather is controlled!"

- "Some of you may be wondering what Aliens and UFO stuff have to do with the Bible. The truth is Aliens and UFOs ARE a BIG part of the Bible, New World Order, and last days deception. Yes they exist, they are the fallen angels who rebelled with Lucifer before and even after the flood, and they are coming back with Lucifer to dominate and control the earth in the last days. To be forewarned, is to be prepared. The Lord has called me forth to inform and warn His people about what is coming."

- "Contrary to all reports about a lone drifter named Mark David Chapman who allegedly shot John Lennon in the back December 8, 1980, you'll find ample evidence in the back issues of *Time*, *Newsweek*, and *U.S. News & World Report* magazines to suggest otherwise. Namely, that John Lennon was not only politically assassinated, but that Richard Nixon, Ronald Reagan and, you'd better sit down, horror novelist Stephen King are the three people who can be proven guilty of the crime."

- "The thought screen helmet blocks telepathic communication between aliens and humans. Aliens cannot immobilize people wearing thought screens nor can they control their minds or communicate with them. Results of the thought screen helmet are preliminary. As of June 2000, aliens have not taken any abductees while they were wearing thought screen helmets using Velostat shielding."

- "Conclusions: 1. Life forms exist on the surface of the moon. 2. Lunar-surface life forms can grow into large forms and shapes. Some shapes assume cylindrical, linear and curved profiles. Others are complicated and entangled. 3. Lunar-surface life forms have the capability of attaching to equipment with a potential ability to cause equipment malfunction. 4. Lunar-surface life forms can change size and shape, and can do so quickly. 5. Pressure of the MET wheels on the surface appears to arouse lunar life forms to a state of luminescence. 6. Some 'rocks' which in macro view appear to be like earth-like rocks really are not but, rather, are a build-up of an accumulation of growing life forms. 7. Apollo 14 did land on the moon."

What do you make of such a conflict between claims? Well, as a good critical thinker, you can know at least this: You have good reason to doubt claim 1 and therefore have no good grounds for accepting it. You have good reason to doubt it because it conflicts with another claim you have good reason to believe (claim 2). When two claims conflict, they simply cannot *both* be true; at least one of them has to be false. So this principle comes into play:

> If a claim conflicts with other claims we have good reason to accept, we have good grounds for doubting it.

With conflicting claims, you are not justified in believing either one of them until you resolve the conflict. Sometimes this job is easy. If, for example, the competing claims are reports of personal observations, you can often decide between them by making further observations. If your friend says that your dog is sleeping atop your car, and you say that your dog is not sleeping atop your car (because you checked a short time ago), you can see who's right by simply looking at the roof of your car. (Remember, though, that even personal observations can sometimes mislead us, as we'll soon see.)

FURTHER THOUGHT

Fact and Opinion

When we evaluate claims, we often are concerned with making a distinction between facts and opinions. But just what is the difference? We normally use the term *fact* in two senses. First, we may use it to refer to a state of affairs—as in, "Examine the evidence and find out the facts." Second, and more commonly, we use *fact* to refer to *true statements*—as in, "John smashed the dinnerware—that's a fact." Thus, we say that some claims, or statements, are facts (or factual) and some are not. We use the word *opinion*, however, to refer to a *belief*—as in, "It's John's opinion that he did not smash the dinnerware." Some opinions are true, so they are facts. Some opinions are not true, so they are not facts.

Sometimes we may hear somebody say, "That's a matter of opinion." What does this mean? Often it's equivalent to something like, "Opinions differ on this issue" or "There are many different opinions on this." But it also frequently means that the issue is not a matter of objective fact but is entirely subjective, a matter of individual taste. Statements expressing matters of opinion in this latter sense are not the kinds of things that people can disagree on, just as two people cannot sensibly disagree about whether they like chocolate ice cream.

Many times, however, sorting out conflicting claims requires a deeper inquiry. You may need to do some research to see what evidence exists for each of the claims. In the best-case scenario, you may quickly discover that one of the claims is not credible because it comes from an unreliable source (a subject taken up in the next few pages).

Now suppose that you're confronted with another type of conflict—this time a conflict between a claim and your **background information**. Background information is that huge collection of very well supported beliefs that we all rely on to inform our actions and choices. A great deal of this lore consists of basic facts about everyday things, beliefs based on overwhelming evidence (including our own reliable personal observations and the statements of excellent authorities), and strongly justified claims that we would regard as "common sense" or "common knowledge." Background beliefs include obvious claims such as "the sun is hot," "the Easter bunny is not real," "humans are mortal," "fire burns," and "George Washington lived in the eighteenth century." Suppose then that you're asked to accept this unsupported claim:

Some babies can bench-press a 500-pound weight.

You are not likely to give much credence to this claim for the simple reason that it conflicts with an enormous number of your background beliefs concerning human physiology, gravity, weight lifting, and who knows what else.

Or how about this claim:

The U.S. president is entirely under the control of the chief justice of the United States.

This claim is not as outlandish as the previous one, but it too conflicts with our background beliefs, specifically those having to do with the structure and workings of the U.S. government. So we would have good reason to doubt this one also.

The principle exemplified here is:

If a claim conflicts with our background information, we have good reason to doubt it.

Other things being equal, the more background information the claim conflicts with, the more reason we have to doubt it. We would normally—and rightfully—assign a low probability to any claim that conflicts with a great deal of our background information.

You would be entitled, for example, to have some doubt about the claim that Joan is late for work if it conflicts with your background information that Joan has never been late for work in the ten years you've known her. But you are entitled to have very strong doubts about, and to assign very low credibility to, the claim that Luis can turn a stone into gold just by touching it. You could even reasonably dismiss the claim out of hand. Such a claim conflicts with too much of what we know about the physical world.

It's always possible, of course, that a conflicting claim is true and some of our background information is unfounded. So many times it's reasonable for us to examine a conflicting claim more closely. If we find that it has no good reasons in its favor, that it is not credible, we may reject it. If, on the other hand, we discover that there are strong reasons for accepting the new claim, we may need to revise our background information. For example, we may be forced to accept the claim about Luis's golden touch (and to rethink some of our background information) if it is backed by strong supporting evidence. Our background information would be in need of some serious revision if Luis could produce this stone-to-gold transformation repeatedly under scientifically controlled conditions that rule out error, fraud, and trickery.

We need to keep in mind that although our background information is generally trustworthy, it is not infallible. What we assume is a strongly justified belief may be nothing more than prejudice or dogma. We should therefore be willing to re-examine background beliefs that we have doubts about—and to be open to reasonable doubts when they arise.

So it is not reasonable to accept a claim if there is good reason to doubt it. And sometimes, if the claim is dubious enough, we may be justified in dismissing a claim out of hand. But what should we believe about a claim that is not quite dubious enough to summarily discard yet not worthy of complete acceptance? We should measure out our belief according to the strength of reasons. That is,

We should proportion our belief to the evidence.

The more evidence a claim has in its favor, the stronger our belief in it should be. Weak evidence for a claim warrants weak belief; strong evidence warrants strong belief. And the strength of our beliefs should vary across this spectrum as the evidence dictates.

Implicit in all of the foregoing is a principle that deserves to be explicit because it's so often ignored:

> *It's not reasonable to believe a claim when there is no good reason for doing so.*

The famous twentieth-century philosopher Bertrand Russell tried hard to drive this idea home. As he put it, "It is undesirable to believe a proposition when there is no ground whatever for supposing it true."[1] Russell claimed that if the use of this principle became widespread, social life and political systems would be transformed.

"A belief which leaves no place for doubt is not a belief; it is a superstition."
—José Bergamín

Experts and Evidence

When an unsupported claim doesn't conflict with what we already know, we are often justified in believing it *because it comes from experts.* An **expert** is someone who is more knowledgeable in a particular subject area or field than most others are. Experts provide us with reasons for believing a claim because, in their specialty areas, they are more likely to be right than we are. They are more likely to be right because (1) they have access to more information on the subject than we do and (2) they are better at judging that information than we are. Experts are familiar with the established facts and existing data in their field *and* know how to properly evaluate that information. Essentially, this means that they have a handle on the information and know how to assess the evidence and arguments for particular claims involving that information. They are true authorities on a specified subject. Someone who knows the lore of a field but can't evaluate the reliability of a claim is no expert.

In a complex world where we can never be knowledgeable in every field, we must rely on experts—a perfectly legitimate state of affairs. But good critical thinkers are careful about expert opinion, guiding their use of experts by some commonsense principles. One such principle is this:

> *If a claim conflicts with expert opinion, we have good reason to doubt it.*

This tenet follows from our definition of experts. If they really are more likely to be right than nonexperts about claims in their field, then any claim that conflicts with expert opinion is at least initially dubious.

Here's the companion principle to the first:

> *When the experts disagree about a claim, we have good reason to doubt it.*

"None of my friends could diagnose the symptoms, Doctor. You're my last hope!"

Medical Economics

If a claim is in dispute among experts, then nonexperts can have no good reason for accepting (or rejecting) it. Throwing up your hands and arbitrarily deciding to believe or disbelieve the claim is not a reasonable response. The claim must remain in doubt until the experts resolve the conflict or you resolve the conflict yourself by becoming informed enough to competently decide on the issues and evidence involved—a course that's possible but usually not feasible for nonexperts.

Sometimes we may have good reason to be suspicious of unsupported claims even when they are purportedly derived from expert opinion. Our doubt is justified when a claim comes from someone deemed to be an expert who in fact is *not* an expert. When we rely on such bogus expert opinion, we commit the fallacy known as the **appeal to authority.**

The fallacious appeal to authority usually happens in one of two ways. First, we may find ourselves disregarding this important rule of thumb: *Just because*

 FURTHER THOUGHT

Are Doctors Experts?

Yes and no. Physicians are certainly experts in the healing arts, in diagnosing and treating disease and injury. They know and understand the relevant facts and they have the wherewithal to make good judgments regarding those facts. But are physicians experts in determining whether a particular treatment is safe and effective? Contrary to what many believe, the answer is, in general, no. Determining the safety and efficacy of treatments is a job for scientists (who may also be physicians). Medical scientists conduct controlled studies to try to ascertain whether treatment X can safely alleviate disease A—something that usually cannot be determined by a doctor interacting with her patients in a clinical

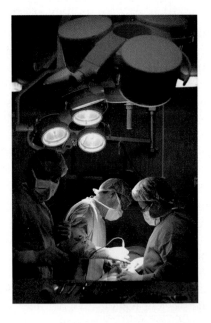

setting. Medical studies are designed to control all kinds of extraneous variables that can skew the study results, the same extraneous variables that are often present in the doctor's office.

Critical thinkers should keep this distinction in mind because they will often hear people assert that treatment Y works just because Dr. Wonderful says so.

someone is an expert in one field, he or she is not necessarily an expert in another. The opinion of experts generally carries more weight than our own—but only in their areas of expertise. Any opinions that they proffer outside their fields are no more authoritative than those of nonexperts. Outside their fields, they are not experts.

We needn't look far for real-life examples of such skewed appeals to authority. Any day of the week we may be urged to accept claims in one field based on the opinion of an expert from an unrelated field. An electrical engineer or Nobel Prize–winning chemist may assert that herbs can cure cancer. A radio talk-show host with a degree in physiology may give advice in psychology. A former astronaut may declare that archaeological evidence shows that Noah's ark now rests on a mountain in Turkey. A botanist may say that the evidence for the existence of ESP is conclusive. The point is not that these experts can't be right, but that their expertise in a particular field doesn't give us reason to believe their pronouncements in another. There is no such thing as a general expert, only experts in specific subject areas.

Second, we may fall into a fallacious appeal to authority by regarding a nonexpert as an expert. We forget that a nonexpert—even one with prestige, status, or sex appeal—is still a nonexpert. Movie stars, TV actors, renowned athletes, and famous politicians endorse products of all kinds in TV and print advertising. But when they speak outside their areas of expertise (which is almost always the case), they give us no good reason for believing that the products are as advertised. Advertisers, of course, know this, but they hope that we will buy the products anyway because of the appeal or attractiveness of the celebrity endorsers.

Historically the regarding of a nonexpert as an expert has probably been the most prevalent form of the appeal to authority—with disastrous results. Political, religious, tribal, and cultural leaders often have been designated as authorities not because they knew the facts and could correctly judge the evidence but because culture, tradition, or whim dictated that they be regarded as authorities. When these "authorities" spoke, people listened and believed—then went to war, persecuted unbelievers, or undertook countless other ill-conceived projects. If we are to avoid this trap, we must look beyond mere labels and titles and ask, "Does this person provide us with any good reasons or evidence?"

This question, of course, is just another way of asking if someone is a true expert. How can we tell? To be considered an expert, someone must have shown that he or she can assess relevant evidence and arguments and arrive at well-supported conclusions in a particular field. What are the indicators that someone has this essential kind of expertise? There are several that provide clues to someone's ability but do not guarantee the possession of true expertise.

In most fields, the following two indicators are considered minimal prerequisites for being considered an expert:

1. Education and training from reputable institutions or programs in the relevant field (usually evidenced by degrees or certificates)
2. Experience in making reliable judgments in the field (generally the more years of experience the better)

> "An expert is a man who has made all the mistakes which can be made in a very narrow field."
> —Niels Bohr

> "An expert is someone who knows some of the worst mistakes that can be made in his subject and who manages to avoid them."
> —Werner Heisenberg

But, unfortunately, people can have the requisite education and experience and still not know what they're talking about in the field in question. Woe be to us, for in the real world there are well-trained, experienced auto mechanics who do terrible work—and tenured Ph.D.s whose professional judgment is iffy. Two additional indicators, though, are more revealing:

1. Reputation among peers (as reflected in the opinions of others in the same field, relevant prestigious awards, and positions of authority)
2. Professional accomplishments

These two indicators are more helpful because they are very likely to be correlated with the intellectual qualities expected in true experts. People with excellent reputations among their professional peers and with significant accomplishments to their credit usually are true experts.

As we've seen, we are often justified in believing an unsupported claim because it's based on expert opinion. But if we have reason to doubt the opinion of the experts, then we are not justified in believing the claim based on that opinion. And chief among possible reasons for doubt (aside from conflicting expert opinion) is bias. When experts are biased, they are motivated by something other than the search for the truth—perhaps financial gain, loyalty to a cause, professional ambition, emotional needs, political outlook, sectarian dogma, personal ideology, or some other judgment-distorting factor. Therefore, if we have reason to believe that an expert is biased, we are not justified in accepting the expert's opinion.

But how can we tell when experts are biased? There are no hard-and-fast rules here. In the more obvious cases, we often suspect bias when an expert is being paid by special-interest groups or companies to render an opinion, or when the expert expresses very strong belief in a claim even though there is no evidence to support it, or when the expert stands to gain financially from the actions or policies that he or she supports.

It's true that many experts can render unbiased opinions and do high-quality research even when they have a conflict of interest. Nevertheless in such situations we have reasonable grounds to suspect bias—unless we have good reason to believe that the suspicion is unwarranted. These good reasons might include the fact that the expert's previous opinions in similar circumstances have been reliable or that he or she has a solid reputation for always offering unbiased assessments.

There are, of course, many other possible reasons to doubt the opinion of experts. Any blatant violation of the critical thinking principles discussed in this text, for example, would give us good reason to question an authority's reliability. Among the more common tip-offs of dubious authority are these:

• The expert is guilty of simple factual or formal errors.
• The expert's claims conflict with what you have good reason to believe.
• The expert does not adequately support his or her assertions.
• The expert's writing contains logical contradictions or inconsistent statements.
• The expert does not treat opposing views fairly.

- The expert is strongly biased, emotional, or dismissive.
- The expert relies on information you know is out of date.
- Most other experts in the same field disagree.

The amount of weight you give to any one of these factors—and the subsequent degree of doubt you attach to an expert's opinion—will vary in each case. In general, a single minor error of fact or style does not justify dismissing an expert's entire article that is otherwise excellent. But doubt is cumulative, and as reasons for doubt are added, you may rightfully decide that you are not justified in believing any part of an expert's testimony, regardless of his or her credentials. Depending on your aims, you may decide to check the expert's assertions against other sources or to consult an authority with much less evidential or rhetorical baggage.

Finally, keep in mind that there are certain kinds of issues that we probably don't want experts to settle for us. Indeed, in most cases the experts *cannot* settle them for us. These issues usually involve moral, social, or political questions. If we're intellectually conscientious, we want to provide our own final answers to such questions, though we may draw heavily on the analyses and arguments provided by experts. We may study what the experts have to say and the conclusions they draw. But we want ultimately to come to our own conclusions. We prefer this approach in large part because the questions are so important and because the answers we give help define who we are. What's more, the experts typically disagree on these issues. So even if we wanted the experts to settle one of these questions for us, they probably couldn't.

 NEWSMAKERS

Fallacious Appeal to (Questionable) Authority

Why do so many people listen to the advice and endorsements of famous people who may be no more knowledgeable than the least informed among us? If you have ever fallen for the celebrity version of the fallacious appeal to authority, maybe the following quotes will do you good. They prove that some really famous people can say some really stupid things—and knowing that might help you think twice before getting stung by this fallacy.

> I love them. Love them. I think the more positive approach you have to smoking, the less harmful it is.
> —Sienna Miller

What is my talent? Well, a bear can juggle and stand on a ball and he's talented, but he's not famous.

—Kim Kardashian

Would you not be so much more interested in finding out that Bigfoot existed than in watching a really good movie? I believe in aliens. I am childlike in my spirit, and I want to believe in fairy tales. Loch Ness monster . . . the Bell Witch. What distracts me from my reality is Bigfoot. They are my celebrities.

—Megan Fox

Sorry losers and haters, but my I.Q. is one of the highest—and you all know it! Please don't feel so stupid or insecure, it's not your fault.

—Donald Trump

I've been noticing gravity since I was very young.

—Cameron Diaz

It's okay to have beliefs, just don't believe in them.

—Guy Ritchie

So where's the Cannes Film Festival being held this year?

—Christina Aguilera

I think that gay marriage is something that should be between a man and a woman.

—Arnold Schwarzenegger

Rarely is the question asked: Is our children learning?

—George W. Bush

 REVIEW NOTES

Conflicting Claims

- If a claim conflicts with other claims we have good reason to accept, we have good grounds for doubting it.
- If a claim conflicts with our background information, we have good reason to doubt it.
- We should proportion our belief to the evidence.
- It's not reasonable to believe a claim when there is no good reason for doing so.
- If a claim conflicts with expert opinion, we have good reason to doubt it.
- When the experts disagree about a claim, we have good reason to doubt it.

Personal Experience

We accept a great many claims because they are based on personal experience—our own or someone else's. Personal experience, broadly defined, arises from our senses, our memory, and our judgment involved in those faculties. In countless cases, personal experience is our evidence (or part of the evidence) that something is or is not the case. You believe that Jack caused the traffic accident because you, or someone else, witnessed it. You think that the herbal tea cured your headache because the pain went away after you drank it. You believe that your friend can bend spoons with her mind because you saw her do it at a party. You're sure that the other guy threw the first punch, not you, because that's how you remember the incident. Or you vote to convict the defendant because eyewitness testimony puts him at the scene of the crime with a gun in his hand. But can you trust personal experience to reveal the truth?

The answer is a *qualified* yes. And here's the qualification in the form of an important principle:

> *It's reasonable to accept the evidence provided by personal experience only if there's no good reason to doubt it.*

If we have no good reason to doubt what our personal experience reveals to us, then we're justified in believing it. This means that if our faculties are working properly and our use of them is unimpeded by anything in our environment, we're entitled to accept what our personal experience tells us. If we seem to see a cat on the mat under good viewing conditions—that is, we have no reason to believe that our observations are impaired by, say, poor lighting, cracked glasses, or too many beers—then we're justified in believing that there's a cat on the mat.

The problem is that personal experience, though generally reliable, is not infallible. Under certain circumstances, our senses, memory, and judgment can't be trusted. It's easy enough to identify these circumstances in an abstract way, as you'll see later. The harder job is (1) determining when they actually occur in real-life situations and (2) avoiding them or taking them into account.

The rest of this section is a rundown of some of the more common factors that can give us good reason to doubt the reliability of personal experience.

Impairment

This should be obvious: If our perceptual powers are somehow impaired or impeded, we have reason to doubt them. The unambiguous cases are those in which our senses are debilitated because we are ill, injured, tired, stressed out, excited, drugged, drunk, distracted, or disoriented. And just as clear are the situations that interfere with sensory input—when our environment is, say, too dark, too bright, too noisy, or too hazy. If any of these factors are in play, the risk of misperception

> ## FURTHER THOUGHT
>
> ## Do Nonexperts Know Best?
>
> Some people have a bias against experts—*all* experts. Their thoughts on the subject might run something like this: "It's the uneducated ones, the simple seekers of knowledge who are the truly wise, for their thinking has not yet been corrupted by ivory-tower learning and highbrow theorizing that's out of touch with the real world. Thus the wisdom of the nonexpert is to be preferred over the expert whenever possible." This attitude is, oddly enough, sometimes embraced by very educated people. There's a strong strain of it, for example, among New Agers and advocates of alternative, or unconventional, medicine.
>
> This nonexpertism is related to the appeal to ignorance discussed in Chapter 5. (The appeal to ignorance says that since there's no evidence refuting a position, it must be true.) The problem is that both tacks, though psychologically compelling, are fallacious. A lack of good reasons—evidence or expert testimony—does not constitute proof of a claim.
>
> The history of science shows that virtually all notable scientific discoveries have been made by true experts—men and women who were fully knowledgeable about their subject matter. There have been many more instances, however, of cocksure nonexperts who proposed theories, cures, and solutions to problems that turned out to be worthless.

"Besides learning to see, there is another art to be learned—not to see what is not."
—Maria Mitchell

is high, which gives us reason to doubt the trustworthiness of what we experience.

Memories can be affected by many of the same factors that interfere with accurate perception. They are especially susceptible to distortion if they are formed during times of stress—which helps explain why the memories of people who witness crimes or alleged ghosts are so often unreliable. These situations are understandably stressful.

The impairment of our faculties is complicated by the peculiar way they operate. Contrary to what many believe, they are not like recording devices that make exact mental copies of objects and events in the world. Research suggests that they are more like artists who use bits of sensory data or memory fragments to concoct creative representations of things, not exact replicas. Our perception and memory are *constructive*, which means that what we perceive and remember is to some degree fabricated by our minds. Some of the more blatant examples: You see a man standing in the shadows by the road—then discover when you get closer that the man is a tree stump. You anxiously await a phone call from Aunt Mary, and when the call comes and you hear the person's voice, you're sure

Tinkering with Your Memory

The memories of eyewitnesses are notoriously unreliable. One reason is that your memory of an event can be altered if you later receive new information regarding the event. Research shows that your memory can be changed in this way, but you won't know it. You will be sincerely convinced that your altered memory is the original memory. Research studies have uncovered this phenomenon again and again. Here's a description of the classic case:

> Once upon a time, a man (whom we'll call Mike) stumbled upon an armed robbery in a hardware store. The robber rummaged around the cluttered store brandishing a silver weapon; finally, he stole all the money. Then, almost as an afterthought, he grabbed a hand calculator and a hammer, placing these in his satchel as he left the store. The police were summoned immediately, but before they arrived, Mike talked to another customer about the robbery. We'll call her Maria. Maria told Mike that she saw the robber grab a calculator and a screwdriver, stuffing them in his satchel as he left the store. The police arrived, and when they questioned Mike, he recounted the robbery at some length: He described in detail the silver weapon, the money, and the calculator. When the police asked him about a tool that they heard had been taken, "Did you see if it was a hammer or a screwdriver?" he said, "Screwdriver."[2]

it's her—then realize that it's some guy asking for a charitable donation. While in the shower you hear the phone ring—but no one is calling, and the ringing is something your mind is making up.

The constructive workings of our minds help us solve problems and deal effectively with our environment. But they can also hinder us by manufacturing too much of our experiences using too little data. Unfortunately, the constructive tendency is most likely to lead us astray precisely when our powers of perception and memory are impaired or impeded. Competent investigators of alleged paranormal phenomena understand this and are rightfully skeptical of paranormal claims based on observations made under dubious conditions like those mentioned here. Under the right conditions, the mind is very good at showing us UFOs and midnight ghosts that aren't there. Likewise, juries are expected to be suspicious of the testimony of eyewitnesses who swear they plainly saw the dirty deed committed but were frightened, enraged, or a little tipsy at the time.

FURTHER THOUGHT

Look! Martian Canals

How easy it is for even trained observers to see what isn't there! This famous example, one of many, is explained by psychologist Terence Hines:

> The constructive nature of perception accounts for a famous astronomical illusion—the canals of Mars. These were first reported in 1877 by the Italian astronomer Schiaparelli. They were popularized in the early twentieth century by the American astronomer Percival Lowell. . . . Lowell argued that the canals were constructed by an advanced Martian civilization. It turns out, however, that the canals of Mars don't exist. [Carl Sagan and P. Fox (1975)] have compared the photos taken by *Mariner 9*, which photographed the entire Martian surface, with maps of the canals. When the actual Martian surface is examined, there are no canals and no other physical features that could account for what Schiaparelli and Lowell reported. So, where did the canals come from? Sagan and Fox state that "the vast majority of the canals appear to be largely self-generated by the visual observers of the canal school, and stand as monuments to the imprecision of the human eye-brain-hand system under difficult observing conditions."[3]

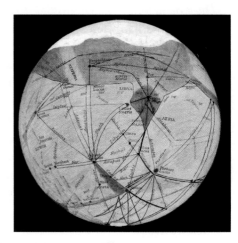

Lowell's drawings of Martian canals.

Expectation

A tricky thing about perception is that we often perceive exactly what we expect to perceive—regardless of whether there's anything there to detect. Ever watch the second hand on an electric clock move—then suddenly realize that the clock is not running at all? Ever been walking through a crowd looking for a friend and hear her call your name—then find out later that she was ten blocks away at the time? Such experiences—the result again of the constructive tendencies of mind—are common examples of how expectation can distort your perceptions.

Scientific research shows that expectation can have a more powerful effect on our experiences than most people think. In numerous studies, subjects

Eyewitness Testimony and Injustice

Eyewitness testimony is unreliable. So says a raft of scientific evidence, including this study that made headlines in 2007:

Because of a misidentification, Jerry Miller was convicted of a crime he did not commit and spent 25 years in prison. In 2007 he became the 200th prisoner in the United States to be exonerated by DNA evidence.

> Brandon L. Garrett, a law professor at the University of Virginia, has, for the first time, systematically examined . . . 200 cases, in which innocent people served an average of 12 years in prison. In each case, of course, the evidence used to convict them was at least flawed and often false—yet juries, trial judges and appellate courts failed to notice.
>
> "A few types of unreliable trial evidence predictably supported wrongful convictions," Professor Garrett concluded in his study, "Judging Innocence," to be published in *The Columbia Law Review* in January.
>
> The leading cause of the wrongful convictions was erroneous identification by eyewitnesses, which occurred 79 percent of the time. In a quarter of the cases, such testimony was the only direct evidence against the defendant.[4]

who expected to see a flash of light, smell a certain odor, or feel an electric shock did indeed experience these things—even though the appropriate stimuli were never present. The mere suggestion that the stimuli would occur was enough to cause the subjects to perceive, or apparently perceive, things that did not exist.

Our tendency to sometimes perceive things that are not really there is especially pronounced when the stimuli are vague or ambiguous. For example, we may perceive completely formless stimuli—clouds, smoke, "white noise," garbled voices, random-patterned wallpaper, blurry photos, lights in the night sky, stains on the ceiling—yet think we observe very distinct images or sounds. In the formlessness we may see ghosts, faces, and words and hear songs, screams, or verbal warnings. We may see or hear exactly what we expect to see or hear. Or the mere suggestion of what we should perceive helps us perceive it. This phenomenon is a kind of illusion known as *pareidolia*. It's the reason some people claim to hear Satanic messages when rock music is played backward, or to observe a giant stone face in fuzzy pictures of the surface of Mars, or to see the perfect likeness of Jesus in the skillet burns on a tortilla.

Scientists are keenly aware of the possible distorting influence of expectancy, so they try to design experiments that minimize it. We too need to minimize it as much as possible. Our strong expectations are a signal that we should double-check our sensory information and be careful about the conclusions we draw from it.

Innumeracy and Probability

When we make an off-the-cuff judgment about the chances of something happening (whether an event in the past or one in the future), we should be extra careful. Why? Because, generally, we humans are terrible at figuring probabilities.

Here's a classic example. Imagine that your classroom has twenty-three students present including yourself. What are the chances that at least two of the students have exactly the same birthday? (Not the same *date of birth,* but the same birthday out of the 365 possible ones.) The answer is neither 1 chance in 365 (1/365), nor 1 in 52 (1/52). It's *1 chance in 2* (1/2, or fifty-fifty)—a completely counterintuitive result.

A common error is the misjudging of coincidences. Many of us often believe that an event is simply too improbable to be a mere coincidence, that something else surely must be going on—such as paranormal or supernatural activity. But we mustn't forget that amazing coincidences occur all the time and, in fact, *must* occur according to elementary laws of statistics. The probability that a particular strange event will occur—say, that an ice cube tossed out of an airplane will hit the roof of a barn—may be extremely low, maybe one in a billion. But that same event given enough opportunities to occur may be highly probable over the long haul. It may be unlikely in any given instance for you to flip a coin and get tails seven times in a row. But this "streak" is virtually certain to happen if you flip the coin enough times.

What are the odds that someone will be thinking of a person she knew, or knew of, from the past twenty-five years then suddenly learn that the person is seriously ill or dead? Believe it or not, such a strange event is likely to occur several times a day. If we make the reasonable assumption that someone would recognize the names of a few thousand people (both famous and not so famous) from the past twenty-five years and that a person would learn of the illness or death of each of those few thousand people in the twenty-five years, then the chances of our eerie coincidence happening to someone somewhere are pretty good. We could reasonably expect that each day several people would have this experience.[5]

Another error is to think that previous events can affect the probabilities in the random event at hand. This mistake is known as the **gambler's fallacy.** Let's say you toss an unbiased coin six times in a row. On the first toss, the odds are, of course, 1 in 2, or fifty-fifty, that it will land tails. It lands tails. Astoundingly, on the other five tosses the coin also lands tails. That's six tails in a row. So what

REVIEW NOTES

Personal Experience

- It's reasonable to accept the evidence provided by personal experience only if there's no good reason to doubt it.
- If our perceptual powers are impaired or impeded, we have reason to doubt them.
- Our perception and memory are *constructive*, which means that our minds are capable of manufacturing what we experience.
- We often perceive exactly what we expect to perceive, and this tendency is enhanced when stimuli are vague or ambiguous.
- The gambler's fallacy is the mistake of thinking that previous events can affect the probabilities in the random event at hand.

are the odds that the coin will land tails on the seventh toss? Answer: fifty-fifty. Each toss has exactly the same probability of landing tails (or heads): fifty-fifty. The coin does not remember previous tosses. To think otherwise is to commit the gambler's fallacy. You see it a lot in casinos, sporting events, and—alas—everyday decision making.

The lesson here is not that we should mistrust all judgment about probabilities, but that we shouldn't rely solely on our intuitive sense in evaluating them. Relying entirely on intuition, or "gut feeling," in assessing probabilities is usually not a reason to trust the assessment, but to doubt it.

If we require greater precision in judging probabilities, we're in luck because mathematicians have worked out how to quantify and evaluate them. In the simplest case, calculating the probability of the occurrence of an event or outcome is a matter of division. For example, the probability of getting heads in the toss of an unbiased coin is one chance out of two—1/2 or 0.50. There is one toss and only two possible outcomes, heads or tails. Likewise the probability of randomly drawing the jack of spades out of a standard deck of 52 cards is 1 chance in 52—1/52, or 0.192. And the probability of drawing one of the hearts out of the deck is 13 in 52, or 0.25 (because there are 13 cards in each suit).

But suppose we want to know the probability of getting a 10 by throwing two dice (two unbiased six-sided dice). Here we are talking about two events that are *independent* of each other—the event of the first die showing a 5, and the event of the second die showing a 5. The one event has no effect on the other. The probability of the first event occurring is 1 chance out of 6—1/6, and the other event has the same probability, 1/6. To determine the probability of *both* events happening in one throw of the dice, we find the mathematical product of the two: $1/6 \times 1/6 = 1/36$. Just as you would expect, the chances of these dual events

"The first principle is that you must not fool yourself—and you are the easiest person to fool."
—Richard P. Feynman

happening (1/36) are much lower than that of just one of them happening (1/6). So to calculate the probability of two independent events happening together, we *multiply* the probability of the first event occurring by the probability of the second event occurring.

Now let's say the events in question are *not independent* of one another— each event can affect the other. Suppose we want to know the probability of drawing two hearts one after another from one standard (shuffled) deck of cards. Note that the deck will be light by one card after the first draw, thereby giving the second draw slightly different odds. The probability of drawing the first heart is 13/52 (13 hearts in the deck of 52), and the probability of drawing the next one is 12/51. To determine the probability of drawing two hearts in a row, we multiply: 13/52 × 12/51 = 1/17. So even when two events *are* affected by each other, to figure the odds of joint occurrence, we still *multiply* the probability of the first event occurring by the probability of the second event occurring.

Sometimes we may want to know the chances of *either* one of two events happening. Here we are not looking merely for two events to occur jointly as in the previous examples. We are interested in the odds of either one happening when they are mutually exclusive (if one occurs, the other cannot). Say we want to know the probability of pulling either a diamond or a club from a 52-card deck in one draw. The odds of drawing a diamond is 1 chance out of 4 (1/4), and the odds of drawing a club is also 1 in 4 (1/4). To figure the odds of drawing either one, we *add* the two probabilities: 1/4 + 1/4 = 1/2.

Fooling Ourselves

As we've seen, it's not reasonable to believe a claim unless we have good reason for doing so. If we care whether our beliefs about the world are reliable, we must base them on the relevant evidence. Beliefs backed by good evidence are more likely to be true, and true beliefs are more likely to help us get what we want out of life.

The kink in this straightforward arrangement is that we too often fail to give evidence its due. We ignore evidence, deny it, manipulate it, and distort it. Somehow there is very little comfort in knowing that everyone occasionally does this dance. What truly is encouraging is that we can learn to be alert to missteps in using and assessing evidence and that we can usually minimize, though not eliminate, the problems. This section looks at three of the most common and most serious mistakes we make when we deal with evidence.

Resisting Contrary Evidence

An all-too-human tendency is to try to resist evidence that flies in the face of our cherished beliefs. We may deny evidence, or ignore it, or reinterpret it so it fits better with our prejudices. Resisting evidence may be psychologically comforting (for a while, anyway), but it thwarts any search for knowledge and stunts our understanding.

A scene from *Fairy Tale: A True Story*. Hoaxed twice—once by the original (and charming) English pranksters and once by Hollywood.

As we will see in Chapter 10, the will to resist contrary evidence is especially strong—and tempting—in forays into the paranormal. Remember the study mentioned in Chapter 2 about researchers who showed subjects both evidence for and evidence against the reality of extrasensory perception (ESP)? The subjects who already had doubts about the existence of ESP accurately recalled both kinds of evidence. But the true believers—the subjects who already believed in ESP—remembered both kinds of evidence as *proving* ESP. They resisted the disconfirming evidence by mentally transforming it into confirming evidence. These results are typical of studies focusing on the paranormal.

Another typical case involves believers in the paranormal who, when confronted with evidence counting against their beliefs, simply refuse to accept it. For example, belief in fairies was given a boost many years ago when two girls presented the world with photographs they had allegedly taken of fairies playing with them in the garden. (The episode was the basis for the 1997 movie *Fairy Tale: A True Story*.) The photos looked fake, with the fairies resembling cutouts from a children's book—which is exactly what they were. But brushing that aside, many (including the renowned writer Sir Arthur Conan Doyle, creator of the fictional Sherlock Holmes) were convinced that the photos showed real fairies. Many years later when the girls were grown, they confessed that the whole thing was a hoax. But some believers—even those who heard the confession firsthand—refused to accept it![6]

But we need not look to the fringes of reality to find instances of the denial of evidence. Scientific research and commonsense experience show that the practice permeates all walks of life. A political activist may refuse to consider evidence that conflicts with his party's principles. A scientist may be so committed to her theory that she refuses to take seriously any data that undermine it. An administrator of a grand program may insist that it is a huge success despite all evidence to the contrary.

Often our resistance to contrary evidence takes a subtle form. If we encounter evidence against our views, we frequently don't reject it outright. We simply apply more critical scrutiny to it than we would to evidence in favor of our views, or we seek out additional confirming information, or we find a way to interpret the data so it doesn't conflict with our expectations.

In one study, proponents and opponents of the death penalty were presented with evidence concerning whether capital punishment deterred crime. Both those opposed to and those in favor of capital punishment were given two types of evidence—(1) some that supported the practice and (2) some that discredited it. Psychologist Thomas Gilovich describes the outcome of the study:

> The results of this experiment were striking. The participants considered the study that provided evidence consistent with their prior beliefs—regardless of what type of study that was—to be a well-conducted piece of research that provided important evidence concerning the effectiveness of capital punishment. In contrast, they uncovered numerous flaws in the research that contradicted their initial beliefs. . . . Rather than ignoring outright the evidence at variance with their expectations, the participants cognitively transformed it into evidence that was considered relatively uninformative and could be assigned little weight.[7]

There is no cure for our tendency to resist opposing evidence. The only available remedy is our commitment to examine critically our favorite claims—which means trying our best to be even-handed in scrutinizing the evidence we like and the evidence we don't.

Looking for Confirming Evidence

We often not only resist conflicting evidence, but also seek out and use only confirming evidence—a phenomenon known as *confirmation bias*. When we go out of our way to find only confirming evidence, we can end up accepting a claim that's not true, seeing relationships that aren't there, and finding confirmation that isn't genuine.

In scientific research on confirmation bias, when subjects are asked to assess a claim, they often look for confirming evidence only, even though disconfirming evidence may be just as revealing. For example, in one study, a group of subjects was asked to assess whether practicing before a tennis match was linked to winning the match; another group, whether practicing before a match was linked to losing the match. All the subjects were asked to select the kind of evidence (regarding practice and winning or losing matches) that they thought would be the most helpful in answering the relevant question. Not surprisingly, the subjects deciding whether pre-game practicing was linked to winning focused on how many times players practiced and then won the match. And subjects assessing whether practicing was associated with losing focused on how many times players practiced and then lost the match.[8]

FURTHER THOUGHT

I Just *Know*!

Suppose you make a claim that you have neither evidence nor argument to back up, and someone asks, "How do you know?" And you say, "I just know," or "My gut (or intuition) tells me it's true." In such situations, do you really know—do you really possess knowledge? Many epistemologists (philosophers who study knowledge) would argue that you do not, unless your

ordinary means of acquiring knowledge (reason and observation) have validated the reliability of your intuition or gut. Nevertheless many people believe that their gut is a reliable way of knowing. Here's a famous case of "gut knowing" that has been criticized by several authors, including the philosopher Stephen Law:

> Notoriously, during George W. Bush's presidency, Bush's gut became the oracle of the state. Bush was distrustful of book learning and those with established expertise in a given area. When he made the decision to invade Iraq, and was subsequently confronted by a skeptical audience, Bush said that ultimately, he just *knew in his gut* that invading was the right thing to do. . . .
>
> The invasion went ahead. A few months later, Senator Joe Biden told Bush of his growing worries about the aftermath. In response, Bush again appealed to the reliability of his "instincts. . . ."
>
> How did Bush suppose his gut was able to steer the ship of state? He supposed it was functioning as a *sort of God-sensing faculty.* Bush believed that by means of his gut he could sense what God wanted of him. . . . Those who, like George W. Bush, place a simple trusting faith in their gut, or wherever else they think their *sensus divinitatis* is located, are being irresponsible and foolish.[9]

Assuming this account of George Bush's thinking is accurate, do you think he really *knew* that invading Iraq was the right thing to do? If so, how does this kind of intuitive knowing work? Exactly how is knowledge gained this way? If not, where do you think Bush's error lies? What is wrong with "knowing in your gut"?

Sometimes we look for confirming evidence even when disconfirming evidence is more telling. For example, take this claim: All swans are white. You can easily find confirming instances; white swans are plentiful and ubiquitous. But even your seeing thousands of white swans will not conclusively confirm that all swans are white because there may be swans in places where you haven't looked. But all you have to do is find one black swan to conclusively show that the claim is false. (People used to believe that the claim was absolutely true—until black swans were discovered in Australia.) In such cases, confirmation bias can lead us way off course.

The moral to this story is that when we evaluate claims, we should look for disconfirming as well as confirming evidence. Doing so requires a conscious effort to consider not only the information that supports what we want to believe but also the information that conflicts with it. We have to seek out disconfirming evidence just as we keep an eye out for confirming evidence—an approach that goes against our grain. We naturally gravitate to people and policies we agree with, to the books that support our views, to the magazines and newspapers that echo our political outlook. Acquiring a broader, smarter, more critical perspective takes effort—and courage.

Preferring Available Evidence

Another common mistake in evaluating evidence is the *availability error*. We commit this blunder when we rely on evidence not because it's trustworthy but because it's memorable or striking—that is, psychologically available. In such cases, we put stock in evidence that's psychologically impressive or persuasive, not necessarily logically acceptable. You fall for the availability error if you vote to convict a murder suspect because he looks menacing, not because the evidence

---

 FURTHER THOUGHT

This Is Lunacy!

When there's a full moon, do people get crazy? Do they behave like *lunatics*? Folklore says that they do, and many people believe that there's a lunar effect on the way people act. But numerous studies have shown that there is absolutely no causal connection between the moon and human behavior. So why do so many people believe in lunar power? Part of the reason is the availability error. Strange behavior is more noticeable (and so more available) than normal behavior, so we tend to think that weird behavior is more frequent. And if we look only for confirming instances (and we do), we're likely to believe that the moon is indeed the cause of a lot of peculiar behavior. Of course, many people behave strangely with or without a full moon.

points to his guilt; or if you decide that a Honda Civic is an unsafe vehicle because you saw one get smashed in a highway accident; or if, just because you watched a TV news report about a mugging in your city, you believe that the risk of being mugged is extremely high.

Being taken in by the availability error can lead to some serious misjudgments about the risks involved in various situations. Some people (are you one of them?) believe that air travel is more dangerous than many other modes of transportation, so they shun travel by airplane in favor of the automobile. Their conclusion is based on nothing more than a few vivid media reports of tragic plane crashes. But research shows that per mile traveled, flying is far safer than automobile travel. Your chances of dying in a plane crash in 2001 were 1 in 310,560, but the odds of your dying in a car accident were only 1 in 19,075. The fact is, there are plenty of less vivid and less memorable (that is, psychologically unavailable) things that are much more dangerous than air travel: falling down stairs, drowning, choking, and accidental poisoning.[10]

Social psychologist John Ruscio provides another example:

> Aside from a close miss by what was reported to be a falling airplane part early in *The Truman Show*, I cannot personally recall ever having heard of such an accident, fictitious or real. Students over the years have told me that they recall stories of people having found fallen airplane parts, but not of an actual fatality resulting from such falling parts. Shark attacks, on the other hand, are easily imagined and widely reported. Moreover, in the first movie that comes to my mind, the shark in *Jaws* actually did cause several fatalities. It may come as some surprise, then, to learn that in an average year in the United States thirty times more people are killed by falling airplane parts than by shark attacks.[11]

The availability error is very likely at work in many controversies regarding environmental hazards. Because the alleged hazard and its effects can be easily and vividly imagined and the scientific data on the issue are not so concrete or memorable, the imagined danger can provoke a public scare even though the fear is completely unwarranted. Brain cancer from the use of cell phones and childhood leukemia from living near power lines—both these putative hazards have provoked fear and public demands for action. But scientific studies have shown these concerns to be groundless. Many environmental hazards are real, of course. But concluding that they exist solely on the basis of scary thoughts is to commit the availability error.

If we're in the habit of basing our judgments on evidence that's merely psychologically available, we will frequently commit the error known as hasty generalization, a mistake discussed in detail in Chapter 8. We're guilty of hasty generalization when we draw a conclusion about a whole group based on an inadequate sample of the group. We fall into this trap when we assert something like this: "Honda Civics are pieces of junk. I owned one for three months, and it gave me nothing but trouble." Our experience with a car is immediate and personal, so for many of us it can be a short step from this psychologically available evidence to a very hasty conclusion. If we give in to the availability error and stick to our guns about lousy Civics in the face of good evidence to the contrary (say, automobile-reliability research done by the Consumers Union or similar organizations), we should get an F in critical thinking.

Evaluating Sources: The Internet and Beyond

So here are the hard, elementary facts about the news media, social media, the Internet, and the print world:

- Alas, not everything you read is true.
- Countless sources on the Internet and in conventional media are unreliable.
- It's often difficult to tell the difference between fake or false news and real news.
- Advertising cannot be trusted to give you unbiased information.
- A great deal of what you read online is false, misleading, vicious, self-serving, clueless, or crazy.

What's a critical thinker to do? For starters, you can try bravely and conscientiously to do the following:

- **Read critically.** Cultivate a skeptical, vigilant, but inquiring attitude toward what you read. Critically examine claims and evidence and be open to changing your mind as the facts warrant. Do not give in to two of the most damaging ideas in contemporary culture—that there's no such thing as truth or that telling fact from fiction is impossible.
- **Size up authors, bloggers, and publishers.** Do not thoughtlessly assume that what a writer says must be true or that every source disseminates trustworthy information. Evaluate the author's credentials, biases, affiliations, assumptions, motives, and sources. Be suspicious if the author demonstrates poor critical thinking. Gauge sources mainly by the claims they convey—do the claims conflict with expert opinion, with what you have good reason to believe, with the assertions of other (reputable) publishers, with logic and common sense?
- **Sort out claims.** Ultimately the credibility of a source comes down to the credibility of its claims, including those used as premises and conclusions of arguments. So correctly judging the plausibility of statements is the essential skill in evaluating sources. Remember: It is reasonable (1) to accept claims that you know are supported independently by authorities or evidence (and that fit well with your background information), (2) to accept claims that are adequately supported by the source itself through citations to other credible sources (experts, research, reports, etc.) or through references to supporting facts, (3) to reject claims when there is good reason for believing them false, and (4) to suspend judgment on claims that you are unsure of, for it is unreasonable to accept a claim without good reasons. The only cure for uncertainty about a source's claims is further research and reflection.

- **Compare sources.** Relying exclusively on one source for information is usually a mistake. Consulting a variety of sources helps you put the information in proper perspective, uncover errors and bias, pinpoint consensus and disagreement among experts, and find out where the preponderance of evidence points. Certainly your hunt for sources should be carefully planned and limited, but examining too few of them can lead to views that are one-sided, incomplete, and wrong.
- **Try to discern the source's purpose.** Is the purpose advertising, fund-raising, opinion, news, advocacy, entertainment, venting, trolling, commerce?
- **Check alternative news sources.** How can you tell if the news you're getting is incomplete—if there's important news you're not seeing? You can't, unless you check alternative news sources for any missing stories. Reading a variety of newspapers, newsmagazines, blogs, websites, and journals of opinion is the best way to ensure that you're getting the big picture. To avoid confirmation bias, and to ensure that you're fully informed, you should read not only those sources that agree with you but also those that don't. Don't get trapped in an echo chamber. The air inside is decidedly unhealthy.

Fake News

Fake news—bogus news stories that masquerade as truthful reporting—has been around for a long time. But thanks to social media, fake news now spreads faster and more cleverly than ever. It was a force to be reckoned with in the 2016 presidential campaign and will continue to deceive, provoke, and harm society indefinitely. Typically it shows up on sites that look legitimate but aren't. The "news" presented can be completely made up, or it can be so partisan that it says only good things about one political perspective and only bad things about another, or it can be a strange but plausible blend of fact and fiction, or it can be satirical—good fun perhaps, except for those who don't get the joke.

It's easy to fall for the misinformation, partly because of the nature of the material and partly because of the way we humans are. We are prone to confirmation bias and to group thinking. You come across a compelling news story that confirms exactly what you want to believe. It reinforces the perspective and prejudices of your group. It seems to be evidence that you have been right all along. So you skip critical thinking and share the story with your like-minded friends, and thousands of people become believers. But for all you know the story may be fake—and you have no good reason for believing it true or false.

Fortunately there are ways to avoid the traps of fake news, and the general strategies for doing so are the same ones highlighted in this chapter. But there are also tips for spotting fake news. Here are some from FactCheck.org:

> **Consider the Source**. . . . Clearly, some [fake news] sites do provide a "fantasy news" or satire warning, like WTOE 5, which

published the bogus headline, "Pope Francis Shocks World, Endorses Donald Trump for President, Releases Statement." Others aren't so upfront, like the Boston Tribune, which doesn't provide any information on its mission, staff members, or physical location—further signs that maybe this site isn't a legitimate news organization. The site, in fact, changed its name from Associated Media Coverage, after its work had been debunked by fact-checking organizations.

Snopes.com, which has been writing about viral claims and online rumors since the mid-1990s, maintains a list of known fake news websites, several of which have emerged in the past two years. . . .

Read beyond the headline. If a provocative headline drew your attention, read a little further before you decide to pass along the shocking information. Even in legitimate news stories, the headline doesn't always tell the whole story. But fake news, particularly efforts to be satirical, can include several revealing signs in the text. That abcnews.com.co story that we checked, headlined "Obama Signs Executive Order Banning The Pledge Of Allegiance In Schools Nationwide," went on to quote "Fappy the Anti-Masturbation Dolphin." We have to assume that the many readers who asked us whether this viral rumor was true hadn't read the full story. . . .

What's the support? Many times these bogus stories will cite official—or official-sounding—sources, but once you look into it, the source doesn't back up the claim. For instance, the Boston Tribune site wrongly claimed that President Obama's mother-in-law was going to get a lifetime government pension for having babysat her granddaughters in the White House, citing "the Civil Service Retirement Act" and providing a link. But the link to a government benefits website doesn't support the claim at all.

The banning-the-pledge [of allegiance] story cites the number of an actual executive order—you can look it up. It doesn't have anything to do with the Pledge of Allegiance. . . .

Check your biases. We know this is difficult. Confirmation bias leads people to put more stock in information that confirms their beliefs and discount information that doesn't. But the next time you're automatically appalled at some Facebook post concerning, say, a politician you oppose, take a moment to check it out.

Try this simple test: What other stories have been posted to the "news" website that is the source of the story that just popped up in your Facebook feed? You may be predisposed to believe that Obama bought a house in Dubai, but how about a story on the same site that carries this headline: "Antarctica 'Guardians' Retaliate Against America With Massive New Zealand Earthquake." That, too, was written by the prolific "Sorcha Faal, and as reported to her Western Subscribers."[12]

FURTHER THOUGHT

When You Don't Trust the Mainstream Media

So you have come to the conclusion that the mainstream media can't be trusted—and that alternative sources of information *can* be trusted. Perhaps you're right. Or wrong. In any case, the crucial question to ask is, What are your *legitimate* reasons for thinking so? Legitimate reasons are those that increase the likelihood of a claim being true. As we've seen, such reasons come from reliable evidence, trustworthy authorities, and critical reasoning. The problem is that we too often reach for illegitimate reasons, those that are *irrelevant* to the truth of a claim. Here are some illegitimate reasons for accepting or rejecting claims from a media source:

- My group (political faction, fans of politician X or pundit Y, online community, etc.) trusts this source. (So I will too.)
- This source contradicts my beliefs. (So it must be fake news or otherwise untrustworthy.)
- An opposing group rejects this source. (So I will accept it because I hate the opposing group.)
- This source reinforces what I'd like to believe. (So I will believe it without question.)
- I reject any claim that comes from sources I don't like. (Because nothing they say can be right.)
- I feel strongly that the claims made by this source are true; therefore they are true. (Because my feelings alone can certify claims.)
- I have faith in my leader, and he or she hates this source. (So I will hate it too, because I believe whatever he or she says.)
- Believing this claim or source makes me feel good. (And feeling good is what matters.)
- I let my intuition or gut tell me whether to trust a source. (It saves time and energy.)

There are times when it's perfectly rational to believe a claim just because a source says it's true. But that attitude is appropriate only when you have previously verified the reliability of the source by checking for legitimate reasons supporting the source's claims.

When critically evaluating media (mainstream or otherwise) for trustworthiness, there is no way around the hard work of checking for good reasons to believe or disbelieve. And there is no denying that doing this often takes tremendous courage. Remember, a good critical thinker is prepared to believe almost anything—given enough good reasons.

> **FURTHER THOUGHT**
>
> ## Man Shoots Neighbor with Machete
>
> Man shoots neighbor with machete? Yes—so says a headline that actually appeared in a large-circulation newspaper. Probably every newspaper in America has been guilty of running such ambiguously goofy headlines. Here are a few more:
>
> - Iraqi Head Seeks Arms
> - Study Finds Sex, Pregnancy Link
> - Kicking Baby Considered to Be Healthy
> - Typhoon Rips Through Cemetery; Hundreds Dead
> - Lack of Brains Hinders Research
> - Panda Mating Fails; Veterinarian Takes Over

Advertising and Persuasion

Advertising is like air: It is everywhere, so pervasive and so natural that we forget it's there, yet penetrating and changing us every day. Advertising messages hit us rapid-fire and nonstop from television, radio, email, websites, podcasts, movie theaters, magazines, newsletters, newspapers, book covers, junk mail, telephones, fax machines, product labels, billboards, vehicle signs, T-shirts, wall posters, flyers, and who knows what else. Ads permeate all media—print, film, video, television, radio, and cyberspace. Caught in this whirl of words and sounds and images, we can easily overlook the obvious and disconcerting facts behind them: (1) All advertising is designed to influence, persuade, or manipulate us; (2) to an impressive degree and in many ways, it *does* successfully influence, persuade, or manipulate us; and (3) we are often oblivious to—or in outright denial about—how effectively advertising influences, persuades, or manipulates us.

The purpose of advertising is to sell products and services, promote causes or candidates, or alter attitudes and opinions. How well advertising does these jobs can be measured in money. Advertising in most media can cost a great deal. A single full-page magazine ad can cost tens of thousands of dollars; a thirty-second TV ad can run into the millions (especially on Super Bowl Sunday). But companies are willing to pay the price because advertising works. The revenues garnered from advertising can outweigh its costs by wide margins; in the case of a magazine ad or a TV spot, the gain could easily be hundreds of thousands or millions of dollars. In addition, advertisers and advertising agencies invest heavily each year in scientific consumer research to determine how to configure ads precisely to elicit the desired response from people. Again, they make these investments because there is a sure payoff: Consumers usually respond just as the research says they will. How do your eyes track across a newspaper ad when you are looking at it? Would you respond better to a TV commercial if the voice-over came from Walter Cronkite or from Jon Bon Jovi? Would the magazine ad be more likely to sell you the cottage cheese if the headline used the word *creamy* instead of *smooth*? Would the ad copy on the junk-mail envelope increase sales if it were red instead of blue? You may not care about any of this, but advertisers do because such seemingly trivial bits of information can help them influence you in ways you barely suspect.

However averse we are (or think we are) to advertising or to its aims, we cannot deny its appeal. We like advertising, at least some of it. We easily can point to ads that annoy us or insult our intelligence, but most of us can also recall ones that are entertaining, funny, inspiring, even informative.

How, then, should good critical thinkers think about advertising? Our guiding principle should be:

> *We generally have good reason to doubt advertising claims and to be wary of advertising's persuasive powers.*

This means that usually the most reasonable response to advertising is a degree of suspicion. If we prefer truth over falsehood, if we would rather not be mistaken or bamboozled, if we want to make informed choices involving our time and money, then a general wariness toward advertising ploys is justified. This principle does not assume that all ad claims are false or that advertising cannot be genuinely informative or useful. It simply says that we should not accept uncritically an ad's message or impact on us.

There are several reasons for this cautious approach. First, recall the purpose of advertising—to *sell or promote something*, whether a product, service, person, or idea. To put the point bluntly, though advertising can be both truthful and helpful, its primary function is *not* to provide objective and accurate information to consumers. Advertisers will tell you many good things about their products but are unlikely to mention all the bad. Their main job is *not* to help consumers make fully informed, rational choices about available options. Advertising is advertising—it is not intended to be an impartial search for facts or a program of consumer protection. We are therefore justified in maintaining the same attitude toward advertising that we would toward a complete stranger who wants to sell us a widget: His motives are obviously pecuniary while his commitment to honesty is unknown.

Second, advertising has a reputation for—and a history of—misleading messages. The world is filled with ads that make dubious or false claims, use fallacious arguments (stated or implied), and employ psychological tricks to manipulate consumer responses.

Some of these methods fit neatly in our rundown of fallacies in Chapters 4 and 5. Ads frequently employ fallacious appeals to authority ("As an Olympic gold medal winner, I can tell you that PowerVitamin 2000 really works!"), appeals to emotion ("Enjoy the goodness and warmth of Big-Brand Soup, just like mother used to make"), appeals to popularity ("CNN, America's number-one source for news"), hasty generalizations ("Mothers everywhere will love Softie Diapers—our test mothers sure did!"), and faulty analogies ("As a businessman, I saved General Motors. As president, I can save this country.").

"Advertising is the rattling of a stick inside a swill bucket."
—George Orwell

But advertisers also use an array of other persuasive techniques, most of which do not involve making explicit claims or providing good reasons for acting or choosing. The following are some of the more common ones.

Identification

Many ads persuade by simply inviting the consumer to identify with attractive people (real or imagined) or groups. Most ads featuring celebrity endorsements use this ploy. The idea is to get you to identify so strongly with a celebrity that you feel his or her product choices are *your* preferred choices. Without providing a single good reason or argument, endorsement ads say, in effect, that if Christina Aguilera prefers Pepsi, if Halle Berry likes Revlon, if Michael Jordan loves Nike, maybe you should, too.

Slogans

Catchy, memorable phrases are the stock-in-trade of advertising. How can we forget "Nike. Just do it" (Nike); "Reach out and touch someone" (AT&T); "Like a rock" (Chevrolet); "Don't leave home without it" (American Express); "Built Ford tough!" (Ford); "Obey your thirst" (Sprite); or "An army of one" (U.S. Army)? Such catchphrases may not say much, but they do get our attention, engender appealing emotions or concepts, and associate them with products or companies— again and again and again. Through repetition that seems to embed themselves in our brains, slogans surreptitiously get us to feel that one product or brand is better than another.

Misleading Comparisons

In advertising, comparisons can mislead in many ways. Consider these examples:

1. BeSure Tampons are 30% more absorbent.
2. Big sale! The SuperX CD Player for less than the suggested retail price!
3. Simply better-tasting tacos. No question.

The problem with example 1 is its vagueness, which is of course deliberate. What does "30% more absorbent" mean? Thirty percent more absorbent than they used to be? Thirty percent more absorbent than similar products are? If the latter, what similar products are we talking about? Are BeSure Tampons being compared to the *least* absorbent tampons on the market? The *30%* may seem impressive—until we know to what it actually refers. (Another relevant question is how absorbency was determined. As you might imagine, there are many ways to perform such tests, some of them likely to yield more impressive numbers than others.)

The claim in example 2 may or may not be touting a true bargain. We would probably view the "Big sale" in a different light if we knew whether the store's *regular* prices are below the suggested retail prices or if *all* stores sell the CD player below the suggested retail.

Example 3 contains the same sort of vagueness we find in example 1 plus an additional sort of emptiness. The phrase "better-tasting tacos" is a claim about a subjective state of affairs—a claim that *anyone* could make about his or her own gustatory experience. You and a thousand other people might try the tacos and think they taste terrible. So the claim tells you nothing about whether you will like the tacos. The claim would be empty even if it were stretched to "The best-tasting tacos on earth!" In the ad world, such exaggerations are known as *puffery*, which is regarded in advertising law as hype that few people take seriously.

Weasel Words

When advertisers want to *appear* to make a strong claim but avoid blatant lying or deception, they use what are known as *weasel words*. Weasel words water down a claim in subtle ways—just enough to ensure that it is technically true but superficially misleading. Consider:

1. You may have already won a new 2007 Ford pickup truck!
2. Some doctors recommend ginseng for sexual dysfunction.
3. Relieves up to 60 percent of headaches in chronic headache sufferers.

Example 1 is typical junk-mail hype that seems to promise a valuable prize. But the weasel word *may* weakens the claim. Technically, you *may* have actually won since your winning is at least (remotely) possible. But in the typical sweepstakes, the odds of your winning anything are millions to one. Yes, you may have already won—and you are just as likely to get hit by an asteroid tomorrow. Example 2 plays on the weasel word *some*. It is probably true that *some* (meaning at least one) doctors recommend ginseng for sexual dysfunction, but a huge majority of them do not. Using *some*, we could craft an infinite number of technically true but misleading (and ridiculous) claims about what doctors do and don't do. In example 3 the weasel words are *up to*. Notice that many states of affairs would be consistent with this (vague) statement. It would be true even if just 1 percent of headaches were relieved in almost all headache sufferers.

Other weasels include *as many as, reportedly, possibly, virtually, many, seems*, and *perhaps*. Such words, of course, can have perfectly respectable uses as necessary qualifiers in many contexts. The problems arise when they are used not to qualify but to misguide.

 KEY WORDS

appeal to authority	**expert**
background information	**gambler's fallacy**

Summary

When Claims Conflict

- Many times we need to be able to evaluate an unsupported claim—a claim that isn't backed by an argument. There are several critical thinking principles that can help us do this. An important one is: *If a claim conflicts with other claims we have good reason to accept, we have good grounds for doubting it.*
- Sometimes there is a conflict between a claim and your background information. Background information is the large collection of very well supported beliefs that we rely on to inform our actions and choices. The relevant principle is: *If a claim conflicts with our background information, we have good reason to doubt the claim.*
- It's not reasonable to accept a claim if there is good reason to doubt it. In the case of claims that we can neither accept nor reject outright: *We should proportion our belief to the evidence.*

Experts and Evidence

- An expert is someone who is more knowledgeable in a particular subject area than most others are. The important principle is: *If a claim conflicts with expert opinion, we have good reason to doubt it.*
- We must couple this principle with another one: *When the experts disagree about a claim, we have good reason to doubt it.* When we rely on bogus expert opinion, we commit the fallacy known as the appeal to authority.

Personal Experience

- Many claims are based on nothing more than personal experience, ours or someone else's. We can trust our personal experience—to a point. The guiding principle is: *It's reasonable to accept the evidence provided by personal experience only if there's no reason to doubt it.*
- Some common factors that can raise such doubts are impairment (stress, injury, distraction, emotional upset, and the like), expectation, and our limited abilities in judging probabilities.

Fooling Ourselves

- Some of the common mistakes we make in evaluating claims are resisting contrary evidence, looking for confirming evidence, and preferring available evidence.
- To counteract these tendencies, we need to take deliberate steps to examine critically even our most cherished claims, search for disconfirming evidence as well as confirming, and look beyond evidence that is merely the most striking or memorable.

Evaluating Sources: The Internet and Beyond

- The news media, social media, the Internet, and the print world are loaded with unreliable sources, fake or false news, and deceptive or misleading claims everywhere.
- The best way to avoid media nonsense is to read critically; size up authors, bloggers, and publishers; sort out claims; compare sources; uncover the source's purpose; and check alternative sources.

Fake News

- Fake news consists of bogus news stories that masquerade as truthful reporting. They deceive, mislead, and misinform. But there are ways to avoid these traps.
- Some tips for spotting fake news: consider the source, read beyond the headline, ask what's the support, and check your own biases.

Advertising and Persuasion

- Advertising is another possible source of unsupported or misleading claims. We should realize that we generally have good reason to doubt advertising claims and to be wary of advertising's persuasive powers.

 EXERCISES

Exercise 4.1

REVIEW QUESTIONS

1. What kinds of beliefs are part of a person's background information?
2. What is the most reasonable attitude toward a claim that conflicts with other claims you have good reason to believe?
3. What degree of probability should we assign to a claim that conflicts with our background information?
* 4. What is the most reasonable attitude toward a claim that is neither worthy of acceptance nor deserving of outright rejection?
5. What is an expert?
6. What should be our attitude toward a claim that conflicts with expert opinion?
7. What should be our attitude toward a claim when experts disagree about it?
8. What is the fallacy of the appeal to authority?
9. According to the text, in most fields, what are the two minimal prerequisites for being considered an expert?
* 10. According to the text, beyond the minimal prerequisites, what are two more telling indicators that someone is an expert?

11. Under what three circumstances should we suspect that an expert may be biased?

12. When is it reasonable to accept the evidence provided by personal experience?

13. What are two factors that can give us good reason to doubt the reliability of personal experience?

14. In what ways are our perception and memory constructive?

15. What are some ways that people resist contrary evidence?

16. What is confirmation bias?

* 17. How can critical thinkers counteract confirmation bias?

18. What is the availability error?

19. What is the connection between availability error and hasty generalization?

20. According to the text, other than reporters and editors themselves, what is the foremost factor influencing the quality of news reporting?

21. According to the text, what are three techniques for critically evaluating the reliability of news reports?

22. What principle should guide our judgments about advertising?

Exercise 4.2

Based on claims you already have good reason to believe, your background information, and your assessment of the credibility of any cited experts, indicate for each of the following claims whether you would accept it, reject it, or proportion your belief to the evidence. Give reasons for your answers. If you decide to proportion your belief to the evidence, indicate generally what degree of plausibility you would assign to the claim.

1. Israeli psychic Uri Geller can bend spoons with his mind.

2. In Russia, some people live to be 150 years old.

3. Every year in the United States over three hundred people die of leprosy.

* 4. According to Dr. Feelgood, the spokesperson for Acme Mattresses, the EasyRest 2000 from Acme is the best mattress in the world for back-pain sufferers.

5. Some bars in the suburbs of Chicago have been entertaining their nightly patrons with pygmy hippo tossing.

* 6. Every person has innate psychic ability that, when properly cultivated, can enable him or her to read another person's mind.

7. The prime minister of Canada works with the government of the United States to suppress the economic power of French Canadians.

8. Molly, a thirty-four-year-old bank manager, says that stock prices will plummet dramatically in two months and will trigger another deep year-long recession.

9. Humans use only about 10 percent of the brain's capacity for thinking and creating.

* 10. Fifteen women have died after smelling a free perfume sample that they received in the mail.

11. A chain letter describing the struggles of a nine-year-old girl with incurable cancer is circulating on the Internet. The more people who receive the letter, the better the little girl's chances of survival.

12. A report from the National Institutes of Health says that there is no evidence that high doses of the herb ephedra can cure cancer.

13. Giant albino alligators crawl through the underground sewers of New York City.

* 14. Crop circles—large-scale geometric patterns pressed into crop fields—are the work of space aliens.

15. Crop circles are the work of human hoaxers.

16. North Korea is a communist paradise where everyone prospers and human rights are respected.

* 17. Dr. Xavier, a world-famous astrologer, says that the position of the sun, planets, and stars at your birth influences your choice of careers and your marital status.

18. Eleanor Morgan, a Nobel Prize–winning economist, says that modern democratic systems (including developed nations) are not viable.

19. Eating meat rots your colon.

20. The highway speed limit in New York is 65 mph.

Exercise 4.3

For each of the following claims, decide whether you agree or disagree with it. If you agree with it, indicate what evidence would persuade you to reject the statement. If you disagree with it, indicate what evidence would persuade you to accept the statement. In each case, ask yourself if you would really change your mind if presented with the evidence you suggested.

1. Affirmative action should be abolished at all state colleges.

2. Same-sex marriage should be legally recognized in all fifty states.

* 3. An alien spacecraft crashed in Roswell, New Mexico, in 1947.

4. Earth is only ten thousand years old.

5. There is life on Mars.

6. Some people can twist their heads around on their necks a complete 360 degrees.

7. On Tuesday, a new computer virus will shut down every network and every PC in the world.

* 8. Meditation and controlled breathing can shrink cancerous tumors.

9. All swans are white.

10. "Corporate welfare"—tax breaks and other special considerations for businesses—should be discontinued.

Exercise 4.4

Examine the following newspaper story and answer the questions that follow.

Work Farce

June 26, 2003—Brazen Department of Education construction employees ripped off the city by clocking in but doing little or no work—instead spending their days at the gym, shopping or moonlighting, a sting operation by Schools Investigator Richard Condon's office found.

Checks of 13 workers—some chosen randomly, others on the basis of complaints—who were monitored beginning last August found eight of them doing little or no work.

The slackers will soon find themselves in handcuffs and unemployment lines, authorities said. . . . Condon charged that time cheating by phantom workers is "common practice."

"Time abuse is a financial drain on the city's public school system. No doubt it plays a role in the overtime that is paid to skilled trade workers," Condon said. . . .

Condon did not release the names of the slackers because they're about to be arrested, he said. Chancellor Joel Klein said they will be fired "immediately."[13]

1. Is the story slanted toward or against a particular group mentioned in the story? How?
2. Are there instances of loaded or biased language or emotional appeals in the story or headline? If so, give examples.
3. What is the main source for this story?

 ## Field Problems

1. Find a controversial newspaper story posted on the Internet and answer the questions in Exercise 4.4 about it.
2. Write down a claim in which you strongly believe. Select one that pertains to an important social, religious, or political issue. Then indicate what evidence would persuade you to change your mind about the claim.
3. Select a news item or press release from a pro-life website (such as www .covenantnews.com or www.prolifeamerica.com) and a pro-choice one (such as www.choiceusa.org or www.prochoiceamerica.org). Analyze each selection, looking for evidence of bias or slanting—loaded or biased language, unsupported opinion, emotional appeals, omission of relevant but opposing information, and undeserved emphasis on aspects of the story.
4. From a magazine select a full-page ad that uses at least two of the following ploys: (1) misleading comparison, (2) catchy slogan, (3) identification with a celebrity, or (4) weasel words.

Self-Assessment Quiz

Answers appear in "Answers to Self-Assessment Quizzes" (Appendix D).

1. How should a critical thinker regard an unsupported claim that conflicts with a great deal of her background information?

2. State in your own words Bertrand Russell's principle regarding unsupported claims.

3. Name four factors to consider in deciding whether someone should be considered an expert.

4. According to the text, what are some telltale signs that an expert may be biased?

5. Name three types of perceptual impairment that can give us good reason to doubt the reliability of our personal experience.

For each of the following situations and the claim associated with it, indicate whether there may be good reasons to doubt the claim and, if so, specify the reasons.

6. Standing on a street corner in heavy fog, Eve thinks that she sees an old friend walking away from her on the other side of the street. She says to herself, "That's Julio Sanchez."

7. While playing an old rock tune backwards, Elton thinks that he hears a sentence on the tape. It's almost inaudible, but he thinks it says, "Hello, Elton, long time no see."

8. Detective Jones views the videotape of the robbery at the 7-Eleven, which occurred last night. He sees the robber look into the camera. "I know that guy," he says. "I put him away last year on a similar charge."

For each of the following claims, indicate whether it is: (a) probably true, (b) probably false, (c) almost certainly true, (d) almost certainly false, or (e) none of the above.

9. "Most people are not aware that the cartoonish 'Bigfoot' figure is a distorted product of ancient and modern stories describing a real but unacknowledged species that is still occasionally observed today in North American forests." [The Bigfoot Field Researchers Organization]

10. "The actual risk of falling ill from a bioterrorist attack is extremely small." [American Council on Science and Health]

11. Nobody in the world is truly altruistic. Everyone is out for himself alone.

12. School violence is caused mainly by hypocrisy on the part of teachers and school administrators.

13. "The world shadow government behind the U.S. government is at it again, destroying U.S. buildings and killing people with staged acts of terrorism [on 9/11/01], the intent of which being—among other things— to start WW III." [Website devoted to 9/11 theories]

14. "What is Pre-Birth Communication? It's something that many people experience, yet very few talk about—the sense that somehow we are

in contact with a being who is not yet born! It may be a vivid dream, the touch of an invisible presence, a telepathic message announcing pregnancy, or many other types of encounter. It is a mystery, one that challenges our ideas about ourselves and our children." [Website on "pre-birth communication"]

15. Physicians, drug companies, the food industry, the National Cancer Institute, and the American Cancer Society are all fighting to prevent "natural" cancer cures such as vitamin supplements and herbs from being used by cancer patients.

16. Medieval history is a lie—or, rather, it doesn't exist. Monks made it up based on a corrupt copy of ancient history.

Read the following news story and then answer questions 17–20.

Soldiers Sweep Up Saddam's Hit Goons

July 1, 2003—WASHINGTON—U.S. troops captured 319 suspected Ba'ath Party murderers as part of a tough new crackdown on regime diehards yesterday, as Defense Secretary Donald Rumsfeld forcefully denied that the United States is getting into a "quagmire" in Iraq.

Military officials said U.S. forces carried out 27 raids and also seized more than $9 million in cash as well as hundreds of machine guns and grenade launchers over the past two days as part of Operation Sidewinder.

The military offensive is a get-tough display of American power aimed at defeating Saddam Hussein's loyalists and outside terrorists responsible for hit-and-run attacks on U.S. troops and sabotage of Iraq's power and water services. But the Iraqi goon squads continued their guerrilla-style campaign yesterday, ambushing a U.S. Avenger air-defense vehicle in the ultra-tense town of Fallujah, wounding Jeremy Little, an Australian-born sound man for NBC news.

The Pentagon says 65 soldiers have been killed and scores more wounded in a series of ambushes and attacks by Saddam loyalists since the war was declared over May 1.

But at a Pentagon briefing, Rumsfeld tried to counter growing criticism in Congress and in the media over the U.S. policy toward Iraq and angrily denied that the U.S. is getting into another Vietnam War quagmire. . . .

Rumsfeld admitted that fighting in Iraq "will go on for some time," but said "more and more Iraqis" are starting to cooperate with coalition forces in their hunt for Saddam's goon squads.[14]

17. Is the story slanted toward or against a particular group mentioned in the story? How?

18. Are there instances of loaded or biased language or emotional appeals in the story or headline? If so, give examples.

19. What is the main source for this story?

20. Is this story lacking another perspective on the events? Is there more to the story that isn't mentioned? If so, explain.

Integrative Exercises

These exercises pertain to material in Chapters 1–4.

1. What is a deductive argument? An inductive one?
2. What is a valid argument? A strong one?
3. What is an expert?
4. What is the appeal to authority?

For each of the following arguments, specify the conclusion and premises and indicate whether it is deductive or inductive. If it's inductive, indicate whether it's strong or weak; if deductive, indicate whether it's valid or invalid. If necessary, add implicit premises and conclusions.

5. "Sentencing reforms have produced some perverse results. For example, the primary goal of sentencing guidelines was to reduce the disparity among criminals who committed the same crime. Yet, by equalizing only prison sentences, the guidelines make it impossible for judges to equalize the 'total' penalty, which can include fines and restitution. How these are imposed can vary dramatically among criminals." [Opinion, John Lott, *USA Today*]

6. "We believe that affirmative action has been good for the country because it creates diverse student populations that give everyone a shot at the top—the American promise." [Editorial, *Times Herald-Record*, Middletown, NY]

7. If the United States attacks Syria, it will lose the support of every nation in the world. Fortunately, it will not attack Syria. So it will not lose worldwide support.

8. No one is going to support the prime minister if he backs the United States again in a war. But it looks like he is going to back the Americans. Thus, no one will support him.

9. For years, the grass simply would not grow, no matter how much watering or fertilizing she did. But after adding Miracle Sprout, the grass started to grow and spread throughout the property. Miracle Sprout did the trick.

10. "Of course, Banzhaf's argument—that so-called 'fast food' fare, like cigarettes, is addictive and causes illness and death—is ludicrous. Food supports life and only contributes to obesity when it is overused, that is, when we consume more calories (regardless of the source) than are expended in exercise. You will become overweight whether your excess calories come from beer, butter, beans, or burgers." [Editorial, *New York Post*]

11. "The dueling arguments about protecting the flag are familiar. One side says, 'Yes, the flag is a revered symbol, and those who insult it are vulgar fools. But in the end it is freedom that the flag represents, even the freedom to denigrate the nation. To limit free expression would dishonor the meaning of the stars and stripes in a way that flag burners never can.'" [Opinion, *Miami Herald*]

12. "'Yes, replies the other side, freedom is what the flag stands for. But the flag is special. It is sacred, consecrated with the blood of patriots recent and remote. America's detractors can say whatever they please about the nation—only not in this one indefensible way.'" [Opinion, *Miami Herald*]

13. If God be for us, no one can stand against us. If God be against us, we will know only defeat. We continue to see only defeat. God is against us.

14. Vitamin X can lower blood pressure in middle-aged adults. At least four well-controlled scientific studies of nearly three thousand people prove it.

15. Franklin is either evil or crazy. He's definitely not crazy, so he must be evil.

16. If Julio doesn't pay his bills, he will be bankrupt. He will pay his bills. Therefore, he will not be bankrupt.

For each of the following unsupported claims, specify whether it seems worthy of acceptance, rejection, or a degree of belief in between.

17. I saw a ghost last night. I awoke in the middle of the night, looked up, and saw the figure of a woman at the foot of my bed. But I was too drowsy to pay much attention then. I fell back into a deep sleep.

18. My doctor says that drinking ten glasses of water every day can prevent heart disease, diabetes, and high blood pressure.

19. Wearing an evil grin on his face when he was captured, the goon had to be the guy who committed the recent Central Park mugging.

20. The contractor for the giant high-rise says that constructing it makes good economic sense.

Writing Assignments

1. Write an outline for Essay 6 ("What's Wrong with Adultery?") in Appendix B. Include a thesis statement, each premise, conclusion, and points supporting each premise.

2. Write a three-page assessment of the argument in Essay 6, touching on the premises and the evidence supporting them.

3. Select one of the following topics and extract an issue from it that you can write about. Investigate arguments on both sides of the issue, and write a three-page paper defending your chosen thesis.

immigration

the morning-after pill

the federal deficit

textbook censorship

media bias

cloning humans

American drone strikes of reputed terrorists in foreign countries

North Korea and nuclear weapons

endangered species

animal rights

date rape

school prayer

Fallacies and Persuaders

CHAPTER OBJECTIVES

FALLACIES: IRRELEVANT PREMISES

- Learn how to recognize fallacies of irrelevant premises (genetic fallacy, composition, division, appeal to the person, equivocation, appeal to popularity, appeal to tradition, appeal to ignorance, appeal to emotion, red herring, and straw man).
- Understand the concept of burden of proof and when it applies.

FALLACIES: UNACCEPTABLE PREMISES

- Learn to recognize fallacies of unacceptable premises (begging the question, false dilemma, slippery slope, hasty generalization, and faulty analogy).

PERSUADERS: RHETORICAL MOVES

- Learn to recognize the rhetorical devices known as innuendo, euphemism, dysphemism, stereotyping, ridicule, and rhetorical definition.

A N ARGUMENT IS MEANT TO PROVE A POINT—TO PROVIDE GOOD REASONS FOR accepting a claim. As you know, sometimes an argument succeeds, and sometimes it doesn't. When it doesn't, the problem will be that the premises are false, the reasoning is faulty, or both. In any case, the argument is defective, bad, or bogus—call it what you will. There are countless ways that an argument can be defective. But there are certain types of defective arguments that recur so frequently that they have names (given to them, in many cases, by ancient philosophers or medieval scholars) and are usually gathered into critical thinking texts so students can become aware of them. Such common, flawed arguments are known as **fallacies**, and they are therefore said to be fallacious.

OUT OUT !!
YOU DEMONS OF
STUPIDITY !!

© 1994 United Feature Syndicate, Inc.

DILBERT: © Scott Adams/Dist. By United Feature Syndicate, Inc.

Fallacies are often beguiling; they can *seem* plausible. Time and again they are *psychologically* persuasive, though *logically* impotent. The primary motivation for studying fallacies, then, is to be able to detect them so you're not taken in by them.

We can divide fallacies into two broad categories: (1) those that have *irrelevant* premises and (2) those that have *unacceptable* premises.[1] Irrelevant premises have no bearing on the truth of the conclusion. An argument may seem to offer reasons for accepting the conclusion, but the "reasons" have nothing to do with the conclusion. Unacceptable premises are relevant to the conclusion but are nonetheless dubious in some way. An argument may have premises that pertain to the conclusion, but they do not adequately support it. Premises can be unacceptable because they are as dubious as the claim they're intended to support, because the evidence they offer is too weak to adequately support the conclusion, or because they're otherwise so defective that they provide no support at all.

Alas, critical thinking is undone by more than just fallacies. It is easily weakened or wrecked by subtler means—by **rhetoric**, the use of nonargumentative, emotive words and phrases to persuade or influence an audience. Arguments try to persuade through logic and reasons, but rhetoric tries to persuade primarily through the artful use of emotion-laden language. Fallacies at least have the semblance of arguments, but rhetorical devices are nonargument persuaders. There's nothing inherently wrong with using rhetoric. Its use can become worrisome, though, when there's an attempt to persuade or coerce through rhetoric alone.

In this chapter we examine numerous fallacies of both types as well as some of the more popular rhetorical ploys. Once again the key to immunizing yourself against manipulation by fallacies or rhetoric is practice in identifying the species and subspecies when you see them.

Fallacies: Irrelevant Premises
Genetic Fallacy

The term **genetic fallacy** has both a general and specific meaning. In the general sense—that is, when it applies to arguments that a claim is true or false solely because of its origin—it refers to nonhuman and abstract origins (such as a group of people or a piece of writing) as well as to particular individuals (such as John Smith). But to avoid confusion, it's best to restrict *genetic fallacy* to nonhuman and abstract origins, and to use the terms *appeal to the person* or *ad hominem* (discussed later) to refer to individual persons.

So the following are examples of the genetic fallacy (restricted sense):

> *You can safely dismiss that alternative energy plan. It's the brainchild of a liberal think tank in Washington.*

"One must accept the truth from whatever source it comes."
—Maimonides

*We should reject that proposal for solving the current Social Security mess. It
  comes straight from the Republican Party.*

*Russell's idea about tax hikes for the middle class came to him in a dream, so it
  must be bunk.*

These arguments fail because they reject a claim based solely on where it
comes from, not on its merits. In most cases, the source of an idea is irrelevant to
its truth. Good ideas can come from questionable sources. Bad ideas can come
from impeccable sources. Generally, judging a claim only by its source is a recipe
for error.

Composition

The fallacy of **composition** is arguing that what is true of the parts must be true
of the whole. The error here is thinking that the characteristics of the parts are
somehow transferred to the whole, something that is not always the case. Likewise, the error is committed whenever we assume that what's true of a member
of a group is true of the group as a whole. For example,

*The atoms that make up the human body are invisible. Therefore, the human
  body is invisible.*

*Each member of the club is productive and effective. So the club will be productive
  and effective.*

Each note in the song sounds great. Therefore, the whole song will sound great.

*Every part of this motorcycle is lightweight; therefore, the whole motorcycle is
  lightweight.*

Sometimes, of course, the parts do share the same characteristics as the
whole. We may safely conclude that since all the parts of the house are made of
wood, the house itself is made of wood. We commit the fallacy of composition,
though, when we assume that a particular case must be like this.

 FURTHER THOUGHT

The High Cost of a Fallacy

Did you know that fallacies can sell cars? Take a look at this conversation:

BRUNO: I really like this car. Looks like a babe magnet. Is it very
expensive?

SALESPERSON: Oh, the price is very reasonable. You can easily afford it.
The payments are only $190 a month.

BRUNO: Wow, I'll take it.

SALESPERSON: (Thinking to himself.) Sucker. He just bought a $30,000 car.

The fallacy of composition strikes again.

The fallacy of composition often shows up in statistical arguments. Consider:

The average small investor puts $2000 into the stock market every year.
The average large investor puts $100,000 into stocks each year. Therefore, the
*   group of large investors as a whole invests more money in the stock market*
*   than the small-investor group does.*

Just because the average small investor invests less than the average large investor does not mean that small investors as a group invest less than large investors as a group. After all, there may be many more small investors than large investors.

Division

The flip side of the fallacy of composition is the fallacy of **division**—arguing that what is true of the whole must be true of the parts. The fallacy is also committed when we assume that what is true of a group is true of individuals in the group.

This machine is heavy. Therefore, all the parts of this machine are heavy.
Since the committee is a powerful force in Washington politics, each member of
*   the committee is a powerful force in Washington politics.*
University students study every conceivable subject. So that university student
*   over there also studies every conceivable subject.*

These arguments are fallacious because they assume that characteristics of the whole must transfer to the parts or that traits of the group must be the same as traits of individuals in the group.

Like the fallacy of composition, the fallacy of division is frequently used in statistical arguments:

The average SAT test score of seniors [as a group] is higher than the average
*   SAT score of sophomores. Therefore, this senior's test score must be higher*
*   than the score of that sophomore.*

 FURTHER THOUGHT

Bamboozling the Taxpayers

Suppose you hear these words in a speech by a national politician: "My tax cut plan will be a windfall for the American taxpayer. Under my plan, the average tax savings will be $1100 per person. Think of what each of you could do with that much extra income."

Sounds like great news—except that this almost surely is an example of the fallacy of division. Just because the politician paired "average" and "per person" in that way doesn't mean that each individual taxpayer will get $1100. It's possible that only a few taxpayers will get $1100 or more while most won't get any tax break at all.

Just because the average score for seniors is higher than the average score for sophomores doesn't mean that any individual senior must have a higher score than any sophomore. The scores of individuals, which make up the average, may vary greatly.

Appeal to the Person

The fallacy of **appeal to the person** (or *ad hominem*, meaning "to the man") is rejecting a claim by criticizing the person who makes it rather than the claim itself. For example:

> Jones has argued for a ban on government-sanctioned prayer in schools and at school-sponsored events. But he's a rabid atheist without morals of any kind. Anything he has to say on the issue is bound to be a perversion of the truth.
>
> We should reject Chen's argument for life on other planets. He dabbles in the paranormal.
>
> You can't believe anything Morris says about welfare reform. He's a bleeding-heart liberal.

Such arguments are fallacious because they attempt to discredit a claim by appealing to something that's almost always irrelevant to it: a person's character, motives, or personal circumstances. Claims must be judged on their own merits; they are not guilty by association. We are never justified in rejecting a claim because of a person's faults unless we can show how a person's faults translate into faults in the claim—and this is almost never the case. Even when a person's character is relevant to the truth of claims (as when we must consider the merits of testimonial evidence), we are not justified in believing a claim false just because the person's character is dubious. If the person's character is dubious, we are left with no reason to think the claim either true *or* false.

The fallacy of appeal to the person comes in several varieties. One is the personal attack (mentioned earlier), often simply consisting of insults. The gist is familiar enough: Reject X's claims, ideas, or theories because X is a radical, reactionary, extremist, right-winger, left-winger, fool, bonehead, moron, nutbar, or scum of the earth. Whatever psychological impact such terms of abuse may have, logically they carry no weight at all.

Another form of this fallacy emphasizes not a person's character but his or her circumstances. Here someone making a claim is accused of inconsistency—specifically, of maintaining a view that is inconsistent with his or her previous views or social or political commitments.

> Edgar asserts that evolution is true, but he's an ordained minister in a fundamentalist church that has taken a firm stand against evolution. So he can't accept this theory; he must reject it.
>
> Madison says she's opposed to abortion, but you can't take her seriously. Her view goes against everything her party stands for.

These arguments are fallacious if they're implying that a claim must be true (or false) just because it's inconsistent with some aspect of the claimant's circumstances. The circumstances are irrelevant to the truth of the claim.

> "The broad mass of a nation . . . will more easily fall victim to a big lie than to a small one."
> —Adolf Hitler

When such arguments are put forth as charges of hypocrisy, we get another *ad hominem* fallacy known as ***tu quoque*** (or "you're another"). The fallacious reasoning goes like this: Ellen claims that X, but Ellen doesn't practice/live by/condone X herself—so X is false. Look:

> Alice, the town liberal, tells us that we shouldn't drive SUVs because the cars use too much gas and are bad for the environment. But she drives an SUV herself. What a hypocrite! I think we can safely reject her stupid pronouncements.

But whether someone is hypocritical regarding their claims can have no bearing on the truth of those claims. We may, of course, condemn someone for hypocrisy, but we logically cannot use that hypocrisy as a justification for rejecting their views. Their views must stand or fall on their own merits.

In another variation of circumstantial *ad hominem* reasoning, someone might deduce that a claim is false because the person making it, given his or her circumstances, would be expected to make it. For example:

> Wilson claims that the political system in Cuba is exemplary. But he has to say that. He's a card-carrying communist. So forget what he says.

But whether Wilson is a communist, and whether he would be expected or required to have certain views because of his connection to communism, is irrelevant to the truth of his claim.

Finally, we have the *ad hominem* tactic known as "poisoning the well." In this one, someone argues like this: X has no regard for the truth or has non-rational motives for espousing a claim, so nothing that X says should be believed—including the claim in question. The idea is that just as you can't get safe water out of a poisoned well, you can't get reliable claims out of a discredited claimant. This tack is fallacious because the fact that someone might have dubious reasons for making a claim does not show that the claim is false, nor does it mean that everything that comes out of the "poisoned well" can be automatically dismissed.

Equivocation

The fallacy of **equivocation** is the use of a word in two different senses in an argument. For example:

> The end of everything is its perfection.
> The end of life is death.
> Therefore, death is the perfection of life.

> Only man is rational.
> No woman is a man.
> Therefore, no woman is rational.

> Laws can only be created by law-givers.
> There are many laws of nature.
> Therefore, there must be a Law-Giver, namely, God.

In the first argument, *end* is used in two different senses. In the first premise it means purpose, but in the second it means termination. Because of this flip-flop in meanings, the conclusion doesn't follow from the premises—but it looks as if it should.

In the second argument, *man* is the equivocal term. In the first premise it means humankind, but in the second, male. So the conclusion doesn't follow, making it appear that a sound argument has banished women's rationality.

In the third argument, *laws* is used in two senses—rules of human behavior in the first premise, regularities of nature (as in "law of gravity") in the second. Consequently, the conclusion trying to establish the existence of God doesn't follow.

The fallacy of equivocation occurs whenever a word has one meaning in one premise and another meaning in another premise or the conclusion. This switch of senses always invalidates the argument.

©ieroen - www.kartoen.be

Appeal to Popularity

The fallacy of the **appeal to popularity** (or to the masses) is arguing that a claim must be true merely because a substantial number of people believe it. The basic pattern of this fallacy is "Everyone (or almost everyone, most people, many people) believes X, so X must be true." For example:

> Most people approve of the government's new security measures, even though innocent people's privacy is sometimes violated. So I guess the measures must be okay.
> Of course the war is justified. Everyone believes that it's justified.
> The vast majority of Americans believe that there's a supreme being, so how could you doubt it?

These arguments are fallacious because they assume that a proposition is true merely because a great number of people believe it. But as far as the truth of a claim is concerned, what many people believe is irrelevant. Many people used to believe that certain women were witches and should be burned, that slavery was perfectly acceptable, that Earth was the center of the universe, and that bleeding and purging were cures for just about every ill. Large groups of people are no more infallible than an individual is. Their belief in a proposition, by itself, is no indication of truth.

What many other people believe, however, can be an indication of truth if they are experts or have expert knowledge in the issue at hand. If almost all farmers say that the fall harvest will be abundant, ordinarily we should believe them.

"The exact contrary of what is generally believed is often the truth."
—Jean de La Bruyère

Appeal to Tradition

The **appeal to tradition** is arguing that a claim must be true just because it's part of a tradition. For example:

Acupuncture has been used for a thousand years in China. It must work.
Of course publishing pornography is wrong. In this community there's a tradition of condemning it that goes back fifty years.

Such appeals are fallacious because tradition, like the masses, can be wrong. Remember that an established tradition barred women from voting, stripped African Americans of their civil rights, promoted the vengeful policy of "an eye for an eye," and sanctioned the sacrifice of innocents to the gods.

Be careful, though. Automatically rejecting a claim because it's traditional is not reasonable either. The point is that a tradition should be neither accepted nor rejected without good reason. Knee-jerk acceptance of tradition is as bad as knee-jerk rejection.

Appeal to Ignorance

The **appeal to ignorance** is arguing that a lack of evidence proves something. In one type of this fallacy, the problem arises by thinking that a claim must be true because it hasn't been shown to be false. For example:

No one has shown that ghosts aren't real, so they must be real.
It's clear that God exists because science hasn't proved that he doesn't exist.
You can't disprove my theory that JFK was killed by LBJ. Therefore, my theory is correct.

The problem here is that a lack of evidence is supposed to prove something—but it can't. A lack of evidence alone can neither prove nor disprove a proposition. A lack of evidence simply reveals our ignorance about something.

In another variation of this fallacy, the breakdown in logic comes when you argue that a claim must be false because it hasn't been proved to be true. Look at these:

No one has shown that ghosts are real, so they must not exist.
It's clear that God doesn't exist because science hasn't proved that he does.
You can't prove your theory that JFK was killed by LBJ. Therefore, your theory is false.

Again, the moral is: Lack of evidence proves nothing. It does not give us a reason for believing a claim.

But what if our moral was wrong? If we could prove something with a lack of evidence, we could prove almost anything. You can't prove that invisible men aren't having a keg party on Mars—does this mean that it's true that invisible men are having a keg party on Mars? You can't prove that Socrates belched at his famous trial—does this prove that he didn't belch?

There are cases, however, that may seem like appeals to ignorance but actually are not. Sometimes when we carefully search for something, and such a

> "Euphemisms are unpleasant truths wearing diplomatic cologne."
> —Quentin Crisp

NEWSMAKERS

Possibly, Maybe, You Never Know

Related to the appeal to ignorance is the argument that because a problem has never been shown not to exist (that is, because the problem is merely possible), we should take steps now to deal with it. Consider this news report:

> The head of a prominent cancer research institute has warned his faculty and staff to limit cell phone use because of a possible cancer risk, The Associated Press reports.
>
> Dr. Ronald B. Herberman, the director of the University of Pittsburgh Cancer Institute, notes that while the evidence about a cell phone–cancer link remains unclear, people should take precautions, particularly for children.
>
> "Really at the heart of my concern is that we shouldn't wait for a definitive study to come out, but err on the side of being safe rather than sorry later," Dr. Herberman told The Associated Press.[2]

Research on cell phone use and cancer has been equivocal, with some studies suggesting an association (not a cause-and-effect relationship) between cancer and cell phone use and others finding no such connection. Scientists know of no plausible way that nonionizing radiation (the kind emitted by cell phones) could cause cancer.

Robert T. Carroll, philosopher and creator of the *Skeptic's Dictionary* website, has this to say about Dr. Herberman's reasoning:

> On July 23, Dr. Ronald B. Herberman, director of the University of Pittsburgh Cancer Institute, warned his faculty and staff to limit cell phone use because of the possible risk of cancer. He even warned them against using their cell phones in public places because they might expose others to dangerous electromagnetic radiation. He might as well have warned them to stop watching television or using a toaster because of the possible risk of cancer. And what about those laptops and hair dryers? Is it possible someone, somewhere could get cancer from the radiation emitted from a toaster, a hair dryer, or a laptop? I suppose so. But it is about as likely as a severed arm reattaching itself to the body it once graced. Likewise for getting cancer from using a cell phone.

Dr. Herberman's reason for issuing the warning is an example of the *precautionary principle* gone amok: it hasn't been proven that cell phone use doesn't cause cancer.[3]

Is it ever reasonable to take action to try to avoid a risk that is merely possible or unknown? If so, under what circumstances would it be reasonable? When would it be unreasonable? Would you be logically inconsistent if you were concerned about the risk of using cell phones but not concerned about the risks of using many other devices whose comparable risks are just as uncertain?

thorough search is likely to uncover it if there is anything to uncover, the failure to find what we're looking for can show that it probably isn't there. A botanist, for example, may scan a forest looking for a rare plant but not find it even though she looks in all the likely places. In this case, her lack of evidence—her not finding the plant after a thorough search—may be good evidence that the plant doesn't exist in that environment. This conclusion would not rest on ignorance, but on the knowledge that in these circumstances any thorough search would probably reveal the sought-after object if it was there at all.

This kind of inductive reasoning is widespread in science. Drugs, for example, are tested for toxicity on rodents or other animals before the drugs are given to humans. If after extensive testing no toxic effects are observed in the animals (which are supposed to be relevantly similar to humans), the lack of toxicity is considered evidence that the drug will probably not cause toxic effects in humans. Likewise, in the realm of extraordinary claims, some scientists regard the failure to find the Loch Ness monster or Bigfoot after decades of searching to be evidence that these creatures do not exist.

Appeals to ignorance involve the notion of **burden of proof.** Burden of proof is the weight of evidence or argument required by one side in a debate or disagreement (in the critical thinking sense). Problems arise when the burden of proof is placed on the wrong side. For example, if Louise declares that "no one has shown that gremlins aren't real, so they must be real," she implicitly puts the burden of proof on those who don't agree with her. She's asserting, in effect, "I say that gremlins are real, and it's up to you to prove I'm wrong." Or to put it another way, "I'm entitled to believe that gremlins are real unless you prove that they're not." But as we saw earlier, this line is just an appeal to ignorance, and the burden of proof for showing that gremlins are real rests with *her*—not with those who don't share her belief. If her claim is unsupported, you need not accept it. If you take the bait and try to prove that gremlins don't exist, you are accepting a burden of proof that should fall on Louise's shoulders, not yours.

Usually, the burden of proof rests on the side that makes a positive claim—an assertion that something exists or is the case, rather than that something does not exist or is not the case. So in general, if a person (the claimant) makes an unsupported positive claim, he or she must provide evidence for it if the claim

FURTHER THOUGHT

Can You Prove a Negative?

As you might imagine, appeals to ignorance can result in strange (and frustrating) conversations.

ALICE: Unicorns exist!

YOU: Oh, yeah, can you prove they exist?

ALICE: Can you prove they don't?

Alice's appeal to ignorance, of course, does not prove that unicorns exist. (The proper response to her unsupported claim is to point out that the claim is unsupported and that you therefore have been offered no good reason to believe it.) Moreover, her demand for proof that unicorns don't exist is unfair because she is asking you to do the impossible. She is asking you to *prove a universal negative*—a claim that nothing of a certain kind exists. To prove that unicorns do not exist, you would have to search throughout all space and time. But no one can do that. So her request is unreasonable.

It is possible, however, to prove a more limited negative claim, such as "There are no baseballs on this table." Some limited negative claims are very difficult to prove, but not impossible—such as "There are no Chevrolet trucks in this state."

is to be accepted. If you doubt the claim, you are under no obligation to prove it wrong. You need not—and should not—accept it without good reasons (which the claimant should provide). Of course, you also should not reject the claim without good reasons. If the claimant does provide you with reasons for accepting the claim, you can either accept them or reject them. If you reject them, you are obligated to explain the reasons for your rejection.

Appeal to Emotion

The fallacy of the **appeal to emotion** is the use of emotions as premises in an argument. That is, it consists of trying to persuade someone of a conclusion solely by arousing his or her feelings rather than presenting relevant reasons. When you use this fallacy, you appeal to people's guilt, anger, pity, fear, compassion,

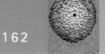

"Phew! Fooling some of the people all of the time is damn hard work."

www.CartoonStock.com

resentment, pride—but not to good reasons that could give logical support to your case. Take a look:

> *You should hire me for this network analyst position. I'm the best person for the job. If I don't get a job soon my wife will leave me, and I won't have enough money to pay for my mother's heart operation. Come on, give me a break.*
>
> *Political ad: If school music programs are cut as part of the new district budget, we will save money—and lose our children to a world without music, a landscape without song. Let the children sing. Vote no on Proposition 13.*

As arguments, these passages are fallacious not just because they appeal to strong emotions, but because they appeal to almost *nothing but* strong emotions. They urge us to accept a conclusion but offer no good reasons for doing so. We may feel compassion for the job hunter and his mother, but those feelings have no bearing on whether he is truly the best person for the job. We may recoil from the idea of children in a stark, tuneless world, but that overblown image and the emotions it evokes in us provide no logical support for the conclusion.

Good writers often combine arguments with emotional persuasion in the same piece of writing, and no fallacy need enter the picture. A strong argument is presented, and it's reinforced by strong feelings. Consider this piece of persuasive prose:

> I am a mother though my child is dead. He did not die of an incurable disease, of a virus beyond the ken of medical science. He was not taken from me by a foreign enemy while defending his country. No, he was needlessly slaughtered on the highway. A drunk driver ran broadside into his motorcycle. My son was shot fifty feet through the air by the collision and hit the blacktop at forty-five miles per hour.
>
> My son's assassin is not yet out of high school and yet that boy was able to walk into a liquor store and purchase two sixpacks of beer, most of which he drank that evening. This boy does not have the mental capability to graduate from high school in the prescribed time (he was held back in his senior year), and yet the law has given him the right to purchase alcohol and decide for himself what is appropriate behavior with regard to alcoholic consumption. I do not trust most of my adult friends to make such mature judgments. How can anyone trust the eighteen-year-old?
>
> The law must change. Statistics have shown that states which have a minimum drinking age of twenty-one years also have significantly fewer automobile accidents caused by drunken teenagers. I lost my son, but why do any of the rest of us have to suffer as I have? Please, support legislation to increase the drinking age to twenty-one.[4]

"Discourse on virtue and they pass by in droves; whistle and dance the shimmy, and you've got an audience."
—Diogenes

This passage evokes sympathy and indignation—but also gives an argument using statistics to support a conclusion about the need for new legislation.

As you would expect, appeals to emotion come in different flavors, some of which are identified by name:

APPEAL TO PITY: the attempt to persuade people to accept a conclusion by evoking their pity, compassion, or empathy. Example: *I should get this merit scholarship. I'm homeless and penniless, so the money would be put to good use.*

APPLE POLISHING: the attempt to persuade people to accept a conclusion by flattering them. Example: *I know you'll vote for me in the upcoming election because you have the true American spirit and the genuine wisdom that comes from faith and hard work.*

SCARE TACTICS: the attempt to persuade people to accept a conclusion by engendering in them an unwarranted fear. Example: *Unless we defeat Proposition 13, the homosexual agenda will be taught in our schools, and more kids will want to become gay.*

Red Herring

Perhaps the most blatant fallacy of irrelevance is the **red herring**, the deliberate raising of an irrelevant issue during an argument. This fallacy gets its name from the practice of dragging a smelly fish across a trail to throw a hunting dog off the scent. The basic pattern is to put forth a claim and then couple it with additional claims that may seem to support it but in fact are mere distractions. For instance:

> *Every woman should have the right to an abortion on demand. There's no question about it. These anti-abortion activists block the entrances to abortion clinics, threaten abortion doctors, and intimidate anyone who wants to terminate a pregnancy.*
>
> *The legislators should vote for the three-strikes-and-you're-out crime control measure. I'm telling you, crime is a terrible thing when it happens to you. It causes death, pain, and fear. And I wouldn't want to wish these things on anyone.*

Notice what's happening here. In the first example, the issue is whether women should have the right to abortion on demand. But the arguer shifts the subject to the behavior of anti-abortion activists, as though their behavior has some bearing on the original issue. Their behavior, of course, has nothing to do with the main issue. The argument is bogus. In the second example, the issue is whether the legislators should vote for a three-strikes crime bill. But the subject gets changed to the terrible costs of crime, which is only remotely related to the main issue. (There's also an appeal to fear.) We can all agree that crime can have awful consequences, but this fact has little to do with the merits and demerits of enacting a three-strikes law.

Straw Man

Related to red herring is the fallacy of the **straw man**—the distorting, weakening, or oversimplifying of someone's position so it can be more easily attacked or

refuted. A straw-man argument works like this: Reinterpret claim X so that it becomes the weak or absurd claim Y. Attack claim Y. Conclude that X is unfounded. For example:

> *David says that he's opposed to the new sodomy laws that make it illegal for consenting adult homosexuals to engage in sex acts in their own homes. Obviously he thinks that gay sex is something special and should be protected so it's allowed to take place just about anywhere. Do you want gays having sex all over town in full view of your children? David does, and he's dead wrong.*

> *Senator Miller is opposed to the military spending bill, saying that it's too costly. Why does he always want to slash everything to the bone? He wants a pint-sized military that couldn't fight off a crazed band of terrorists, let alone a rogue nation.*

> *Lawyers for the ACLU have sued to remove the massive Ten Commandments monument from the lobby of the courthouse. As usual, they are as anti-religious as ever. They want to remove every vestige of religion and faith from American life. Don't let them do it. Don't let them win yet another battle in their war to secularize the whole country.*

In the first passage, David is opposed to laws prohibiting sexual activity between consenting, homosexual adults in their own homes. His opponent, however, distorts his view, claiming that David is actually in favor of allowing gay sex virtually anywhere, including in public. David, of course, is not asserting this (few people would). This distorted version of David's position is easy to ridicule and reject, allowing his actual view to be summarily dismissed.

In the second passage, Senator Miller is against the military spending bill on the grounds that it costs too much. His position, though, is twisted into the claim that the military should be pared down so drastically that it would be ineffective even against small groups of terrorists. The senator's views on military spending are thus made to appear extreme or ludicrous. But it is unlikely that Senator Miller (or any other senator) wants to see the U.S. military reduced to such a level. He simply wants a less expensive military—not necessarily an ineffective one.

REVIEW NOTES

Fallacies with Irrelevant Premises

- **Genetic fallacy:** Arguing that a claim is true or false solely because of its abstract or nonhuman origins
- **Composition:** Arguing that what is true of the parts must be true of the whole
- **Division:** Arguing that what is true of the whole must be true of the parts or that what is true of a group is true of individuals in the group
- **Appeal to the person:** Rejecting a claim by criticizing the person who makes it rather than the claim itself
- **Equivocation:** The use of a word in two different senses in an argument
- **Appeal to popularity:** Arguing that a claim must be true merely because a substantial number of people believe it
- **Appeal to tradition:** Arguing that a claim must be true or good just because it's part of a tradition
- **Appeal to ignorance:** Arguing that a lack of evidence proves something
- **Appeal to emotion:** The use of emotions as premises in an argument
- **Red herring:** The deliberate raising of an irrelevant issue during an argument
- **Straw man:** The distorting, weakening, or oversimplifying of someone's position so it can be more easily attacked or refuted
- **Two wrongs make a right:** Arguing that your doing something morally wrong is justified because someone else has done the same (or similar) thing

The third passage is typical of the kind of fallacious arguments that crop up in debates over church-state separation. Here, the ACLU wants a monument displaying the Ten Commandments removed from the lobby of a government building, a view that is characterized as anti-religious. But a request that a religious symbol be removed from a government context is not, in itself, necessarily anti-religious. Many have argued, for example, that such requests should be made to protect freedom of religion by preventing the government from giving preferential treatment to one religion over another. Also, wanting to get rid of a religious display on public property is a far cry from wanting to remove "every vestige of religion and faith from American life." Characterizing the ACLU suit as anti-religious, though, is a way to generate strong opposition to it. Note that in church-state debates, the straw-man tack is also used to bolster the other side of the dispute. Those who favor religious displays on government property are sometimes characterized as fanatics who want to turn the government into a theocracy. But, of course, from the fact that people want to allow such a religious display it does not follow that they want anything like a theocracy.

Two Wrongs Make a Right

Two wrongs make a right is a piece of fallacious reasoning that we are all probably guilty of. It is arguing that your doing something morally wrong is justified because someone else has done the same (or similar) thing:

I have a clear conscience. I stole his laptop because he took mine a month ago.
My wife had an affair, so I'm within my rights to have one too.
Okay, I snatched a few of those little Brach candies at the supermarket. So what?
  Three other people did too.

The idea is that someone else's wrong acts can somehow make yours right. But if your action is morally impermissible, someone else's deed cannot make it otherwise. If your action lacks justification, it cannot acquire justification by what someone else does.

That is not to say that justification for your behavior is impossible to obtain. Most ethicists would say that self-defense against other people's injurious actions can be a legitimate reason for your doing something that normally would be wrong. It surely must be permissible, they would argue, to knock down a mugger who is busy trying to knock you down. Likewise, a nation surely must be justified in going to war against a foreign power that first made war against it. And to many, in the name of justice, punishment by the state for criminal acts can also be justified.

But what about "an eye for an eye" justice? Can't we avenge a wrong done to us by someone else—can't we do unto him as he has done to us? In many cultures, the answer is an emphatic *yes*. If a man kills your goat, you are justified in killing his. If a woman steals your coat, you can legitimately steal hers. But most ethicists would probably say *no*: this "eye for an eye" principle (and similar "two wrongs make a right" views) is not justice but personal vengeance, which is immoral.

Fallacies: Unacceptable Premises
Begging the Question

The fallacy of **begging the question** (or arguing in a circle) is the attempt to establish the conclusion of an argument by using that conclusion as a premise. To beg the question is to argue that a proposition is true because the very same proposition supports it:

p
Therefore, p.

The classic question-begging argument goes like this:

God exists. We know that God exists because the Bible says so, and we should
  believe what the Bible says because God wrote it.

Or, more formally:

The Bible says that God exists.
The Bible is true because God wrote it.
Therefore, God exists.

This argument assumes at the outset the very proposition ("God exists") that it is trying to prove. Any argument that does this is fallacious.

Unfortunately, most question-begging arguments are not as obviously fallacious as "*p* is true because *p* is true." They may be hard to recognize because they are intricate or confusing. Consider this argument:

> *It is in every case immoral to lie to someone, even if the lie could save a life. Even in extreme circumstances a lie is still a lie. All lies are immoral because the very act of prevarication in all circumstances is contrary to ethical principles.*

At first glance, this argument may seem reasonable, but it's not. It reduces to this circular reasoning: "Lying is always immoral because lying is always immoral."

Among the more subtle examples of question-begging is this famous one, a favorite of critical thinking texts:

> *To allow every man unbounded freedom of speech must always be, on the whole, advantageous to the state; for it is highly conducive to the interests of the community that each individual should enjoy a liberty, perfectly unlimited, of expressing his sentiments.*[5]

This argument, as well as the one preceding it, demonstrates the easiest way to subtly beg the question: Just repeat the conclusion as a premise, but use different words.

False Dilemma

The fallacy of **false dilemma** is asserting that there are only two alternatives to consider when there are actually more than two. For example:

> *Look, either you support the war or you are a traitor to your country. You don't support the war. So you're a traitor.*

This argument contends that there are only two alternatives to choose from: Either you back the war, or you are a traitor. And since you don't back the war, you must be a traitor. But this argument works only if there really are just two

"Truth, like light, is blinding. Lies, on the other hand, are a beautiful dusk, which enhances the value of each object."
—Albert Camus

 FURTHER THOUGHT

Are We Begging the Question Yet?

In everyday usage, the phrase "beg the question" often refers to the famous fallacy. But many times it does not. It is sometimes used (some would say misused) to mean something like "prompts the question" or "raises the question," as in, "The rise in the crime rate begs the question of whether we have enough police officers on the job." As a critical thinker, you need to make sure you don't get these two uses confused.

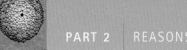

alternatives. Actually there are other plausible possibilities here. Maybe you are loyal to your country but don't want to see it get involved in a costly war. Maybe you are a patriot who simply disagrees with your government's rationale for going to war. Because these possibilities are excluded, the argument is fallacious.

Again:

> *Either those lights you saw in the night sky were alien spacecraft (UFOs), or you were hallucinating. You obviously weren't hallucinating. So they had to be UFOs.*

This argument says that there are only two possibilities: The lights were UFOs, or you hallucinated the whole thing. And they must have been UFOs because you weren't hallucinating. But as is the case with the majority of alleged paranormal events, there are many more possible explanations than most people realize. The lights could have been commercial aircraft, military aircraft, meteors, atmospheric conditions, or the planet Venus (which, believe it or not, is often mistaken for a UFO). Since the argument ignores these reasonable possibilities, it's fallacious.

 FURTHER THOUGHT

False Dilemmas, Evolution, and Creationism

False dilemmas seem to crop up in all kinds of controversies, including debates in science and philosophy. The following is an example of how the fallacy is thought to arise in the ongoing dispute between creationism and evolution.

> Creationists also assume that any data that counts against evolution counts in favor of creationism. But to argue in this way is to commit the fallacy of *false dilemma*; it presents two alternatives as mutually exclusive when, in fact, they aren't. Gish sets up the dilemma this way: "Either the Universe arose through naturalistic, mechanistic evolutionary processes, or it was created supernaturally." This argument is a false dilemma for a number of reasons. In the first place, there is no need to assume that the universe was created even if evolution is not supported. The universe, as many non-Western peoples believe, may be eternal, that is, without beginning or end. . . . Second, evolution is not the only natural account of creation, and Genesis is not the only supernatural account. Theories of creation are as varied as the cultures that conceived them. Some believe that the universe developed naturally from the void (the Vikings) while others believe that it's the supernatural work of the devil (the Gnostics). Thus, even if the creationists could totally discredit evolution, they would not thereby prove their own position, for there are many other alternatives.[6]

Finally:

> *We must legalize drugs. We either legalize them or pay a heavy toll in lives and the taxpayer's money to continue the war on drugs. And we cannot afford to pay such a high price.*

At first glance, these two alternatives may seem to exhaust the possibilities. But there is at least one other option—to launch a massive effort to prevent drug use and thereby reduce the demand for illegal drugs. The argument does not work because it fails to consider this possibility.

Note that these three arguments are expressed in disjunctive (either-or) form. But they can just as easily be expressed in a conditional (if-then) form, which says the same thing:

> *Look, if you don't support the war, then you are a traitor to your country. You don't support the war. So you're a traitor.*
>
> *If those lights you saw in the night sky were not alien spacecraft (UFOs), then you were hallucinating. You obviously weren't hallucinating. So they had to be UFOs.*
>
> *We must legalize drugs. If we don't legalize them, then we will pay a heavy toll in lives and the taxpayer's money to continue the war on drugs. And we cannot afford to pay such a high price.*

Sometimes we encounter stand-alone disjunctive phrases, rather than full-blown false dilemma arguments. These are false choices often presented as one-liners or headlines in tabloid newspapers, TV news programs, and magazines. For example:

> *Iraq: Quagmire or Failure?*
> *Microsoft: Bad Cop or Evil Giant?*
> *Is the Administration Incompetent or Just Evil?*

By limiting the possibilities, these headlines can imply that almost any outlandish state of affairs is actual—without even directly asserting anything.

People are often taken in by false dilemmas because they don't think beyond the alternatives laid before them. Out of fear, the need for simple answers, or a failure of imagination, they don't ask, "Is there another possibility?" To ask this is to think outside the box and reduce the likelihood of falling for simplistic answers.

Decision-Point Fallacy

Finally, here's a variation on the false dilemma ploy that you will encounter sooner or later, if you haven't already: the **decision-point fallacy** (also called the line-drawing fallacy). For the sake of clarity, let's start with a silly example:

> *Joe lost the hair on his head. When he had a full head of hair and he lost just a hair or two, he clearly was not bald. If we are to say truthfully that he is bald, there must have been a point in the hair-loss process (a decision point) in which he became bald. (Maybe the loss of one more hair was enough to render*

him bald.) But obviously there is no such point at which we can legitimately decide that Joe went from not being bald to being bald. Therefore, we must infer that Joe did not become bald at all.

And here are two opposing arguments that are far more serious:

The abortion-rights version: *At conception, an embryo is not a person (not an entity with full moral rights, including a right to life). And in the long process of gestation, there is no precise point at which we can definitively say that the fetus has gone from being a nonperson to being a person. Therefore, the fetus does not become a person at any point in gestation—the fetus is simply not a person.*

The right-to-life version: *In the long process of gestation, there is no point at which we can definitively say that the fetus has become a person. People have suggested different points at which personhood arises (at viability, for example), but none of these is plausible. Conception, however, is plausible as the beginning of personhood, for at that instant the embryo receives what will make it fully human—DNA. Therefore, personhood arises at the moment of conception.*

What's wrong with these decision-point arguments? In many processes, there is no decision point, no dynamic moment that suddenly transforms something into something else—and our concepts are fuzzy to reflect this fact. *Bald* and *hairy* are such terms. But none of this means that those concepts don't sometimes apply. Even though we can't say at what point a man becomes bald, we can normally use the word *bald* just fine to accurately describe a man who has hair loss.

The decision-point fallacy would have us assume that there must be a specific transforming point even though no such point exists or needs to exist. It is often an easy assumption to make—and to avoid.

Slippery Slope

The fallacy of **slippery slope** is arguing, without good reasons, that taking a particular step will inevitably lead to a further, undesirable step (or steps). The idea behind the metaphor, of course, is that if you take the first step on a slippery slope, you will have to take others because, well, the slope is slippery. A familiar slippery-slope pattern is "Doing action A will lead to action B, which will lead to action C, which will result in calamitous action D. Therefore, you should not do action A." It's fallacious when there is no good reason to think that doing action A will actually result in undesirable action D. Take a look at this classic example:

We absolutely must not lose the war in Vietnam. If South Vietnam falls to the communists, then Thailand will fall to them. If Thailand falls to them, then South Korea will fall to them. And before you know it, all of Southeast Asia will be under communist control.

REVIEW NOTES

Fallacies with Unacceptable Premises

- **Begging the question:** The attempt to establish the conclusion of an argument by using that conclusion as a premise
- **False dilemma:** Asserting that there are only two alternatives to consider when there are actually more than two
- **Slippery slope:** Arguing, without good reasons, that taking a particular step will inevitably lead to a further, undesirable step (or steps)
- **Hasty generalization:** The drawing of a conclusion about a target group based on an inadequate sample size
- **Faulty analogy:** An argument in which the things being compared are not sufficiently similar in relevant ways
- **Decision-point fallacy:** Arguing that because a line or distinction cannot be drawn at any point in a process, there are no differences or gradations in that process.

This argument was commonplace during the Cold War. It was known as the domino theory because it asserted that if one country in Southeast Asia succumbed to communism, they all would succumb, just as a whole row of dominoes will fall if the first one is pushed over. It was fallacious because there was no good evidence that the dominoes would inevitably fall as predicted. In fact, after South Vietnam was defeated, they did not fall as predicted.

Here are some more examples:

> If assault rifles are banned in this country, then handguns will be next. Then sporting rifles will be banned. And ultimately all guns will be banned, and our fundamental freedom to own guns will be canceled out altogether. So if assault rifles are banned, we might as well strike the Second Amendment from the Constitution because it will be worthless.
>
> We must ban pornography in all forms. Otherwise, rape and other sex crimes will be as common as jaywalking.
>
> All Americans should be against laws permitting consensual homosexual sex in one's own home. If that kind of thing is allowed, before you know it anything goes—bestiality, prostitution, illegal drug use, and violence.

These arguments follow the basic slippery-slope pattern. They are fallacies not because they assert that one event or state of affairs can inevitably lead to others, but because there is no good reason to believe the assertions. Some arguments may look like slippery-slope fallacies but are not because there is good reason to think that the steps are connected as described. Observe:

> If you have Lyme disease, you definitely should get medical treatment. Without treatment, you could develop life-threatening complications. Man, you could die. You should see your doctor now.

Whose Pants Are On Fire?

In case you wanted more convincing that critical thinking is badly needed in political discourse, here is some unsettling evidence. Every day PolitiFact.com, a project of the *Tampa Bay Times*, fact-checks the statements of politicians, lobbyists, and others making assertions about political issues. The project then rates the statements using the Truth-O-Meter scale: an assertion is either True, Mostly True, Half True, Mostly False, False, and—for the really outrageously wrong—Pants On Fire. Here are a few statements that earned the latter rating. (For a more detailed analysis of them, go to PolitiFact.com.)

Facebook posts: "Congress includes 36 people accused of spousal abuse, 84 arrested for drunk driving in the past year, 71 with terrible credit and more."

asamericanasapplepie.org: "Hillary (Clinton) caught on tape laughing about (hurricane) Irma 'wiping out all of those Florida hillbillies.'"

Bloggers: "Human meat found in McDonald's meat factory."

Tucker Carlson: "The United States ended slavery around the world, and maybe we should get some credit for that, too."

Roy Moore: "There are communities under Sharia law right now in our country. Up in Illinois . . . There's Sharia law, as I understand it, in Illinois, Indiana—up there. I don't know."

J. K. Rowling: Says Donald Trump was seen "looking deliberately over a disabled child's head, ignoring his outstretched hand."

Pat Robertson: Margaret Sanger "wanted a black Christian leader to be like a Judas goat and lead the blacks to genocide. Remember that? And they picked Martin Luther King as their spokesman."

Feministing: "Missouri Votes to Let Employers Fire People Who Use Birth Control."

Rick Perry: "More than 3,000 homicides were committed by 'illegal aliens' over the past six years."

Harry Reid: There was a "loss of eight million jobs during the Bush eight years."

Democratic Congressional Campaign Committee: "Seniors will have to find $12,500 for health care because Republicans voted to end Medicare."

Bill O'Reilly: "We researched to find out if anybody on Fox News had ever said you're going to jail if you don't buy health insurance. Nobody's ever said it."

Rudy Giuliani: "We had no domestic attacks under Bush."

Rush Limbaugh: "President Obama . . . wants to mandate circumcision."

This is not a fallacious slippery-slope argument. There are good reasons to believe that the series of events mentioned would actually happen.

Hasty Generalization

In Chapter 4 we pointed out the connection between the availability error and the fallacy known as **hasty generalization.** In Chapter 8 we will examine hasty generalizations at length. Here we need only recall that we are guilty of hasty generalization when we draw a conclusion about a whole group based on an inadequate sample of the group. This mistake is a genuine fallacy of unacceptable premises because the premises stating the sample size are relevant to the conclusion, but they provide inadequate evidence. For example:

> *You should buy an iPhone. They're great. I bought one last year, and it has given me nothing but flawless performance.*
>
> *The only male professor I've had this year was a chauvinist pig. All the male professors at this school must be chauvinist pigs.*
>
> *Psychology majors are incredibly ignorant about human psychology. Believe me, I know what I'm talking about: My best friend is a psych major. What an ignoramus!*
>
> *The French are snobby and rude. Remember those two high-and-mighty guys with really bad manners? They're French. I rest my case.*
>
> *The food at Pappie's Restaurant is awful. I had a sandwich there once, and the bread was stale.*

> "One cool judgment is worth a thousand hasty counsels."
> —Woodrow Wilson

Faulty Analogy

We will also discuss **arguments by analogy** in Chapter 8. Like hasty generalizations, defective arguments by analogy, or faulty analogies, are also fallacies involving unacceptable premises. An analogy is a comparison of two or more things alike in specific respects. An argument by analogy reasons this way: Because two or more things are similar in several respects, they must be similar in some further respect. For example:

> *In the Vietnam War, the United States had not articulated a clear rationale for fighting there, and the United States lost. Likewise, in the present war the United States has not articulated a clear rationale for fighting. Therefore, the United States will lose this war too.*
>
> *A watch is a mechanism of exquisite complexity with numerous parts precisely arranged and accurately adjusted to achieve a purpose—a purpose imposed by the watch's designer. Likewise the universe has exquisite complexity with countless parts—from atoms to asteroids—that fit together precisely and accurately to produce certain effects as though arranged by plan. Therefore, the universe must also have a designer.*

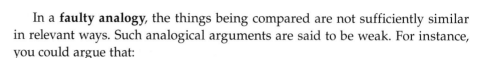

In a **faulty analogy**, the things being compared are not sufficiently similar in relevant ways. Such analogical arguments are said to be weak. For instance, you could argue that:

> *Dogs are warm-blooded, nurse their young, and give birth to puppies.*
> *Humans are warm-blooded and nurse their young. Therefore, humans give birth*
> *to puppies too.*

This argument by analogy is about as weak as they come—and a little silly. Dogs and humans are not sufficiently similar in relevant ways (in physiology, for one thing) to justify such a strange conclusion.

Persuaders: Rhetorical Moves

Rhetoric presents us with a large repertoire of techniques for influencing hearts and minds through emotion—while proving nothing through reason. Very often rhetorical devices do nothing more than promote a negative (or positive) attitude toward someone or something, but this ploy can be extraordinarily persuasive. Here are a few of the better known examples.

Innuendo

Innuendo is suggesting something denigrating about a person without explicitly stating it. Through innuendo you can indirectly convey the false claim that someone is bad, though you make only true statements. For example:

> *I'm fairly sure that Senator Johnson's youthful indiscretions involving alcohol, mari-*
> *juana, and crack cocaine probably have no influence on her current public service.*
> *I think we can assume that Mr. Abernathy absolutely does not embezzle—*
> *anymore.*

Innuendo was employed in a notorious smear of Senator John McCain in the South Carolina Republican primary in 2000. In a sham telephone survey, voters were asked, "Would you be more or less likely to vote for John McCain if you knew he had fathered an illegitimate black child?"

Euphemisms and Dysphemisms

Euphemisms are words used to convey positive or neutral attitudes or emotions in place of more negative ones; **dysphemisms** are words used to convey negative attitudes or emotions in place of neutral or positive ones. These rhetorical devices work by using the persuasive force of a word's *connotations*, the feelings and attitudes linked to the word's literal meaning. The devices can mislead, obscure, and confuse. To hide the truth, political, economic, or military leaders might use the euphemism *meaningful downturn in aggregate output* for *recession*; *revenue enhancement* for *tax increase*; *downsizing* for *firing*; *armed reconnaissance* for *bombing*; *neutralize* for *kill*; *enhanced interrogation methods* for *torture*; *collateral damage* for *civilian casualties*; or *soft targets* for *people to kill*.

In debates about gun ownership, those who want to restrict gun ownership may characterize their position as "anti-assault weapon." Those opposed to this position may label it as "anti-self-defense." Both these labels are meant to provoke certain attitudes toward the subject matter—attitudes that may not be supported by any evidence or argument.

Consider the disparate impact on the reader of these pairs of terms, both of which refer to the same thing:

full-figured	fat
guerrillas	freedom fighters
routed the enemy	made a strategic withdrawal
resolute	pigheaded
emphatic	pushy
sweat	perspire

But keep in mind that euphemisms often perform a useful social purpose by allowing us to discuss sensitive subjects in an unoffensive way. We may spare people's feelings by saying that their loved ones "have passed on" rather than that they "have died," or that their dog "was put to sleep" rather than "killed." Nevertheless, as critical thinkers, we should be on guard against the deceptive use of connotations. As critical writers, we should rely primarily on argument and evidence to make our case.

Stereotyping

A **stereotype** is an unwarranted conclusion or generalization about an entire group of people. To stereotype someone is to judge her not as an individual, but as part of a group whose members are thought to be all alike. We think because she is a member of the group, and we assume without good reason that all the members are rude and arrogant, that she must also be rude and arrogant. We wrongly assume that because all members of _____ (insert name of any political, ethnic, or class group) are _____ (insert name of any negative attribute), the member of that group standing before us also must have that attribute.

By asserting that someone is part of a hated stereotyped group, a speaker or writer can induce others to form a baseless, negative opinion of that person. This slanted opinion in turn can cause people to react dismissively, disdainfully, or angrily to any member of the disparaged group. This is the well-worn path of bigots of all stripes—and a painful indication that critical thinking is needed.

Stereotypes are especially prevalent in politics, where they are often mixed in with dysphemisms, the straw man fallacy, innuendo, appeal to the person, and other fallacious thinking. A few examples:

We all know that the Democrats are pro-taxes and anti-rich.
All the Republicans want is a free ride for rich people and no entitlements for the less well off.
Don't elect Southerners. They're all anti-government, states-rights fanatics.

Ridicule

Ridicule is the use of derision, sarcasm, laughter, or mockery to disparage a person or idea. Ridicule succeeds when it gets an emotional reaction from you that leads you to dismiss people or their claims for no good reason. Its aim is to put people or beliefs in a ridiculous or absurd light, to make them a laughing-stock. Look:

> Trust the New York Times *to report the news fairly? Right, just like I trust the airlines to be always on time.*
> *You think Fox News is fair and balanced? Ha!*

Remember, when ridicule does its work, it makes no appeal to evidence or argument. It may be interesting or amusing, but it gives you no good reason to believe anything. When the credibility of claims is at stake, ridicule is best seen as an emotional trick.

Rhetorical Definitions

One of the more subtle means of persuasion uses **rhetorical definition**. The point of this tactic is not to accurately define but to influence through an emotion-charged skewed definition. Usually we are most interested in what is called a *lexical definition*, which reports the meaning that a term has among those who use the language. For example, among English-speaking people, the word "rain" is used to refer to (or mean) condensed atmospheric moisture falling in drops, which is the lexical definition. A *stipulative definition* reports a meaning that a term is deliberately assigned, often for the sake of convenience or economy of expression. If you assign a meaning to a familiar term or to a term that you invent, you give a stipulative definition. A *precising* definition reports a meaning designed to decrease ambiguity or vagueness. It qualifies an existing term by giving it a more precise definition. Someone, for example, might offer a precising definition for the word "old" (as it applies to the age of humans) by specifying that "old" refers to anyone over eighty. A rhetorical definition, on the other hand, wants to sway you toward particular attitudes or beliefs.

Someone who opposes abortions for any reason, for example, might rhetorically define "abortion" as "the murder of innocent human beings and the rejection of God." Someone who believes that some abortions are morally permissible might define "abortion" as "the termination of a human embryo or fetus."

Now take a look at these politically motivated rhetorical definitions:

> *Government entitlements should be discontinued. They're just handouts to people who don't want to work.*
> *For conservatives, tax reform means making the rich richer and the middle class poorer.*
> *Gun control is code for "Let's get rid of every gun in America."*
> *Capital punishment is legalized murder.*

🔑 KEY WORDS

ad hominem	composition	innuendo
appeal to emotion	decision-point (line-drawing) fallacy	red herring
appeal to ignorance		rhetoric
appeal to pity	division	rhetorical definitions
appeal to popularity (or to the masses)	dysphemism	ridicule
	equivocation	scare tactics
appeal to the person	euphemism	slippery slope
appeal to tradition	fallacy	stereotyping
apple polishing	false dilemma	straw man
argument by analogy	faulty analogy	*tu quoque*
begging the question	genetic fallacy	two wrongs make a right
burden of proof	hasty generalization	

Summary
Fallacies: Irrelevant Premises

- Certain types of defective arguments that occur frequently are known as fallacies. Fallacies are often psychologically persuasive but logically flawed.
- We can divide fallacies into two broad categories: (1) those that have *irrelevant* premises and (2) those that have *unacceptable* premises.
- Fallacies with irrelevant premises include the genetic fallacy (arguing that a claim is true or false solely because of its origin), composition (arguing that what is true of the parts must be true of the whole), division (arguing that what is true of the whole must be true of the parts or that what is true of a group is true of individuals in the group), appeal to the person (rejecting a claim by criticizing the person who makes it rather than the claim itself), equivocation (the use of a word in two different senses in an argument), appeal to popularity (arguing that a claim must be true merely because a substantial number of people believe it), appeal to tradition (arguing that a claim must be true or good just because it's part of a tradition), appeal to ignorance (arguing that a lack of evidence proves something), appeal to emotion (the use of emotions as premises in an argument), red herring (the deliberate raising of an irrelevant issue during an argument), straw man (the distorting, weakening, or oversimplifying of someone's position so it can be more easily attacked or refuted), and two wrongs make a right (arguing that your doing something morally wrong is justified because someone else has done the same thing).

Fallacies: Unacceptable Premises

- Fallacies with unacceptable premises include begging the question (the attempt to establish the conclusion of an argument by using that conclusion as a premise), false dilemma (incorrectly asserting that only two alternatives exist), decision-point fallacy (arguing that because a line or distinction cannot be drawn at any point in a process, there are no differences or gradations in that process), slippery slope (arguing, without good reasons, that taking a particular step will inevitably lead to a further, undesirable step or steps), hasty generalization (the drawing of a conclusion about a group based on an inadequate sample of the group), and faulty analogy (an argument in which the things being compared are not sufficiently similar in relevant ways).

Persuaders: Rhetorical Moves

- Critical thinking is also undermined by rhetoric, the use of nonargumentative, emotive words and phrases to persuade or influence an audience.
- Rhetorical devices include innuendo (suggesting something denigrating about a person without explicitly stating it), euphemisms (words used to convey positive or neutral attitudes or emotions in place of more negative ones), dysphemisms (words used to convey negative attitudes or emotions in place of neutral or positive ones), stereotyping (drawing an unwarranted conclusion or generalization about an entire group of people), ridicule (the use of derision, sarcasm, laughter, or mockery to disparage a person or idea), and rhetorical definition (influencing opinion through an emotion-charged definition).

 EXERCISES

Exercise 5.1

REVIEW QUESTIONS

1. What are fallacies of irrelevant premises? What makes them irrelevant?
2. What is the genetic fallacy?
3. Can the origin of a claim ever be relevant to deciding its truth or falsity?
* 4. What is the fallacy of composition?
5. What are the two forms of the fallacy of division?
6. Why are appeals to the person fallacious?
7. What type of *ad hominem* argument is put forth as a charge of hypocrisy?
8. What is the fallacy of poisoning the well?

9. What is the fallacy of equivocation?

* 10. Why are appeals to popularity fallacious?

11. Why are appeals to tradition fallacious?

12. What are the two forms of the appeal to ignorance?

13. What is the proper response to an appeal to ignorance?

14. What is rhetoric?

* 15. According to the text, is it ever legitimate to use rhetoric and argument together?

16. What is the fallacy of red herring?

17. Why is an argument that relies on the straw-man fallacy a bad argument?

18. What is the fallacy of begging the question?

* 19. Why are people often taken in by false dilemmas?

20. What is the burden of proof?

21. What is the fallacy of slippery slope? Can the argument used in the slippery-slope fallacy ever be used legitimately? Why or why not?

22. What is the rhetorical device of innuendo?

23. What is the rhetorical device of stereotyping?

Exercise 5.2

In the following passages, identify any fallacies of irrelevance (genetic fallacy, composition, division, appeal to the person, equivocation, appeal to popularity, appeal to tradition, appeal to ignorance, appeal to emotion, red herring, and straw man). Some passages may contain more than one fallacy, and a few may contain no fallacies at all. Also identify any rhetorical devices highlighted in this chapter.

* 1. "Seeing that the eye and hand and foot and every one of our members has some obvious function, must we not believe that in like manner a human being has a function over and above these particular functions?" [Aristotle]

2. The federal budget deficits are destroying this country. Just ask any working stiff; he'll tell you.

3. The hippies of the sixties railed against the materialistic, capitalistic system and everyone who prospered in it. But all their bellyaching was crap because they were a bunch of hypocrites, living off their rich mothers and fathers.

4. Anthony argues that capital punishment should be abolished. But why should we listen to him? He's a prisoner on death row right now.

* 5. The *New York Times* reported that one-third of Republican senators have been guilty of Senate ethics violations. But you know that's false—the *Times* is a notorious liberal rag.

6. Geraldo says that students who cheat on exams should not automatically be expelled from school. But it's ridiculous to insist that students should never be punished for cheating.

7. Of course the death penalty is a just punishment. It has been used for centuries.

8. My sweater is blue. Therefore, the atoms that make up the sweater are blue.

9. The prime minister is lying about his intelligence briefings since almost everyone surveyed in national polls thinks he's lying.

* 10. Kelly says that many women who live in predominantly Muslim countries are discriminated against. But how the heck would she know? She's not a Muslim.

11. A lot of people think that football jocks are stupid and boorish. That's a crock. Anyone who had seen the fantastic game that our team played on Saturday, with three touchdowns before halftime, would not believe such rubbish.

12. Does acupuncture work? Can it cure disease? Of course. It has been used in China by folk practitioners for at least three thousand years.

13. The arguments of right-to-lifers cannot be believed. They're hypocrites who scream about dead babies but then murder abortion doctors.

* 14. "The only proof capable of being given that an object is visible, is that people actually see it. The only proof that a sound is audible, is that people hear it: and so of the other sources of our experience. In like manner, I apprehend, the sole evidence it is possible to produce that anything is desirable, is that people actually desire it." [John Stuart Mill]

15. The new StratoCar is the best automobile on the road. Picture the admiring glances you'll get when you take a cruise in your StratoCar through town. Imagine the power and speed!

16. Gremlins exist, that's for sure. No scientist has ever proved that they don't exist.

17. "The most blatant occurrence of recent years is all these knuckleheads running around protesting nuclear power—all these stupid people who do not research at all and who go out and march, pretending they care about the human race, and then go off in their automobiles and kill one another." [Ray Bradbury]

18. Is the theory of evolution true? Yes. Polls show that most people believe in it.

* 19. The former mayor was convicted of drug possession, and he spent time in jail. So you can safely ignore anything he has to say about legalizing drugs.

20. I don't believe in heaven and hell because no one—not even scientists—has ever produced proof that they exist.

21. Professor, I deserve a better grade than a D on my paper. Look, my parents just got a divorce. If they see that I got a D, they will just blame each other, and the fighting will start all over again. Give me a break.

22. Only man has morals. No woman is a man. Therefore, no woman has morals.

23. Every player on the team is the best in the league. So the team itself is the best in the league.

* 24. Why are Asians so good at math?

25. I'm sure Senator Braxton would never take a large bribe.

* 26. Our administration may need to consider trying some form of revenue enhancement.

Exercise 5.3

In the following passages, identify any fallacies of unacceptable premises (begging the question, false dilemma, slippery slope, hasty generalization, and faulty analogy). Some passages may contain more than one fallacy, and a few may contain no fallacies at all.

1. Random drug testing in schools is very effective in reducing drug use because the regular use of the testing makes drug use less likely.

2. If today you can make teaching evolution in public schools a crime, then tomorrow you can make it a crime to teach it in private schools. Then you can ban books and other educational materials that mention evolution. And then you can ban the very word from all discourse. And then the anti-science bigots will have won.

3. Three thieves are dividing up the $7000 they just stole from the First National Bank. Robber number one gives $2000 to robber number two, $2000 to robber number three, and $3000 to himself. Robber number two says, "How come you get $3000?" Robber number one says, "Because I am the leader." "How come you're the leader?" "Because I have more money."

* 4. Either God exists or he does not exist. If he exists, and you believe, you will gain heaven; if he exists and you don't believe, you will lose nothing. If he does not exist, and you believe, you won't lose much. If he does not exist, and you don't believe, you still won't lose much. The best gamble then is to believe.

5. John is now on trial for murder, but the proceedings are a waste of time and money. Everyone knows he's guilty.

* 6. I used to work with this engineering major. And, man, they are really socially inept.

7. I met these two guys on a plane, and they said they were from Albuquerque. They were total druggies. Almost everyone in that city must be on drugs.

8. Some people are fools, and some people are married to fools.

9. Bill is an investment banker, drives a Cadillac, is overweight, and votes Republican. John is also an investment banker, drives a Cadillac, and is overweight. So John probably votes Republican too.

* 10. Either we fire this guy or we send a message to other employees that it's okay to be late for work. Clearly, we need to fire him.

Exercise 5.4

For each of the following claims, devise an argument using the fallacy shown in parentheses. Make the argument as persuasive as possible.

1. The federal budget deficit will destroy the economy. (red herring)
2. *The Hunger Games* is the best movie ever made. (appeal to popularity)
* 3. Mrs. Anan does not deserve the Nobel Prize. (appeal to the person)
4. Vampires—the blood-sucking phantoms of folklore—are real. (appeal to ignorance)
5. Internet pornography can destroy this country. (slippery slope)
* 6. The Boy Scouts of America should allow gay kids to be members. (begging the question)
7. The United States should attack Iran. (false dilemma)
8. That economics seminar is absolutely the worst course offered at the university. (hasty generalization)
9. Pope John Paul II was a moral giant. (appeal to emotion)
10. The Nigerian court was right to sentence that woman to be stoned to death for adultery. (appeal to popularity)
* 11. There are too many guns on the streets because our politicians are controlled by the National Rifle Association and other gun nuts. (red herring)
12. All efforts should be made to ban trade in exotic pets such as tigers. (genetic fallacy)

 Field Problems

1. Find a magazine or newspaper letter to the editor that contains at least one fallacy. Identify the fallacy and rewrite the passage to eliminate the fallacy and strengthen the argument. (To effectively rework the argument, you may have to make up some facts.)

2. Select an editorials/letters page from a newspaper (it should contain several opinions on various issues). Scan the entire page, circling and labeling any examples of fallacies. Locate at least three examples.

3. Tune into a TV or radio political talk show—preferably one in which you usually find yourself in strong agreement with the opinions expressed— and identify at least three instances of fallacious reasoning.

Self-Assessment Quiz

Answers appear in "Answers to Self-Assessment Quizzes" (Appendix D). Identify the fallacies or rhetorical devices in the following passages.

1. "[The senator] Dean has leapt beyond criticizing [the president] and is now embracing terrorists. He has called Hamas terrorists 'soldiers in a war' and said the U.S. should not take sides between Israel and Palestinian suicide bombers." [Ann Coulter]

2. You think that welfare mothers would actually prefer to have jobs? Prove it, and until you do they are all lazy moochers.

3. Civil rights legislation was furiously opposed by Dixiecrat Strom Thurmond—which proves that it was reasonable and moral.

4. "The president lies about important things like the economy, his tax cuts, his education, our reasons for going to war and drunk driving. But I think he lies only when he feels he has to. He knows that most of the time Fox News, the *Wall Street Journal,* and Rush Limbaugh are only too glad to do it for him." [Al Franken]

5. "Jews are part of the Soviet people. They are a fine people, intelligent, very valued in the Soviet Union. Therefore, the problem for the Jews in the Soviet Union does not exist." [Mikhail Gorbachev]

6. You can safely ignore Helena's argument for the rights of women because she's a member of the National Organization for Women.

7. You advocate a woman's right to abortion because you do not understand how hideous and monstrous an abortion procedure is, how it tears a living fetus away from the uterine wall, crushes it to bleeding pieces, and sucks it away into oblivion.

8. That is a lousy book. It did not sell well at all.

9. All of us cannot be loved because all of us cannot be the focus of deep affection.

10. "If the parts of the Universe are not accidental, how can the whole Universe be considered as the result of chance? Therefore the existence of the Universe is not due to chance." [Moses Maimonides]

11. This administration is either one of the best or one of the worst. It is certainly not one of the best, so we must count it among those at the bottom of the heap.

12. Atheistic philosophers have been trying for thousands of years to prove that there is no God, and they haven't succeeded yet. This shows that there is indeed a God after all.

13. How can you, with a straight face, argue that animals have rights and expect me to believe you? You eat meat!

14. Judges should not hand down anything but maximum sentences for all convicted criminals. If you start making exceptions, prosecutors will start

asking for lighter sentences. Next thing you know, every criminal will be getting off with mere warnings.

15. America—love it or leave it!

16. "I cannot wait until Andy Rooney starts acting his age and retires. What a waste of editorial space. His op-ed column in the Sept. 28 *News* was so silly." [Letter to the editor, *Buffalo News*]

17. The biggest threat to the Constitution these days is the destroy-all-guns left.

18. Children were asked to recite the Pledge of Allegiance every day and to include the phrase "under God." That was dead wrong. No child should have to submit to such brainwashing.

19. Ranjit was caught cheating on his final exam. But why should he be punished when a dozen other people cheated last year in the same course?

20. We all know what "abortion rights activists" really means—it means baby killers.

 Integrative Exercises

These exercises pertain to material in Chapters 1–5.

For each of the following passages, indicate whether it contains an argument. If it does, specify the conclusion and premises, whether it is deductive or inductive, whether it is a good argument (sound or cogent), and whether it is a fallacy. Some passages may contain no argument.

1. Andrea denies that she is an atheist, so she must be a theist.

2. You say that there are no such things as ghosts, but can you prove that they don't exist?

3. "Didn't Tom Cruise make a stock-car movie in which he destroyed thirty-five cars, burned thousands of gallons of gasoline, and wasted dozens of tires? If I were given the opportunity, I'd say to Tom Cruise, 'Tom, most people don't own thirty-five cars in their *life*, and you just trashed thirty-five cars for a movie. Now you're telling other people not to pollute the planet? Shut up, sir.'" [Rush Limbaugh]

4. "The large number of female voters for Arnold Schwarzenegger in California announces one thing: the death of feminism. That so many women would ignore his sexual misconduct and vote for him bespeaks the re-emergence of the reckless phallus." [Letter to the editor, *Newsday*]

5. Hillary Clinton supports gun-control legislation. As you know, all fascist regimes of the twentieth century passed gun-control legislation. We are forced to conclude that Hillary Clinton is a fascist.

6. If Congress bans automatic weapons, America will slide down a slippery slope leading to the banning of all guns, the shredding of the Bill of Rights, and a totalitarian police state.

7. Affirmative action makes for a better society. Everybody knows that, even if they won't admit it.

8. Thinking is like swimming. Just as in swimming it's easy to float on the top but hard to dive deep, it's easy in thinking to float along on the surface of an issue but difficult to use your intellect to delve down into the layers.

9. "If a cell, under appropriate conditions, becomes a person in the space of a few years, there can surely be no difficulty in understanding how, under appropriate conditions, a cell may, in the course of untold millions of years, give origin to the human race." [Herbert Spencer]

10. The chancellor is either a crook or a nut. He is a crook. Thus, he is no nut.

11. Everything must either happen by random accident or by divine intervention. Nothing happens by pure accident, so everything must happen because of divine intervention.

12. Children should never be spanked. Spanking is harmful. I've talked to three mothers about this issue, and they all agree that spanking harms a child's self-esteem and development.

13. The Eagles are the most popular rock group in history because they have sold the most records.

14. My professor says that telling a lie is never morally permissible. But that's ridiculous. The other day I heard him tell a bald-faced one to one of his students.

15. "Not all forms of gender discrimination are unethical. There are a number of exclusively male or female fitness clubs around the country utilized by religious individuals who shun the meat market scene. If a woman wants to spare herself the embarrassment of being ogled in her sports bra while doing thigh-thrusts, it is her right to work out with women only. Similarly, if a man wants to spare himself the temptation of working out with lingerie models, he should be allowed membership to strictly male fitness clubs. It would be unreasonable to require non-discrimination of these private clubs, or to make them build separate facilities to accommodate everyone." [Letter to the editor, *Arizona Daily Wildcat*]

16. "Highway checkpoints, drug testing, ubiquitous security cameras and now the government's insistence on the use of sophisticated software tools to spy on the American people all point to a single vision. This vision was shared with us years ago, in George Orwell's book *1984*. Big Brother is indeed watching." [Letter to the editor, *Buffalo News*]

17. There are those on campus who would defend a student's right to display a Confederate flag on his or her dorm room door. But there is no such right. Slavery was wrong, is wrong, and always will be wrong.

18. "It is impossible to make people understand their ignorance; for it requires knowledge to perceive it and therefore he that can perceive it hath it not." [Jeremy Taylor]

19. If you give that homeless guy fifty cents today, tomorrow he will want a dollar, then five dollars, then ten, and where will it stop? Before you know it, *you're* homeless.

20. The biblical story of Adam and Eve in the garden of Eden is true. If it weren't true, it would not be in the Bible.

Writing Assignments

1. In a one-page essay argue that women are more nurturing and caring than men are. Avoid fallacies. Then write a one-page critique of the first paper, paying special attention to any fallacies you uncover.

2. Write a one-page paper arguing that the speed limit on all U.S. highways should be raised to 70 mph. Include at least three fallacies in the paper. Exchange your paper with a classmate who has done the same assignment. Pinpoint the fallacies in each other's papers.

3. Study Essay 7 ("A Pat-Down Is Better Than a Blow-Up"). Identify the conclusion and premises of the essay's argument, and write a rebuttal to it.

Deductive Reasoning: Propositional Logic

 CHAPTER OBJECTIVES

CONNECTIVES AND TRUTH VALUES

- Understand the purpose and uses of propositional logic.
- Understand the meaning, the symbols, and the uses of the four logical connectives—conjunction, disjunction, negation, and conditional.
- Know the definition of *statement* and the distinction between simple and compound statements.
- Know how to translate simple statements into symbolic form.
- Know how to construct a truth table and how to use it to test the validity of arguments.
- Know the situations in which conjunctions, disjunctions, negations, and conditionals are true or false.
- Understand the structure of conditional statements and the various ways in which they can be expressed.

CHECKING FOR VALIDITY

- Know how to determine the validity of very simple arguments using truth tables.
- Be able to use parentheses to express statements in symbolic form.
- Be able to use the short method to evaluate complex arguments.

PROOF OF VALIDITY

- Be able to use the rules of inference to confirm the validity of complex arguments.
- Know the rules of replacement.

FOR CENTURIES PHILOSOPHERS, MONKS, SCIENTISTS, LINGUISTS, AND STUDENTS have been enthralled by logic. Yes, logic. For many people—including some great thinkers such as Aristotle, Gottfried Leibniz, and Bertrand Russell—logic has been, ironically, a passion, something deemed worthy of deep study and long devotion. For hundreds of years, logic (along with philosophy) was a required course in universities and was regarded as one of the grand pillars upon which a liberal arts education was based (the others were grammar, rhetoric, arithmetic, music, astronomy, and geometry). Even today scholars continue to be drawn into logic's depths, never seeming to tire of exploration and application.

But why do they bother? Why do they seem to think that logic is anything other than the dry and dusty preoccupation of dry and dusty philosophers? Well, maybe they bother because the study and use of logic, like the study and use of mathematics, is an exercise in exactitude, precision, clarity, and—above all—definite answers. All of which can be very satisfying. Or perhaps they bother because logic is the study of good reasoning or thinking and is therefore concerned with every decision and every judgment we make.

Logic also labors. Out of the study of logic have come discoveries now used in electronic engineering, set theory, linguistics, mathematics, and, of course, philosophy. Investigations in logic have yielded insights that made the invention of digital computers possible.

Of course, what you really want to know is what coursework in logic can do for *you*. Well, in this chapter you get a preliminary answer to that question. Here we take up an exploration of **propositional logic** (or truth-functional logic)—the branch of deductive reasoning that deals with the logical relationships among statements. In propositional logic, we use symbols to represent and clarify these relationships. If you master this material, you should reap at least two rewards right off. The first is a more thorough understanding of the power, precision, and dynamics of deductive reasoning. The second is the ability to evaluate the validity of very complex arguments.

How complex? Take a look at this deductive argument. Can you tell if it's valid?

(1) *The United States will be secure and prosperous only if it shares more of its resources with the impoverished or discontented peoples of the world.*

(2) *The United States will share more of its resources with the impoverished or discontented peoples of the world only if doing so will not significantly reduce Americans' standard of living.*

(3) *If Americans' standard of living is significantly reduced, then either the United States will not be secure and prosperous or it will not share more of its resources with the impoverished or discontented peoples of the world.*

"My lawyer says I can sue the school because they're violating my right to be stupid."

© 1996 by Randy Glasbergen.

(4) The United States will not share more of its resources with the impoverished or discontented peoples of the world.

(5) Therefore, the United States will not be secure and prosperous.

If you don't know anything about propositional logic, the only way you can check this argument for validity is to use brute brainpower. You just have to noodle it out, and the noodling will not be easy. But with a grounding in propositional logic, you can figure this one out in straightforward fashion.

Connectives and Truth Values

As we've seen, arguments are composed of statements. In Chapter 3 we used symbols to represent the statements. Each symbol stood not for a logical relationship between statements but for a single statement. Propositional logic takes this symbolization to another level by using symbols to stand not just for statements but also for the *relationships between statements*—relationships that we specified previously with logical connective words, or connectives, such as "if . . . then" and "or." Propositional logic gets this work done by using the symbol language of **symbolic logic**, a branch of logic in its own right.

Because these logical connectives specify the relationships between statements, they shape the *form* of the argument. Recall that the validity of an argument is a matter of the argument's form, which is why we can judge the validity of an argument apart from any consideration of the truth of its premises. So propositional logic helps us assess the validity of an argument without being distracted by nonformal elements such as the language used to express content.

So the symbols used to express an argument are of two types. The first you're already familiar with; they're the letters, or **variables,** you use to represent propositions. For example: If p, then q. (There's no particular distinction in the letters p and q; any letters will do, as long as you use them consistently. That is, once you've chosen p to represent, say, "Alice rode her bike," p must consistently represent this same statement throughout the argument.) The second kind are the symbols for the logical connectives that indicate relationships between statements.

The following table presents the symbols for, and the meaning of, four logical connectives.

Symbol	Meaning	Example
&	Conjunction (and)	$p \mathbin{\&} q$ Alice rode her bike, and John walked.
v	Disjunction (or)	$p \lor q$ Either Alice rode her bike, or John walked.
~	Negation (not)	$\sim p$ Alice did not ride her bike. (or) It is not the case that Alice rode her bike.
→	Conditional (if-then)	$p \to q$ If Alice rode her bike, then John walked.

These connectives are used in compound statements such as "The air is clean, and the sky is blue" or "If you stay up late, you will sleep in tomorrow." Remember that a **statement** (or claim) is an assertion that something is or is not the case. In other words, it is the kind of thing that can be either true or false. A **simple statement** is one that doesn't contain any other statements as constituents. And a **compound statement** is composed of at least two simple statements.

Every statement has a truth value. That is, a statement is either true or false. Or to be more precise, a true statement has a truth value of *true*, and a false statement has a truth value of *false*. In contrast, questions and exclamations don't have truth values.

Now let's say that we've converted an argument into its symbolic form, and we know all the *possible* truth values of the argument's variables (statements). In other words, we know under what circumstances a statement is true or false due to the influence of the logical connectives. How would this information help us?

It could help us quickly uncover the validity or invalidity of the whole argument. Given the possible truth values of some statements in the argument, and given the statements' relationships with one another as governed by the logical connectives, we could infer the possible truth values of all the other statements. Then we would have to answer just one question: *Is there a combination of truth values in the argument such that the premises could be true and the conclusion false?* If the answer is yes, then the argument is invalid. If there is no such circumstance, the argument is valid.

If you're a little fuzzy on all this, don't worry. It will become clearer to you as you digest the following examples and learn more about the dance between connectives and truth values.

Conjunction

Two simple statements joined by a connective to form a compound statement are known as a **conjunction**. Each of the component statements is called a **conjunct**. For example:

Julio is here, and Juan is here.

Which we symbolize like this:

p & q

The grammatical conjunction *and* is one of several terms that can express logical conjunction. Others include *but, yet, nevertheless, while, also,* and *moreover*. In propositional logic, all these are logically equivalent; they are therefore properly symbolized by the ampersand (&). *Caution:* Make sure the connective really is conjoining two distinct statements and not a set of compound nouns as in "We went to Jack's Bar *and* Grill" or "Juanita *and* Maria were a team."

To identify the possible truth values of a conjunction, we can create a **truth table,** which is just a graphic way of displaying all the possibilities. Here's the truth table for the conjunction p & q:

p	q	p & q
T	T	T
T	F	F
F	T	F
F	F	F

Above the line in the table, you see a column for each of the component statements and the conjunction itself. The T's and F's below the line are abbreviations for true and false. The first two columns of T's and F's represent the four possible sets of truth values for the variables. The table shows, in other words, that there are only four combinations of truth values for the pair of variables p and q: T T, T F, F T, and F F. These are the only combinations possible for a conjunction, which is a two-variable compound.

The last column of T's and F's (under p & q) shows the truth values for the conjunction given the four possible combinations of truth values of the pair of variables. This means that if you plug into the conjunction every possible pair of truth values, the conjunction will yield only these four truth values: T, F, F, and F.

In ordinary language, this is what each of the rows is saying:

Row 1: When p is true and q is true, p & q is true.
Row 2: When p is true and q is false, p & q is false.
Row 3: When p is false and q is true, p & q is false.
Row 4: When p is false and q is false, p & q is false.

Maybe you've already guessed (by studying the truth table) an important fact about the truth value of a conjunction: *If just one statement in the conjunction is false, the whole conjunction is false; only if both conjuncts are true is the whole conjunction true.* The previous truth table reflects this state of affairs. In the table, we see that p & q is true only when p is true and q is true (in the first row)—and that p & q is false whenever at least one of the component statements is false (in the other three rows). This should make perfect sense to you because in everyday speech, if one-half of a conjunction is false, we would normally regard the *whole* conjunction as false.

It's a good idea to remember the exact sequence of T's and F's in the first two columns of the previous truth table. That way you won't have to guess to make

PENGUINS ARE BLACK AND WHITE. SOME OLD TV SHOWS ARE BLACK AND WHITE. THEREFORE, SOME PENGUINS ARE OLD TV SHOWS.

GLASBERGEN

Logic: another thing that penguins aren't very good at.

© 2002 by Randy Glasbergen.

sure you include every possible combination of truth values. The first few columns in any truth table are usually entered automatically as guides.

Disjunction

In a conjunction we assert that *p* and *q* are both true and that if just one conjunct is false, the whole conjunction is false. But in a **disjunction**, we assert that either *p* or *q* is true (though both might be) and that even if one of the statements is false, the whole disjunction is still true. Each statement in a disjunction is called a **disjunct**. For example:

> *Either Joan is angry, or Ann is serene.*

which we symbolize as

> *p* v *q*

or

> *Either Joan or Ann will row the boat.*

which we also symbolize as

> *p* v *q*

The symbol for disjunction (v) is called a wedge, which is roughly equivalent to the word *or*. The word *unless* is also sometimes used in place of *or* to form a disjunction, as in "I will be tired at the game unless I drink coffee." The words *either* and *neither* usually signal the beginning of a disjunction.

The truth table for a disjunction looks like this:

p	*q*	*p* v *q*
T	T	T
T	F	T
F	T	T
F	F	F

The table shows us that *p* v *q* is true in every possible combination of T's and F's—except one, where both *p* and *q* are false (in the last row). This situation just reflects the fact that for a disjunction to be true, only one of the disjuncts must be true. The disjunction here, for example, is true if (1) Joan is angry or (2) Ann is serene or (3) Joan is angry and Ann is serene.

An important point to keep in mind is that in English the word "or" has two meanings. It can mean "one or the other, or both," which is called the *inclusive* sense. In this sense, *p* v *q* means "*p* or *q* or both" ("If he's sick or tired, he won't go jogging"). But "or" can also mean "either but not both," which is called the *exclusive* sense. In the exclusive sense, *p* v *q* means "*p* or *q* but not both" ("Either the baby is a boy or a girl"). Standard practice in logic is to assume the inclusive

"Logic is not a body of doctrine, but a mirror-image of the world. Logic is transcendental."
—Ludwig Wittgenstein

FURTHER THOUGHT

Arguments We Have Known and Loved

Virtually every field has its share of well-worn arguments used to establish this theory or that proposition. But the discipline of philosophy—because it is, well, philosophy—is studded from end to end with influential arguments, including some especially famous ones.

If all that exists is matter in motion, then there are no disembodied spirits.
All that exists is matter in motion.
Therefore, there are no disembodied spirits.

Whatever begins to exist has a cause.
The universe began to exist.
Therefore, the universe had a cause, namely God.

There is unnecessary evil in the world.
If there were an all-powerful, all-knowing, all-good being, there would be no unnecessary evil in the world.
Therefore, there is no all-powerful, all-knowing, all-good being.

If it's true that all our actions are determined by an indefinitely long chain of prior events, then people cannot perform free actions.
It's true that all our actions are determined by an indefinitely long chain of prior events.
Therefore, people cannot perform free actions.

We can't be certain that we are not dreaming.
If we can't be certain that we are not dreaming, we cannot be certain that what we sense is real.
If we cannot be certain that what we sense is real, we cannot acquire knowledge through sense experience.
Therefore, we cannot acquire knowledge through sense experience.

sense when dealing with disjunctions. This approach is reflected in the truth table for a disjunction, and it simplifies the evaluation of disjunctive arguments. It has no effect on our evaluation of disjunctive syllogisms (discussed in Chapter 3); they would be valid forms regardless of whether the disjunction was construed as inclusive or exclusive. Look:

Either p *or* q.
Not p.
Therefore, q.

In the disjunctive syllogism, one of the disjuncts is denied, so the argument is valid in any case. But if one of the disjuncts is affirmed, the argument is invalid when the disjunction is inclusive:

Either p *or* q.
p.
*Therefore, not-*q.

Obviously, if the disjunction means "*p* or *q* or both," then by affirming *p* we cannot conclude not-*q*.

If we know that the disjuncts in a disjunctive premise really are exclusive options ("either a boy or a girl"), then we can safely assume the exclusive meaning of "or" and examine the argument accordingly. Otherwise it's safest to stick to the inclusive sense.

Negation

A negation is the denial of a statement, which we indicate with the word "not" or a term that means the same thing. For example, the negation of the statement "The price of eggs in China is steep" is

The price of eggs in China is not steep.

or

It is not the case that the price of eggs in China is steep.

or

It is false that the price of eggs in China is steep.

Assuming we use *p* to represent the foregoing statement, here's how we would symbolize its negation:

$\sim p$

The symbol $\sim$ is called a "tilde," and when we state $\sim p$ aloud, we say "not-*p*." When it appears in front of a statement, it indicates the reversal of the statement's truth value. A true statement becomes false; a false statement becomes true. One interesting consequence of this reversal is that a *double negation* is the same thing as *no* negation. For example, take the foregoing negation ("The price of eggs in China is not steep"). If you negate this negation ("It is not the case that the price of eggs in China is not steep"), you end up with the positive statement, "The price of eggs in China is steep." The truth table for a negation explains why such reversals can happen:

p	$\sim p$
T	F
F	T

Conditional

Remember conditional statements? We looked at them when we discussed valid and invalid argument forms (*modus ponens*, denying the antecedent, etc.). The basic form of a conditional is "if . . . then . . ." For example: "If the cat is on the mat, then the rat will stay home." Symbolized, a conditional looks like this: $p \rightarrow q$, where an arrow represents the connective. Recall also that in a conditional, the first part (p) is the antecedent, and the second part (q) is the consequent.

Notice that a conditional asserts only that if the antecedent is true, then the consequent must be true. It does not assert that the antecedent is actually true or that the consequent is actually true—but only that under specified conditions a certain state of affairs will be actual.

At first, you may find that the truth table for conditionals seems a little odd. But it makes good sense when you think about it:

p	q	$p \rightarrow q$
T	T	T
T	F	F
F	T	T
F	F	T

The table shows that a conditional is false in only one situation—when the antecedent is true and the consequent is false. Put more precisely, a conditional statement is false if and only if its antecedent is true and its consequent is false. In all other possible combinations of truth values, a conditional is true—and this is the part that may strike you as odd.

Let's take each of the four combinations in turn and see how they work in this conditional statement: "If George is paid a dollar, then he'll jump out the window." The question we can ask is this: "Under what circumstances is the conditional statement (the whole statement, antecedent and consequent together) true?" Well, it should be clear that if George is indeed paid a dollar, and if he does jump out the window, then the whole conditional would be true. This is the situation in the first row of the truth table.

What about the last row—what if the antecedent is false and the consequent is false? If it is false that George is paid a dollar, and it's false that he jumps out the window, there is no reason to think that the conditional itself is false. George could reasonably assert that the conditional statement isn't false if he isn't paid a dollar and doesn't jump out the window.

George could also reasonably assert that the conditional isn't false even when the antecedent is false and the consequent is true (the situation in the third row). If George isn't paid a dollar, and he still jumps out the window, that doesn't prove that the conditional is false.

This path brings us back to the fact that a conditional statement is false *only* when the antecedent is true and the consequent is false.

"The art of reasoning becomes of first importance. In this line antiquity has left us the finest models for imitation."

—Thomas Jefferson

Statements and Connectives

- A simple statement, or claim, is one that does not contain any other statements as constituents. A compound statement is one composed of at least two simple statements.
- Logical connectives

  Conjunction (and): & If just one statement in a conjunction is false, the whole conjunction is false.

  Disjunction (or): v A disjunction is true even if one of the disjuncts is false.

  Negation (not): ~ A negation "reverses" the truth value of any statement.

  Conditional (if-then): → A conditional is false if and only if its antecedent is true and its consequent is false.

- Words used in conditionals

  if—introduces the antecedent; If p, then $q = p \rightarrow q$
  only if—introduces the consequent; p only if $q = p \rightarrow q$
  provided—introduces the antecedent; p provided $q = q \rightarrow p$
  unless—introduces the antecedent; p unless $q = {\sim}q \rightarrow p$
  whenever—introduces antecedent; whenever p, $q = p \rightarrow q$

Conditional statements can be expressed in ways other than the if-then configuration, the standard form. Here are some conditionals in various patterns with each one paired with the standard-form version:

1. You will fall off that ladder if you're not careful.
   If you're not careful, you will fall off that ladder.
2. Gregory will excel in school, provided that he studies hard.
   If Gregory studies hard, then he will excel in school.
3. Jenna would not have wrecked the car if she had not tried to beat that light.
   If Jenna had not tried to beat that light, she would not have wrecked the car.
4. I'll ride the bus only if I'm late.
   If I ride the bus, then I'm late.
5. Whenever I think, I get a headache.
   If I think, I get a headache.
6. I will walk the dog unless it's raining.
   If it's not raining, I will walk the dog.

Among these patterns, pair 4 and pair 6 are likely to cause you the most trouble. In pair 4, "only if" is the troublesome term. Just remember that "only if" introduces the *consequent* of a conditional. So in "I'll ride the bus only if I'm late," "only if" indicates that the consequent is "I'm late." So the antecedent is "If I ride the bus."

You have to move "if" to the front of the antecedent to put the statement in standard form. In pair 6, "unless" is the sticking point. You need to understand that "unless" introduces the antecedent and means "if not." So here "unless it's raining" becomes "if it's not raining" in the antecedent position.

Because of such variations in conditional statements, it's important to translate conditionals into standard form before you try to assess their validity. To do that, you must identify the antecedent and consequent and put them in proper order (antecedent before consequent).

 EXERCISES

Exercise 6.1

Identify each of the following statements as a conjunction, disjunction, or conditional; identify its component statements; and indicate the symbol used to represent the connective.

* 1. The Democrats raised taxes, and the Republicans cut programs.
  2. Either I walk home, or I drive Ralph's car.
  3. If the Yankees win, they will be in the World Series.
  4. It is not the case that the Yankees won.
* 5. If Taslima can read your mind, then you're in trouble.
  6. The newspaper ad was either misleading, or it was meant as a joke.
* 7. If God is all-powerful, then he can prevent evil in the world.
  8. He supported the revolution, and he was arrested without being charged.

Exercise 6.2

Translate each of the following statements into symbolic form. Use the letters in parentheses to represent each component statement. (Assume that the letters stand for positive statements so that a negated statement is indicated by adding a ~ in front of a letter.)

* 1. Either Herman does his homework, or he goofs off. (*p, q*)
  2. If Herman does his homework, he will have time to go to the party. (*s, t*)
  3. It is not the case that Hans had access to the murder weapon. (*a*)
* 4. People die, but books live forever. (*e, f*)
  5. Aiming that loaded gun at someone is not a good idea. (*c*)
  6. Provided Alex returns the money, he will not be prosecuted. (*x, y*)
  7. Human cloning will become widespread, unless the government interferes. (*p, q*)
* 8. He will not benefit from instruction, and he will not learn on his own. (*g, h*)
  9. Buffalo gets a lot of snow in winter, and everybody hates it. (*j, k*)
  10. His tampering with the judicial system is not appropriate. (*b*)

11. You will eventually discover the correct formula if you work systemati-cally. (*x*, *y*)
12. He's either a nut or a brilliant eccentric. (*p*, *q*)
13. If Socrates is a man, he is mortal. (*d*, *e*)
* 14. It is not the case that the zoo won't accept any more mammals. (*p*)
15. Either disembodied spirits exist, or psychic hoaxes are rampant. (*s*, *t*)
16. Mickey Mouse wanted to get married, but Minnie demurred. (*p*, *q*)

Exercise 6.3

Indicate which of the following statements are true and which are false.

1. Dogs are mammals v Snakes are marsupials
* 2. Alligators are reptiles & Dogs are reptiles
3. ~ Dogs are reptiles & ~ Alligators are mammals
4. Dogs can bark → Dogs can talk
5. Dogs can talk → Dogs are reptiles
* 6. ~ Dogs are mammals v Snakes are reptiles
7. ~ Alligators are reptiles → Alligators are mammals
* 8. Alligators can bark & ~ Dogs are reptiles
9. ~ ~ Dogs are mammals v Snakes are reptiles
10. ~ ~ Dogs are mammals → ~ ~ Snakes are reptiles

Exercise 6.4

Indicate which of the following symbolized statements are true and which are false. Assume that the variables *a*, *b*, and *c* are true, and *p*, *q*, and *r* are false.

1. *a* & *p*
* 2. *b* v *r*
3. *c* → *q*
4. ~*b* v *c*
* 5. ~*b* → ~*q*
6. *a* & ~*q*
7. *b* v ~*p*
8. *a* & *c*
9. *b* → ~*c*
* 10. *p* → ~*r*

Exercise 6.5

Translate each of the symbolic statements in Exercise 6.4 into a statement in English. Assume that the letters stand for positive statements. Answers are pro-vided for 2, 5, and 10.

Exercise 6.6

Translate each of the following statements into symbolic form. Assume that the letters you use stand for positive statements.

1. If Joshua fought the battle of Jericho, then the walls must have come tumbling down.
* 2. Either democracy is losing ground in the United States, or it is being enhanced in Third World countries.
3. Either the ancient Greek temples were built by ancient Greeks, or they were built by Romans who imitated the Greeks.
4. The Egyptian pyramids were not built by ancient alien visitors from space, and they certainly were not built by Egyptians taught by alien visitors from space.
* 5. Science will never triumph over religion unless science can offer a spiritual experience.
6. If World War II was a just war, then the Gulf War was a just war.
7. I will fly to Detroit, but I will not meet you in Dallas.
8. It is not the case that philosophy is dead, and it is not true that science has replaced it.
* 9. Provided I pass my logic course, I will finally be able to fathom political arguments.
10. The federal deficit is out of control, but most Americans are not worried.

Checking for Validity

Now you're ready to put what you've learned about truth tables to use in determining the validity of arguments. The truth-table test of validity is based on an elementary fact about validity that you've already encountered: *It's impossible for a valid argument to have true premises and a false conclusion.* So any procedure that allows us to easily check if the premises are true and the conclusion is false will help us test an argument for validity. Truth tables can do this. Devising truth tables for arguments, then, can reveal the underlying structure—the form—of the arguments, even those that are fairly complex.

Simple Arguments

Let's start by analyzing a very simple argument involving a conjunction:

Ducks have webbed feet.
Ducks have feathers.
Therefore, ducks have webbed feet and ducks have feathers.

We symbolize the argument like this:

p

q

∴ *p & q*

Here we have each premise and the conclusion represented by variables, giving us a good look at the argument's logical form. The symbol ∴ indicates that a conclusion follows (it's often translated as "therefore"). The argument is, of course, valid—a fact that you can quickly see without the aid of a truth table. But it makes for a simple illustration:

p	*q*	*p & q*
T	T	T
T	F	F
F	T	F
F	F	F

This truth table is a repeat of the one we looked at in the section on conjunctions. The top line of the table shows the argument's two premises and its conclusion with their truth values listed below. Like all truth tables, this one shows every possible combination of truth values for the premises and conclusion.

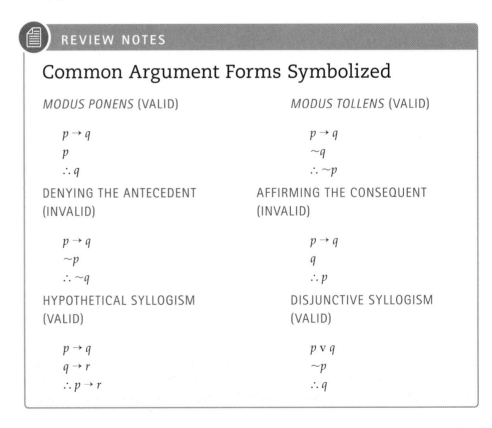

REVIEW NOTES

Common Argument Forms Symbolized

MODUS PONENS (VALID)

p → q

p

∴ *q*

MODUS TOLLENS (VALID)

p → q

~*q*

∴ ~*p*

DENYING THE ANTECEDENT
(INVALID)

p → q

~*p*

∴ ~*q*

AFFIRMING THE CONSEQUENT
(INVALID)

p → q

q

∴ *p*

HYPOTHETICAL SYLLOGISM
(VALID)

p → q

q → r

∴ *p → r*

DISJUNCTIVE SYLLOGISM
(VALID)

p ∨ *q*

~*p*

∴ *q*

When dealing with simple arguments, the first two columns of a truth table are guide columns in which the variables, or letters, of the argument are listed, followed by a column for each premise and then a column for the conclusion. In this case, though, the guide columns happen to be identical to the premise columns, so we won't repeat them.

Now we can ask the big question: "Does the truth table show (in any row) a state of affairs in which the premises of the argument are true and the conclusion false?" If we can find even *one* instance of this arrangement, we will have shown that the argument is invalid. Remember that we are trying to judge the *validity* of an argument, which is a matter of argument *form*. So if we can discover that it's *possible* for a particular argument form to have true premises and a false conclusion, we will know without further investigation that the argument is invalid. Not only that, but we will know that *any* argument of the same pattern is invalid. The truth table can tell us definitively whether an argument is invalid because the table includes every possible combination of truth values. If the truth table doesn't reveal a situation in which the argument has true premises and a false conclusion, then the argument is valid.

As you can see in the previous table, there is no row in which the premises are true (T-T) and the conclusion false (F). Therefore, the argument is valid.

Here's a slightly more complex argument:

If the icebergs melt, the lowlands will flood.
The icebergs will not melt.
Therefore, the lowlands will not flood.

You should recognize this argument as an instance of denying the antecedent. Here it is symbolized, with negation and conditional connectives:

$p \rightarrow q$
$\sim p$
$\therefore \sim q$

And here's the argument's truth table:

p	q	$p \rightarrow q$	$\sim p$	$\sim q$
T	T	T	F	F
T	F	F	F	T
F	T	T	T	F
F	F	T	T	T

You can begin checking for validity in a couple of different ways. You can first inspect all rows that have a false conclusion and then see if the premises in that row are true, indicating an invalid argument. Or you can zero in on rows showing all true premises and then check to see if they have false conclusions.

> "Logic takes care of itself; all we have to do is to look and see how it does it."
> —Ludwig Wittgenstein

In this case, the third row tells the tale: Both premises are true and the conclusion is false. So the argument is invalid, and we need not check any other rows.

As we saw earlier, the truth value of a compound statement depends on the truth value of its components. That's why it's a good idea to start out with guide columns in a truth table. The truth value of these variables (letters) determines the truth value of statements that are comprised of the variables. The truth value of these compound units in turn determines the truth value of any larger compound units.

In the truth table just given, the truth value of ~p is the contradictory of p, and the truth value of ~q is the contradictory of q. So whatever the truth value of a statement, the tilde (~) reverses it, from true to false or false to true.

Now let's try this one:

Either we fight for freedom or we give in to tyranny.
We won't fight for freedom.
Therefore, we will give in to tyranny.

 FURTHER THOUGHT

From Here to Absurdity

One kind of powerful argument that you frequently encounter is known as *reductio ad absurdum* (reduction to absurdity). The idea behind it is that if the contradictory (negation) of a statement leads to an absurdity or falsehood, then the negation of the statement is false and the statement itself must be true. You must accept the statement because denying it gets you into logical trouble. So if you want to demonstrate that a statement is true (or false), you assume the statement's negation and show that it leads to an absurd or false statement. Here's the form of this type of argument:

p
$p \rightarrow q$
$\sim q$
$\therefore \sim p$

In plain English, this says: Let's suppose that p is true. If p is true, then q must be true. But there's no way that q can be true. (Or, q being true is absurd.) So it must not be the case that p is true. For example:

Suppose that water cannot freeze.
If water cannot freeze, then ice cannot exist.
But obviously ice does exist.
Therefore, water can freeze.

Symbolized, it looks like this:

$p \lor q$
$\sim p$
$\therefore q$

And here is its truth table:

p	q	$p \lor q$	$\sim p$	q
T	T	T	F	T
T	F	T	F	F
F	T	T	T	T
F	F	F	T	F

Is this argument valid? To find out, we need to check the table for any row that shows true premises and a false conclusion. The third row is the only one in which both premises are true—but the conclusion is also true. So this argument is valid.

Tricky Arguments

Arguments can get more complicated when variables and connectives are intricately combined into larger compounds and when the number of variables increases. In both these situations, truth tables can help you unravel the complexities. Let's examine an argument that has both these wrinkles. We'll go right to the symbolized form:

$p \rightarrow \sim(q \& r)$
p
$\therefore \sim(q \& r)$

Notice in these premises the use of parentheses to join variables. The parentheses enable us to symbolize arguments more precisely and to avoid confusion. In math, there is an obvious difference between $2 \times (3 + 4)$, which equals 14, and $(2 \times 3) + 4$, which equals 10. Likewise, there is a crucial difference between $p \rightarrow \sim(q \& r)$ and $(p \rightarrow \sim q) \& r$. The former symbolization would express a conditional such as "If it rains tomorrow, then Alice and Eric will not go to the movies." But the latter symbolization would represent a very different conditional, such as "If it rains tomorrow, then Alice will not go to the movies, and Eric will go to the movies." Such differences, of course, can affect the truth values of a statement and require a different truth table.

Here's a distinction involving parentheses that's worth committing to memory. Consider these two statements:

$\sim(q \& r)$
It is not the case that Leo sings the blues and Fats sings the blues.

$\sim q$ & $\sim r$
Leo does not sing the blues, and Fats does not sing the blues.

The first statement asserts that it is not the case that *both* Leo and Fats sing the blues. That is, it's not true that Leo and Fats are concurrently in the habit of singing the blues. Maybe Leo sings the blues, and Fats doesn't, or vice versa. On the other hand, the second statement says that Leo doesn't sing the blues and neither does Fats. If we hope that at least one of these guys sings the blues, we're out of luck.

Here's another distinction worth knowing. Look at these two statements:

$\sim(q \lor r)$
It is not the case that either Leo sings the blues or Fats sings the blues.

$\sim q \lor \sim r$
Either Leo does not sing the blues or Fats does not sing the blues.

The first statement says that neither Leo nor Fats sings the blues. The second statement says that it is not the case that Leo *and* Fats sing the blues.

Correctly symbolizing statements with parentheses is a straightforward business, but it requires close attention to what's being said. Your best clues to where to insert parentheses come from the words *either* and *neither*, conjunction and disjunction words such as *and* and *or*, and the punctuation of the sentences. Notice how the sentence clues in the following statements inform how the statements are symbolized:

If the gods intervene, then neither peace nor war can change the destiny of the nation.

We can symbolize the statements with the following variables:

p—The gods intervene.
q—Peace can change the destiny of the nation.
r—War can change the destiny of the nation.

$p \rightarrow \sim(q \lor r)$

And:

Either Jay Leno is funny or the show is rigged, or the network has made a bad investment.

p—Jay Leno is funny.
q—The show is rigged.
r—The network has made a bad investment.

$(p \lor q) \lor r$

Arguments like these that have three variables instead of two may look formidable, but they're not. The steps you use to check the validity of a three-variable argument are the same ones you apply in two-variable arguments. You devise a truth table, calculate truth values, and check for true premises with a

"Reason in man is rather like God in the world."
—Thomas Aquinas

false conclusion. The truth table, of course, has an additional guide column for the third variable, and there are more rows to accommodate the larger number of possible true-false combinations. In a two-variable table there are four rows; in a three-variable table there are eight and thus eight combinations of truth values. Notice how the guide columns are laid out:

p	q	r
T	T	T
T	T	F
T	F	T
T	F	F
F	T	T
F	T	F
F	F	T
F	F	F

To remember the truth values in each guide column, think: The first column is four T's, then four F's; the second column is alternating pairs of truth values beginning with T T; and the third column is alternating T's and F's starting with T.

Now let's test this argument for validity:

If Billy shot the sheriff but he didn't shoot the deputy, then he's guilty of only one crime. But it's not true that he shot the sheriff but didn't shoot the deputy. Therefore, it's not the case that he's guilty of only one crime.

p—Billy shot the sheriff.
q—He shot the deputy.
r—He's guilty of only one crime.

$(p \mathbin{\&} \sim q) \rightarrow r$
$\sim(p \mathbin{\&} \sim q)$
$\therefore \sim r$

And here's the argument's truth table:

	1 p	2 q	3 r	4 $p \mathbin{\&} \sim q$	5 $(p \mathbin{\&} \sim q) \rightarrow r$	6 $\sim(p \mathbin{\&} \sim q)$	7 $\sim r$
1	T	T	T	F	T	T	F
2	T	T	F	F	T	T	T
3	T	F	T	T	T	F	F
4	T	F	F	T	F	F	T
5	F	T	T	F	T	T	F
6	F	T	F	F	T	T	T
7	F	F	T	F	T	T	F
8	F	F	F	F	T	T	T

This truth table has seven columns, and you can guess why six of them are there: The first three are the guide columns, and the last three are for the two premises and the conclusion. Column 4 is there because it simplifies the assigning of truth values to columns 5, 6, and 7—it's a component of the two premises. If we wanted, we could add more columns for other components if the additions would make creating the truth table easier.

The truth values for p & $\sim q$ are, of course, determined by the truth values of its conjuncts. If just one conjunct is false, the conjunction is false (as it is in rows 1, 2, and 5 through 8). Only in rows 3 and 4 is the conjunction true. The truth value of the conditional $(p$ & $\sim q) \rightarrow r$ is based on the truth values of $(p$ & $\sim q)$ and r, with the conditional being false only when $(p$ & $\sim q)$ is true and r is false (row 4). In all other rows the conditional is true. The truth value of the premise $\sim(p$ & $\sim q)$ is the contradictory of the truth value for $(p$ & $\sim q)$. Likewise, the truth value of $\sim r$ is the contradictory of r.

Is there any row in which the premises are true and the conclusion false? Yes, that's the situation in rows 1, 5, and 7, so the argument is invalid.

Streamlined Evaluation

With truth tables, you can accurately assess the validity of any propositional argument, even some fairly complicated ones. But as the arguments get more complicated (when they have more than two or three variables, for example), you may want a more efficient technique for calculating validity. Here's a good alternative method—one that just happens to be easier to master if you already know the ins and outs of truth tables.

In this approach—what we'll call the *short method*—we don't bother to produce a whole truth table, but we do try to construct some truth-table rows (maybe only one if we're lucky). The basic strategy is based on the same fact we relied on in the truth-table test: It's impossible for a valid argument to have true premises and a false conclusion. So we try to discover if there's a way to make the conclusion false and the premises true by assigning various truth values to the argument's components. That is, we try to prove that the argument is invalid. If we can do this, then we'll have the proof we need.

Let's try the short method on this argument:

$\sim q$
$p \rightarrow (q \vee r)$
r
$\therefore p$

First we write out the argument so that the premises and conclusion are in a single row:

$$\sim q \qquad p \rightarrow (q \vee r) \qquad r \qquad p$$

Now we examine the conclusion. What truth value must we assign to it to ensure that it's false? Obviously the answer is *false*—because there is only one variable in the conclusion, and the conclusion must be false. So we label p with

> ## REVIEW NOTES
>
> ## The Short Method: Step by Step
>
> 1. Write out the symbolized argument in a single row.
> 2. Assign truth values to the variables in the conclusion to make the conclusion false. (Write the appropriate T's or F's below the row.) Assign these truth values to the same variables elsewhere.
> 3. Consistently assign truth values to variables in the premises. Assign truth values first to premises where specific truth values are "locked in."
> 4. Try to make assignments that yield a false conclusion and true premises. If you can, the argument is invalid. If not, the argument is valid.

an F in the conclusion and everyplace else in the argument. Then our row looks like this:

$$\sim q \qquad p \to (q \lor r) \qquad\qquad r \qquad\qquad p$$
$$ $$

~q	p → (q v r)	r	p
	F		F

Just one caution: As you work through the short method, you must remember that the truth values you mark under the argument row *apply to the variables (letters) only, not the premises.* To avoid any confusion, if you want you can write the truth values for the premises *above* the argument row. In this way you can indicate either (1) the premise truth values that you're trying for or (2) the premise truth values that result from your truth value assignments.

In this argument we can also tell right away that *r must* be true because it's a premise in the argument, and we're trying to see if we can make all the premises true (and the conclusion false). Then we have:

~q	p → (q v r)	r	p
	F T	T	F

Now we look at the first premise because it will be easy to determine its truth value. Since the first premise must be true, and it's a negation, *q* must be false. This fills out the whole argument with truth values:

~q	p → (q v r)	r	p
F	F F T	T	F

We've shown then that the first and third premises are true. And we can now see that the second premise must also be true: The disjunction (*q* v *r*) is true because one of the disjuncts is true (*r*). And the conditional (made up of *p* and the disjunction) is true because a false antecedent (*p*) and a true consequent (*q* v *r*) yields a true conditional.

We have thus shown that this argument can have a false conclusion and true premises—the sign of an invalid argument.

Now let's try the short method on this argument:

$p \rightarrow q$
$q \rightarrow r$
$\sim r$
$\therefore \sim p$

$p \rightarrow q$	$q \rightarrow r$	$\sim r$	$\sim p$

Again, we start with the conclusion. Since the conclusion is a negation ($\sim p$), we know that there's only one way that the conclusion could be false—if p is true. We then must make p true everyplace else in the argument:

$p \rightarrow q$	$q \rightarrow r$	$\sim r$	$\sim p$
T			T

We now turn to the first premise, a simple conditional. The antecedent (p) is true, which means that if the conditional is to be true, its consequent (q) cannot be false (a true antecedent and a false consequent yields a false conditional). So we're forced to assign these truth values:

$p \rightarrow q$	$q \rightarrow r$	$\sim r$	$\sim p$
T T	T		T

That leaves just r to deal with. Again we are forced to assign a truth value to it. Because the premise is a negation, and it must be true, r has to be false. But if r is false, the second premise (another simple conditional) must be false (truth values for the premises are shown *above* the argument row):

T	F	T	F
$p \rightarrow q$	$q \rightarrow r$	$\sim r$	$\sim p$
T T	T F	F	T

So we see that since there is only one way for the conclusion to be false, we are locked into truth values that prevented us from having all true premises. We simply cannot consistently assign truth values to this argument that will give us a false conclusion and true premises. Therefore, this argument is valid.

In using the short method like this, your overall goal is to see if you can prove invalidity in the most efficient way possible. You want to get the job done without a lot of unnecessary steps. The best strategy for doing this is to look for truth value assignments *that cannot be any other way* given the truth value assignments in the conclusion. That is, focus on premises with assignments that are "locked into" the argument by the truth values you've given the conclusion. Make assignments in those premises first, regardless of which premise you start with.

In the foregoing arguments, the conclusions could be made false in only one way, and that made the rest of the work easier. But sometimes a conclusion can be made false in more than one way. In such cases, your strategy should be to try each possibility—each way that the conclusion can be false—until you get what you're after: an argument with true premises and a false conclusion. As soon as you get it, stop. You've proven that the argument form is invalid, and there's no reason to continue making assignments. If you try all the possibilities and still can't prove invalidity, the argument is valid.

Let's take a look at one of these multiple-possibility arguments:

$p \rightarrow q$
$q \lor r$
$\sim q$
$\therefore p \& r$

$p \rightarrow q$	$q \lor r$	$\sim q$	$p \& r$

In this argument the conclusion is a conjunction, which means that it can be made false by any one of these combinations of truth values: F-T, T-F, and F-F. If we make separate rows for each of these possibilities, they look like this:

	$p \rightarrow q$	$q \lor r$	$\sim q$	$p \& r$	
1					
	F	T		F	T
2	$p \rightarrow q$	$q \lor r$	$\sim q$	$p \& r$	
	T	F		T	F
3	$p \rightarrow q$	$q \lor r$	$\sim q$	$p \& r$	
	F	F		F	F

So can we consistently assign truth values to make the premises true and the conclusion false in any of these rows? We can forget about row 2 because in the first premise, q must be true (to avoid making the conditional false). And if q is true, the third premise would be false. Likewise, we must throw out row 3 because q again must be true (to ensure that the disjunction is true). And if true, we run into the same problem we have in row 2—the third premise must be false. Row 1, though, works. To make the third premise true, we must make q false. And when we assign a truth value of false to q in the rest of the argument, we make the premises true and the conclusion false. Therefore, the argument is invalid.

 EXERCISES

Exercise 6.7

Construct a truth table for each of the statements in Exercise 6.3. Answers are provided for 2, 6, and 8.

Exercise 6.8

Construct a truth table for each of the following arguments and indicate whether the argument is valid or invalid.

1. $a \& b$
   $\therefore a$

* 2. $p \rightarrow q$
   p
   $\therefore q$

3. $p \lor q$
p
$\therefore \sim q$

4. $p \to q$
$\sim p$
$\therefore q$

5. $a \,\&\, b$
$\sim a$
$\therefore b$

6. $p \to q$
$q \to r$
$\therefore q$

* 7. $p \to q$
$\sim q \,\&\, r$
$\therefore r$

8. $a \lor (b \,\&\, c)$
$\sim (b \,\&\, c)$
$\therefore a$

9. $x \to y$
$y \to z$
$\therefore x \to z$

10. $p \to q$
$\therefore p \to (p \,\&\, q)$

11. $a \to b$
$b \to c$
$\therefore (b \,\&\, c) \lor (a \,\&\, b)$

12. $a \lor (b \to c)$
$b \,\&\, \sim c$
$\therefore \sim a$

13. $(p \lor q) \to (p \,\&\, q)$
$p \,\&\, q$
$\therefore p \lor q$

* 14. $p \to q$
$\sim (q \lor r)$
$\therefore \sim p$

15. $d \to e$
$e \lor f$
e
$\therefore d \,\&\, f$

16. $(p \rightarrow q) \rightarrow (p \rightarrow r)$
    $\sim(p \rightarrow q)$
    $\sim r$
    $\therefore p$

17. $(d \lor e) \rightarrow f$
    $f \rightarrow (d \& e)$
    $\therefore (d \& e) \rightarrow (d \lor e)$

18. $\sim(d \& e)$
    $e \lor f$
    $\therefore \sim d \& e$

19. $d \& (\sim e \rightarrow \sim d)$
    $f \rightarrow \sim e$
    $\therefore f$

20. $d \lor \sim e$
    $f \rightarrow e$
    $\therefore d \rightarrow \sim f$

Exercise 6.9

For each of the following arguments, translate it into symbols, construct a truth table, and determine its validity.

1. If there is no rain soon, the crops will die. If the crops die, there will be no food for the coming winter. The crops will not die. Therefore, there will be rain soon.

2. If we give kidnappers the money that they demand, then further kidnappings will be encouraged. If we do not give kidnappers the money that they demand, the kidnappers will kill the hostages. We will not give kidnappers the money that they demand. Therefore, the kidnappers will kill the hostages.

* 3. Jake is the plumber or Jake is the carpenter. Jake is not the carpenter. Therefore, Jake is the plumber.

4. "Men, it is assumed, act in economic matters only in response to pecuniary compensation or to force. Force in the modern society is largely, although by no means completely, obsolete. So only pecuniary compensation remains of importance." [John Kenneth Galbraith, *The New Industrial State*]

5. If the lake freezes, then the lake-effect snow will stop. If the lake-effect snow stops, the streets will be easier to plow. Therefore, the streets will be easier to plow.

6. Either Emilio walks or he takes the train. And either Joann takes the train or she does not take the train. If Emilio walks, then Joann takes the train. Emilio takes the train. So Joann will not take the train.

7. UN peacekeepers will not attack the local militants, provided that the militants behave themselves. The militants will not make trouble if the UN peacekeepers don't attack. Therefore, UN peacekeepers will not attack the local militants, and the militants will not make trouble.

8. "If then, it is agreed that things are either the result of coincidence or for an end, and these cannot be the result of coincidence or spontaneity, it follows that they must be for an end." [Aristotle, *Physics*]

9. Either there is evidence that women of supernatural powers (i.e., witches) exist, or there is no such evidence. If there is no such evidence, then we have no reason to believe in witches. If there is evidence, we do have reason to believe in witches. There is no such evidence. Therefore, we have no reason to believe in witches.

10. Either the herbal remedy alleviated the symptoms, or the placebo effect alleviated the symptoms. If the placebo effect is responsible for easing the symptoms, then the herbal remedy is worthless. The herbal remedy alleviated the symptoms. So the herbal remedy is not worthless.

* 11. Unless both Mary goes and Henry goes, the party will be a disaster. The party will be a disaster. Therefore, both Mary and Henry will not go.

Exercise 6.10

Use the short method to check the validity of the following arguments in Exercise 6.8: 1, 3, 5, 9, 10, 15, 16, and 18. Write the symbolized argument in one row and assign truth values to each variable. Then above the argument row, assign truth values to the premises and conclusion. Answers are provided for 3, 10, and 15.

Proof of Validity

When arguments are very complex—when they consist of several variables and many premises—the truth-table method of checking for validity may be unwieldy and tedious. In such cases, the method of proof is a more efficient procedure. The **method of proof** is a way to confirm the validity of an argument by using simple, valid argument forms to deduce its conclusion from its premises. Most valid complex arguments consist of several of these valid sub-arguments (most of which you may already know). Determining the validity of the larger argument then is a matter of moving step by step from premises to conclusion, identifying the valid, component arguments along the way. If these component arguments are valid, we know that the larger argument is also valid. Thus, the method of proof can show that an argument is valid (it cannot, however, prove an argument invalid).

To demonstrate that an argument consists of valid steps from premises to conclusion is to provide a *proof* of its validity, much as valid mathematical operations can serve as proofs in geometry. The steps in the proof—the valid arguments—can be expressed as *rules of inference*. Being familiar with the most common of these rules is a prerequisite for successfully working through a proof.

Rules of Inference

Here are nine of the most common rules of inference. You may have already encountered at least five of them in earlier chapters, and the other four will likely seem obvious or familiar. (*Note:* The rules themselves are set out in lower-case letters; capital letters, though, are used to symbolize statements in a proof.)

1. *Modus Ponens* (MP)

    $p \rightarrow q$

    p

    $\therefore q$

2. *Modus Tollens* (MT)

    $p \rightarrow q$

    $\sim q$

    $\therefore \sim p$

3. Hypothetical Syllogism (HS)

    $p \rightarrow q$

    $q \rightarrow r$

    $\therefore p \rightarrow r$

4. Simplification (SIMP)

$p \& q$	or	$p \& q$
$\therefore p$		$\therefore q$

5. Conjunction (CONJ)

    p

    q

    $\therefore p \& q$

6. Addition (ADD)

p	or	q
$\therefore p \vee q$		$\therefore p \vee q$

7. Disjunctive Syllogism (DS)

$p \vee q$	or	$p \vee q$
$\sim p$		$\sim q$
$\therefore q$		$\therefore p$

8. Constructive Dilemma (CD)

    $(p \rightarrow q) \& (r \rightarrow s)$

    $p \vee r$

    $\therefore q \vee s$

9. Destructive Dilemma (DD)

$(p \rightarrow q) \& (r \rightarrow s)$

$\sim q \vee \sim s$

$\therefore \sim p \vee \sim r$

How do we use these rules? Here is a sample argument followed by its proof:

If Trish fails math or gets an incomplete in English, then she will not be attending college in the future.
Unfortunately, she will in fact fail math.
Therefore, she will not be attending college in the future.

1. $(M \vee E) \rightarrow \sim C$ Premise
2. $M / \sim C$ Premise/Conclusion
3. $M \vee E$ 2, ADD
4. $\sim C$ 1, 3, MP

Each step is numbered. The column on the right consists of *annotations* for the proof—notes that describe each line and how it was derived. Line 1 states the first premise, and line 2 states the second. After the forward slash comes a mention of the conclusion ($\sim C$), not as another line in the proof but as a reminder of what the premises are supposed to justify.

Line 3 is an inference from the preceding premise; the line's annotation says that $M \vee E$ was derived from line 2 using the addition rule of inference. Line 4 (the conclusion) was derived from lines 1 and 3 by applying the *modus ponens* rule (MP): $(M \vee E) \rightarrow \sim C$; $M \vee E$; therefore, $\sim C$. This proof, then, demonstrates that the argument is valid, that the conclusion can be validly deduced from its premises.

Keep in mind that you must always apply the inference rules to *entire* lines in the proof. Applying a rule to only a portion of a line will result in a faulty proof. Also you must apply only one rule at a time. Each line should be derived by just one rule.

Now consider the proof for this more involved argument:

$P \rightarrow Q$

$Q \rightarrow R$

$R \rightarrow S$

$\sim S$

$P \vee T$

$\therefore T$

1. $P \rightarrow Q$ Premise
2. $Q \rightarrow R$ Premise
3. $R \rightarrow S$ Premise
4. $\sim S$ Premise
5. $P \vee T / T$ Premise/Conclusion
6. $P \rightarrow R$ 1, 2, HS

7. $P \rightarrow S$ 6, 3, HS

8. $\sim P$ 7, 4, MT

9. T 5, 8, DS

Notice that the rules are not used jointly but are applied one at a time and once per line. They can, however, be applied multiple times in the same proof, either sequentially or occasionally.

Rules of Replacement

Another set of rules distinct from the rules of inference can also help us prove the validity of arguments. These are known as the *rules of replacement* (or equivalence). They stipulate that some statements are logically equivalent—they have precisely the same truth value even though they are expressed differently. This means that in working through a proof, we can replace certain statements with any others that are logically equivalent, and this procedure can make proofs easier to construct. For example, any statement p can be replaced with its equivalent, the double negation of that statement: $\sim\sim p$. To say that p is not the case is to say that it is not the case that p. To say that we are happy is to affirm that we are not unhappy (not not happy). This may be a clumsy way of speaking, but in logic such equivalences can be very useful.

Logical equivalence is indicated by the symbol $\equiv$, like this: $\sim\sim p \equiv p$, or $p \equiv \sim\sim p$. Logicians call such a compound statement a *biconditional* because it asserts that one part of the statement (left or right of the $\equiv$) is true if and only if the other part is true. If one is true (or false), the other must be true (or false). Proofs using rules of replacement are constructed in much the same way as proofs using the rules of inference, with one exception. Rules of inference are applied only to entire lines; rules of replacement can be applied to the constituent parts of a line.

Here are nine of the most useful rules of replacement with some examples in ordinary language for the less obvious ones.

10. Tautology (TAUT)

    $p \equiv (p \ \& \ p)$

    $p \equiv (p \ v \ p)$

11. Double Negation (DN)

    $\sim\sim p \equiv p$

    $p \equiv \sim\sim p$

12. Commutation (COM)

    $(p \ \& \ q) \equiv (q \ \& \ p)$

    $(p \ v \ q) \equiv (q \ v \ p)$

13. Association (ASSOC)

    $[p \ \& \ (q \ \& \ r)] \equiv [(p \ \& \ q) \ \& \ r]$

    $[p \ v \ (q \ v \ r)] \equiv [(p \ v \ q) \ v \ r]$

14. Distribution (DIST)

$[p \mathbin{\&} (q \vee r)] \equiv [(p \mathbin{\&} q) \vee (p \mathbin{\&} r)]$

$[p \vee (q \mathbin{\&} r)] \equiv [(p \vee q) \mathbin{\&} (p \vee r)]$

Example: "I'll wash dishes and either dry them myself or ask my sister to help." ≡ "I'll wash dishes and dry them myself, or I'll wash dishes and ask my sister to help."

15. De Morgan's Law (DM)

$\sim(p \mathbin{\&} q) \equiv (\sim p \vee \sim q)$

$\sim(p \vee q) \equiv (\sim p \mathbin{\&} \sim q)$

Example: "You can't commit a crime and go unpunished." ≡ "You either can't commit a crime or you can't go unpunished."

16. Contraposition (CONTRA)

$(p \rightarrow q) \equiv (\sim q \rightarrow \sim p)$

Example: "If John is home, then he is doing his homework." ≡ "If John is not home, then he is not doing his homework."

17. Implication (IMP)

$(p \rightarrow q) \equiv (\sim p \vee q)$

$(p \rightarrow q) \equiv \sim(p \mathbin{\&} \sim q)$

Example: "If I pay my dues, then I'll succeed." ≡ "Either I don't pay my dues or I'll succeed."

18. Exportation (EXP)

$[(p \mathbin{\&} q) \rightarrow r] \equiv [p \rightarrow (q \rightarrow r)]$

Example: "If I fail to take skiing lessons and still try to ski, then I'll break my neck." ≡ "If I fail to take skiing lessons, then if I try to ski I'll break my neck."

Consider this proof using three rules of replacement:

1.	$(P \rightarrow Q) \vee R$	Premise
2.	$P \mathbin{/} Q \vee R$	Premise/Conclusion
3.	$(\sim P \vee Q) \vee R$	1, IMP
4.	$\sim P \vee (Q \vee R)$	3, ASSOC
5.	$\sim\sim P$	2, DN
6.	$Q \vee R$	4, 5, DS

Here is a slightly more complex proof featuring three premises and four rules.

1.	$(P \mathbin{\&} Q) \vee R$	Premise
2.	$R \rightarrow S$	Premise
3.	$P \rightarrow \sim Q \mathbin{/} S$	Premise/Conclusion
4.	$\sim P \vee \sim Q$	3, IMP
5.	$\sim(P \mathbin{\&} Q)$	4, DM
6.	R	1, 5, DS
7.	S	2, 6, MP

EXERCISES

Exercise 6.11

For each of the following arguments, use the rules of inference and replacement to construct a proof.

1. $P \rightarrow Q$
   $P \vee (R \,\&\, S)$
   $\sim Q \,\&\, \sim T$
   $\therefore R$

*2. $P \rightarrow Q$
   $\sim Q \vee R$
   P
   $\therefore R$

3. $P \rightarrow Q$
   $\sim P \rightarrow R$
   $\sim Q$
   $\therefore R$

4. $\sim(A \,\&\, B)$
   $\sim B \rightarrow C$
   $\therefore A \rightarrow C$

5. $A \vee (B \rightarrow A)$
   $\sim A \,\&\, C$
   $\therefore \sim B$

6. $D \rightarrow F$
   $F \rightarrow G$
   $\therefore \sim D \vee G$

7. $P \rightarrow (Q \rightarrow R)$
   $\sim R$
   $\therefore \sim P \vee \sim Q$

8. $P \rightarrow \sim Q$
   $\therefore \sim P$

*9. $E \vee F$
   $\sim G \vee H$
   $\sim(E \vee H)$
   $\therefore F \,\&\, \sim G$

10. $\sim P$
    $\therefore P \rightarrow Q$

KEY WORDS

compound statement	disjunction	statement
conjunct	method of proof	symbolic logic
conjunction	propositional logic	truth table
disjunct	simple statement	variables

Summary
Connectives and Truth Values

- In propositional logic we use symbols to stand for the relationships between statements—that is, to indicate the form of an argument. These relationships are made possible by logical connectives such as conjunction (and), disjunction (or), negation (not), and conditional (If . . . then . . .). Connectives are used in compound statements, each of which is composed of at least two simple statements. A statement is a sentence that can be either true or false.
- To indicate the possible truth values of statements and arguments, we can construct truth tables, a graphic way of displaying all the truth value possibilities.
- A conjunction is false if at least one of its statement components (conjuncts) is false. A disjunction is still true even if one of its component statements (disjuncts) is false. A negation is the denial of a statement. The negation of any statement changes the statement's truth value to its contradictory (false to true and true to false). A conditional statement is false in only one situation—when the antecedent is true and the consequent is false.

Checking for Validity

- The use of truth tables to determine the validity of an argument is based on the fact that it's impossible for a valid argument to have true premises and a false conclusion. A basic truth table consists of two or more guide columns listing all the truth value possibilities, followed by a column for each premise and the conclusion. We can add other columns to help us determine the truth values of components of the argument.
- You can check the validity of arguments not only with truth tables but also with the short method. In this procedure we try to discover if there is a way to make the conclusion false and the premises true by assigning various truth values to the argument's components.

Proof of Validity

- The *method of proof* is a way to confirm the validity of an argument by deducing its conclusion from its premises using simple, valid argument forms. Most valid complex arguments consist of several of these valid sub-arguments (most of which you may already know). Determining the validity of the larger argument then is a matter of moving step by step from premises to conclusion, identifying the valid component arguments along the way.
- The method of proof uses nine rules of inference and nine rules of replacement. By properly applying them, you can confirm an argument's validity.

 ## Field Problems

1. Find three deductive arguments on the Internet or in a college newspaper. Symbolize the arguments and determine the validity of each one by making a truth table.
2. Find a deductive argument in one of your textbooks (excluding this one). Symbolize it and create a truth table to test its validity. Then devise a different argument that uses the same argument form as the one you found.

 ## Self-Assessment Quiz

Answers appear in "Answers to Self-Assessment Quizzes" (Appendix D).
1. What are the four logical connectives used in this chapter? How is each one symbolized?
2. Construct the truth table for each logical connective.
3. Under what circumstances is a conjunction false?
4. Under what circumstances is a conditional false?
5. Which of the following symbolized statements are true and which are false? Assume that a, b, and c are true, and p, q, and r are false.

$c \rightarrow q$
$a \,\&\, {\sim}q$
$a \vee {\sim}c$

6. Put the following statement into symbolic form:

You will go far if you study hard.

7. Put the following statement into symbolic form:

Either the Earth is flat or it is hollow.

8. Construct a truth table for each of the following arguments and indicate whether the argument is valid or invalid.

$p \rightarrow q$
$q \rightarrow r$
$\therefore q$

$p \text{ v } (q \text{ \& } r)$
$\sim(q \text{ \& } r)$
$\therefore p$

9. Translate this argument into symbols, construct its truth table, and indicate whether the argument is valid.

If the temperature rises, then the water will rise. If the water rises, the dam will break. Either the water rises, or it doesn't rise. The water will not rise. Therefore, the dam will not break.

10. Translate this argument into symbols, construct its truth table, and indicate whether the argument is valid.

Either Joe goes to the movie, or Julia goes to the movie. If the movie is Gone with the Wind, *then Julia goes to the movie. So if Joe goes to the movie, the movie is not* Gone with the Wind.

Construct arguments in English for each of the following symbolized arguments.

11. $x \rightarrow y$
    $y \rightarrow z$
    $\therefore x \rightarrow z$

12. $a \rightarrow b$
    $\therefore a \rightarrow (a \text{ \& } b)$

13. $a \text{ \& } b$
    $\sim b$
    $\therefore a$

14. $(p \text{ v } q) \rightarrow (p \text{ \& } q)$
    $p \text{ \& } q$
    $\therefore p \text{ v } q$

15. $p \rightarrow q$
    $\sim p$
    $\therefore q$

Use the short method to check the validity of the following arguments. Write out the argument in a single row and assign truth values to each variable.

16. $p \rightarrow q$
    $\sim q$
    $\therefore \sim p$

17. $p \& q$

   $q \to r$

   $\sim q$

   $\therefore r$

18. $p \to q$

   $q \to r$

   $\therefore q \to r$

19. $p \lor (q \& r)$

   $\sim p$

   $\sim q$

   $\therefore r$

20. $a \to b$

   $b \to c$

   $\therefore (b \& c) \lor (a \& b)$

Use the method of proof to demonstrate the validity of the following arguments.

21. $P \to Q$

   $R \to S$

   $P \lor R$

   $\therefore Q \lor S$

22. $P \lor Q$

   $R \to S$

   $\sim P \& \sim S$

   $\therefore Q \& \sim R$

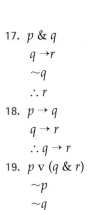 Integrative Exercises

These exercises pertain to material in Chapters 1–6.

1. What is critical thinking?
2. What is an argument?
3. What are the symbols for the four logical connectives, and what do they mean?
4. True or false: A mere assertion or statement of beliefs constitutes an argument.
5. Can a deductive argument guarantee the truth of its conclusion?

For each of the following arguments, specify the conclusion and premises and indicate any argument indicator words. Symbolize the argument and construct a truth table to determine the argument's validity.

6. If there are no clouds tonight, I will be able to see Venus and you will be able to see Saturn. There will be clouds tonight, so you will not be able to see Saturn.

7. If the bill is passed, the public will demand the resignations of all senators involved. The public, though, will never demand the resignations of an elected official. The bill will not be passed.

8. Either the crippled economy or the sex scandals will drive the prime minister from office. If inflation rises, then we will have a crippled economy. Inflation will not rise. Therefore, the sex scandals will drive the prime minister from office.

9. Jones is either crazy or very shrewd. He definitely isn't very shrewd, so he's not crazy either.

10. I will go to market unless the farmer objects, and I will stay home if the cows are sick. The cows aren't sick; therefore, I will go to market.

For each of the following arguments, determine whether it is deductive or inductive, valid or invalid, and strong or weak.

11. Either Ellen is shy or she is not. If her cheeks turn red, she's shy. If they don't turn red, she's not shy. Her cheeks are red. Ellen is shy.

12. Assad graduated from Harvard. If he graduated from Harvard, he's probably very competitive. He's probably very competitive.

13. "And certainly if its essence and power are infinite, its goodness must be infinite, since a thing whose essence is finite has finite goodness." [Roger Bacon, *The Opus Majus*]

14. The comet has appeared in the sky every sixty years for the past four centuries. It will appear in the sky again, right on schedule.

15. Use the short method to check the validity of this argument:

$a \rightarrow b$
$\sim b$
$\therefore \sim a$

16. Use the short method to check the validity of this argument:

$p \rightarrow q$
p
$\therefore \sim q$

For each of the following arguments, identify the implicit premise that will make the argument valid.

17. The conflict to combat terrorism involves the killing of human beings. Therefore, the conflict cannot be morally justified.

18. The movie *Harry Potter* is a huge box office success. Obviously it is a great film.

Identify the following rules of inference.

19. $p \rightarrow q$
$q \rightarrow r$
$\therefore p \rightarrow r$

20. $(p \rightarrow q) \ \& \ (r \rightarrow s)$
$p \lor r$
$\therefore q \lor s$

Writing Assignments

1. In a one-page essay, devise a deductive argument in which you argue for (or against) the idea that freedom of speech or the press should be restricted on college campuses.

2. Write a one-page essay defending the argument in Essay 8 ("The Cohabitation Epidemic"). Then write a one-page essay rebutting the argument.

3. Select an issue from the following list and write a two-page paper defending a claim pertaining to the issue. Use one or more deductive arguments to make your case.

   • Should there be restrictions on who can speak or what can be said at college graduation ceremonies?
   • Should private clubs be permitted to ban members of the opposite sex from membership?
   • Should "In God We Trust" be removed from U.S. currency?
   • Should there be restrictions on what college professors can say in the courses they teach?
   • Should privately owned businesses have the right to refuse to sell to any person they don't like?

Deductive Reasoning: Categorical Logic

CHAPTER OBJECTIVES

STATEMENTS AND CLASSES

- Understand how categorical logic differs from propositional logic.
- Learn the definitions of subject term, predicate term, copula, quantifier, quantity, and quality.
- Memorize the four standard-form categorical statements.

TRANSLATIONS AND STANDARD FORM

- Know how to translate ordinary statements into standard categorical form.
- Know how to translate singular statements into standard form.

DIAGRAMMING CATEGORICAL STATEMENTS

- Be able to construct a Venn diagram for any categorical statement.
- Memorize the Venn diagrams for the four standard-form categorical statements.
- Know how to use Venn diagrams to tell if two statements are, or are not, equivalent.

SIZING UP CATEGORICAL SYLLOGISMS

- Understand the structure of categorical syllogisms.
- Know the definition of major term, minor term, middle term, major premise, and minor premise.
- Know how to check the validity of a categorical argument by drawing Venn diagrams.

THE SQUARE OF OPPOSITION

- Understand how standard-form statements are related to one another, as illustrated in the square of opposition.
- Know how to use the square of opposition to deduce the truth values of standard-form categorical claims.

CATEGORICAL EQUIVALENCE

- Understand the three types of categorical equivalence—conversion, obversion, and contraposition— and know when different categorical claims are equivalent.

A S WE'VE SEEN, IN PROPOSITIONAL LOGIC THE BASIC UNIT OF OUR CONCERN is the statement. Simple statements make up compound statements joined by logical connectives. And the truth value of a compound statement is a function of the truth values of the *component statements*. This important fact is the reason propositional logic is also called *truth-functional logic*. In truth-functional logic we ignore the deeper relationships among the internal parts of a statement.

Categorical logic is different. The basic unit of concern in categorical logic is the *statement component*. We study the relationships not between statements but between the subject and predicate of a statement.

Both types of reasoning are deductive, and in both our ultimate goal is the evaluation of arguments. In propositional logic this task is made easier with truth tables and truth table–like calculations. In categorical logic the primary tools are diagrams and calculation rules.

In categorical reasoning the statements, or claims, of interest are **categorical statements**—those that make simple assertions about categories, or classes, of things. They say how certain classes of things are, or are not, included in other classes of things. For example: "All cows are herbivores," "No gardeners are plumbers," or "Some businesspeople are cheats." Categorical statements like these play their part without the complexities that arise from conjunctive, disjunctive, or conditional statements.

Like propositional logic, categorical logic is inescapable in daily life. Without thinking much about the process, we often use arguments composed of categorical statements. We may reason, for example, that no pocketknives are things permitted on a commercial airplane because no sharp instruments are things allowed on a commercial airplane, and all pocketknives are sharp instruments. In a real-life situation, we wouldn't state the argument so formally (and awkwardly), and we would probably make one of these premises implicit because it's too obvious to mention. Also, this whole process would likely happen in seconds, with the argument zipping through our heads at top speed.

There are several good reasons why categorical logic—first formulated by Aristotle over two thousand years ago—is still around. Chief among these are that (1) we cannot avoid it and (2) we need it. If so, then learning how to use it well can only help us.

"Bad reasoning as well as good reasoning is possible; and this fact is the foundation of the practical side of logic."
—Charles Sanders Peirce

Statements and Classes

The words in categorical statements that name classes, or categories, of things are called *terms*. Each categorical statement has both a **subject term** and a **predicate term.** For example:

All cats are carnivores.

"MEMO: It has come to my attention that every time we solve one problem, we create two more. From now on, all problem solving is forbidden."

© 2001 by Randy Glasbergen.

The subject term here is *cats,* and the predicate term is *carnivores.* The statement says that the class of *cats* is included in the class of *carnivores.* We can express the form of the statement like this:

All S *are* P.

By convention, S stands for the subject term in a categorical statement; P, the predicate term.

This kind of statement—All S are P—is one of four **standard forms of categorical statements.** Here are all four of them together:

1. All S are P. (All cats are carnivores.)
2. No S are P. (No cats are carnivores.)
3. Some S are P. (Some cats are carnivores.)
4. Some S are not P. (Some cats are not carnivores.)

Standard-form statement 2, "No S are P," asserts that no member of the S class is included in the P class (no members of the class of cats are part of the class of carnivores). Statement 3, "Some S are P," asserts that some members of the S class are also members of the P class (some members of the class of cats are also members of the class of carnivores). Statement 4, "Some S are not P," asserts that some members of the S class are not members of the P class (some members of the class of cats are not members of the class of carnivores).

For the sake of simplicity, the terms in these statements about cats are single words, just nouns naming a class. But subject and predicate terms can also consist of noun phrases and pronouns. Noun phrases are used because several words may be needed to specify a class. Sometimes a noun like cats won't do, but a noun phrase like "cats that live outdoors and hunt mice" will.

In standard-form categorical statements, subject and predicate terms can't be *anything but* nouns, pronouns, and noun phrases. Only nouns, pronouns, and noun phrases can properly designate classes. So the statement "All cats are carnivores" is in standard form, but "All cats are carnivorous" is not.

As you might guess, many categorical statements you'll run into don't strictly fit any of these four patterns. But they should—if you want to easily evaluate the validity of arguments containing these statements. So part of the job of assessing such arguments is translating the categorical statements found "in the wild" into the tamer and clearer configurations of the standard forms. The challenge is to do these translations while being faithful to the meaning of the original.

Now, to accurately translate categorical statements, you need to know more about how they're put together. Categorical statements have four parts and several characteristics expressed in these parts. You already know about two of these parts, the subject term and the predicate term. They're joined together by a third part called the **copula,** a linking verb—either "are" or "are not."

The fourth part is the **quantifier,** a word that expresses the **quantity,** or number, of a categorical statement. The acceptable quantifiers are "all," "no," or "some." The quantifiers "all" and "no" in front of a categorical statement tell us that it's *universal*—it applies to every member of a class. The quantifier "some" at

Aristotle (384–322 B.C.E.), the father of formal logic.

the beginning of a categorical statement says that the statement is *particular*—it applies to at least one member of a class.

Categorical statements can vary not only in quantity, but also in the characteristic of **quality,** being either *affirmative* or *negative*. A categorical statement that *affirms* that a class is entirely or partly included in another class is said to be affirmative in quality. A categorical statement that *denies* that a class is entirely or partly included in another class is said to be negative in quality.

With this technical vocabulary we can describe each of the standard forms of statements noted earlier.

1. All *S* are *P*. (All cats are carnivores.)

This standard-form statement has a universal quantity and an affirmative quality. It *affirms* that *all* cats are included in the class of carnivores. So we characterize it as a *universal affirmative* statement, or claim.

2. No *S* are *P*. (No cats are carnivores.)

This one *denies* that *all* cats are included in the class of carnivores. Put another way, the whole class of cats is *excluded* from the class of carnivores. It's a *universal negative* statement.

3. Some *S* are *P*. (Some cats are carnivores.)

This one *affirms* that only *some* cats are included in the class of carnivores. It's a *particular affirmative* statement.

4. Some *S* are not *P*. (Some cats are not carnivores.)

This one *denies* that only *some* cats are included in the class of carnivores. It doesn't refer to the whole class of cats, just as statement 3 doesn't refer to the whole class. But it denies, instead of affirms, that the partial class of cats is included in the class of carnivores. It's a *particular negative* statement.

Here are the four standard forms of categorical statements again with their quality and quantity listed:

A: All *S* are *P*. (universal affirmative)
E: No *S* are *P*. (universal negative)
I: Some *S* are *P*. (particular affirmative)
O: Some *S* are not *P*. (particular negative)

Notice that this time the statements are preceded not by numbers but by the letters A, E, I, and O. These letters are the traditional designations for the four logical forms of categorical statements. We can say then, for example, that this or that statement is an A-statement or an O-statement, indicating the pattern of the arguments in an easy shorthand.

Something important to remember, even if it's obvious: All categorical statements should fit into one of these four standard forms, and all statements that do fit into one of these have the *same* form.

EXERCISES

Exercise 7.1

For each of the following statements, identify the subject and predicate terms and the name of the form (universal affirmative, universal negative, particular affirmative, or particular negative). Also, state the traditional letter designation for each form (A, E, I, O).

* 1. No scientists are Baptists.
  2. Some plants are trees.
  3. No cats that have lived over fifteen years in a domestic setting are pets free of all health problems.
  4. Some mammals are not whales.
* 5. All theologians who have studied arguments for the existence of God are scholars with serious misgivings about the traditional notion of omnipotence.
  6. No football players are A students.
  7. All refugees from unstable countries are poor people.
* 8. Some who play the stock market are not millionaires.
  9. No taxpayers from the 2003 tax year are embezzlers.
  10. No U.S. prosecutors who have reviewed the cases of death and injury at the Ace-Westinghouse foundry are friends of corporate America.
  11. All cancer survivors in the clinical study are coffee drinkers.
* 12. Some terrorists are Saudi citizens.
  13. No pro-democracy students in China are outside agitators.
  14. Some congressional Republican leaders are pro-lifers.
  15. Some health care programs proposed in the Senate are not viable options.
* 16. No death-row inmates are death-penalty supporters.
  17. All child-abuse caseworkers are overburdened civil servants.

Translations and Standard Form

This is worth repeating: We translate ordinary statements into standard-form categorical statements so we can handle them more efficiently. We want to handle them efficiently so we can more easily evaluate the validity of arguments composed of categorical statements. Translation is necessary to bring out the underlying structure of statements. It's also important because ordinary language is too imprecise and ambiguous to use in the analysis of statements and arguments. You'll appreciate this fact more as you work with categorical statements.

Translating statements into standard form is a straightforward process consisting of a few simple steps and some rules of thumb. Knowing the steps and the rules is important, but *practice* translating statements is vital if you want to

FROM THE WEB

Logic Help!

The Web may be big and crazy, but sanity is always nearby: Many websites offer help in the study of logic. (For a good list of such resources, visit *EpistemeLinks* at http://www.epistemelinks.com/Main/Topics .aspx?TopiCode=Logi.) Here are three that include solid treatment of categorical logic:

- *The Logic Toolbox* (http://philosophy.lander.edu/~jsaetti/Welcome.html); interactive lessons in categorical logic, propositional logic, and formal proofs, by John Saetti

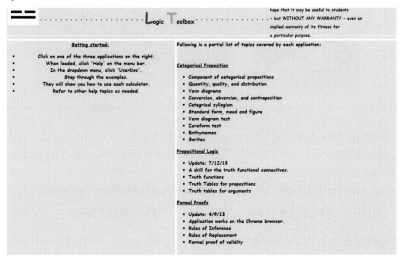

- An interactive tutorial on categorical syllogisms and Venn diagrams (http://www.math.wsu.edu/mathlessons/html/venndiagrams/Logic/ vennDiagram.html), from Washington State University

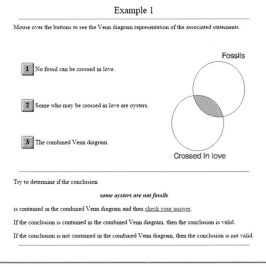

- A review of the basics of categorical syllogisms and Venn diagrams at *The Philosophy Pages* (http://www.philosophypages.com/lg/e08a.htm)

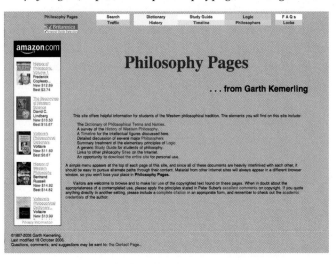

know how to translate fast and accurately. If you don't understand a particular point, you'll have an easier time if you go over it until you do rather than skipping it and looking at it later.

Just as a reminder, here's the pattern of all standard-form categorical statements:

Quantifier . . . Subject Term . . . Copula . . . Predicate Term

You need to know how to handle each of these parts. The copula must always be either "are" or "are not," so you don't have to spend a lot of time trying to determine the correct verb. But pinning down the terms and quantifiers is a little more challenging.

Terms

In translating statements, your first order of business is usually identifying the terms and ensuring that they designate classes. Once you identify the terms and distinguish the subject term from the predicate term, you'll know in what order the terms must appear in the statement because the subject term must always precede the predicate term. Identifying the terms, though, often involves rewording them so they actually name classes. Consider these translations:

[Original] All dogs are loyal.
[Translation] All dogs are loyal animals.

[Original] Some bachelors waste money.
[Translation] Some bachelors are people who waste money.

[Original] No nations can survive without secure borders.
[Translation] No nations are things that can survive without secure borders.

The Four Standard-Form Categorical Statements

A: All *S* are *P*. (universal affirmative)   "All cats are felines."

E: No *S* are *P*. (universal negative)   "No cats are felines."

I: Some *S* are *P*. (particular affirmative)   "Some cats are felines."

O: Some *S* are not *P*. (particular negative)   "Some cats are not felines."

Sometimes it's easy to locate statement terms but not as easy to tell which is the subject term and which is the predicate term. This can happen when the order of the subject and predicate is reversed:

Beyond the mountains stood the redwood trees.

Here the subject is "the redwood trees." The sentence has a normal variation of subject-predicate order, common in English. If you understand the structure of such grammatical reversals, then you should be able to identify the true subject and predicate terms.

Difficulty distinguishing subject and predicate terms can also arise when the word "only" is in a statement. For example, which is the subject term and which is the predicate in these A-statements?

1. Only palm readers are wise counselors.
2. Only if something is a dance is it a minuet.
3. Hamburgers are the only entrées.
4. The only crimes prosecuted are murders.

We can figure out statements 1 and 2 by using this formula: *The words "only" and "only if" precede the predicate term in an A-statement.* So the correct translations are:

1. All wise counselors are palm readers.
2. All minuets are dances.

The translations of statements 3 and 4 follow this formula: *The words "the only" precede the subject term in an A-statement.* Therefore the correct translations are:

3. All entrées are hamburgers.
4. All prosecuted crimes are murders.

Now, what are the terms in these statements?

5. Harrison Ford is an actor.
6. Toronto is Canada's finest city.
7. Sunday is the first day of the week.
8. *The Matrix* is an amazing movie.
9. Alicia is not a good student.

FURTHER THOUGHT

Standard Form Versus Fuzziness

We take the trouble to translate categorical statements into standard form for several reasons—one of them being that language is fuzzy, fuzzy, fuzzy. The famed logician Bertrand Russell agreed: "Because language is misleading, as well as because it is diffuse and inexact when applied to logic (for which it was never intended) logical symbolism is absolutely necessary to any exact or thorough treatment of our subject" (*Introduction to Mathematical Philosophy*).

We can see a good example of language fuzziness in this type of categorical statement: "All *S* are not P." Take the statement "All Bigfoot monsters are not apes." Does this mean that (1) no Bigfoot monsters are apes or (2) that some Bigfoot monsters are not apes? Statement 1 is an E-statement; statement 2 is an O-statement. To defeat fuzziness, we have to apply some categorical logic and translate the original sentence into either an E- or O-statement.

These are known as **singular statements.** Each one asserts something about a single person or thing, including objects, places, and times. Each subject term is a noun (including proper names), pronoun, or noun phrase referring to an individual, particular item. In a way, the predicate terms specify classes but, alas, the subject terms don't. We can transform such statements, though, into universal statements (A-statements or E-statements). The trick is to think of each subject term as naming a class in which there's just one member. We can, for example, treat the subject term in statement 5 ("Harrison Ford") as designating a class with Harrison Ford as one member of that class, like this:

5. All persons identical with Harrison Ford are actors.

We can translate our other singular statements in similar fashion:

6. All places identical with Toronto are places that are Canada's finest city.
7. All days identical with Sunday are the first days of the week.
8. All things identical with the film *The Matrix* are amazing movies.
9. No persons identical with Alicia are good students.

Now we can see more clearly that statements 5–8 are A-statements and statement 9 is an E-statement.

Granted, translations of ordinary statements into standard-form categorical statements can sometimes sound awkward, as the preceding translations surely do. But when we translate statements, we put them into a form that makes their logical connections transparent—an agreeable state of affairs when we're trying to check the validity of complex arguments.

FURTHER THOUGHT

Let Us Count the Ways . . .

Plenty of nonstandard statements are equivalents of categorical statements in standard form.

A-STATEMENT: "ALL *S* ARE *P*"

Only celebrities are spoiled brats.
Mathematicians are good acrobats.
Every general is a leader.
Only if something is a plant is it a flower.
Any car is a vehicle.
Something is a breakfast only if it is a meal.
Whatever is a revolver is a weapon.
Every pediatrician is a doctor.
If something is not a vegetable, then it is not a potato.
All dictators are thugs.

E-STATEMENT: "NO *S* ARE *P*"

If anything is a weapon, then it is not a flower.
All humans are nonreptiles.
Pontiacs are not doctors.
Nothing that is a mind is a body.
Nothing red is a banana.
None of the vegetables are fruits.
It is false that some vegetables are fruits.

I-STATEMENT: "SOME *S* ARE *P*"

There are engineers who are painters.
Most criminals are morons.
Several diplomats are egomaniacs.
At least one survivor is a hero.
A few lotteries are scams.
Many Europeans are Germans.

O-STATEMENT: "SOME *S* ARE NOT *P*"

Some philosophers are nonreptiles.
Some nonreptiles are philosophers.
Not all judges are rock stars.
Many conservatives are not Republicans.
Most liberals are not hawks.
There are nonreptile philosophers.
Americans are not always patriots.
A few rock stars are not maniacs.

Quantifiers

Some quantifiers may be in nonstandard form, and some may be unexpressed. Consider these statements:

1. Every soldier is a warrior.
2. Whoever is an artist is a genius.
3. Sharks are good swimmers.
4. Nothing breakable is a warehouse item.
5. Comets are ice balls.

Each is a universal statement with a nonstandard or unexpressed quantifier. Here are the translations with the proper quantifiers:

1. All soldiers are warriors.
2. All artists are geniuses.
3. All sharks are good swimmers.
4. No breakable things are warehouse items.
5. All comets are ice balls.

Statements 1, 2, and 4 have nonstandard quantifiers; statements 3 and 5 have unexpressed quantifiers. Fortunately, most nonstandard quantifiers are fairly easy to decipher. "Every soldier," for example, obviously means all the soldiers. "Nothing" and "none" mean not any, which refers to all of them, whatever they are. Usually, unexpressed quantifiers are readily understood because of the nature of the terms. The statement "Sharks are good swimmers" clearly refers to all sharks, not just some of them. In some statements, though, the unexpressed quantifier is not obvious—for example, "Berkeley students are liberals." Is it *"All* Berkeley students" or *"Some* Berkeley students"? When in doubt, assume the quantifier that you think would make the statement most likely to be true. In this case, "All Berkeley students . . ." is a sweeping generalization that's unlikely to apply to every single Berkeley student. The claim more likely to be true is "Some Berkeley students . . ."

Now consider these statements:

6. There are government workers who are spies.
7. Most movie stars are snobs.
8. Several politicians are space aliens.

These are all particular categorical statements. Their translations are:

6. Some government workers are spies.
7. Some movie stars are snobs.
8. Some politicians are space aliens.

The quantifier "some" is appropriate in all these statements because, in logic, it means "at least one." We therefore have only two options for expressing quantity in categorical statements: *all* and *less than all*. "Most," "a few," "several," "almost all," and similar terms are all translated as "some." Part of the reason for logic's restrictive definition of "some" is that, in everyday language, "some" is extremely vague. The word could mean "most," "two or three," "ten or more," "many," who knows? Logic, though, needs precision—more precision than is found in ordinary discourse.

 EXERCISES

Exercise 7.2

Translate each of the following statements into standard categorical form and indicate whether the form is A, E, I, or O.

* 1. All Giants fans are fanatical.
  2. Some government programs are wasteful.
  3. Brave are the soldiers who give their all.
  4. "People who whisper lie." [Swedish proverb]
* 5. Only cell phone companies that keep up with the latest technology are good investments.
  6. Only if something has a backbeat is it a rock-and-roll song.
  7. "People with pinched faces often have poisonous hearts." [Chinese proverb]
  8. Nothing that is a snake is a mammal.
* 9. "All intelligent thoughts have already been thought." [Johann Wolfgang von Goethe]
  10. "The only good human is a dead human." [*Planet of the Apes*]
  11. Gregory is a Republican.
  12. Soldiers who broke their legs didn't finish their training.
* 13. Some things are meant to be forgotten.
  14. "There is no excellence without difficulty." [Ovid]
  15. Jonathan is not a very brave pilot.
  16. "All men have sinned." [New Testament]

Exercise 7.3

Follow the instructions given for Exercise 7.2.

* 1. Only poets are guardians of the soul.
  2. Any earthquake is a potential disaster.
  3. "People who wish to salute the free and independent side of their evolutionary character acquire cats." [Anna Quindlen]
* 4. All androids like Commander Data are nonhuman.
* 5. Nothing that satisfies the heart is a material thing.
  6. Some young people are non-Catholics.
  7. Every political party that gets at least 50 percent of the vote in a presidential election is a major player in American politics.
* 8. Most treatments said to be part of "alternative medicine" are unproven.

9. There are products advertised on the Internet that are unsafe devices.
10. "People who love only once in their lives are . . . shallow people." [Oscar Wilde]
11. Some of the members of the Daughters of the American Revolution are from Canada.
* 12. Friday is the only day that gives her any joy.
13. Many socialists are not communists.
14. "All prejudices may be traced to the intestines." [Friedrich Nietzsche]
* 15. The picture hanging on the wall is crooked.
16. Whoever seeks the truth through philosophy is a free person.
17. "He that is born to be hanged shall never be drowned." [French proverb]
18. Only artists are visionaries.
19. Not all writers are poets.
* 20. "A nation without a conscience is a nation without a soul." [Winston Churchill]

Diagramming Categorical Statements

If you want more help in understanding the relationships between subject and predicate terms, you're in luck. You can graphically represent such relationships with the use of **Venn diagrams** (named after British logician and mathematician John Venn). The diagrams consist of overlapping circles, each one representing a class specified by a term in a categorical statement. Here's an example:

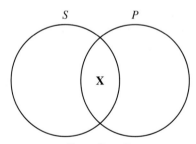

Some *S* are *P*.

This is the diagram for an I-statement: "Some *S* are *P*." The circle on the left represents the class of *S*; the circle on the right, the class of *P*. The area on the left contains only members of the *S* class. The area on the right contains only members of the *P* class. The area where the circles overlap indicates that both *S* members and *P* members are present. The X in the overlapped area, however, gives more specific information: It shows that *at least one S member is a P member*. That is, there is at least one *S* that also is a *P*. This diagram, of course, represents *any* statement of the form "Some *S* are *P*"—like, for instance, "Some cars are Fords." The X on the diagram where the circles overlap, then, would indicate that at least one car is a Ford.

Now here's the diagram for an O-statement—"Some *S* are not *P*":

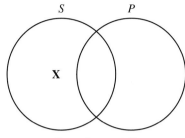

Some *S* are not *P*.

Here the X is in the *S* circle but outside the *P* circle, indicating that at least one *S* is not a *P*. In our car example (in which the *S* circle represents the class of cars and the *P* circle represents the class of Fords), this diagram would indicate that at least one car is not a Ford.

Here's the diagram for an A-statement—"All *S* are *P*":

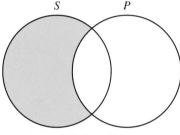

All *S* are *P*.

This diagram asserts that all members of the *S* class are also members of the *P* class. ("All cars are Fords.") Notice that the part of the diagram where the *S* circle does not overlap the *P* circle is shaded, showing that that area is "empty," or without any members. And this means that there are no members of *S* that are not also members of *P*. The remaining part of the *S* circle overlaps with the *P* circle, showing that *S* members are also *P* members.

Finally, the diagram for an E-statement—"No *S* are *P*":

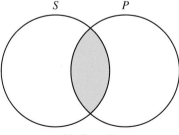

No *S* are *P*.

Here the area where the *S* circle and the *P* circle overlap is shaded (empty), meaning that there is no situation in which *S* overlaps with *P* (in which members of *S* are also members of *P*). So no members of *S* are also members of *P* ("No cars are Fords").

Venn diagrams can come in handy when you want to know whether two categorical statements are equivalent—whether they say the same thing. If the diagrams for the statements are identical, then the statements are equivalent.

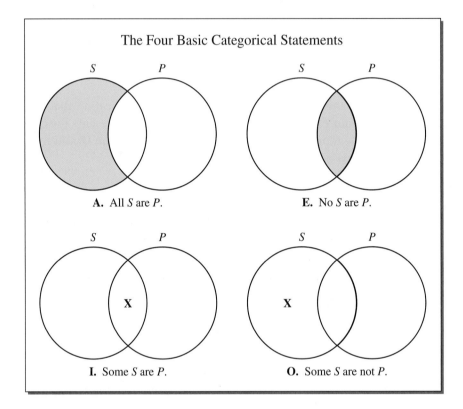

The Four Basic Categorical Statements

A. All *S* are *P*.

E. No *S* are *P*.

I. Some *S* are *P*.

O. Some *S* are not *P*.

Let's say that you want to know whether the following two statements say the same thing:

No *S* are *P*.
No *P* are *S*.

If you diagram them both, you get your answer:

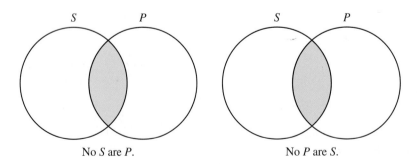

No *S* are *P*.

No *P* are *S*.

REVIEW NOTES

Three Steps to Diagramming a Categorical Statement

1. Draw two overlapping circles, each one representing a term in the statement.
2. Label the circles with the terms.
3. Shade an area of a circle to show that an area is empty; insert an X to show that at least one member of a class is also a member of another class.

You can see that the diagrams are identical—they both show the area of overlap between the two circles as shaded, signifying that there are no members of *S* that are also members of *P*, and vice versa. So the first statement ("No *S* are *P*," an E-statement) says the same thing as the second statement ("No *P* are *S*").

Likewise, if we compare the diagrams for "Some *S* are *P*" (I-statement) and "Some *P* are *S*," we can see that these statements are also equivalent:

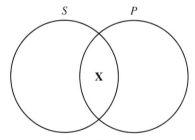

Some *S* are *P*.

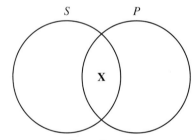

Some *P* are *S*.

On the other hand, by comparing diagrams we can see that A-statements and E-statements are *not* equivalent (something you knew already, of course):

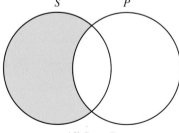

All *S* are *P*.

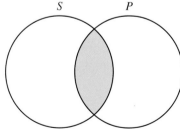

No *S* are *P*.

Let's examine one final pair of statements:

All *S* are *P*.
No *S* are non-*P*.

The diagrams clearly show that these are equivalent:

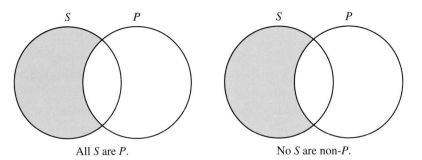

All *S* are *P*.   No *S* are non-*P*.

 EXERCISES

Exercise 7.4

Construct Venn diagrams for each of the following statements. Specify both the subject and predicate terms. If necessary, translate the statement into standard form before diagramming (A, E, I, or O).

* 1. No one is exempt from the draft in times of war.
2. No creed can be inviolable.
3. No one can join the army at the age of sixteen.
4. Some birds are flightless.
* 5. Nothing is more pitiable than the reasons of an unreasonable man.
6. Abraham Lincoln is one of the few writers whose words helped turn the world.
7. Some snakes are not poisonous.
* 8. Some good talkers are good listeners.
9. It is false that some businessmen are crooks.
10. Some people with excellent reputations are not persons of excellent character.
11. Black dogs didn't get fed.
* 12. "Every commander is alone." [Michael Powell]
13. Rainbows are always misleading.
14. There are bad apples in every barrel.
15. "Few friendships could survive the moodiness of love affairs." [Mason Cooley]

Exercise 7.5

Construct Venn diagrams for each statement in the following pairs, then indicate whether the statements are equivalent.

* 1. No P are S; No S are P.
2. Some *S* are *P*; Some *P* are *S*.

* 3. All *S* are *P*; All *P* are *S*.
  4. No *S* are *P*; All *P* are non-*S*.
  5. All *S* are *P*; Some *P* are non-*S*.
* 6. All *P* are non-*S*; All *S* are non-*P*.
  7. No non-*S* are *P*; No non-*P* are *S*.
  8. No *S* are *P*; No *P* are *S*.
* 9. Some *S* are not *P*; Some *P* are not *S*.
 10. All *S* are non-*P*; No *P* are *S*.

Sizing Up Categorical Syllogisms

Once you understand the workings of categorical statements, you're ready to explore the dynamics of categorical arguments, or—more precisely—categorical syllogisms. As we saw in Chapter 3, a syllogism is a deductive argument made up of three statements: two premises and a conclusion. A categorical syllogism is one consisting of three categorical statements (A, E, I, or O) interlinked in a specific way. You can see the interlinking structure in this categorical syllogism:

(1) All egomaniacs are warmongers.
(2) All dictators are egomaniacs.
(3) Therefore, all dictators are warmongers.

If we diagram this argument as we did in Chapter 3, we come up with this structure:

$$1 + 2$$
$$\downarrow$$
$$3$$

But this kind of diagram, though handy in truth-functional logic, isn't much help here because it doesn't reveal the internal components and interlinking structure of the statements. Observe: Each categorical statement has, as usual, two terms. But there are a total of only three terms in a categorical syllogism, each term being mentioned twice but in different statements. So in the preceding argument, *dictators* appears in statements 2 and 3; *egomaniacs,* in 1 and 2; and *warmongers,* in 1 and 3.

In a categorical syllogism, the *major term* of the argument is the predicate term in the conclusion (*warmongers,* in this case). It also appears in one of the premises (premise 1), which is therefore called the *major premise.* The *minor term* (*dictators*) occurs as the subject term in the conclusion. It also occurs in one of the premises (premise 2), which is therefore called the *minor premise.* And the *middle term* (*egomaniacs*) appears once in each premise but not in the conclusion. If we map out the argument with the terms labeled in this way, here's what we get:

Major Premise: (1) [middle term] [major term].
Minor Premise: (2) [minor term] [middle term].
Conclusion: (3) Therefore, [minor term] [major term].

> "Logical consequences
> are the scarecrows
> of fools and the
> beacons of wise men."
> —Thomas Henry Huxley

(We could have placed the minor premise first and the major premise second because, logically, the order doesn't matter. But by convention we always position the major premise first and the minor premise next.)

We can symbolize this argument form with letters:

(1) All *M* are *P*.
(2) All *S* are *M*.
(3) Therefore, all *S* are *P*.

Here, *M* stands for the middle term; *P* for the major term; and *S* for the minor term. So a categorical syllogism, then, is one that has:

1. Three categorical statements—two premises and a conclusion.
2. Exactly three terms, with each term appearing twice in the argument.
3. One of the terms (the middle term) appearing in each premise but not the conclusion.
4. Another term (the major term) appearing as the predicate term in the conclusion and also in one of the premises (the major premise).
5. Another term (the minor term) appearing as the subject term in the conclusion and also in one of the premises (the minor premise).

A valid categorical syllogism, like a valid deductive argument of any other sort, is such that if its premises are true, its conclusion *must* be true. (That is, if the premises are true, the conclusion cannot possibly be false.) This fact, of course, you already know. Of more interest now is how we can *check the validity* of categorical syllogisms. Fortunately, there are several ways, the simplest of which is the Venn diagramming method. This technique involves drawing a circle for each term in the argument (giving us three overlapping circles), then diagramming the premises on these circles. If the resulting diagram reflects the assertion in the conclusion, the argument is valid.

If you know how to diagram categorical statements, then you can diagram a categorical argument. Remember that since a categorical statement has two terms, we need two circles to diagram it—one circle for each term. And since a categorical syllogism has three terms, we need three circles, overlapping like this:

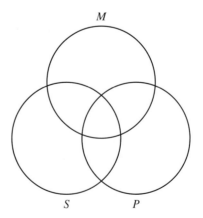

The top circle represents the class designated by the middle term (*M*); the bottom left circle, the minor term (*S*); and the bottom right circle, the major term

(*P*). The two lower circles together represent the conclusion since they stand for the relationship between the minor and major terms (*S* and *P*).

Let's diagram our syllogism about dictators and warmongers, diagramming one statement, or premise, at a time. We can start by labeling the diagram like this:

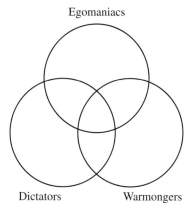

Now, we diagram the first premise ("All egomaniacs are warmongers"). To represent premise 1, we shade the part of the egomaniacs circle that does *not* overlap with the warmongers circle. This signifies that all the existing egomaniacs are also warmongers:

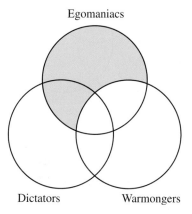

Then we diagram premise 2 ("All dictators are egomaniacs") by shading the part of the dictators circle that does not overlap with the egomaniacs circle:

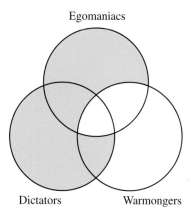

The resulting combined diagram is supposed to reflect the information in the conclusion ("Therefore, all dictators are warmongers"). We can see that the dictators circle is shaded everywhere—except in the area that overlaps the egomaniac circle. And this is how the syllogism's diagram *should* be shaded to depict the statement "all dictators are warmongers." So the diagram does express what's asserted in the conclusion. The argument is therefore valid. If you diagram the premises of a categorical syllogism and the resulting combined diagram says the same thing as the conclusion, the syllogism is valid. If the diagram does not "contain" the conclusion (if information is missing), the syllogism is invalid.

This syllogism has two universal ("All") premises (both A-statements). Let's diagram one that has a particular ("Some") premise:

> All robots are drudges.
> Some professors are robots.
> Therefore, some professors are drudges.

Here's the diagram properly labeled:

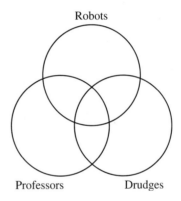

We'll diagram the major premise first ("All robots are drudges")—but not just because it happens to be the first premise. In categorical syllogisms with both a universal and a particular premise, we should always diagram the universal premise first. The reason is that diagramming the particular premise first can lead to confusion. For example, in the argument in question, if we were to diagram the particular premise first ("Some professors are robots"), we would end up with an X in the area where the robots and professors circles overlap. That section, however, is split into two subsections by the drudges circle:

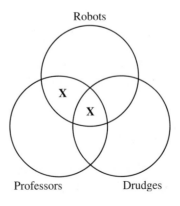

REVIEW NOTES

Five Steps to Checking Validity with Venn Diagrams

1. Draw three overlapping circles, each circle representing a term in the syllogism, with the two circles representing the major and minor terms placed on the bottom.
2. Label the circles with the terms.
3. Diagram the first premise. (Diagram universal premises first. When diagramming a particular premise, if it's unclear where to place an X in a circle section, place it on the dividing line between subsections.)
4. Diagram the second premise.
5. Check to see if the diagram represents what's asserted in the conclusion. If it does, the argument is valid; if not, it's invalid.

So then the question arises, In which subsection should we place the X? Should we plunk the X into the area overlapping with the drudges circle—or into the part not overlapping with the drudges circle? Our choice *does* affect what the diagram says about the validity of the argument. But if we diagram the universal premise first, then the decision of where to insert the X is made for us because there would be only one relevant subsection left (and we can't place an X in a shaded area):

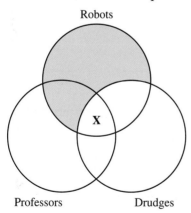

The resulting diagram represents the statement that some professors are drudges, which is what the conclusion asserts. The syllogism, then, is valid.

But sometimes, diagramming the universal premise first still leaves us with a question about where the X should go. Consider this syllogism:

All barbers are singers.
Some Italians are singers.
Therefore, some Italians are barbers.

When we diagram the universal premise first, we see that the section where the Italians and singers circles overlap is divided between a subsection including barbers and a subsection excluding barbers. So the X could go in either subsection, and we have no way of knowing which:

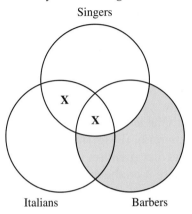

In situations like this, the best approach is to indicate our lack of information by placing the X on the border between the two subsections, like this:

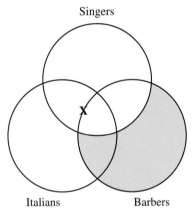

An X placed in this position means that among things that are both Italians and singers, something is either a barber or not a barber. Now, the conclusion says that some Italians are barbers. This conclusion is represented in the diagram only if there's an X *unquestionably* in the area where the barbers and Italians circles overlap. But we don't have an X unquestionably in that region; we have only an X that *may or may not be there.* That is, there's a question of just where the X is. Therefore, the diagram does not assert what the conclusion does, and the argument is invalid.

 EXERCISES

Exercise 7.6

For each of the following arguments, label the minor term, major term, and middle term. Then translate each syllogism into symbolic form using *S, P,* and *M* to represent the terms.

1. No apples are vegetables. Some plants are vegetables. So some plants are not apples.

* 2. All horses are mammals, and no mammals are lizards. Therefore, no lizards are horses.

3. All cars are self-propelled vehicles, and all motorcycles are self-propelled vehicles. Thus, all motorcycles are cars.

4. Some roses are yellow flowers. All roses are plants. Therefore, some plants are yellow flowers.

5. All roads are highways to Rome, but no mere paths are roads. So no mere paths are highways to Rome.

* 6. Some videotapes are not film classics, but all black-and-white movies are film classics. Therefore, some black-and-white movies are not videotapes.

7. All presidents are leaders, but some statesmen are not presidents. So some statesmen are not leaders.

8. All politicians are campaigners. All campaigners are money-grubbers. Therefore all politicians are money-grubbers.

* 9. No elm trees are cacti. Some tall plants are elm trees. So some tall plants are not cacti.

10. All thieves are criminals. All thieves are dangers to society. Therefore, all dangers to society are criminals.

Exercise 7.7

Draw Venn diagrams to test the validity of each of the arguments in Exercise 7.6. Answers are given for 2, 6, and 9.

Exercise 7.8

Translate each of the following arguments into categorical syllogistic form (major premise, minor premise, conclusion), symbolize the argument (using the conventional *S*, *P*, *M* variables), and draw a Venn diagram to test its validity.

* 1. Some architectural structures are nontraditional designs, for all houses are architectural structures, and some houses are nontraditional designs.

2. All bacon burgers are heart attack–inducing foods because all bacon burgers are high-fat foods, and some heart attack–inducing foods are not high-fat foods.

* 3. All worshippers of God are spiritual giants because all worshippers of God are redeemed souls, and all redeemed souls are spiritual giants.

4. Some famous men are not racists since all racists are enemies of justice, and some famous men are not enemies of justice.

5. No persons who are true to the values of this republic are politicians because all politicians are self-promoting egoists. And no self-promoting egoists are persons true to the values of this republic.

6. Some philosophers are musicians. Therefore, some trumpet players are philosophers since all trumpet players are musicians.

7. All opponents of the United States going to war against terrorist states are people opposed to anti-terrorist security arrangements. Some people opposed to anti-terrorist security arrangements are Leftist extremists. Therefore, some opponents of the United States going to war against terrorist states are not Leftist extremists.

* 8. No wimps are social activists because no wimps are people of honest and strong conviction. And all social activists are people of honest and strong conviction.

9. Most people who drive SUVs (sport utility vehicles) are instant-gratification freaks who don't care about the environment or environmental issues. Instant-gratification freaks who don't care about the environment or environmental issues are the true enemies of the planet. Therefore, people who drive SUVs are the true enemies of the planet.

10. Vitamin pills are useless gimmicks promoted as sure-cures for a variety of illnesses. Some useless gimmicks promoted as sure-cures, though, are placebos that can make people feel good. So some vitamin pills are placebos that can make people feel good even if they don't cure anything.

The Square of Opposition

Logicians discovered centuries ago that the four standard-form categorical statements (A, E, I, and O) are related in interesting—and useful—ways. They found that standard-form statements with the same subject and predicate but different quantity or quality will have truth values that are predictably correlated. By tradition, this connection is described as one of *opposition*, and it is formalized and illustrated in the **square of opposition**. (The Venn diagrams of the four statements give a clear demonstration of these relationships.)

Notice in the diagram that each corner of the square represents one of the four standard-form statements, with A and E at the top and I and O at the bottom. The A- and E-statements are known as *contraries* because they cannot both be true, but they both can be false. Compare these two statements:

A: All wombats are marsupials. (All *S* are *P*.)
E: No wombats are marsupials. (No *S* are *P*.)

Note that if either statement is true, the other one must be false. But *both* statements can be false: It can at the same time be false that all wombats are marsupials and false that no wombats are marsupials. After all, it can still be true that at least *some* wombats are marsupials.

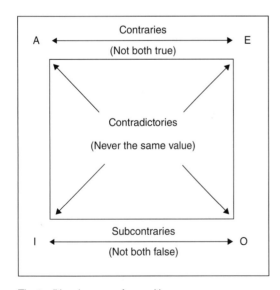

The traditional square of opposition.

Along the bottom of the square we see the I- and O-statements, which are known as *subcontraries* because both can be true, but both cannot be false. Consider this pair:

I: Some wombats are marsupials. (Some *S* are *P*.)
O: Some wombats are not marsupials. (Some *S* are not *P*.)

It should be easy to see how *both* an I- and O-statement can be true. Some wombats are marsupials and some aren't. But it cannot be the case that *both* these statements are false—if it's false that some wombats are marsupials, it cannot also be false that some wombats are not marsupials.

Now study the relationship between A- and O-statements, and between E- and I-statements. These pairs are known as *contradictories*—both cannot be true, and they *both* cannot be false. Look at our A- and O-statements:

A: All wombats are marsupials. (All *S* are *P*.)
O: Some wombats are not marsupials. (Some *S* are not *P*.)

Can it be the case that all wombats are marsupials yet some wombats are *not* marsupials? Of course not. Alternatively, can it be false that all wombats are marsupials (that some wombats are not marsupials) yet also false that some wombats are not marsupials (that all wombats are marsupials)? Clearly not.

The E- and I-statements are also contradictories: they cannot both be true, and they cannot both be false.

E: No wombats are marsupials. (No *S* are *P*.)
I: Some wombats are marsupials. (Some *S* are *P*.)

It cannot be the case that both propositions are true—that *no* wombats are marsupials and that some wombats *are* marsupials. And it cannot be the case that both these statements are false—that some wombats are marsupials and that no wombats are marsupials.

Now say you want to refute someone's universal claim (for example, that all politicians are thieves). You wouldn't need to take on the very difficult job of proving that *no* politicians are thieves (the contrary proposition). You would need to prove only that *some* (at least one) politicians are thieves (the contradictory claim), a much easier task. To prove that not all crows are black, you need to find only one crow that isn't black.

With the square of opposition, we can in some cases deduce the truth value of three of the standard-form categorical claims just by knowing the truth value of one of them. For example, if it's true that all politicians are thieves (an A-statement), then we can infer that the E- and O-statements are false and that the I-statement is true. The pattern works out like this:

TRUE A: All politicians are thieves. (All *S* are *P*.)
FALSE O: Some politicians are not thieves. (Some *S* are not *P*.)
FALSE E: No politicians are thieves. (No *S* are *P*.)
TRUE I: Some politicians are thieves. (Some *S* are *P*.)

Likewise, if it's true that no politicians are thieves (E: No *S* are *P*), then we can deduce the truth values of the other three statements:

TRUE E: No politicians are thieves. (No *S* are *P*.)
FALSE A: All politicians are thieves. (All *S* are *P*.)
TRUE O: Some politicians are not thieves. (Some *S* are not *P*.)
FALSE I: Some politicians are thieves. (Some *S* are *P*.)

And if either an I- or an O-statement is false, we can infer the truth values of the other three statements.

Categorical Equivalence

The square of opposition shows us how categorical statements can contrast with one another and what we can deduce from those contrasts. But there are also instances in which different categorical claims are equivalent, and knowing when they are equivalent can help us evaluate categorical inferences.

Conversion. A useful kind of equivalence is that of *conversion*. You obtain the converse of an E- or I-claim by reversing the positions of the subject and predicate terms. The converse of the E-statement "No students are sloths" is "No sloths are students," which means the same thing. The converse of the I-statement "Some students are geniuses" is "Some geniuses are students"—again an equivalent claim. In both these examples, taking the converse of an E- or I-statement does not change the basic structure of the statement. The converse of an E-statement is an E-statement, and the converse of an I-statement is an I-statement.

Obversion. This kind of equivalence is based on the idea that by designating a class of things, we are implicitly describing a class consisting of *everything that is not in the original class*. This everything-but class is the *complement* of the first class, or the *complementary* class. Thus, if there is a class *P*, there is also a class non-*P*. The complement of "rabbits" is "non-rabbits"; the complement of "red things" is "non-red things."

For every A-, E-, I-, or O-statement, there is a complementary obverse statement, and each obverse statement is equivalent to its complementary partner. We derive the obverse of a statement by (1) replacing the predicate term with the term's complement and (2) switching the statement from affirmative to negative, or negative to affirmative. Obversion, then, yields equivalent statements for each of the four standard-form claims:

A: All wombats are marsupials. (All *S* are *P*.)
Obverse: No wombats are non-marsupials.

E: No wombats are marsupials. (No *S* are *P*.)
Obverse: All wombats are non-marsupials.

I: Some wombats are marsupials. (Some *S* are *P*.)
Obverse: Some wombats are not non-marsupials.

O: Some wombats are not marsupials. (Some *S* are not *P*.)
Obverse: Some wombats are non-marsupials.

Contraposition. We form the *contrapositive* of a statement by (1) reversing the positions of the subject and predicate terms and (2) substituting complement terms for the subject and predicate terms. Only A- and O-statements are equivalent to their contrapositive versions; E- and I-statements are not equivalent to their contrapositives. Look:

A: All carrots are vegetables. (All *S* are *P*.)
Contrapositive: All non-vegetables are non-carrots.

O: Some horses are not thoroughbreds. (Some *S* are not *P*.)
Contrapositive: Some non-thoroughbreds are non-horses.

 EXERCISES

Exercise 7.9

For each of the following pairs of standard-form statements, determine the truth value of the second statement assuming that the first one is true.

1. No *S* are *P*. Some *S* are not *P*.
2. All *S* are *P*. Some *S* are *P*.
3. All *S* are *P*. No *S* are *P*.
* 4. Some *S* are *P*. No *S* are *P*.
5. Some *S* are not *P*. All *S* are *P*.
6. No *S* are *P*. Some *S* are *P*.
7. Some *S* are not *P*. No *S* are *P*.
* 8. All *S* are *P*. Some *S* are not *P*.
9. Some *S* are *P*. Some *S* are not *P*.
10. Some *S* are not *P*. Some *S* are *P*.
11. No *S* are *P*. All *S* are *P*.
12. Some *S* are *P*. All *S* are *P*.

Exercise 7.10

I. For each of the following statements, state its converse and indicate whether the two statements are equivalent.

1. Some men are students. Converse: Some students are men.
2. All writers are storytellers. Converse: All storytellers are writers.
* 3. No Buddhists are voters. Converse: No voters are Buddhists.
4. Some wars are unjust conflicts. Converse: Some unjust conflicts are wars.
5. No moral persons are criminals. Converse: No criminals are moral persons.
6. Some promises are lies. Converse: Some lies are promises.
7. No elephants are dangerous beasts. Converse: No dangerous beasts are elephants.

* 8. Some legislators are not brilliant persons. Converse: Some brilliant persons are not legislators.

9. Some great artists are poor people. Converse: Some poor people are great artists.

10. Some remote deserts are not picturesque landscapes. Converse: Some picturesque landscapes are not remote deserts.

II. Write the obverse of each of the following statements.

1. Some men are morons.
* 2. No runners are acrobats.
3. All cars are gas-guzzlers.
4. Some conservatives are not Republicans.
* 5. All humans are mammals.
6. Some writers are not journalists.

III. For each of the following statements, derive its converse, obverse, or contrapositive as indicated and determine if the two statements are equivalent.

1. No *S* are *P*. Converse.
2. All *S* are *P*. Obverse.
3. No non-*S* are non-*P*. Contrapositive.
* 4. All non-*S* are *P*. Converse.
5. Some *S* are not *P*. Obverse.
6. Some non-*S* are non-*P*. Converse.
7. Some *S* are non-*P*. Converse.
* 8. No *S* are non-*P*. Obverse.
9. Some *S* are *P*. Contrapositive.
10. All *S* are non-*P*. Contrapositive.
11. No *S* are non-*P*. Obverse.
* 12. All non-*S* are non-*P*. Converse.

🔑 **KEY WORDS**

categorical logic	quantifier	standard-form categorical statement
categorical statement	quantity	
copula	singular statements	subject term
predicate term	square of opposition	Venn diagram
quality		

Summary

Statements and Classes

- Every categorical statement has a subject term and a predicate term. There are four standard forms of categorical statements: (1) universal affirmative (All dogs are mammals), (2) universal negative (No dogs are mammals), (3) particular affirmative (Some dogs are mammals), and (4) particular negative (Some dogs are not mammals).

Translations and Standard Form

- Categorical statements must be translated into standard form before you can work with them.
- Translating involves identifying terms and ensuring that they designate classes and determining the quantifiers.

Diagramming Categorical Statements

- Drawing Venn diagrams is a good way to visualize categorical statements and to tell whether one statement is equivalent to another.

Sizing Up Categorical Syllogisms

- A categorical syllogism is an argument consisting of three categorical statements (two premises and a conclusion) that are interlinked in a structured way.
- The syllogism consists of a major term, minor term, and middle term. The middle term appears once in each premise. The major term appears in one premise and the conclusion, and the minor term appears in the other premise and the conclusion.
- The easiest way to check the validity of a categorical syllogism is to draw a three-circle Venn diagram—three overlapping circles with the relationship between terms graphically indicated. If, after diagramming each premise, the diagram reflects what's asserted in the conclusion, the argument is valid. If not, the argument is invalid.

The Square of Opposition

- Standard-form statements with the same subject and predicate but different quantity or quality have truth values that are predictably correlated. This relationship is formalized and illustrated in the square of opposition.
- With the square of opposition, we can in some cases deduce the truth value of three of the standard-form categorical claims by knowing the truth value of just one of them.

Categorical Equivalence

- There are instances in which different categorical claims are equivalent, and knowing when there is equivalence can help us evaluate categorical inferences.
- There are three types of equivalence: conversion, obversion, and contraposition.

 Field Problems

1. Do a search on the Internet for the term "rant" or "rants." You will get an enormous list of web pages featuring off-the-cuff opinions and tirades on countless topics—everything from religion and politics to celebrity fashion, cheese, bad drivers, Rice Krispies, and many unmentionables. From this mélange, pick out an *invalid* categorical syllogism and write a 100- to 150-word paragraph assessing the soundness of the argument (both its truth and validity) and how it might be rewritten to be made valid.

2. Check recent news reports to find one categorical statement made by the president of the United States, the U.S. attorney general, or the chairman of the Joint Chiefs of Staff. Translate the statement into standard form. (1) Construct a *valid* categorical syllogism using the statement as the conclusion and supplying whatever premises you deem appropriate. Assume that your premises are true. (2) Then construct an *invalid* syllogism using the same statement as the conclusion and supplying premises, also assumed to be true. In both arguments, try to keep the statements as realistic as possible (close to what you may actually read in a news magazine, say).

 Self-Assessment Quiz

Answers appear in "Answers to Self-Assessment Quizzes" (Appendix D).

1. What is a quantifier? What are the two quantities that can be expressed in categorical statements?
2. What are the two qualities that can be expressed in categorical statements?
3. What are the four standard-form categorical statements? (Specify them by quality and quantity and by letter designation.)

For each of the following statements, identify the subject and predicate terms, the quality, the quantity, and the name of the form (universal affirmative, universal negative, particular affirmative, or particular negative).

4. Some tax cuts are economic mistakes.
5. No philosophers are five-year-old kids.

6. All patients treated with herbal medicine are Chinese.

7. Some ghost stories are not fabrications devised by true believers.

Translate each of the following statements into standard categorical form and indicate whether the form is A, E, I, or O.

8. Only if something is a watercraft is it a canoe.

9. "Baseball is pastoral." [George Carlin]

10. Sheila is the finest scholar in the department.

11. No one with any sense would drive a car without headlights on a rainy night.

12. "Slow and steady wins the race." [Aesop]

13. A politician is someone who firmly believes that getting elected makes one smart.

14. "A fanatic is someone who can't change his mind and won't change the subject." [Winston Churchill]

Construct Venn diagrams to test the validity of each of the following syllogisms.

15. All *M* are *P.* Some *S* are *M.* Therefore, some *S* are *P.*

16. No *M* are *P.* No *S* are *M.* Therefore, all *S* are *P.*

17. All *P* are *M.* No *S* are *M.* Therefore, no *S* are *P.*

For each of the following pairs of standard-form statements, assume that the first one is true and determine the truth value of the second (either true, false, or undetermined).

18. Some *S* are not *P.* All *S* are *P.*

19. No *S* are *P.* All *S* are *P.*

20. All *S* are *P.* Some *S* are *P.*

 Integrative Exercises

These exercises pertain to material in Chapters 3–7.

For each of the following arguments, determine whether it is deductive or inductive, valid or invalid, strong or weak. Then diagram it using the lines-and-arrows method discussed in Chapter 3. Also indicate whether the argument contains any appeals to popularity or common practice.

1. "[Sen. John Edwards (D-NC)] brings enough solid assets to the wide-open race [for Democratic presidential nomination] that his credentials are worth examining—even if his shortcomings are also apparent. The first of those assets is geographical. He is currently the only Southerner in the field, and Democrats know their only successful presidential candidates in the past 40 years came from Texas, Georgia, and Arkansas. . . . The second asset is personal. The Democratic field is longer on

competence than on charisma. Edwards can light up a room, and he bonds with voters more easily than, say, Sen. John Kerry of Massachusetts." [David S. Broder]

2. "Encouragement of contempt for laws is more dangerous to society than occasional use of marijuana. Severe laws against marijuana do not discourage use of marijuana, but rather breed this contempt not only for drug laws, but for laws in general. Therefore severe laws against marijuana are more dangerous to society than the activity which they are designed to prevent." [A. Blakeslee]

3. Psychic powers (ESP, telepathy, and clairvoyance) are a myth. Hundreds of studies have failed to detect any genuine effects of such phenomena. Numerous case histories and other research over the past one hundred years reveal that most putative "psychics" have turned out to be frauds or incapable of reliably producing the desired results. And no researchers in this field have ever devised a plausible theory that explains how psychic powers work.

4. It is ridiculous for the Supreme Court or any other branch of the government to ban the reciting of school-sponsored (or school-allowed) prayers before football games. In areas of the country where this practice is prevalent, the communities involved are overwhelmingly in favor of such prayers. These recitations are thus the right thing to do—morally and legally.

For each of the following arguments, identify the argument pattern—*modus ponens, modus tollens,* affirming the consequent, denying the antecedent, or none of these.

5. If minds are identical to bodies, then whatever is true of minds is true of bodies, and vice versa. But minds are indivisible (they cannot be divided into parts) and bodies are divisible (we can break down a body into many parts and in many ways). Therefore, minds are not identical to bodies.

6. If Vaughn is boring, then no student can stand to listen to his lectures for more than sixty seconds. Vaughn is not boring, so students can stand to listen to him for more than a minute.

7. If there were structures in nature that were so complex that they could not possibly have evolved through natural selection, then the theory of evolution must be false. There are such structures, however—like the human eye. Consequently evolution cannot be the right explanation for the existence of the peculiar life forms found on Earth.

Indicate which of the following symbolized statements are true and which are false. Assume that the variables a, b, and c are true, and p, q, and r are false.

8. $\sim b \vee r$

9. $a \mathbin{\&} \sim p$

10. $p \rightarrow \sim a$

11. $b \rightarrow r$

For each of the following arguments, specify the conclusion and premises (including any implied premises). Symbolize the argument and construct a truth table to determine the argument's validity.

12. If the nuclear power industry improves its safety record and solves the nuclear waste problem, then it will become the number-one source of energy in the world. But it will never be able to change its safety record or solve the waste problem. Consequently the industry will not become the primary source of the world's energy.

13. Either Katharine inherited money from her grandparents or she won the lottery. But she certainly did not inherit money from her grandparents. So she won the lottery.

14. The surgery will be a success if blood loss can be controlled. The surgery is a success and the patient has spoken to the press. So blood loss must have been controlled.

15. If racial justice and equal opportunity are ever to be achieved in the United States, then affirmative action must be instituted in higher education and in civil service employment. If affirmative action is instituted in higher education and in civil service jobs, the income gap between whites and African Americans will disappear. The income gap between whites and African Americans will disappear, so affirmative action will be instituted in higher education and in civil service jobs.

Translate each of the following arguments into categorical syllogistic form (major premise, minor premise, conclusion), symbolize the argument (using the conventional *S, P, M* variables), and draw a Venn diagram to test its validity.

16. Some Muslims are not Sunni Muslims, for some Muslims are Shiite Muslims, and no Shiite Muslims are Sunni Muslims.

17. Some Army soldiers are Rangers, and no Army Rangers are Marine pilots. So some Army soldiers are not Marine pilots.

18. Some sociopaths are not criminals, but all serial killers are criminals. It follows that some sociopaths are not serial killers.

19. Senator Bullhorn will not back any civil rights legislation. He's a former Dixiecrat. And former Dixiecrats never back civil rights legislation.

20. Some Bible believers are fundamentalist Christians, and fundamentalist Christians are always pro-lifers. So some Bible believers are pro-lifers.

 Writing Assignments

1. Write a two-page essay arguing either for or against capital punishment. Cast your argument as a categorical syllogism.

2. Read Essay 9 ("Not Being Vaccinated Is Not Acceptable") in Appendix B, noting the premises and conclusions of any arguments. Write a three-page rebuttal to it.

3. Write a two-page essay arguing for or against same-sex marriage. Use research to back up your premises.

Inductive Reasoning

ENUMERATIVE INDUCTION

- Know what enumerative induction is and how it's used.
- Learn the definitions of *target population, sample,* and *relevant property.*
- Understand the two ways in which an enumerative induction can fail to be strong.
- Understand the error known as hasty generalization and know how to avoid it.
- Understand the basics of opinion polls and know the definitions of *random sampling, self-selecting sample, margin of error,* and *confidence level.*

ANALOGICAL INDUCTION

- Know how to formulate and evaluate an argument by analogy.
- Know how to use the following criteria to evaluate arguments by analogy: relevant similarities, relevant dissimilarities, the number of instances compared, and diversity among cases.

CAUSAL ARGUMENTS

- Know what causal claims and arguments are.
- Be able to apply Mill's methods to the evaluation of causal arguments.
- Be aware of the ways in which people can make errors in causal reasoning.
- Recognize and know how to avoid the post hoc fallacy.
- Learn the definitions of *necessary* and *sufficient conditions.*
- Be able to distinguish between necessary and sufficient conditions in everyday contexts.

W E NOW PASS FROM AN EXPLORATION OF DEDUCTIVE ARGUMENTS TO A close examination of inductive ones—a very small step since both these argument types are common features of our everyday lives. Recall that a deductive argument is intended to provide logically conclusive support for its conclusion, being valid or invalid, sound or unsound. An inductive argument, on the other hand, is intended to supply only probable support for its conclusion, earning the label of "strong" if it succeeds in providing such support and "weak" if it fails. The conclusion of an inductively strong argument is simply more likely to be true than not. If the argument's premises are true, it is said to be cogent. Unlike valid deductive arguments, an inductively strong argument cannot guarantee that the conclusion is true—but it can render the conclusion probably true, even highly likely to be true. Inductive arguments, then, cannot give us certainty, but they can give us high levels of probability—high enough at least to help us acquire knowledge in everything from physics to bird watching.

Deductive logic is the invisible framework on which much of our reasoning hangs and the solid bond that holds together the logical lattices of mathematics, computer science, and other theoretical or abstract disciplines. Inductive reasoning, though, gives us most of what we know about the empirical workings of the world, allowing us in science and in ordinary experience to soar reliably from what we know to what we don't. It allows us to reason "beyond the evidence"— from bits of what is already known to conclusions about what those bits suggest is probably true.

Inductive arguments come in several forms. In this chapter we will examine three of them and focus, as in previous chapters, on how to evaluate their merits in real-life contexts.

> "The rules of probable inference are the most difficult part of logic, but also the most useful."
>
> —Bertrand Russell

Enumerative Induction

As you may have noticed in Chapter 3, sometimes an inductive argument reasons from premises about a group, or class, of things to a conclusion about a single member of the group—that is, from the general to the particular, or the whole to the part. For example:

> *Almost all of the students attending this college are pacifists.*
> *Wei-en attends this college.*
> *Therefore, Wei-en is probably a pacifist.*

> *Eighty-two percent of residents in this neighborhood have been victims of crimes.*
> *Samuel is a resident of this neighborhood.*
> *Therefore, Samuel will probably be a victim of a crime.*

Such an inductive argument has been known traditionally as a *statistical syllogism*. The word *syllogism*—which is usually reserved for deductive arguments—refers to the fact that this argument consists of three statements: two premises and a conclusion. *Syllogism* is used to indicate that the generalization expressed in one of the premises is less than universal. But the

"There are lies, damn lies, and statistics. We're looking for someone who can make all three of these work for us."

www.CartoonStock.com

defining feature of this argument is that its line of reasoning goes from a statement about a group of things to a conclusion about a single member of that group.

Our main concern in this section, however, is a more common inductive argument that reasons from premises about individual members of a group to conclusions about the group as a whole (from particular to general, or the part to the whole). In such cases we begin with observations about some members of the group and end with a generalization about all of them. This argument pattern is called **enumerative induction**, and it's a way of reasoning that we all find both natural and useful:

> *Most peace activists I know are kind-hearted. So probably all peace activists are kind-hearted.*

> *Every Gizmo computer I've bought in the last two years has had a faulty monitor. Therefore all Gizmo computers probably have faulty monitors.*

> *Forty percent of the pickles that you've pulled out of the barrel are exceptionally good. So 40 percent of all the pickles in the barrel are probably exceptionally good.*

More formally, enumerative induction has this form:

> *X percent of the observed members of group A have property P.*
> *Therefore, X percent of all members of group A probably have property P.*

In this formal guise, our pickle argument looks like this:

> *Forty percent of the observed pickles from the barrel are exceptionally good.*
> *Therefore, 40 percent of all the pickles in the barrel are probably exceptionally good.*

Enumerative induction comes with some useful terminology. The group as a whole—the whole collection of individuals in question—is called the **target population** or **target group.** The observed members of the target group are called the **sample members** or **sample.** And the property we're interested in is called the **relevant property** or **property in question**. In the foregoing example, the target group is the pickles in the barrel. The sample is the observed pickles. And the property is the quality of being exceptionally good.

Now, using this terminology we can study arguments by enumeration a little closer. Remember that an inductive argument can not only be strong or weak, but it can also vary in its strength—in the degree of support that the premises give to the conclusion. So argument strength depends on the premises as well as on how much is claimed in the conclusion. Let's look at some examples.

Argument 1
All the corporate executives Jacques has worked for have been crooks.
Therefore, all corporate executives are probably crooks.

The target group is corporate executives, the sample is the corporate executives Jacques has worked for, and the relevant property is being a crook. We don't know how many corporate executives Jacques has worked for, but we must assume from what we know about career paths in corporate America that the number is small, probably no more than a dozen. Neither do we know exactly how many corporate executives there are, but we can safely guess that there are thousands or hundreds of thousands. It should be obvious then that this enumerative inductive falls short on at least one score: The sample is too small. We simply cannot draw reliable conclusions about all corporate executives based on a mere handful of them. The argument is weak.

We can fault this argument on another count: The sample is not representative of the target group. With thousands of corporate executives working for thousands of corporations, we must assume that corporate executives—in temperament, morality, demographics, and many other factors—are a diverse lot. It is therefore highly unlikely that Jacques's former bosses are representative of all corporate executives in their crookedness (the relevant property). And if the sample is not representative of the whole, we cannot use it to draw accurate conclusions about the whole. Argument 1 is weak for this additional reason.

Consider this one:

Argument 2
All of the blue herons that we've examined at many different sites in the nature
*   preserve (about two hundred birds) have had birth defects.*
Therefore, most of the blue herons in the nature preserve probably have birth
*   defects.*

In this argument the target group is the blue herons in the nature preserve, the sample is the two hundred blue herons examined, and the relevant property is having birth defects. We would normally consider this a very strong enumerative induction. Assuming that the premise is true, we would probably be surprised to discover that only a tiny minority of the target group had birth defects. Since the sample was drawn from many parts of the preserve, we would deem it representative of the target group. And due to the general uniformity of characteristics among birds in the wild, we would assume that a sample of two hundred birds would be large enough to strongly support the conclusion. As it stands, argument 2 is strong.

On the other hand, a conclusion asserting that *all* of the target group had birth defects would normally go beyond what the evidence in the premise would support. There could easily be at least some blue herons in the preserve (assuming it to be sufficiently large) that don't have birth defects, even if most do.

So you can see that an enumerative inductive argument can fail to be strong in two major ways: Its sample can be (1) too small or (2) not representative.

"The deductive method is the mode of using knowledge, and the inductive method the mode of acquiring it."
—Henry Mayhew

Of course, it's possible for an enumerative induction to be perfectly strong—but have false premises, in which case the argument isn't cogent. That is, the data (or evidence) stated in the premises could have been misinterpreted, fabricated, or misstated.

Sample Size

Let's say that you decide to conduct a survey of college students to determine their attitude toward federal deficits. So you stand around in the student center and query the first five students that pass by. Four out of the five say that deficits don't matter. You conclude: Eighty percent of the student body believe that deficits don't matter. Should you send your findings to the school newspaper—or to CNN?

No way. This survey is a joke—the sample is much too small to yield any reliable information about the attitudes of the students as a whole. This verdict may seem obvious, but just about everyone at one time or another probably makes this kind of mistake, an error known as **hasty generalization.** We're guilty of hasty generalization whenever we draw a conclusion about a target group based on an inadequate sample size. People regularly make this mistake when dealing with all sorts of enumerative inductive evidence—political polls, consumer opinion surveys, scientific studies (especially medical research), quality-control checks, anecdotal reports, and many others.

In our everyday experience, we may casually make, hear, or read hasty generalizations like this:

> *You should buy a Dell computer. They're great. I bought one last year, and it has given me nothing but flawless performance.*

> *The only male professor I've had this year was a chauvinist pig. All the male professors at this school must be chauvinist pigs.*

> *Psychology majors are incredibly ignorant about human psychology. Believe me, I know what I'm talking about: My best friend is a psych major. What an ignoramus!*

> *The French are snobby and rude. Remember those two high-and-mighty guys with really bad manners? They're French. I rest my case.*

> *The food at Pappie's Restaurant is awful. I had a sandwich there once, and the bread was stale.*

In general, the larger the sample, the more likely it is to reliably reflect the nature of the larger group. In many cases our common sense tells us when a sample is or is not large enough to draw reliable conclusions about a particular target group. A good rule of thumb is this: *The more homogeneous a target group is in traits relevant to the property in question, the smaller the sample can be; the less homogeneous, the larger the sample should be.*

For example, if we want to determine whether cottontail rabbits have teeth, we need to survey only a tiny handful of cottontail rabbits (maybe even just one)

FURTHER THOUGHT

Do You Really Need to Know This?

Here's a little reminder—in case you needed one—that many inductive general-izations you come across *are just not worth knowing*, whether they're well founded or not. Consider the following, compliments of DumbFacts.com:

- In the course of a lifetime the average person will grow two meters of nose hair.
- The average American makes six trips to the bathroom every day; that's about two and one-half years of your life down the drain.
- More people use blue toothbrushes than red ones.
- The average adult male shaves off one pound of beard per year.
- Men get hiccups more often than women do.
- In the United States, 55,700 people are injured by jewelry each year.
- According to the World Health Organization, there are approximately 100 million acts of sexual intercourse each day.

because cottontail rabbits are fairly uniform in their physical characteristics. In this sense, if you've seen one cottontail rabbit, you've seen them all. On the other hand, if we want to know the sexual preferences of Hispanics who live in North American suburbs, surveying just a few won't do. Questioning a sample of two or twenty or even two hundred North American suburban Hispanics will not give us a reliable read on the sexual preferences of the target group. In social, psychological, and cultural properties, people are too diverse to judge a large target group by just a few of its members. In biological properties, however, *Homo sapiens* is relatively uniform. We need to survey only one normal member of the species to find out if humans have ears.

Representativeness

In addition to being the proper size, a sample must be a **representative sample**—it must resemble the target group in all the ways that matter. If it does not properly represent the target group, it's a **biased sample.** An enumerative inductive argu-ment is strong only if the sample is representative of the whole.

Many arguments using unrepresentative samples are ludicrous; others are more subtle.

> *College students are glad that Congress is controlled by Republicans. Surveys of the members of Young Republican clubs on dozens of college campuses prove this.*

> *Most nurses in this hospital are burned out, stressed out, and overworked. Just ask the ones who work in the emergency department. They'll tell you they're absolutely miserable.*

No one is happy. Almost everyone is complaining about something. Just look at the letters to the editor in any big-city newspaper. Complaints, complaints, complaints.

To be truly representative, the sample must be like the target group by (1) having all the same relevant characteristics and (2) having them in the same proportions that the target group does. The "relevant characteristics" are features that could influence the property in question. For example, let's say that you want to survey adult residents of Big City to determine whether they favor distributing condoms in high schools. Features of the residents that could influence whether they favor condom distribution include political party affiliation, ethnic background, and being Catholic. So the sample of residents should have all of these features and have them in the same proportions as the target group (residents of Big City). If half the adult residents of Big City are Catholic, for example, then half the sample should consist of residents who are Catholic.

Say that we want to determine how the ten thousand eligible voters in a small town intend to vote in an upcoming presidential election. We survey one thousand of them, which should be more than enough for our purposes. But the voters we poll are almost all over seventy years old and live in nursing homes. Our sample is biased because it does not reflect the makeup of the target group, most of whom are people under forty-five who live in their own homes, work in factories or offices, and have school-age children. Any enumerative argument based on this survey would be weak.

We are often guilty of biased sampling in everyday situations. One way this happens is through a phenomenon called *selective attention* (see Chapters 2 and 4), the tendency to observe and remember things that reinforce our beliefs and to gloss over and dismiss things that undercut those beliefs. We may tell our friends that *The Sopranos* is a lousy TV series because we remember that three episodes were boring—but we conveniently forget the four other episodes that we thought were superb. Or we may be convinced that Dr. Jones is one of the legendary "absent-minded professors." But this generalization seems plausible to us only because we're on the lookout for instances in which the professor's behavior seems to fit the stereotype, and we don't notice instances that contradict the stereotype.

Opinion Polls

Enumerative inductions reach a high level of sophistication in the form of opinion polls conducted by professional polling organizations. Opinion polls are used to arrive at generalizations about everything from the outcome of presidential elections to public sentiments about cloning babies to the consumer's appetite for tacos. But as complex as they are, opinion polls are still essentially inductive arguments (or the basis of inductive arguments) and must be judged accordingly.

So as inductive arguments, opinion polls should (1) be strong and (2) have true premises. More precisely, any opinion poll worth believing must (1) use a large

FURTHER THOUGHT

How Survey Questions Go Wrong

Many opinion polls are untrustworthy because of flaws in the way the questions are asked. The sample may be large enough and representative in all the right ways, but the poll is still dubious. Here are a few of the more common problems.

QUESTION PHRASING

Poll results can be dramatically skewed simply by the way the questions are worded. A poll might ask, for example, "Are you in favor of a woman's right to kill her unborn child?" The question is ostensibly about a woman's right to terminate a pregnancy through abortion and is supposed to be a fair measure of attitudes on the question. But the wording of the question practically guarantees that a very large percentage of respondents will answer "no." The controversial and emotionally charged characterization of abortion as the killing of an unborn child would likely persuade many respondents to avoid answering "yes." More neutral wording of the question would probably elicit a very different set of responses.

Another example: A 1995 poll of African Americans discovered that 95 percent of the sample group approved of a local school voucher program. To get this huge approval rating, the survey question was worded like this: "Do you think that parents in your area should or should not have the right to choose which local schools their children will attend?" Who would want to give up such a right? No wonder the question elicited an overwhelming number of "shoulds."

Such biased wording is often the result of pollster sloppiness. Many other times it's a deliberate attempt to manipulate the poll results. The crucial test of polling questions is whether they're likely to bias responses in one direction or another. Fair questions aren't skewed this way—or are skewed as little as possible.

QUESTION ORDERING

The order in which questions are asked in a poll can also affect the poll results. Pollsters know that if the economy is in bad shape and they ask people about the economic mess first and then ask them how they like the president, the respondents are likely to give the president lower marks than if the order of the questions was reversed. Likewise, if you're asked specific questions about crimes that have been committed in your home town and then you're asked if you feel safe from crime, you're more likely to say no than if you're asked the questions in reverse order.

> "Facts do not cease to exist because they are ignored."
>
> —Aldous Huxley

Opinion polls frequently condense broad spectrums of opinions on issues into a few convenient choices. Some of this condensation is necessary to make the polling process manageable. But some of it is both unnecessary and manipulative, seriously distorting the opinions of those polled. Daniel Goleman of the *New York Times* offers this example: "In one survey . . . people were asked if they felt 'the courts deal too harshly or not harshly enough with criminals.' When offered just the two options, 6 percent said 'too harshly' and 78 percent answered 'not harshly enough.' But when a third alternative was added—'don't have enough information about the courts to say'—29 percent took that option, and 60 percent answered 'not harshly enough.'"

enough sample that accurately represents the target population in all the relevant population features and (2) generate accurate data (the results must correctly reflect what they purport to be about). A poll can fail to meet this latter requirement through data-processing errors, botched polling interviews, poorly phrased questions, and the like. (See the box "How Survey Questions Go Wrong.")

In national polling, samples need not be enormous to be accurate reflections of the larger target population. Modern sampling procedures used in national polls can produce representative samples that are surprisingly small. Polling organizations such as Gallup and Harris regularly conduct polls in which the target group is American adults (more than 187 million), and the representative sample consists of only one thousand to fifteen hundred individuals.

How can a sample of one thousand be representative of almost two hundred million people? By using **random sampling.** To ensure that a sample is truly representative of the target group, the sample must be selected *randomly* from the target group. In a simple random selection, every member of the target group has an equal chance of being selected for the sample. Imagine that you want to select a representative sample from, say, one thousand people at a football game, and you know very little about the characteristics of this target population. Your best bet for getting a representative sample of this group is to choose the sample members at random. Any nonrandom selection based on preconceived notions about what characteristics are representative will likely result in a biased sample.

Selecting a sample in truly random fashion is easier said than done (humans have a difficult

"I don't have any political opinions - would you like to hear about my symptoms?"

www.CartoonStock.com

FURTHER THOUGHT

Mean, Median, and Mode

If you read enough opinion polls, you will surely encounter one of these terms: mean, median, or mode. These concepts are invaluable in expressing statistical facts, but they can be confusing. Mean is simply an average. The mean of these four numbers—6, 7, 4, and 3—is 5 (6 + 7 + 4 + 3 = 20 divided by 4 = 5). The median is the middle point of a series of values, meaning that half the values are above the point and half the values are below the point. The median of these eleven values—3, 5, 7, 13, 14, 17, 21, 23, 24, 27, 30—is 17 (the number in the middle). The mode is the most common value. The mode in this series of values—7, 13, 13, 13, 14, 17, 21, 21, 27, 30, 30—is 13 (the most frequently appearing value).

The notions of mean, median, and mode are often manipulated to mislead people. For example, let's say that the dictator of Little Island Nation (population one thousand) proposes a big tax cut for everyone, declaring that the mean tax savings will be $5000 (the total tax cut divided by one thousand taxpayers). The Islanders begin to gleefully envision how they will spend their $5000. But then they learn that the mean figure has been skewed higher because of a few millionaires whose tax savings will be $100,000 or more. The tax savings for the vast majority of taxpayers is actually less than $500. The $5000 figure that the dictator tossed out is the true mean—but painfully misleading. To the Islanders, the median tax savings is much more revealing: The median is $400. The mode, the most common figure, is $300. When they get all the facts, the Islanders stage a revolt—the first one in history caused by a better understanding of statistics.

> "The so-called science of poll-taking is not a science at all but a mere necromancy. People are unpredictable by nature, and although you can take a nation's pulse, you can't be sure that the nation hasn't just run up a flight of stairs."
> —E. B. White

time selecting anything in a genuinely random way). Even a simple process such as your trying to arbitrarily pick names off a list of registered voters is not likely to be truly random. Your choices may be skewed, for example, by unconscious preferences for certain names or by boredom and fatigue. Researchers and pollsters use various techniques to help them get close to true randomization. They may, for instance, assign a number to each member of a population, then use a random-number generator to make the selections.

One approach that definitely does *not* yield a random sample is allowing survey subjects to choose themselves. The result of this process is called a **self-selecting sample**—a type of sample that usually tells you very little about the target population. We would get a self-selecting sample if we publish a questionnaire in a magazine and ask readers to fill it out and mail it in or if during a TV or radio news broadcast, we ask people to cast their vote on a particular issue by clicking options on a website or emailing their responses. In such cases, the sample is likely to be biased in favor of subjects who, for example, just happen to be especially opinionated or passionate; who may have strong views about the topic of the survey and are eager to spout off; or who may simply like to fill out questionnaires. Magazines, newspapers, talk shows, and news programs sometimes acknowledge the use of self-selecting samples by labeling the survey in question as "unscientific." But whether or not that term is used, the media frequently tout the results of such distorted surveys as though the numbers actually proved something.

So a well-conducted poll using a random sample of one thousand to fifteen hundred people can reliably reflect the opinions of the whole adult population. Even so, if a second well-conducted poll is done in exactly the same way, the results will not be identical to that of the first poll. The reason is that every instance of sampling is only an approximation of the results that you would get if you polled every single individual in a target group. And, by chance, each attempt at sampling will yield slightly different results. If you dipped a bucket into a pond to get a one gallon sample of water, each bucketful would be slightly different in its biological and chemical content—even if the pond's content was very uniform.

NEWSMAKERS

Is Barack Obama the Antichrist?

A 2010 Harris poll said that 14 percent of Americans believed Barack Obama may be the antichrist. Really? Some sharp observers at *Newsweek* didn't buy it. Their reason, they say, is that the survey has built-in biases. According to *Newsweek*,

> The poll started by telling people "Here are some things people have said about President Obama" and then asked them to agree or disagree with a series of pejorative statements—from "Obama wants the terrorists to win," to "Obama may be the antichrist." Respondents were not given a set of alternative statements to consider. As ABC's award-winning pollster Gary Langer explains, presenting the questions like that practically guarantees a skewed result. "'Some people have said' is a biasing introductory phrase," he writes. "It imbues the subsequent statements with an air of credibility—particularly when you don't note that others say something else."[1]

Sample selection was also a problem: It was self-selecting. Participants agreed to take an online survey concerning adverse characterizations of the president and to accept cash and prizes for doing so. The result was a nonrandom sample and an unreliable poll.

Such differences are referred to as the **margin of error** for a particular sampling or poll. Competently executed opinion polls will state their results along with a margin of error. A presidential poll, for example, might say that Candidate X will receive 62 percent of the popular vote, plus or minus 3 points (a common margin of error for presidential polls). The usual way of expressing this number is 62 percent ±3. This means that the percentage of people in the target population who will likely vote for Candidate X is between 59 and 65 percent.

Connected to the concept of margin of error is the notion of **confidence level.** In statistical theory, the confidence level is the probability that the sample will accurately represent the target group within the margin of error. A confidence level of 95 percent (the usual value) means that there is a 95 percent chance that the results from polling the sample (taking into account the margin of error) will accurately reflect the results that we would get if we polled the entire target population. So if our aforementioned presidential poll has a 95 percent confidence level, we know that there's a 95 percent chance that the sampling results of 62 percent ±3 points will accurately reflect the situation in the whole target group. Of course, this confidence level also means that there's a 5 percent chance that the poll's results will *not* be accurate.

Note that "confidence level" refers only to sampling error, the probability of the sample not accurately reflecting the true values in the target population. It doesn't tell you anything about any other kinds of polling errors such as bias that can occur because of poorly worded questions or researchers who may consciously or unconsciously influence the kinds of answers received.

Sample size, margin of error, and confidence level are all related in interesting ways.

- Up to a point, the larger the sample, the smaller the margin of error because the larger the sample, the more representative it is likely to be. Generally, for national polls, a sample size of six hundred yields a margin of error of 65 points; a sample of one thousand, 64 points; and a sample of fifteen hundred, 63 points. But increasing the sample size substantially to well beyond one thousand does not substantially decrease the margin of error. Boosting the sample from fifteen hundred to ten thousand, for example, pushes the margin of error down to only 1 percent.
- The lower the confidence level, the smaller the sample size can be. If you're willing to have less confidence in your polling results, then a smaller sample will do. If you can accept a confidence level of only 90 percent (a 10 percent chance of getting inaccurate

Thank you for taking part in this poll, sir. Here's the first question: What the heck makes you so arrogant to think your opinion could have any kind of importance, sir?

www.CartoonStock.com

FURTHER THOUGHT

Polling the Clueless

Sometimes polls end up surveying not the views of people with genuine opinions but what has been called "non-attitudes." This happens when respondents answer polling questions even though they have no real opinion on the subject or no idea what the questions are really about. Presumably, people—being people—would rather give a bogus answer than admit that they are clueless.

In one landmark poll conducted many years ago, respondents were asked, "Some people say that the 1975 Public Affairs Act should be repealed. Do you agree or disagree with this idea?" One-third of those polled offered their opinion on the issue. Trouble was, the Public Affairs Act did not exist. The pollsters made it up.

results), then you don't need a sample size of fifteen hundred to poll the adult population.

- The larger the margin of error, the higher the confidence level can be. With a large margin of error (68, for example), you will naturally have more confidence that your survey results will fall within this wide range. This idea is the statistical equivalent of a point made earlier: You can have more confidence in your enumerative inductive argument if you qualify, or decrease the precision of, the conclusion.

REVIEW NOTES

Enumerative Induction

- Target group: The class of individuals about which an inductive generalization is made
- Sample: The observed members of a target group
- Relevant property: The property under study in a target group
- Hasty generalization: The drawing of a conclusion about a target group based on an inadequate sample size
- Biased sample: A sample that is not representative of its target group
- Simple random sampling: The selecting of a sample to ensure that each member of the target group has an equal chance of being chosen
- Margin of error: The variation between the values derived from a sample and the true values of the whole target group
- Confidence level: The probability that the sample will accurately represent the target group within the margin of error

To sum up: An enumerative induction, like any other inductive argument, must be strong and have true premises for us to be justified in accepting the conclusion. A strong enumerative induction must be based on a sample that is both large enough and representative. An opinion poll, as a sophisticated enumerative induction, must use a sufficiently large and representative sample and ensure that the gathered data accurately reflect what's being measured.

 EXERCISES

Exercise 8.1

For each of the following enumerative inductions, (1) identify the target group, sample, and relevant property; (2) indicate whether the argument is strong or weak; and (3) if it's weak, say whether the problem is a sample that's too small, not representative, or both. Assume that the information provided in the premises of each argument is true.

* 1. Two-thirds of the adults in New York City identify themselves as "pro-choice" in the abortion debate. And almost 70 percent of adults in San Francisco do. This makes the situation perfectly clear: A large majority of the people in this country are pro-choice.

2. Most people are fed up with celebrities who get on their soapbox and air their political opinions. When people on the street have been asked by TV reporters how they feel about this issue, they almost always say that they wish celebrities would keep their opinions to themselves.

3. Doctors used to think that anti-arrhythmic drugs were the cure for irregular heartbeats. They overprescribed these drugs and fifty thousand patients died. Doctors used to believe that the cure for ulcers was a bland diet, but that turned out to be wrong too. Every new treatment we see these days sounds great. But history tells us that they will all turn out to be worthless.

* 4. I've asked at least a dozen first-year students at this university whether the United States should go to war with "terrorist" countries, and they all have said no. So most of the students at this university are against such a militant policy.

5. A randomized Gallup poll of Berkeley students shows that 90 percent of them are in favor of immigration reform. Thus, we can safely say that Americans definitely want immigration reform.

6. In every winter for the past twenty years Buffalo has received several feet of snow. Therefore, assuming that the effects of global warming are minimal, Buffalo is likely to get several feet of snow in the next fifty winters.

7. Most newspaper reports of crimes in Chicago involve alleged perpetrators who belong to racial minorities. Therefore, most crimes in Chicago are committed by racial minorities.

* 8. Eighty-five percent of dentists who suggest that their patients chew gum recommend Brand X gum. Therefore, 85 percent of dentists recommend Brand X gum.

9. Two hundred samples of water taken from many sites all along the Charles River show unsafe concentrations of toxic chemicals. Obviously the water in the Charles River is unsafe.

10. Clearly there is an epidemic of child abductions in this country. In the past year, major network news organizations have reported five cases of children who were abducted by strangers.

11. University fraternities are magnets for all sorts of illegal activity. Last year several frat brothers were arrested at a frat-house party. And this year a fraternity was actually kicked off campus for violating underage drinking laws.

* 12. Most Americans are happy with their jobs and derive a great deal of satisfaction from them. A survey of fifteen hundred adults with an annual income of $48,000 to $60,000, employed in various occupations, supports this assertion. When these subjects were asked if they were happy and satisfied with their jobs, 82 percent said yes.

Exercise 8.2

For each of the enumerative inductions in Exercise 8.1, indicate whether the argument is strong or weak. If it's strong, explain how the sample could be modified to make the argument weak. If it's weak, explain how the sample could be modified to make the argument strong. Keep the modifications as realistic as possible. Answers are supplied for 1, 4, 8, and 12.

Exercise 8.3

For each of the following opinion polls, (1) determine whether the poll results offer strong support for the pollster's conclusion, and, if they don't, (2) specify the source of the problem (sample too small, unrepresentative sample, or nonrandom sampling). Assume that the conducting of each survey is free of technical errors such as mistakes in data processing or improper polling interviews.

* 1. An Internet site featuring national and world news asks visitors to participate in the site's "instant daily poll" of hot topics. The current polling question is: "Should the words 'under God' be stricken from the Pledge of Allegiance if its recitation is required of public school children?" Twelve thousand people visit the site on the day that the poll is taken. Of those, seven thousand answer no to the question. The site concludes that 58 percent of Americans oppose modifying the Pledge.

2. Anita conducts a survey to determine if Americans are willing to support the arts by contributing money directly to local theater groups. One night she and her assistants interview five hundred people who are attending a performance of a musical at the city's biggest theater. To help ensure random selection, they purposely select every other patron they encounter for interviewing. There is only one interview question: "Are you

willing to support the arts by giving money to local theater groups?"
Ninety-four percent of the interviewees answer yes. Anita later reports
that a large majority of Americans are willing to support the arts by
giving money to local theater groups.

3. A prominent sociologist wants to determine the sexual attitudes of
women aged twenty-five to forty-five. The main question to be explored
is whether heterosexual women in this age group feel satisfied with their
partners' sexual performance. The sociologist interviews two hundred of
her friends who belong to the target group. She also asks two hundred of
her female colleagues at her college to complete and return a survey asking the key question. She gets 78 completed surveys back from women in
the target group. She finds that 75 percent of all the interviewees say that
they are not satisfied with their partners' performance. She concludes
that most heterosexual women aged twenty-five to forty-five aren't
happy with the sexual performance of their partners.

4. A national polling organization surveys fifteen hundred obstetrician-
gynecologists chosen randomly from a national registry of this medical specialty. The survey question is whether obstetrician-gynecologists
provide quality care for pregnant women. Ninety-eight percent of those
surveyed say yes. The pollsters conclude that almost all physicians think
that obstetrician-gynecologists provide quality care for pregnant women.

5. A national women's magazine publishes a questionnaire on sexual
harassment in the workplace. Respondents are asked to complete the
questionnaire and mail it in to the magazine. The magazine receives over
twenty thousand completed questionnaires in the mail. Sixty-two percent
of the respondents say that they've been sexually harassed at work. The
magazine reports that most women have been sexually harassed at work.

Exercise 8.4

For each of the following arguments, indicate which conclusions from the accompanying list would be strongly supported by the premise given. Assume
that all statements are true.

* 1. Seventy-two percent of the three hundred university students who
responded to a questionnaire published in the campus newspaper are
opposed to the U.S. president's economic policies.

   a. Some readers of the campus newspaper are opposed to the U.S. president's economic policies.

   b. Seventy-two percent of the students attending this school are opposed
   to the U.S. president's economic policies.

   c. Some students attending this school are opposed to the U.S. president's economic policies.

   d. Most readers of the campus newspaper are opposed to the U.S.
   president's economic policies.

   e. Seventy-two percent of the readers of the campus newspaper are
   opposed to the U.S. president's economic policies.

2. By listening to music, 43 percent of arthritis patients at the Drexell Clinic experience a decrease in pain in their knee and finger joints.
   a. By listening to music, 43 percent of arthritis patients can experience a decrease in pain in their knee and finger joints.
   b. By listening to music, some arthritis patients can experience a decrease in pain in their knee and finger joints.
   c. By listening to music, some arthritis patients at the Drexell Clinic can experience a decrease in pain in their knee and finger joints.
   d. By listening to music, many arthritis patients can experience a decrease in pain in their knee and finger joints.

3. Four out of five of the college's English majors hate anything written by William Faulkner.
   a. Eighty percent of the college's English majors hate anything written by William Faulkner.
   b. Most students at this college hate anything written by William Faulkner.
   c. Most college students hate anything written by William Faulkner.
   d. English majors at this college hate anything written by William Faulkner.

4. Alonzo has been driving his Dodge Spirit for seven years without any problems. His friend has the same kind of car and has been driving it for five years trouble-free.
   a. Dodge Spirits are trouble-free cars.
   b. Most Dodge Spirits are trouble-free cars.
   c. Some Dodge Spirits are trouble-free cars.
   d. Many Dodge Spirits are trouble-free cars.

5. Seventy-seven percent of adults interviewed in three Philadelphia shopping malls (650 people) say they will vote Democratic in the next presidential election.
   a. Most people will vote Democratic in the next presidential election.
   b. Seventy-seven percent of adult residents of Philadelphia will vote Democratic in the next presidential election.
   c. Many people in Philadelphia will vote Democratic in the next presidential election.
   d. A substantial percentage of people who shop at malls in Philadelphia will vote Democratic in the next presidential election.

Exercise 8.5

The following statements suggest modifications to each of the opinion polls in Exercise 8.3. In each case, determine whether the modification (and any associated change in poll results) would make the pollster's conclusion more likely to be true or not more likely to be true.

* 1. Twenty-one thousand people visit the site on the day that the poll is taken (instead of 12,000), and of those, 12,600 answer no to the question (instead of 7000).

2. Anita supplements her research by conducting phone interviews of a random sample of eight hundred adult residents of her city (population one million), asking a slightly modified question: "Are you willing to support the arts by giving money to local theater groups?" She conducts a similar poll in another large city. In both polls, at least 60 percent of respondents say yes.

3. The sociologist interviews three hundred of her friends (instead of two hundred) who belong to the target group, and she asks four hundred (instead of two hundred) of her female colleagues at her college to complete and return a survey asking the key question. Again, 75 percent of respondents say that they are not satisfied with their partners' performance.

4. The national polling organization surveys fifteen hundred physicians of various specialties chosen randomly from a national registry. Ninety-five percent of the respondents say that obstetrician-gynecologists provide quality care for pregnant women.

5. The magazine receives over thirty thousand completed questionnaires in the mail (instead of twenty thousand). Fifty-five percent of the respondents say that they've been sexually harassed at work.

Analogical Induction

An **analogy** is a comparison of two or more things alike in specific respects. In literature, science, and everyday life, analogies are used to explain or describe something. Analogies (often in the form of similes) can be powerful literary devices, both unforgettable and moving:

> . . . the evening is spread out against the sky
> Like a patient etherized upon a table . . .
>   [T. S. Eliot]

> As cold waters to a thirsty soul,
> so is good news from a far country.
>   [Proverbs 25:25]

> . . . Out, out brief candle!
> Life's but a walking shadow, a poor player
> That struts and frets his hour upon the stage
> And then is heard no more. It is a tale
> Told by an idiot, full of sound and fury,
> Signifying nothing.
>   [Macbeth, Act V]

But an analogy can also be used to *argue inductively for a conclusion*. Such an argument is known as an **analogical induction,** or simply an **argument by analogy.**

"All perception of truth is the detection of an analogy."
—Henry David Thoreau

An analogical induction reasons this way: Because two or more things are similar in several respects, they must be similar in some further respect. For example:

> Humans can move about, solve mathematical equations, win chess games, and feel pain.
>
> Robots are like humans in that they can move about, solve mathematical equations, and win chess games.
>
> Therefore, it's probable that robots can also feel pain.

This argument says that because robots are like humans in several ways (ways that are already known or agreed on), they must be like humans in yet another way (a way that the argument is meant to establish).

So analogical induction has this pattern:

> Thing A has properties P_1, P_2, P_3 plus the property P_4.
> Thing B has properties P_1, P_2, and P_3.
> Therefore, thing B probably has property P_4.

Argument by analogy, like all inductive reasoning, can establish conclusions only with a degree of probability. The greater the degree of similarity between the two things being compared, the more probable the conclusion is.

Arguments by analogy are probably used (and misused) in every area of human endeavor—but especially in law, science, medicine, ethics, archeology, and forensics. Here are a few examples.

Argument 3: Medical Science

> Mice are mammals, have a mammalian circulatory system, have typical mammalian biochemical reactions, respond readily to high blood pressure drugs, and experience a reduction in blood cholesterol when given the new Drug Z. Humans are mammals, have a mammalian circulatory system, have typical mammalian biochemical reactions, and respond readily to high blood pressure drugs. Therefore, humans will also experience a reduction in blood cholesterol when given the new Drug Z.

Argument 4: Religion

> A watch is a mechanism of exquisite complexity with numerous parts precisely arranged and accurately adjusted to achieve a purpose—a purpose imposed by the watch's designer. Likewise the universe has exquisite complexity with countless parts—from atoms to asteroids—that fit together precisely and accurately to produce certain effects as though arranged by plan. Therefore, the universe must also have a designer.

Argument 5: Law

> The case before the court involves a school-sponsored charity drive at which school officials led a public prayer. At issue is whether the school officials were in violation of the constitutional ban on government support of religion. A similar case—a relevant precedent—involved school-sponsored prayer at a school soccer game, and again at issue was whether the school

was in violation of the constitutional ban on government support of religion. In that case, the high court ruled that the school-sponsored prayer was unconstitutional. Therefore, the high court should also rule in the charity-drive case that the officially led prayer is unconstitutional.

Argument 6: Forensics

Whenever we have observed this pattern in the spatter of blood, we have subsequently learned that the gunshot victim was about 4 feet from the gun when it was fired and that the victim was facing away from the assailant. In this crime scene, we have exactly the same pattern of blood spatter. Therefore, the victim was about 4 feet from the gun when it was fired and was facing away from the assailant.

Arguments by analogy are easy to formulate—perhaps too easy. To use an analogy to support a particular conclusion, all you have to do is find two things with some similarities and then reason that the two things are similar in yet another way. You could easily reach some very loopy conclusions. You could argue this, for instance: Birds have two legs, two eyes, breathe air, and fly; and humans have two legs, two eyes, and breathe air; therefore, humans can also fly. So the question is, how do we sort out the worthy analogical inductions from

---

 FURTHER THOUGHT

Analogical Induction in Moral Reasoning

In Chapter 11 we'll study in detail the uses of argument and critical thinking in moral reasoning. For now, it's sufficient to know this: When we try to show that a particular action is right or wrong , we often rely on argument by analogy. We argue that since an action is relevantly similar to another action, and the former action is clearly right (or wrong), then we should regard the latter action in the same way. For example, we might propose an argument like this:

> Premise 1: Caring more for the members of one's own family than outsiders is morally permissible.
> Premise 2: America's policy of giving more aid to its own citizens than those of other countries is relevantly similar to caring more for the members of one's own family than outsiders.
> Conclusion: Therefore, America's policy of giving more aid to its own citizens than those of other countries is probably morally permissible.

Here, as in any argument by analogy, the conclusion can be established only with a degree of probability. And we would evaluate its strength the same way we would any other analogical argument.

the unworthy (or really wacky)? How do we judge which ones have conclusions worth accepting and which ones don't?

Fortunately, there are some criteria we can use to judge the strength of arguments by analogy:

1. Relevant similarities
2. Relevant dissimilarities
3. The number of instances compared
4. Diversity among cases

If you find yourself thinking that they make perfect sense, that's probably because you already use these criteria in your own arguments by analogy.

Relevant Similarities

The more relevant similarities there are between the things being compared, the more probable the conclusion. Consider this argument:

> *In the Vietnam War, the United States had not articulated a clear rationale for fighting there, and the United States lost. Likewise, in the present war the United States has not articulated a clear rationale for fighting. Therefore, the United States will lose this war too.*

There is just one relevant similarity noted here (the lack of rationale). As it stands, this argument is weak; the two wars are only dimly analogous. A single similarity between two wars in different eras is not enough to strongly support the conclusion. But watch what happens if we add more similarities:

> *In the Vietnam War, the United States had not articulated a clear rationale for fighting, there was no plan for ending the involvement of U.S. forces (no exit strategy), U.S. military tactics were inconsistent, and the military's view of enemy strength was unrealistic. The United States lost the Vietnam War. Likewise, in the present war, the United States has not articulated a clear rationale for fighting, there is no exit strategy, U.S. tactics are inconsistent, and the military's view of enemy strength is naive. Therefore, the United States will also lose this war.*

With these additional similarities between the Vietnam War and the current conflict, the argument is considerably stronger. (The premises, of course, may be false, rendering the argument not cogent, even if the inferences were strong.) Arguments 3–6 (medical science, religion, law, and forensics) can also be strengthened by citing additional relevant similarities between the things compared.

Notice that this first criterion involves *relevant* similarities. The similarities cited in an analogical induction can't strengthen the argument at all if they have nothing to do with the conclusion. A similarity (or dissimilarity) is relevant to an argument by analogy if it has an effect on whether the conclusion is probably true. The argument on war that was just given mentions five different similarities between the Vietnam War and the present war, and each similarity is relevant because it has some bearing on the probability of the conclusion. But what if we added these similarities?

1. In both wars, some combatants have green eyes.
2. In both wars, some soldiers are taller than others.
3. In both wars, ticket sales to movies in the United States increase.

These factors would make no difference to the probability of the conclusion. They're irrelevant and can neither strengthen nor weaken the argument.

Relevant Dissimilarities

Generally, the more relevant dissimilarities, or disanalogies, there are between the things being compared, the less probable the conclusion. Dissimilarities weaken arguments by analogy. Consider argument 3 (regarding Drug Z). What if we discover that cholesterol-lowering drugs that work in mice almost never work in humans? This one dissimilarity would severely weaken the argument and make the conclusion much less probable.

Pointing out dissimilarities in an analogical induction is a common way to undermine the argument. Sometimes finding one relevant dissimilarity is enough to show that the argument should be rejected. A familiar response to argument 4 (the watch argument) is to point out a crucial dissimilarity between a watch and the universe: The universe may resemble a watch (or mechanism) in some ways, but it also resembles a living thing, which a watch does not.

The Number of Instances Compared

The greater the number of instances, or cases, that show the relevant similarities, the stronger the argument. In the war argument, for example, there is only one instance that has all the relevant similarities: the Vietnam War. But what if there were five additional instances—five different wars that have the relevant similarities to the present war? The argument would be strengthened. The Vietnam War, though it is relevantly similar to the present war, may be an anomaly, a war with a unique set of properties. But citing other cases that are relevantly similar to the present war shows that the relevant set of similarities is no fluke.

Argument 6 (the forensics induction) is an especially strong argument in part because it cites numerous cases. It implies the existence of such instances when it says "Whenever we have observed this pattern. . . ."

Diversity Among Cases

As we've seen, dissimilarities between the things being compared weaken an argument by analogy. Such dissimilarities suggest that the things being compared are not strongly analogous. And we've noted that several cases (instead of just one) that exhibit the similarities can strengthen the argument. In this criterion, however, we focus on a very different point: The greater the diversity among the cases that exhibit the relevant similarities, the stronger the argument.

Take a look at this argument:

(1) In the 1990s a U.S. senator, a Republican from Virginia, was chairman of the commerce committee, had very close ties to Corporation X, had previously worked for Corporation X before coming to office, and was found to have been taking bribes from Corporation X.

(2) In the 1980s another U.S. senator, a Democrat from Texas, was chairman of the commerce committee, had very close ties to Corporation X, had previously worked for Corporation X before coming to office, and was found to have been taking bribes from Corporation X.

(3) In the 1970s another U.S. senator, an Independent from Arkansas with strong religious values, was chairman of the commerce committee, had very close ties to Corporation X, had previously worked for Corporation X before coming to office, and was found to have been taking bribes from Corporation X.

(4) Now the newly elected Senator Jones, a Democrat from New York with strong support from labor unions, is chairman of the commerce committee, has very close ties to Corporation X, and has previously worked for Corporation X before coming to office.

(5) Therefore, Senator Jones will take bribes from Corporation X.

Here we have several similarities in question, and they exist between the Senator Jones situation (described in premise 4) and three other cases (detailed in premises 1–3). But what makes this argument especially strong is that the cases are diverse despite the handful of similarities—one case involves a Republican senator from Virginia; another, a Democratic senator from Texas; and finally a religious Independent senator from Arkansas. This state of affairs suggests that the similarities are not accidental or contrived but are strongly linked even in a variety of situations.

 REVIEW NOTES

Analogical Induction

ANALOGICAL ARGUMENT PATTERN

Thing A has properties P_1, P_2, P_3 plus the property P_4.
Thing B has properties P_1, P_2, and P_3.
Therefore, thing B probably has property P_4.

CRITERIA FOR JUDGING ARGUMENTS BY ANALOGY

1. The number of relevant similarities
2. The number of relevant dissimilarities
3. The number of instances compared
4. The diversity among cases

As you know, an inductive argument cannot guarantee the truth of the conclusion, and analogical inductions are no exception. But by carefully applying the foregoing criteria, we can increase our chances of arriving at well-supported conclusions (or of identifying those conclusions that are not). This is happily the case—even though there is no magic formula for using the criteria in real-life situations.

 EXERCISES

Exercise 8.6

Evaluate each of the following passages and indicate whether it contains (a) an argument by analogy, (b) a literary analogy, or (c) an enumerative induction. If the passage contains an argument by analogy, indicate the total number of things (instances) being compared, the relevant similarities mentioned or implied, the conclusion, and whether the argument is strong or weak.

1. "The moon was a ghostly galleon tossed upon cloudy seas." [Alfred Noyes]

* 2. "Duct tape is like the force. It has a light side, a dark side, and it holds the universe together." [Carl Zwanzig]

3. Girls are smarter than boys. Girls in the debate club always argue better than boys. And the mean grade-point average of the girls in the glee club is higher than that of the boys in the club.

4. "Howard Hughes was able to afford the luxury of madness, like a man who not only thinks he is Napoleon but hires an army to prove it." [Ted Morgan]

5. "Look around the world: contemplate the whole and every part of it: you will find it to be nothing but one great machine, subdivided into an infinite number of lesser machines, which again admit of subdivisions, to a degree beyond what human senses and faculties can trace and explain. All these various machines, and even their most minute parts, are adjusted to each other with an accuracy, which ravishes into admiration all men who have ever contemplated them. The curious adapting of means to ends, throughout all nature, resembles exactly, though it much exceeds, the production of human contrivance; of human design, thought, wisdom, and intelligence. Since therefore the effects resemble each other, we are led to infer, by all the rules of analogy, that the causes also resemble; and that the Author of Nature is somewhat similar to the mind of men; though possessed of much larger faculties, proportioned to the grandeur of the work, which he has executed. By this argument *a posteriori*, and by this argument alone, do we prove at once the existence of a Deity, and his similarity to human mind and intelligence." [David Hume]

* 6. My brother was always good at arithmetic, so he'll be a whiz at algebra.

7. Tolerating a vicious dictator is like tolerating a bully on the block. If you let the bully push you around, sooner or later he will beat you up and take everything you have. If you let a dictator have his way, he will

abuse his people and rob them of life and liberty. If you stand up to the bully just once or—better yet—knock him senseless with a stick, he will never bother you again. Likewise, if you refuse to be coerced by a dictator or if you attack him, his reign will be over. Therefore, the best course of action for people oppressed by a dictator is to resist and attack.

* 8. I like sausage, and I like ham, and I like pork chops. So I will like chitlins.

9. "The brain secretes thought as the stomach secretes gastric juice, the liver bile, and the kidneys urine." [Karl Vogt]

10. "Vigorous writing is concise. A sentence should contain no unnecessary words, a paragraph no unnecessary sentences, for the same reason that a drawing should have no unnecessary lines and a machine no unnecessary parts." [E. B. White]

11. How does one know that there exist in the world other minds—that is, others having feelings and other subjective experiences? One can observe that one's own experiences are connected to publicly observable phenomena, that other people exhibit publicly observable phenomena, and therefore other people also must have subjective experiences. For example, one may observe that when one stubs a toe, one feels pain and cries "ouch." Then if other people—who are physically similar to oneself—also stub their toes and cry "ouch," one can conclude that they also experience pain.

* 12. "Character is the foundation stone upon which one must build to win respect. Just as no worthy building can be erected on a weak foundation, so no lasting reputation worthy of respect can be built on a weak character." [R. C. Samsel]

Exercise 8.7

Evaluate each of the following arguments by analogy, indicating (1) the things (instances) being compared, (2) the relevant similarities mentioned or implied, (3) whether diversity among multiple cases is a significant factor, (4) the conclusion, and (5) whether the argument is strong or weak.

* 1. Like former president Ronald Reagan, president George W. Bush is a staunch conservative, has strong Christian values, and adheres almost dogmatically to certain conservative principles. President Reagan allowed his fierce fidelity to his principles and values to lead him into a foreign policy disaster, the Iran-Contra debacle. President Bush will likely be involved in a similar foreign policy mess for similar reasons.

2. The United Nations failed to intervene in Bosnia to prevent massive human rights violations and ethnic cleansing. It also failed to act to stop the murders of close to a million innocent people in Rwanda. The UN will not intervene to stop any widespread slaughter of innocents in Nigeria.

3. "If a single cell, under appropriate conditions, becomes a person in the space of a few years, there can surely be no difficulty in understanding

how, under appropriate conditions, a cell may, in the course of untold millions of years, give origin to the human race." [Herbert Spencer]

4. The casinos in Atlantic City have brought a tremendous amount of revenue into both area businesses and local government, without inviting the evils of organized crime and causing the degradation of law and order or quality of life. The same can be said for the Turning Stone casino in upstate New York, as well as for Casino Niagara in Niagara Falls, Canada. A casino built in Buffalo, New York, will provide all the same benefits without the disadvantages.

* 5. A well-established moral principle is that one is morally justified in using deadly force in self-defense when one is threatened with death or great pain from an assailant. A disease such as terminal cancer can also threaten one with death or great pain. So suicide—a use of deadly force—must sometimes be morally justified when it is an act of self-defense against an assailant (terminal disease) that threatens death or great pain.

6. "If we survey the universe, so far as it falls under our knowledge, it bears a great resemblance to an animal or organized body, and seems actuated with a like principle of life and motion. A continual circulation of matter in it produces no disorder: a continual waste in every part is incessantly repaired: The closest sympathy is perceived throughout the whole system. And each part or member, in performing its proper offices, operates both to its own preservation and to that of the whole. The world, therefore, I infer, is an animal, and the Deity is the soul of the world, activating it and activated by it." [Philo, in Hume's *Dialogues Concerning Natural Religion*]

7. "The mass of men serve the State thus, not as men mainly, but as machines, with their bodies. They are the standing army, and the militia, jailers, constables, *posse comitatus*, &c. In most cases there is no free exercise whatever of the judgment or of the moral sense; but they put themselves on a level with wood and earth and stones, and wooden men can perhaps be manufactured that will serve the purpose as well. Such command no more respect than men of straw, or a lump of dirt." [Henry David Thoreau]

Causal Arguments

Our world is a shifting, multifarious, complicated web of causes and effects—and that's an oversimplification. Incredibly, the normal human response to the apparent causal chaos is to jump in and ask what causes what. What causes breast cancer? What made Malcolm steal the car? What produced that rash on Norah's arm? What brought the universe into existence? When we answer such questions (or try to), we make a **causal claim**—a statement about the causes of things. And when we try to prove or support a causal claim, we make a **causal argument**—an inductive argument whose conclusion contains a causal claim.

"I would rather discover a single causal connection than win the throne of Persia."

—Democritus

"This is a little embarrassing to admit, but everything that happens happens for no real reason."

Causal arguments, being inductive, can give us only probable conclusions. If the premises of a strong causal argument are true, then the conclusion is only probably true, with the probability varying from merely likely to highly probable. The probabilistic nature of causal arguments, however, is not a failing or weakness. Causal reasoning is simply different from deductive reasoning, and it is our primary method of acquiring knowledge about the workings of the world. The great human enterprise known as science is concerned mainly with causal processes and causal arguments, and few people would consider this work inferior or unreliable because it was not deductively unshakeable.

Causal arguments can come in several inductive forms, some of which you already know about. For example, we sometimes reason about cause and effect using enumerative induction:

> *One time, when I made the aluminum rod come in contact with the rotating circular-saw blade, sparks flew.*
> *Another time, when I made the aluminum rod come in contact with the rotating circular-saw blade, sparks flew.*
> *Many other times, when I made the aluminum rod come in contact with the rotating circular-saw blade, sparks flew.*
> *Therefore, making the aluminum rod come in contact with the rotating circular-saw blade always causes sparks to fly.*

Occasionally, we may argue to a causal conclusion using analogical induction:

> *Ten years ago a massive surge in worldwide oil prices caused a recession.*
> *Five years ago a massive surge in worldwide oil prices caused a recession.*
> *Therefore, the current massive surge in worldwide oil prices will cause a recession.*

Most often, though, we use another type of induction in which we reason to a causal conclusion by pinpointing the best explanation for a particular effect. Let's say that after a hailstorm you discover that the roof of your car, which you had left parked outside in the driveway, has a hundred tiny dents in it. You might reason like this: The dents could have been caused by the mischievous kids next door, or by a flock of lunatic woodpeckers, or by the hailstorm. After considering these options (and a few others), you decide that the best explanation (or hypothesis) for the dents is the hailstorm. So you conclude that the hailstorm caused the dents in your car's roof.

This is a very powerful and versatile form of inductive reasoning called **inference to the best explanation.** It's the essence of scientific thinking and a mainstay of our everyday problem-solving and knowledge acquisition (whether causal or noncausal). Because of the importance and usefulness of such reasoning, this text devotes three chapters to it in Part 4. So we won't try to cover the same ground here. Instead, we'll concentrate on some other inductive patterns of reasoning that have traditionally been used to assess causal connections.

Testing for Causes

English philosopher John Stuart Mill (1806–1873) noted several ways of evaluating causal arguments and formulated them into what are now known as "Mill's methods" of inductive inference. Despite their fancy name, however, the methods are basically common sense and are used by just about everyone. They also happen to be the basis of a great deal of scientific testing. Let's look at a few of the more important ones.

Agreement or Difference

A modified version of Mill's *Method of Agreement* says that if two or more occurrences of a phenomenon have only one relevant factor in common, that factor must be the cause.

Imagine that dozens of people stop into Elmo's corner bar after work as they usually do and that ten of them come down with an intestinal illness one hour after leaving the premises. What caused them to become ill? There are a lot of possibilities. Maybe a waiter who had a flu-like illness sneezed into their drinks, or the free tacos had gone bad, or another patron had a viral infection and passed it along via a handshake. But let's say that there is only one relevant factor that's common to all ten people who got sick: They all had a drink from the same bottle of wine. We could then plausibly conclude that something in the wine probably caused the illness.

Public health officials often use the Method of Agreement, especially when they're trying to determine the cause of an unusual illness in a population of several thousand people. They might be puzzled, say, by an unusually large number of cases of rare liver disease in a city. If they discover that all the affected people have the same poison in their bloodstreams—and this is the only common relevant factor—they have reason to believe that the poison is the cause of the liver disease. In such situations, the poison may turn out to have an industrial or agricultural source.

Here's a schematic of an argument based on the Method of Agreement:

Instance 1: Factors *a, b,* and *c* are followed by *E.*
Instance 2: Factors *a, c,* and *d* are followed by *E.*
Instance 3: Factors *b* and *c* are followed by *E.*
Instance 4: Factors *c* and *d* are followed by *E.*
Therefore, factor *c* is probably the cause of *E.*

There's only one factor—factor *c*—that consistently accompanies effect *E*. The other factors are sometimes present and sometimes not. We conclude then that factor *c* brings about *E*.

Mill's (modified) *Method of Difference* says that the relevant factor present when a phenomenon occurs, and absent when the phenomenon does not occur, likely is the cause. Here we look not for factors that the instances of the phenomenon have in common, but for factors that are points of difference among the instances.

Suppose that the performance of football players on a major league team has been consistently excellent except for six players who've recently been playing the worst games of their careers. The only relevant difference between the high- and low-performing players is that the latter have been taking daily doses of Brand X herbal supplements. If the supplement dosing is really the only relevant difference, we could plausibly conclude that the supplements are causing the lousy performance. (Finding out if the supplements are indeed the only relevant difference, of course, is easier said than done.)

So arguments based on the Method of Difference have this form:

Instance 1: Factors *a, b,* and *c* are followed by *E*.
Instance 2: Factors *a* and *b* are not followed by *E*.
Therefore, factor *c* is probably the cause of *E*.

Both Agreement and Difference

If we combine these two reasoning patterns, we get a modified version of what Mill called the *Joint Method of Agreement and Difference*. Using this joint method is, obviously, just a matter of applying both methods simultaneously—a procedure that generally increases the probability that the conclusion is true. This combined method, then, says that the likely cause is the one isolated when you (1) identify the relevant factors common to occurrences of the phenomenon (the Method of Agreement) and (2) discard any of these that are present even when there are no occurrences (the Method of Difference).

Let's apply this combined method to the mystery illness at Elmo's bar. Say that among the ten patrons who become ill, the common factors are that they all drank from the same bottle of wine, and they all had the free tacos. So we reason that the likely cause is either the wine or the tacos. After further investigation, though, we find that other patrons who ate the tacos did not become ill. We conclude that the wine is the culprit.

The schematic for arguments based on the Joint Method of Agreement and Difference is:

Instance 1: Factors *a, b,* and *c* are followed by *E*.
Instance 2: Factors *a, b,* and *d* are followed by *E*.
Instance 3: Factors *b* and *c* are not followed by *E*.
Instance 4: Factors *b* and *d* are not followed by *E*.
Therefore, factor *a* is probably the cause of *E*.

Factors *a* and *b* are the only relevant factors that are accompanied by *E*. But we can eliminate *b* as a possibility because when it's present, *E* doesn't occur. So *b* can't be the cause of *E*; *a* is most likely the cause.

You can see the Joint Method of Agreement and Difference at work in modern "controlled trials" used to test the effectiveness of medical treatments. In these experiments, there are two groups of subjects—one known as the experimental group; the other, the control group. The experimental group receives the treatment being tested, usually a new drug. The control group receives a bogus, or inactive, treatment (referred to as a placebo). This setup helps ensure that the two groups are as similar as possible and that they differ in only one respect—the use of the genuine treatment. A controlled trial, then, reveals the relevant factor *common* to the occurrence of the effect, which is the subjects' response to the treatment (Method of Agreement). And it shows the only important difference between the occurrence and nonoccurrence of the effect: the use of the treatment being tested.

Correlation

In many cases, relevant factors aren't merely present or absent during occurrences of the phenomenon—they are closely *correlated* with the occurrences. The cause of an occurrence varies as the occurrence (effect) does. For such situations Mill formulated the *Method of Concomitant Variation*. This method says that when two events are correlated—when one varies in close connection with the other—they are probably causally related.

If you observe that the longer you boil eggs, the harder they get (and no other relevant factors complicate this relationship), you can safely conclude that this correlation between boiling and hardening is a causal connection. You have good evidence that the boiling causes the hardening.

In medical science, such correlations are highly prized because direct evidence of cause and effect is so hard to come by. Correlations are often indirect evidence of one thing causing another. In exploring the link between cigarette smoking and lung cancer, for example, researchers discovered first that people who smoke cigarettes are more likely to get lung cancer than those who don't smoke. But later research also showed that the more cigarettes people smoke, the higher their risk of lung cancer. Medical scientists call such a correlation a *dose-response relationship*. The higher the dose of the element in question (smoking), the higher the response (the more cases of lung cancer). This dose-response relationship between cigarette smoking and lung cancer is, when combined with other data, strong evidence that smoking causes lung cancer.

We can represent arguments based on the Method of Concomitant Variation like this:

Instance 1: Factors *a*, *b*, and *c* are correlated with *E*.
Instance 2: Factors *a*, *b*, and increased-*c* are correlated with increased *E*.
Instance 3: Factors *a*, *b*, and decreased-*c* are correlated with decreased *E*.
Therefore, factor *c* is causally connected with *E*.

A very important cautionary note must accompany this discussion of correlation: Correlation, of course, does not always mean that a causal relationship is present. A correlation could just be a coincidence (see later). An increase in home PC sales is correlated with a rise in the incidence of AIDS in Africa, but this doesn't mean that one is in any way causally linked with the other.

 FURTHER THOUGHT

Is It Causal Confusion or ESP?

For over two decades, scientist-writer Susan Blackmore (with degrees in psychology, physiology, and parapsychology) has been investigating the psychology of "psychic," or paranormal, experience. Her central hypothesis has been that people's supposed experience of extrasensory perception, or ESP (telepathy, clairvoyance, and precognition), is the result of errors in causal thinking. Specifically, people tend to mistake coincidence for causal connection. She writes:

Scientist-writer Susan Blackmore

> My hypothesis is that psychic experiences are comparable to visual illusions. The experience is real enough, but its origin lies in internal processes, not peculiarities in the observable world. Like visual illusions they arise from cognitive processes that are usually appropriate but under certain circumstances give rise to the wrong answer. In other words, they are a price we pay for using efficient heuristics.
>
> In the case of vision, illusions arise when, for example, depth is seen in two-dimensional figures and constancy mechanisms give the answer that would be correct for real depth. The equivalent in the case of psychic experiences may be the illusion that a cause is operating and an explanation is required when in fact none is. In other words, psychic experiences are illusions of causality. . . .
>
> Experiences of telepathy, clairvoyance, and precognition imply a coincidence that is "too good to be just chance." This is so whether the experience involves dreaming about a person's death and that person dies within a few

hours, feeling the urge to pick up one's partner from the station and in fact he was stranded and needed help, or betting on a horse that later wins a race.

Some people's response to such events is to say, "That was just a chance coincidence"; while others' is to say, "That cannot be chance." In the latter case the person will then look for a causal explanation for the coincidence. If none can be found, a "cause," such as ESP, may be invoked. Alternatively, some kind of noncausal but meaningful connection may be sought, such as Jung's "acausal connecting principle."

There are two possible types of error that may be made here. First, people may treat connected events as chance coincidences, thereby missing real connections between events and failing to look for explanations. Second, they may treat chance events as connected and seek for explanations where none is required. In the real world of inadequate information and complex interactions one would expect errors of both types to occur. It is the latter type that, I suggest, gives rise to experiences of ESP. . . .

One prediction of this approach is that those people who more frequently look for explanations of chance coincidences are more likely to have psychic experiences. Therefore, sheep [believers in ESP] should be those who underestimate the probability of chance coincidences.

It has long been known that probability judgments can be extremely inaccurate. Kahneman and Tversky (1973) have explored some of the heuristics, such as "representativeness" and "availability," that people find coincidences surprising (Fall 1982; Falk and McGregor 1983). Adding specific but superfluous detail can make coincidences seem more surprising, and things that happen to subjects themselves seem more surprising to them than the same things happening to other people. . . .

There is, however, little research relating these misjudgments to belief in the paranormal or to having psychic experiences. Blackmore and Troscianko (1985) found that sheep performed worse than goats [skeptics about ESP] on a variety of probability tasks. For example, in questions testing for responsiveness to sample size, sheep did significantly worse than goats. The well-known birthday question was asked: How many people would you need to have at a party to have a 50:50 chance that two have the same birthday? . . . As predicted, goats got the answer right significantly more often than sheep.

Subjects also played a coin-tossing computer game and were asked to guess how many hits they would be likely to get by chance. The correct answer, 10 hits in 20 trials, seems to be rather obvious. However, the sheep gave a significantly lower mean estimate of only 7.9, while goats gave a more accurate estimate of 9.6.[2]

Causal Confusions

Mill's methods and other forms of causal reasoning may be common sense, but they're not foolproof. No inductive procedure can guarantee the truth of the conclusion. More to the point, it's easy to commit errors in cause-and-effect reasoning—regardless of the method used—by failing to take into account pertinent aspects of the situation. This section describes some of the more common causal blunders to which we're all prey.

Misidentifying Relevant Factors

A key issue in any type of causal reasoning is whether the factors preceding an effect are truly relevant to that effect. In the Method of Agreement, for example, it's easy to find a preceding factor common to all occurrences of a phenomenon. But that factor may be irrelevant. In the case of Elmo's bar, what if all those who became ill had black hair? So what? We know that hair color is very unlikely to be related to intestinal illness. *Relevant* factors include only those things that could possibly be causally connected to the occurrence of the phenomenon being studied. We could reasonably judge that factors relevant to the intestinal illness would include all the conditions that might help transmit bacteria or viruses.

Your ability to identify relevant factors depends mostly on your background knowledge—what you know about the kinds of conditions that could produce the occurrences in which you're interested. Lack of background knowledge might lead you to dismiss or ignore relevant factors or to assume that irrelevant factors must play a role. The only cure for this inadequacy is deeper study of the causal possibilities in question.

Mishandling Multiple Factors

Most of the time, the biggest difficulty in evaluating causal connections is not that there are so few relevant factors to consider—but that there are so many. Too often the Method of Agreement and the Method of Difference are rendered useless because they cannot, by themselves, narrow the possibilities to just one. At the same time, ordinary causal reasoning is frequently flawed because of the failure to consider *all* the relevant antecedent factors. (Later chapters will refer to this problem as the failure to consider alternative explanations.)

Sometimes this kind of oversight happens because we simply don't look hard enough for possible causes. At other times, we miss relevant factors because we don't know enough about the causal processes involved. This again is a function of skimpy background knowledge. Either way, there is no countermeasure better than your own determination to dig out the whole truth.

"In reality, the most astonishingly incredible coincidence imaginable would be the complete absence of all coincidences."

—John Allen Paulos

Being Misled by Coincidence

Sometimes ordinary events are paired in unusual or interesting ways: You think of Hawaii, then suddenly a TV ad announces low-cost fares to Maui; you receive some email just as your doorbell sounds and the phone rings; or you stand in the

FURTHER THOUGHT

Coincidence, Birth Dates, and U.S. Presidents

When we're tempted to say that the conjunction of two events "couldn't be just coincidence," we should think twice. People are often lousy at determining the true likelihood of events. Recall the birth-date problem mentioned in Chapter 4. It's the classic example of misjudged probabilities: In a random selection of twenty-three people, what is the probability that at least two of them will have the same birth date? The answer: 50 percent, or 50-50. People are usually shocked when they hear the answer. Part of the reason is that they typically underestimate how often oddball coincidences occur and fail to see that such strange conjunctions *must* occur from time to time. Here's a succinct explanation of the problem from social psychologist David G. Myers:

> We've all marveled at such coincidences in our own lives. Checking out a photocopy counter from the Hope College library desk, I confused the clerk when giving my six-digit department charge number—which just happened at that moment to be identical to the counter's six-digit number on which the last user had finished. Shortly after my daughter, Laura Myers, bought two pairs of shoes, we were astounded to discover that the two brand names on the boxes were "Laura" and "Myers."

> And then there are those remarkable coincidences that, with added digging, have been embellished into really fun stories, such as the familiar Lincoln–Kennedy coincidences (both with seven letters in their last names, elected 100 years apart, assassinated on a Friday while beside their wives, one in Ford's theater, the other in a Ford Motor Co. car, and so forth). We also have enjoyed newspaper accounts of astonishing

happenings, such as when twins Lorraine and Levinia Christmas, driving to deliver Christmas presents to each other near Flitcham, England, collided.

My favorite is this little known fact: In Psalm 46 of the King James Bible, published in the year that Shakespeare turned 46, the 46th word is "shake" and the 46th word from the end is "spear." (More remarkable than this coincidence is that someone should have noted this!) . . .

"In reality," says mathematician John Allen Paulos, "the most astonishingly incredible coincidence imaginable would be the complete absence of all coincidences." When Evelyn Marie Adams won the New Jersey lottery twice, newspapers reported the odds of her feat as 1 in 17 trillion—the odds that a given person buying a single ticket for two New Jersey lotteries would win both. But statisticians Stephen Samuels and George McCabe report that, given the millions of people who buy U.S. state lottery tickets, it was "practically a sure thing" that someday, somewhere, someone would hit a state jackpot twice. Consider: An event that happens to but one in a billion people in a day happens 2000 times a year. A day when nothing weird happened would actually be the weirdest day of all.[3]

lobby of a hotel thinking of an old friend—then see her walk by. Plenty of interesting pairings can also show up in scientific research. Scientists might find, for example, that men with the highest rates of heart disease may also have a higher daily intake of water. Or women with the lowest risk of breast cancer may own Toyotas. Such pairings are very probably just coincidence, merely interesting correlations of events. A problem arises, though, when we think that there nevertheless must be a causal connection involved.

For several reasons, we may very much want a coincidence to be a cause-and-effect relationship, so we come to believe that the pairing is causal. Just as often we may mistake causes for coincidences because we're impressed or excited about the conjunction of events. The pairing of events may seem "too much of a coincidence" to be coincidence, so we conclude that one event must have caused the other. You may be thinking about how nice it would be for your sister to call you from her home in Alaska—then the phone rings, and it's her! You're tempted to conclude that your wishing caused her to call. But such an event, though intriguing and seemingly improbable, is not really so extraordinary. Given the ordinary laws of statistics, incredible coincidences are common and must occur. Any event, even one that seems shockingly improbable, is actually very probable over the long haul. Given enough opportunities to occur, events like this surprising phone call are virtually certain to happen to *someone*.

People are especially prone to "it can't be just coincidence" thinking because, for several psychological reasons, they misjudge the probabilities involved. They may think, for example, that a phone call from someone at the moment they're thinking of that person is incredible—but only because they've forgotten about all the times they've thought of that person and the phone *didn't* ring. Such probability misjudgments are a major source of beliefs about the paranormal or supernatural, topics that we address in Chapter 10. (See also the box "Is It Causal Confusion or ESP?" in this chapter.)

Unfortunately, there is no foolproof way to distinguish coincidence from cause and effect. But this rule of thumb can help:

> *Don't assume that a causal connection exists unless you have good reason for doing so.*

Generally, a good reason consists of the passing of one or more standard causal tests (such as the ones we've been discussing)—and being able to rule out any relevant factors that might undermine the verdict of those tests. Usually, when a cause-effect connection is uncertain, only further evaluation or research can clear things up.

Confusing Cause with Temporal Order

A particularly prevalent type of misjudgment about coincidences is the logical fallacy known as ***post hoc, ergo propter hoc*** ("after that, therefore because of that"). We believe that a cause must precede its effect. But just because one event precedes another that doesn't mean that the earlier one *caused* the later. To think so is to be taken in by this fallacy. Outrageous examples of post hoc arguments include: "The rooster crowed, then the sun came up, so the rooster's crowing caused sunrise!" and "Jasmine left her umbrella at home Monday, and this caused it to rain." You can clearly see the error in such cases, but consider these arguments:

> *Argument 7*
> After the training for police officers was enhanced, violent crime in the city decreased by 10 percent. So enhanced training caused the decline in violent crime.

> *Argument 8*
> An hour after Julio drank the cola, his headache went away. The cola cured his headache.

> *Argument 9*
> As soon as Smith took office and implemented policies that reflected his conservative theory of economics, the economy went into a downward slide characterized by slow growth and high unemployment. Therefore, the Smith policies caused the current economic doldrums.

> *Argument 10*
> I wore my black shirt on Tuesday and got an F on a math quiz. I wore the same shirt the next day and flunked my psych exam. That shirt's bad luck.

The conclusion of argument 7 is based on nothing more than the fact that the enhanced training preceded the reduction in violent crime. But crime rates can decrease for many reasons, and the enhanced training may have had nothing to do with the decline in crime. For the argument to be strong, other considerations besides temporal order would have to apply—for example, that other possible causes or antecedent factors had been ruled out; that there was a close correlation between amount of training and decline in crime rates; or that in previous years (or in comparable cities) enhanced training was always followed by decreased violent crime (or no change in training was always followed by steady crime rates).

Argument 8 is also purely post hoc. Such reasoning is extremely common and underlies almost all folk remedies and a great deal of quackery and bogus self-cures. You take a vitamin E capsule, and eight hours later your headache is gone. But was it really the vitamin E that did the trick? Or was it some other overlooked factor such as something you ate, the medication you took (or didn't take), the nap you had, the change in environment (from, say, indoors to outdoors), or the stress reduction you felt when you had pleasant thoughts? Would your headache have gone away on its own anyway? Was it the *placebo effect*—the tendency for people to feel better when treated even when the treatment is fake or inactive? A chief function of controlled medical testing is to evaluate cause-and-effect relationships by systematically ruling out post hoc thinking and irrelevant factors.

Argument 9 is typical post hoc reasoning from the political sphere. Unless there are other good reasons for thinking that the economic policy is causally connected to specific economic events, the argument is weak and the conclusion unreliable.

Argument 10 is 100 percent post hoc and undiluted superstition. There is no difference in kind between this argument and much of the notorious post hoc reasoning of centuries ago: "That girl gave me the evil eye. The next day I broke my leg. That proves she's a witch, and the Elders of Salem should have her put to death!"

Confusing Cause and Effect

Sometimes we may realize that there's a causal relationship between two factors—but we may not know which factor is the cause and which is the effect. We may be confused, in other words, about the answers to questions like these:

> Does your coffee drinking cause you to feel stressed out—or do your feelings of being stressed out cause you to drink coffee?
> Does participation in high school sports produce desirable virtues such as courage and self-reliance—or do the virtues of courage and self-reliance lead students to participate in high school sports?
> Does regular exercise make people healthy—or are healthy people naturally prone to regular exercise?

As you can see, it's not always a simple matter to discern what the nature of a causal link is. Again, we must rely on our rule of thumb: *Don't assume that a causal connection exists unless you have good reason for doing so.* This tenet applies not only to our ordinary experience but to all states of affairs involving cause and effect, including scientific investigations.

In everyday life, sorting cause from effect is often easy because the situations we confront are frequently simple and familiar—as when we're trying to

The Deadly *Post Hoc* Fallacy

Despite a growing body of scientific research showing no connection between a measles vaccine and autism in young children, many people have insisted that the vaccine causes the disorder. Some parents of autistic children reasoned that since autism symptoms arose after the children were vaccinated, the vaccine was to blame. As evidence builds against a causal link, the reasoning looks more and more *post hoc*—and dangerous. Here's a recent statement from the National Institutes of Health:

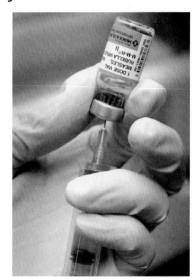

> Study after study has found no link between autism spectrum disorders (ASD) and the measles-mumps-rubella (MMR) vaccine—or any vaccine for that matter. Yet many parents still refuse or delay vaccinations for their young children based on misplaced fear of ASD, which can be traced back to a small 1998 study that's since been debunked and retracted. Such decisions can have a major negative impact on public health. With vaccination rates in decline, we've recently seen the resurgence of measles and other potentially fatal childhood infectious diseases.
>
> Among the parents most likely to avoid getting their kids vaccinated are those who already have a child with ASD. So, it's especially important and timely news that researchers have once again found no link between MMR vaccines and ASD—even among children known to be at greater risk for autism because an older sibling has the developmental brain disorder.[4]

What are the dangers for children of their parents' *post hoc* reasoning? Why do you think some parents would hold to their belief in the vaccine-autism link in the face of contrary scientific evidence? Is the availability error at work here?

discover what caused the kettle to boil over. Here, we naturally rely on Mill's methods or other types of causal reasoning. But as we've seen, in many other common circumstances, things aren't so simple. We often cannot be sure that we've identified all the relevant factors, or ruled out the influence of coincidence, or correctly distinguished cause and effect. Our rule of thumb, then, should be our guide in all the doubtful cases.

Science faces all the same kinds of challenges in its pursuit of causal explanations. And despite its sophisticated methodology and investigative tools, it must expend a great deal of effort to pin down causal connections. Identifying the cause of a disease, for example, usually requires not one study or experiment, but many. The main reason is that uncovering relevant factors and excluding irrelevant or misleading factors is always tough. This is why we should apply our rule of thumb even to scientific research that purports to identify a causal link. In Chapters 9 and 10, we'll explore procedures for evaluating scientific research and for applying our rule of thumb with more precision.

Necessary and Sufficient Conditions

To fully appreciate the dynamics of cause and effect and to be able to skillfully assess causal arguments, you must understand two other important concepts: **necessary conditions** and **sufficient conditions**. Causal processes always occur under specific conditions. So we often speak of cause and effect in terms of *the conditions for the occurrence of an event*. Scientists, philosophers, and others go a step further and emphasize a distinction between necessary and sufficient conditions for the occurrence of an event:

> *A necessary condition for the occurrence of an event is one without which the event cannot occur.*
> *A sufficient condition for the occurrence of an event is one that guarantees that the event occurs.*

Suppose you drop a water-filled balloon from atop a building (aiming it at your least favorite professor, of course), and it breaks on the pavement. What are the *necessary conditions* for the breaking of the balloon (the effect)? There are several, including (1) your releasing the balloon, (2) the force of gravity acting on the water, (3) the weakness of the material that the balloon is made of (its breakability), and (4) the hardness of the pavement. If any one

> "Shallow men believe in luck. Strong men believe in cause and effect."
> —Ralph Waldo Emerson

REVIEW NOTES

Causal Confusions

- Misidentifying relevant factors
- Overlooking relevant factors
- Confusing coincidence with cause
- Confusing cause with temporal order (*post hoc* fallacy)
- Confusing cause and effect

of these conditions is not present, the water balloon will not break. To state the obvious: If you don't release the balloon, it won't drop. If gravity is not in force, the balloon won't fall. If the balloon material isn't breakable, it won't, well, break. If the pavement isn't hard enough, even a breakable balloon won't rupture. (For the sake of illustration, this list of necessary conditions is incomplete. Many, if not most, events in nature have large numbers of necessary conditions.)

What are the *sufficient* conditions for the balloon's breaking? Not one of the four conditions by itself is sufficient to cause the balloon to break. None *guarantees* the occurrence of the effect; none suffices to produce the event. But all the necessary conditions combined (these four and others) are sufficient to guarantee the balloon's breaking.

Failing to feed a healthy goldfish for a few weeks is a sure way to kill it. So this deprivation is a sufficient condition for its death, as is removing the water from its fishbowl. But neither taking away the fish's food nor draining its bowl is a necessary condition for a goldfish's death because its death can be caused without resorting to either of these methods. On the other hand, necessary conditions for *sustaining* the fish's life include feeding it, providing it with water to live in, ensuring that the water is properly oxygenated, and so on. Again, in this instance, the whole set of the necessary conditions would constitute a sufficient condition for sustaining the fish's life.

In cases in which a complete set of necessary conditions constitutes a sufficient condition for an event, we say that the conditions are *individually necessary and jointly sufficient* for an event to occur. As the previous examples suggest, however, it's possible to have a set of conditions that are individually necessary but not jointly sufficient. Say some of the conditions necessary for sustaining the goldfish's life are present, but not all of them are. Because some necessary conditions are missing, the sufficient condition for keeping the fish alive would not exist. On the other hand, it's also possible to have a set of conditions that are jointly sufficient but *not* individually necessary. By not feeding a goldfish for weeks we would create a set of conditions sufficient for the death of the fish. But these conditions aren't necessary for the death of a goldfish because we could ensure its death in other ways.

So there are conditions that are necessary but not sufficient for the occurrence of an event, and conditions that are sufficient but not necessary. There are also conditions that are both necessary and sufficient for an event. The Earth's being more massive than the moon is *both* a necessary and sufficient condition for the moon's being less massive than the Earth. A piece of paper's being heated to a sufficiently high temperature in the presence of oxygen is both a necessary and sufficient condition for the combustion of the paper.

In some situations, depending on our interests or practical concerns, we may focus on necessary causal conditions; in other situations, sufficient causal conditions. When we're interested in preventing or eliminating a state of affairs, we often zero in on necessary causal conditions. If you were a scientist trying to discover how to prevent mosquito infestations, you would try to determine the necessary conditions for the occurrence of mosquito infestations.

Uncovering and understanding just one necessary condition could give you everything you need to control the problem. If you found out, for example, that a necessary condition for mosquito breeding is standing water, you would need to look no further for an answer. Eliminating the standing water would prevent infestations.

When we're interested in *bringing about* a state of affairs, we're likely to focus on sufficient causal conditions. If you were a doctor devoted to treating clogged arteries in your patients, you would seek out treatments scientifically proven to be sufficient for alleviating the condition. The treatments might include surgery to remove the blockage or a procedure called balloon angioplasty to widen artery passageways.

Your success in appraising causal arguments often depends heavily on your ability to distinguish between statements expressing causes as necessary conditions and statements expressing causes as sufficient conditions. Consider:

> *In the current situation, the president will send in U.S. troops if the United Nations refuses to act.*

This statement says that the condition required for the deployment of U.S. troops is the United Nations' refusing to act. But is this a necessary or sufficient condition? The use of the word "if" by itself signals a sufficient condition. If sufficient condition is what's meant, then the statement says that the UN's refusing to act will automatically trigger the troop deployment. This outcome is assured if the UN refuses.

But if the statement is meant to express the idea that the UN refusal is a necessary condition, then we're talking about a very different situation. If the UN refusal is a necessary condition, then it *will not* unavoidably trigger the troop deployment because the refusal may not be the *only* necessary condition. The idea of necessary condition is expressed by the phrase "only if" before the stipulated condition. To express necessary condition, the statement should read:

> *In the current situation, the president will send in U.S. troops only if the United Nations refuses to act.*

So depending on the kind of causal condition meant, the statement could describe a war that's sure to happen if the condition obtains—or a war that may not occur even if the condition does obtain.

As you might expect, conditions that are *both* necessary and sufficient are indicated by the phrase "if and only if." For example:

> *The paper will combust if and only if it's heated to a sufficiently high temperature in the presence of oxygen.*

None of this discussion, however, should lead you to think that a causal condition must be *either* necessary or sufficient. It could be neither:

> *Late delivery of the package caused John to miss his deadline.*

> *Ricardo's stubbornness caused the negotiations to break down.*

EXERCISES

Exercise 8.8

Analyze each of the following causal arguments. Identify the conclusion and whether the argument appeals to the method of agreement, the method of difference, the joint method of agreement and difference, or correlation. In some cases the conclusion may be implied but not stated. Indicate whether the argument is strong or weak.

1. Forty-five patients were admitted to Mercy Hospital for pneumonia in December. They were all given standard treatment for pneumonia. After five days, thirty of them were well enough to go home. The other fifteen, however, somehow acquired other infections and were not well enough to be released for fourteen days. The only relevant factor common to these fifteen is this: They all stayed in the same ward (different from the ward that the other group stayed in). Something about staying in that ward is the cause of the prolonged illness.

* 2. Research suggests that eating lots of fruits and vegetables may provide some protection against several types of cancer. Studies have revealed that the risk of getting cancer associated with the lowest intakes of fruits and vegetables is twice as high as that associated with the highest intakes. This association holds for several types of cancer, including cancers of the breast, colon, pancreas, and bladder.

3. "An experimental vaccine prevented women from becoming persistently infected with a [type of human papillomavirus called HPV-16] that is associated with half of all cervical cancers, researchers reported. . . . The study involved 2,392 women from 16 to 23 years in age. Participants were randomly assigned to receive three shots of either an HPV-16 vaccine or a placebo (a dummy substance). The study was double-blinded—that is, neither the investigators nor the study participants knew who got the vaccine and who got the placebo. Participants were followed for an average of 17 months after getting the third shot. . . . [Forty-one] women developed HPV-16 infection—all of these women were in the placebo group. . . . By comparison, no one who got all three vaccine shots developed an HPV-16 infection." [National Cancer Institute]

4. Getting the endorsement of the teachers union in this town is absolutely essential to being elected to the school board in this city. No one has ever won a seat on the school board without an endorsement from the teachers union.

5. For most of the school year the number of disciplinary actions taken weekly because of student misconduct at North High School has remained about the same—roughly ten a week. But for the last month the number of actions per week has gone down considerably—to about six per week. There can be only one reason: Last month the Ten Commandments were posted in the hallway outside the principal's office. This posting was the only significant recent change in the school.

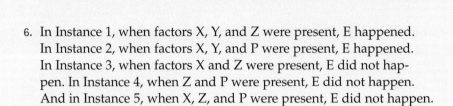

6. In Instance 1, when factors X, Y, and Z were present, E happened. In Instance 2, when factors X, Y, and P were present, E happened. In Instance 3, when factors X and Z were present, E did not happen. In Instance 4, when Z and P were present, E did not happen. And in Instance 5, when X, Z, and P were present, E did not happen. Therefore, Y caused E.

* 7. Educators have frequently noted the connection between education level and salary. The higher a person's education level is, the higher his or her annual salary is likely to be. Education increases people's earning power.

8. "On the 20th May, 1747, I took twelve patients [with] scurvy on board the *Salisbury* at sea. Their cases were as similar as I could have them. They all in general had putrid gums, the spots and lassitude, with weakness of their knees. They lay together in one place, being a proper apartment for the sick in the fore-hold; and had one diet in common to all. . . . Two of these were ordered each a quart of cider a day. Two others took [twenty-five drops of] vitriol three times a day. . . . Two others took two spoonfuls of vinegar three times a day. . . . Two of the worst patients [were given a half pint of sea water daily]. . . . Two others had each two oranges and one lemon given them everyday. . . . The two remaining patients took [small doses of nutmeg, garlic, mustard seed, and a few other ingredients]. The consequence was that the most sudden and visible good effects were perceived from the use of the oranges and lemons; one of those who had taken them being at the end of six days fit for duty. . . . The other was the best recovered of any in his condition, and being now deemed pretty well was appointed nurse to the rest of the sick. As I shall have occasion elsewhere to take notice of the effects of other medicines in this disease, I shall here only observe that the result of all my experiments was that oranges and lemons were the most effectual remedies for this distemper at sea." [James Lind, *Of the Prevention of the Scurvy,* 1753]

9. On Tuesday fifty-two people ate ham sandwiches at Johnny's Deli, and half of these came down with hepatitis. The board of health discovered that the people who became ill had their ham sandwiches made by Johnny's brother, who had hepatitis at the time. This was the only relevant common element among those who got sick. Seems Johnny's brother was the cause of this outbreak.

10. Scientists wanted to see whether giving pre-puberty children dietary supplements of calcium could significantly increase the density of the children's bones. (Bone density is a key part of bone strength.) So they selected seventy-one pairs of identical twins and gave one twin of each pair a daily supplement of extra calcium and the other twin a sugar pill (placebo). All the twins had diets that contained adequate amounts of all nutrients. The investigators monitored the

twins and their diets for three years. The only relevant difference between the twins was the extra calcium that half of them received. At the end of the three years, the scientists found that the twins who had received the extra calcium had significantly greater bone density. They concluded that the extra calcium caused the increased density.

11. For years vehicular accidents at the intersection of Fifth and Main Streets have consistently averaged two to four per month. Since a traffic light was installed there, the rate has been one or two accidents every three months. That new traffic light has made quite a difference.

12. The risk of atherosclerosis (a.k.a. hardening of the arteries) is linked to the amount of cholesterol in the bloodstream (called serum cholesterol). The higher the serum cholesterol levels, the greater the risk of athero-sclerosis. There's a causal connection between serum cholesterol levels and risk of atherosclerosis.

* 13. Investigators tested the performance of four gasoline-powered lawn-mowers before and after a tune-up. The machines differed in age, manu-facturer, engine type, and controls. The performance of every mower was better after the tune-up, leading the testers to conclude that tune-ups can improve the performance of lawnmowers.

14. The reason there have been so many terrorist attacks in Western coun-tries in the past ten years is that the rights of Palestinians have been vio-lated by Westerners. Every time large numbers of innocent Palestinians have been jailed, persecuted, or killed in Western countries, there has been a terrorist attack in the West.

15. Charlie was pretty happy all week, but then he started moping around like he'd lost his dog or something. I think he's upset be-cause he got word that his grades weren't good enough to get into med school.

* 16. The price of a barrel of oil on the world market has hit $40 only twelve times in the last thirty years. Sometimes major world econo-mies were in recession, and sometimes they weren't. Sometimes oil production was down; sometimes up. U.S. oil reserves were sometimes sold off; sometimes not. But one thing that was always present when oil hit $40 was that there was a major war going on somewhere in the world.

17. Sometimes my television reception is excellent, and sometimes it's ter-rible. There's only one important factor that seems to make a difference. When the reception is excellent, no other major appliances are running in the house. When it's terrible, at least one major appliance—like the dishwasher—is running. For some reason, running a major appliance interferes with my TV reception.

18. In our test, after people washed their hands with Lather-Up Germicidal Soap, no germs whatsoever could be detected on their hands. But under

exactly the same conditions, after they washed their hands with Brand X germicidal soap, plenty of germs were found on their hands. Lather-Up is better.

* 19. Just five people got As on the midterm exam. The only common factor in their success is that they all studied the night before and reviewed their notes just before walking into class to take the test.

20. The cause of Jackie M's criminal behavior—his involvement in petty theft and assaults—is no mystery. Jackie commits most of his criminal acts when the outdoor temperatures are highest. When outdoor temperatures are lowest, he behaves himself. In fact, the incidence of his criminal behavior rises as the temperature rises. Jackie's problem is that he has a heat-sensitive personality.

Exercise 8.9

For each argument in Exercise 8.8, identify errors in causal reasoning that are most likely to occur in the circumstances indicated. The possibilities include (a) misidentifying or overlooking relevant factors, (b) being misled by coincidence, (c) falling for the *post hoc* fallacy, and (d) confusing cause and effect. Answers are provided for 2, 7, 13, 16, and 19.

Exercise 8.10

For each of the following causal statements, indicate whether the specified cause is (a) a necessary condition, (b) a sufficient condition, (c) a necessary and sufficient condition, or (d) neither a necessary nor a sufficient condition.

* 1. Sylvia's being exposed to the influenza virus caused her to get the flu.

2. Sergio's eagerness to get to the airport caused him to get a speeding ticket.

3. James died of a heart attack because he drank too much and ate a high-fat diet.

* 4. Chopping off the head of the king put an end to him.

5. The mighty Casey hit the ball out of the park, winning the game by one run.

6. The straw broke the camel's back.

7. The war in Iraq started because the president feared that Saddam Hussein had weapons of mass destruction.

8. Johann got a good grade on the exam because he studied the night before.

* 9. A single spark started the internal combustion engine.

10. Simone lost weight by exercising regularly.

KEY WORDS

analogy	enumerative induction	random sample
argument by analogy (analogical induction)	hasty generalization	relevant property
	inference to the best explanation	representative sample
biased sample	margin of error	sample (members)
causal argument	necessary condition	self-selecting sample
causal claim	*post hoc, ergo propter hoc*	sufficient condition
confidence level		target group

Summary
Enumerative Induction

- An inductive argument is intended to provide only probable support for its conclusion, being considered strong if it succeeds in providing such support and weak if it does not.
- Inductive arguments come in several forms, including enumerative, analogical, and causal. In enumerative induction, we argue from premises about some members of a group to a generalization about the entire group. The entire group is called the target group; the observed members of the group, the sample; and the group characteristics we're interested in, the relevant property.
- An enumerative induction can fail to be strong by having a sample that's too small or not representative. When we draw a conclusion about a target group based on an inadequate sample size, we're said to commit the error of hasty generalization.
- Opinion polls are enumerative inductive arguments, or the basis of enumerative inductive arguments, and must be judged by the same general criteria used to judge any other enumerative induction.

Analogical Induction

- In analogical induction, or argument by analogy, we reason that since two or more things are similar in several respects, they must be similar in some further respect. We evaluate arguments by analogy according to several criteria: (1) the number of relevant similarities between things being compared, (2) the number of relevant dissimilarities, (3) the number of instances (or cases) of similarities or dissimilarities, and (4) the diversity among the cases.

Causal Arguments

- A causal argument is an inductive argument whose conclusion contains a causal claim. There are several inductive patterns of reasoning used to assess causal connections. These include the Method of Agreement, the Method of Difference, the Method of Agreement and Difference, and the Method of Concomitant Variation.
- Errors in cause-and-effect reasoning are common. They include misidentifying relevant factors in a causal process, overlooking relevant factors, confusing cause with coincidence, confusing cause with temporal order, and mixing up cause and effect.
- Crucial to an understanding of cause-and-effect relationships are the notions of necessary and sufficient conditions. A necessary condition for the occurrence of an event is one without which the event cannot occur. A sufficient condition for the occurrence of an event is one that guarantees that the event occurs.

 Field Problems

1. Design an opinion poll to determine the percentage of people on campus who believe that individuals under age seventeen who commit crimes that carry the death penalty for adults should likewise get the death penalty. Specify all the following parameters: (1) the target group, (2) the makeup and size of the sample, (3) the methods for ensuring a random sample, (4) the methods for ensuring a representative sample, (5) the exact phrasing of the polling question(s), (6) the method for gathering the responses (telephone survey, "man on the street" poll, email questionnaire, etc.), and (7) the acceptable margin of error. Explain the reasons for your choices.

2. Devise an extended argument by analogy (two hundred to three hundred words) to support the proposition that Earth is not a mere planet of rock and soil but is a living organism, a notion that has come to be known as the gaia theory. You'll need to research this term on the Internet. (The original idea that inspired this view was not that the planet was an organism, but that it *could be usefully viewed* as an organism that is self-regulating.) People who take the idea literally might say, for example, that just as billions of cells in the human body perform the functions that sustain the body, so billions of organisms on Earth perform the functions that sustain the life of Earth. Use several relevant similarities in your argument. Then write a critique of your argument, focusing especially on relevant dissimilarities and the number of relevant similarities.

3. Select a causal argument on a political issue from recent op-ed pages (in newspapers or on websites). Then critique it, explaining why it's strong or weak, specifically noting whether it misidentifies or overlooks relevant factors, confuses cause with coincidence, commits the *post hoc* fallacy, confuses cause and effect, or mishandles or misunderstands necessary and sufficient conditions.

Self-Assessment Quiz

Answers appear in "Answers to Self-Assessment Quizzes" (Appendix D).

1. What is the logical form of enumerative induction, indicated schematically?

2. In enumerative induction, what are the target group, the sample, and the relevant property?

3. What are the two major ways in which an enumerative induction can fail to be strong?

4. What is the logical form of analogical induction, indicated schematically?

For each of the following enumerative inductions, indicate whether the argument is strong or weak. If it's weak, say whether the problem is a sample that's too small, not representative, or both.

5. All the women in my yoga class are against the war. Ninety percent of the members of a national women's group (twelve thousand members) are against the war. And all my women friends are against the war. The fact is, almost all American women oppose this war.

6. Recently there was a racially motivated murder in Texas. Two white men killed a black man. Then another murder of a black man by some racist whites occurred in Louisiana. And in Mississippi an admitted racist finally was convicted of the murder of a black man that occurred years ago. The South has more racist killers than any other part of the country.

7. Most professors at this college are not grading as strictly as they used to. They now give Bs for work to which they used to assign Cs. The grading standards in American colleges are dropping.

8. The first time Ariana encountered trigonometry, she couldn't understand it. And the first time she read Shakespeare, she didn't get it. She will never understand anything.

9. Americans are quite satisfied with the administration's recent foreign policy decisions. An "instant poll" conducted yesterday on the CNN website got fifteen thousand responses from site visitors—and 95 percent of them said that American foreign policy was on the right track.

10. Judging from what I've seen, anti-war demonstrators are just a bunch of peaceniks left over from the Vietnam War era.

Evaluate each of the following arguments by analogy, indicating (1) the two things being compared, (2) the conclusion, and (3) whether the argument is strong or weak.

11. "Suppose that someone tells me that he has had a tooth extracted without an anaesthetic, and I express my sympathy, and suppose that I am then asked, 'How do you know that it hurt him?' I might reasonably reply, 'Well, I know that it would hurt me. I have been to the dentist and know how painful it is to have a tooth stopped without an anaesthetic, let alone taken out. And he has the same sort of nervous system as I

have. I infer, therefore, that in these conditions he felt considerable pain, just as I should myself.'" [Alfred J. Ayer]

12. "As for one who is choosy about what he learns . . . we shall not call him a lover of learning or a philosopher, just as we shall not say that a man who is difficult about his food is hungry or has an appetite for food. We shall not call him a lover of food but a poor eater. . . . But we shall call a philosopher the man who is easily willing to learn every kind of knowledge, gladly turns to learning things, and is insatiable in this respect." [Socrates]

13. "Let us begin with a parable [showing that statements about God have no meaning]. . . . Once upon a time two explorers came upon a clearing in the jungle. In the clearing were growing many flowers and many weeds. One explorer says, 'Some gardener must tend this plot.' The other disagrees, 'There is no gardener.' So they pitch their tents and set a watch. No gardener is ever seen. 'But perhaps he is an invisible gardener.' So they set up a barbed-wire fence. They electrify it. . . . But no shrieks ever suggest that some intruder has received a shock. No movements of the wire ever betray an invisible climber. . . . Yet still the Believer is not convinced. 'But there is a gardener, invisible, intangible, insensible.' . . . At last the Sceptic despairs, 'But what remains of your original assertion? Just how does what you call an invisible, intangible, eternally elusive gardener differ from an imaginary gardener or even from no gardener at all?'" [Antony Flew]

Analyze each of the following causal arguments. Identify the conclusion and whether the argument is weak or strong. If it's weak, explain why with reference to the material in this chapter.

14. School violence is caused mainly by teens playing violent video games. Incidents of violence in schools have increased as more and more teens are playing violent video games, as the video games themselves have become more graphically and realistically violent, and as the number and variety of video games have expanded dramatically.

15. Smoking and exposure to secondhand smoke among pregnant women pose a significant risk to both infants and the unborn. According to numerous studies, each year the use of tobacco causes thousands of spontaneous births, infant deaths, and deaths from SIDS. Death rates for fetuses are 35 percent higher among pregnant women who smoke than among pregnant women who don't smoke.

16. Why are crime rates so high, the economy so bad, and our children so prone to violence, promiscuity, and vulgarity? These social ills have arisen—as they always have—from the "moral vacuum" created when Americans turn away from religion. Our current slide into chaos started when prayer was banned from public schools and secular humanism swooped in to replace it. And as God has slowly faded from public life, we have got deeper in the hole.

17. The twelve of us went on a hike through the mountains. We all drank bottled water except Lisa, who drank from a stream. Later she got really sick. Some intestinal thing. But the rest of us were fine. We've repeated this adventure many times on other hikes, with all but one of us drinking bottled water and one drinking from a stream. Everything else was the same. Each time, the person who drank from the stream got really ill. Drinking from streams on these hikes causes intestinal illness. Don't do it.

18. Ever since I started drinking herbal tea in the morning, my energy level has improved and I'm a lot calmer during the day. That stuff works.

19. Yesterday my astrological chart—prepared by a top astrologer—said that I would meet an attractive person today, and I did. Last week, it said I'd come into some money, and I did. (Jack paid me that hundred dollars he owed me.) Now I'm a believer. The stars really do rule.

20. Most of the terminal cancer patients in this ward who had positive attitudes about their disease lived longer than expected. Most of the negative-attitude patients didn't live as long as expected. A positive attitude can increase the life expectancy of people with terminal cancer.

 Integrative Exercises

These exercises pertain to material in Chapters 3 and 6–8.
For each of the following arguments, specify the conclusion and premises and indicate whether it is deductive or inductive. If it's deductive, use Venn diagrams or truth tables to determine its validity. If it's inductive, indicate whether it's an enumerative, analogical, or causal induction and whether it's strong or weak. If necessary, add implicit premises and conclusions.

1. It's clear that if the allies accidentally damage any holy sites when they attack enemy forces, the local people will never give the allies any respect or cooperation. The allies, though, will not damage any holy sites. Therefore, the locals will respect the allies and cooperate with them.

2. "By removing the exact-change-only lane at the Black Rock toll barrier, the New York State Thruway Authority has created artificial traffic jams. For 20 years, I have rarely encountered traffic problems at this toll barrier. Now it is a daily occurrence." [Letter to the editor, *Buffalo News*]

3. If people have free will, then they can be held morally responsible for what they do. But—as our judicial system demonstrates—people cannot really be held morally responsible for their actions. Thus, people do not have free will.

4. "If we take in hand any volume; of divinity or school metaphysics, for instance; let us ask, *Does it contain any abstract reasoning concerning quantity*

or number? No. *Does it contain any experimental reasoning concerning matter of fact and existence?* No. Commit it then to the flames; for it can contain nothing but sophistry and illusion." [David Hume]

5. No philosophy majors are persons without a brain. All students without a brain are persons who spend most of their time partying. So no philosophy majors are persons who spend most of their time partying.

6. "The decision to have or not to have a child is mine and mine alone. I am not cattle for the government to order about, demanding that I bring an unwanted child to term. Stripping me of the right to control my own destiny dehumanizes me, period. Anything less than my choice, on my terms, reduces me to property." [Guest opinion, The Onion.com]

7. All politicians are corrupt manipulators, so some corrupt manipulators are effective leaders, since some effective leaders are politicians.

8. If we increase security in the country because of terrorist attacks, then our personal freedoms will be curtailed. If we do not increase security in the country, then terrorist attacks will increase. So either our personal freedoms will be curtailed or terrorist attacks will increase.

9. "A well regulated militia being necessary to the security of a free State, the right of the people to keep and bear arms shall not be infringed." [U.S. Constitution]

10. "World War II would still be going on had we adhered to the rules we now find our troops having to operate under. War is brutal, and innocent folks are going to die in the process. The time has come to realize that we, as a nation, cannot afford another Vietnam. Let's use what means are necessary to win now and deal with the public outcry afterward." [Letter to the editor, *Buffalo News*]

11. [Be careful: This one has an unstated conclusion.] "The U.S. is the only nation-state to have been condemned by the World Court for international terrorism. The U.S. vetoed a UN Security Council resolution calling on governments to observe international law. After deliberately targeting the civilian public health infrastructure, the U.S. military imposes a continuing economic blockade on Iraq which has directly resulted in the deaths of hundreds of thousands of children. The U.S. government is the primary financier and arms supplier for the decades-old Israeli war against the entire Palestinian people." [Editorial, *Alternative Press Review*]

12. Almost all of the owners of restaurants, bars, and clubs in New York City are opposed to the city's total ban on smoking in indoor public places. The vast majority of New Yorkers simply do not like this law.

13. Every student Maria knows who wears glasses also has a high grade-point average. So most students who wear glasses probably have high grade-point averages.

14. "The evils of the world are due to moral defects quite as much as to lack of intelligence. But the human race has not hitherto discovered any

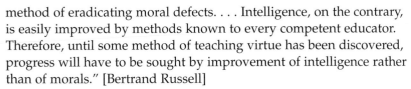

method of eradicating moral defects. . . . Intelligence, on the contrary, is easily improved by methods known to every competent educator. Therefore, until some method of teaching virtue has been discovered, progress will have to be sought by improvement of intelligence rather than of morals." [Bertrand Russell]

15. Television is destroying morality in this country. As TV violence, sex, and vulgarity have increased, so have violent crimes, sexual assaults, and violations of obscenity laws.

16. Several Navy planes and a number of ships have disappeared in the Bermuda Triangle. These odd vanishings cannot be mere coincidence. The Bermuda Triangle is the epicenter of mysterious forces unknown to science.

17. "The idea that mainstream corporate media—the broadcast networks and newspaper chains, both those under consolidated ownership and those few that still cling to independence—is consistently liberal is laughable on its face. . . . [The] raft of Bush endorsements from the 'undeniably liberal' papers . . . seems to provide some deniability. Add in the past and current presence of avowed conservatives like Jack Welch at the top of these organizations, look over to the regular political forums of the Sunday talk shows, scan the editorial pages of the supposedly liberal *Washington Post* (where conservative pundits overshadow their left colleagues in both numbers and vehemence) and the argument is clearly bogus." [Letter to the editor, Salon.com]

18. Eighty-three percent of the letters to the editor received by this newspaper are adamantly pro-life. And since the *Daily Planet* is the only major newspaper in the city, and it provides the primary forum for discussion of local issues, we must conclude that this town is also overwhelmingly pro-life.

19. The big grandfather clock in the hallway struck midnight—and then the old man died. This doesn't prove that the striking of the clock killed him, but it does show that the two events—the clock's striking and the death of the old man—were somehow causally linked.

20. If the recession continues, people will lose billions of dollars in failed investments. People will indeed lose billions of dollars in failed investments, so the recession will continue.

 Writing Assignments

1. Write a two-page rebuttal to Essay 10 ("Women and the Afghanistan Peace Process").

2. Study Essay 16 ("Torture: Time for Congress to End the Debate") and Essay 17 ("Torture: Severe Interrogations Work"). Decide which essay presents the stronger arguments, and write a paper defending your view.

3. In a two-page essay argue for or against one of these claims:
    - Men are better at science than women are.
    - Everyone does what is in his or her own best interests.
    - It's wrong for the government to tax citizens to support people who are poor and needy.
    - Deadbeat dads (fathers who don't or won't pay child support that they are legally obligated to pay) should be put in jail.
    - Sexual harassment is not a problem on this campus.
    - Competition is always a good thing.
    - Pornography should never be banned on a college campus.

PART FOUR

EXPLANATIONS

Inference to the Best Explanation

 CHAPTER OBJECTIVES

EXPLANATIONS AND INFERENCE

- Understand what inference to the best explanation is and how it differs from other kinds of induction.
- Know what an explanation (including theoretical explanation) is and how it differs from an argument.
- Appreciate how inference to the best explanation is used in all disciplines and in everyday life.
- Be able to demonstrate how to use inference to the best explanation in many different situations.

THEORIES AND CONSISTENCY

- Know how to check an explanation for internal and external consistency.

THEORIES AND CRITERIA

- Understand the importance of using criteria to judge the adequacy of theories.
- Be able to list and explain the five criteria of adequacy.
- Be able to apply the criteria of adequacy to simple causal theories.
- Know what an ad hoc hypothesis is.

TELLING GOOD THEORIES FROM BAD

- Memorize and explain the four steps in the TEST formula.
- Recognize the importance of considering alternative explanations.
- Be able to use the TEST formula to evaluate theories.

LET'S TAKE STOCK OF THE INDUCTIVE TERRAIN TRAVELED THUS FAR. IN CHAPTER 8 WE closely examined the nature and uses of inductive reasoning. We were reminded that a deductive argument, unlike an inductive one, is intended to provide logically conclusive support for its conclusion. If it succeeds in providing such support, it's said to be valid; if not, invalid. If a valid argument has true premises, it's said to be sound. But an inductive argument is intended to supply only probable support for its conclusion. If it manages to provide such support, it's said to be strong; if not, weak. The conclusion of an inductively strong argument is simply more likely to be true than not. If a strong argument has true premises, it's said to be cogent.

We also saw that inductive arguments come in several forms. One of them is enumerative induction, in which we reason from premises about *some* members of a group to a conclusion, or generalization, about the group *as a whole.* All the swans you have ever seen are white, so *all* swans must be white. Forty percent of the students at your college have a driver's license, so 40 percent of all students everywhere must have a driver's license. (Whether these enumerative inductive arguments are strong or cogent is another matter.)

Another kind of inductive argument is argument by analogy (or analogical induction), in which we reason that since two or more things are similar in several respects, they must be similar in some additional respect. In an analogical induction you might argue that (1) since humans can move about, solve mathematical equations, win chess games, and feel pain, *and* (2) since computers (or robots) are like humans in that they can move about, solve mathematical equations, and win chess games, it's therefore probable that computers can also feel pain. Analogical induction, like all inductive reasoning, can establish conclusions only with a degree of probability.

Finally, we saw that causal arguments—inductive arguments whose conclusions contain causal claims—can be enumerative inductions, analogical inductions, or arguments that rely on Mill's methods and similar kinds of inferences.

 REVIEW NOTES

A Look Back at the Basics

- **Statement (claim):** An assertion that something is or is not the case
- **Premise:** A statement given in support of another statement
- **Conclusion:** A statement that premises are intended to support
- **Argument:** A group of statements in which some of them (the premises) are intended to support another of them (the conclusion)
- **Indicator words:** Words that frequently accompany arguments and signal that a premise or conclusion is present
- **Deductive argument:** An argument intended to provide conclusive support for its conclusion
- **Inductive argument:** An argument intended to provide probable support for its conclusion

Reasoning well about causal connections means avoiding numerous common errors, including misidentifying or overlooking relevant factors, confusing coincidence with cause, and committing the post hoc fallacy.

We noted only in passing that there is another kind of inductive reasoning that is so important that a whole section in this text (Part 4) is devoted to it: **inference to the best explanation.** Well, here we are in Part 4, and it's time to delve deep into this kind of inductive reasoning, perhaps the most commonly used form of inference and arguably the most empowering in daily life.

Explanations and Inference

Recall from Chapter 1 that an explanation is a statement (or statements) asserting why or how something is the case. For example: The bucket leaks because there's a hole in it. He was sad because his dog died. She broke the pipe by hitting it with a wrench. These explanations and all others are intended to clarify and elucidate, to increase our understanding. Remember too our discussion of the important distinction between an explanation and an argument. While an explanation tells us *why or how something is the case,* an argument gives us reasons for believing *that something is the case.*

As you've probably already guessed, there are also different kinds of explanations. (See the box "The Lore of Explanations.") For instance, some explanations are what we might call procedural—they try to explain how something is done or how an action is carried out. ("She opened up the engine, then examined the valves, then checked the cylinders.") Some are interpretive—they try to explain the meaning of terms or states of affairs. ("This word means 'dashing' or 'jaunty.'") And some are functional—they try to explain how something functions. ("The heart circulates and oxygenates the blood.")

But the kind of explanation we're concerned with here—and the kind we bump into most often—is what we'll call, for lack of something snappier, a **theoretical explanation.** Such explanations are theories, or hypotheses, that try to explain why something is the way it is, why something is the case, why something happened. In this category we must include all explanations intended to explain the cause of events—the causal explanations that are so important to both science and daily life. Theoretical explanations, of course, are claims. They assert that something is or is not the case.

Now, even though an explanation is not an argument, an explanation can be *part* of an argument. It can be the heart of the kind of inductive argument known as inference to the best explanation. And in this kind of inference, the explanations we use are theoretical explanations.

In inference to the best explanation, *we reason from premises about a state of affairs to an explanation for that state of affairs.* The premises are statements about observations or other evidence to be explained. The explanation is a claim about why the state of affairs is the way it is. The key question that this type of inference tries to answer is, What is the best explanation for the existence or nature of this state of affairs? The best explanation is the one most likely to be true, even though there is no guarantee of its truth as there is in deductive inference.

"There is nothing more practical than a good theory."
—Leonid Ilich Brezhnev

Let's look briefly at the other kinds of inductive inferences we have studied. Recall that *enumerative induction* has this pattern:

> *X percent of the observed members of group A have property P.*
> *Therefore, X percent of all members of group A probably have property P.*

Remember:

> *Forty percent of the pickles that you've pulled out of the barrel are exceptionally good. So 40 percent of all the pickles in the barrel are probably exceptionally good.*

> *All of the blue herons that we've examined at many different sites in the nature preserve (about two hundred birds) have had birth defects. Therefore, most of the blue herons in the nature preserve probably have birth defects.*

> *Every Gizmo computer I've bought in the last two years has had a faulty monitor. Therefore all Gizmo computers probably have faulty monitors.*

Analogical induction has this pattern:

> *Thing A has properties P_1, P_2, P_3 plus the property P_4.*
> *Thing B has properties P_1, P_2, and P_3.*
> *Therefore, thing B probably has property P_4.*

For example:

> *Character is the foundation stone upon which one must build to win respect. Just as no worthy building can be erected on a weak foundation, so no lasting reputation worthy of respect can be built on a weak character.* [R. C. Samsel]

> *As for one who is choosy about what he learns . . . we shall not call him a lover of learning or a philosopher, just as we shall not say that a man who is difficult about his food is hungry or has an appetite for food. We shall not call him a lover of food but a poor eater. . . . But we shall call a philosopher the man who is easily willing to learn every kind of knowledge, gladly turns to learning things, and is insatiable in this respect.* [Plato]

> *Mice are mammals, have a mammalian circulatory system, have typical mammalian biochemical reactions, respond readily to high blood pressure drugs, and experience a reduction in blood cholesterol when given the new Drug Z. Humans are mammals, have a mammalian circulatory system, have typical mammalian biochemical reactions, and respond readily to high blood pressure drugs. Therefore, humans will also experience a reduction in blood cholesterol when given the new Drug Z.*

Inference to the best explanation, however, has this pattern:

> *Phenomenon Q.*
> *E provides the best explanation for Q.*
> *Therefore, it is probable that E is true.*

For example:

> *The new quarterback dropped the ball again. The best explanation for that screw-up is that he's nervous. So he's definitely nervous.*

> *The best explanation for Maria's absence today is that she's angry at the boss. Yep, she's mad at the boss.*

> *The defendant's fingerprints were all over the crime scene, the police found the victim's blood on his shirt, and he was in possession of the murder weapon. The only explanation for all this that makes any sense is that the defendant actually committed the crime. He's guilty.*

If the explanations in these arguments really are the best, then the arguments are inductively strong. And if the premises are also true, then the arguments are cogent. If cogent, we are justified in believing that the explanations for the phenomena are in fact correct.

Notice that an inference to the best explanation always goes "beyond the evidence"—it tries to explain facts but does so by positing a theory that is not derived entirely from those facts. It tries to understand the known by putting forth—through inference and imagination—a theoretical pattern that encompasses both the known and unknown. It proposes a plausible pattern that expands our understanding.

The fact that there are *best* explanations, of course, implies that not all explanations for a state of affairs are created equal; some are better than others. Just because you've devised an explanation for something doesn't mean that you're justified in believing that the explanation is the right one. If other explanations are just as good, your explanation is in doubt. If other explanations are better than yours, you are not justified in believing it. But much of the time, after further study or thought, you can reasonably conclude that a particular explanation really is the best explanation. (More on how to evaluate the relative worth of explanations later.) In this way you can come to understand the state of affairs more than you did before.

Inference to the best explanation probably seems very familiar to you. That's because you use it all the time—and need it all the time. Often when we try to understand something in the world, we construct explanations for why this something is the way it is, and we try to determine which of these is the best. Devising explanations helps increase our understanding by fitting our experiences and background knowledge into a coherent pattern. At every turn we are confronted with phenomena that we can only fully understand by explaining them.

Sometimes we're barely aware that we're using inference to the best explanation. If we awaken and see that the streets outside are wet, we may immediately posit this explanation: It's been raining. Without thinking much about it, we may also quickly consider whether a better explanation is that a street-sweeper machine has wet the street. Just as quickly we may dismiss this explanation because we see that the houses and cars are also wet. After reasoning in this fashion, we may decide to carry an umbrella that day.

The Lore of Explanations

An explanation is a statement (or statements) asserting why or how something is the case. In traditional terminology, that which is to be explained in an explanation is called the *explanandum,* and that which does the explaining is called the *explanans.* Take this explanation: "The dog barked because a prowler was nearby." The explanandum is "the dog barked," and the explanans is "a prowler was nearby."

You can categorize explanations in many ways, depending on the kind of explanandum in which you're interested. Here are a few of the more common categories:

- Teleological explanations try to explain the purpose of something, how it functions, or how it fits into a plan. (*Telos* is a Greek word meaning "end" or "purpose.")

    Example: The wall switch is there so you can turn off the lamp from across the room.
    Example: These wildflowers are here as a blessing from God.

- Interpretive explanations concern the meaning of terms or states of affairs. These explanations seek to understand not something's purpose or cause, but rather its sense or semantic meaning.

    Example: When Mary smiled, she was signaling her agreement.
    Example: "Effect" means to accomplish, but "affect" means to influence.

- Procedural explanations try to explain how something is done or how an action is carried out.

    Example: To stop the chemical reaction, Ariana added sulfur.
    Example: He paid his taxes online by downloading the forms, then using his credit card number.

Let's consider a more elaborate example. Say that you discover that your car won't start in the morning (the phenomenon to be explained). You would like to know why it won't start (the explanation for the failure) because you can't repair the car unless you know what the problem is. You know that there are several possible explanations or theories.

1. The battery is dead.
2. The fuel tank is empty.
3. The starter has malfunctioned.

4. A vandal has sabotaged the car.
5. All or several of the above.

So you try to figure out which theory is the most plausible, that is, most likely to be true. You see right away that there is snow around the car from yesterday's snowstorm—but there are no tracks (not even yours) and no signs of tampering anywhere. So you dismiss theory 4. You remember that you filled up the gas tank yesterday, the fuel gauge says that the tank is full, and you don't see any signs of leakage. So you can safely ignore theory 2. You notice that the lights, heater, and radio work fine, and the battery gauge indicates a fully charged battery. So you discard theory 1. When you try to start the car, you hear a clicking sound like the one you heard when the starter had failed previously. Among the theories you started with, then, theory 3 now seems the most plausible. This means that theory 5 cannot be correct since it entails two or more of the theories.

If you wanted to, you could state your argument like this:

"WELL WHICH DO YOU THINK IS MORE LIKELY, YOUR PILLOW IS GROWING HAIR OR YOU'RE LOSING YOURS?"

www.CartoonStock.com

(1) *Your car won't start in the morning.*
(2) *The theory that the starter has malfunctioned is the best explanation for the car's not starting in the morning.*
(3) *Therefore, it's probable that the malfunctioning starter caused the car not to start in the morning.*

In science, where inference to the best explanation is an essential tool, usually the theories of interest are causal theories, in which events are the things to be explained and the proposed causes of the events are the explanations. Just as we do in everyday life, scientists often consider several competing theories for the same event or phenomenon. Then—through scientific testing and careful thinking—they systematically eliminate inadequate theories and eventually arrive at the one that's rightly regarded as the best of the bunch. Using this form of inference, scientists discover planets, viruses, cures, subatomic particles, black holes—and many things that can't even be directly observed.

> "A superstition is a premature explanation that overstays its time."
> —George Iles

And then there are all those other professionals who rely on inference to the best explanation. Physicians use it to pinpoint the cause of multiple symptoms in patients. Police detectives use it to track down lawbreakers. Judges and juries use it to determine the guilt or innocence of accused persons. And philosophers use it to assess the worth of conceptual theories.

With so many people in so many areas of inquiry using inference to the best explanation, you'd expect the world to be filled with countless theories proposed by innumerable people looking to explain all sorts of things. And so there are.

FURTHER THOUGHT

Darwin and the Best Explanation

Charles Darwin (1809–1882) offered the theory of evolution by natural selection as the best explanation for a wide variety of natural phenomena. He catalogued an extensive list of facts about nature and showed that his theory explains them well. He argued, however, that the alternative theory of the day—the view that God independently created species—does not explain them. Darwin declared:

Charles Darwin (1809–1882).

> It can hardly be supposed that a false theory would explain, in so satisfactory a manner as does the theory of natural selection, the several large classes of facts above specified. It has recently been objected that this is an unsafe method of arguing; but it is a method used in judging of the common events of life, and has often been used by the greatest natural philosophers.[1]

Here's a very brief table of notable or interesting proposed theories and the phenomena they are meant to explain:

Theory	To Explain . . .
Atomic	Behavior of subatomic particles
Germ	Spread of disease
HIV	Cause of AIDS
Oedipus complex	Behavior of men and boys
Placebo effect	Apparent cure of disease
The lone gunman	Assassination of John F. Kennedy
Violent video games	Violence in children
No official prayer in school	High crime and low morals
El Niño	Bad weather
El Niño	Good weather
Incumbent politicians	A bad economy
Political sex scandals	Immoral behavior of young people

FURTHER THOUGHT

Sherlock Holmes and Inference to the Best Explanation

Sherlock Holmes owed his great success as a detective primarily to inference to the best explanation. He was so good at this kind of inference that people (especially Watson) were frequently astonished at his skill. Holmes, however, was guilty of spreading some confusion about his ability. He called his method deduction, though it was clearly inductive. Holmes in action:

> I knew you came from Afghanistan. From long habit the train of thoughts ran so swiftly through my mind that I arrived at the conclusion without being conscious of intermediate steps. There were such steps, however. The train of reasoning ran, "Here is a gentleman of medical type, but with the air of a military man. Clearly an army doctor, then. He has just come from the tropics, for his face is dark, and that is not the natural tint of his skin, for his wrists are fair. He has undergone hardship and sickness, as his haggard face says clearly. His left arm has been injured. He holds it in a stiff and unnatural manner. Where in the tropics would an English army doctor have seen much hardship and got his arm wounded? Clearly in Afghanistan."[2]

Here Holmes explains how he knew that a man had "gone about in fear of some personal attack within the last twelve-month":

> "You have a very handsome stick," I answered. "By the inscription I observed that you had not had it more than a year. But you have taken some pains to bore the head of it and pour melted lead into the hole so as to make it a formidable weapon. I argued that you would not take such precautions unless you had some danger to fear."[3]

Of course, it's often easy to make up theories to explain things we don't understand. The harder job is sorting out good theories from bad, and that's the topic of the next few pages.

Exercise 9.1

1. What is an explanation?
2. What is inference to the best explanation?
3. Is inference to the best explanation inductive or deductive?
* 4. According to the text, what is a theoretical explanation?
5. What is the basic logical pattern of inference to the best explanation? for enumerative induction? for analogical induction?
6. According to the text, under what circumstances can an inference to the best explanation be deemed strong? cogent?
7. Did the fictional Sherlock Holmes use deduction or induction in his crime-solving?
* 8. What is a causal explanation? Are causal explanations used in inference to the best explanation?
9. How does the kind of explanation used in inference to the best explanation differ from a teleological explanation or an interpretive explanation?
10. Have you used inference to the best explanation today? If so, how did you use it? (Supply an example from the events of your day.)

Exercise 9.2

For each of the following explanations, indicate what state of affairs is being explained and what the explanation is.

1. Most students drop Professor Graham's class because he is so boring.
* 2. We all know that the spotted owl is endangered, and the only explanation for that is the political clout of the logging industry.
3. Why did James say that he saw a ghost in his bedroom? Because he drinks too much and has a vivid imagination.
4. Crimes committed by high school students are increasing because school districts refuse to mandate harsh punishments for criminal acts.
* 5. I'll tell you why the incidence of robbery is up: There aren't enough gun owners in the population.
6. Binge drinking is on the rise at women's colleges. This can best be explained by the permissive attitudes of the deans.
7. Americans are fond of the death penalty, but Europeans are not. Americans just never got over the old Wild West eye-for-an-eye mentality. Europeans never had a Wild West.
* 8. I believe that psychics really can predict the future because many things that psychics have told me have come true.

9. Rock stars make more money than teachers because they are smarter than teachers.

10. Global terrorism is caused by worldwide injustice and deprivation.

Exercise 9.3

For each of the following, determine whether the type of explanation offered is theoretical (the kind used in inference to the best explanation) or nontheoretical (e.g., teleological, interpretive, procedural). Be careful to note any borderline cases (explanations that could be either theoretical or nontheoretical).

1. There is no peace in the Middle East—and there never will be—due to the stubbornness of both sides in the conflict.

2. "Creation science" is controversial because mainstream scientists hate it.

* 3. Ethics is the critical study of morality.

4. John built himself a solar house so he could thumb his nose at the power company.

5. Jack is soaking wet because he stood in the rain.

6. When Jill raises her hand, that means she's going to ask a question that no one can answer.

* 7. When you experience memory loss, that can only mean one thing: Alzheimer's disease.

8. I wear this medallion for good luck.

9. He got the information through a complicated process of downloading it from the hard drive and putting it on multiple flash drives.

10. Evil exists in the world because God allows it.

11. You are always sick because you don't take care of yourself.

* 12. That painting is without vibrancy or cohesion. Just look at the dull colors and mishmash of forms.

13. Jill flunked her courses because she liked to party too much.

14. Sam has been weight training, so he's pretty buff.

15. Jane is studying hard so she can get a better job.

16. No one noticed the comet before because of cloud cover.

17. He broke the lock and pushed open the door—that's how he got in.

Exercise 9.4

In each of the following examples, a state of affairs is described. Devise two theories to explain each one. Include one theory that you consider plausible and one theory that you think is not plausible.

1. Mutilated cows have been found in several pastures in the western United States. In each case organs are missing from the carcasses. There are never any signs of vehicle tracks or footprints. The cause of death

is unknown. The method used to remove the organs is also unknown, although the wounds show indications of precision surgical tools.

* 2. When Jack came home, he noticed the window in the kitchen was broken, there were muddy footprints on the kitchen floor, and some valuable silverware was missing.

3. Maria awoke yesterday and found that the furniture in her room had been completely rearranged while she slept.

4. José discovered this morning that the roof and hood of his car bore dozens of tiny dents.

5. In the 1980s the number of homeless people in the United States increased dramatically.

* 6. Alice has been taking vitamin C every day for a year, and during that time she has not had a cold or a sore throat.

7. Teenagers are now having sex at earlier ages.

8. Scientists have discovered that there is a direct correlation between fat in people's diets and heart disease. The more fat, the greater the risk of heart disease.

9. The incidence of violent crimes in the United States has decreased in recent years.

Exercise 9.5

Read each of the following passages and answer these questions:

1. What is the phenomenon being explained?
2. What theory is suggested as a possible explanation for the phenomenon?
3. Is the theory plausible? If not, why not?
4. Is there a plausible theory that the writer has overlooked? If so, what is it?

PASSAGE 1

Many people believe that drinking a warm glass of milk at bedtime helps them fall asleep. The reason must be the tryptophan in the milk. Tryptophan is an essential amino acid that is converted into serotonin. Serotonin affects sleep patterns and the perception of pain.

PASSAGE 2

"Shark attacks around the world declined in 2003 for a third straight year, partly because swimmers and surfers grew more accustomed to thinking of the ocean as a wild and dangerous place. . . .

"The University of Florida, which houses the International Shark Attack File, said there were 55 unprovoked attacks worldwide, down from 63 reported in 2002 and lower than the previous year's 68 attacks.

"Four people were killed, compared to three in 2002, four in 2001 and 11 in the year 2000.

"Normally, scientists do not put much stock in year-to-year fluctuations in the number of attacks because they can be affected by such things as the weather and oceanographic conditions that drive bait fish closer to shore.

"But the third consecutive year of decline could indicate a longer term trend, the university said.

"'I think people are beginning to get a little more intelligent about when and where they enter the water,' George Burgess, director of the International Shark Attack File, said in a statement.

"'There seems to be more of an understanding that when we enter the sea, it's a wilderness experience and we're intruders in that environment.'"[4]

PASSAGE 3

"Women who have been coloring their hair for 24 years or more have a higher risk of developing a cancer called non-Hodgkin lymphoma, researchers reported.

"They said their study of 1,300 women could help explain a mysterious rise in the number of cases of the cancer that affects the lymphatic system.

"Writing in the *American Journal of Epidemiology*, they said women who dyed their hair starting before 1980 were one-third more likely to develop non-Hodgkin lymphoma, or NHL, and those who used the darkest dyes for more than 25 years were twice as likely to develop the cancer.

"'Women who used darker permanent hair coloring products for more than 25 years showed the highest increased risk,' Tongzhang Zheng, associate professor of epidemiology and environmental health at Yale School of Medicine, said in a statement.

"Cancer experts note that a person's absolute risk of developing lymphoma is very low, so doubling that risk still means a woman who dyes her hair is very unlikely to develop lymphoma."[5]

PASSAGE 4

Spontaneous human combustion (SHC) is the theory that under certain rare circumstances, a human body mysteriously ignites, burns, and is almost entirely consumed. Investigators have encountered a few cases in which the burnt remains of a human body (usually only a limb or two) are found in an enclosed room, with nearby flammable objects completely unaffected by fire. The other parts of the body, including the torso, are entirely incinerated. There is usually, or always, a source of flame in the room—a lit pipe or candle, for example. And the victim is often elderly, alcoholic, or in some way incapacitated. SHC is the only reasonable explanation for these strange facts.

Theories and Consistency

Very often we may propose a theory as an explanation for a phenomenon, or we may have a theory thrust upon us for consideration. In either case, we will likely be dealing with an argument in the form of inference to the best explanation. The conclusion of the argument will always say, in effect, *this* theory is the best

"In making theories, keep a window open so that you can throw one out if necessary."
—Béla Schick

> ### REVIEW NOTES
>
> ## Minimum Requirement: Consistency
>
> - Internal consistency: A theory that is internally consistent is free of contradictions
> - External consistency: A theory that is externally consistent is consistent with the data it's supposed to explain

explanation of the facts. And we will be on the hot seat trying to decide if it really is. How do we do that?

The work is not always easy, but there are special criteria we can use to get the job done. Before we apply these criteria, though, we have to make sure that the theory in question meets the minimum requirement of *consistency*. A theory that does not meet this minimum requirement is worthless, so there is no need to use the special criteria to evaluate the theory. A theory that meets the requirement is eligible for further consideration. Here we are concerned with both *internal* and *external* consistency. A theory that is internally consistent is consistent with itself—it's free of contradictions. A theory that is externally consistent is consistent with the data it's supposed to explain—it fully accounts for the phenomenon to be explained.

If we show that a theory contains a contradiction, we have refuted it. A theory that implies that something both is and is not the case cannot possibly be true. By exposing an internal contradiction, Galileo once refuted Aristotle's famous theory of motion, a venerable hypothesis that had stood tall for centuries. He showed that the theory implied that one falling object falls both faster and slower than another one.

If a theory is externally inconsistent, we have reason to believe that it's false. Suppose you leave your car parked on the street overnight and the next morning discover that (1) the windshield is broken, (2) there's blood on the steering wheel, and (3) there's a brick on the front seat. And let's say that your friend Charlie offers this theory to explain these facts: Someone threw a brick through your windshield. What would you think about this theory?

You would probably think that Charlie had not been paying attention. His theory accounts for the broken windshield and the brick—but not the blood on the steering wheel. You would likely toss his theory out and look for one that was complete. Like this one: A thief broke your windshield with a brick then crawled through the broken window, cutting himself in the process.

Theories and Criteria

For a moment let's return to our example of the car that won't start. Recall that we examined five possible explanations for the non-start phenomenon:

1. The battery is dead.
2. The fuel tank is empty.

"The Universe is not obliged to conform to what we consider comfortable or plausible."
—Carl Sagan

3. The starter has malfunctioned.
4. A vandal has sabotaged the car.
5. All or several of the above.

But what if someone suggested that our analysis of this problem was incomplete because we failed to consider several other possible theories that are at least as plausible as these five? Consider these, for example:

6. Each night, you are sabotaging your own car while you sleepwalk.
7. Your ninety-year-old uncle, who lives a thousand miles away from you, has secretly been going for joyrides in your car, damaging the engine.
8. A poltergeist (a noisy, mischievous ghost) has damaged the car's carburetor.
9. Yesterday, you accidentally drove the car through an alternative space-time dimension, scrambling the electrical system.

What do you think of these theories? More specifically, are the last four theories *really* at least as plausible as the first five? If you think so, *why?* If you think not, *why not?* Remember that a theory's strangeness is no good reason to discount it. It will not do to say that theories 6–9 are too weird to be true. In the history of science plenty of bizarre theories have turned out to be correct. (Quantum theory in physics, for example, is about as weird as you can get.) Earlier we concluded that theory 3 was better (more likely to be true) than 1, 2, 4, and 5. But what criteria did we use to arrive at this judgment? And on the basis of what criteria can we say that theory 3 is any better than theories 6–9? There must be *some* criteria because it is implausible that every theory is equally correct. Surely there is a difference in quality between a theory that explains rainfall by positing some natural meteorological forces and one that alleges that Donald Duck causes weather phenomena.

A simplified answer to the problem of theory choice is this: Just weigh the evidence for each theory, and the theory with the most evidence wins. As we will soon see, the amount or degree of evidence that a theory has is indeed a crucial factor—but it cannot be the sole criterion by which we assess explanations. Throughout the history of science, major theories—from the heliocentric theory of the solar system to Einstein's general theory of relativity—have never been established by empirical evidence alone.

The task of determining the best explanation has another complication. If we accept such extraordinary theories as 6–9 as legitimate possibilities, there must be no end to the number of theories that we could devise to explain the data at hand. In fact, we could come up with an infinite number of possible theories for any phenomenon simply by repeatedly adding one more element. For example, we could propose the one-poltergeist theory (a single entity causing the trouble), a two-poltergeist theory, a three-poltergeist theory, and so on.

Fortunately, despite these complications, there are reasonable criteria and reliable procedures for judging the merits of eligible theories and for arriving at a defensible judgment of which theory is best. Enter: the **criteria of adequacy.** The criteria of adequacy are the essential tools of science and have been used by scientists throughout history to uncover the best explanations for all sorts

Inference to the Best Explanation and the External World

In Chapters 10 and 11 we will explore in detail how inference to the best explanation can be used to tackle some big issues. Here we just want to mention one of the "big questions" to which philosophers and other thinkers have applied inference to the best explanation.

A problem that has historically occupied thinkers in the history of philosophy is whether we have any good reasons to believe that there is a world outside our own thoughts. That is, is there an *external world* independent of the way we represent it to ourselves? Some people, called skeptics, have denied that we have any such good reasons because we can never get "outside our skins" to objectively compare our subjective experiences with reality. All we know is the nature of our perceptions—which may or may not be linked to the "real world" in any way.

To this puzzle many philosophers have applied inference to the best explanation. They argue that we can indeed know that there is an external reality because that belief is the best explanation of the peculiar pattern of our perceptions. In other words, the best explanation of why we seem to see a tree in front of us is that there *really is a real tree in front of us.*

of events and states of affairs. Science, though, doesn't own these criteria. They are as useful—and as used—among nonscientists as they are among men and women of science.

Applying the criteria of adequacy to a set of theories constitutes the ultimate test of a theory's value, for *the best theory is the eligible theory that meets the criteria of adequacy better than any of its competitors.* Here, "eligible" means that the theory has already met the minimum requirement for consistency.

All of this implies that the evaluation of a particular theory is not complete until alternative, or competing, theories are considered. As we've seen, there is an indefinite number of theories that could be offered to explain a given set of data. The main challenge is to give a fair assessment of the relevant theories in relation to each other. To fail to somehow address the alternatives is to overlook or deny relevant evidence, to risk biased conclusions, and to court error. Such failure is probably the most common error in the appraisal of theories.

A theory judged by these criteria to be the best explanation for certain facts is worthy of our belief, and we may legitimately claim to know that such a theory is true. But the theory is not then necessarily or certainly true in the way that a sound deductive argument's conclusion is necessarily or certainly true. Inference to the best explanation, like other forms of induction, cannot guarantee the truth of the best explanation. That is, it is not truth-preserving. The best theory we have may actually be false. Nevertheless we would have excellent reasons for supposing our best theory to be a true theory.

The criteria of adequacy are *testability, fruitfulness, scope, simplicity,* and *conservatism.* Let's examine each one in detail.

Testability

Most of the theories that we encounter every day and all the theories that scientists take seriously are **testable**—*there is some way to determine whether the theories are true or false.* If a theory is untestable—if there is no possible procedure for checking its truth—then it is of little or no help in increasing our understanding. Suppose someone says that an invisible, undetectable spirit is causing your headaches. What possible test could we perform to tell if the spirit actually exists? None. So the spirit theory is entirely empty. We can assign no weight to such a claim.

Here's another way to look at it. Theories are explanations, and explanations are designed to increase our understanding of the world. But an untestable theory does not—and cannot—explain anything. It is equivalent to saying that an unknown thing with unknown properties acts in an unknown way to cause a phenomenon—which is the same thing as offering no explanation at all.

We often run into untestable theories in daily life, just as scientists sometimes encounter them in their work. Many practitioners of alternative medicine claim that health problems are caused by an imbalance in people's *chi,* an unmeasurable form of mystical energy that is said to flow through everyone. Some people say that their misfortunes are caused by God or the Devil. Others believe that certain events in their lives happen (and are inevitable) because of fate. And parents may hear their young daughter say that she did not break the lamp, but her invisible friend did.

Many theories throughout history have been untestable. Some of the more influential untestable theories include the theory of witches (some people called witches are controlled by the Devil), the moral fault theory of disease (immoral behavior causes illness), and the divine placement theory of fossils (God created geological fossils to give the false impression of an ancient Earth).

 REVIEW NOTES

Criteria of Adequacy

- Testability: whether there is some way to determine if a theory is true
- Fruitfulness: the number of novel predictions made
- Scope: the amount of diverse phenomena explained
- Simplicity: the number of assumptions made
- Conservatism: how well a theory fits with existing knowledge

But what does it mean for a theory to be testable or untestable? A theory is testable *if it predicts something other than what it was introduced to explain.* Suppose your electric clock stops each time you touch it. One theory to explain this event is that there is an electrical short in the clock's wiring. Another theory is that an invisible, undetectable demon causes the clock to stop. The wiring theory predicts that if the wiring is repaired, the clock will no longer shut off when touched. So it is testable—there is something that the theory predicts other than the obvious fact that the clock will stop when you touch it. But the demon theory makes no predictions about anything, *except* the obvious, the very fact that the theory was introduced to explain. It predicts that the clock will stop if you touch it, but we already know this. So our understanding is not increased, and the demon theory is untestable.

Now, if the demon theory says that the demon can be detected with x-rays, then there is something the theory predicts other than the clock's stopping when touched. You can x-ray the clock and examine the film for demon silhouettes. If the theory says that the demon can't be seen but can be heard with sensitive sound equipment, then you have a prediction, something to look for other than clock stoppage.

So other things being equal, testable theories are superior to untestable ones; they may be able to increase our understanding of a phenomenon. But an untestable theory is just an oddity.

Fruitfulness

Imagine that we have two testable theories, theory 1 and theory 2, that attempt to explain the same phenomenon. Theory 1 and theory 2 seem comparable in most respects when measured against the criteria of adequacy. Theory 1, however, successfully predicts the existence of a previously unknown entity, say, a star in an uncharted part of the sky. What would you conclude about the relative worth of these two theories?

If you thought carefully about the issue, you would probably conclude that theory 1 is the better theory—and you would be right. Other things being equal, theories that perform this way—that successfully predict previously unknown phenomena—are more credible than those that don't. They are said to be **fruitful**, to yield new insights that can open up whole new areas of research and discovery. This fruitfulness suggests that the theories are more likely to be true.

If a friend of yours is walking through a forest where she has never been before, yet she seems to be able to predict exactly what's up ahead, you would probably conclude that she possessed some kind of accurate information about the forest, such as a map. Likewise, if a theory successfully predicts some surprising state of affairs, you are likely to think that the predictions are not just lucky guesses.

All empirical theories are testable (they predict something beyond the thing to be explained). But fruitful theories are testable and then some. They not only predict something, they predict something that no one expected. The element of surprise is hard to ignore.

The Importance (and Fun) of Crazy Theories

Many theories proposed throughout the history of science have been, well, crazy. That is, they have been unorthodox or heretical, with a shockingly different take on the world. The heliocentric theory of our solar system is a prime example. Some of these crazy theories have turned out to be good theories—they measured up to the criteria of adequacy very well. So a crazy theory is not necessarily a bad theory. Science as a whole has always been open to offbeat explanations, but they had to be judged to have merit. Most crazy theories in science or the fringes of science, though, usually fail the criteria of adequacy miserably. The challenge for scientists and other critical thinkers is to remain open to unorthodox theories but not be afraid to test them through criti-

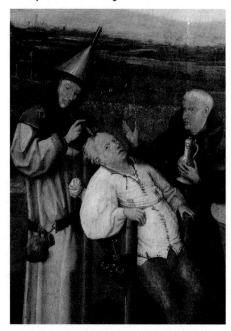

Trepanation: formerly for the release of evil spirits and later for the achievement of enlightenment.

cal reasoning. Besides, offbeat theories are fun. These following theories were gleaned from the Web.

- "I personally feel that the Crystal Skulls [sculptures resembling the human skull, some of which were made by the Aztecs] are not only here to share ancient knowledge and wisdom, but to assist in awakening our race to higher spiritual laws and understanding of itself. . . . If the Crystal Skulls were not brought by extraterrestrials then certainly we must conclude their [*sic*] have been civilizations much more technologically or spiritually advanced than our own today."
- "It is my belief that Mars was once a beautiful, fertile planet capable of sustaining life, much like our own, until some cataclysmic, global event changed everything. I believe that the survivors went searching for another planet, on which to live, and that they chose the Earth. We are their descendants. They were an advanced civilization who brought their technology with them. Upon reaching Earth, they proceeded to build the same type structures that were familiar to them on Mars. That way, if there were more survivors they'd recognize the structures and know where the others were."

- "Trepanation is the practice of making a hole in the skull. It is sometimes spelled trephination. . . . trepanation was practiced on every continent through every time period and by every race of mankind until the advent of brain surgery in this century. Doctors, today, have been taught that trepanation was done in past centuries for superstitious, magical or religious reasons. They generally look on trepanation as a practice akin to blood letting. They scoff at it. . . . The risk to benefit ratio would have to have been very favorable for the practice to have been so widely practiced but official investigators haven't been able to see that there is both a rationale and a benefit to this procedure."

- "There is without any doubt whatsoever scientific evidence for the existence of the afterlife. . . . Some of the technical evidence includes: The Electronic Voice Phenomenon (Spirit Voices on Tape), Instrumental Transcommunication (two-way communication with those who crossed over), the SCOLE Experiments, Out of Body Experiences, Near Death Experiences, Empirical Materialisation, Trans and Mental Mediumship; Poltergeists, Xenoglossy and Reincarnation, the Cross-Correspondences, Proxy Sittings."

- Have you ever dreamed of traveling in time? Now you can experience what you have only dreamed of. With the Hyper Dimensional Resonator you can travel into the past or explore the future. The world will be at your beck and call and you will have all the time in the world to explore it. . . . I sell an instrument which can be used for both, out of the body time travel and can also be used to help heal the sick."

Decades ago Einstein's theory of relativity gained a great deal of credibility by successfully predicting a phenomenon that was extraordinary and entirely novel. The theory predicts that light traveling close to massive objects (such as stars) will appear to be bent because the space around such objects is curved. The curve in space causes a curve in nearby light rays. At the time, however, the prevailing opinion was that light always travels in straight lines—no bends, no curves, no breaks. In 1919 the physicist Sir Arthur Eddington devised a way to test this prediction. He managed to take two sets of photographs of exactly the same portion of the sky—when the sun was overhead (in daylight) and when it was not (at night). He was able to get a good photo of the sky during daylight because there was a total eclipse of the sun at the time. If light rays really were bent when they passed near massive objects, then stars whose light passes near the sun should appear to be shifted slightly from their true position (as seen at night). Eddington discovered that stars near the sun did appear to have moved and that the amount of their apparent movement was just what the theory predicted. This novel prediction then demonstrated the fruitfulness of Einstein's theory, provided a degree of confirmation for the theory, and opened up new areas of research.

So the moral is that other things being equal, fruitful theories are superior to those that aren't fruitful. Certainly many good theories make no novel predictions but are accepted nonetheless. The reason is usually that they excel in other criteria of adequacy.

Scope

Suppose theory 1 and theory 2 are two equally plausible theories to explain phenomenon X. Theory 1 can explain X well, and so can theory 2. But theory 1 can explain or predict *only* X, whereas theory 2 can explain or predict X—as well as phenomena Y and Z. Which is the better theory?

We must conclude that theory 2 is better because it explains more diverse phenomena. That is, it has more **scope** than the other theory. The

www.CartoonStock.com

more a theory explains or predicts, the more it extends our understanding. And the more a theory explains or predicts, the less likely it is to be false because it has more evidence in its favor.

A major strength of Newton's theory of gravity and motion, for example, was that it explained more than any previous theory. Then came Einstein's theory of relativity. It could explain everything that Newton's theory could explain plus many phenomena that Newton's theory could not explain. This increased scope of Einstein's theory helped convince scientists that it was the better theory.

Here's a more down-to-earth example. For decades psychologists have known about a phenomenon called *constructive perception* (discussed in Chapter 4). In constructive perception what we perceive (see, hear, feel, etc.) is determined in part by what we expect, know, or believe. Studies have shown that when people expect to perceive a certain stimulus (say, a flashing light, a certain color or shape, a shadow), they often *do* perceive it, even if there is no stimulus present. The phenomenon of constructive perception then can be used to explain many instances in which people seem to perceive something when it is not really there or when it is actually very different from the way people think it is.

One kind of case that investigators sometimes explain as an instance of constructive perception is the UFO sighting. Many times people report seeing lights in the night sky that look to them like alien spacecraft, and they explain their perception by saying that the lights were caused by alien spacecraft. So we have two theories to explain the experience: constructive perception and UFOs from space. If these two theories differ only in the degree of scope provided by each one, however, we must conclude that the constructive-perception theory is better. (In reality, theories about incredible events usually differ on several criteria.) The constructive-perception theory can explain not only UFO sightings but all kinds of ordinary and extraordinary experiences—hallucinations, feelings of an unknown "presence," misidentification of crime suspects, contradictory reports in car accidents, and more. The UFO theory, however, is (usually) designed to explain just one thing: an experience of seeing strange lights in the sky.

Scope is often a crucial factor in a jury's evaluation of theories put forth by both the prosecution and the defense. The prosecution will have a very powerful case against the defendant if the prosecutor's theory (that the defendant did it)

 NEWSMAKERS

The Best Explanation for Hurricanes Katrina and Harvey?

Some explanations are definitely newsworthy. In 2008 John Hagee, a prominent evangelical leader and author, publicly endorsed the presidential candidacy of John McCain, immediately thrusting both men into a media-heightened controversy involving some of Hagee's previously stated views. Receiving a large share of the attention was his explanation (later retracted) for the devastation of New Orleans by Hurricane Katrina:

> All hurricanes are acts of God, because God controls the heavens. I believe that New Orleans had a level of sin that was offensive to God, and they were recipients of the judgment of God for that.
>
> The newspaper carried the story in our local area, that was not carried nationally, that there was to be a homosexual parade there on the Monday that the Katrina came. And the promise of that parade was that it was going to reach a level of sexuality never demonstrated before in any of the other gay pride parades.
>
> So I believe that the judgment of God is a very real thing. I know there are people who demur from that, but I believe that the Bible teaches that

when you violate the law of God, that God brings punishment sometimes before the Day of Judgment, and I believe that the Hurricane Katrina was, in fact, the judgment of God against the city of New Orleans.[6]

More recently, Hurricane Harvey devastated Houston, and again some people offered up the wrath of God as an explanation. For example:

> Seeing the devastation of Hurricane Harvey, conservative Christian pastor John McTernan argued recently that "God is systematically destroying America" out of anger over "the homosexual agenda."
>
> There were others who disagreed over the reasons for God's anger but not necessarily with the assumption that God can be wrathful. . . . And, from the other side of the political spectrum, a Tampa University professor tweeted that God had punished Texans for voting Republican. He subsequently expressed regret but was fired.[7]

As an explanation for a physical phenomenon, this theory is as subject to evaluation using the criteria of adequacy as any other theory. What is the leading alternative theory to explain the natural disaster? Which theory, as judged by the criteria, is better?

explains all the evidence and many other things while the defense theory (innocence) does not. The defendant would be in big trouble if the prosecutor's theory explains the blood on the defendant's shirt, the eyewitness accounts, the defendant's fingerprints on the wall, and the sudden change in his usual routine—*and* the innocence theory renders these facts downright mysterious.

Other things being equal, then, the best theory is the one with the greatest scope. And if other things aren't equal, a theory with superior scope doesn't necessarily win the day because it may do poorly on the other criteria—or another theory might do better.

"I cannot help fearing that men may reach a point where they look on every new theory as a danger, every innovation as a toilsome trouble, every social advance as a first step toward revolution, and that they may absolutely refuse to move at all for fear of being carried off their feet."

—Alexis de Tocqueville

Simplicity

Let's return one last time to the scenario about the nonstarting car. Recall that the last four theories are:

6. Each night, you are sabotaging your own car while you sleepwalk.
7. Your ninety-year-old uncle, who lives a thousand miles away from you, has secretly been going for joyrides in your car, damaging the engine.
8. A poltergeist (a noisy, mischievous ghost) has damaged the car's carburetor.
9. Yesterday, you accidentally drove the car through an alternative space-time dimension, scrambling the electrical system.

 FURTHER THOUGHT

There's No Theory Like a Conspiracy Theory

Conspiracy theories try to explain events by positing the secret participation of numerous conspirators. The assassination of JFK, the terrorist attacks of 9/11, international banking, the Watergate scandal, the inner workings of the U.S. government—all these and more have been the subject of countless conspiracy theories, both elaborate and provocative. Some conspiracy theories, of course, have been found to be true after all. But most of them are implausible. The main problem with them is that they usually fail the criterion of simplicity. They would have us make numerous assumptions that raise more questions than they answer: How do the conspirators manage to keep their activities secret? How do they control all the players? Where is the evidence that all the parts of the conspiracy have come together just so?

Nonetheless, the United States seems to be Conspiracy Central. Here's a short list of things that, we are told, are the center of a massive conspiracy:

The death of Elvis Presley
The assassination of Martin Luther King, Jr.
The Oklahoma City bombing
The death of Princess Diana
The terrorist attacks of September 11, 2001

And here are a few of the alleged cabals that are doing all the dirty deeds:

The U.S. government
The Vatican
The CIA
The Illuminati, a secret society controlling the government
Doctors
The Freemasons

By now you probably suspect that these explanations are somehow unacceptable, and so they are. One important characteristic that they each lack is **simplicity**. Other things being equal, the best theory is the one that is the simplest—that is, the one that makes the fewest assumptions. The theory making the fewest assumptions is less likely to be false because there are fewer ways for it to go wrong. Another way to look at it is that since a simpler theory is based on fewer assumptions, less evidence is required to support it.

Explanations 8 and 9 lack simplicity because they each must assume the existence of an unknown entity (poltergeists and another dimension that scrambles electrical circuits). Such assumptions about the existence of unknown objects, forces, and dimensions are common in occult or paranormal theories. Explanations 6 and 7 assume no new entities, but they do assume complex chains of events. This alone makes them less plausible than the simple explanation of 3, starter malfunction.

The criterion of simplicity has often been a major factor in the acceptance or rejection of important theories. For example, simplicity is an important advantage that the theory of evolution has over creationism, the theory that the world was created at once by a divine being (see Chapter 10). Creationism must assume the existence of a creator and the existence of unknown forces (supernatural forces used by the creator). But evolution does not make either of these assumptions.

Scientists eventually accepted Copernicus's theory of planetary motion (heliocentric orbits) over Ptolemy's (Earth-centered orbits) because the former was simpler (see Chapter 10). In order to account for apparent irregularities in the movement of certain planets, Ptolemy's theory had to assume that planets have extremely complex orbits (orbits within orbits). Copernicus's theory, however, had no need for so much extra baggage. His theory could account for the observational data without so many orbits-within-orbits.

Sometimes a theory's lack of simplicity is the result of constructing ad hoc hypotheses. An **ad hoc hypothesis** is one that cannot be verified independently of the phenomenon it's supposed to explain. If a theory is in trouble because it is not matching up with the observational data of the phenomenon, you might be able to rescue it by altering it—by positing additional entities or properties that can account for the data. Such tinkering is legitimate (scientists do it all the time) if there is an independent way of confirming the existence of these proposed entities and properties. But if there is no way to verify their existence, the modifications are ad hoc hypotheses. Ad hoc hypotheses always make a theory less simple—and therefore less credible.

Conservatism

What if a trusted friend told you that—believe it or not—some dogs lay eggs just as chickens do? Let's assume that your friend is being perfectly serious and believes what she is saying. Would you accept this claim about egg-laying dogs? Not likely. But why not?

Probably your main reason for rejecting such an extraordinary claim would be that it fails the criterion of **conservatism**, though you probably wouldn't state it that way. (Note: This sense of "conservatism" *has nothing to do with political* *parties.*) This criterion says that other things being equal, *the best theory is the one that fits best with our well-established beliefs*—that is, with beliefs backed by excellent evidence or very good arguments. We would reject the canine-egg theory because, among other things, it conflicts with our well-founded beliefs about mammals, evolution, canine anatomy, and much more. Humans have an enormous amount of experience with dogs (scientific and otherwise), and none of it suggests that dogs can lay eggs. In fact, a great deal of what we know about dogs suggests that they *cannot* lay eggs. To accept the canine-egg theory despite its conflicting with a mountain of solid evidence would be irrational—and destructive of whatever understanding we had of the subject.

Perhaps one day we may be shocked to learn that—contrary to all expectations and overwhelming evidence—dogs do lay eggs. But given that this belief is contrary to a massive amount of credible experience, we must assign a very low probability to it.

What kind of beliefs fall into the category of "well-established" knowledge? For starters, we can count beliefs based on our own everyday observations that we have no good reasons to doubt (such as "It's raining outside," "The parking lot is empty," and "The train is running late today"). We can include basic facts about the world drawn from excellent authority ("the Earth is round," "men have walked on the moon," and "Cairo is the capital of Egypt"). And we can include a vast array of beliefs solidly supported by scientific evidence, facts recognized as such by most scientists ("cigarettes cause lung cancer," "vaccines prevent disease," "dinosaurs existed," and "germs cause infection").

Many of our beliefs, however, cannot be regarded as well established. Among these, of course, are all those we have good reasons to doubt. But there is also a large assortment of beliefs that occupy the middle ground between those we doubt and those we have excellent reasons to believe. We may have some reasons in favor of these beliefs, but those reasons are not so strong that we can regard the beliefs as solid facts. We can only proportion our belief to the evidence and be open to the possibility that we may be wrong. Very often such claims reside in areas that are marked by controversy—politics, religion, ethics, economics, and more. Among these notions, we must walk cautiously, avoid dogmatism, and follow the evidence as best we can. We should not assume that the claims we have absorbed from our upbringing and culture are beyond question.

That being said, there are good reasons for respecting the criterion of conservatism, properly understood. We are naturally reluctant to accept explanations that conflict with what we already know, and we should be. Accepting beliefs that fly in the face of our knowledge has several risks:

1. The chances of the new belief being true are not good (because it has no evidence in its favor, while our well-established beliefs have plenty of evidence on their side).
2. The conflict of beliefs undermines our knowledge (because we cannot know something that is in doubt, and the conflict would be cause for doubt).
3. The conflict of beliefs lessens our understanding (because the new beliefs cannot be plausibly integrated into our other beliefs).

Was the Moon Landing a Hoax?

A stunning conspiracy theory says yes. NASA faked the whole thing, you see. Here's NASA's side of the story:

All the buzz about the Moon began on February 15th when Fox television aired a program called *Conspiracy Theory: Did We Land on the Moon?* Guests on the show argued that NASA technology in the 1960s wasn't up to the task of a real Moon landing. Instead, anxious to win the Space Race any way it could, NASA acted out the Apollo program in movie studios. Neil Armstrong's historic first steps on another world, the rollicking Moon Buggy rides, even Al Shepard's arcing golf shot over Fra Mauro—it was all a fake! . . .

According to the show NASA was a blundering movie producer thirty years ago. For example, *Conspiracy Theory* pundits pointed out a seeming discrepancy in Apollo imagery: Pictures of astronauts transmitted from the Moon don't include stars in the dark lunar sky—an obvious production error! What happened? Did NASA film-makers forget to turn on the constellations?

Most photographers already know the answer: It's difficult to capture something very bright and something else very dim on the same piece of film—typical emulsions don't have enough "dynamic range." Astronauts striding across the bright lunar soil in their sunlit spacesuits were literally dazzling. Setting a camera with the proper exposure for a glaring spacesuit would naturally render background stars too faint to see.

Here's another one: Pictures of Apollo astronauts erecting a U.S. flag on the Moon show the flag bending and rippling. How can that be? After all, there's no breeze on the Moon. . . .

Not every waving flag needs a breeze—at least not in space. When astronauts were planting the flagpole they rotated it back and forth to better penetrate the lunar soil (anyone who's set a blunt tent-post will know how this works). So of course the flag waved! Unfurling a piece of rolled-up cloth with stored angular momentum will naturally result in waves and ripples—no breeze required! . . .

The best rebuttal to allegations of a "Moon Hoax," however, is common sense. Evidence that the Apollo program really happened is compelling: A dozen astronauts (laden with cameras) walked on the Moon between 1969 and 1972. Nine of them are still alive and can testify to their experience. They didn't return from the Moon empty-handed, either. Just as Columbus carried a few hundred natives back to Spain as evidence of his trip to the New World, Apollo astronauts brought 841 pounds of Moon rock home to Earth.

"Moon rocks are absolutely unique," says Dr. David McKay, Chief Scientist for Planetary Science and Exploration at NASA's Johnson Space Center (JSC). McKay is a member of the group that oversees the Lunar Sample Laboratory Facility at JSC where most of the Moon rocks are stored. "They differ from Earth rocks in many respects," he added.

"For example," explains Dr. Marc Norman, a lunar geologist at the University of Tasmania, "lunar samples have almost no water trapped in their crystal structure, and common substances such as clay minerals that are ubiquitous on Earth are totally absent in Moon rocks."

"We've found particles of fresh glass in Moon rocks that were produced by explosive volcanic activity and by meteorite impacts over 3 billion years ago," added Norman. "The presence of water on Earth rapidly breaks down such volcanic glass in only a few million years. These rocks must have come from the Moon!"[8]

So everything considered, the more conservative a theory is, the more plausible it is.[9]

Here's another example. Let's say that someone claims to have built a perpetual motion machine. A perpetual motion machine is supposed to function without ever stopping and without requiring any energy input from outside the machine; it is designed to continuously supply its own energy.

Now, this is an intriguing idea—that we shouldn't take too seriously. The problem is that the notion of a perpetual motion machine is not conservative at all. It conflicts with a very well-established belief—namely, one of the scientific laws of thermodynamics. The law of conservation of mass-energy says that mass-energy cannot be created or destroyed. A perpetual motion machine, though, would have to create energy out of nothing. Like any law of nature, however, the law of conservation of mass-energy is supported by a vast amount of empirical evidence. We must conclude, then, that it is extremely unlikely that anyone could escape the law of conservation of mass-energy through the use of any machine. (This fact, however, has not stopped countless optimistic inventers from claiming that they've invented such devices. When the devices are put to the test, they invariably fail to perform as advertised.)

It's possible, of course, that a new theory that conflicts with what we know could turn out to be right and a more conservative theory wrong. But we would need good reasons to show that the new theory was correct before we would be justified in tossing out the old theory and bringing in the new.

Science looks for conservative theories, but it still sometimes embraces theories that are departures (sometimes *radical* departures) from the well-worn, accepted explanations. When this dramatic change happens, it's frequently because other criteria of adequacy outweigh conservatism. We'll explore the creation and evaluation of scientific theories in the next chapter.

Occult or paranormal theories often run afoul of the criterion of conservatism. Take *dowsing*, for instance. Dowsing is the practice of detecting underground water by using a Y-shaped stick (known as a divining rod or dowsing rod), a pendulum, or another device. It's a folk tradition that's hundreds of years old. Dowsers claim to be able to detect the presence of underground water by walking over a given terrain and holding the two branches of the dowsing rod (one in each hand) with its point facing skyward away from the body. (This claim, as it turns out, is unsupported.) When the point of the rod dips toward the ground, that's supposed to indicate that water is beneath the dowser. It seems to the dowser (and sometimes to observers) that the rod moves on its own, as though under the influence of some hidden force.

One theory to account for the rod's movements is this: an unknown form of radiation emanating from the underground water pulls on the diving rod, causing it to move. (A well-supported alternative theory is that the movement of the divining rod in the dowser's hands is caused by suggestion and unconscious muscular activity in the dowser.) As it stands, the radiation theory is not testable, fruitful, or simple. But its major failing is its lack of conservatism. The claim about the strange, occult radiation conflicts with what scientists know about energy, radiation, and human sensory systems. It is possible that the dowser's radiation exists, but there is no reason to believe that it does and good reason to doubt it.

We will look at many more examples shortly, but before we go any further, you need to fully understand two crucial points about the nature of theory appraisal.

First, there is no strict formula or protocol for applying the criteria of adequacy. In deductive arguments there are rules of inference that are precise and invariable. But inference to the best explanation is a different animal. There are no precise rules for applying the criteria, no way to quantify how a theory measures up according to each criterion, and no way to rank each criterion according to its importance. Sometimes we may assign more weight to the criterion of scope if the theory in question seems comparable

The art of dowsing. What makes the rod dip?

to other theories in terms of all the remaining criteria. Other times we may weight simplicity more when considering theories that seem equally conservative or fruitful. The process of theory evaluation is not like solving a math problem—but more like diagnosing an illness or making a judicial decision. It is rational but not formulaic, and it depends on the dynamics of human judgment. The best we can do is follow some guidelines for evaluating theories generally and for applying the criteria of adequacy. Fortunately, this kind of help is usually all we need. (You'll get this kind of guidance in the following pages.)

Second, despite the lack of formula in theory assessment, the process is far from subjective or arbitrary. There are many distinctions that we successfully make every day that are not quantifiable or formulaic—but they are still objective. We cannot say exactly when day turns into night or when a person with a full head of hair becomes bald or when a puddle in the rain becomes a pond, but our distinctions between night and day or baldness and hirsuteness or puddles and ponds are clearly objective. Of course, there are cases that are not so clear-cut that give rise to reasonable disagreement among reasonable people. But there are also many instances that are manifestly unambiguous. Pretending that these states of affairs are unclear would be irrational. It would simply be incorrect to believe that broad daylight is nighttime or that a puddle is a pond.

EXERCISES

Exercise 9.6

1. When you are trying to decide between two theories, can you just rely on evidence alone to determine which theory is better?
* 2. In theory evaluation, what is the minimum requirement of consistency?
3. According to the text, what is a "best theory"?
4. According to the text, what are the criteria of adequacy?
5. What does it mean for a theory to be testable? fruitful? conservative?
* 6. What does it mean to say that a theory does not have much scope?
7. According to the text, are theories that posit paranormal entities simple? If not, why not?
8. What are the risks involved in accepting a nonconservative theory?

Exercise 9.7

Following are several pairs of theories used to explain various phenomena. For each pair, determine (1) which theory is simpler and (2) which one is more conservative.

1. Phenomenon: A sudden remission of cancer in a patient.
   Theories: Part of the natural cycle of the disease; the result of taking an elixir with "healing properties" unknown to science.

* 2. Phenomenon: The survival of a group of sailors whose ship sank at sea.
  Theories: Quick action by a group of magic dolphins; quick action by the Coast Guard rescue team.

3. Phenomenon: The winning of an election by a relatively unknown candidate.
  Theories: A last-minute blitz of TV ads; the candidate's endorsement by a famous convicted murderer.

* 4. Phenomenon: A "precognitive" dream (having one's dream come true).
  Theories: Coincidence; psychic energy emanating from the dreamer.

5. Phenomenon: The sudden friendliness of the North Korean government toward the United States.
  Theories: A big change in the leadership of the government; North Korea's realization that democratic capitalism is the way to go.

6. Phenomenon: The bizarre and dangerous behavior of your best friend.
  Theories: An allergy attack; the result of taking LSD.

* 7. Phenomenon: A hurricane hitting south Florida.
  Theories: El Niño; radiation from outer space.

8. Phenomenon: A huge drop in the incidence of childhood disease over the last fifty years.
  Theories: Mandatory immunization; lower levels of air pollution.

Telling Good Theories from Bad

Many (perhaps most) explanatory theories that you run into every day are easy to assess. They are clearly the best (or not the best) explanations for the facts at hand. The dog barked because someone approached the house. Your friend blushed because he was embarrassed. The senator resigned because of a scandal. In such cases, you may make inferences to the best explanation (using some or all of the criteria of adequacy) without any deep reflection. But at other times, you may need and want to be more deliberate, to think more carefully about which explanation is really best. In either case, it helps to have a set of guidelines that tells you how your inquiry *should* proceed if you're to make cogent inferences. Here, then, is the **TEST formula,** four steps to finding the best explanation:

> "For any scientific theory is born into a life of fierce competition, a jungle red in tooth and claw. Only the successful theories survive—the ones which in fact latched on to the actual regularities in nature."
>
> —Bas Van Fraassen

Step 1. State the **T**heory and check for consistency.
Step 2. Assess the **E**vidence for the theory.
Step 3. **S**crutinize alternative theories.
Step 4. **T**est the theories with the criteria of adequacy.

(In the next chapter, you will see that this formula is also one way of describing the general approach used in science to evaluate sets of theories.)

Step 1. State the theory and check for consistency. Before you can evaluate an explanatory theory, you must express it in a statement that's as clear and specific as possible. Once you do this, you can check to see if the theory meets the minimum requirement for consistency. If it fails the consistency test, you can have no good grounds for believing that it's correct. And, obviously, if the theory fails step 1, there's no reason to go to step 2.

Step 2. Assess the evidence for the theory. To critically evaluate any theory, you must understand any reasons in its favor—the empirical evidence or logical arguments that may support or undermine it. Essentially, this step involves an honest assessment of the empirical evidence relevant to the truth (or falsity) of the theory. To make this assessment, you must put to use what you already know about the credibility of sources, causal reasoning, and evidence from personal and scientific observations (topics covered in Chapters 4 and 8).

In this step, you may discover that the evidence in favor of a theory is strong, weak, or nonexistent. You may find that there is good evidence that seems to count against the theory. Or you may learn that the phenomenon under investigation did not occur at all. Whatever the case, you must have the courage to face up to reality. You must be ready to admit that your favorite theory has little to recommend it.

Step 3. Scrutinize alternative theories. Inference to the best explanation will not help us very much if we aren't willing to consider alternative explanations. Simply examining the evidence relevant to an eligible theory is not enough.

Theories can often appear stronger than they really are if we don't bother to compare them with others. To take an outrageous example, consider this theory designed to explain the popularity and seeming omnipresence of an American icon: Mickey Mouse is not an animated character but a living, breathing creature that lives in Hollywood. The evidence for this explanation is the following: (1) Millions of people (mostly children) worldwide believe that Mickey is real; (2) Walt Disney (Mickey's alleged creator) always talked about Mickey as if the mouse was real; (3) millions of ads, books, movies, and TV shows portray Mickey as real; (4) it's possible that through millions of years of Earth history a biological creature with Mickey's physical characteristics could have evolved; and (5) some say that if enough people believe that Mickey is real, then—through psychic wish fulfillment or some other paranormal process—he will become real.

Now, you don't believe that Mickey is real (do you?), even in the face of reasons 1–5. But you might admit that the Mickey theory is starting to sound more plausible. And if you never hear any alternative explanations, you might eventually become a true believer. (Anthropologists can plausibly argue that various cultures have come to believe in many very unlikely phenomena and exotic deities in large part because of *a lack of alternative explanations.*)

When you do consider an alternative explanation—for example, that Mickey is an imaginary character of brilliant animation marketed relentlessly to the world—the Mickey-is-real theory looks a little silly. And once you consider the evidence for this alternative theory (for example, documentation that Walt Disney created Mickey with pen and ink and that countless marketing campaigns have been launched to promote his creation), the other explanation looks even sillier.

Step 3 requires us to have an open mind, to think outside the box, to ask if there are other ways to explain the phenomenon in question and to consider the evidence for those theories. Specifically, in this step we must conscientiously look for competing theories, *then apply both step 1 and step 2 to each one of them.* This process may leave us with many or few eligible theories to examine. In any case, it's sure to tell us something important about the strength or weakness of competing theories.

Many times the criteria of adequacy can help us do a preliminary assessment of a theory's plausibility without our surveying alternative theories. For example, a theory may do so poorly regarding a particular criterion that we can conclude that, whatever the merits of alternative explanations, the theory at hand is not very credible. Such a clear lack of credibility is often apparent when a theory is obviously neither simple nor conservative.

Skipping step 3 is an extremely common error in the evaluation of explanations of all kinds. It is a supreme example of many types of errors discussed in earlier chapters—overlooking evidence, preferring available evidence, looking only for confirming evidence, and denying the evidence.

Step 3 goes against our grain. The human tendency is to grab hold of a favorite theory—and to halt any further critical thinking right there. Our built-in bias is to seize on a theory immediately—because we find it comforting or because we just "know" it's the right one—then ignore or resist all other possibilities. The result is a greatly increased likelihood of error and delusion and a significantly decreased opportunity to achieve true understanding.

Failure to consider alternative theories is the archetypal mistake in inquiries into the paranormal or supernatural (a topic we discuss in Chapter 10). The usual pattern is this: (1) You come across an extraordinary or impressive phenomenon, (2) you can't think of a natural explanation of the facts, and (3) you conclude that the phenomenon must not be natural but paranormal or supernatural. This conclusion, however, would be unwarranted. Just because you can't think of a natural explanation doesn't mean that there isn't one. You may simply be unaware of the correct natural explanation. In the past, scientists have often been confronted with extraordinary phenomena that they couldn't explain—phenomena that were later found to have a natural explanation.

Step 4. Test the theories with the criteria of adequacy. As we've seen, simply toting up the evidence for each of the competing theories and checking to see which one gets the highest score will not do. We need to measure the plausibility of the theories using the criteria of adequacy. The criteria can help us put any applicable evidence in perspective and allow us to make a judgment about theory plausibility even when there's little or no evidence to consider.

By applying the criteria to all the competing theories, we can often accomplish several important feats. We may be able to eliminate some theories immediately, assign more weight to some than others, and distinguish between theories that at first glance seem equally strong.

The best way to learn how to do step 4, as well as steps 1–3, is by example. Watch what happens when we assess the plausibility of theories for the following two phenomena.

Evaluating Theories: The TEST Formula

Step 1: State the **T**heory and check for consistency.

Step 2: Assess the **E**vidence for the theory.

Step 3: **S**crutinize alternative theories.

Step 4: **T**est the theories with the criteria of adequacy.

A Doomed Flight

In 1996, a Boeing 747 jetliner known famously as TWA flight 800 crashed in the Atlantic Ocean off Long Island, New York, killing all 230 people onboard. The incident, like most airline disasters, prompted a search for explanations for the crash and the proliferation of numerous explanatory theories, some of them alleging conspiracy, cover-up, and dark deeds. The FBI, the National Transportation Safety Board (NTSB), and others launched investigations, relying heavily on the criteria of adequacy to sort through competing theories. After many months of inquiry and debate, experts concluded that the probable cause of the crash was mechanical failure.

Using this incident as inspiration and guide, let's devise another story of a mysterious jetliner crash and examine the main theories to explain it. We will assume that all the facts in the case are known, that all relevant reports are honest (no intent to deceive), and that no other information is forthcoming. In other words, this is a very contrived case. But it suits our purposes here just fine. Here goes.

The (made-up) facts of the case are these: At 7:30 p.m. flight 200, a Boeing 747, departed JFK airport in New York on its way to London and then crashed into the Atlantic about thirty miles off the coast. While in flight, the plane exploded, sending debris over a wide area. The crash happened during a time of heightened awareness of possible terrorist attacks on aircraft.

Now let's try steps 1–4 on a supposedly popular theory and some of its leading alternatives. Here's the pop theory in question. Theory 1: *A missile fired by a terrorist brought down the plane.* This one meets the requirement

A Boeing 747 in trouble; from the movie *Eraser.*

for consistency, so our first concern is to assess the evidence for the theory. Those who favor this theory point to several pieces of evidence. Eyewitnesses said that they had seen a bright streak of light or flame speeding toward the plane. A few people said that they thought they were watching a missile intercept the plane. And a journalist reported on the Internet that the plane had been shot down by a missile fired from a boat.

There are, however, some problems with this evidence. Eyewitness reports of the movements of bright lights in a dark sky are notoriously unreliable, even when the eyewitnesses are experts. Under such viewing conditions, the actual size of a bright object, its distance from the observer, its speed, and even whether it's moving are extremely difficult to accurately determine by sight. Also another phenomenon could have easily been mistaken for a speeding missile: It's known that an explosion rupturing a fuel tank on a 747's wing can ignite long streams of fuel, which from the ground may look like a missile heading toward the plane. In addition, U.S. Coast Guard and Navy ships were in sight of every ship and boat in the area and report no firing of missiles or any other pyrotechnics. Because of the distances involved and other factors, firing a missile from the ground at flight 200 and hitting it was virtually impossible. Finally, an unsupported allegation—whether from a journalist or anyone else—is not good evidence for anything.

Then we have this explanation. Theory 2: *An alien spacecraft shot down the plane.* For the sake of illustration, we will assume that this explanation meets the consistency requirement. The evidence is this: Several people say that they saw a UFO fly near the plane just before the plane exploded. And tapes of radar images show an unknown object flying close to the 747.

These eyewitness accounts suffer from the same weakness as those mentioned in theory 1. Observations under the conditions described are not reliable. Thus, many alleged alien craft have turned out to be airplanes, helicopters, blimps, meteors, and even the planet Venus, an extremely bright object in the sky. Radar tapes may show many objects that are "unknown" to untrained observers but are identified precisely by experts. The radar evidence would be more impressive if flight controllers could not account for an object flying close to flight 200.

Theory 3: *A bomb on board the plane exploded, bringing the aircraft down.* This explanation is internally and externally consistent. The main evidence for it is the existence of trace amounts of explosive residue on a few of the recovered aircraft parts. Also, the story of the crash of flight 200 resembles the media account of the crash of another jetliner that's known to have been brought down by an onboard bomb.

This resemblance, though, is only that—it's not evidence that counts in favor of the bomb theory. And the explosive residue is not so telltale after all. Investigators determined that the residues are most likely left over from a security training exercise conducted on the plane a week earlier. Moreover, examination of the wreckage and patterns of damage to it suggests that a bomb was not detonated inside the aircraft.

Theory 4: *A mechanical failure involving the fuel tanks caused the explosion that brought the plane down.* This is an eligible theory. It's backed by evidence showing that an explosion occurred in one of the plane's fuel tanks. Experts know that a short circuit in wiring outside a fuel tank can cause excess voltage in wiring that's inside the tank, igniting the fuel. Investigators found that there was indeed a short circuit in some of the fuel tank wiring. In addition, explosions in several other 747s, some smaller planes, and various machine engines have been linked to faulty wiring in fuel tanks.

Theory 5: *A solar flare disrupted electrical circuits in the plane, releasing a spark that made the fuel tanks explode.* This too is an eligible theory. Solar flares are massive electromagnetic explosions on the surface of the sun. They can sometimes disrupt radio communications, even cause radio blackouts. Theory 5 says that a solar flare so dramatically affected electrical circuits in the plane that a spark was emitted that ignited the fuel. The rationale behind this theory is that flying planes, being closer to the sun, are more susceptible to the powerful effects of solar flares.

The evidence for this theory, however, is nil. There is no good reason to believe that a solar flare could ever cause a spark in an electrical circuit.

Now let's apply the criteria of adequacy to these explanations. We can see right away that all the theories do equally well in terms of testability and fruitfulness. They're all testable, and none has yielded any surprising predictions. Except for theory 4, they also have equal scope because they explain only the phenomenon they were introduced to explain, the crash of flight 200 (and perhaps similar airline crashes). Theory 4, however, has a slight edge because it can explain certain airline crashes as well as explosions in other systems that have wired fuel tanks. So if we are to distinguish between the theories, we must rely on the other criteria.

This is bad news for theories 2 and 5 because they fail the criteria of simplicity and conservatism. The evidence in favor of the alien spacecraft theory is extremely weak. Even worse, it conflicts with a great deal of human experience regarding visitors from outer space. We simply have no good evidence that anyone has ever detected any beings or technology from outer space. Moreover, the probability of Earth being visited by beings from outer space must be considered low (but not zero) in light of what we know about the size of the universe and the physical requirements of space travel. Likewise, the solar flare theory has no evidence to support it, and it too conflicts with what we know. There are no documented cases of solar flares causing sparks in electrical wiring. And neither theory is simple. Theory 2 assumes an unknown entity (aliens), and theory 5 assumes unknown processes (solar flares causing sparks in wiring). These are excellent grounds for eliminating theories 2 and 5 from the running.

That leaves theories 1, 3, and 4, which we must also sort out using the criteria of simplicity and conservatism. They fare equally well in terms of simplicity because none assumes any unknown or mysterious entities or processes. Conservatism, though, is a different story. Neither theory 1 nor 3 accords with the evidence. In each case, existing evidence counts *against* the theory. Theory 4, though, accords well with the evidence. It not only doesn't conflict with what we know, but the evidence also supports the theory in important ways. Theory 4, then, is the best explanation for the crash of flight 200 and the theory most likely to be true. And the explanation we started with, theory 1, is implausible.

An Amazing Cure

Homeopathy is an old theory that currently occupies an honored place among advocates of what is often called "alternative medicine"—health practices and hypotheses that are, for the most part, outside the realm of conventional medicine and medical science. Homeopathy is based on the idea that extremely tiny doses of substances that cause disease symptoms in a healthy person can alleviate similar symptoms in a sick person. Samuel Hahnemann (1755–1843), a German physician, was the first to apply this notion systematically. He also added what he called the "law of infinitesimals," the proposition that—contrary to the findings of science—the smaller the dose, the more powerful the medicine. So he treated people with drastically diluted substances—so diluted that, in many homeopathic medicines, not even one molecule of the substance remained. Hahnemann acknowledged this fact but believed that the substances somehow left behind an imperceptible "spirit-like" essence, or memory, that effected cures. This essence was supposed to revitalize the "vital force" in the body.

To be more precise, we can state the homeopathic theory like this: *Extremely dilute solutions of substances that produce symptoms in a healthy person can cure those same symptoms in a sick person.* This hypothesis is offered as an explanation of why people taking homeopathic remedies seem to get better. They get better because homeopathy works.

The leading alternative theory is this: *People taking homeopathic remedies feel better because of the placebo effect.* That is, homeopathy does not work as advertised, but people think that it does because of the power of placebos (inactive or fake treatments). The placebo effect is a very well-documented phenomenon in which people given a placebo respond with improvements in the way they feel. Scientists disagree over how much placebos can affect clinical conditions, but there is little doubt that placebos can have at least a modest impact on how people feel, especially their experience of pain.[10] Because placebos can have an effect, they are used in all well-designed clinical trials—that is, studies testing the effectiveness of treatments. (More on clinical testing and placebos in the next chapter.) There are other plausible alternative theories (such as the idea that people feel better because of the natural course of the disease), but we will restrict our analysis to the homeopathy and placebo theories.

Both are eligible theories. They are also both testable, so we must turn to the other criteria to help us judge their worth. The homeopathy theory has yielded no observable, surprising predictions, so it has no advantage in fruitfulness. The placebo theory has yielded several predictions (that a certain percentage of people who suffer from a particular illness and who get a placebo will feel better), but none of these are particularly surprising. The homeopathy theory has no scope because it tries to explain events by positing unknown forces and processes—which doesn't explain anything. The placebo theory, though, does have scope, explaining why people may feel better after trying a homeopathic remedy as well as why people with a variety of illnesses feel better after taking a placebo.

"Science is organized common sense where many a beautiful theory was killed by an ugly fact."

—Thomas H. Huxley

But in terms of simplicity, the homeopathy theory is in trouble. Homeopathy postulates both an undetectable essence and an unknown mysterious force. These assumptions alone are serious problems for the theory. The placebo theory, on the other hand, assumes no unknown forces, entities, or processes.

Finally, homeopathy runs afoul of the criterion of conservatism. It conflicts with a massive amount of scientific evidence in biochemistry and pharmacology. There is no verified instance of any substance having a stronger effect the more diluted it becomes. There isn't a single documented case of an extremely diluted solution (one in which not one molecule of the original substance remains) affecting any biological system. In addition, all available scientific evidence on the question gives little or no support to homeopathy. (Many studies have been conducted on homeopathic remedies, but several scientific reviews have concluded that the studies are seriously flawed or weak, offering no significant support to the theory.[11])

We can lay out these assessments as in the following table:

Criteria	Homeopathy	Placebo
Testable	Yes	Yes
Fruitful	No	No
Scope	No	Yes
Simple	No	Yes
Conservative	No	Yes

In the absence of a formula for weighting or ranking criteria, what plausible judgments can we make about the relative strengths of these two theories? It seems that we can ignore the criteria of testability and fruitfulness because both theories seem roughly even on these criteria—or at least no theory has a clear advantage over the other. We have decided, however, that homeopathy has no scope, while the placebo theory does.

Things become more clear when we consider the remaining criteria. There are stark differences between the two theories in simplicity and conservatism. Homeopathy is not simple, and any theory that posits an unknown entity is less plausible than one that does not—unless the other criteria of adequacy can somehow offset this disadvantage. But the other criteria are not much help for homeopathy. This judgment—the lack of simplicity and the resulting lower plausibility—seems clear-cut and is based on an unambiguous state of affairs. The homeopathy theory's lack of conservatism is also evident. The plausibility of any theory that flies in the face of such a mountain of established fact is near zero. So homeopathy's score must also be near zero. It is, therefore, a very poor explanation and strikingly inferior to the alternative explanation.

Without a detailed formula, without a weighting system, and without quantifying any criteria, we have arrived at a verdict regarding two competing theories. Deciding among theories is not always so straightforward, of course. But this lack of clear-cut answers is what gives rise to more research and more critical thinking.

EXERCISES

Exercise 9.8

Based on what you already know and the criteria of adequacy, determine which theory in each group is most plausible.

1. Phenomenon: A deadly illness striking everyone in a small town.
   Theories: (1) Resurgence of smallpox, (2) poison in the drinking water, (3) a failure to think positively.

2. Phenomenon: A sudden and dramatic drop in the price of most corporate stocks.
   Theories: (1) Rumors of a recession, (2) manipulation of the stock market by one powerful stockholder, (3) particularly nasty weather on the East Coast.

* 3. Phenomenon: Extraordinarily large humanlike footprints in the snow on a mountainside.
   Theories: (1) The legendary man-beast known as the Yeti, (2) falling rocks from the sky, (3) a very big human mountain climber.

4. Phenomenon: The construction of the Egyptian pyramids.
   Theories: (1) The work of clever Egyptian engineers and many slaves, (2) the work of Egyptians with the help of extraterrestrial beings, (3) the work not of the Egyptians but the ancient Romans.

5. Phenomenon: A large increase in the incidence of heart disease among middle-aged women.
   Theories: (1) The result of an increase in violence against women, (2) an increase in the amount of fat consumed by women over age forty-five, (3) an increase in the number of women who marry late in life.

6. Phenomenon: A peaceful march by hundreds of people in the streets of Washington, DC.
   Theories: (1) A group of activists protesting the killing of animals for food, (2) hundreds of people sleepwalking at the same time, (3) people going to a festival on the White House lawn.

Exercise 9.9

Evaluate the following theories using the TEST formula. As part of your evaluation:

a. State the claim to be evaluated.
b. Indicate what phenomenon is being explained.
c. Specify at least one alternative theory.
d. Use the criteria of adequacy to assess the two theories and determine which one is more plausible.
e. Write a paragraph detailing your reasons for your choice. Use your background knowledge to fill in any information about the theories and how well they do regarding each criterion.

1. A religious sect based in Boston predicts that the end of the world will occur on January 1, 2001. The world, of course, did not end then. The leader of the sect explains that the prophesy failed to come true because members of the sect did not have enough faith in it.

2. A small, secret society of corporate CEOs and international bankers runs the economies of the United States and Europe. For its own benefit and for its own reasons the society decides when these nations go into and come out of recession, what levels of production will be achieved by the oil industry, and what each country's gross national product will be. Members of the society are so rich and powerful that they are able to hide the society's activities from public view and operate without the knowledge of governments and ordinary citizens.

3. What is the greatest influence on the course of human history, its social and cultural development? Some say it's powerful ideas like socialism, democracy, human dignity, and scientific method. Some say it's the social movements that embody and promote these ideas. But the greatest influences are wrought by great leaders, who are not necessarily great thinkers. Throughout history, every time a great leader appeared—Moses, Alexander, Caesar, Napoleon, and the like—the world was irrevocably changed regardless of what ideas or social movements were in existence.

4. The primary cause of all wars is fear. When people are afraid of others—because of ignorance or perceived threats—they naturally respond with belligerence and acts of violence. If they have no fear of others, they tend to react rationally and calmly and to seek some sort of fair accommodation.

5. Scientists studied twenty terminal cancer patients, taking note of the overall mental attitudes of the patients. Some of them were characterized as having negative attitudes; they were often angry at their situation and experienced feelings of hopelessness and regret. But other patients were thought to have positive attitudes; they were generally upbeat, optimistic about their treatment, and hopeful. Most of those with positive attitudes lived longer than most of those with negative attitudes. A positive attitude can lengthen cancer patients' lives.

6. Anaïs said farewell to her favorite uncle as he boarded a plane for Paris. That night she dreamed that he was flying in a jetliner that suddenly ran into a powerful thunderstorm and extreme turbulence. The plane rocked from side to side, then descended rapidly into the night. The jetliner crashed into a mountain, killing all onboard. When she awoke the next day, she learned that her uncle's plane had encountered violent turbulence on the way to Paris and that several passengers, including her uncle, had been injured during the flight. She had just had one of those rare experiences known as a prophetic dream.

Exercise 9.10

Read the following passages and answer these questions for each one:

1. What is the phenomenon being explained?
2. What theories are given to explain the phenomenon? (Some theories may be unstated.)
3. Which theory seems the most plausible and why? (Use the criteria of adequacy.)
4. Which theory is the least plausible and why?
5. Regarding the most credible theory, what factors would convince you to regard it as even more plausible?
6. Regarding the least credible theory, what factors would convince you to regard it as much more plausible?

PASSAGE 1

"Since Venus rotates so slowly, we might be tempted to conclude that Venus, like Mercury, keeps one face always toward the Sun. If this hypothesis were correct we should expect that the dark side would be exceedingly cold. Pettit and Nicholson have measured the temperature of the dark side of Venus. They find that the temperature is not low, its value being only 29F degrees, much warmer than our stratosphere in broad daylight. It is unlikely that atmospheric currents from the bright side of Venus could perpetually heat the dark side. The planet must rotate fairly often to keep the dark side from cooling excessively."[12]

PASSAGE 2

"Parapsychologists claim man's ability to know when he is being stared at has existed since the time of primitive man and served, in those days, to warn him of impending danger and attack from savage beasts. They also believe this ability still exists in modern men and women today. Skeptics deny this claim and believe it is nothing more than superstition and/or a response to subtle signals from the environment that are not strong enough to let us know exactly what caused them. For example, if we are in a very dark room and we suddenly sense the presence of another person—even though we do not see or hear him—we may know he is there because of the person's shaving lotion, movement of air currents in the room, body heat, etc. In other words if we are warned of another's presence, it is likely due to subtle physical cues in the environment that we normally do not attend to—not to any so-called 'psychic' or paranormal ability!

"To determine if people can tell when they are being stared at, two demonstrations were completed. In the first, forty individuals were stared at for an average time of 8.6 minutes while they were eating, reading, or watching a computer screen or television. When they finished they were asked if they were aware they were being stared at. Of the forty a total of thirty-five reported they were 'totally unaware that anyone was looking at them.' For the other five there is good reason to believe they also were not aware they were being viewed.

In the second demonstration fifty students sat at a table in front of a one-way mirror and were observed by two experimenters, one minute at a time, five times during a twenty-minute observation period. The students' task was to try to guess when they were being stared at and report their degree of certainty. None of the fifty were able to correctly guess when they were being stared at. The mean accuracy score for the group was 1.24; the chance score for guessing was 1.25 out of a total of five guesses."[13]

KEY WORDS

ad hoc hypothesis	inference to the best explanation	testability
conservatism		TEST formula
criteria of adequacy	scope	theoretical explanation
fruitfulness	simplicity	

Summary
Explanations and Inference

- Even though an explanation is not an argument, an explanation can be part of an argument—a powerful inductive argument known as inference to the best explanation.
- In inference to the best explanation, we reason from premises about a state of affairs to an explanation for that state of affairs.

Theories and Consistency

- To be worthy of consideration, a theory must meet the minimum requirement for consistency.

Theories and Criteria

- We use the criteria of adequacy to judge the plausibility of a theory in relation to competing theories.
- The best theory is the one that meets the criteria of adequacy better than any of its competitors.
- The criteria of adequacy are testability (whether there is some way to determine if a theory is true), fruitfulness (the number of novel predictions made), scope (the amount of diverse phenomena explained), simplicity (the number of assumptions made), and conservatism (how well a theory fits with existing knowledge).

Telling Good Theories from Bad

- Judging the worth of a theory is a four-step process called the TEST formula: (1) Stating the theory and checking for consistency, (2) assessing the evidence for the theory, (3) scrutinizing alternative theories, and (4) testing the theories with the criteria of adequacy.

 ## Field Problems

1. Many companies have recently marketed products that are supposed to relieve various ills (arthritis, lower back pain, migraine headaches, tennis elbow, etc.) through the use of simple magnets. This "magnetic therapy" is said to work because magnetic fields generated by the magnets act on the body's processes or structures. Look at ads in magazines, on TV, or on the Internet to find a health claim made for one of these products. Then in a 150-word paragraph evaluate the claim in light of the criteria of simplicity and conservatism. Check for any relevant scientific research and information at www.quackwatch.com or www.hcrc.org/sram (*The Scientific Review of Alternative Medicine*).

2. Using the TEST formula, evaluate the theory that people are more likely to behave strangely or violently during a full moon than at other times. Do some research to uncover any evidence pertaining to this theory. Write a 200-word report summarizing your findings.

3. Do Internet research on conspiracy theories concerning the September 11, 2001, attack on the United States. They posit explanations of why or how the attack happened—explanations that are usually shockingly different from the explanations accepted by most Americans. Select one of these alternative theories and compare it to the prevailing standard explanation. Using the TEST formula, decide which theory is more plausible.

 ## Self-Assessment Quiz

Answers appear in "Answers to Self-Assessment Quizzes" (Appendix D).

1. What is the basic pattern of inference to the best explanation? How does this pattern differ from that of enumerative induction? analogical induction?

2. What is the minimum requirement for consistency?

3. What are the criteria of adequacy?

4. According to the text, what does it mean for a theory to be testable or untestable?

5. What is the TEST formula?

6. According to the text, in theory evaluation, when is a theory properly considered the best?

Each of the following theories is offered to explain John's apparently prophetic dream that a distant cousin would die in a plane crash. Indicate which theory (a) lacks simplicity, (b) is not conservative, (c) is untestable, and (d) has the most scope. (Some theories may merit more than one of these designations.)

7. The fact that John's dream happened to be about a plane crash involving his cousin was coincidence. We have many dreams, and some are likely to match real events from time to time.

8. In his dream, John was able to see into the future and "view" the plane crash.

9. The incident was an example of "synchronicity," in which events are paired in unusual but predetermined ways by cosmic forces.

10. John had calculated the odds of the crash even before he dreamed about it, so the dream was not a prophesy, but a memory of his calculation.

Indicate which theory in each of the following groups is most plausible.

11. Phenomenon: The rise in popularity of a newly elected president.
Theories: (1) The so-called honeymoon effect in which a new president enjoys popularity until he or she is involved in serious or controversial decisions, (2) the systematic manipulation of all polling organizations by the president's staff, (3) the influence of a powerful secret society controlling the media.

12. Phenomenon: Your friend has been skipping class, and you haven't seen her in days.
Theories: (1) She's in bed with the flu, (2) she has been kidnapped, (3) she has inherited millions of dollars and has decided to hang out with a better class of friends.

13. Phenomenon: Ships, boats, and planes have been disappearing off the coast of Florida for years.
Theories: (1) Considering the meteorological and atmospheric conditions of the area, it's normal for some craft to be lost from time to time; (2) the craft have been hijacked; (3) the ships, boats, and planes are simply off course.

14. Phenomenon: The rapid spread of an unknown, dangerous, viral disease throughout North America.
Theories: (1) The lack of awareness and defenses against a new mutated virus, (2) bureaucratic bungling at the Centers for Disease Control and Prevention, (3) a massive conspiracy of doctors who want higher fees for treating seriously ill patients.

Evaluate the following theories using the TEST formula. As part of your evaluation, (1) state the claim to be evaluated, (2) indicate what phenomenon is being explained, (3) specify at least one alternative theory, and (4) use the criteria of adequacy to assess the two theories and determine which one is more plausible.

15. People buy high-ticket merchandise because of subliminal advertising—their minds are being influenced by imperceptible stimuli designed by ad execs.

16. Skeptical scientists have never been able to find evidence for cold fusion, try as they may. That's because their skepticism skews their observations.

17. Eleanor won the state lottery twice in nine months. She must have a system that enables her to pick winning numbers.

18. He embezzled that money because his parents were divorced when he was very young.

19. Schoolchildren who do poorly in school are not dumb or handicapped. They perform poorly for one reason only: low or negative expectations of their teachers.

20. The woman has been displaying bizarre behavior for years, but recently she seems worse than ever. She sometimes suddenly begins screaming, saying that there are snakes crawling on the walls. She shakes uncontrollably at the slightest noise. And she has started to bleed from her palms. The priest says that she's possessed by demons, and he's right.

 Integrative Exercises

These exercises refer to lessons in Chapters 3 and 6–9.

1. What is a deductive argument?
2. What is a valid argument?
3. What is an inductive argument?
4. What is the logical pattern of *modus ponens*?

For each of the following arguments, specify the conclusion and premises and indicate whether it is deductive or inductive. If it's deductive, use Venn diagrams or truth tables to determine its validity. If it's inductive, indicate whether it's an enumerative, analogical, or causal induction and whether it's strong or weak. If necessary, add implicit premises and conclusions.

5. The problem is that if people realize that they can do their own buying and selling of stocks, they won't use brokers anymore. But people don't realize that yet. So people will continue to use brokers.

6. "After days of talking to Shiites in Karbala and Najaf, it is clear to this reporter that there is virtually no undercurrent of anti-Americanism in the heartland of Iraqi Shi'ism. Even some clerics who have just returned from exile in Iran were keen to advertise their goodwill toward the United States." [Amir Taheri, *New York Post*]

7. Every man I know has some kind of hangup about sex. What is it with men? They're all a bunch of sexual neurotics.

8. Either the prime minister sent troops into Iraq to grab the oil there, or he sent them to get rid of Saddam. Obviously, the point was not to take the oil, so the real reason must have been to oust Saddam.

9. "Hence a young man is not a proper hearer of lectures on political science; for he is inexperienced in the actions that occur in life, but its discussions start from these and are about these; and, further, since he tends to follow his passions, his study will be vain and unprofitable, because the end aimed at is not knowledge but action." [Aristotle, *Nichomachean Ethics*]

10. "For every needy illegal immigrant, there is a needy legal immigrant or U.S. citizen who could greatly benefit from educational assistance. Granting in-state tuition to illegal aliens is hardly fair when there are plenty of U.S. citizens and legal immigrants who cannot obtain the same benefits." [Letter to the editor, *Newsday*]

11. No kings are persons without power. All people without power are persons who spend their days being victims. Therefore, no kings are victims.

12. Vulgarity is abroad upon the land, and Hollywood is to blame. As vulgar, sexually explicit, tasteless movies have proliferated, so has the amount of vulgarity increased.

13. He's afraid of her. He avoids her all the time, and he won't look her in the eye.

14. Most teens arrested for committing some act of violence also play a lot of violent video games. These games are causing violent behavior among our youth.

Evaluate each of the following theories and indicate whether it is plausible or implausible.

15. The positions and movements of the stars and planets at the time of your birth can have a powerful effect on your life.

16. Clyde Moran was sent to prison for raping and murdering a woman in her home, and he spent fifteen years behind bars. He was convicted on the testimony of three witnesses who say that they saw him near the woman's house on the night of the murder. The district attorney now says that recent DNA evidence shows that the man who committed the crime is not Moran. But the word of three good witnesses is good enough for me. Moran killed that woman, and he should stay in prison where he belongs.

17. In Area 51, the famous portion of a military base near Groom Dry Lake in Nevada, the government is concealing real alien visitors or an actual space vehicle used by the visitors to reach Earth.

18. If people are homeless, it's because they chose to be homeless. In America, there are a hundred ways to get out of poverty—if you want to.

19. The large network news organizations have ignored most of the anti-war protests staged since 9/11. Coverage of any anti-war sentiment seems to be against media policy. This can only mean that top network execs have decided together that such coverage is not in their best interests.

20. When the street lights shined on the side of the building, a vague image appeared on the wall, a mixture of shadows and light. Most people say that the image shows the face of Jesus. This image is a holy sign from God.

Writing Assignments

1. In a one-page essay evaluate the theory that all major decisions made by the current U.S. president are politically motivated and have very little to do with the merits of ideas or programs. Use the TEST formula.

2. Think of the last time you caught a cold or the flu. Write a one-page paper evaluating at least two theories that explain how you first came in contact with the virus. Use the TEST formula.

3. Write a three-page paper in which you use the TEST formula to assess two theories meant to explain the existence of the pictures, videos, and rocks that NASA says were acquired on the moon.

4. Study Essay 18 ("Freedom of Expression: Protect Student Speech—Even 'Unwise' Bong Banner") and Essay 19 ("Freedom of Expression: Policy Reflects Common Sense"). Decide which essay presents the stronger arguments, and write a paper defending your view.

Judging
Scientific Theories

 CHAPTER OBJECTIVES

SCIENCE AND NOT SCIENCE

- Understand why science is not the same thing as technology, ideology, and scientism.

THE SCIENTIFIC METHOD

- Know the five steps of the scientific method.
- Understand the logic of scientific testing.
- Learn why no scientific hypothesis can be conclusively confirmed or conclusively confuted.

TESTING SCIENTIFIC THEORIES

- Using the steps of the scientific method, be able to explain how a scientist would go about testing a simple hypothesis in medical science.
- Understand why scientists use control groups, make studies double-blind, include placebos in testing, and seek replication of their work.

JUDGING SCIENTIFIC THEORIES

- Be able to list the five criteria of adequacy and explain what they mean.
- Understand how to apply the criteria of adequacy to the theories of evolution and creationism and why the text says that evolution is the better theory.

SCIENCE AND WEIRD THEORIES

- Be able to explain why evaluating weird claims might be worthwhile.

MAKING WEIRD MISTAKES

- Understand why it can be so easy to err when trying to evaluate weird theories.
- Be prepared to explain three major errors that people often make when they are trying to assess extraordinary experiences and theories.
- Learn the distinction between logical and physical possibility.

JUDGING WEIRD THEORIES

- Be able to use the TEST formula to evaluate extraordinary theories.
- Understand why eyewitness testimony is often unreliable.

S O THE WORLD IS CHOCKABLOCK WITH CLAIMS IN THE FORM OF EXPLANATIONS— *theoretical explanations*, to be more precise, about why something is the case or why something happens. An overwhelming number of such theories are offered to explain the cause of events: why the window broke, why the moon looks so pale, why Ralph stole the bike, why the stock market tanked. As critical thinkers, we do the best we can in evaluating these theories that come our way, testing them if possible, looking for alternative theories, and applying the criteria of adequacy. As it turns out, science is in the same line of work.

Science seeks to acquire knowledge and understanding of reality, and it does so through the formulation, testing, and evaluation of theories. When this kind of search for answers is both systematic and careful, science is being done. And when we ourselves search for answers by scrutinizing possible theories—and we do so systematically and carefully—we are searching scientifically.

Let's examine the scientific process more closely.

"The aim of science is not to open the door to infinite wisdom, but to set a limit to infinite error."

—Bertolt Brecht

Science and Not Science

First, let's explore what science is *not*.[1]

Science is not technology. Science is a way of searching for truth—a way that uses what's often referred to as *the scientific method.* Technology is not a search for truth; it's the production of products—DVDs, cell phones, wireless computers, robots that sweep the carpet, better mousetraps. Technology applies knowledge acquired through science to practical problems that science generally doesn't care about, such as the creation of electronic gadgets. Technology seeks facts to use in producing stuff. Science tries to understand how the world works not by merely cataloging specific facts but by identifying general principles that both explain and predict phenomena.

This nice distinction gets blurry sometimes when technologists do scientific research in order to build a better product or scientists create gadgets in order to do better scientific research. But, in general, science pursues knowledge; technology makes things.

Science is not ideology. Some people say that science is not a way of finding out how the world works, but a worldview affirming how the world is, just as Catholicism or socialism affirms a view of things. To some, science is not only an

Seven Warning Signs of Bogus Science

What would a distinguished scientist tell trial judges who must try to discern whether scientific testimony by an expert is credible? Robert L. Park is that scientist (as well as an author and professor of physics), and he has identified the following clues "that a scientific claim lies well outside the bounds of rational scientific discourse." He cautions, though, that "they are only warning signs—even a claim with several of the signs could be legitimate."

Claims for the existence of Bigfoot rest largely on the shaky underpinning of anecdotal evidence.

1. **The discoverer pitches the claim directly to the media.** The integrity of science rests on the willingness of scientists to expose new ideas and findings to the scrutiny of other scientists. Thus, scientists expect their colleagues to reveal new findings to them initially. An attempt to bypass peer review by taking a new result directly to the media, and then to the public, suggests that the work is unlikely to stand up to close examination by other scientists.

2. **The discoverer says that a powerful establishment is trying to suppress his or her work.** The idea is that the establishment will presumably stop at nothing to suppress discoveries that might shift the balance of wealth and power in society. Often, the discoverer describes mainstream science as part of a larger conspiracy that includes industry and government. Claims that the oil companies are frustrating the invention of an automobile that runs on water, for instance, are a sure sign that the idea of such a car is baloney.

3. **The scientific effect involved is always at the very limit of detection.** Alas, there is never a clear photograph of a flying saucer, or the Loch Ness monster. All scientific measurements must contend with some level of background noise or statistical fluctuation. But if the signal-to-noise ratio cannot be improved, even in principle, the effect is probably not real and the work is not science.

   Thousands of published papers in parapsychology, for example, claim to report verified instances of telepathy, psychokinesis, or precognition. But those effects show up only in tortured analyses of statistics. The researchers can find no way to boost the signal, which suggests that it isn't really there.

4. **Evidence for a discovery is anecdotal.** If modern science has learned anything in the past century, it is to distrust anecdotal evidence. Because anecdotes have a very strong emotional impact, they serve to keep superstitious beliefs alive in an age of science. The most important discovery of modern medicine is not vaccines or antibiotics; it is the randomized double-blind test, by means of which we know what works and what doesn't. Contrary to the saying, the word "data" is not the plural of "anecdote."

5. **The discoverer says a belief is credible because it has endured for centuries.** There is a persistent myth that hundreds or even thousands of years ago, long before anyone knew that blood circulates throughout the body or that germs cause disease, our ancestors possessed miraculous remedies that modern science cannot understand. Much of what is termed "alternative medicine" is part of that myth.

6. **The discoverer has worked in isolation.** The image of a lone genius who struggles in secrecy in an attic laboratory and ends up making a revolutionary breakthrough is a staple of Hollywood's science-fiction films, but it is hard to find examples in real life. Scientific breakthroughs nowadays are almost always syntheses of the work of many scientists.

7. **The discoverer must propose new laws of nature to explain an observation.** A new law of nature, invoked to explain some extraordinary result, must not conflict with what is already known. If we must change existing laws of nature or propose new laws to account for an observation, it is almost certainly wrong.[2]

ideology, but a most objectionable one—one that posits a universe that is entirely material, mechanistic, and deterministic. On this "scientific view," the world—including us—is nothing more than bits of matter forming a big machine that turns and whirs in predetermined ways. This mechanistic notion is thought to demean humans and human endeavors by reducing us to the role of cogs and sprockets.

But we can't identify science with a specific worldview. At any given time, a particular worldview may predominate in the scientific community, but this fact doesn't mean that the worldview is what science is all about. Predominant worldviews among scientists have changed over the centuries, but the general nature of science as a way of searching for truth has not. For example, the mechanistic view of the universe, so common among scientists in the seventeenth century, has now given way to other views. Discoveries in quantum mechanics (the study of subatomic particles) have shown that the old mechanistic perspective is incorrect.

Science is not scientism. One definition of *scientism* is the view that science is the only reliable way to acquire knowledge. Put another way, science is the only reliable road to truth. But in light of the reliability of our sense experience under

> "Science is not gadgetry. The desirable adjuncts of modern living, although in many instances made possible by science, certainly do not constitute science."
>
> —Warren Weaver

standard, unhindered conditions (see Chapter 4), this claim is dubious. We obviously do know many things without the aid of scientific methodology.

But there is a related point that is not so dubious. Science may not be the only road to truth, but it is an extremely reliable way of acquiring knowledge about the empirical world. (Many philosophers of science would go a step further and say that science is our *most reliable* source of knowledge about the world.) Why is science so reliable? Science embodies to a high degree what is essential to reliable knowing of empirical facts: systematic consideration of alternative solutions or theories, rigorous testing of them, and careful checking and rechecking of the conclusions.

Some would say that science is reliable because it is self-correcting. Science does not grab hold of an explanation and never let go. Instead, it looks at alternative ways to explain a phenomenon, tests these alternatives, and opens up the conclusions to criticism from scientists everywhere. Eventually, the conclusions may turn out to be false, and scientists will have to abandon the answers they thought were solid. But usually, after much testing and thinking, scientists hit upon a theory that does hold up under scrutiny. They are then justified in believing that the theory is true, even though there is some chance that it is flawed.

The Scientific Method

> "The essence of science: ask an impertinent question, and you are on the way to a pertinent answer."
> —Jacob Bronowski

The scientific method cannot be identified with any particular set of experimental or observational procedures because there are many different methods to evaluate the worth of a hypothesis. In some sciences such as physics and biology, hypotheses can be assessed through controlled experimental tests. In other sciences such as astronomy and geology, hypotheses usually must be tested through observations. For example, an astronomical hypothesis may predict the existence of certain gases in a part of the Milky Way, and astronomers can use their telescopes to check whether those gases exist as predicted.

The scientific method, however, does involve several steps, regardless of the specific procedures involved:

1. Identify the problem or pose a question.
2. Devise a hypothesis to explain the event or phenomenon.
3. Derive a test implication or prediction.
4. Perform the test.
5. Accept or reject the hypothesis.

Scientific inquiry begins with a problem to solve or a question to answer. So in step 1 scientists may ask: What causes X? Why did Y happen? Does hormone therapy cause breast cancer? Does aspirin lower the risk of stroke? How is it possible for whales to navigate over long distances? How did early hominids communicate with one another? Was the Big Bang an uncaused event?

In step 2 scientists formulate a hypothesis that will constitute an answer to their question. In every case there are facts to explain, and the hypothesis is an explanation for them. The hypothesis guides the research, suggesting what kinds of observations or data would be relevant to the problem at hand. Without a hypothesis, scientists couldn't tell which data are important and which are worthless.

Where do hypotheses come from? One notion is that hypotheses are generated through induction—by collecting the data and drawing a generalization from them to get a hypothesis. But this can't be the way that most hypotheses are formulated because they often contain concepts that aren't in the data. (Remember, theories generally reach beyond the known data to posit the existence of things unknown.) The construction of hypotheses is not usually based on any such mechanical procedure. In many ways, they are created just as works of art are created. Scientists dream them up. They, however, are guided in hypothesis creation by certain criteria—namely, the criteria of adequacy we examined in the last chapter. With testability, fruitfulness, scope, simplicity, and conservatism as their guide, they devise hypotheses from the raw material of the imagination.

Remember, though, that scientists must consider not just their favorite hypothesis, but alternative hypotheses as well. The scientific method calls for consideration of competing explanations and for their examination or testing at some point in the process. Sometimes applying the criteria of adequacy can immediately eliminate some theories from the running, and sometimes theories must be tested along with the original hypothesis.

In step 3 scientists derive implications, or consequences, of the hypothesis to test. As we've seen, sometimes we can test a theory directly, as when we simply check the lawnmower's gas tank to confirm the theory that it won't run because it's out of gas. But often theories cannot be tested directly. How would we directly test, for example, the hypothesis that chemical X is causing leukemia in menopausal women? We can't.

So scientists test indirectly by first deriving a test implication from a hypothesis and then putting that implication to the test. Deriving such an observational consequence involves figuring out what a hypothesis implies or predicts. Scientists ask, "If this hypothesis were true, what consequences would follow? What phenomena or events would have to obtain?"

Recall that we derived test implications in the problem of the car that wouldn't start in Chapter 9. One hypothesis was that the car wouldn't start because a vandal had sabotaged it. We reasoned that if a vandal had indeed sabotaged the car, there would be tracks in the snow around it. But there were no tracks, disconfirming the sabotage hypothesis.

The logic of hypothesis testing, then, works like this. When we derive a test implication, we know that if the hypothesis to be tested (H) is true, then there is a specific predicted consequence (C). If the consequence turns out to be false (it does not obtain as predicted), then the hypothesis is probably false, and we can reject it. The hypothesis, in other words, is disconfirmed. We can represent this outcome in a conditional, or hypothetical, argument:

If H, then C.
not-C.
Therefore, not-H.

This is, remember, an instance of *modus tollens,* a valid argument form. In this case, H would be false even if only one of several of its consequences (test implications) turned out to be false.

> "The whole of science is nothing more than a refinement of everyday thinking."
> —Albert Einstein

Are You Scientifically Literate?

Surveys conducted by the National Science Foundation (NSF) have consistently shown that Americans' understanding of science and the scientific process is limited and that belief in such things as psychic powers and UFOs is more widespread than we might expect in a scientifically advanced culture. For

years the NSF has been gauging public understanding of science using a nine-question knowledge survey. In 2012 Americans scored a 5.8 out of the 9 questions (65 percent). Here's the survey so you can test your own scientific literacy. Answers are at the end. (*Note:* More than 25 percent of respondents got question 3 wrong!)

1. The center of the Earth is very hot. True or false?
2. The continents have been moving their location for millions of years and will continue to move. True or false?
3. Does the Earth go around the sun, or does the sun go around the Earth?
4. All radioactivity is man-made. True or false?
5. Electrons are smaller than atoms. True or false?
6. Lasers work by focusing sound waves. True or false?
7. It is the father's gene that decides whether the baby is a boy or a girl. True or false?
8. Antibiotics kill viruses as well as bacteria. True or false?
9. Human beings, as we know them today, developed from earlier species of animals. True or false?

Answers: 1. True; 2. True; 3. The Earth goes around the sun; 4. False; 5. True; 6. False; 7. True; 8. False; 9. True.

On the other hand, we would get a very different situation if *C* turned out to be true:

If *H,* then *C.*
C.
Therefore, *H.*

Notice that this is an instance of affirming the consequent, an invalid argument form. So just because C is true, that doesn't necessarily mean that H is true. If a consequence turns out to be true, that doesn't *prove* that the hypothesis is correct. In such a result, the hypothesis is confirmed, and the test provides at least some evidence that the hypothesis is true. But the hypothesis isn't then established. If other consequences for the hypothesis are tested, and all the results are again positive, then there is more evidence that the hypothesis is correct. As more and more consequences are tested, and they are shown to be true, we can have increasing confidence that the hypothesis is in fact true. As this evidence accumulates, the likelihood that the hypothesis is actually false decreases—and the probability that it's true increases.

In step 4 scientists carry out the testing. Usually this experimentation is not as simple as testing one implication and calling it quits. Scientists may test many consequences of several competing hypotheses. As the testing proceeds, some hypotheses are found wanting, and they're dropped. If all goes well, eventually one hypothesis remains, with considerable evidence in its favor. Then step 5 can happen, as the hypothesis or hypotheses are accepted or rejected.

Because scientists want to quickly eliminate unworthy hypotheses and zero in on the best one, they try to devise the most telling tests. This means that they are on the lookout for situations in which competing hypotheses have different test consequences. If hypothesis 1 says that C is true, and hypothesis 2 says that C is false, a test of C can then help eliminate one of the hypotheses from further consideration.

As we've seen, implicit in all this is the fact that no hypothesis can ever be *conclusively* confirmed. It's always possible that we will someday find evidence that undermines or conflicts with the evidence we have now.

Likewise, no hypothesis can ever be *conclusively* confuted. When scientists test hypotheses, they never really test a single hypothesis—they test a hypothesis together with a variety of background assumptions and theories. So a hypothesis can always be saved from refutation by making changes in the background claims. (As we detailed in the previous chapter, sometimes these changes are made by constructing ad hoc hypotheses—by postulating unverifiable entities or properties.) In such situations, no amount of evidence logically compels us to conclusively reject a hypothesis.

 REVIEW NOTES

Steps in the Scientific Method

1. Identify the problem or pose a question.
2. Devise a hypothesis to explain the event or phenomenon.
3. Derive a test implication or prediction.
4. Perform the test.
5. Accept or reject the hypothesis.

But our inability to conclusively confirm or confute a hypothesis does not mean that all hypotheses are equally acceptable. Maintaining a hypothesis in the face of mounting negative evidence is unreasonable, and so is refusing to accept a hypothesis despite accumulating confirming evidence. Through the use of carefully controlled experiments, scientists can often affirm or deny a hypothesis with a high degree of confidence.

Testing Scientific Theories

Let's see how we might use the five-step procedure to test a fairly simple hypothesis. Suppose you hear reports that some terminal cancer patients have lived longer than expected because they received high doses of vitamin C. And say that the favored hypothesis among many observers is that the best explanation for the patients' surviving longer is that vitamin C is an effective treatment against cancer. So you decide to test this hypothesis: High doses of vitamin C can increase the survival time of people with terminal cancer. (Years ago, this hypothesis was actually proposed and tested in three well-controlled clinical trials.[3]) An obvious alternative hypothesis is that vitamin C actually has no effect on the survival of terminal cancer patients and that any apparent benefits are due mainly to the placebo effect (the tendency for people to temporarily feel better after they're treated, even if the treatment is a fake). The placebo effect could be leading observers to believe that people taking vitamin C are being cured of cancer and are thus living longer. Or the placebo effect could be making patients feel better, enabling them to take better care of themselves (by eating right or complying with standard medical treatment, for example), increasing survival time.

Now, if your hypothesis is true, what would you expect to happen? That is, what test implication could you derive? If your hypothesis is true, you would expect that terminal cancer patients given high doses of vitamin C would live longer than terminal cancer patients who didn't receive the vitamin (or anything else).

How would you conduct such a test? To begin with, you could prescribe vitamin C to a group of terminal cancer patients (called the experimental group) but not to another group of similar cancer patients (called the control group) and keep track of their survival times. Then you could compare the survival rates of the two groups. But many people who knowingly receive a treatment will report feeling better—even if the treatment is an inactive placebo. So any positive results you see in the treated group might be due not to vitamin C but to the placebo effect.

To get around this problem, you would need to treat both groups, one with vitamin C and the other with a placebo. That way, if most of the people getting the vitamin C live longer than expected and fewer of those in the placebo group do, you can have slightly better reason for believing that vitamin C works as advertised.

But even this study design is not good enough. It's possible for the people conducting the experiment, the experimenters, to unknowingly bias the results. Through subtle behavioral cues, they can unconsciously inform the test subjects which treatments are real and which ones are placebos—and this, of course, would allow the placebo effect to have full rein. Also, if the experimenters know

"The grand aim of all science is to cover the greatest number of empirical facts by logical deduction from the smallest number of hypotheses or axioms."
—Albert Einstein

"Science is an edged tool, with which men play like children, and cut their fingers."
—Arthur Eddington

FURTHER THOUGHT

Nonintervention (Population) Studies

Not all medical hypotheses are tested by treating (or not treating) groups of patients and analyzing the results (as in the vitamin C example). Many are tested without such direct intervention in people's lives. The former type of study is known as an intervention, or controlled, trial, while the latter is called, not surprisingly, a *nonintervention* study (also an *observational* or *population* study). The basic idea in a nonintervention study is to track the interplay of disease and related factors in a specified population, uncovering associations among these that might lead to better understanding or control of the disease process.

A typical nonintervention study might go like this: For seven years scientists monitor the vitamin E intake (from food and supplements) and the incidence of heart disease of 90,000 women. Evaluation of this data shows that the women with the highest amounts of vitamin E in their diets have a 40 percent lower incidence of heart disease. That is, for reasons unknown, a lower risk of heart disease is associated with a higher intake of vitamin E in women. This study does not show that higher intakes of vitamin E *cause* less heart disease, only that there is a link between them. Perhaps some other factor merely associated with vitamin E is the true protector of hearts, or maybe women who take vitamin E are more likely to do other things (such as exercise) that lower their risk of heart disease.

Generally, nonintervention studies cannot establish cause-and-effect relationships, though they may hint that a causal relationship is present. And sometimes multiple nonintervention studies yielding the same results can make a strong case for a causal connection. Intervention trials, however, *can* establish cause and effect.

Nonintervention studies have led scientists to some of the most important findings in preventive health. It was a series of such studies done over decades, coupled with other kinds of scientific data, that revealed that cigarette smoking caused cancer. And it was such investigations that showed that high blood pressure, high cholesterol, overweight, and smoking are risk factors for heart disease.

Note to critical thinkers: Very often the media misreport the results of nonintervention studies, reading cause and effect into a mere association. For example, if a single nonintervention study finds a link between chewing gum and better eyesight, a headline in the morning paper (or a TV newscaster) may proclaim that "Gum-chewing improves your eyesight!" Maybe, maybe not—but the study would not justify that conclusion.

which treatment is the real one, they can unintentionally misinterpret or skew the study results in line with their own expectations.

This problem can be solved by making the study *double-blind*. In double-blind experiments, neither the subjects nor the experimenters know who receives the real treatment and who the inactive one. A double-blind protocol for your vitamin study would ensure that none of the subjects would know who's getting vitamin C, and neither would the experimenters.

What if you have a double-blind setup but most of the subjects in the vitamin C group were sicker to begin with than those in the placebo control group? Obviously, this would bias the results, making the vitamin C treatment look less effective—even if it *is* effective. To avoid this skewing, you would need to ensure that each group is as much alike as possible to start—with all subjects being around the same age, same physical condition, same stage of cancer, and so on.

Finally, you would need to run some statistical tests to ensure that your results are not a fluke. Even in the most tightly controlled studies, it's possible that the outcome is the result of random factors that cannot be controlled. Statisticians have standard methods for determining when experiment results are likely, or not likely, to be due to chance.

Suppose you design your study well and you conduct it. The results: The patients receiving the high doses of vitamin C did not live longer than the placebo group. In fact, all the subjects lived about the same length of time. Therefore, your hypothesis is disconfirmed. On the other hand, the alternative hypothesis—that vitamin C has no measurable effect on the survival of terminal cancer patients—is confirmed.

Should you now reject the vitamin C theory? Not yet. Even apparently well-conducted studies can have hidden mistakes in them, or there can be factors that the experimenters fail to take into account. This is why scientists insist on study *replication*—the repeating of an experiment by different groups of scientists. If the study is replicated by other scientists, and the study results hold up, then you can be more confident that the results are solid. In such a case, you could safely reject the vitamin C hypothesis. (This is, in fact, what scientists did in the real-life studies of vitamin C and cancer survival.)

At this point, when evidence has been gathered that can bear on the truth of the hypothesis in question, good scientific judgment is crucial. It's here that consideration of other competing hypotheses and the criteria of adequacy again come into play. At this stage, scientists need to decide whether to reject or accept a hypothesis—or modify it to improve it.

Judging Scientific Theories

As you can see, theory testing is part of the broader effort to assess the merits of one theory against a field of alternatives. And as you know by now, this broader effort will always involve, explicitly or implicitly, the application of the criteria of adequacy to the theories in question:

- Testability: Whether there's some way to determine if a theory is true
- Fruitfulness: The number of novel predictions made

> "When, however, the lay public rallies around an idea that is denounced by distinguished but elderly scientists and supports that idea with great fervour and emotion—the distinguished but elderly scientists are then, after all, probably right."
> —Isaac Asimov

- Scope: The amount of diverse phenomena explained
- Simplicity: The number of assumptions made
- Conservatism: How well a theory fits with existing knowledge

Let's study two important examples to see how scientists manage this task: The first is a classic case from the history of science; the second, a contemporary tale of what many perceive as a battle between science and religion. Notice that the steps itemized by the TEST formula are implicit in the evaluation process.

Copernicus Versus Ptolemy

Consider the historic clash between the geocentric (Earth-centered) and the heliocentric (sun-centered) theories of planetary motion. It's difficult to imagine two rival theories that have more profoundly influenced how humanity views itself and its place in the universe.

In the beginning was the geocentric view. Aristotle got things going by putting forth the theory that a spherical Earth was at the center of a spherical universe consisting of a series of concentric, transparent spheres. On one celestial sphere we see the sun, the moon, and the known planets. On the outermost sphere we behold the stars. All the heavenly bodies rotate in perfect circles around the stationary Earth. The heavenly bodies are pure, incorruptible, and unchanging; the Earth, impure, corruptible, and transient.

 FURTHER THOUGHT

Copernicus on Ptolemy's System

Copernicus was shocked at how complex and seemingly arbitrary Ptolemy's revered system was. He thought that Ptolemy, through countless revisions and additions, had created not a beautiful model—but a kind of monster. As Copernicus put it,

> It is as though an artist were to gather the hands, feet, head and other members for his images from diverse models, each part excellently drawn, but not related to a single body, and since they in no way match each other, the result would be a monster rather than a man.

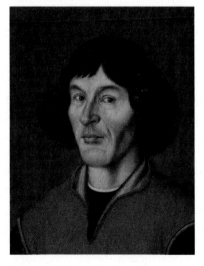

Nicolaus Copernicus (1473–1543).

"IT'S BLACK, AND IT LOOKS LIKE A HOLE. I'D SAY IT'S A BLACK HOLE."

Then came the great astronomer and mathematician Ptolemy, who flourished in Alexandria between 127 and 148 C.E. He discovered inconsistencies in the traditional geocentric system between the predicted and observed motions of the planets. He found, in other words, that Aristotle's theory was not conservative, a crucial failing. So he fine-tuned the old view, adding little circular motions (called epicycles) along the planet orbits and many other minor adjustments. He also allowed for an odd asymmetry in which the center of planet orbits was not exactly the center of Earth—all this so the theory would match up to astronomical observations. By the time Ptolemy finished tinkering he had posited eighty circles and epicycles—eighty different planetary motions—to explain the movements of the sun, moon, and five known planets.

The result was a system far more complex than Aristotle's was. But the revised theory worked well enough for the times, and it agreed better than the earlier theory did with observational data. Despite the complications, learned people could use Ptolemy's system to calculate the positions of the planets with enough accuracy to effectively manage calendars and astrological charts. So for fifteen centuries astronomers used Ptolemy's unwieldy, complex theory to predict celestial events and locations. In the West, at least, Earth stood still in the center of everything as the rest of the universe circled around it.

The chief virtue of the Ptolemaic system, then, was conservatism. It fit, mostly, with what astronomers knew about celestial goings-on. It was also testable, as any scientific theory should be. Its biggest failing was simplicity—or the lack thereof. The theory was propped up by numerous assumptions for the purpose of making the theory fit the data.

Enter Nicolaus Copernicus (1473–1543). He was disturbed by the complexity of Ptolemy's system. It was a far cry from the simple theory that Aristotle bequeathed to the West. Copernicus proposed a heliocentric theory in which Earth and the other planets orbit the sun, the true center of the universe. In doing so, he greatly simplified both the picture of the heavens and the calculations required to predict the positions of planets.

Copernicus's theory was simpler than Ptolemy's on many counts, but one of the most impressive was retrograde motion, a phenomenon that had stumped astronomers for centuries. From time to time, certain planets seem to reverse

"[Natural selection] has no vision, no foresight, no sight at all. If it can be said to play the role of watchmaker in nature, it is the blind watchmaker."

—Richard Dawkins

their customary direction of travel across the skies—to move backward! Ptolemy explained this retrograde motion by positing yet more epicycles, asserting that planets orbiting Earth will often orbit around a point on the larger orbital path. Seeing these orbits within orbits from Earth, an observer would naturally see the planets sometimes backing up.

But the Copernican theory could easily explain retrograde motion without all those complicated epicycles. As the outer planets (Mars, Jupiter, Saturn) orbit the sun, so does Earth, one of the inner planets. The outer planets, though, move much slower than Earth does. On its own orbital track, Earth sometimes passes the outer planets as they lumber along on their orbital track, just as a train passes a slower train on a parallel track. When this happens, the planets appear to move backward, just as the slower train seems to reverse course when the faster train overtakes it.

Copernicus's theory, however, was not superior on every count. It explained a great many astronomical observations, but Ptolemy's theory did too, so they were about even in scope. It had no big advantage in fruitfulness over the Ptolemaic system. It made no impressive predictions of unknown phenomena. Much more troubling, it seemed to conflict with some observational data.

One test implication of the Copernican theory is the phenomenon known as *parallax*. Critics of the heliocentric view claimed that if the theory were true, then as Earth moved through its orbit, stars closest to it should seem to shift their position relative to stars farther away. There should, in other words, be parallax. But no one had observed parallax.

Copernicus and his followers responded to this criticism by saying that stars were too far away for parallax to occur. As it turned out, they were right about this, but confirmation didn't come until 1832 when parallax was observed with more powerful telescopes.

Another test implication seemed to conflict with the heliocentric model. Copernicus reasoned that if the planets rotate around the sun, then they should show phases just as the moon shows phases due to the light of the sun falling on it at different times. But in Copernicus's day, no one could see any such planetary phases. Fifty years later, though, Galileo used his new telescope to confirm that Venus had phases.

Ultimately, scientists accepted the Copernican model over Ptolemy's because of its simplicity—despite what seemed at the time like evidence against the theory. As Copernicus said, "I think it is easier to believe this [sun-centered view] than to confuse the issue by assuming a vast number of Spheres, which those who keep the Earth at the center must do."[4]

Evolution Versus Creationism

Few scientific theories have been more hotly debated among nonscientists than evolution and its rival, creationism (or creation science). Both theories purport to explain the origin and existence of biological life on Earth, and each claims to be a better explanation than the other. Can science decide this contest? Yes. Despite the complexity of the issues involved and the mixing of religious themes

"Science is an integral part of culture. It's not this foreign thing, done by an arcane priesthood. It's one of the glories of human intellectual tradition."

—Stephen Jay Gould

"It is a good morning exercise for a research scientist to discard a pet hypothesis every day before breakfast. It keeps him young."
—Konrad Lorenz

💡 **FURTHER THOUGHT**

Can You See Evolution?

Critics of the theory of evolution often ask, "If evolution occurs, why can't we see it?" Here's how the National Academy of Sciences responds to this objection (http://books.nap.edu/html/creationism/evidence.html):

> Special creationists argue that "no one has ever seen evolution occur." This misses the point about how science tests hypotheses. We don't see Earth going around the sun or the atoms that make up matter. We "see" their consequences. Scientists infer that atoms exist and Earth revolves because they have tested predictions derived from these concepts by extensive observation and experimentation.
>
> Furthermore, on a minor scale, we "experience" evolution occurring every day. The annual changes in influenza viruses and the emergence of antibiotic-resistant bacteria are both products of evolutionary forces. . . . On a larger scale, the evolution of mosquitoes resistant to insecticides is another example of the tenacity and adaptability of organisms under environmental stress. Similarly, malaria parasites have become resistant to the drugs that were used extensively to combat them for many years. As a consequence, malaria is on the increase, with more than 300 million clinical cases of malaria occurring every year.

with the nonreligious, good science can figure out which theory is best. Remember that the best theory is the one that explains the phenomenon and measures up to the criteria of adequacy better than any of its competitors. There is no reason that the scientific approach cannot provide an answer here—even in this thorniest of thorny issues.

Neither the term "evolution" nor the concept began with Charles Darwin (1809–1882), the father of evolutionary theory. The word showed up in English as early as 1647. The ancient Greek philosopher Anaximander (c. 611–547 B.C.E.) was actually the first evolutionary theorist, inferring from some simple observations that humans must have evolved from an animal and that this evolution must have begun in the sea. But in his famous book *On the Origin of Species* (1859), Darwin distilled the theory of evolution into its most influential statement.

Scientists have been fine-tuning the theory ever since, as new evidence and new insights pour in from many different fields, such as biochemistry and genetics. But the basic idea has not changed: Living organisms adapt to their environments through inherited characteristics, which results in changes in succeeding generations. Specifically, the offspring of organisms differ physically from their parents in various ways, and these differences can be passed on genetically to their offspring. If an offspring has an inherited trait (such as sharper vision or a larger brain) that increases its chances of surviving long enough to reproduce, the individual is more likely to survive and pass the trait on to the next generation. After several generations, this useful trait, or adaptation, spreads throughout a whole population of individuals, differentiating the population from its ancestors. *Natural selection* is the name that Darwin gave to this process.

Creation science, on the other hand, maintains that (1) the universe and all life was created suddenly, out of nothing, only a few thousand years ago (six thousand to ten thousand is the usual range); (2) natural selection could not have produced living things from a single organism; (3) species change very little over time; (4) man and apes have a separate ancestry; and (5) the Earth's geology can be explained by catastrophism, including a worldwide flood.[5]

© 2002 by Sidney Harris. www.ScienceCartoonsPlus.com

The first thing we should ask about these two theories is whether they're testable. The answer is yes. Recall that a theory is testable if it predicts or explains something other than what it was introduced to explain. On this criterion, evolution is surely testable. It explains, among other things, why bacteria develop resistance to antibiotics, why there are so many similarities between humans and other primates, why new infectious diseases emerge, why the chromosomes of closely related species are so similar, why the fossil record shows the peculiar progression of fossils that it does, and why the embryos of related species have such similar structure and appearance.

Creationism is also testable. It too explains something other than what it was introduced to explain. It claims that Earth's geology was changed in a worldwide flood, that the universe is only a few thousand years old, that all species were created at the same time, and that species change very little over time.

Innumerable test implications have been derived from evolutionary theory, and innumerable experiments have been conducted, confirming the theory. For example, if evolution is true, then we would expect to see systematic change in the fossil record from simple creatures at the earlier levels to more complex individuals at the more recent levels. We would expect not to see a reversal of this configuration. And this sequence is exactly what scientists see time and time again.

Creationism, however, has not fared as well. Its claims have not been borne out by evidence. In fact, they have consistently conflicted with well-established scientific findings.

This latter point means that creationism fails the criterion of conservatism—it conflicts with what we already know. For example, the scientific evidence shows that Earth is not six thousand to ten thousand years old—but billions of years old. According to the National Academy of Sciences:

> There are no valid scientific data or calculations to substantiate the belief that Earth was created just a few thousand years ago. [There is a] vast amount of evidence for the great age of the universe, our galaxy, the Solar system, and Earth from astronomy, astrophysics, nuclear physics, geology, geochemistry, and geophysics. Independent scientific methods consistently give an age for Earth and the Solar system of about 5 billion years, and an age for our galaxy and the universe that is two to three times greater.[6]

Creationism also fails the criterion of conservatism on the issue of a geology-transforming universal flood. Again, the National Academy of Sciences:

> Nor is there any evidence that the entire geological record, with its orderly succession of fossils, is the product of a single universal flood that occurred a few thousand years ago, lasted a little longer than a year, and covered the highest mountains to a depth of several meters. On the contrary, intertidal and terrestrial deposits demonstrate that at no recorded time in the past has the entire planet been under water. . . . The belief that Earth's sediments, with their fossils, were deposited in an orderly sequence in a year's time defies all geological observations and physical principles concerning sedimentation rates and possible quantities of suspended solid matter.[7]

Has either theory yielded any novel predictions? Evolution has. It has predicted, for example, that new species should still be evolving today; that the fossil record should show a movement from older, simpler organisms to younger, more complex ones; that proteins and chromosomes of related species should be similar; and that organisms should adapt to changing environments. These and many other novel predictions have been confirmed. Creationism has made some novel claims, as we saw earlier, but none of these have been supported by good evidence. Creationism is not a fruitful theory.

The criterion of simplicity also draws a sharp contrast between the two theories. Simplicity is a measure of the number of assumptions that a theory makes. Both theories make assumptions, but creationism assumes much more. Creationism assumes the existence of a creator and unknown forces. Proponents of creationism readily admit that we do not know how the creator created nor what creative processes were used.

In this contest of theories, the criterion of scope—the amount of diverse phenomena explained—is probably more telling than any of the others. Biological evolution explains a vast array of phenomena in many fields of science. In fact, a great deal of the content of numerous scientific fields—genetics, physiology, biochemistry, neurobiology, and more—would be deeply perplexing without

"If we are going to teach creation science as an alternative to evolution, then we should also teach the stork theory as an alternative to biological reproduction."
—Judith Hayes

Gaps in the Fossil Record?

Creationists hold that if evolution were true, then there should be fossil remains of transitional organisms. But, they insist, there are gaps where transitional fossils should be, so evolution didn't happen. But this claim is incorrect. There are transitional fossils:

In 2006 scientists discovered this 375-million-year-old fossil of a species that spans the gap between fish and land animals.

Gaps in the fossil record are not even a critical test of evolution vs. progressive creation, as evolution also predicts gaps. There are some 2 million described species of living animals, but only 200,000 described fossil species. Thus, it is impossible to provide a minutely detailed history for every living species. This is because, first, the fossil record has not been completely explored. It is pretty hard to overlook a dinosaur bone! Yet, though dinosaurs have been excavated for over 150 years, 40% of the known species were found in the last 20 years or so (*Discover*, March 1987, p. 46). It is likely many more dinosaur species remain to be found. Second, sedimentary rocks were formed locally in lakes, oceans, and river deltas, so many upland species were never fossilized. Third, many deposits that were formed have been lost to erosion. Thus, a complete record is impossible.

However, there is a critical test. Evolution predicts that some complete series should be found, while [creationists predict] that none should ever be found. In fact, many excellent series exist. The evolution of the horse is known in exquisite detail from *Hyracotherium* (*Eohippus*) to the modern horse (G. G. Simpson, *Horses*, 2nd ed. Oxford, 1961). Scientific creationists have been forced to claim that the series is but an allowed variation within a created "kind." If so, then rhinoceroses, tapirs, and horses are all the same "kind," as they can be traced to ancestors nearly identical to *Hyracotherium*! All of these fossils lie in the correct order by both stratigraphic and radioisotope dating.

Another critical test is Darwin's prediction that ". . . our early ancestors lived on the African continent. . . ." (*The Descent of Man*, p. 158). An excellent, detailed series of skulls and some nearly complete skeletons now connect modern man to African australopithecines. Some of the extinct australopithecines had brains about the size and shape of those of chimpanzees.[8]

the theory of evolution. As the eminent geneticist Theodosius Dobzhansky put it, "Nothing in biology makes sense except in the light of evolution."[9]

Virtually all scientists would agree—and go much further:

> It helps to explain the emergence of new infectious diseases, the development of antibiotic resistance in bacteria, the agricultural relationships among wild and domestic plants and animals, the composition of Earth's atmosphere, the molecular machinery of the cell, the similarities between human beings and other primates, and countless other features of the biological and physical world.[10]

"My theory of evolution is that Darwin was adopted."
—Steven Wright

Creationism, however, can explain none of this. And it provokes, not solves, innumerable mysteries: What caused the worldwide flood? Where did all that water come from? Where did it all go? Why does Earth seem so ancient (when it's said to be so young)? How did the creator create the entire universe suddenly—out of nothing? Why does the fossil record seem to suggest evolution and not creation? So many questions are an indication of diminished scope and decreased understanding.

Good scientists must be prepared to admit this much: If creationism meets the criteria of adequacy as well as evolution does, then creationism must be as good a theory as evolution. But creationism fails to measure up to the criteria of adequacy. On every count it shows itself to be inferior. Scientists then are justified in rejecting creationism in favor of evolution. And this is exactly what they do.

 FURTHER THOUGHT

The Clash over "Intelligent Design"

A controversial view known as intelligent design (ID) is the latest conceptual challenge to evolution, maintaining that biological life is much too complex to be fully explained by evolutionary processes. Take a moment to reflect on this synopsis of part of the debate:

> The proponents of intelligent design, a school of thought that some have argued should be taught alongside evolution in the nation's schools,

say that the complexity and diversity of life go beyond what evolution can explain.

Biological marvels like the optical precision of an eye, the little spinning motors that propel bacteria and the cascade of proteins that cause blood to clot, they say, point to the hand of a higher being at work in the world.

In one often-cited argument, Michael J. Behe, a professor of biochemistry at Lehigh University and a leading design theorist, compares complex biological phenomena like blood clotting to a mousetrap: Take away any one piece—the spring, the baseboard, the metal piece that snags the mouse—and the mousetrap stops being able to catch mice.

Similarly, Dr. Behe argues, if any one of the more than 20 proteins involved in blood clotting is missing or deficient, as happens in hemophilia, for instance, clots will not form properly.

Such all-or-none systems, Dr. Behe and other design proponents say, could not have arisen through the incremental changes that evolution says allowed life to progress to the big brains and the sophisticated abilities of humans from primitive bacteria.

These complex systems are "always associated with design," Dr. Behe, the author of the 1996 book *Darwin's Black Box*, said in an interview. "We find such systems in biology, and since we know of no other way that these things can be produced, Darwinian claims notwithstanding, then we are rational to conclude they were indeed designed."

It is an argument that appeals to many Americans of faith.

But mainstream scientists say that the claims of intelligent design run counter to a century of research supporting the explanatory and predictive power of Darwinian evolution, and that the design approach suffers from fundamental problems that place it outside the realm of science. For one thing, these scientists say, invoking a higher being as an explanation is unscientific.

"One of the rules of science is, no miracles allowed," said Douglas H. Erwin, a paleobiologist at the Smithsonian Institution. "That's a fundamental presumption of what we do."

That does not mean that scientists do not believe in God. Many do. But they see science as an effort to find out how the material world works, with nothing to say about why we are here or how we should live.

And in that quest, they say, there is no need to resort to otherworldly explanations. So much evidence has been provided by evolutionary studies that biologists are able to explain even the most complex natural phenomena and to fill in whatever blanks remain with solid theories.

This is possible, in large part, because evolution leaves tracks like the fossil remains of early animals or the chemical footprints in DNA that have been revealed by genetic research.

For example, while Dr. Behe and other leading design proponents see the blood-clotting system as a product of design, mainstream scientists see it as a result of a coherent sequence of evolutionary events.

Early vertebrates like jawless fish had a simple clotting system, scientists believe, involving a few proteins that made blood stick together, said Russell F. Doolittle, a professor of molecular biology at the University of California, San Diego.

Scientists hypothesize that at some point, a mistake during the copying of DNA resulted in the duplication of a gene, increasing the amount of protein produced by cells.

Most often, such a change would be useless. But in this case the extra protein helped blood clot, and animals with the extra protein were more likely to survive and reproduce. Over time, as higher-order species evolved, other proteins joined the clotting system. For instance, several proteins involved in the clotting of blood appear to have started as digestive enzymes.

By studying the evolutionary tree and the genetics and biochemistry of living organisms, Dr. Doolittle said, scientists have largely been able to determine the order in which different proteins became involved in helping blood clot, eventually producing the sophisticated clotting mechanisms of humans and other higher animals. The sequencing of animal genomes has provided evidence to support this view.

For example, scientists had predicted that more primitive animals such as fish would be missing certain blood-clotting proteins. In fact, the recent sequencing of the fish genome has shown just this.

"The evidence is rock solid," Dr. Doolittle said. . . .

Dr. Behe, however, said he might find it compelling if scientists were to observe evolutionary leaps in the laboratory. He pointed to an experiment by Richard E. Lenski, a professor of microbial ecology at Michigan State University, who has been observing the evolution of *E. coli* bacteria for more than 15 years. "If anything cool came out of that," Dr. Behe said, "that would be one way to convince me."

Dr. Behe said that if he was correct, then the *E. coli* in Dr. Lenski's lab would evolve in small ways but never change in such a way that the bacteria would develop entirely new abilities.

In fact, such an ability seems to have developed. Dr. Lenski said his experiment was not intended to explore this aspect of evolution, but nonetheless, "We have recently discovered a pretty dramatic exception, one where a new and surprising function has evolved," he said.

Dr. Lenski declined to give any details until the research is published. But, he said, "If anyone is resting his or her faith in God on the outcome that our experiment will not produce some major biological innovation, then I humbly suggest they should rethink the distinction between science and religion."

Dr. Behe said, "I'll wait and see."[11]

As it turned out, Dr. Lenski's experiment showed that the bacteria did indeed evolve, acquiring many significant mutations and new abilities.

 EXERCISES

Exercise 10.1

REVIEW QUESTIONS

1. How does science differ from technology?
2. What is the scientific method?
3. Can science be identified with a particular worldview?
4. According to the text, what is scientism?
5. According to the text, why is science such a reliable way of knowing?
* 6. What are the five steps of the scientific method?
7. Can hypotheses be generated through induction? Why or why not?
8. What does it mean to derive a test implication from a theory?
* 9. What is the conditional argument reflecting the fact that a theory is disconfirmed?
10. What is the conditional argument reflecting the fact that a theory is confirmed?
11. Can theories be conclusively confirmed? Why or why not?
* 12. Can theories be conclusively disconfirmed? Why or why not?
13. According to the text, is creationism as good a scientific theory as evolution? Why or why not?

Exercise 10.2

For each of the following phenomena, devise a hypothesis to explain it and derive a test implication to test the hypothesis.

1. In a recent study of scientific literacy, women performed better than men in understanding the scientific process and in answering questions about basic scientific facts and concepts.

* 2. Jamal found giant footprints in his backyard and mysterious tufts of brown fur clinging to bushes in the area. Rumors persist that Bigfoot, the giant primate unknown to science, is frequenting the area. Two guys living nearby also claim to be perpetrating a hoax about the existence of the creature.

3. A man with a gun entered a mall in Chicago and began shooting randomly at shoppers, shouting something about demons using his body to commit horrible acts.

4. For years after the tragedy of September 11, 2001, there were no major terrorist attacks in the United States.

5. The CIA reviewed the president's State of the Union speech before he made it and verified that the intelligence information in the speech was correct. Later it was found that some of the information was erroneous and based on dubious sources.

* 6. Weight trainers swear that the supplement creatine dramatically increases their performance.

7. Many people who take B vitamins for their headaches report a lower incidence of headaches.

8. Recent research confirms a link between diets high in saturated fat and a higher risk of coronary artery disease.

9. When John got home, he found that the lock on his door had been broken and his color TV was missing.

10. The economic gap between the very rich and the very poor widened considerably in 2014.

Exercise 10.3

Using your background knowledge and any other information you may have about the subject, devise a competing theory for each of the following and then apply the criteria of adequacy to both of them—that is, ascertain how well each theory does in relation to its competitor on the criteria of testability, fruitfulness, scope, simplicity, and conservatism.

1. Phenomenon: People report feeling less pain after trying acupuncture.
   Theory: Treatment with acupuncture needles can alleviate pain.

2. Phenomenon: In the United States in 2014, a few people contracted the Ebola virus even though none of them had traveled recently to places in Africa known to be the source of the virus.
   Theory: The virus was carried from Africa to the United States by trade winds in the Atlantic Ocean.

* 3. Phenomenon: The unexpected melting of massive chunks of the world's glaciers.
   Theory: Local climate changes.

4. Phenomenon: A rare species of fungus grows in only one place in the world—the wing tips of a beetle that inhabits caves in France.
Theory: Evolution.

5. Phenomenon: As the job market worsens, blacks lose jobs faster than whites.
Theory: Racial prejudice.

6. Phenomenon: The psychic was able to recount a number of personal details about a recently deceased person he never met.
Theory: Psychic ability.

* 7. Phenomenon: Almost all of the terrorist attacks in the world in the past five years have been perpetrated by religious fanatics.
Theory: Religion fosters terrorism.

8. Phenomenon: Twenty patients with severe arthritis pain were prayed for by fifty people, and fourteen out of those twenty reported a significant lessening of pain.
Theory: Prayer heals.

9. Phenomenon: Over the past year, two terminally ill cancer patients in Broderick Hospital were found to be cancer free.
Theory: Treatment with a new type of chemotherapy works.

10. Phenomenon: Air pollution levels in San Francisco are at their highest levels in years.
Theory: Increased numbers of SUVs being driven in the San Francisco area.

Exercise 10.4

For each of the following theories, derive a test implication and indicate whether you believe that such a test would likely confirm or disconfirm the theory.

1. Elise has the power to move physical objects with her mind alone.

" 2. Ever since the city installed brighter street lights, the crime rate has been declining steadily.

3. The Ultra-Sonic 2000 pest-control device can rid a house of roaches by emitting a particular sound frequency that humans can't hear.

4. The Dodge Intrepid is a more fuel-efficient car than any other on the road.

5. Practitioners of transcendental meditation (TM) can levitate—actually ascend unaided off the ground without physical means of propulsion.

* 6. Eating foods high in fat contributes more to overweight than eating foods high in carbohydrates.

7. Lemmings often commit mass suicide.

8. The English sparrow will build nests only in trees.

Exercise 10.5

Read the following passages and answer the following questions for each one:

1. What is the phenomenon being explained?
2. What theories are advanced to explain the phenomenon? (Some theories may be unstated.)
3. Which theory seems the most plausible and why? (Use the criteria of adequacy.)
4. Regarding the most credible theory, is there a test implication mentioned? If so, what is it? If not, what would be a good test implication for the theory?
5. What test results would convince you to change your mind about your preferred theory?

PASSAGE 1

"In the past several years, a researcher named David Oates has been advocating his discovery of a most interesting phenomenon. Oates claims that backward messages are hidden unintentionally in all human speech. The messages can be understood by recording normal speech and playing it in reverse. . . . [According to Oates] 'Any thought, any emotion, any motive that any person has can appear backwards in human speech. The implications are mind boggling because reverse speech opens up the Truth.'. . . To our knowledge there is not one empirical investigation of reverse speech in any peer-reviewed journal. If reverse speech did exist it would be, at the very least, a noteworthy scientific discovery. However, there are no data to support the existence of reverse speech or Oates's theories about its implications."[12]

PASSAGE 2

"Michael Behe, a Lehigh University biochemist, claims that a light-sensitive cell, for example, couldn't have arisen through evolution because it is 'irreducibly complex.' Unlike the scientific creationists, however, he doesn't deny that the universe is billions of years old. Nor does he deny that evolution has occurred. He only denies that every biological system arose through natural selection.

"Behe's favorite example of an irreducibly complex mechanism is a mouse trap. A mouse trap consists of five parts: (1) a wooden platform, (2) a metal hammer, (3) a spring, (4) a catch, and (5) a metal bar that holds the hammer down when the trap is set. What makes this mechanism irreducibly complex is that if any one of the parts were removed, it would no longer work. Behe claims that many biological systems, such as cilia, vision, and blood clotting, are also irreducibly complex because each of these systems would cease to function if any of their parts were removed.

"Irreducibly complex biochemical systems pose a problem for evolutionary theory because it seems that they could not have arisen through natural selection. A trait such as vision can improve an organism's ability to survive only if it works. And it works only if all the parts of the visual system are present. So, Behe concludes, vision couldn't have arisen through slight modifications of a previous system. It must have been created all at once by some intelligent designer. . . .

"Most biologists do not believe that Behe's argument is sound, however, because they reject the notion that the parts of an irreducibly complex system could not have evolved independently of that system. As Nobel Prize–winning biologist H. J. Muller noted in 1939, a genetic sequence that is, at first, inessential to a system may later become essential to it. Biologist H. Allen Orr describes the processes as follows: 'Some part (A) initially does some job (and not very well, perhaps). Another part (B) later gets added because it helps A. This new part isn't essential, it merely improves things. But later on A (or something else) may change in such a way that B now becomes indispensable.' For example, air bladders—primitive lungs—made it possible for certain fish to acquire new sources of food. But the air bladders were not necessary to the survival of the fish. As the fish acquired additional features, however, such as legs and arms, lungs became essential. So, contrary to what Behe would have us believe, the parts of an irreducibly complex system need not have come into existence all at once."[13]

Exercise 10.6

Read the following passage about a study conducted on the use of vitamin C to treat cancer. Identify the hypothesis being tested, the consequences (test implication) used to test it, and whether the hypothesis was confirmed or disconfirmed.

PASSAGE 1

"In 1978, the Mayo Clinic embarked on a prospective, controlled, double-blind study designed to test Pauling and Cameron's claims [for the effectiveness of vitamin C]. Each patient in this study had biopsy-proven cancer that was considered incurable and unsuitable for further chemotherapy, surgery, or radiation. The patients were randomized to receive 10 grams of vitamin C per day or a comparably flavored lactose placebo. All patients took a glycerin-coated capsule four times a day.

"The patients were carefully selected so that those vitamin C and placebo groups were equally matched. There were 60 patients in the vitamin C group and 63 in the placebo group. The age distributions were similar. There was a slight predominance of males, but the ratio of males to females was virtually identical. Performance status was measured using the Eastern Cooperative Oncology Group Scale, a clinical scale well recognized by cancer researchers. Most study patients had some disability from their disease, but only a small proportion were bedridden. Most patients had advanced gastrointestinal or lung cancer. Almost all had received chemotherapy, and a smaller proportion had undergone radiation therapy.

"The results were noteworthy. About 25% of patients in both groups showed some improvement in appetite. Forty-two percent of the patients on placebo alone experienced enhancement of their level of activity. About 40% of the patients experienced mild nausea and vomiting, but the two groups had no statistically significant differences in the number of episodes. There were no survival differences between patients receiving vitamin C and those receiving the placebo. The median survival time was approximately seven weeks from the onset of therapy. The longest surviving patient in this trial had received the placebo. Overall, the study showed no benefit from vitamin C."[14]

Science and Weird Theories

"I maintain there is much more wonder in science than in pseudoscience. And in addition, to whatever measure this term has any meaning, science has the additional virtue, and it is not an inconsiderable one, of being true."
—Carl Sagan

What good is science and inference to the best explanation in the realm that seems to lie *beyond* common sense and scientific inquiry—the zone of the extraordinary, the paranormal, and the supernatural? In this land of the wonderfully weird—the interesting and mysterious domain of UFOs, ESP, ghosts, psychic predictions, tarot card readings, and the like—exactly what work can science do?

From reading Chapter 9, you probably have already guessed that science and critical reasoning can be as useful in assessing weird claims as they are in sizing up mundane ones. Inference to the best explanation—whether wielded in science or everyday life—can be successfully applied to extraordinary theories of all kinds. Fortunately for critical thinkers, the TEST formula outlined in Chapter 9 for finding the best theoretical explanation is not afraid of ghosts, monsters, or space aliens. In the next few pages, we will get a good demonstration of these points by examining some extraordinary theories in much greater detail than we have previously.

Science has always been interested in the mysterious, and from time to time it has also ventured into the weird. In the past 150 years, scientists have tested spiritualism, clairvoyance, telepathy, telekinesis (moving physical objects with the mind alone), astrology, dowsing, the Loch Ness monster, faith healing, fire walking, and more. Among these we should also count some bizarre phenomena that scientists never tire of studying—black holes, alternative dimensions of space, and the microworld of subatomic particles (the weirdest of the weird) where the laws of physics are crazy enough to make Alice in Wonderland scream.

But why should anyone bother to learn how to evaluate weird claims in the first place? Well, for one thing, they are widely believed (see accompanying box) and often difficult to ignore. They are, after all, heavily promoted in countless television programs, movies, books, magazines, and tabloids.

And—like claims in politics, medicine, and many other fields—they can dramatically affect people's lives, for better or worse. It's important then for anyone confronted with such popular and influential claims to be able to assess them carefully.

In addition, if you really care whether an extraordinary claim is true or false, there is no substitute for the kind of critical evaluation discussed here. Accepting (or rejecting) a weird claim solely because it's weird will not do. A horselaugh is not an argument, and neither is a sneer. Weird claims often turn out to be false, and, as the history of science shows, they sometimes surprise everyone by being true.

Making Weird Mistakes

So in science and in our own lives, the critical assessment of weird theories is possible—but that doesn't mean the process is without risks. It's easy for a scientist or anyone else to err when thinking about extraordinary claims. Weird claims and experiences have a way of provoking strong emotions, preconceived attitudes, and long-held biases. In the world of the weird, people (including scientists and other experts) are often prone to the kinds of errors in reasoning we discussed in Chapter 4, including resisting contrary evidence, looking for confirming evidence, and preferring available evidence. Those who contemplate extraordinary things also seem to be especially susceptible to the following errors.

Leaping to the Weirdest Theory

When people have an extraordinary experience, they usually try to make sense of it. They may have a seemingly prophetic dream, see a ghostly shape in the dark, watch their astrologer's prediction come true, think that they've witnessed a miracle, or feel that they have somehow lived another life centuries ago. Then they cast about for an explanation for such experiences. And when they cannot think of a natural explanation, they often conclude that the explanation must be paranormal or supernatural. This line of reasoning is common but fallacious. *Just because you can't think of a natural explanation doesn't mean that there isn't one.* You may just be ignorant of the correct explanation. Throughout history, scientists have often been confronted with astonishing phenomena that they could not explain in natural terms at the time. But they didn't assume that the phenomena must be paranormal or supernatural. They simply kept investigating—and they eventually found natural explanations. Comets, solar eclipses, meteors, mental illness, infectious diseases, and epilepsy were all once thought to be supernatural or paranormal but were later found through scientific investigation to have natural explanations. When confronted then with a phenomenon that you don't understand, the most reasonable response is to search for a natural explanation.

"TELL THEM ABOUT YOUR PSORIASIS, BETTY. MAYBE THEY CAN CURE IT."

Harley Schwadron.

The fallacious leap to a nonnatural explanation is an example of the appeal to ignorance discussed in Chapter 5. People think that since a paranormal or supernatural explanation has not been shown to be false, it must be true. This line, though logically fallacious, can be very persuasive.

The failure to consider alternative explanations is probably the most common error in assessing paranormal claims. As we've seen, this failure can be willful: People can refuse to consider seriously a viable alternative. But honest and intelligent people can also simply be unaware of possible natural explanations. Looking for alternative explanations requires imagination and a deliberate attempt to "think outside the box."

Mixing What Seems with What Is

Sometimes people leap prematurely to an extraordinary theory by ignoring this elementary principle: *Just because something seems real doesn't mean that it is.* Because of the nature of our perceptual equipment and processes, we

 REVIEW NOTES

Common Errors in Evaluating Extraordinary Theories

1. Believing that just because you can't think of a natural explanation, a phenomenon must be paranormal.
2. Thinking that just because something *seems* real, it *is* real. (A better principle: It's reasonable to accept the evidence provided by personal experience only if there's no good reason to doubt it.)
3. Misunderstanding logical possibility and physical possibility. Also, believing that if something is logically possible, it must be actual.

humans are bound to have many experiences in which something appears to be real but is not. The corrective for mistaking the unreal for the real is applying another important principle that we discussed in Chapter 4: It's reasonable to accept the evidence provided by personal experience only if there's no good reason to doubt it. We have reason to doubt if our perceptual abilities are impaired (we are under stress, drugged, afraid, excited, etc.), we have strong expectations about a particular experience (we strongly expect to see a UFO or hear spooky noises, for example), and observations are made under poor conditions (the stimuli are vague and ambiguous or the environment is too dark, too noisy, too hazy, etc.). Scientists can falter here just as anyone else can, which is why they try to use research methods that minimize reasons for doubt.

Misunderstanding the Possibilities

Debates about weird theories often turn on the ideas of possibility and impossibility. Skeptics may dismiss a weird theory by saying, "That's impossible!" Believers may insist that a state of affairs is indeed possible, or they may proclaim, "*Anything* is possible!" Such protestations, however, are often based on misunderstandings.

The experts on the subject of possibility (namely, philosophers) often talk about *logical possibility* and *logical impossibility*. Something is logically impossible if it violates a principle of logic (that is, it involves a logical contradiction). Something is logically possible if it does not violate a principle of logic (does not involve a logical contradiction). Anything that is logically impossible can't exist. We know, for example, that there are no married bachelors because these things involve logical contradictions (male humans who are both married and not married). Likewise we know that there are no square circles because they involve logical contradictions (things that are both circles and not circles). We must conclude from all this that, despite what some people sincerely believe, it is not the case that anything is possible. If a weird phenomenon is logically impossible, we needn't investigate it further because it can't exist. Most alleged paranormal phenomena, however, are not logically impossible. ESP, UFOs, reincarnation, dowsing, spontaneous human combustion, out-of-body experiences, and many more generally do not involve any logical contradiction.

Philosophers also refer to *physical possibility* and *physical impossibility*. Something is said to be physically impossible if it violates a law of science. We know that traveling faster than the speed of light is physically impossible because such an occurrence violates a law of science. Perpetual motion machines are physically impossible because they violate the law of science known as the conservation of mass-energy. Thus, scientists are skeptical of any extraordinary phenomenon that is said to be physically impossible.

People have been faking UFO photos for decades, insisting the pictures showed the genuine article and attracting a lot of publicity and true believers. This, despite the ease of making fakes. Astronomer Tom Callen created these two with a camera, some UFO models, and Paint Shop Pro. Do these images look as authentic as those you've seen in TV documentaries purporting to have photographic proof of UFOs?

Yet whether an event violates a law of nature is very difficult—perhaps impossible—to prove. The philosopher of science Theodore Schick, Jr., explains why:

No event . . . can provide sufficient grounds for believing that a miracle [a violation of scientific law] has occurred, because its seeming impossibility may simply be due to our ignorance of the operative laws. . . . We would be justified in believing that an apparent violation of a natural law was a miracle only if we were justified in believing that no natural law would ever be discovered to explain the occurrence. But we can never be justified in believing that, because no one can be sure what the future will bring. We can't rule out the possibility that a natural explanation will be found for an event, no matter how incredible.[15]

Some things that are logically possible are physically impossible. It's logically possible for Vaughn's dog to fly to another galaxy in sixty seconds. This astounding performance does not violate a principle of logic. But it does violate laws of science pertaining to speed-of-light travel and gravitation. It is therefore physically impossible. The upshot of all this is that, contrary to what some people would have us believe, if something is logically possible, that doesn't mean it's physically possible. That is, if something is logically possible, that doesn't mean it's actual. Many logically possible things may not be real.

Judging Weird Theories

Now let's do a detailed evaluation of two extraordinary theories using the TEST formula from Chapter 9. Recall the procedure's four steps:

Step 1. State the theory and check for consistency.
Step 2. Assess the evidence for the theory.
Step 3. Scrutinize alternative theories.
Step 4. Test the theories with the criteria of adequacy.

Science uses such a procedure to assess all manner of extraordinary explanations, and—by proceeding carefully and systematically—so can you.

Crop Circles

Crop circles are large-scale geometric designs pressed or stamped into fields of grain. They are often circular but can be almost any shape, ranging from simple patterns to complex pictograms or symbols. They can measure a few feet in diameter or span the length of several football fields. Interest in crop circles began in the 1970s when they started mysteriously appearing overnight in the grain fields of southern England. The crops

would be neatly flattened with the stalks pressed together and sometimes impressively interlaced. In the 1980s and 1990s, interest in the phenomenon grew as crop circles proliferated throughout the world, showing up in Europe, Africa, Australia, the United States, and elsewhere. In 2002 Hollywood got into the act by releasing the movie *Signs* starring Mel Gibson. He plays a Pennsylvania farmer who discovers massive crop circles in his fields and is soon drawn into encounters with extraterrestrial beings.

From the beginning, crop circles have been both intriguing and controversial. The controversy has centered mostly on one question: What theory best explains the existence of crop circles? Many explanations for the cause of the phenomenon have been offered and debated, with plenty of people making the case for their favorite theory through books, magazine articles, and, of course, the Internet. Let's examine some of these theories and see if we can separate the good from the bad.

Step 1. We begin with a theory that has gotten a great deal of attention from skeptics and believers alike.

Theory 1: Crop circles are created by small whirlwinds of electrified air (a.k.a. wind vortices). The idea here is that crop circles are made by columns of whirling, charged air similar to dust devils or miniature tornadoes. These vortices form above grain fields and then plunge to the ground, discharging the electricity and flattening the grain in swirled patterns. But unlike tornadoes, wind vortices leave the stalks of grain undamaged.

Step 2. What is the evidence for this theory? The evidence is indirect. Natural crop-circle vortices are unknown to science, but similar vortices are reported to have been produced artificially in laboratories. A few people claim to have seen the vortices in open fields. An electrified vortex might produce

FURTHER THOUGHT

The Art of Crop Circles

To many people, crop circles are the work of space aliens, or the result of natural processes, or the mischievous doings of pranksters. But to some, crop circles are an art form. Every year in Britain, serious artists hit the fields and, under cover of darkness, create crop-circle formations that are elegant enough to hang in a museum—if they would fit. John Lundberg, a graphic design artist, is one of these artistic circle makers.

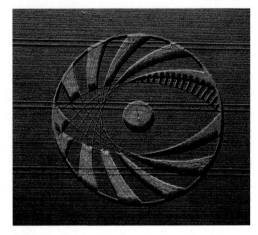

Who—or what—is the artist?

[Lundberg's] group, known as the Circlemakers, considers their practice an art. Lundberg estimates that there are three or four dedicated crop circle art groups operating in the United Kingdom today, and numerous other small groups that make one or two circles a year more or less as a lark.

Circlemakers [www.circlemakers.org] now does quite a bit of commercial work; in early July, the group created a giant crop formation 140 feet (46 meters) in diameter for the History Channel. But they also still do covert work in the dead of night.

Formulating a design and a plan, from original concept to finished product, can take up to a week. "It has to be more than a pretty picture. You have to have construction diagrams providing the measurements, marking the center, and so on," said Lundberg. Creating the art is the work of a night. . . .

"You think about art in terms of authorship and signature," he said. But circle makers never claim credit for specific formations they created. "To do so would drain the mystery of crop circles," he explained. "The art form isn't just about the pattern making. The myths and folklore and energy [that] people give them are part of the art."

Over the last 25 years, the formations have evolved from simple, relatively small circles to huge designs with multiple circles, elaborate pictograms, and shapes that invoke complex non-linear mathematical principles. A formation that appeared in August 2001 at Milk Hill in Wiltshire contained 409 circles, covered about five hectares, and was more than 800 feet (243 meters) across.[16]

light during discharge, and sure enough eyewitnesses have reported seeing "balls of light" and other light phenomena in or near crop circles. Many crop-circle enthusiasts (known as "cereologists" or "croppies") have photographed what they claim are mysterious lights near crop circles, and the photographs show impressive balls of light and strange glowing arcs. Some croppies also report hearing strange sounds near crop circles (humming noises, for example). Finally, some cereologists have reported that the plants in crop circles differ anatomically from those outside the circles. The joints in stalks, for example, may be bigger in crop-circle plants than in plants growing elsewhere.

This evidence, however, is weak. Producing a vortex in a laboratory does not prove that it exists "in the wild." In fact, there is no good evidence that crop-circle vortices exist in nature. As with most unfamiliar and provocative phenomena, eyewitness accounts of vortices are generally unreliable, especially since people generally don't know what a true crop-circle vortex looks like. Sightings of various light phenomena are not direct evidence for the existence of vortices because they can be explained in alternative ways. The lights could come from many other sources, including ball lightning (a documented phenomenon), commercial aircraft, military aircraft, the parachute flares of pranksters, and the flashlights of people making crop circles (there are plenty of people who make crop circles as hoaxes or works of art). The photographs of light phenomena also have alternative explanations. The arcs and balls of light in these photos can be easily produced when the flash reflects off of the camera strap, insects, droplets of water, and the like. Photos of weird lights are also easily faked. Reports of strange sounds, like the reports of weird lights, are not good evidence of vortices at work because the sounds could have several alternative causes (farm machinery, wind, etc.). And even if there are anatomical differences between crop-circle plants and non-circle plants, this would not show that crop circles are made by vortices. At most, it would suggest only that crop-circle plants are different, however the circles are made. (This same point applies to claims about other kinds of differences between crop-circle areas and non-circle locations, including alleged magnetic or soil anomalies. The anomalies, if they exist, do not confirm that crop circles are made in any particular way.)

"Bloody hell! Crap circles."

The biggest problem for the crop-circle vortex theory is that it doesn't explain the evidence. The theory seems adequate to explain circular crop-circle designs (a whirlwind would seem to be just the thing to make a circle on the ground), but not all crop circles are circular. Many are incredibly complex amalgams of squares, triangles, straight lines, and shapes that have no names.

Step 3. Now let's examine a popular alternative theory.

Theory 2: Crop circles are made by extraterrestrial beings (space aliens). This explanation asserts only that crop circles

FURTHER THOUGHT

I Confess: I'm a Crop-Circle Prankster

Other than to make great art, why would anyone want to go skulking around in the night to make crop circles in someone's wheat field? Maybe this confession from an unrepentant circle-maker will clear things up:

I made my first crop circle in 1991. My motive was to prove how easy they were to create, because I was convinced that all crop circles were man-made. It was the only explanation nobody seemed interested in testing. Late one August night, with one accomplice—my brother-in-law from Texas—I stepped into a field of nearly ripe wheat in northern England, anchored a rope into the ground with a spike and began walking in a circle with the rope held near the ground. It did not work very well: the rope rode up over the plants. But with a bit of help from our feet to hold down the rope, we soon had a respectable circle of flattened wheat.

Two days later there was an excited call to the authorities from the local farmer: I had fooled my first victim. I subsequently made two more crop circles using far superior techniques. A light garden roller, designed to be filled with water, proved helpful. Next, I hit on the "plank walking" technique that was used by the original circle makers, Doug Bower and the late Dave Chorley, who started it all in 1978. It's done by pushing down the crop with a plank suspended from two ropes. To render the depression circular is a simple matter of keeping an anchored rope taut. I soon found that I could make a sophisticated pattern with very neat edges in less than an hour.

Getting into the field without leaving traces is a lot easier than is usually claimed. In dry weather, and if you step carefully, you can leave no footprints or tracks at all. There are other, even stealthier ways of getting into the crop. One group of circle makers uses two tall bar stools, jumping from one to another.

But to my astonishment, throughout the early 1990s the media continued to report that it was impossible that all crop circles could be man-made. They cited "cereologists"—those who study crop circles—and never checked for themselves. There were said to be too many circles to be the work of a few "hoaxers" (but this assumed that each circle took many hours to make), or that circles appeared in well-watched crops (simply not true), or that circle creation was accompanied by unearthly noises (when these sounds were played back, even I recognized the nocturnal song of the grasshopper warbler).[17]

are the work of aliens; it does not specify how the aliens do it. The circles could be created by alien spacecraft, energy beams from space, or "thought energy" from places unknown. This theory has seemed plausible to some people in light of the intricacy and beauty of crop-circle pictograms, with a few croppies insisting that aliens must be communicating in geometrical language. To some, the circles have seemed much too complicated and elegant to be the result of human ingenuity.

The evidence for this alien explanation? The elegant complexity of crop circles has been thought to be pretty good support for the theory. Who else but aliens would create such brilliant masterpieces on such a large scale—masterpieces that are best viewed from the air or space itself? A few people have announced that they found very intricate mathematics in the more elaborate crop-circle designs. Also, some have reported seeing odd lights in the vicinity of crop circles, and others have claimed that they saw actual alien craft in the night sky not far from the crop-circle fields. A few cereologists have even claimed that they caught sight of UFOs in the process of making crop circles.

This evidence, however, is problematic and has some of the same weaknesses as the wind vortex evidence. The complexity and beauty of crop circles do not lend support to the alien theory because the artistry of the crop formations has an obvious alternative explanation: Humans made them. There are numerous documented cases of humans—either hoaxers or artists—creating stunningly exquisite and elaborate crop circles, some with plenty of mathematics built in. Because the human artist explanation is at least as plausible as the alien artist one, the artistic or intellectual impressiveness of crop circles can give no weight to the alien theory. As mentioned earlier, light phenomena near crop circles also have alternative explanations. Nighttime UFO sightings might seem to be good evidence that aliens are up to something. But they are susceptible to many of the doubt-producing factors that we discussed in Chapter 4: darkness, ambiguous stimuli, lack of cues to the true position and size of moving objects, perceptual construction, stress, strong emotions, expectancy, and more. Eyewitness reports of aliens actually constructing crop circles constitute very weak evidence for theory 2. Such extraordinary reports require reliable corroborating evidence, but no alien activity of any kind has ever been scientifically documented, despite allegations to the contrary.

Many people favor a more down-to-earth theory.

Theory 3: Crop circles are made by humans using ordinary means. This explanation encompasses the creation of crop circles by hoaxers, artists, or any other humans. The relevant evidence suggests that many crop circles have indeed been produced by humans. In 1991 two English artists with a sense of humor, Doug Bower and Dave Chorley, declared that they had been making crop circles for years to fool gullible people who believed in UFOs. They demonstrated their circle-making skills for reporters and television audiences, easily producing very elaborate crop circles in a short time. To create their designs,

"It is easier to attribute UFO sightings to the known irrationalities of terrestrials than to the unknown efforts of extraterrestrials."
—Richard Feynman

they used only ropes and planks. They showed that crop circles thought to be way beyond human ability were in fact made by humans using incredibly simple techniques. Their formations fooled many people including at least one prominent cereologist. Many circle-watchers conceded that human hoaxers were making crop circles and that distinguishing "true" circles from fake ones is no cinch. A leading cereologist admitted that 80 percent of crop circles in Britain were made by humans.

It is clear, however, that Bower and Chorley could not have created all the known crop circles. From southern England, crop-circle creation spread all over the globe, appearing in increasing numbers. This spread of the phenomenon, though, seemed to correlate with increased international media coverage of crop circles, suggesting that other humans may have been inspired to copy English circle-making. In addition, many artists have been fascinated by the aesthetics of crop circles and have generated their own masterpieces in grain.

Croppies have argued that humans can't be responsible for some crop circles because there are often no signs of human activity at formation sites (no footprints, paths through the grain, etc.). But as the circle-building of hoaxers suggests, crop circles can be produced by humans without leaving evidence of human activity behind. Hoaxers, for example, can often avoid leaving footprints in a grain field by walking along tramlines, the narrow footpaths created by farm machinery.

Also, as suggested earlier, physical anomalies in crop-circle plants or soil do not prove that crop circles are made in any particular way. It's possible that anomalies are produced by the techniques used in human circle-making. Some have suggested, for example, that enlarged joints in grain stalks are the result of the bent stalks baking in the hot sun.

Step 4. Now let's see what happens when we apply the criteria of adequacy to these three theories. Theories 1 and 3 seem equal in terms of testability. Both predict something other than what they were introduced to explain. Theory 1, for example, predicts that in the creation of a crop circle, an electrified vortex forms above the formation area—something that should be detectable by the right kind of scientific instruments. Theory 3 is certainly testable because human activity is detectable and measurable. Theory 2 (aliens) may or may not be testable, depending on how alien activity is construed. We will give the theory the benefit of the doubt and say that it too is testable.

Theories 1 and 2 are not fruitful, for they have yielded no surprising predictions. We could argue, though, that theory 3 is fruitful because the creation of specific crop circles at designated times and places has been successfully predicted by hoaxers (the ones who created the circles).

In terms of scope, neither theory 1 nor 2 gets any points. The vortex theory does not explain anything other than the creation of crop circles. Theory 2 could be construed as explaining many things in which aliens are involved (UFO sightings, abductions, UFO crashes, etc.). But positing the existence of mysterious beings that act in mysterious ways for mysterious reasons does not seem to explain much of anything. Theory 3, on the other hand, can be used to explain many strange phenomena because humans, after all, are responsible for many hoaxes and bizarre happenings.

As far as simplicity is concerned, theories 1 and 2 are in deep trouble. Like most paranormal explanations, they both posit the existence of unknown entities (charged, naturally occurring vortices and space aliens). Theory 3 sticks with known entities and processes.

On the criterion of conservatism, theories 1 and 2 are again in trouble. There is no good evidence that the hypothesized vortex has ever occurred anywhere. And we have no good reason to believe that either space aliens or alien technology has ever visited Earth, let alone created some nice designs in a wheat field.

FURTHER THOUGHT

Eyewitness Testimony and Extraordinary Things

A great deal of the evidence for paranormal phenomena is eyewitness testimony. Unfortunately, research suggests that eyewitness testimony generally can't be trusted—especially when the testimony concerns the paranormal. For example, in some studies people who had participated in séances later gave wildly inaccurate descriptions of what had transpired. Researchers have found that people's beliefs and expectations seem to play a big role in the unreliability of testimony about the paranormal.

> Different people clearly have different beliefs and expectations prior to observing a supposed psychic—skeptics might expect to see some kind of trickery; believers may expect a display of genuine psi [parapsychological phenomena]. Some seventy years ago Eric Dingwall in Britain speculated that such expectations may distort eyewitness testimony: The frame of mind in which a person goes to see magic and to a medium cannot be compared. In one case he goes either purely for amusement or possibly with the idea of discovering "how it was done," whilst in the other he usually goes with the thought that it is possible that he will come into direct contact with the other world.
>
> Recent experimental evidence suggests that Dingwall's speculations are correct.
>
> Wiseman and Morris in Britain carried out two studies investigating the effect that belief in the paranormal has on the observation of conjuring tricks. Individuals taking part in the experiment were first asked several questions concerning their belief in the paranormal. On the basis of their answers they were classified as either believers (labeled "sheep") or skeptics (labeled "goats").

In both experiments individuals were first shown a film containing fake psychic demonstrations. In the first demonstration the "psychic" apparently bent a key by concentrating on it; in the second demonstration he supposedly bent a spoon simply by rubbing it.

After they watched the film, witnesses were asked to rate the "paranormal" content of the demonstrations and complete a set of recall questions. Wiseman and Morris wanted to discover if, as Hodgson and Dingwall had suggested, sheep really did tend to misremember those parts of the demonstrations that were central to solving the tricks. For this reason, half of the questions concerned the methods used to fake the phenomena. For example, the psychic faked the key-bending demonstration by secretly switching the straight key for a pre-bent duplicate by passing the straight key from one hand to the other. During the switch the straight key could not be seen. This was clearly central to the trick's method; and one of the "important" questions asked was whether the straight key had always remained in sight. A second set of "unimportant" questions asked about parts of the demonstration that were not related to the tricks' methods. Overall, the results suggested that sheep rated the demonstrations as more "paranormal" than goats did, and that goats did indeed recall significantly more "important" information than sheep. There was no such difference for the recall of the "unimportant" information.[18]

We can summarize these judgments as in the following table:

Criteria	Vortices	Aliens	Humans
Testable	Yes	Yes	Yes
Fruitful	No	No	Yes
Scope	No	No	Yes
Simple	No	No	Yes
Conservative	No	No	Yes

We can see immediately that the three theories are equal in testability, but theory 3 wins on all other counts. It is clearly the superior theory. Both the vortex theory and the alien theory fail the test of fruitfulness, scope, simplicity, and conservatism. Of these four criteria, simplicity and conservatism carry the most weight here. In general, the plausibility of a theory is weakened considerably when it posits unknown entities and processes. Likewise, a theory that doesn't fit with what we already know takes a hit in credibility. An unconservative theory, of course, can acquire some credibility if it excels in the other criteria of adequacy. But theories 1 and 2 fall short in all the criteria except testability.

We can see then that theories 1 and 2 are not good explanations for crop circles. They are most likely false. Theory 3—human creation of crop circles—is a much better theory.

There are other crop-circle theories that we haven't examined. None of them seem to measure up to the criteria of adequacy as well as theory 3 does. If this is the case, then we can give an even stronger endorsement of theory 3: Crop circles are probably human-made.

Talking with the Dead

Some people claim that they can communicate with the dead, providing impressive and seemingly accurate information about a person's dead loved ones. They are called psychics (a century ago they were called mediums), and they have gained the respect of many who have come to them in search of messages from the deceased. They have appeared on television programs, published books, and offered seminars to thousands. The most famous among these modern-day mediums are psychics James Van Praagh and John Edward. Their performances assure many people that their loved ones who "have passed over" are fine and that any unsettled issues of guilt and forgiveness can be resolved.

Psychic John Edward.

What is the best explanation for these otherworldly performances in which the psychics appear to be in contact with the dead? Several theories have been proposed. One is that the psychics are getting information about the dead and their loved ones ahead of time (before the performances begin). Another is that the psychics are using telepathy to read the minds of the living to discover facts about the dead. But for simplicity's sake let's narrow the list of theories down to the two leading ones.

Step 1. Here's the psychics' theory.

Theory 1: The psychics are communicating information or messages to and from the disembodied spirits of people who have died. In other words, the psychics are doing exactly what they claim to be doing. They are somehow identifying the appropriate deceased spirit, receiving and decoding transmissions from that spirit, conveying the information to the living, and sending messages back to the dead.

Step 2. The main evidence in support of this theory is the psychics' performance. They typically perform before an audience and talk to audience members who have lost loved ones. The psychics appear to know facts about the dead that they could only know if they were actually communicating with the dead. They also seem to inexplicably know things about members of the audience. Often they also provide incorrect information (such as saying that a member of the audience has lost her mother when in fact the mother is very much alive). But their "hits" (times when they produce correct information) occur often enough and seem to be specific enough to impress.

Psychics have rarely been tested scientifically. The few experiments conducted to date have been severely criticized for sloppy methodology. So there is no good scientific evidence to support theory 1. Investigators who have seen the psychics' live

". . . we [psychics] are here to heal people and to help people grow . . . skeptics . . . they're just here to destroy people. They're not here to encourage people, to enlighten people. They're here to destroy people."
—James Van Praagh

FURTHER THOUGHT

Why People Believe Psychic Readings

Ray Hyman was professor emeritus of psychology at the University of Oregon and an expert on the scientific investigation of paranormal claims, including psychic readings. Years of research led him to be skeptical of the validity of psychic readings, but he used to be a true believer. He explained why he went from believer to skeptic:

> Now it so happens that I have devoted more than half a century to the study of psychic and cold readings. I have been especially concerned with why such readings can seem so concrete and compelling, even to skeptics. As a way to earn extra income, I began reading palms when I was in my teens. At first, I was skeptical. I thought that people believed in palmistry and other divination procedures because they could easily fit very general statements to their particular situation. To establish credibility with my clients, I read books on palmistry and gave readings according to the accepted interpretations for the lines, shape of the fingers, mounds, and other indicators. I was astonished by the reactions of my clients. My clients consistently praised me for my accuracy even when I told them very specific things about problems with their health and other personal matters. I even would get phone calls from clients telling me that a prediction that I had made for them had come true. Within months of my entry into palm reading, I became a staunch believer in its validity. My conviction was so strong that I convinced my skeptical high school English teacher by giving him readings and arguing with him. I later also convinced the head of the psychology department where I was an undergraduate.
>
> When I was a sophomore, majoring in journalism, a well-known mentalist and trusted friend persuaded me to try an experiment in which I would deliberately read a client's hand opposite to what the signs in her hand indicated. I was shocked to discover that this client insisted that this was the most accurate reading she had ever experienced. As a result, I carried out more experiments with the same outcome. It dawned on me that something important was going on. Whatever it was, it had nothing to do with the lines in the hand. I changed my major from journalism to psychology so that I could learn why not only other people, but also I, could be so badly led astray. My subsequent career has focused on the reasons why cold readings can appear to be so compelling and seemingly specific.

Psychologists have uncovered a number of factors that can make an ambiguous reading seem highly specific, unique, and uncannily accurate. And once the observer or client has been struck with the apparent accuracy of the reading, it becomes virtually impossible to dislodge the belief in the uniqueness and specificity of the reading. Research from many areas demonstrates this finding. The principles go under such names as the fallacy of personal validation, subjective validation, confirmation bias, belief perseverance, the illusion of invulnerability, compliance, demand characteristics, false uniqueness effect, foot-in-the-door phenomenon, illusory correlation, integrative agreements, self-reference effect, the principle of individuation, and many, many others. Much of this is facilitated by the illusion of specificity that surrounds language. All language is inherently ambiguous and depends much more than we realize upon the context and nonlinguistic cues to fix its meaning in a given situation.[19]

HEART

HEAD

LIFE

What is this palm saying? Psychologists think they know.

performances (not just the edited versions of the TV programs) report that the hit rates (the percentage of hits out of the total number of statements or questions) are actually much lower than most people realize. They have found hit rates as low as 5 percent with the highest being well under 50 percent. The low hit rate, though, may not be apparent on TV shows because misses are often edited out. Psychics tend to explain their misses with ad hoc hypotheses (explanations that cannot be verified).

Step 3. Here's the main alternative to the psychics' theory.

Theory 2: The psychics are doing "cold reading." Cold reading is a very old skill practiced by fortune-tellers, tarot-card readers, and mentalists (performers who pretend to read minds). When done well, cold reading can astonish and appear to be paranormal. In cold reading, the psychic reader surreptitiously acquires information from people (the subjects) by asking them questions, making statements, observing how people behave, and listening to what they say. Good cold readers always give the impression that the information actually comes from some mysterious source such as the spirits of the departed. Anyone can

"Ahh.. I see your future. Get up, go to work go to bed. Get up, go to work, go to bed. Get..."

www.CartoonStock.com

learn to do cold reading. It doesn't require any exotic skills or special powers. All that's needed is the practiced ability to deftly manipulate a conversation to elicit information from the subject.

Note that theory 2 does not say that the cold reading is necessarily done to deliberately deceive an audience. Cold reading can be done either consciously or unconsciously. It's possible for people to do cold reading while believing that they are getting information via their psychic powers.

To get the relevant information (or appear to have it), a psychic reader can use several cold-reading techniques. These include the following.

1. The reader encourages the subject to fill in the blanks.

   READER: I'm sensing something about the face or head or brow.
   SUBJECT: You're right, my father used to have terrible headaches.

   READER: I'm feeling something about money or finances.
   SUBJECT: Yes, my mother always struggled to pay the bills.

2. The reader makes statements with multiple variables so that a hit is very likely.

   READER: I'm feeling that your father was dealing with a lot of frustration, anguish, or anger.
   SUBJECT: Yes, he was always arguing with my brother.

3. The reader makes accurate and obvious inferences from information given by the subject.

   READER: Why was your father in the hospital?
   SUBJECT: He had had a heart attack.
   READER: Yes, he struggled with heart disease for years and had to take heart medication for a long time. You were really worried that he would have another heart attack.

4. The reader asks many questions and treats answers as though they confirmed the reader's insight.

   READER: Who was the person who got a divorce?
   SUBJECT: That was my daughter. She divorced her husband in 1992.
   READER: Because I feel that the divorce was very painful for her, that she was sad and depressed for a while.

5. The reader makes statements that could apply to almost anyone.

> READER: I'm sensing something about a cat or a small animal.
> SUBJECT: Yes, my mother owned a poodle.

With such cold-reading techniques a reader can appear to read minds. Theory 2 is bolstered by the fact that the psychics' amazing performances can be duplicated by anyone skilled in the use of cold reading. In fact, magicians, mentalists, and other nonpsychic entertainers have used cold-reading techniques to give performances that rival those of the top psychics. Regardless of their authenticity, the performances of Van Praagh, Edward, and other psychics seem to be indistinguishable from those based on cold reading. The psychics may indeed be communicating with the dead, but they look like they're using cold-reading techniques.

Step 4. Now we can apply the criteria of adequacy to these two competing explanations. Both theories are testable, and neither has yielded any novel predictions. So we must judge the theories in terms of scope, simplicity, and conservatism. And on each of these criteria, theory 2 is clearly superior. Theory 1 explains only the psychics' performances as described earlier, but theory 2 explains these performances plus other kinds of seemingly psychic readings, including tarot-card reading, fortune-telling, mentalist acts, and old-fashioned spiritualist séances. Theory 1, of course, fails the criterion of simplicity because it assumes unknown entities (disembodied spirits with certain abilities) and unknown processes (communication to and from the dead). Theory 2 makes no such assumptions. Finally, theory 1 is not conservative. It conflicts with everything we know about death, the mind, and communication. Theory 2, though, fits with existing knowledge just fine.

Here are these judgments in table form:

Criteria	Theory 1	Theory 2
Testable	Yes	Yes
Fruitful	No	No
Scope	No	Yes
Simple	No	Yes
Conservative	No	Yes

We must conclude that theory 1 is a seriously defective theory. It is unlikely to be true. Theory 2, however, is strong. It is not only superior to theory 1, but it is also a better explanation than other competing theories we haven't discussed in that it can explain most or all of the psychics' hits. If the cold-reading theory really is better than all these others, then we have good reasons to believe that Van Praagh, Edward, and other psychics perform their amazing feats through simple cold reading.

 EXERCISES

Exercise 10.7

1. Is it reasonable to accept or reject an extraordinary claim solely because of its weirdness?
2. What are the five steps of the scientific method?
3. Is it reasonable to conclude that a phenomenon is paranormal just because you cannot think of a natural explanation?
* 4. The fallacious leap to a nonnatural explanation is an example of what logical fallacy?
5. According to the text, what is the critical thinking principle that can help you avoid mistaking how something seems for how something is?
* 6. What is logical possibility? logical impossibility?
7. What is physical possibility? physical impossibility?
8. Are dogs that lay eggs logically possible?
9. Is anything possible? If not, why not?
10. What is the four-step method for evaluating a theory?
11. What is the difference between science and technology?
12. What is scientism?
13. What is a placebo, and how is it used in scientific experiments?
14. What is the Copernican theory of planetary motion?
15. How reliable is eyewitness testimony? Under what circumstance are eyewitness accounts most likely to be inaccurate?

Exercise 10.8

In each of the following examples, a state of affairs is described. Devise three theories to explain each one. Include two plausible theories that are natural explanations and one competing theory that is paranormal.

1. Jack spent the night in a hotel that had a reputation for being haunted. He slept in the very room (number 666) in which a horrible murder had been committed in the 1930s. He fell asleep thinking about the crime. At 3:00 a.m. he awoke to see the apparition of a man sitting at the foot of his bed.
* 2. Jacques lived in a house built back in the 1940s which was now in disrepair. As he sat reading in the parlor, he heard creaking sounds coming from upstairs.
3. Selena found herself thinking about the camping trip that she went on in Pennsylvania. She was remembering the morning she woke up to find her tent crawling with ladybugs. As she was pondering the ladybugs, she suddenly noticed a ladybug on the windowsill near her chair.

4. Some people report that in the past when they needed help in a risky situation (for example, when they were in a car accident or when they were lost in a crime-ridden neighborhood), they were aided by a stranger who never gave his or her name and who left the scene quickly after rendering assistance. They claim that the stranger must have been their guardian angel.

5. According to a recent survey, 38 percent of Americans believe in ghosts or spirits of the dead.

6. Lil's horoscope said that she would meet someone interesting. Three days after reading it, she did.

* 7. Leroy dreamed that his uncle was killed in Iraq when he stepped on a land mine. When Leroy woke up, he got a call from his mother saying that his uncle had been injured in a car accident in Baghdad.

8. Eleanor has a reputation for acting strangely. Recently when her priest came to visit her in her home, she fell to the floor writhing with convulsions.

9. Nelly made a fresh batch of tortillas. On one of them she noticed that the scorch marks were unusual. She was sure that she could see the face of Jesus in the design made by the scorch marks.

10. Ali was not feeling well. He heard that a crazy woman in his village had put a curse on him because he called her a witch. The next day Ali broke his arm when he slipped and fell against some rocks.

Exercise 10.9

Using your background knowledge and any other information you may have about the subject, devise a competing, naturalistic theory for each paranormal theory that follows, and then apply the criteria of adequacy to both of them—that is, ascertain how well each theory does in relation to its competitor on the criteria of testability, fruitfulness, scope, simplicity, and conservatism.

1. Phenomenon: George and Jan have been married for twenty years. Many times George seems to know exactly what Jan is thinking, as though he could read her mind.
   Theory: George is telepathic.

2. Phenomenon: Yolanda awoke one morning and remembered having a strange dream. She dreamed that space aliens came into her bedroom while she was sleeping and abducted her. The dream seemed extremely vivid. Later in the day, she noticed some scratches on her ankle. She didn't know how they got there.
   Theory: Yolanda was abducted by aliens.

* 3. Phenomenon: In 1917 in Cottingley, England, three girls claimed to have taken photos of fairies who played with them in the garden. The photos showed the girls in the garden with what appeared to be tiny fairies dancing around them. (The 1997 movie *Fairy Tale* was about the girls and their story.)
   Theory: Fairies really do exist, and the girls photographed them.

4. Phenomenon: The Loch Ness monster is alleged to be a large aquatic creature that inhabits one of Scotland's lochs. The creature is unknown to science. People have been reporting sightings of Nessie for hundreds of years. There is no hard evidence proving the existence of the monster.
Theory: The Loch Ness monster actually exists.

5. Phenomenon: The famous Israeli psychic Uri Geller seems to be able to bend spoons and keys with his mind. He has been performing this feat for audiences for years. Magicians claim that Geller is a fraud and that they can also bend spoons and keys with simple sleight-of-hand magic tricks.
Theory: Geller's psychic powers enable him to bend metal with his mind.

6. Phenomenon: When there's a full moon, people seem to act weird. All you have to do to confirm this is to go downtown and observe people when there's a full moon.
Theory: Through some unknown force, the moon exerts influence on people's behavior.

7. Phenomenon: Some people claim to be psychic detectives, psychics who help law enforcement agencies solve crimes. The psychics sometimes mention the police departments that they have assisted. This psychic detective work is hard to verify, and skeptics claim that either the psychics lie about their successes or they hit upon a solution to a crime by chance.
Theory: The psychic abilities of psychic detectives enable them to solve crimes.

Exercise 10.10

Read the following passages and answer these questions for each one:

1. What is the phenomenon being explained?
2. What theories—stated or implied—are used to explain the phenomenon?
3. Which theory seems the most plausible and why? (Base your judgment on the evidence cited in the passage as well as any other information you might have on the subject, and use the criteria of adequacy.)
4. What kind of evidence would convince you to change your mind about your preferred theory?

PASSAGE 1

"A Ouija board is used in divination and spiritualism. The board usually has the letters of the alphabet inscribed on it, along with words such as 'yes,' 'no,' 'good-bye' and 'maybe.' A planchette (a slidable 3-legged device) or pointer of some sort is manipulated by those using the board. The users ask the board a question and together or one of them singly moves the pointer or the board until a letter is 'selected' by the pointer. The selections 'spell' out an answer to the question asked.

"Some users believe that paranormal or supernatural forces are at work in spelling out Ouija board answers. Skeptics believe that those using the board either consciously or unconsciously select what is read. To prove this, simply try it blindfolded for some time, having an innocent bystander take notes on what letters are selected. Usually, the result will be unintelligible nonsense.

"The movement of the planchette is not due to paranormal forces but to un-noticeable movements by those controlling the pointer, known as the *ideomotor effect*. The same kind of unnoticeable movement is at work in dowsing.

"The Ouija board was first introduced to the American public in 1890 as a parlor game sold in novelty shops."[20]

PASSAGE 2

"Most scientists discount the existence of Bigfoot because the evidence supporting belief in the survival of a prehistoric bipedal apelike creature of such dimensions is scant. The only notable exception is Grover S. Krantz (1931–2002), an anthropologist at Washington State University. For nearly forty years, Krantz argued for the probable existence of Bigfoot, but was unable to convince the majority of scientists. The evidence for Bigfoot's existence consists mainly of testimony from Bigfoot enthusiasts, footprints of questionable origin, and pictures that could easily have been of apes or humans in ape suits. There are no bones, no scat, no artifacts, no dead bodies, no mothers with babies, no adolescents, no fur, no nothing. There is no evidence that any individual or community of such creatures dwells anywhere near any of the 'sightings.' In short, the evidence points more towards hoaxing and delusion than real discovery. Some believers dismiss all such criticism and claim that Bigfoot exists in another dimension and travels by astral projection. Such claims reinforce the skeptic's view that the Bigfoot legend is a function of passionate fans of the paranormal, aided greatly by the mass media's eagerness to cater to such enthusiasm."[21]

PASSAGE 3

"Trickery aside, what about reports of apparent animal ESP? Anecdotal evidence suggests some animals may have precognitive awareness of various types of natural catastrophes, becoming agitated before earthquakes, volcanic eruptions, cyclones, and other events. However, the creatures may actually be responding to subtle sensory factors—like variations in air pressure and tremors in the ground—that are beyond the range of human perception.

"Something of the sort may explain some instances of apparent animal prescience. For example, a Kentucky friend of mine insists that his dogs seem to know when he has decided to go hunting, exhibiting a marked excitement even though they are lodged some distance away from the house. However, it seems possible that they are either responding to some unintended signal (such as recognizing certain noises associated with his getting ready for a hunting trip) or that he is selectively remembering those occasions when the dogs' excitement happens to coincide with his intentions. Another friend says he once had dogs who seemed to know when he was going to take them for a walk, but he decided he must have unconsciously signaled them (such as by glancing in the direction of their hanging leashes)."[22]

PASSAGE 4

"Ever since humans gained the ability to look down at the Earth from airplanes, space shuttles, and satellites, we've discovered a number of unusual markings. We know very little about them. [There are some] mysterious lines that are found on the Nazca Desert of Peru. They stretch for several miles, crossing over cliffs and hills. A Swiss author named Erich von Daniken claims in his book, *Chariots of the Gods,* that these lines were made by aliens who visited the Earth long ago. A German scientist, Maria Reicher, says that von Daniken's idea is ridiculous, and she has her own theory. . . .

"Von Daniken claims that aliens landed in the Nazca Desert back when humans were still evolving from primitive beings. When the alien vehicles touched down, they gouged tracks into the desert plain. According to his theory, the ancient Nazcan natives would have believed that these lines were made by the 'fiery chariots of the sky gods.' They carefully preserved the tracks the 'gods' chariots' had made and even extended them in all directions.

"Maria Reicher believes that the Nazca lines were created by ancient Peruvians to form a kind of calendar. She found that the lines aren't formed by marks in the earth, but by dark, purplish rocks that form borders and rows. The Nazcan people separated these rocks, which litter the desert, from the yellowish sand. Ancient Peruvians depended on the annual spring rains for their very existence. Since they needed time to prepare their fields before rainy season began, they made a point of learning when the seasons changed. Reicher noticed that the lines of rocks point to a place on the horizon where the sun rose and set during the winter and summer solstice—the times when the seasons change. Her theory is that the Nazcans used these lines as a sort of grand astronomical calendar, to help them get ready for the all-important change of seasons."[23]

PASSAGE 5

The renowned prophet Michel Nostradamus (1503–1566) composed a thousand verses that foretold historical events. Here's proof. Verse XXVII reads like this:

> Underneath the cord, Guien struck from the sky,
> Near where is hid a great treasure,
> Which has been many years a gathering,
> Being found, he shall die, the eye put out by a spring.[24]

This is a clear reference to World War II. It means "paratroopers alight near the Nazi's plunder hoard and, captured, they are executed." Some people think that the verses are so vague that anyone can read anything they want into them. But they're not ambiguous at all.

Summary

Science and Not Science

- Science seeks knowledge and understanding of reality, and it does so through the formulation, testing, and evaluation of theories. Science is a way of searching for truth.
- Science is not a worldview, and we can't identify it with a particular ideology. Science is also not scientism—it is not the only way to acquire knowledge. It is, however, a highly reliable way of acquiring knowledge of empirical facts.

The Scientific Method

- The scientific method cannot be identified with any particular set of experimental or observational procedures. But it does involve several general steps: (1) identifying the problem, (2) devising a hypothesis, (3) deriving a test implication, (4) performing the test, and (5) accepting or rejecting the hypothesis.
- No hypothesis can be *conclusively* confirmed or confuted. But this fact does not mean that all hypotheses are equally acceptable.

Testing Scientific Theories

- Following the steps of the scientific method, scientists test hypotheses in many fields, including medical science. One example is the testing of the hypothesis that taking high doses of vitamin C can cure cancer.
- To minimize errors in testing, scientists use control groups, make studies double-blind, include placebos in testing, and seek replication of their work.

Judging Scientific Theories

- Theory testing is part of a broader effort to evaluate a theory against its competitors. This kind of evaluation always involves, implicitly or explicitly, the criteria of adequacy.
- The criteria are testability, fruitfulness, scope, simplicity, and conservatism.
- The criteria of adequacy played a major role in settling the historic debate about planetary motion, and they are used today to effectively judge the relative merits of the theories of evolution and creationism.

Science and Weird Theories

- Inference to the best explanation can be used to assess weird theories as well as more commonplace explanations in science and everyday life.
- Scientifically evaluating offbeat theories can often be worthwhile in determining their truth or falsity and (sometimes) in discovering new phenomena.

Making Weird Mistakes

- When people try to evaluate extraordinary theories, they often make certain typical mistakes. They may believe that because they can't think of a natural explanation, a paranormal explanation must be correct. They may mistake what *seems* for what *is*, forgetting that we shouldn't accept the evidence provided by personal experience if we have good reason to doubt it. And they may not fully understand the concepts of logical and physical possibility.
- The distinction between logical and physical possibility is crucial. Some things that are logically possible may not be physically possible, and things that are physically possible may not be actual.

Judging Weird Theories

- In both science and everyday life, the TEST formula enables us to fairly appraise the worth of all sorts of weird theories, including those about crop circles and communication with the dead, the two cases examined in this chapter.

 Field Problems

1. Find a controversial health or medical theory on the Internet and design a study to test it. Indicate the makeup and characteristics of any group in the study, whether a placebo group is used, whether the study is double-blind, and what study results would confirm and disconfirm the theory.

2. Find a controversial theory in the social sciences on the Internet and design a study to test it. Indicate the makeup and characteristics of any group in the study, whether a placebo group is used, whether the study is double-blind, and what study results would confirm and disconfirm the theory. If the theory is one that you strongly believe, indicate the kind and level of evidence that could convince you to change your mind about it.

3. Do research on the Internet to find information on spontaneous human combustion, the theory that a human body can catch on fire due to an unknown internal chemical or biological process. Apply the TEST formula to evaluate the theory. Consider at least one plausible alternative theory. Look for background information at The Skeptic's Dictionary (http://skepdic.com), the Committee for the Scientific Investigation of Claims of the Paranormal (CSICOP) (www.csicop.org), or *Skeptic Magazine* (www.skeptic.com).

 Self-Assessment Quiz

Answers appear in "Answers to Self-Assessment Quizzes" (Appendix D).

1. What is a test implication?

2. Are hypotheses generated purely through induction? Why or why not?

3. When a test implication is disconfirmed, what conditional argument is exemplified?

4. When a test implication is confirmed, what conditional argument is exemplified?

5. Why can't scientific hypotheses be conclusively confirmed?

6. Why can't scientific hypotheses be conclusively disconfirmed?

For each of the following phenomena, devise a hypothesis to explain it and derive a test implication to test the hypothesis.

7. Automobile accidents on Blind Man's Curve have increased lately, especially since the street light was broken and not replaced.

8. Juan was found two hours after the fatal stabbing, sitting in Central Park with blood on his shirt.

9. Mysterious lights appeared in the night sky. They looked like alien spacecraft.

For each of the following phenomena, indicate (1) a possible hypothesis to explain it, (2) a possible competing hypothesis, (3) a test implication for each hypothesis, and (4) what testing results would confirm and disconfirm the hypothesis.

10. While camping in the state park, Maria came down with a gastrointestinal illness.

11. The students who were put in a class with two teachers instead of one showed an improvement in their grades.

12. Public health officials report a significant increase in levels of stress in people who live or work in New York City.

13. Since the Vaughn family started using Super Cold-Stopper With Beta-Carotene they have suffered 50 percent fewer colds.

For each of the following hypotheses, specify a test implication and indicate what evidence would convince you to accept the hypothesis.

14. Esther stole the book from the library.

15. Most people—both white and black—are economically better off now than their parents were thirty years ago.

16. The health care system in this country is worse now than it was when Bill Clinton was president.

Each of the theories that follow is offered to explain why an astrological reading by a famous astrologer turned out to be wildly inaccurate. Based on a person's horoscope, he had predicted that the person was a nice man who could work with other people very well. The person turned out to be Josef Mengele, the Nazi mass murderer. Indicate which theory (a) lacks simplicity, (b) is not conservative, (c) is untestable, and (d) has the most scope. (Some theories may merit more than one of these designations.)

17. Theory: Astrology—the notion that the position of the stars and planets at your birth controls your destiny—has no basis in fact.

18. Theory: Astrology works, but the astrologer read the horoscope wrong.

19. Theory: An unknown planetary force interfered with the astrological factors that normally determine a person's destiny.

Evaluate the following theory using the TEST formula. Indicate what phenomenon is being explained. Use your background knowledge to assess the evidence. Specify one alternative theory, use the criteria of adequacy to assess the two theories, and determine which one is more plausible.

20. Joseph has acted strangely for years—always wearing black clothes and sometimes having seizures in public. He's possessed.

 Integrative Exercises

These exercises pertain to material in Chapters 3–5 and 8–10.

1. What is an enumerative induction?

2. What is an analogical induction?

3. What is a necessary condition? a sufficient condition?

4. What is the appeal to ignorance?

For each of the following arguments, specify the conclusion and premises. If necessary, add implicit premises and conclusions.

5. "While the time may be right for more privacy in our bedrooms and civil rights protection for gays in the workplace, we don't think most people want our laws rewritten to accommodate same-sex marriage. Instead, they probably agree with *Boston Globe* columnist Jeff Jacoby, who wrote, 'Sometimes, change destroys. No structure can stand for long when its bearing wall is removed. The bearing wall of marriage—its central and universal characteristic—is its heterosexuality. Knock that down and what is left is ruin.'" [Editorial, *The Tribune-Star*, Terre Haute, IN]

6. "Today in Western New York, more than 46,000 people suffer from Alzheimer's disease or a related dementia. Without a research breakthrough or the development of new treatments in the next few years, 14 million baby boomers nationwide will be victims of the disease, and the cost of their care alone will bankrupt both Medicaid and Medicare. We urge voters to call their senators and representatives to ask them to commit more funding for Alzheimer's research." [Letter to the editor, *Buffalo News*]

7. "OK, I've been shilly-shallying around here, hesitant to come right out and say what I think, but I'm becoming convinced that our president, the man with his finger on the nuclear trigger, is a bona fide nutcase. I really do. For him to say God told him to strike al-Qaida is just nutso. For him to say God told him to strike at Saddam, ditto. This guy is not dealing with a full deck." [Editorial, SFGate.com]

8. "As to his [Braxton's] reasoning that 'perhaps there is a public-health basis for anti-sodomy laws' since ' . . . scores of thousands of American homosexuals died from engaging in same sexual acts,' there is a bit of a problem. Since heterosexuals also have died from diseases that have directly resulted from sex, then, by Braxton's logic, the Supreme Court would have to ban heterosexual unions as well. With all the conservatives' carping about the intrusiveness of government, one would think that the elimination of laws concerning one's private life would be cause for celebration for a conservative like Braxton." [Letter to the editor, *Newsday*]

For each of the following phenomena, indicate (1) a possible hypothesis to explain it, (2) a possible competing hypothesis, and (3) a test implication for each hypothesis.

9. The accident rate on I-295 has been very high but was reduced considerably after the speed limit was lowered to 60 mph and billboards urged drivers to obey the law.

10. In stressful situations, women appear to adapt better and quicker to the emotional demands of the situation than men do.

11. The percentage of high school seniors engaging in sexual intercourse has risen dramatically in the past six years.

12. The mosquito population in the county has decreased drastically in the past year even though county workers have curtailed the use of insecticides and have stopped urging residents to get rid of standing water on their property, which is a breeding ground for the insects.

Evaluate each of the following theories and indicate whether it is plausible or implausible.

13. Treatment for HIV/AIDS is much more effective than it used to be because of global warming.

14. Six thousand years ago a worldwide flood devastated Earth, killing all but a handful of human beings, who survived by building an ark.

15. The universe is so vast, with billions of stars that could have planets that will sustain life, that it is probable that intelligent life exists in other places besides Earth.

16. Transcendental meditation shows us that if enough people meditate together on the prevention of crime, the crime rate in an area will decrease.

Evaluate each of the following theories using the TEST formula. Use your background knowledge to assess the evidence. Specify one alternative theory, use the criteria of adequacy to assess the two theories, and determine which one is more plausible.

17. The United States lost the Vietnam War because the Americans' weapons were inferior to those of the North Vietnamese.

18. The federal deficit is astronomically high because of accounting errors.

19. The conflict between the Israelis and Palestinians is caused by the meddling of the United States and Britain.

20. Everyone who has ever beaten cancer—that is, been cured—has done so because of a wholesome diet.

 Writing Assignments

1. In a one-page essay evaluate the following theories using the TEST formula:

   a. **Phenomenon:** People report feeling less arthritis pain after taking fish oil capsules.
      Theory 1: Fish oil relieves joint pain.
      Theory 2: The placebo effect.

   b. **Phenomenon:** A temporary drop in the crime rate in Des Moines, Iowa, just after a transcendental meditation (TM) group meditated for three days on a lower crime rate.
      Theory 1: TM meditation lowers crime rates.
      Theory 2: Normal fluctuations in Des Moines crime rate.

   c. **Phenomenon:** Fifty patients with severe arthritis pain were prayed for by one hundred people, and twenty-five out of those fifty patients reported a significant lessening of pain.
      Theory 1: Prayer heals.
      Theory 2: Normal pain remission that is characteristic of arthritis.

2. Read Essay 14 ("Fighting Islamic Terrorists Who Stifle Free Speech") in Appendix B and write a two-page essay assessing the strength or validity of its argument.

3. Devise two theories to explain the low test scores of most of the students in your calculus course, and then write a two-page paper evaluating the worth of the two theories.

4. Write a three-page essay evaluating the arguments in Essay 19 ("Freedom of Expression: Policy Reflects Common Sense") and Essay 18 ("Freedom of Expression: Protect Student Speech—Even 'Unwise' Bong Banner"). Explain which essay contains the stronger argument and why.

Critical Thinking in Morality and the Law

 ## CHAPTER OBJECTIVES

MORAL ARGUMENTS

- Understand the distinction between moral statements, arguments, and theories.
- Learn the difference between moral and nonmoral statements.
- Be familiar with the structure of moral arguments.
- Know the reason why a moral argument requires at least one moral premise.
- Know how to supply the missing moral premise in a moral argument.
- Know how to use the counterexample method to evaluate moral premises.

MORAL PREMISES

- Be able to define moral principle, moral theory, and considered moral judgment.
- Understand how moral premises can be supported or undermined by moral principles, moral theories, and considered moral judgments.
- Know how to use the counterexample method to assess a moral premise.

MORAL THEORIES

- Recognize the differences among moral judgments, principles, and theories.
- Recognize that everyone has a moral theory and that it's important to ensure that your moral theory is coherent.
- Understand the similarities between moral theories and scientific theories.
- Know the three moral criteria of adequacy.
- Know how to apply the moral criteria of adequacy to moral theories.

LEGAL REASONING

- Understand how arguments and inference are used in the law and how inductive reasoning in particular is applied to determine facts and causes.

- Explain why reasoning by analogy is so important in judicial decision-making and how judges apply it to decide cases in light of previous settled cases.

A COHERENT WORLDVIEW

- Understand what a worldview is and why having a coherent worldview is so important.
- Understand how a worldview can fail to be coherent.
- Know how and why the criterion of internal consistency is applied to worldviews.

W E HAVE COME FAR. WE HAVE SEEN THAT WE CAN PRODUCTIVELY APPLY critical thinking to everyday claims, arguments, and problems; to explanations in a wide range of subject areas; to scientific theories of all sorts; and to offbeat theories of the paranormal and supernatural kind. Now we can go even further. We can now venture into a vast and complex sphere that is often thought to be off limits to critical reasoning: *morality*. Morality concerns beliefs about right and wrong, good and bad, and just and unjust. It's an aspect of life that we deal with every day because we have little choice. In countless situations we must decide what we ought to do or not do, what is moral or immoral, and what is good or bad. To do these things, we are forced to accept or reject moral statements, make and criticize moral arguments, and wrestle with moral theories.

In this process of contending with moral issues, we inevitably formulate our own moral theory—our own beliefs about what morality is or is not, what actions are right or wrong, and what things are good or bad. To an astonishing degree, our moral theory charts the course of our lives. If the course matters, then we must try to fashion the best moral theory we can.

If we are to be intellectually mature, we also must try to integrate the results of these moral analyses and deliberations into a comprehensive picture of reality, what is known as a worldview. A **worldview** is a philosophy of life, a set of beliefs and theories that helps us make sense of a wide range of issues in life. It defines for us what exists, what should be, and what we can know. We all have a worldview, and our notions about morality are an important part of it. A good critical thinker tries to ensure that his or her worldview contains no internal contradictions and that it offers reliable guidance in dealing with the world.

So in this chapter, we set out to apply critical thinking to some big ideas and broad questions. We explore procedures for evaluating moral discourse—specifically, moral judgments, principles, arguments, and theories—and look at ways that we can incorporate our understanding into a coherent worldview.

Moral Arguments

A moral argument, like any other kind of argument, has premises and a conclusion. The premises (and sometimes the conclusion) may be implied, not stated, and they may be simple or complex—just as in other arguments. Moral arguments, however, differ from nonmoral ones in that their conclusions are moral

FURTHER THOUGHT

Is Moral Reasoning Possible?

Some people claim that reasoning about morality is not possible because moral statements are not statements at all. This view is a moral theory known as *emotivism*. Emotivism says that moral statements are just not the kinds of things that can be true or false. They are more like exclamations such as "Hooray!" or "Bah!" They are expressions of emotion, not statements of fact. So according to emotivism, the sentence "Capital punishment is wrong" means something like "Capital punishment—boo!"

But this theory has been severely criticized by moral philosophers. They contend, for example, that in several ways the theory conflicts with our experience of the moral life. Our everyday moral experience seems to suggest that we sometimes have moral disagreements with others. The notion that we do have disagreements seems to most people like a simple matter of common sense. But according to emotivism, moral disagreements are impossible. Since moral utterances are not statements, they cannot contradict one another. If you say "ice cream—yes!" and someone else says "ice cream—yuk!" the two of you are not disagreeing; you're just venting. But our moral experience seems to show that in moral disagreements we are doing much more than expressing emotion. In addition, emotivism says that nothing is good or bad, right or wrong, because these terms don't refer to anything. But our moral experience appears to suggest that some things really are good or bad, right or wrong. Many moral philosophers believe that these considerations show that emotivism must be mistaken.

Critics who take this line of argument against emotivism admit that our commonsense moral experience may be misleading. It's possible that emotivism is correct after all. Commonsense views of the world have been wrong in the past. But, these critics assert, we are justified in believing what common sense tells us unless we have good reason to doubt it.

> "A system of morality which is based on relative emotional values is a mere illusion, a thoroughly vulgar conception which has nothing sound in it and nothing true."
> —Socrates

statements. In general, a **moral statement** is a statement asserting that an action is right or wrong (moral or immoral) or that something (such as a person or motive) is good or bad. Here are some moral statements:

- Serena should keep her promise to you.
- It is wrong to treat James so harshly.
- Abortion is immoral.
- We ought to protect Liu from the angry mob.
- My father is a good man.

Moral statements are plainly different from nonmoral, or descriptive, statements. Nonmoral statements do not assert that something is right or wrong, good or bad—they simply describe a state of affairs without giving it a value one way or the other. Compare these nonmoral statements with the moral statements just given:

- Serena did not keep her promise to you.
- James was treated harshly.
- Some people think abortion is immoral.
- Liu was protected from the angry mob.
- My father tried to be a good man.

The standard moral argument is a mixture of moral and nonmoral statements. At least one premise is a moral statement that asserts a general moral principle or moral standard. At least one premise makes a nonmoral claim. And the conclusion is a moral statement, or judgment, about a particular case (usually a particular kind of action). For example:

Argument 1
(1) It is wrong to inflict unnecessary pain on a child.
(2) Spanking inflicts unnecessary pain on a child.
(3) Therefore, spanking is wrong.

In this simple argument, premise 1 is a moral statement, affirming a general moral principle. Premise 2 is a nonmoral statement describing the nature of a specific kind of action. And the conclusion is the moral statement that the argument is intended to establish. It is about a specific kind of action.

A standard moral argument has this form for good reason. In a moral argument, we simply cannot establish the conclusion (a moral statement) without a moral premise. A moral argument with only nonmoral premises does not work. To put it another way, we cannot infer what *should be* or *ought to be* (in the conclusion) from statements about *what is*. Suppose the previous argument reads like this (and there are no missing premises):

Spanking inflicts unnecessary pain on a child.
Therefore, spanking is wrong.

 FURTHER THOUGHT

Moral and Nonmoral Statements

Is this a moral statement: "I am opposed to abortion"? How about this one: "I feel very strongly that abortion is wrong"? Actually in many contexts, statements like these are not meant to be moral statements at all; they are not meant to assert that an action is right or wrong or that a person is good or bad. They are used instead to report on someone's state of mind. Saying that you feel a certain way toward an action is not the same thing as stating that the action is wrong. But be careful. Sometimes statements like these really are meant as moral statements. Context will usually tell you which kind of statement is intended.

The premise doesn't say anything about right or wrong; it just makes a descriptive claim. The conclusion, though, does assert something about right or wrong. So the conclusion is not supported by the premise; it does not follow from the descriptive statement.

Here's another example:

Torturing prisoners of war is a case of intentional mistreatment.
Prisoners of war should not be tortured.

This argument fails because the moral premise is missing. We need a moral premise to connect the nonmoral premise to the conclusion, like this:

Argument 2
No prisoner of war should ever be intentionally mistreated.
Torturing prisoners of war is a case of intentional mistreatment.
Prisoners of war should not be tortured.

 FURTHER THOUGHT

Can't We All Just Get Along?

Despite the prevalence of moral disagreements on countless issues, there is a surprising amount of agreement on basic moral principles. Often, the bone of contention in moral arguments is not the moral premises (which may be widely accepted), but the nonmoral ones. In debates about "pulling the plug" on severely comatose patients, for example, all parties may agree that murder is wrong but disagree about the nature of comatose patients. Some may insist that comatose patients are entities that can be murdered (because they are fully human, true persons, etc.); others, that comatose patients are not the kind of entities that can be murdered (because they are not persons, for example). So there may not be as much moral disagreement in the world as you might think. Here's a list of moral principles that both parties in moral debates often accept:

- **Personal benefit:** Acknowledge the extent to which an action produces beneficial consequences for the individual in question.
- **Principle of benevolence:** Help those in need.
- **Principle of harm:** Do not harm others.
- **Principle of honesty:** Do not deceive others.
- **Principle of lawfulness:** Do not violate the law.
- **Principle of autonomy:** Acknowledge a person's freedom over his/her actions or physical body.
- **Principle of justice:** Acknowledge a person's right to due process, fair compensation for harm done, and fair distribution of benefits.
- **Rights:** Acknowledge a person's rights to life, information, privacy, free expression, and safety.[1]

In the standard moral argument, we also need a nonmoral premise. Remember that the conclusion is a moral statement (judgment) about a particular kind of action. The moral premise, however, is a statement expressing a general moral principle about a much broader class of actions. In order to infer the narrower conclusion from a much broader premise, we need a nonmoral statement to bridge the gap. For example, from the general moral principle that "no prisoner of war should ever be intentionally mistreated," we cannot conclude that "prisoners of war should not be tortured" unless there is a nonmoral premise stating that torturing prisoners of war is a type of intentional mistreatment. Likewise from the general moral principle that "murder is wrong," we cannot conclude that "abortion is wrong" unless there's a factual premise telling us that abortion is murder.

Now, very often when you encounter moral arguments, they are abbreviated and missing the moral premise (the general moral principle), like the arguments discussed earlier:

Spanking inflicts unnecessary pain on a child.
Therefore, spanking is wrong.

Torturing prisoners of war is a case of intentional mistreatment.
Prisoners of war should not be tortured.

Usually, the moral premise is missing because it's implicit. In such cases, to make sense of the argument, you must supply the implicit premise. Sometimes you may automatically add the implicit premise in your head without bothering to properly fill out the argument. But if you want to carefully evaluate moral arguments, it's best to spell out any missing premises. Implicit moral premises are often dubious and need to be studied closely. General moral principles that are taken for granted may turn out to be unfounded or incomplete. Also, laying everything out on the table like this is essential if you want to improve the argument—an important exercise if you care that your positions on moral issues are well supported.

The simplest approach to identifying implicit premises is to treat moral arguments as deductive. (Notice that arguments 1 and 2 are valid deductive arguments.) Your task, then, is to supply plausible premises that will make the argument valid. (We used this same procedure in Chapter 3 for finding implicit premises.) Consider this argument:

Cloning humans is unnatural.
Therefore, cloning humans is morally
wrong.

As it stands, this argument is not valid, and we can see right away that the missing premise is a general moral principle. A plausible premise to make this argument valid,

"Do everything ethically ... within reason, of course."

then, is "Anything unnatural is morally wrong," a general moral principle. The revised version is:

Argument 3
Anything unnatural is morally wrong.
Cloning humans is unnatural.
Therefore, cloning humans is morally wrong.

Here's another incomplete argument:

Meg lied to her sister for no good reason.
Therefore, Meg should not have lied to her sister.

To make this argument valid and to supply a general moral principle, we can add this premise:

Argument 4
One should not lie without good reason.
Meg lied to her sister for no good reason.
Therefore, Meg should not have lied to her sister.

Another advantage to treating moral arguments as deductive (and to supplying explicit premises that will make the arguments valid) is ease of analysis. Generally, moral arguments are easier to appraise and modify when they are deductive. And if they are deductively valid, you know that any flaws in the arguments will likely be the result of false premises. For example, if you have a deductively valid argument, and the conclusion is false, you know that at least one of the premises is false.

> "So, if we can support our [moral] judgments with good reasons, and provide explanations of why these reasons matter, and show that the case on the other side is weak, what more in the way of 'proof' could anyone possibly want?"
> —James Rachels

Moral Premises

In good arguments the inferences are valid or strong and the premises—whether nonmoral or moral—are true. This latter stipulation means that to make good arguments, you must ensure that the premises are backed by good reasons and are not simply assumed without warrant. To evaluate arguments, you must check the premises for these same qualities. As noted in previous chapters, accurately assessing the truth of nonmoral premises depends mostly on your knowledge of the subject matter, including the results of relevant scientific research, the analyses of reliable experts, and the content of your background information. Gauging the truth of moral premises (moral principles) mostly involves examining the support they get from three sources: (1) other moral principles, (2) moral theories, and (3) considered moral judgments.

The appeal to another moral principle (usually a more general or higher-level principle) is probably the most common way to support a moral premise. Often the more general principle is extremely credible or accepted by all parties so that further support for it is unnecessary. Sometimes it is controversial so that it too is in need of support. Suppose the moral premise in question is, "A dying patient in intolerable and untreatable pain should be allowed to commit suicide with a

"BUT ISN'T IT MORE IMPORTANT TO LEARN HOW TO BE A DECENT HUMAN BEING?"

www.CartoonStock.com

physician's help." Some would say that this claim is derived from, or is based on, the higher (and more widely accepted) principle of autonomy—the notion that a person has an inherent right of self-determination, a right to make autonomous choices about his or her own life and death. Others would support the premise by appealing to the principle of beneficence, or mercy: If we are in a position to relieve the severe suffering of another without excessive cost to ourselves, we have a duty to do so. They would interpret this principle as sanctioning the physician's role in helping a competent, hopelessly ill patient to die. To try to show that the premise is false, someone might appeal to a sanctity-of-life principle, asserting that human life is sacred and should be preserved at all costs. When such higher principles are brought in, the truth of the original premise often becomes clear—or not. They cannot be the court of final appeal in ethics, for they too can be tested by reasoned argument showing why they should or should not be believed.

Reasons for accepting or rejecting a moral premise can also come from a moral theory, a general explanation of what makes an action right or what makes a person or motive good (see the next section). For example, traditional utilitarianism is a moral theory asserting that right actions are those that produce the greatest happiness for all concerned. To support the assisted suicide premise, you could appeal to the theory, arguing that the least amount of unhappiness (pain and suffering) for all concerned (patient, physician, and family) would result if the physician helped the patient die. To counter your argument, someone would need to show that your happiness calculations were incorrect (for example, that assisted suicide actually causes more unhappiness in the long run), or that utilitarianism itself is an inadequate theory, or that other theories or considerations are more important or relevant than utilitarian factors.

A moral premise can also be supported or undermined by our *considered moral judgments*. These are moral judgments that we consider credible after we carefully and dispassionately reflect on them. Pertaining to either specific cases or general statements, they constitute what philosophers have called our moral common sense. They are not infallible guides to morality, but unless we have good reasons for doubting their soundness, we are entitled to trust them. Some of our considered judgments may seem undeniable, even self-evident—for example: "Inflicting unnecessary, undeserved suffering on someone is wrong"; "Torturing children for the fun of it is immoral"; "Treating people harshly merely because of the color of their skin is unjust."

Moral principles, theories, and judgments relate to one another in interesting ways (a topic we explore in the following pages). For now, it's enough to note that we can evaluate moral premises by seeing if they conflict with principles, theories, or judgments that we have good reason to trust. Specifically, we can assess a moral premise the same way we might assess any other kind of universal generalization—by trying to think of counterexamples to it. Consider this deductively valid argument, a modified version of argument 3:

Argument 5
(1) The medical cloning of humans is unnatural because it is something that would not occur without human intervention.
(2) All actions that are unnatural and that are not done for religious reasons should not be done.
(3) The medical cloning of humans is never done for religious reasons.
(4) Therefore, cloning humans should not be done.

Premise 2 is the general moral principle here. Is it true? At the very least it is questionable. We know that it's questionable because we can think of counterexamples to it. That is, we can think of instances in which the principle seems not to hold. For example, what about the use of antibiotics to treat infections? The use of antibiotics is unnatural as defined in the argument (they are a good example of human intervention in the natural course of illness), and few would claim that antibiotics are employed for religious reasons. (The term "for religious reasons" is vague, but we will assume for the sake of this example that it means something like "as an integral part of established religious practice.") But despite its unnaturalness, the use of antibiotics seems to be morally acceptable to almost everyone. At any rate, it is difficult to imagine what a plausible argument against antibiotics would be like. So premise 2 appears to be false. We could probably refute premise 2 by using many other counterexamples, such as wearing clothes, drinking bottled water, and riding a bicycle.

Moral Theories

Very often when we assess moral arguments and in other ways think critically about morality, we are trying to come to a moral judgment about a particular issue or kind of action. We deliberate because we want to understand what's right or wrong, good or bad. Our moral judgments may appear as premises or conclusions in our arguments or as sturdy pillars of our moral common sense. They may be justified by appeals to general moral principles, which in turn may gain credibility from the most reliable of our moral judgments. But what of moral theories? In the previous section we saw how a moral theory can strengthen or weaken a moral premise. Yet that's only part of the story.

As we have seen, theories of morality are attempts to explain what makes an action right or what makes a person or motive good. They try to specify what all right actions and all good things have in common. As such, they can give support, guidance, or validation to our moral decision making, shaping our moral principles, judgments, and arguments. Traditional utilitarianism (mentioned earlier) is a

well-known example of a moral theory. Another is the divine command theory, the view that what makes an action right is that God commands it or wills it. Ethical egoism asserts that right actions are those that promote one's own best interests.

Interestingly enough, we all have a moral theory. Whether we articulate it or not, we all have some kind of view of what makes actions right or persons good. Even the notion that there is no such thing as right or wrong is a moral theory. Even the idea that all moral theories are worthless or that all moral judgments are subjective, objective, relative, or meaningless is a moral theory. The critical question, then, is not whether you have a moral theory but whether the theory you have is a good one.

Moral theorizing is a fact of the moral life. We do moral theorizing when we ponder what rightness or goodness means, or try to furnish basic justification for a moral standard, or resolve a conflict between principles, or gauge the credibility of moral intuitions, or explain why an action is right or wrong. To theorize is to step back from the specifics of a case and try to see the larger pattern that can help us make sense of it all.

Despite the importance of moral theories, they are not the ultimate authority or sole referee in moral reasoning. A theory gives us very general norms, but morality is about more than just generalities—it's also about the particulars of individual moral judgments. How do the general and the particular fit together? Here is one way. Suppose you must decide whether an action is morally permissible. From a plausible moral theory, you draw general guidance in the form of moral principles that apply to the case. If the principles appear to sanction conflicting decisions, you turn again to the theory for understanding in how to resolve the inconsistency. At the same time you consult your considered moral judgments. If your theory and your considered judgments lead you to the same conclusion, you have good reason to believe that the conclusion is correct. If your theory and considered judgments diverge, you must decide which is more credible. If the implications of your theory seem more plausible, you may decide to revise your considered judgments to cohere better with the theory. If your judgments seem more plausible, you may decide to alter your theory accordingly. If your credible judgments conflict drastically with your theory, you may be justified in giving up the theory altogether.

> "In my view moral theorizing is something that real people do in everyday life. It is not just the domain of professors, expounding in their lecture halls. Moral theorizing can be found on the highways and byways, practiced by everyone from bartenders to politicians."
> —Dale Jamieson

Evaluating Moral Theories

As you may have gathered, several moral theories vie for our allegiance, each one with a distinctive take on morality and with different implications for moral issues. Moral philosophers remind us that theories also differ in quality: All moral theories are not created equal. Some theories are better than others. This fact immediately prompts two questions: Which moral theory is best, and how can we judge that it is the best? Recall that we asked this type of question in Chapters 9 and 10 when we discussed inference to the best explanation and several types of theories (everyday, scientific, and weird). The answer in this chapter is the same as the answer in those chapters: To identify the best theory, we must compare competing theories and use the criteria of adequacy to appraise their worth. The criteria of adequacy that we use in judging moral theories are a little different from those we

FURTHER THOUGHT

Critiquing Moral Theories

Most moral philosophers don't buy the idea that one moral theory is as good as any other. They spend a good deal of time evaluating moral theories to gauge their worth, and some theories don't fare very well under this scrutiny. Here, for example, are some typical criticisms of four controversial moral theories.

Note on relativism: In Chapter 2, we discussed relativism as it applies to truth generally, and we saw that it comes in two varieties—subjective and social. But relativism is very often restricted to the sphere of morality and is thus termed, as you would expect, *moral relativism.* And like general relativism, moral relativism can apply to individuals (*subjective moral relativism*) or to societies (*social moral relativism*). When the context is clear, these long names are usually shortened to subjective relativism or social relativism, or just relativism.

SUBJECTIVE MORAL RELATIVISM

This view states that what makes an action right for someone is that it is approved by that person. Moral judgments are relative to what each person believes. If you say that stealing is wrong, then it's wrong (for you). If someone else says that stealing is right, then it's right (for her). Moral philosophers, though, think that the theory has several problematic implications. For example, the theory implies that each person is morally infallible. If you truly approve of an action, then it's right, and you cannot be wrong. Subjective relativism also makes moral disagreement nearly impossible. You disagree with others when you think they are mistaken. But according to subjective relativism, no one could be mistaken. These and other implications, critics say, render the theory implausible.

SOCIAL MORAL RELATIVISM

This view claims that what makes an action right is that it's approved by one's society. If your society deems something to be right, it's right. Moral truth is relative to societies, or cultures. As you might expect, this view is criticized for many of the same problems that plague subjective relativism. It implies that societies are infallible. This means that if most people living in Nazi Germany during World War II had approved of the extermination of the Jews, then the Holocaust was morally right. It seems, though, that societies are no more infallible than individuals are. What's more, social relativism implies that it would be impossible to disagree with one's society and be right. Social reformers such as Martin Luther King, Jr., or Gandhi could not claim that an action approved by society is wrong, for if society approves of it, the action is right. For these and other reasons, most moral philosophers view social relativism as a questionable moral theory.

ETHICAL EGOISM

In this view, what makes an action right is that it promotes one's own best interests. It doesn't imply that you should do anything you want because, in the long run, that may not be in your own best interest. Ethical egoism could even condone altruism on the grounds that being nice to other people is in your best interest. Critics, however, say that the theory is implausible because it sanctions all sorts of abominable acts. For example, if it's in your best interest to kill your boss, and if you could do it without suffering any negative consequences (such as getting caught), then ethical egoism says that your moral duty is to kill him.

DIVINE COMMAND THEORY

This is the idea that God *makes* morality; right and wrong are constituted by the will of God. Right actions are those commanded by God; wrong actions are those prohibited by God. The problem here as most philosophers see it is that the doctrine forces a troubling dilemma on us: Are actions right because God commands them, or does God command them because they are right? To choose the first option is to say that God makes morality and to accept the divine command theory. To choose the second is to say that morality exists independently of God's will, and even he must obey it. For many theists, the second option (the denial of the divine command theory) is far more palatable than the first, for the first one implies that morality is completely arbitrary. These critics argue that if an action is morally right only because God says so, then *any* action at all could be morally right. If God so willed, the torture and slaughter of innocents would be morally right. As the divine command theory would have it, there could be no reasons for God's willing one way or the other. He just commands, and that makes an action right (or wrong). But if God has no reasons for his commands, no standards other than his say-so, his commands are arbitrary. This arbitrariness makes morality a cruel joke and reveals God as less than perfect. It has led both theists and nontheists to reject the divine command theory and to accept the second option of the dilemma, the view that morality is not dependent on God's will.

use to assess other types of theories, though the two sets of criteria have much in common. In significant ways, too, moral theories are much like scientific theories, and the process of theory evaluation is similar in both cases.

How are moral theories like scientific theories? Recall that scientific theories try to explain the causes of events, everything from tumor growth to exploding stars. A plausible scientific theory is one that's consistent with all the relevant data. A theory explaining the cause of a fatal illness, for example, must take into account facts about patient symptoms, medical test results, medical histories, environmental factors, and more. Moral theories, on the other hand, try to explain what makes an action right or what makes a person good. A plausible moral theory must also be consistent with the relevant data. The data that moral theories try to explain are our considered moral judgments, the moral judgments we accept after we reason about them carefully. Any plausible moral theory must be consistent with those considered moral judgments. As we have seen, they are fallible and revisable, but we are entitled to believe them unless we have good reason to doubt them. If a moral theory is seriously inconsistent with them—if, for example, it approves of obviously immoral acts (such as inflicting pain on innocent children for no good reason or treating equals unequally)—it is dubious, perhaps even fatally flawed, and deserving of radical revision or rejection. So the first criterion of adequacy for moral theories is: *consistency with considered moral judgments.*

In science (and many other fields of inquiry) there is an interesting relationship between theory and data. The data have an impact on the theory because the theory explains the data. A good theory, on the other hand, can lead scientists to reject certain data. Scientists want the data and theory to match up as closely as possible. They want the match to be so close that significant changes in either the data or theory aren't necessary. Moral theories work this way too. As suggested earlier, our moral data (our considered moral judgments) influence our moral theory. And our moral theory can lead us to accept or reject certain data. Ideally, we want the fit between data and theory to be as close as possible. In other words, we want to achieve what moral philosophers refer to as a "reflective equilibrium" between facts and theory. We want the fit to be so close that significant adjustments in either data or theory are not necessary.

In addition to being consistent with the data, a plausible scientific theory must also be conservative. It must be consistent with background information—that is, with well-founded beliefs such as reliable scientific findings and well-established theories. Plausible moral theories must also be consistent with the relevant background information—that is, with our experience of the moral life. Whatever else our moral experience involves, it certainly includes (1) making moral judgments (we do this constantly), (2) having moral disagreements (we occasionally do this), and (3) sometimes acting immorally (we recognize that we are not morally perfect). If a moral theory suggests that we do not have these experiences, we must view the theory with suspicion. Another criterion of adequacy for moral theories, then, is *consistency with our experience of the moral life.*

Now, it's possible that our experience of the moral life is an illusion, only seeming to involve making moral judgments, having moral disagreements, and getting into moral disagreements. But unless we have good reason to believe that our moral experience is an illusion, we are justified in accepting it at face value.

A scientific theory gains in credibility if it helps to solve problems (has fruitfulness and scope). A plausible moral theory must also help to solve problems. That is, it must help us make moral decisions, especially those that involve

 REVIEW NOTES

Moral Criteria of Adequacy

1. Consistency with our considered moral judgments
2. Consistency with our experience of the moral life
3. Workability in real-life situations

moral dilemmas, instances where moral principles or moral judgments are in conflict. After all, the reason we want a moral theory is that it helps guide our actions and reconcile clashing moral beliefs. A moral theory that offers no help with such moral problems is said to be *unworkable*. Unworkable moral theories are inferior. So a final criterion of adequacy for moral theories is *workability in real-life situations*.

Two Important Theories

Now let's see how we can use these criteria to take the measure of two fundamentally different theories: traditional utilitarianism and Kantian ethics.

Traditional utilitarianism was founded by Jeremy Bentham (1748–1832) and later refined by John Stuart Mill (1806–1873). Bentham's idea was that

 NEWSMAKERS

Relativism and Honor Killings

In recent years, stories like this one have been appearing in the news with shocking frequency:

> Fawaz later recalled that his wife, Zahra, was sleeping soundly on her side and curled slightly against the pillow when he rose at dawn and readied himself for work at his construction job on the outskirts of Damascus. It was a rainy Sunday morning in January and very cold; as he left, Fawaz turned back one last time to tuck the blanket more snugly around his 16-year-old wife. Zahra slept on without stirring, and her husband locked the door of their tiny apartment carefully behind him.
>
> Zahra was most likely still sleeping when her older brother, Fayyez, entered the apartment a short time later, using a stolen key and carrying a dagger. His sister lay on the carpeted floor, on the thin, foam mattress she shared with her husband, so Fayyez must have had to kneel next to Zahra as he raised the dagger and stabbed her five times in the head and back: brutal, tearing thrusts

Zahra's grave in Damascus.

that shattered the base of her skull and nearly severed her spinal column. Leaving the door open, Fayyez walked downstairs and out to the local police station. There, he reportedly turned himself in, telling the officers on duty that he had killed his sister in order to remove the dishonor she had brought on the family by losing her virginity out of wedlock nearly 10 months earlier.

"Fayyez told the police, 'It is my right to correct this error,'" Maha Ali, a Syrian lawyer who knew Zahra and now works pro bono for her husband, told me not long ago. "He said, 'It's true that my sister is married now, but we never washed away the shame.'"[2]

Fayyez had committed an honor killing, a murder for the sake of a family's honor, usually involving the slaying of a sister, wife, or daughter thought to have disgraced the family by immoral behavior. Nowadays women are killed for having an extramarital affair, having premarital sex, being flirtatious, being raped or sexually abused, or otherwise violating some cultural taboo. The United Nations Population Fund estimates that each year about 5000 honor killings are committed in countries all over the globe. They have occurred in the United States, Europe, Africa, and the Middle East, mostly in Muslim communities where they are generally approved of or at least tolerated to some degree.

Fawaz, Zahra's widower.

Honor killings have presented a disquieting challenge to Western social moral relativists, who are committed to saying that the murders are morally permissible if they are approved by the culture involved. But this view often conflicts with that of the relativists' own culture, which may endorse universal human rights (including women's rights) and strongly condemn such murders.

Do you believe that honor killings are wrong—even in those cultures that approve of them? On what grounds? If you are a relativist, are you a consistent one, conceding that honor killings are right if one's society sanctions them? If you think they are objectively wrong, do you also judge other heinous acts wrong even though they are culturally sanctioned?

right actions are those that achieve the greatest happiness for the greatest number. He declared that by this simple standard all actions could be judged. Many people embraced the theory, for it seemed so much more rational than moral theories of the time, which often rested on dubious assumptions. In the nineteenth century, traditional utilitarianism inspired reformers who worked to abolish slavery, eliminate child labor, and increase recognition of women's rights.

To be more precise, traditional utilitarianism says that what makes an action right is that it maximizes overall happiness, everyone considered. Acting morally in any given situation, then, involves calculating how much happiness can be produced by several possible actions, identifying the persons who will be affected by those actions, and opting for the one action that produces the greatest amount of happiness in the world. Notice that what matters in utilitarianism is the *consequences* of an action—not whether the action breaks a rule or violates some abstract principle. If happiness is maximized by a particular action, then the action is morally right, regardless of any other considerations. By the lights of utilitarianism, the end justifies the means.

How does traditional utilitarianism fare when judged by the moral criteria of adequacy? For starters, the theory does seem to be consistent with key aspects of our experience of the moral life. The theory assumes that we can and do make moral judgments, have moral disagreements, and act immorally.

Some critics, however, have questioned whether traditional utilitarianism is a workable theory because calculating amounts of happiness seems to be extremely difficult or impossible. For example, each action we perform has consequences indefinitely into the future. If this is the case, then at what point should we make our calculation of the happiness produced? Should we figure into our calculations the happiness that will accrue by next Tuesday? next year? next decade? Some actions may produce very little happiness in the short run but a great deal of happiness over the long haul. Some actions work the other way round—big short-term benefits, no long-term payback. Traditional utilitarianism offers no help in resolving this problem, and so critics have accused the theory of being unworkable.

Many moral philosophers think that the theory faces a much bigger problem than unworkability: It seems to conflict with many of our considered moral judgments. For instance, the theory seems inconsistent with our considered moral judgments involving rights. We tend to think that certain things should not be done to people even if doing them would produce the greatest amount of happiness in the world. We would not think it right to falsely accuse and punish an innocent person just because doing so would make a whole town of people happy. We would not think it right to torture one person just because the action would make a dozen other people extremely happy. Our considered moral judgments say that such actions are wrong, but traditional utilitarianism says they may be right.

FURTHER THOUGHT

Critical Thinking and Racism

Critical thinking makes moral reasoning possible, helping us use and evaluate arguments and evidence, theories and principles, and moral and nonmoral facts. But how useful—really—is critical thinking in the vital work of making sense of the large, weighty, and seemingly intractable social issues of our time?

In many cases, *very* useful. Consider the issue of racism, a monstrous evil to dispel from society and often a hard topic to discuss without provoking raised voices and elevated blood pressures. But what is racism—and who exactly is a racist?

The distinguished philosopher Lawrence Blum, author of the book *"I'm Not a Racist But . . ." The Moral Quandary of Race,* uses critical reasoning to try to answer this question. He draws attention to the "conceptual inflation" of the terms *racist* and *racism.* He and other scholars observe that the words are so overused and misapplied that they are losing their moral power to indict and to shame. Their reckless use causes misunderstanding and resentment. Blum says,

> Some feel that the word [racist] is thrown around so much that anything involving "race" that someone does not like is liable to castigation as "racist." . . . A local newspaper called certain blacks "racist" for criticizing other blacks who supported a white over a black candidate for mayor. A white girl in Virginia said that it was "racist" for an African American teacher in her school to wear African attire. . . . Merely mentioning someone's race (or racial designation), using the word "Oriental" for Asians without recognizing its origins and its capacity for insult, or socializing only with members of one's own racial group are called "racist."[3]

Blum cuts through popular confusion about racism by offering a plausible definition of the word. All forms of racism, past and present, he says, involve two key elements: (1) an attitude or belief that another race is *inferior* or (2) *antipathy* (hatred, hostility) toward that race.

> Inferiorization is linked to historical racist doctrine and racist social systems. Slavery, segregation, imperialism, apartheid, and Nazism all treated certain groups as inferior to other groups. . . .
>
> Though race-based antipathy is less related to the original concept of "racism," today the term unequivocally encompasses racial bigotry, hostility, and hatred. Indeed, the racial bigot is many people's paradigm image of a "racist." . . .
>
> Historical systems of racism did of course inevitably involve racial antipathy as well as inferiorization. Hatred of Jews was central to Nazi philosophy; and it is impossible to understand American racism without seeing hostility to blacks and Native Americans as integral to the nexus of attitudes and emotions that shored up slavery and segregation.[4]

> But if racism always involves either inferiorization or antipathy, as Blum argues, then many actions that people call racist may actually be something else.
>
> Not every instance of racial conflict, insensitivity, discomfort, miscommunication, exclusion, injustice, or ignorance should be called "racist." Not all *racial* incidents are *racist* incidents. . . . We need a more varied and nuanced moral vocabulary for talking about the domain of race. . . . All forms of racial ills should elicit concern from responsible individuals. If someone displays racial insensitivity, but not racism, people should be able to see that for what it is.[5]
>
> Blum is careful to point out that we can't conclude from this "conceptual inflation" that racism and inequality have been overstated. Indirect or veiled racism, he says, is likely worse than we might think.
>
> The point here is not that Blum is right about racism (although he most likely is), but that critical thinking like this (using conceptual analysis and argument) is powerful and can yield very useful insights into real problems.

Suppose two possible actions will produce exactly the same amount of overall happiness. But one of the actions involves the violation of someone's rights or causes a serious injustice. According to utilitarianism, the two actions are equally right. But to many, this evaluation of the situation seems to conflict with our considered moral judgments.

The same kind of conflict arises in regard to moral duties. Most of us believe that we have certain duties to other people that often seem more weighty than considerations of happiness. For example, we believe that in general we have a duty to keep our promises to people. But traditional utilitarianism does not recognize any such duties. It says that our only goal should be to maximize happiness—regardless of whether we have to break a promise to do it.

So for these reasons (and a few others), many critics have accused the theory of being acutely inconsistent with relevant moral data. They believe that any theory that runs afoul of the criterion of consistency in this way cannot be correct.

But take note: Even the fiercest critics of utilitarianism have admitted that the theory does seem to capture something essential to moral theories—the notion that the consequences of actions are indeed relevant to moral judgments. Probably very few people would want to say that in moral decision making the consequences of their actions never matter.

For the record, the sketch of traditional utilitarianism given here has been oversimplified so we can focus on the process of theory assessment. Over the years, utilitarians have modified the theory to make it more plausible. Critics, however, still claim that the theory is flawed . . . but that's another story.

In radical contrast to utilitarianism and other theories basing rightness on the consequences of actions, the moral theory of Immanuel Kant (1724–1804) says that rightness does not depend at all on the production of happiness or on the satisfaction of human desires. For Kant, rightness is not defined by an action's results, but by its form—that is, by the nature of the action itself. Harming the innocent is wrong not because it causes unhappiness, but because of the kind of action it is. Morality is about conforming your actions to universal moral rules derived from reason and doing so for duty's sake alone. Your actions are right only if they are consistent with such rules, and you deserve praise for right actions only if you act solely from a sense of duty.

In Kantian ethics, the moral rules (or duties) are expressed as categorical imperatives—that is, as commands that apply without exception (categorically, or absolutely) and without regard to a person's preferences or goals. Kant says that we can infer all our duties from one moral principle, the ultimate categorical imperative. He formulates it in several ways but supposes that they are all equivalent. His first formulation says, "Act only on that maxim through which you can at the same time will that it should become a universal law."[6] On Kant's view, our actions imply general moral rules, or maxims. To tell a lie for personal gain is essentially to act according to a maxim that says something like, "It's morally permissible to lie to someone to promote your own interests." To determine if an action is permissible, we need to ask ourselves if we could consistently will that the maxim of our action become a universal moral law that applies to everyone. We must ask, "Could all humankind, with logical consistency, act on the maxim, and would we be willing to have them do that?" If the answer is yes on both counts, the action is morally permissible; if not, it is prohibited.

Here is Kant's illustration of properly applying this formulation. Suppose that to borrow money from a friend (money that you know you will never pay back), you falsely promise to repay the loan. Is this behavior permissible? To find out, you must ask if you could consistently will that the maxim of your action become a universal law. The maxim of your action is, "Whenever you need money that you know you cannot pay back, make a lying promise to obtain the loan." What would happen if everyone acted according to this maxim? Everyone would make lying promises to get a loan, but everyone would also know that the promises were empty—and the practice of loaning money based on a promise would cease to exist. The result is a contradiction: The universal making of lying promises would end the practice of promising. Thus, you cannot consistently will that the maxim of your action become a universal law, so making a lying promise to borrow money is prohibited.

This bare sketch of only one formulation of the categorical imperative does not do justice to Kant's theory, but it's enough for an illustration of how we might apply the moral criteria of adequacy.

One fact that seems obvious is that the theory easily passes the second criterion: It is generally consistent with our experience of the moral life. According to Kantian ethics, we do form moral judgments, have moral disagreements, and err in our moral beliefs. Any flaws in the theory are more likely to arise from the first criterion; sure enough, critics insist that the theory is not consistent with our considered moral judgments. One argument for this conclusion starts from Kant's claim that the moral rules are absolute—that is, they must be obeyed without exception (or as he says, we have "perfect" duties). He asserts, for example, that we have an absolute duty not to lie or to kill the innocent, regardless of the consequences of observing the rule. Suppose a crazed killer wants to murder an innocent man who takes refuge in your house. The killer knocks at your door and asks you if the man is hiding inside. If you tell the truth, the innocent man will be murdered; if you lie, he will be saved. What would Kant have you do in a case like this? His answer is unequivocal: You must tell the truth though it leads to the murder of an innocent person. How does this absolutism fit with our moral common sense? Not very well, critics say. Our considered moral judgments seem to suggest that, in general, saving an innocent life has far more moral value than blindly adhering to an absolute rule. Moral common sense seems to affirm that doing our duty for duty's sake—though generally a worthy aim—is sometimes less important than avoiding tragic consequences. Kant would have us do our duty though the heavens fall, but that view appears inconsistent with moral judgments that we have good reasons to trust.

 FURTHER THOUGHT

Moral Dilemmas

Moral dilemmas are situations in which moral duties, or principles, are in conflict. Suppose you cannot feed your family without stealing a loaf of bread. Your duty to take care of your family conflicts with your duty not to steal. Or imagine that you cannot save a drowning child without breaking a solemn promise to drive your friend to a very important appointment. Your duty to preserve life is inconsistent with your duty to keep promises.

In Kant's theory, some duties are absolutist (exceptionless). So when these conflict, there is no way to resolve the inconsistency. You have a duty not to kill and not to lie (and you can't forgo deciding the issue), but you cannot fulfill one duty without failing to fulfill the other. The dilemma is irresolvable.

But other moral theories are nonabsolutist, and they are often able to resolve dilemmas because their principles are prima facie. Prima facie principles apply unless exceptions are warranted, and exceptions are warranted when two principles conflict. In such cases, you must decide which principle carries the most weight. Making that decision is often straightforward; our considered judgments or moral theory show us the way. For example, in the scenarios just mentioned, it seems clear that the more important duty is to feed your family, even if the only way to do that is to steal. And in the case of the drowning child, surely the weightier moral duty is to save the child.

In many other situations, however, deciding which duty is more important is not so easy. Consider these two cases:

> You have witnessed a man rob a bank, but then he did something completely unusual and unexpected with the money: he donated it to an orphanage that was poor, rundown, and lacking in proper food, care, water, and amenities. The sum

of money would be a great benefit to the orphanage, and the children's lives would turn from poor to prosperous. Would you (a) Call the police and report the robber, even though they would likely take the money away from the orphanage, or (b) Do nothing and leave the robber and the orphans alone?

Your best friend is about to get married. The ceremony will be performed in one hour, but you have seen, just before coming to the wedding, that your friend's fiancée has been having an affair. If your friend marries this woman, she is unlikely to be faithful, but on the other hand, if you tell your friend about the affair, you will ruin his wedding. Would you, or would you not, tell your friend of the affair?[7]

Such cases demand careful moral deliberation, which involves at least these four steps:

1. Learn as much as you can about the *nonmoral* facts of the case. Sometimes the really important facts are hidden below the surface.
2. Minimize bias, self-interest, prejudice, or strong emotions (especially fear, anger, and hatred).
3. Identify the relevant moral principles. Think: What duties apply in this situation?
4. Determine the relative importance of the principles in the situation.

There is no formula, algorithm, or standard ranking of duties to help you in weighing the importance of the relevant principles. You must rely on your considered judgments, a sound moral theory, and your experience.

Given enough space, we could review the responses that Kant's defenders have offered to this criticism (and to others). And we could dwell on the formulation of the categorical imperative that some consider Kant's greatest insight—the principle of respect for persons. But this brief treatment will have to do.

Between utilitarianism and Kantian ethics, which theory is better and why? An adequate answer to that question would be anything but brief. Comparing the virtues and vices of these two theories, and then deciding which one is preferable, would require a great deal of careful analysis and critical thinking. But however the task proceeds, it is sure to involve applying to both theories some telling criteria of adequacy (either the three criteria discussed here, or variations on them, and perhaps others). Such an investigation would show that neither theory is perfect (no theory is) and would likely yield an edifying conclusion such as (1) one theory is more plausible than the other, or (2) both theories are seriously defective, or (3) the best elements of both can be blended into a new theory, or (4) one of the theories is an especially good candidate for modification to eliminate shortcomings.

Applying the criteria is not like solving a mathematical equation or following a set of instructions to build a gasoline engine. There is no rigid rubric for using or weighting the criteria to sort good theories from bad. But like the scientific criteria of adequacy, these standards do give us guidance in making reasonable judgments about the objective strengths and weaknesses of theories.

Legal Reasoning

As noted in Chapter 3, argument and inference play a dynamic role in legal reasoning of all sorts. They are regularly put to use in debates about the making of new laws, in criminal and civil proceedings, and in judicial decision-making. And as in any other field, deductive and inductive patterns form the foundation of the reasoning used. The application of these two forms of argument, however, is not as mechanical or formulaic as some might assume.

Usually when judges decide particular cases, the overarching pattern in their reasoning is deductive (although there is much more to it than that). In a given case, the judge ascertains a relevant rule of law, identifies the facts to which the rule pertains, and applies the rule to the facts. The result is a judicial decision, a ruling, that should reflect both the rule and the facts. When explicitly stated, this line of reasoning might look like this:

> *Those who fail to meet the nation's citizenship requirements cannot be citizens. (the rule)*
> *Victor has failed to meet the nation's citizenship requirements. (the facts)*
> *Therefore, Victor is not a citizen. (the conclusion, or ruling)*

Or in a conditional mode:

> *If someone fails to meet the nation's citizenship requirements, he or she cannot be a citizen. (the rule)*
> *Victoria has failed to meet the nation's citizenship requirements. (the facts)*
> *Therefore, Victoria is not a citizen. (the conclusion, or ruling)*

Such deductive arguments constitute only the general framework of judicial decision-making. Inside this framework other kinds of inferences and considerations are at work. First, to reach a verdict, a judge cannot simply apply the rule to the facts and get the right answer, as if by formula or computer calculation. Often the rules contain unclear or conflicting statements, or they are inconsistent with other rules, or how the rules are to be applied to the facts may not be apparent, or there may be no rules at all that are relevant to the case at hand. So a judge must interpret the rules or make do when no rule applies. The facts too require some interpretation, for there are usually several different ways to describe them, and it's not always obvious which way is appropriate. Moreover, inductive inference plays an even larger role than deduction does in judicial reasoning.

How so? For one thing, courts must determine what the facts are in cases, and that task must involve inductive reasoning. They have to reason inductively to derive the facts from eyewitness testimony, the testimony of expert witnesses, and physical evidence. Such inferences are often very straightforward: Expert X says that the defendant's DNA was left on the murder weapon; therefore, the defendant's DNA was probably left on the murder weapon.

Also, very often the dominant question before a court is that of causality. Did the driver of the truck cause the accident? Did Johnson burglarize the house? Did the chemical company cause toxic waste to flow into the ground water and did that waste make the residents ill? The main reason that such questions are important is that they are linked to legal responsibility. Those who cause an injury to someone are held legally responsible for it and therefore must face the legal consequences—a judgment of the court that goes against them.

Inductive inferences in the form of arguments from analogy are both common and essential in judicial reasoning. In trial courts, analogical arguments are often used to establish the facts. Expert testimony is assessed by referring to the expert's previous experience in circumstances analogous to those of the present. Evaluating circumstantial evidence requires comparing familiar experiences of the past with analogous experiences relevant to the present case.

More important, reasoning by analogy is central to judicial decision-making. In many systems of justice (notably those of the United States and the United Kingdom), judges must decide cases in light of previous settled cases—in accordance with precedent, especially precedent established by higher courts. That is, courts are required to let their judgments be controlled by decisions handed down in relevantly similar cases. Thus, arguments by analogy arise naturally and take the familiar form discussed in Chapter 8:

1. Cases A through Y have properties P_1, P_2, and P_3 plus the property P_4.
2. Case Z has properties P_1, P_2, and P_3.
3. Therefore, case Z probably has property P_4.

For example:

1. In the cases relevant to the present case, persons with lung cancer sue cigarette manufacturers for causing their cancer, and the courts rule that the persons must be compensated for their illness.
2. In the present case, a person with lung cancer sues a cigarette manufacturer for causing her cancer.
3. Therefore, in the present case, the person with lung cancer should probably be compensated.

As with any other analogical argument, the strength of such inferences depends on relevant similarities and differences. Judges must decide whether prior cases are similar enough (or different enough) in relevant ways to the case at hand. They will follow precedent and treat the cases the same if they think the cases are relevantly similar enough. They will depart from precedent and treat the cases differently if they decide the cases are too dissimilar in relevant aspects.

A Coherent Worldview

Making a coherent and powerful worldview for yourself is the work of a lifetime, requiring reflection, critical thinking, and (often) personal anguish. So there is no way that this chapter—or *any* chapter, book, or person—can provide you with ready-made content for your worldview. But we can trace out some characteristics that any good worldview should possess.

A worldview is a massive intellectual construct with many elements. We can get a handle on it, though, by thinking of it as primarily a composite

"The Answer to the Great Question of . . . Life, the Universe and Everything . . . [is] Forty-Two."
—Douglas Adams

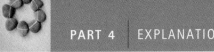

© 2002 by Sidney Harris. www.ScienceCartoonsPlus.com

of theories—theories about morality, God, science, mind, personhood, society, knowledge, and much more. We all have our own beliefs about these things, and our most general beliefs often congeal into theories. Since worldviews are framed out of theories, good worldviews will, as a minimum requirement, consist of good theories. So much of the job of devising a good worldview consists of ensuring that our theories are the best theoretical explanations available. We do that, of course, by putting our theories to the test as we have in previous chapters.

But there's more to crafting a plausible worldview than that. Recall our discussion of theories and inference to the best explanation in Chapter 9. We saw that a theory helps increase our understanding by fitting our beliefs into a coherent pattern. When some of our most fundamental beliefs conflict with one another, the relevant theory is in trouble and our understanding is decreased. After all, if two of our beliefs are inconsistent with one another, we know that at least one of them must be false. To achieve true understanding, we must somehow resolve the inconsistency. Likewise, if the theories that make up our worldview are inconsistent with one another, there is obviously something wrong with our worldview. At least one of our theories must be flawed, and some of our beliefs must be wrong. Our understanding of the world is decreased, and our prospects for success (however we define it) are dimmed. A crucial criterion, then, for judging a worldview is *internal consistency*—the requirement that the theories composing our worldview do not conflict.

> "Reason and free inquiry are the only effectual agents against error."
> —Thomas Jefferson

How can our best theories conflict? Here are some ways:

- *Our moral theory can conflict with our view of human freedom.* Most people believe that persons can be held morally responsible for their actions—as long as they act freely. That is, persons can be praised or blamed only for those actions over which they have control. But many people also think that humans *cannot* act freely, that they do not have free will. They believe in causal determinism, the view that every event in the universe has a cause (is determined). This means that everything that happens (including human actions) has a preceding cause, so that the chain of causes stretches back into the indefinite past—out of our control. Many would see this situation as an unacceptable conflict between their moral theory and their view of the way the world is.
- *Our theory about the existence of God can conflict with our scientific theory about the nature of the universe.* Some people argue that God must exist because

everything has a cause, including the universe, and the only thing that could have caused the universe is God. Modern physics, however, shows that some things in the universe (namely, certain subatomic particles) often occur uncaused, so it's not true that everything has a cause. Thus, in this instance science seems to be at odds with a certain brand of theology.

• *Our theory about the mind can be in conflict with theories of personal survival after death.* Some believe that people can live on in some ethereal form (as souls or disembodied minds, for example) after death. This notion accords well with the idea that the mind (our true essence) is the kind of thing that can exist independently of the body. But this kind of survival after death would not be possible if the mind is identical to the body, as some people believe.

The work of building plausible worldviews will always involve eliminating inconsistencies. If you really want to understand the world and your place in it, you must wrestle with these inconsistencies. Reconciling conflicting beliefs (by eliminating them or modifying them) is a necessary condition for creating theories and a worldview that can successfully guide your thinking, your choices, and your deeds.

With this discussion, we now come full circle to a theme that bubbles up in the first few pages of this book and flows through each chapter to this final paragraph: Every statement, every theory, and every worldview is fair game for critical thinking. No claim can be considered immune to critical inquiry, revision, and rejection. We will probably never be able to evaluate the truth of all our beliefs, but we violate the spirit of critical reasoning and do ourselves a disfavor if we cordon them off and post a sign that says "Off Limits!" If truth is what we seek, if knowledge is our goal, we should be willing to turn the light of critical thinking on any dark corner anywhere. This point is especially relevant to the development of worldviews, which too often are thought to be the unalterable givens of clan and culture, ideologies carved in the pillars of the mind forever. Our worldviews are far too important not to subject them to intelligent, reasoned reflection.

KEY WORDS

moral statement   worldview

Summary
Moral Arguments

• A moral argument is an argument in which the conclusion is a moral statement. A moral statement is a statement asserting that an action is right or wrong (moral or immoral) or that a person or motive is good or bad.

• In a moral argument, we cannot establish the conclusion without a moral premise. A standard moral argument has at least one premise that asserts a general moral principle, at least one premise that is a nonmoral claim, and a conclusion that is a moral statement.

- Often a moral premise in a moral argument is implicit. The best approach to identifying the implicit premises is to treat moral arguments as deductive. Your job then is to supply plausible premises that will make the argument valid.

Moral Premises

- Gauging the truth of moral premises (moral principles) mostly involves examining the support they get from three sources: (1) other moral principles, (2) moral theories, and (3) considered moral judgments.
- We can assess the truth of a moral premise the same way we might assess any other kind of universal generalization—by trying to think of counterexamples to it.

Moral Theories

- Theories of morality are attempts to explain what makes an action right or what makes a person good. We test moral theories the same way we test any other theory—by applying criteria of adequacy to a theory and its competitors.
- The criteria of adequacy for moral theories are (1) consistency with considered moral judgments, (2) consistency with our experience of the moral life, and (3) workability in real-life situations.

Legal Reasoning

- Arguments and inference are widely used in the law. Inductive reasoning predominates. Courts must determine what the facts are in cases, and that task must involve inductive reasoning. When the question before a court is about causality, inductive arguments must provide answers.
- Reasoning by analogy is central to judicial decision making. It is usually applied when judges must decide cases in light of previous settled cases— in accordance with precedent, especially precedent established by higher courts.

A Coherent Worldview

- Worldviews are composites of theories, including theories of morality. A good worldview must consist of good theories. But it also must have internal consistency—the theories composing our worldview must not conflict.
- Our worldviews are far too important not to subject them to intelligent, reasoned reflection.

EXERCISES

Exercise 11.1

REVIEW QUESTIONS

1. What is a moral theory?
2. According to the text, what is a worldview?
3. What is a moral statement?
4. What is the basic structure of a standard moral argument?
* 5. Why can't we infer a moral statement from nonmoral statements alone?
6. Why is it important to spell out implicit premises in a moral argument?
7. What technique can we use to determine whether a general moral principle is true?
8. What is a moral judgment?
* 9. According to the text, what precisely does a moral theory try to explain?
10. According to the text, what are the criteria of adequacy for appraising moral theories?
11. According to the text, how are moral theories like scientific theories?
12. Who founded the moral theory known as traditional utilitarianism?
* 13. According to the text, what is a crucial criterion for judging a worldview?
14. How do judges use analogical argument in deciding cases?
15. Why can't judges use deductive reasoning alone in their deliberations?
16. What is emotivism? What arguments do critics make against emotivism?
17. What are some of the moral principles that both parties in a moral debate are likely to agree on?
18. What are considered moral judgments? Are they infallible? How are they used in moral deliberations?
19. What is subjective relativism? What is social relativism? What criticisms have been launched against these moral theories?
20. What is Kant's theory of ethics?

Exercise 11.2

Specify whether the following statements are moral or nonmoral.

* 1. Joan worries whether she's doing the right thing.
2. When the government restricts freedom of the press, it harms every citizen.

3. The government should not restrict freedom of the press.
4. Paul was sure that he saw Gregory steal the book from the library.
5. Because of the terrible results of the bombing, it's clear that the entire war effort was immoral.
* 6. The Church should never have allowed pedophile priests to stay in the priesthood.
7. The officer was justified in using deadly force because his life was threatened.
8. The officer used deadly force because his life was threatened.
* 9. Lying is wrong unless the lie involves trivial matters.
10. The officials should never have allowed the abuse to continue.

Exercise 11.3

In each of the following passages, add a moral premise to turn it into a valid moral argument.

1. Noah promised to drive Thelma to Los Angeles, so he should stop bellyaching and do it.
2. The refugees were shot at and lied to, and the authorities did nothing to stop any of this. The authorities should have intervened.
3. There was never any imminent threat from the Iraqi government, so the United States should not have invaded Iraq.
* 4. The Indian government posed an imminent threat to Pakistan and the world, so the Pakistanis were justified in attacking Indian troops.
5. Burton used a gun in the commission of a crime; therefore, he should get a long prison term.
6. Ellen knew that a murder was going to take place. It was her duty to try to stop it.
7. Ahmed should never have allowed his daughter to receive in vitro fertilization. Such a procedure is unnatural.
8. The doctors performed the experiment on twenty patients without their consent. Obviously, that was wrong.
* 9. What you did was immoral. You hacked into a database containing personal information on thousands of people and invaded their privacy.
10. Ling spent all day weeding Mrs. Black's garden for no pay. The least Mrs. Black should do is let Ling borrow some gardening tools.

Exercise 11.4

Use counterexamples to test each of the following general moral principles.

1. Anything that is unnatural is immoral.
2. It is always and everywhere wrong to tell a lie.

* 3. In all circumstances the killing of a human being is wrong.

4. In all situations in which our actions can contribute to the welfare, safety, or happiness of others, we should treat all persons equally.

5. Any action that serves one's own best interests is morally permissible.

6. Any action that is approved of by one's society is moral.

* 7. Assisted suicide is never morally justified.

8. Whatever action a person approves of is morally right.

9. Making a promise to someone incurs a moral obligation to keep the promise in all circumstances.

10. Any action done for religious reasons is morally acceptable because religious reasons carry more weight than secular ones.

Exercise 11.5

Identify the moral argument in each of the following passages. Specify the premises and the conclusion, adding implicit premises where needed.

1. The movie *Lorenzo's Oil* is about a family's struggle to find a cure for their young son's fatal genetic disease, an illness that usually kills boys before they reach their eleventh birthday. The script is based on the true story of a family's attempt to save Lorenzo, their son, from this fatal genetic disease through the use of a medicinal oil. The movie is a tear-jerker, but it ends on a hopeful note that suggests that the oil will eventually cure Lorenzo and that the oil is an effective treatment for the genetic disease. The problem is, there is no cure for the disease and no good scientific evidence showing that the oil works. But the movie touts the oil anyway—and gives false hope to every family whose son suffers from this terrible illness. Worse, the movie overplays the worth of the oil, seriously misleading people about the medical facts. The movie, therefore, is immoral. It violates the ageless moral dictum to, above all else, "do no harm." *Lorenzo's Oil* may be just a movie, but it has done harm nonetheless.

2. "I, like many of my fellow Muslims, was appalled by the latest bombings in Saudi Arabia ('Among the Saudis, Attack Has Soured Qaeda Supporters,' front page, Nov. 11). Yet I was disturbed to get the sense that Saudis were angered by this latest act of barbarity because the targets were mainly Arab and Muslim.

"You quote one person as saying of the bombing in Riyadh in May, 'At that time it was seen as justifiable because there was an invasion of a foreign country, there was frustration.' Another says, 'Jihad is not against your own people.'

"Regardless of whether the victims are Muslim or not, the vicious murder of innocent human beings is reprehensible and repugnant, an affront to everything Islam stands for. Any sympathy for Al Qaeda among the minority of Saudis should have evaporated after the May bombings in Riyadh, and it should have surprised no one in Saudi Arabia that Al Qaeda would attack a housing complex full of Arabs and Muslims.

"That is what Al Qaeda is: a band of bloodthirsty murderers."
[Letter to the editor, *New York Times*]

3. John and Nancy Jones had a two-year-old son who suffered from a serious but very curable bowel obstruction. For religious reasons, the Joneses decided to treat their son with prayer instead of modern medicine. They refused medical treatment even though they were told by several doctors that the child would die unless medically treated. As it turned out, the boy did die. The Joneses were arrested and charged with involuntary manslaughter. Were the Joneses wrong to refuse treatment for their son? The answer is yes. Regardless of what faith or religious dogma would have the Joneses do, they allowed their child to die. According to just about any moral outlook, the care of a child by the parents is a fundamental obligation. Above all other concerns, parents have a duty to ensure the health and safety of their children and to use whatever means are most likely to secure those benefits. The Joneses ignored this basic moral principle. They were wrong—and deserve whatever punishment the state deems appropriate.

Exercise 11.6

Read the following description of a moral theory and answer the questions that follow.

The Ethics of Love Theory

According to the ethics of love theory, what makes an action right is that it is based on love toward others. Love is the only universal moral good. In any situation where a moral choice must be made, this theory says that we must ask ourselves: "Which action would demonstrate the greatest degree of love for others, everyone considered?" So in this theory, actions that demonstrate love (such as respecting others, telling the truth, treating people equally, caring for them, protecting them from harm) would always be preferred over actions that do not demonstrate love (discriminating against persons, lying to them, harming them, stealing from them, ignoring them if they ask for help). Also, actions that demonstrate great love (such as risking your life to save theirs) would be preferred over those that exhibit only small degrees of love (such as being courteous).

1. Is this theory consistent with our considered moral judgments? Is it consistent with our judgments regarding the punishment of criminals? acts of war? providing for one's family as opposed to providing for all persons equally? If the theory conflicts with our considered moral judgments, provide an example demonstrating the conflict.

2. Is this theory consistent with our experience of the moral life? According to this theory, are moral judgments possible? Can we have moral disagreements? Can we ever act immorally?

3. Is this theory workable? Does it help you make moral decisions in these situations?

   a. Your beloved mother has a terminal illness, which causes her unimaginable pain, and she begs you to kill her.

   b. You promise to buy your beloved spouse a car, but a half-dozen homeless people beg you to give them the money that you had set aside for the car.

   c. You are a doctor who must decide which of one hundred patients should receive a life-saving organ transplant. You can choose only one, though you love all of them. Some are elderly; some, in great pain; some, very young; and some, Nobel laureates.

4. What is your final assessment of the ethics of love theory? Is it a good theory? Is it a better theory than traditional utilitarianism?

 Field Problems

1. Check the Internet to find out about rule-utilitarianism, a moral theory meant to be an improvement over traditional utilitarianism. (A place to start is The Internet Encyclopedia of Philosophy, www.iep.utm.edu/. See the entry "Ethics.") Write a three-hundred-word assessment of the theory, using the moral criteria of adequacy.

2. From a newspaper opinion/editorial page (including letters to the editor) select a passage containing a moral argument. Write a brief assessment of the argument, identifying the premises and conclusion, adding implicit premises (to make the argument valid), and stating whether the revised argument is sound or unsound.

3. Go to the opinion/editorial section of www.usatoday.com and select a short article on an important moral issue. Analyze the article's argument, identifying premises and the conclusion, and determine whether the argument is a good one.

 Self-Assessment Quiz

Answers appear in "Answers to Self-Assessment Quizzes" (Appendix D).

1. What is a moral statement?
2. What are the elements of a standard moral argument?

3. According to the text, what are the moral criteria of adequacy?

4. According to the text, how can you test whether a general moral principle is true?

5. Is it possible to derive a moral statement from a nonmoral statement?

In each of the following passages, add a moral premise to turn it into a valid moral argument.

6. Of course we should have offered protection to the Kurds. They were in grave danger and they asked for our help.

7. The supplement manufacturers knew that the herb ephedra was dangerous, so they should have removed it from the market.

8. The Democrats insulted the president. They should have never been allowed to do that.

9. The Smiths were consenting adults who were having sex in the privacy of their own home. These actions by the Smiths are morally permissible.

10. Randi killed his neighbor, and the killing was not in self-defense. He should not have committed such an act.

Use counterexamples to test each of the following general moral principles.

11. Lying is wrong under all circumstances.

12. People who commit crimes should not be punished—they should be retrained to act legally.

13. All humans, whatever their circumstances, have full moral rights.

14. All creatures that are alive and sensitive to stimulation are equally valuable and should be accorded equal respect.

15. The morally right action is the one that produces the most happiness, everyone considered.

16. Right actions are those that are in one's own self-interest.

Defend the following actions from a utilitarian standpoint.

17. Medical experimentation on a patient without her consent.

18. Taking food, shelter, and other resources from rich people and distributing them equally among poor people.

Evaluate each of the following arguments.

19. Any form of expression or speech that offends people of faith should not be tolerated. *Penthouse* magazine definitely offends people of faith. Ban it!

20. Anyone who disagrees with the basic moral dictums of the prevailing culture should be censored. Dr. Tilden's graduation speech clearly was inconsistent with the prevailing moral opinions on campus. She should be reprimanded.

Integrative Exercises

These exercises pertain to material in Chapters 3, 5, and 8–11.

For each of the following arguments, specify the conclusion and premises and indicate where possible whether it is cogent or sound. Also, determine whether any fallacies are used and, if so, name them.

1. Ninety percent of famous scientists do not believe in God, so 90 percent of all scientists probably do not believe in God.

2. If Vaughn buys that flat-screen TV, he will spend all of his time watching television. And if he spends all of his time watching television, he will get fat. Well, Vaughn did buy that flat-screen TV. Therefore, he will get fat.

3. Anyone who runs away from an automobile accident should be arrested. Janet ran away from an automobile accident. She should be arrested.

4. I found five jellybeans in the yard this morning, and I found thirty more in the kitchen this afternoon. So I've found thirty-five jellybeans today.

5. Ann is taller than Jacob, and Jacob is taller than Jane. Therefore, Ann is taller than Jane.

6. "I write in response to the Nov. 4 *News* article, 'Plans for group home, storage facility opposed.' As the sister and guardian of a profoundly retarded woman who lives in a group home, I can assure the gentlemen quoted that their fears are very much unfounded. The home in which my sister resides is large, lovely, brand new, well staffed and well maintained. It does nothing but enhance the community, bring neighbors together and create a wonderfully diverse neighborhood." [Letter to the editor, *Buffalo News*]

7. "Scrawling 'Rape all Asian bitches and dump them' on classroom walls is not a hate crime, and graffiti should be protected by the First Amendment, according to assistant professor of communication Laura Leets. This is outrageous. I hope Ms. Leets is simply arguing from a narrow legalistic interpretation and is merely insensitive to the tremendous hurt such graffiti can inflict, not to mention the additional damage caused when a professor on campus defends it. Words can be just as destructive as physical violence. Drawing a technical distinction between the two is at best insensitive, at worst evil." [Letter to the editor, *Stanford Magazine*]

8. We have interviewed one hundred NBA players, and seventy of them admit to extramarital affairs. So most NBA players are adulterers.

9. You think you're going to drive cross-country in that 1978 Chevy disaster-on-wheels? Forget it. It's old, has 150,000 miles on it, and has worn belts and bad cylinders.

10. Take it easy. Joyce will arrive soon to give you a lift into town, just as she promised. She has never broken a promise, and her car is in excellent shape.

11. Yolanda took the money from petty cash even though she had plenty of money in her pocket. People shouldn't steal unless they are destitute. She shouldn't have taken that money.

12. There is one principle we can never avoid: We should never do anything to disrespect human life. The artificial use of human cells—as scientists are now doing in stem cell research—shows a complete disregard for human life. Stem cell research is immoral.

13. Hank is a Harvard grad. Therefore, he's probably intelligent and well educated.

14. This new BMW will give you a sense of style, assurance, and class. See your BMW dealer today.

15. The depiction of Hollywood stars in movies puffing away on cigarettes is teaching our kids to smoke. Recent research reveals a cause-and-effect relationship between exposing children to movie smoking and their subsequent decision to take up the habit.

For each of the following phenomena, (1) devise two theories to explain it, and (2) apply the criteria of adequacy to them to determine which theory is best.

16. The number of delayed and canceled flights in the airline industry has tripled in the last year.

17. After taking a new food supplement known as Max10, hundreds of people have reported having more energy, feeling more alert, and having an enhanced sense of well-being.

18. Ever since the average classroom size at Wellington High dropped from forty-two to twenty-five, grades have improved dramatically and discipline problems are at an all-time low.

19. Over the past ten years there has been a surprising rise in the incidence of leukemia in children who live in the Saxton area.

20. Multiracial neighborhoods seem much friendlier than neighborhoods that are segregated or are dominated by one ethnic or cultural group.

 Writing Assignments

1. Complete Exercise 11.6 and then write a two-page essay assessing the worth of the ethics of love theory. Use the moral criteria of adequacy.

2. Write a one-paragraph summary of the moral argument put forth in Essay 20 ("It's Irresponsible to Spread Fear of Vaccine") in Appendix B. Be sure to identify clearly the argument's premises and conclusion.

3. Write a two-page assessment of the moral theory known as ethical egoism (discussed in the box "Critiquing Moral Theories"). Use the moral criteria of adequacy.

4. Read Essay 17 ("Torture: Severe Interrogations Work") and outline its argument. Decide whether you agree with the author and write a two-page essay giving reasons for your view.

The Truth About Philosophy Majors

Here's the inaccurate, old-school way of thinking:

- Philosophy majors have no marketable skills; they are unemployable.
- They are unprepared for professional careers in anything but teaching philosophy.
- They are useless in an economy built on exploding tech, speed-of-light innovation, and market-wrenching globalization.
- They are destined to earn low salaries.

Here's the new reality: All these assumptions are FALSE.

Careers

A wide range of data suggest that philosophy majors are not just highly employable; they are thriving in many careers that used to be considered unsuitable for those holding "impractical" philosophy degrees. The unemployment rate for recent BA philosophy graduates is 4.3 percent, lower than the national average and lower than that for majors in biology, chemical engineering, graphic design, mathematics, and economics.[1]

Nowadays most philosophy majors don't get PhDs in philosophy; they instead land jobs in many fields outside academia. They work in business consulting firms, guide investors on Wall Street, lead teams of innovators in Silicon Valley, do humanitarian work for nongovernment organizations, go into politics, and cover the world as journalists. They teach, write, design, publish, create. They go to medical school, law school, and graduate school in everything from art and architecture to education, business, and computer science. (Of course, besides majoring in philosophy, students can also minor in it, combining a philosophy BA with other BA programs, or take philosophy courses to round out other majors or minors.)

Many successful companies—especially those in the tech world—don't see a philosophy degree as impractical at all. To be competitive, they want more than just engineers, scientists, and mathematicians. They also want people with broader, big-picture skills—people who can think critically, question assumptions, formulate and defend ideas, develop unique perspectives, devise and evaluate arguments, write effectively, and analyze and simplify complicated problems. And these competencies are abundant in people with a philosophy background.

Plenty of successful business and tech leaders say so. Speaking of her undergraduate studies, Carly Fiorina, philosophy major and eventual chief executive

of Hewlett-Packard, says, "I learned how to separate the wheat from the chaff, essential from just interesting, and I think that's a particularly critical skill now when there is a ton of interesting but ultimately irrelevant information floating around."[2]

Flickr and Slack cofounder Stewart Butterfield, who has both bachelor's and master's degrees in philosophy, says, "I think if you have a good background in what it is to be human, an understanding of life, culture and society, it gives you a good perspective on starting a business, instead of an education purely in business. You can always pick up how to read a balance sheet and how to figure out profit and loss, but it's harder to pick up the other stuff on the fly."[3]

Sheila Bair got her philosophy degree from the University of Kansas and went on to become chair of the Federal Deposit Insurance Corporation from 2006 to 2011. She says that philosophy "helps you break things down to their simplest

Photo 1: Carly Fiorina, businessperson and political figure
Photo 2: Stewart Butterfield, cofounder of Flickr and Slack
Photo 3: Sheila Bair, nineteenth chair of the FDIC

Philosophy: A Natural Segue to Law and Medicine

Law schools will tell you that a major in philosophy provides excellent preparation for law school and a career in law. Philosophy excels as a pre-law major because it teaches you the very proficiencies that law schools require: developing and evaluating arguments, writing carefully and clearly, applying principles and rules to specific cases, sorting out evidence, and understanding ethical and political norms. Philosophy majors do very well on the LSAT (Law School Admission Test), typically scoring higher than the vast majority of other majors.

Philosophy has also proven itself to be good preparation for medical school. Critical reasoning is as important in medicine as it is in law, but the study and practice of medicine requires something else—expertise in grappling with the vast array of moral questions that now confront doctors, nurses, medical scientists, administrators, and government officials. These are, at their core, philosophy questions.

David Silbersweig, a Harvard Medical School professor, makes a good case for philosophy (and all the liberal arts) as an essential part of a well-rounded medical education. As he says,

If you can get through a one-sentence paragraph of Kant, holding all of its ideas and clauses in juxtaposition in your mind, you can think through most anything. . . . I discovered that a philosophical stance and approach could identify and inform core issues associated with everything from scientific advances to healing and biomedical ethics.[4]

elements. My philosophy training really helps me with that intellectual rigor of simplifying things and finding out what's important."[5]

Philosophy major and NBC journalist Katy Tur says, "I would argue that for the vast majority of people, an education of teaching you to think critically about the world you are in and what you know and what you don't know is useful for absolutely everything that you could possibly do in the future."[6]

It's little wonder, then, that the top ranks of leaders and innovators in business and technology have their share of philosophy majors, a fair number of whom credit their success to their philosophy background. The list is long, and it includes:[7]

Patrick Byrne, entrepreneur, e-commerce pioneer, founder and CEO of Overstock.com
Damon Horowitz, entrepreneur, in-house philosopher at Google
Carl Icahn, businessman, investor, philanthropist. . . .
Larry Sanger, Internet project developer, cofounder of Wikipedia
George Soros, investor, business magnate, philanthropist
Peter Thiel, entrepreneur, venture capitalist, cofounder of PayPal
Jeff Weiner, CEO of LinkedIn

Of course, there are also many with a philosophy background who are famous for their achievements outside the business world. This list is even longer and includes:

Wes Anderson, filmmaker, screenwriter (*The Royal Tenenbaums*, The *Grand Budapest Hotel*)
Stephen Breyer, Supreme Court justice
Mary Higgins Clark, novelist (*All By Myself, Alone*)
Ethan Coen, filmmaker, director
Stephen Colbert, comedian, TV host
Angela Davis, social activist
Lana Del Rey, singer, songwriter
Dessa, rapper, singer, poet
Ken Follett, author (*Eye of the Needle, Pillars of the Earth*)
Harrison Ford, actor
Ricky Gervais, comedian, creator of *The Office*
Philip Glass, composer
Rebecca Newberger Goldstein, author (*Plato at the Googleplex*)
Matt Groening, creator of *The Simpsons* and *Futurama*
Chris Hayes, MSNBC host
Kazuo Ishiguro, Nobel Prize–winning author (*The Remains of the Day*)
Phil Jackson, NBA coach
Thomas Jefferson, U.S. president
Charles R. Johnson, novelist (*Middle Passage*)
Rashida Jones, actor

Photo 4: Katy Tur, author and broadcast journalist for NBC News
Photo 5: Damon Horowitz, entrepreneur and in-house philosopher at Google
Photo 6: Larry Sanger, Internet project developer, cofounder of Wikipedia
Photo 7: Stephen Breyer, Supreme Court justice
Photo 8: Stephen Colbert, comedian, TV host
Photo 9: Angela Davis, social activist
Photo 10: Lana Del Rey, singer and songwriter

Martin Luther King Jr., civil rights leader
John Lewis, civil rights activist, congressman
Terrence Malick, filmmaker, director (*The Thin Red Line*)
Yann Martel, author (*Life of Pi*)
Deepa Mehta, director, screenwriter (*Fire, Water*)
Iris Murdoch, author (*Under the Net*)
Robert Parris Moses, educator, civil rights leader
Stone Phillips, broadcaster
Susan Sarandon, actor
Susan Sontag, author, (*Against Interpretation*) MacArthur Fellow
David Souter, Supreme Court justice
Alex Trebek, host of *Jeopardy!*
George F. Will, journalist, author (*Men at Work: The Craft of Baseball*)
Juan Williams, journalist

Philosophy Majors and the GRE

Philosophy majors score higher than *all other majors* on the Verbal Reasoning and Analytical Writing sections of the GRE (Graduate Record Examinations).

	Verbal Reasoning	Quantitative Reasoning	Analytic Writing
Philosophy	160	154	4.3
Average	149.97	152.57	3.48

Educational Testing Service, 2017 GRE Scores, between July 1, 2013 and June 30, 2016.

Salaries

According to recent surveys by PayScale, a major source of college salary information, philosophy majors can expect to earn a median starting salary of $44,800 and a median mid-career salary of $85,100. As you might expect, most of the higher salaries go to STEM graduates (those with degrees in science, technology, engineering, or mathematics). But in a surprising number of cases, salaries for philosophy majors are comparable to those of STEM graduates. For example, while the philosophy graduate earns $85,100 at mid-career, the mid-career salary for biotechnology is $82,500; for civil engineering, $83,700; for chemistry, $88,000; for industrial technology, $86,600; and for applied computer science, $88,800. Median end-of-career salaries for philosophy majors (10–19 years' experience) is $92,665—not the highest pay among college graduates, but far higher than many philosophy-is-useless critics would expect.[8]

Another factor to consider is the increase in salaries over time. On this score, philosophy majors rank in the top ten of all majors with the highest salary increase from start to mid-career at 101 percent. The major with the highest

Photo 11: Chris Hayes, MSNBC host
Photo 12: Rashida Jones, actor
Photo 13: Martin Luther King Jr., civil rights leader
Photo 14: John Lewis, civil rights activist, congressman
Photo 15: Terrence Malick, filmmaker, director
Photo 16: Yann Martel, author (*Life of Pi*)

Salary Potential for Bachelor's Degrees

Major	Median Early Pay	Median Mid-Career Pay
	(0–5 yrs. work experience)	(10+ yrs. work experience)
Mechanical Engineering	$58,000	$90,000
Applied Computer Science	$53,100	$88,800
Information Technology	$52,300	$86,300
Civil Engineering	$51,300	$83,700
Business and Finance	$48,800	$91,100
Biotechnology	$46,100	$82,500
Business Marketing	$45,700	$78,700
Philosophy	**$44,800**	**$85,100**
History	$42,200	$75,700
Advertising	$41,800	$84,200
General Science	$41,600	$75,200
Telecommunications	$41,500	$83,700
English Literature	$41,400	$76,300
Marine Biology	$37,200	$76,000

PayScale, "Highest Paying Bachelor Degrees by Salary Potential," *2017–2018 College Salary Report*, https://www.payscale.com/college-salary-report/majors-that-pay-you-back/bachelors.

increase: government, at 118 percent. Molecular biology is the fifth highest at 105 percent.[9]

And among liberal arts majors, philosophy salaries are near the top of the list. All liberal arts majors except economics earn lower starting and mid-career pay than philosophy does.

Salary Potential for Liberal Arts Bachelor Degrees

Major	Median Early Pay	Median Mid-Career Pay
	(0–5 yrs. work experience)	(10+ yrs. work experience)
Economics	$54,100	$103,200
Philosophy	**$44,800**	**$85,100**
Political Science	$44,600	$82,000

Photo 17: Deepa Mehta, director, screenwriter (*Fire*)
Photo 18: Susan Sontag, author, MacArthur Fellow

	(0–5 yrs. work experience)	(10+ yrs. work experience)
Modern Languages	$43,900	$77,400
Geography	$43,600	$72,700
History	$42,200	$75,700
English Literature	$41,400	$76,300
Anthropology	$40,500	$63,200
Creative Writing	$40,200	$68,500
Theatre	$39,700	$63,500
Psychology	$38,700	$65,300
Fine Art	$38,200	$62,200

PayScale, "Highest Paying Bachelor Degrees by Salary Potential," *2017–2018 College Salary Report*, https://www.payscale.com/college-salary-report/majors-that-pay-you-back/bachelors.

Meaning

In all this talk about careers, salaries, and superior test scores, we should not forget that for many students, the most important reason for majoring in philosophy is the meaning it can add to their lives. They know that philosophy, after two-and-one-half millennia, is still alive and relevant and influential. It is not only for studying but also for living—for guiding our lives toward what's true and real and valuable. They would insist that philosophy, even with its ancient lineage and seemingly remote concerns, applies to your life and your times and your world. The world is full of students and teachers who can attest to these claims. Perhaps you will eventually decide to join them.

Resources

American Philosophical Association, "Who Studies Philosophy?" http://www.apaonline.org/?whostudiesphilosophy.

BestColleges.com, "Best Careers for Philosophy Majors," 2017, http://www.bestcolleges.com/careers/philosophy-majors/.

The University of North Carolina at Chapel Hill, Department of Philosophy, "Why Major in Philosophy?" http://philosophy.unc.edu/undergraduate/the-major/why-major-in-philosophy/.

University of California, San Diego, Department of Philosophy, "What Can I Do with a Philosophy Degree?" https://philosophy.ucsd.edu/undergraduate/careers.html.

University of Maryland, Department of Philosophy, "Careers for Philosophy Majors," http://www.philosophy.umd.edu/undergraduate/careers.

George Anders, "That 'Useless' Liberal Arts Degree Has Become Tech's Hottest Ticket," *Forbes*, July 29, 2015, https://www.forbes.com/sites/georgeanders/2015/07/29/liberal-arts-degree-tech/#5fb6d740745d.

Laura Tucker, "What Can I Do with a Philosophy Degree?" TopUniversities.com, March 2, 2015, https://www.topuniversities.com/student-info/careers-advice/what-can-you-do-philosophy-degree.

Appendix B

Essays for Evaluation

CONTENTS

Essay 1 Death Penalty Discriminates Against Black Crime Victims *USA Today* 458

Essay 2 Marine Parks *Bill Daly* 459

Essay 3 A Feminist Defense of Pornography *Wendy McElroy* 461

Essay 4 A Defense of Homosexuality *John Corvino* 466

Essay 5 More Innocents Die When We Don't Have Capital Punishment *Dennis Prager* 479

Essay 6 What's Wrong with Adultery? *Bonnie Steinbock* 480

Essay 7 A Pat-Down Is Better Than a Blow-Up *Caroline Baum* 484

Essay 8 The Cohabitation Epidemic *Neil Clark Warren* 486

Essay 9 Not Being Vaccinated Is Not Acceptable *David Ropeik* 488

Essay 10 Women and the Afghanistan Peace Process *Ann Jones* 490

Essay 11 A Deviance from God's Norm *Richard Land* 493

Essay 12 Marriage Still Evolving, as Ever *Buffalo News* 494

Essay 13 Slouching Toward Chimeras *Jeremy Rifkin* 495

Essay 14 Fighting Islamic Extremists Who Stifle Free Speech *Ayaan Hirsi Ali and Daniel Huff* 497

Essay 15 Is Sluttishness a Feminist Statement? *Wendy Kaminer* 499

Essay 16 Torture: Time for Congress to End the Debate *USA Today* 501

Essay 17 Torture: Severe Interrogations Work *Trent Franks* 502

Essay 18 Freedom of Expression: Protect Student Speech—Even "Unwise" Bong Banner *USA Today* 503

Essay 19 Freedom of Expression: Policy Reflects Common Sense *Kenneth W. Starr* 504

Essay 20 It's Irresponsible to Spread Fear of Vaccine *USA Today* 505

Essay 21 Flag Amendment: Flag Needs Protection *Dianne Feinstein* 507

Essay 1

Death Penalty Discriminates Against Black Crime Victims

USA TODAY
April 29, 2003

Death penalty opponents have long complained that minorities are more likely to be executed than whites convicted of the same crime. Now a new study points up another troubling racial difference between who lives and who dies: the color of the victim.

While blacks and whites are murdered in roughly equal numbers in the USA, the killers of white people are six times as likely to be put to death, according to a statistical analysis released last week by the anti–death penalty human rights organization Amnesty International USA. It found that of 845 people executed since the U.S. resumed capital punishment in 1977, 80% were put to death for killing whites, while only 13% were executed for killing blacks.

The findings point to one chilling conclusion: The criminal justice system places a higher value on the lives of whites than on the lives of blacks and other minorities. That means minorities who are victims of violent crimes are also victimized by a legal system that fails to provide them the "equal protection of the laws" they are guaranteed under the 14th Amendment to the Constitution.

The report adds to the troubling evidence of racial discrimination against minority victims that has surfaced in other, state-level studies over the past year:

- In Illinois, juries have been three times as likely to sentence a person to death if the victim is white rather than black. Then-Gov. George Ryan cited those findings in January, when he commuted 167 death sentences to life imprisonment.
- In Maryland, the death penalty is four times as likely to be imposed when the victim is white rather than black. But a moratorium on executions imposed by the outgoing governor has been revoked by his successor.

Other studies in New Jersey, North Carolina, Pennsylvania, Texas and Virginia have shown similar results, as did a review a decade ago by the U.S. General Accounting Office, the investigative arm of Congress.

Other research suggests race-based differences in administering justice are not unique to the death penalty. A major study published by Stanford University in 1995 found that prosecutors tended to stereotype nonwhite crime victims as less-convincing witnesses, and cases involving nonwhite victims were more likely to be dismissed or result in plea-bargains to lesser penalties.

The Supreme Court banned the death penalty in 1972 after finding it was imposed arbitrarily. Five years later executions resumed based on the court's 1976 ruling that new laws would guide judges and juries to mete out death sentences evenhandedly.

The record since then shows the court was right the first time. When a victim's skin color is key in deciding who is put to death, the system not only violates constitutional protections but also is corrupt.

A better alternative to the death penalty is life imprisonment without parole. It protects society from those who commit heinous crimes without perpetuating a deadly system of unequal justice based on race.

1. Outline the argument in this essay, specifying the premises and conclusion. Then write the outline of an argument that contradicts the essay's argument.

2. Write a two-page essay in which you defend a claim that contradicts the conclusion in Essay 1. For the purposes of this exercise, you may cite imaginary, but reasonable, evidence.

3. Write a three-page essay in which you assess the merits of Essay 1's argument, examining the truth of its premises and whether the conclusion follows from those premises. Take into account any possible objections to your view.

Essay 2
Marine Parks
Bill Daly

The issue of whether we should allow marine parks to stay open has been widely debated in our community recently. It is an important issue because it concerns fundamental moral and economic questions about the way we use our native wildlife. A variety of different arguments have been put forward about this issue. This essay will consider arguments for having marine parks and point to some of the problems with these views. It will then put forward reasons for the introduction of laws which prohibit these unnecessary and cruel institutions.

It has been argued that dolphin parks provide the only opportunity for much of the public to see marine mammals (Smith, 1992). Most Australians, so this argument goes, live in cities and never get to see these animals. It is claimed that marine parks allow the average Australian to appreciate our marine wildlife. However, as Smith states, dolphins, whales and seals can be viewed in the wild at a number of places on the Australian coast. In fact, there are more places where they can be seen in the wild than places where they can be seen in captivity. Moreover, most Australians would have to travel less to get to these locations than they would to get to the marine parks on the Gold Coast. In addition, places where there are wild marine mammals do not charge an exorbitant entry fee—they are free.

Dr. Alison Lane, the director of the Cairns Marine Science Institute, contends that we need marine parks for scientific research (*The Age,* 19.2.93). She argues that much of our knowledge of marine mammals comes from studies which were undertaken at marine parks. The knowledge which is obtained at marine parks, so this argument goes, can be useful for planning for the conservation of marine mammal species. However, as Jones (1991) explains, park research is only useful for understanding captive animals and is not useful for learning about animals in the wild. Dolphin and whale biology changes in marine park conditions. Their diets are different, they have significantly lower life spans and they are more prone to disease. In addition, marine mammals in dolphin parks are trained and this means that their patterns of social behaviour are changed. Therefore research undertaken at marine parks is generally not reliable.

It is the contention of the Marine Park Owners Association that marine parks attract a lot of foreign tourists (*The Sun-Herald,* 12.4.93). This position goes on to assert that these tourists spend a lot of money, increasing our foreign exchange earnings and assisting our national balance of payments. However, foreign tourists would still come to Australia if the parks were closed down. Indeed, surveys of overseas tourists show that they come here for a variety of other reasons and not to visit places like Sea World (*The Age, Good Weekend,* 16.8.93). Tourists come here to see our native wildlife in its natural environment and not to see it in cages and cement pools. They can see animals in those conditions in their own countries. Furthermore, we should be promoting our beautiful natural environment to tourists and not the ugly concrete marine park venues.

Dolphin parks are unnecessary and cruel. The dolphins and whales in these parks are kept in very small, cramped ponds, whereas in the wild they are used to roaming long distances across the seas. Furthermore, the concrete walls of the pools interfere with the animals' sonar systems of communication. In addition, keeping them in pools is a terrible restriction of the freedom of fellow creatures who may have very high levels of intelligence and a sophisticated language ability. Moreover, there are many documented cases of marine mammals helping humans who are in danger at sea or helping fisherman with their work.

In conclusion, these parks should be closed, or at the very least, no new animals should be captured for marine parks in the future. Our society is no longer prepared to tolerate unnecessary cruelty to animals for science and entertainment. If we continue with our past crimes against these creatures we will be remembered as cruel and inhuman by the generations of the future.

Bibliography

The Age, 19.2.93.

The Age, Good Weekend, 16.8.93.

Jones, G. (1991). "The Myths About Animal Research in Marine Parks." In *Scientific Australian,* Vol. 12, No. 3.

Smith, H. (1992). "Marine Parks: Good for Business, Good for Australia." In *Leisure Business Review,* Vol. 24, No. 4.

The Sun-Herald, 12.4.93.

1. Study the argument presented in this essay. Identify the conclusion and the premises and objections considered. Then write a two-page rebuttal to the essay. That is, defend the claim that marine mammals *should* continue to be kept in marine parks. Cite real evidence to support your argument.

2. Write an alternative opening for Essay 2. If you want, you may invent quotes or stories.

3. Write a three-page essay in which you assess the merits of Essay 2's argument, examining the truth of its premises and whether the conclusion follows from those premises.

Essay 3

A Feminist Defense of Pornography

Wendy McElroy

"Pornography benefits women, both personally and politically." This sentence opens my book *XXX: A Woman's Right to Pornography*, and it constitutes a more extreme defense of pornography than most feminists are comfortable with. I arrived at this position after years of interviewing hundreds of sex workers.

Feminist Positions

Feminist positions on pornography currently break down into three rough categories. The most common one—at least, in academia—is that pornography is an expression of male culture through which women are commodified and exploited. A second view, the liberal position, combines a respect for free speech with the principle "a woman's body, a woman's right" and thus produces a defense of pornography along the lines of, "I don't approve of it, but everyone has the right to consume or produce words and images." A third view—a true defense of pornography—arises from feminists who have been labeled "pro-sex" and who argue that porn has benefits for women.

Little dialogue occurs between the three positions. Anti-pornography feminists treat women who disagree as either brainwashed dupes of patriarchy or as apologists for pornographers. In the anthology *Sexual Liberals and the Attack on Feminism* (1990), editor Dorchen Leidholdt claims that feminists who believe women make their own choices about pornography are spreading "a felicitous lie" (p. 131). In the same work, Sheila Jeffreys argues that "pro-sex" feminists are "eroticizing dominance and subordination." Wendy Stock accuses free speech feminists of identifying with their oppressors "much like . . . concentration camp prisoners with their jailors" (p. 150). Andrea Dworkin accuses them of running a "sex protection racket" (p. 136) and maintains that no one who defends pornography can be a feminist.

The liberal feminists who are personally uncomfortable with pornography tend to be intimidated into silence. Those who continue to speak out, like American Civil Liberties Union President Nadine Strossen (*Defending Pornography*) are ignored. For example, Catharine MacKinnon has repeatedly refused to share a stage with Strossen or any woman who defends porn. "Pro-sex" feminists—many of whom are current or former sex-workers—often respond with anger, rather than arguments.

Peeling back the emotions, what are the substantive questions raised by each feminist perspective?

Anti-porn feminism. Page Mellish of Feminists Fighting Pornography has declared, "There's no feminist issue that isn't rooted in the porn problem." In her book *Only Words*, MacKinnon denies that pornography consists of words and images, both of which would be protected by the First Amendment. She considers pornography—in and of itself—to be an act of sexual violence.

Why is pornography viewed as both the core issue of modern feminism and an inherent act of violence? The answer lies in radical feminist ideology, which Christina Hoff Sommers calls "gender feminism."

Gender feminism looks at history and sees an uninterrupted oppression of women by men that spans cultural barriers. To them, the only feasible explanation is that men and women are separate and antagonistic classes whose interests necessarily conflict. Male interests are expressed through and maintained by a capitalistic structure known as "patriarchy."

The root of the antagonism is so deep that it lies in male biology itself. For example, in the watershed book *Against Our Will*, Susan Brownmiller traces the inevitability of rape back to Neanderthal times when men began to use their penises as weapons. Brownmiller writes: "From prehistoric times to the present, I believe, rape has played a critical function. It is nothing more or less than a conscious process of intimidation by which all men keep all women in a state of fear." How Brownmiller acquired this knowledge of prehistoric sex is not known.

Another tenet of gender oppression is that sex is a social construct. Radical feminists reject what they call "sexual essentialism"—the notion that sex is a natural force based on biology that inclines women toward natural tendencies, such as motherhood. Even deeply felt sexual preferences, such as heterosexuality, are not biological. They spring from ideology.

Men construct women's sexuality through the words and images of society, which the French philosopher Foucault called the "texts" of society. After such construction, men commercialize women's sexuality and market it back in the form of pornography. In other words, through porn man defines woman sexually—a definition that determines every aspect of her role in society. To end the oppression, patriarchy and its texts must be destroyed.

Liberal feminism.   Liberal feminism is a continuation of 1960s feminism that called for equality with men, who were not inherent oppressors so much as recalcitrant partners to be enlightened. Equality did not mean destroying the current system, but reforming it through such measures as affirmative action. The liberal principle "a woman's body, a woman's right" underlay arguments ranging from abortion rights to lifestyle freedoms like lesbianism. The stress was upon the act of choosing, rather than upon the content of any choice.

Liberal feminists share the general liberal bias toward free speech, but they are in flux on pornography. Some liberal organizations like Feminists for Free Expression (FFE) have consistently opposed censorship in any form. Some liberal feminists like Sallie Tisdale (*Talk Dirty to Me*) have staunchly defended sexual freedom. But many liberal feminists commonly reason as follows: "As a woman I am appalled by *Playboy* . . . but as a writer I understand the need for free expression."

Such arguments are not pro-pornography. They are anti-censorship ones based on several grounds, including: great works of art and literature would be banned; the First Amendment would be breached; political expression would be suppressed; and a creative culture requires freedom of speech.

Other liberal feminists, who have accepted many of the ideological assumptions of the anti-porn position, seem willing to sacrifice free speech for the greater good of protecting women. For example, they also condemn the free market for commercializing women as "body parts," which demeans women. In "A Capital Idea," an essay defending pornography, which sometimes seems to be an attack, Lisa Steel comments:

> Sexist representation of women . . . is all part of the same system that, in the service of profits, reduces society to "consumer groups." And marketing is every bit as conservative as the military . . . we pay dearly for the "rights" of a few to make profits from the rest of us.

Such muddled and ambivalent "defenses" often offend the sex workers they are intended to protect.

Pro-sex feminism.   Over the past decade, a growing number of feminists—labeled "pro sex"—have defended a woman's choice to participate in and to consume pornography. Some of these women, such as Nina Hartley, are current or ex–sex-workers who know firsthand that posing for pornography is an uncoerced choice that can be enriching. Pro-sex feminists retain a consistent interpretation of the principle "a woman's body, a woman's right" and insist that every peaceful choice a woman makes with her own body must be accorded full legal protection, if not respect.

Pro-sex arguments sometimes seem to overlap with liberal feminist ones. For example, both express concern over who will act as censor because subjective words, such as "degrading," will be interpreted to mean whatever the censor wishes.

The statute that banned Margaret Sanger because she used the words *syphilis* and *gonorrhea* is no different, in principle, than the one that interprets obscenity today. There will be no protection even for the classics of feminism, such as *Our Bodies, Ourselves*, which provided a generation of women with the first explicit view of their own biology. Inevitably, censorship will be used against the least popular views, against the weakest members of society . . . including feminists and lesbians. When the Canadian Supreme Court decided in 1992 to protect women by restricting the importation of pornography, one of the first victims was the lesbian/gay Glad Day Bookstore, which had been on a police hit list. Among the books seized by Canadian customs were two books by Andrea Dworkin, *Pornography: Men Possessing Women* and *Women Hating*. Such an event should not have surprised Dworkin who declared in *Take Back the Night*, "There is not a feminist alive who could possibly look to the male legal system for real protection from the systematized sadism of men" (p. 257).

On the dangers of censoring pornography, pro-sex and liberal feminists often agree. On the possible benefits of pornography to women, they part company.

Dissecting Anti-Porn
Do the specific accusations hurled at pornography stand up under examination?

Pornography is degrading to women.   *Degrading* is a subjective term. I find commercials in which women become orgasmic over soapsuds to be tremendously degrading. The bottom line is that every woman has the right to define what is degrading and liberating for herself.

The assumed degradation is often linked to the "objectification" of women: that is, porn converts them into sexual objects. What does this mean? If taken literally, it means nothing because objects don't have sexuality; only beings do. But to say that porn portrays women as "sexual beings" makes for poor rhetoric. Usually, the term *sex objects* means showing women as body parts, reducing them to physical objects. What is wrong with this? Women are as much their bodies as they are their minds or souls. No one gets upset if you present women as "brains" or as spiritual beings. If I concentrated on a woman's sense of humor to the exclusion of her other characteristics, is this degrading? Why is it degrading to focus on her sexuality?

Pornography leads to violence against women.   A cause-and-effect relationship is drawn between men viewing pornography and men attacking women, especially in the form of rape. But studies and experts disagree as to whether any relationship exists between pornography and violence, between images and behavior. Even the pro-censorship Meese Commission Report admitted that the data connecting pornography to violence was unreliable.

Other studies, such as the one prepared by feminist Thelma McCormick in 1983 for the Metropolitan Toronto Task Force on Violence Against Women, find no pattern to connect porn and sex crimes. Incredibly, the Task Force suppressed the study and reassigned the project to a pro-censorship male, who returned the "correct" results. His study was published.

What of real-world feedback? In Japan, where pornography depicting graphic and brutal violence is widely available, rape is much lower per capita than in the United States, where violence in porn is severely restricted.

Pornography is violence because women are coerced into pornography.   Not one of the dozens of women depicted in pornographic materials with whom I spoke reported being coerced. Not one knew of a woman who had been. Nevertheless, I do not dismiss reports of violence: every industry has its abuses. And anyone who uses force or threats to make a woman perform should be charged with kidnapping, assault, and/or rape. Any such pictures or films should be confiscated and burned because no one has the right to benefit from the proceeds of a crime.

Pornography is violence because women who pose for porn are so traumatized by patriarchy they cannot give real consent.   Although women in pornography appear to be willing, anti-porn feminists know that no psychologically healthy woman would agree to the degradation of pornography. Therefore, if agreement seems to be present, it is because the women have "fallen in love with their own oppression" and must be rescued from themselves. A common characteristic of the porn actresses I have interviewed is a love of exhibitionism. Yet if such a woman declares her enjoyment in flaunting her body, anti-porn feminists claim she is not merely a unique human being who reacts from a different background or personality. She is psychologically damaged and no longer responsible for her actions. In essence, this is a denial of a woman's right to choose anything outside the narrow corridor of choices offered by political/sexual correctness. The right to choose hinges on the right to make a "wrong" choice, just as freedom of religion entails the right to be an atheist. After all, no one will prevent a woman from doing what she thinks she should do.

A Pro-Sex Defense

As a "pro-sex" feminist, I contend: Pornography benefits women, both personally and politically. It provides sexual information on at least three levels:

- It gives a panoramic view of the world's sexual possibilities. This is true even of basic sexual information such as masturbation. It is not uncommon for women to reach adulthood without knowing how to give themselves pleasure.
- It allows women to "safely" experience sexual alternatives and satisfy a healthy sexual curiosity. The world is a dangerous place. By contrast, pornography can be a source of solitary enlightenment.
- It offers the emotional information that comes only from experiencing something either directly or vicariously. It provides us with a sense how it would "feel" to do something.

Pornography allows women to enjoy scenes and situations that would be anathema to them in real life. Take, for example, one of the most common fantasies reported by women—the fantasy of "being taken." The first thing to understand is that a rape fantasy does not represent a desire for the real thing. Why would a healthy woman daydream about being raped? Perhaps by losing control, she also sheds all sense of responsibility for and guilt over sex. Perhaps it is the exact opposite of the polite, gentle sex she has now. Perhaps it is flattering to imagine a particular man being so overwhelmed by her that he must have her. Perhaps she is curious. Perhaps she has some masochistic feelings that are vented through the fantasy. Is it better to bottle them up?

Pornography breaks cultural and political stereotypes, so that each woman can interpret sex for herself. Anti-feminists tell women to be ashamed of their appetites and urges. Pornography tells them to accept and enjoy them.

Pornography can be good therapy. Pornography provides a sexual outlet for those who—for whatever reason—have no sexual partner. Perhaps they are away from home, recently widowed, isolated because of infirmity. Perhaps they simply choose to be alone. Couples also use pornography to enhance their relationships. Sometimes they do so on their own, watching videos and exploring their reactions together. Sometimes, the couples go to a sex therapist who advises them to use pornography as a way of opening up communication on sex. By sharing pornography, the couples are able to experience variety in their sex lives without having to commit adultery.

Pornography benefits women politically in many ways. Historically, pornography and feminism have been fellow travelers and natural allies. Although it is not possible to draw a cause-and-effect relationship between the rise of pornography and that of feminism, they both demand the same social conditions—namely, sexual freedom.

Pornography is free speech applied to the sexual realm. Freedom of speech is the ally of those who seek change: it is the enemy of those who seek to maintain control. Pornography, along with all other forms of sexual heresy, such as homosexuality, should have the same legal protection as political heresy. This protection is especially important to women, whose sexuality has been controlled by censorship through the centuries.

Viewing pornography may well have a cathartic effect on men who have violent urges toward women. If this is true, restricting pornography removes a protective barrier between women and abuse.

Legitimizing pornography would protect female sex-workers, who are stigmatized by our society. Anti-pornography feminists are actually undermining the safety of sex workers when they treat them as "indoctrinated women." Dr. Leonore Tiefer, a professor of psychology, observed in her essay "On Censorship and Women": "These women have appealed to feminists for support, not rejection. . . . Sex industry workers, like all women, are striving for economic survival and a decent life, and if feminism means anything it means sisterhood and solidarity with these women."

The Purpose of Law

The porn debate is underscored by two fundamentally antagonistic views of the purpose of law in society.

The first view, to which pro-sex feminists subscribe, is that law should protect choice. "A woman's body, a woman's right" applies to every peaceful activity a woman chooses to engage in. The law should come into play only when a woman initiates force or has force initiated against her. The second view, to which both conservatives and anti-porn feminists subscribe, is that law should protect virtue. It should come into play whenever there has been a breach of public morality, or a breach of "women's class interests."

This is old whine in new battles. The issue at stake in the pornography debate is nothing less than the age-old conflict between individual freedom and social control.

1. Create an outline for this essay. Specify the thesis statement, each premise, support for the premises, any objections considered, and the conclusion.
2. Write a summary of Essay 3 in 75 to 100 words, specifying the premises and conclusion.
3. Write a three-page assessment of the argument, evaluating the truth of the premises and conclusion and the logic of the argument as a whole. Address possible objections to your view.

Essay 4
A Defense of Homosexuality
John Corvino

Tommy and Jim are a homosexual couple I know.[1] Tommy is an accountant; Jim is a botany professor. They are in their forties and have been together fourteen years, the last five of which they've lived in a Victorian house that they've lovingly restored. Although their relationship has had its challenges, each has made sacrifices for the sake of the other's happiness and the relationship's long-term success.

I assume that Tommy and Jim have sex with each other (although I've never bothered to ask). Furthermore, I contend that they probably *should* have sex with each other. For one thing, sex is pleasurable. But it is also much more than that: a sexual relationship can unite two people in a way that virtually nothing else can. It can be an avenue of growth, of communication, and of lasting interpersonal fulfillment. These are reasons why most heterosexual couples have sex even if they don't want children, don't want children yet, or don't want additional children. And if these reasons are good enough for most heterosexual couples, then they should be good enough for Tommy and Jim.

Of course, having a reason to do something does not preclude there being an even better reason for not doing it. Tommy might have a good reason for drinking orange juice (it's tasty and nutritious) but an even better reason for not doing so (he's allergic). The point is that one would need a pretty good reason for denying a sexual relationship to Tommy and Jim, given the intense benefits widely associated with such relationships. The question I shall consider in this paper is thus quite simple Why shouldn't Tommy and Jim have sex?

Homosexual Sex Is "Unnatural"

Many contend that homosexual sex is "unnatural." But what does that mean? Many things that people value—clothing, houses, medicine, and government, for example—are unnatural in some sense. On the other hand, many things that people detest—disease, suffering, and death, for example—are "natural" in the sense that they occur "in nature." If the unnaturalness charge is to be more than empty rhetorical flourish, those who levy it must specify what they mean. Borrowing from Burton Leiser, I will examine several possible meanings of "unnatural."[2]

What is unusual or abnormal is unnatural.   One meaning of "unnatural" refers to that which deviates from the norm, that is, from what most people do. Obviously, most people, engage in heterosexual relationships. But does it follow that it is wrong to engage in homosexual relationships? Relatively few people read Sanskrit, pilot ships, play the mandolin, breed goats, or write with both hands, yet none of these activities is immoral simply because it is unusual. As the Ramsey Colloquium, a group of Jewish and Christian scholars who oppose homosexuality, writes, "The statistical frequency of an act does not determine its moral status."[3] So while homosexuality might be unnatural in the sense of being unusual, that fact is morally irrelevant.

What is not practiced by other animals is unnatural. Some people argue, "Even animals know better than to behave homosexually; homosexuality must be wrong." This argument is doubly flawed. First, it rests on a false premise. Numerous studies—including Anne Perkins's study of "gay" sheep and George and Molly Hunt's study of "lesbian" sea gulls—have shown that some animals do form homosexual pair-bonds.[4] Second, even if animals did not behave homosexually, that fact would not prove that homosexuality is immoral. After all, animals don't cook their food, brush their teeth, participate in religious worship, or attend college; human beings do all these without moral censure. Indeed, the idea that animals could provide us with our standards—especially our sexual standards—is simply amusing.

What does not proceed from innate desires is unnatural.   Recent studies suggesting a biological basis for homosexuality have resulted in two popular positions. One side proposes that homosexual people are "born that way" and that it is therefore natural (and thus good) for them to form homosexual relationships. The other side maintains that homosexuality is a lifestyle choice, which is therefore unnatural (and thus wrong). Both sides assume a connection between the origin of homosexual orientation, on the one hand, and the moral value of homosexual activity, on the other. And insofar as they share that assumption, both sides are wrong.

Consider first the pro-homosexual side: "They are born that way; therefore it's natural and good." This inference assumes that all innate desires are good ones (i.e., that they should be acted upon). But that assumption is clearly false. Research suggests that some people are born with a predisposition toward violence, but such people have no more right to strangle their neighbors than anyone else. So while people like Tommy and Jim may be born with homosexual tendencies, it doesn't follow that they ought to act on them. Nor does it follow that they ought *not* to act on them, even if the tendencies are not innate. I probably do not have any innate tendency to write with my left hand (since I, like everyone else in my family, have always been right-handed), but it doesn't follow that it would be immoral for me to do so. So simply asserting that homosexuality is a lifestyle choice will not show that it is an immoral lifestyle choice.

Do people "choose" to be homosexual? People certainly don't seem to choose their sexual *feelings*, at least not in any direct or obvious way. (Do you? Think about it.) Rather, they find certain people attractive and certain activities arousing, whether they "decide" to or not. Indeed, most people at some point in their lives wish that they could control their feelings more—for example, in situations of unrequited love—and find it frustrating that they cannot. What they *can* control to a considerable degree is how and when they act upon those feelings. In that sense, both homosexuality and heterosexuality involve lifestyle choices. But in either case, determining the origin of the feelings will not determine whether it is moral to act on them.

What violates an organ's principal purpose is unnatural.   Perhaps when people claim that homosexual sex is unnatural they mean that it cannot result in procreation. The idea behind the argument is that human organs have various natural purposes: eyes are for seeing, ears are for hearing, genitals are for procreating. According to this argument, it is immoral to use an organ in a way that violates its particular purpose.

Many of our organs, however, have multiple purposes. Tommy can use his mouth for talking, eating, breathing, licking stamps, chewing gum, kissing women, or kissing Jim; and it seems rather arbitrary to claim that all but the last use are "natural."[5] (And if we say that some of the other uses are "unnatural, but not immoral," we have failed to specify a morally relevant sense of the term "natural.")

Just because people can and do use their sexual organs to procreate, it does not follow that they should not use them for other purposes. Sexual organs seem very well suited for expressing love, for giving and receiving pleasure, and for celebrating, replenishing, and enhancing a relationship—even when procreation is not a factor. Unless opponents of homosexuality are prepared to condemn heterosexual couples who use contraception or individuals who masturbate, they must abandon this version of the unnaturalness argument. Indeed, even the Roman Catholic Church, which forbids contraception and masturbation, approves of sex for sterile couples and of sex during pregnancy, neither of which can lead to procreation. The Church concedes here that intimacy and pleasure are morally legitimate purposes for sex, even in cases where procreation is impossible. But since homosexual sex can achieve these purposes as well, it is inconsistent for the Church to condemn it on the grounds that it is not procreative.

One might object that sterile heterosexual couples do not *intentionally* turn away from procreation, whereas homosexual couples do. But this distinction doesn't hold. It is no more possible for Tommy to procreate with a woman whose uterus has been removed than it is for him to procreate with Jim.[6] By having sex with either one, he is intentionally engaging in a nonprocreative sexual act.

Yet one might press the objection further and insist that Tommy and the woman *could* produce children if the woman were fertile: whereas homosexual relationships are essentially infertile, heterosexual relationships are only incidentally so. But what does that prove? Granted, it might require less of a miracle for a woman without a uterus to become pregnant than for Jim to become pregnant, but it would require a miracle nonetheless. Thus it seems that the real difference here is not that one couple is fertile and the other not, nor that one couple "could" be fertile (with the help of a miracle) and the other not, but rather that one couple is male-female and the other male-male. In other words, sex between Tommy and Jim is wrong because it's male-male—i.e., because it's homosexual. But that, of course, is no argument at all.[7]

What is disgusting or offensive is unnatural.   It often seems that when people call homosexuality "unnatural" they really just mean it's disgusting. But plenty of morally neutral activities—handling snakes, eating snails, performing autopsies, cleaning toilets, and so on—disgust people. Indeed, for centuries, most people found interracial relationships disgusting, yet that feeling—which has by no means disappeared—hardly proves that such relationships are wrong. In sum, the charge that homosexuality is unnatural, at least in its most common forms, is longer on rhetorical flourish than on philosophical cogency. At best it expresses an aesthetic judgment, not a moral judgment.

Homosexual Sex Is Harmful

One might instead argue that homosexuality is harmful. The Ramsey Colloquium, for instance, argues that homosexuality leads to the breakdown of the family and, ultimately, of human society, and it points to the "alarming rates of sexual promiscuity, depression, and suicide and the ominous presence of AIDS within the homosexual subculture."[8] Thomas Schmidt marshals copious statistics to show that homosexual activity undermines physical and psychological health.[9]

Such charges, if correct, would seem to provide strong evidence against homosexuality. But are the charges correct? And do they prove what they purport to prove?

One obvious (and obviously problematic) way to answer the first question is to ask people like Tommy and Jim. It would appear that no one is in a better position to judge the homosexual lifestyle than those who know it firsthand. Yet it is unlikely that critics would trust their testimony. Indeed, the more homosexual people try to explain their lives, the more critics accuse them of deceitfully promoting an agenda. (It's like trying to prove that you're not crazy. The more you object, the more people think, "That's exactly what a crazy person would say.")

One might instead turn to statistics. An obvious problem with this tack is that both sides of the debate bring forth extensive statistics and "expert" testimony, leaving the average observer confused. There is a more subtle problem as well. Because of widespread antigay sentiment, many homosexual people won't acknowledge their romantic feelings to themselves, much less to researchers.[10] I have known a number of gay men who did not "come out" until their forties and fifties, and no amount of professional competence on the part of interviewers would have been likely to open their closets sooner. Such problems compound the usual difficulties of finding representative population samples for statistical study.

Yet even if the statistical claims of gay rights opponents were true, they would not prove what they purport to prove, for several reasons. First, as any good statistician realizes, correlation does not equal cause. Even if homosexual people were more likely to commit suicide, be promiscuous, or contract AIDS than the general population, it would not follow that their homosexuality causes them to do these things. An alternative—and very plausible—explanation is that these phenomena, like the disproportionately high crime rates among African Americans, are at least partly a function of society's treatment of the group in question. Suppose you were told from a very early age that the romantic feelings that you experienced were sick, unnatural, and disgusting. Suppose further that expressing these feelings put you at risk of social ostracism or, worse yet, physical violence. Is it not plausible that you would, for instance, be more inclined to depression than you would be without such obstacles? And that such depression could, in its extreme forms, lead to suicide or other self-destructive behaviors? (It is indeed remarkable that couples like Tommy and Jim continue to flourish in the face of such obstacles.)

A similar explanation can be given for the alleged promiscuity of homosexuals.[11] The denial of legal marriage, the pressure to remain in the closet, and the overt hostility toward homosexual relationships are all more conducive to transient, clandestine encounters than they are to long-term unions. As a result, that which is challenging enough for heterosexual couples—settling down and building a life together—becomes far more challenging for homosexual couples.

Indeed, there is an interesting tension in the critics' position here. Opponents of homosexuality commonly claim that "marriage and the family . . . are fragile institutions in need of careful and continuing support."[12] And they point to the increasing prevalence of divorce and premarital sex among heterosexuals as evidence that such support is declining. Yet they refuse to concede that the complete absence of similar support for homosexual relationships might explain many of the alleged problems of homosexuals. The critics can't have it both ways: if heterosexual marriages are in trouble despite the various social, economic, and legal incentives for keeping them together, society should be little surprised that homosexual relationships—which not only lack such supports, but face overt hostility—are difficult to maintain.

One might object that if social ostracism were the main cause of homosexual people's problems, then homosexual people in more "tolerant" cities like New York and San Francisco should exhibit fewer such problems than their small-town counterparts; yet statistics do not seem to bear this out. This objection underestimates the extent of antigay sentiment in our society. By the time many gay and lesbian people move to urban centers, they have already been exposed to (and may have internalized) considerable hostility toward homosexuality. Moreover, the visibility of homosexuality in urban centers makes gay and lesbian people there more vulnerable to attack (and thus more likely to exhibit certain difficulties). Finally, note that urbanites *in general* (not just homosexual urbanites) tend to exhibit higher rates of promiscuity, depression, and sexually transmitted disease than the rest of the population.

But what about AIDS? Opponents of homosexuality sometimes claim that even if homosexual sex is not, strictly speaking, immoral, it is still a bad idea, since it puts people at risk for AIDS and other sexually transmitted diseases. But that claim is misleading: it is infinitely more risky for Tommy to have sex with a woman who is HIV-positive than with Jim, who is HIV-negative. Obviously, it's not homosexuality that's harmful, it's the virus; and the virus may be carried by both heterosexual and homosexual people.

Now it may be true (in the United States, at least) that homosexual males are statistically more likely to carry the virus than heterosexual females and thus that homosexual sex is *statistically* more risky than heterosexual sex (in cases where the partner's HIV status is unknown). But opponents of homosexuality need something stronger than this statistical claim. For if it is wrong for men to have sex with men because their doing so puts them at a higher AIDS risk than heterosexual sex, then it is also wrong for women to have sex with men because their doing so puts them at a higher AIDS risk than homosexual sex (lesbians as a group have the lowest incidence of AIDS). Purely from the standpoint of AIDS risk, women ought to prefer lesbian sex.

If this response seems silly, it is because there is obviously more to choosing a romantic or sexual partner than determining AIDS risk. And a major part of the decision, one that opponents of homosexuality consistently overlook, is considering whether one can have a mutually fulfilling relationship with the partner. For many people like Tommy and Jim, such fulfillment—which most heterosexuals recognize to be an important component of human flourishing—is only possible with members of the same sex.

Of course, the foregoing argument hinges on the claim that homosexual sex can only cause harm indirectly. Some would object that there are certain activities—anal sex, for instance—that for anatomical reasons are intrinsically harmful. But an argument against anal intercourse is by no means tantamount to an argument against homosexuality: neither all nor only homosexuals engage in anal sex. There are plenty of other things for both gay men and lesbians to do in bed. Indeed, for women, it appears that the most common forms of homosexual activity may be less risky than penile-vaginal intercourse, since the latter has been linked to cervical cancer.[13]

In sum, there is nothing *inherently* risky about sex between persons of the same gender. It is only risky under certain conditions: for instance, if they exchange diseased bodily fluids or if they engage in certain "rough" forms of sex that could cause tearing of delicate tissue. Heterosexual sex is equally risky under such conditions. Thus, even if statistical claims like those of Schmidt and the Ramsey Colloquium were true, they would not prove that homosexuality is immoral. At best, they would prove that homosexual people—like everyone else—ought to take great care when deciding to become sexually active.

Of course, there's more to a flourishing life than avoiding harm. One might argue that even if Tommy and Jim are not harming each other by their relationship, they are still failing to achieve the higher level of fulfillment possible in a heterosexual relationship, which is rooted in the complementarity of male and female. But this argument just ignores the facts: Tommy and Jim are homosexual *precisely because* they find relationships with men (and, in particular, with each other) more fulfilling than relationships with women. Even evangelicals (who have long advocated "faith healing" for homosexuals) are beginning to acknowledge that the choice for most homosexual people is not between homosexual relationships and heterosexual relationships, but rather between homosexual relationships and celibacy.[14] What the critics need to show, therefore, is that no matter how loving, committed, mutual, generous, and fulfilling the relationship may be, Tommy and Jim would flourish more if they were celibate. Given the evidence of their lives (and of others like them), this is a formidable task indeed.

Thus far I have focused on the allegation that homosexuality harms those who engage in it. But what about the allegation that homosexuality harms other, non-consenting parties? Here I will briefly consider two claims: that homosexuality threatens children and that it threatens society.

Those who argue that homosexuality threatens children may mean one of two things. First, they may mean that homosexual people are child molesters. Statistically, the vast majority of reported cases of child sexual abuse involve young girls and their fathers, stepfathers, or other familiar (and presumably heterosexual) adult males.[15] But opponents of homosexuality argue that when one adjusts for relative percentage in the population, homosexual males appear more likely than heterosexual males to be child molesters. As I argued above, the problems with obtaining reliable statistics on homosexuality render such calculations difficult. Fortunately, they are also unnecessary.

Child abuse is a terrible thing. But when a heterosexual male molests a child (or rapes a woman or commits assault), the act does not reflect upon all heterosexuals. Similarly, when a homosexual male molests a child, there is no reason why that act should reflect upon all homosexuals. Sex with adults of the same sex is one thing; sex with *children* of the same sex is quite another. Conflating the two not only slanders innocent people, it also misdirects resources intended to protect children. Furthermore, many men convicted of molesting young boys are sexually attracted to adult women and report no attraction to adult men.[16] To call such men "homosexual," or even "bisexual," is probably to stretch such terms too far.[17]

Alternatively, those who charge that homosexuality threatens children might mean that the increasing visibility of homosexual relationships makes children more likely to become homosexual. The argument for this view is patently circular. One cannot prove that doing X is bad by arguing that it causes other people to do X, which is bad. One must first establish independently that X is bad. That said, there is not a shred of evidence to demonstrate that exposure to homosexuality leads children to become homosexual.

But doesn't homosexuality threaten society? A Roman Catholic priest once put the argument to me as follows; "Of course homosexuality is bad for society. If everyone were homosexual, there would be no society." Perhaps it is true that if everyone were homesexual, there would be no society. But if everyone were a celibate priest, society would collapse just as surely, and my friend the priest didn't seem to think he was doing anything wrong simply by failing to procreate. Jeremy Bentham made the point somewhat more acerbically roughly 200 years ago: "If then merely out of regard to population it were right that [homosexuals] should be burnt alive, monks ought to be roasted alive by a slow fire."[18]

From the fact that the continuation of society requires procreation, it does not follow that *everyone* must procreate. Moreover, even if such an obligation existed, it would not preclude homosexuality. At best, it would preclude *exclusive* homosexuality: homosexual people who occasionally have heterosexual sex can procreate just fine. And given artificial insemination, even those who are exclusively homosexual can procreate. In short, the priest's claim—if everyone were homosexual, there would be no society—is false; and even if it were true, it would not establish that homosexuality is immoral.

The Ramsey Colloquium commits a similar fallacy.[19] Noting (correctly) that heterosexual marriage promotes the continuation of human life, it then infers that homosexuality is immoral because it fails to accomplish the same.[20] But from the fact that procreation is good, it does not follow that childlessness is bad—a point that the members of the colloquium, several of whom are Roman Catholic priests, should readily concede.

I have argued that Tommy and Jim's sexual relationship harms neither them nor society. On the contrary, it benefits both. It benefits them because it makes them happier—not merely in a short-term, hedonistic sense, but in a long-term, "big picture" sort of way. And, in turn, it benefits society, since it makes Tommy and Jim more stable, more productive, and more generous than they would otherwise be. In short, their relationship—including its sexual component—provides the same kinds of benefits that infertile heterosexual relationships provide (and perhaps other benefits as well). Nor should we fear that accepting their relationship and others like it will cause people to flee in droves from the institution of heterosexual marriage. After all, as Thomas Williams points out, the usual response to a gay person is not "How come *he* gets to be gay and I don't?"[21]

Homosexuality Violates Biblical Teaching

At this point in the discussion, many people turn to religion. "If the secular arguments fail to prove that homosexuality is wrong," they say, "so much the worse for secular ethics. This failure only proves that we need God for morality."

Since people often justify their moral beliefs by appeal to religion, I will briefly consider the biblical position.

At first glance, the Bible's condemnation of homosexual activity seems unequivocal. Consider, for example, the following two passages, one from the "Old" Testament and one from the "New":[22]

> You shall not lie with a male as with a woman; it is an abomination. (Lev. 18:22)
>
> For this reason God gave them up to degrading passions. Their women exchanged natural intercourse for unnatural, and in the same way also the men, giving up natural intercourse with women, were consumed with passion for one another. Men committed shameless acts with men and received in their own persons the due penalty for their error. (Rom. 1:26–27)

Note, however, that these passages are surrounded by other passages that relatively few people consider binding. For example, Leviticus also declares,

> The pig . . . is unclean for you. Of their flesh you shall not eat, and their carcasses you shall not touch; they are unclean for you. (11:7–8)

Taken literally, this passage not only prohibits eating pork, but also playing football, since footballs are made of pigskin. (Can you believe that the University of Notre Dame so flagrantly violates Levitical teaching?)

Similarly, St. Paul, author of the Romans passage, also writes, "Slaves, obey your earthly masters with fear and trembling, in singleness of heart, as you obey Christ" (Eph. 6:5)—morally problematic advice if there ever were any. Should we interpret this passage (as Southern plantation owners once did) as implying that it is immoral for slaves to escape? After all, God himself says in Leviticus,

> [Y]ou may acquire male and female slaves . . . from among the aliens residing with you, and from their families that are with you, who have been born in your land; and they may be your property. You may keep them as a possession for your children after you, for them to inherit as property. (25:44–46)

How can people maintain the inerrancy of the Bible in light of such passages? The answer, I think, is that they learn to interpret the passages *in their historical context*.

Consider the Bible's position on usury, the lending of money for interest (for *any* interest, not just excessive interest). The Bible condemns this practice in no uncertain terms. In Exodus God says that "if you lend money to my people, to the poor among you, you shall not exact interest from them" (22:25). Psalm 15 says that those who lend at interest may not abide in the Lord's tent or dwell on his holy hill (1–5). Ezekiel calls usury "abominable"; compares it to adultery, robbery, idolatry, and bribery; and states that anyone who "takes advanced or accrued interest . . . shall surely die; his blood shall be upon himself" (18:13).[23]

Should believers therefore close their savings accounts? Not necessarily. According to orthodox Christian teaching, the biblical prohibition against usury no longer applies. The reason is that economic conditions have changed substantially since biblical times, such that usury no longer has the same negative consequences it had when the prohibitions were issued. Thus, the practice that was condemned by the Bible differs from contemporary interest banking in morally relevant ways.[24]

Yet are we not in a similar position regarding homosexuality? Virtually all scholars agree that homosexual relations during biblical times were vastly different from relationships like Tommy and Jim's. Often such relations were integral to pagan practices. In Greek society, they typically involved older men and younger boys. If those are the kinds of features that the biblical authors had in mind when they issued their condemnations, and such features are no longer typical, then the biblical condemnations no longer apply. As with usury, substantial changes in cultural context have altered the meaning and consequences—and thus the moral value—of the practice in question. Put another way, using the Bible's condemnations of homosexuality against contemporary homosexuality is like using its condemnations of usury against contemporary banking.

Let me be clear about what I am *not* claiming here. First, I am not claiming that the Bible has been wrong before and therefore may be wrong this time. The Bible may indeed be wrong on some matters, but for the purpose of this argument I am assuming its infallibility. Nor am I claiming that the Bible's age renders it entirely inapplicable to today's issues. Rather, I am claiming that when we do apply it, *we must pay attention to morally relevant cultural differences between biblical times and today*. Such attention will help us distinguish between specific time-bound prohibitions (for example, laws against usury or homosexual relations) and the enduring moral values they represent (for example, generosity or respect for persons). And as the above argument shows, my claim is not very controversial. Indeed, to deny it is to commit oneself to some rather strange views on slavery, usury, women's roles, astronomy, evolution, and the like.

Here, one might also make an appeal to religious pluralism. Given the wide variety of religious beliefs (e.g., the Muslim belief that women should cover their faces, the Orthodox Jewish belief against working on Saturday, the Hindu belief that cows are sacred and should not be eaten), each of us inevitably violates the religious beliefs of others. But we normally don't view such violations as occasions for moral censure, since we distinguish between beliefs that depend on particular revelations and beliefs that can be justified independently (e.g., that stealing is wrong). Without an independent justification for condemning homosexuality, the best one can say is, "My religion says so." But in a society that cherishes religious freedom, that reason alone does not normally provide grounds for moral or legal sanctions. That people still fall back on that reason in discussions of homosexuality suggests that they may not have much of a case otherwise.

Conclusion

As a last resort, opponents of homosexuality typically change the subject: "But what about incest, polygamy, and bestiality? If we accept Tommy and Jim's sexual relationship, why shouldn't we accept those as well?" Opponents of interracial marriage used a similar slippery-slope argument in the 1960s when the Supreme Court struck down antimiscegenation laws.[25] It was a bad argument then, and it is a bad argument now.

Just because there are no good reasons to oppose interracial or homosexual relationships, it does not follow that there are no good reasons to oppose incestuous, polygamous, or bestial relationships. One might argue, for instance, that incestuous relationships threaten delicate familial bonds, or that polygamous relationships result in unhealthy jealousies (and sexism), or that bestial relationships—do I need to say it?—aren't really "relationships" at all, at least not in the sense we've been discussing.[26] Perhaps even better arguments could be offered (given much more space than I have here). The point is that there is no logical connection between homosexuality, on the one hand, and incest, polygamy, and bestiality, on the other.

Why, then, do critics continue to push this objection? Perhaps it's because accepting homosexuality requires them to give up one of their favorite arguments: "It's wrong because we've always been taught that it's wrong." This argument—call it the argument from tradition—has an obvious appeal: people reasonably favor tried-and-true ideas over unfamiliar ones, and they recognize the foolishness of trying to invent morality from scratch. But the argument from tradition is also a dangerous argument, as any honest look at history will reveal.

I conclude that Tommy and Jim's relationship, far from being a moral abomination, is exactly what it appears to be to those who know them: a morally positive influence on their lives and on others. Accepting this conclusion takes courage, since it entails that our moral traditions are fallible. But when these traditions interfere with people's happiness for no sound reason, they defeat what is arguably the very point of morality: promoting individual and communal well-being. To put the argument simply, Tommy and Jim's relationship makes them better people. And that's not just good for Tommy and Jim: that's good for everyone.

Notes

1. Although my central example in the paper is a gay male couple, much of what I say will apply mutatis mutandis to lesbians as well, since many of the same arguments are used against them. This is not to say gay male sexuality and lesbian sexuality are largely similar or that discussions of the former will cover all that needs to be said about the latter. Furthermore, the fact that I focus on a long-term, committed relationship should not be taken to imply any judgment about homosexual activity outside of such unions. If the argument of this paper is successful, then the evaluation of homosexual activity outside of committed unions should be largely (if not entirely) similar to the evaluation of *heterosexual* activity outside of committed unions.

2. Burton M. Leiser, *Liberty, Justice, and Morals: Contemporary Value Conflicts* (New York: Macmillan, 1986), 51–57.

3. The Ramsey Colloquium, "The Homosexual Movement," *First Things* (March 1994), 15–20.

4. For an overview of some of these studies, see Simon LeVay, *Queer Science* (Boston: MIT Press, 1996), chap. 10.

5. I have borrowed some items in this list from Richard Mohr's pioneering work *Gays/Justice* (New York: Columbia University Press, 1988), 36.

6. I am indebted to Andrew Koppelman and Stephen Macedo for helpful discussions on this point. See Andrew Koppelman's argument in Chapter 4

of this volume, and Stephen Macedo's article "Homosexuality and the Conservative Mind," *Georgetown Law Journal* 84, no. 2 (1995), 261, 276.

7. For a fuller explication of this type of natural law argument, see John Finnis, "Law, Morality, and 'Sexual Orientation,'" *Notre Dame Law Review* 69, no. 5 (1994), 1049–76; revised, shortened, and reprinted in Chapter 3 of this volume. For a cogent and well-developed response, see Chapter 4, and Stephen Macedo, "Homosexuality and the Conservative Mind," *Georgetown Law Journal* 84, no. 2 (1995), 261–300.

8. The Ramsey Colloquium, "Homosexual Movement," 19.

9. Thomas Schmidt, "The Price of Love" in *Straight and Narrow? Compassion and Clarity in the Homosexuality Debate* (Downers Grove, IL: InterVarsity Press, 1995), chap. 6.

10. Both the American Psychological Association and the American Public Health Association have conceded this point: "Reliable data on the incidence of homosexual orientation are difficult to obtain due to the criminal penalties and social stigma attached to homosexual behavior and the consequent difficulty of obtaining representative samples of people to study" (*Amici Curiae* Brief in *Bowers v. Hardwick*, Supreme Court No. 85–140 [October Term 1985]).

11. It is worth noting that allegations of promiscuity are probably exaggerated. The study most commonly cited to prove homosexual male promiscuity, the Bell and Weinberg study, took place in 1978, in an urban center (San Francisco), at the height of the sexual revolution—hardly a broad sample. See Alan P. Bell and Martin S. Weinberg, *Homosexualities* (New York: Simon & Schuster, 1978). The far more recent and extensive University of Chicago study agreed that homosexual and bisexual people "have higher average numbers of partners than the rest of the sexually active people in the study," but it concluded that the differences in the mean number of partners "do not appear very large." See Edward O. Laumann et al., *The Social Organization of Sexuality: Sexual Practices in the United States* (Chicago: University of Chicago Press, 1994), 314, 316. I am grateful to Andrew Koppelman for drawing my attention to the Chicago study.

12. The Ramsey Colloquium, "Homosexual Movement," 19.

13. See S. R. Johnson, E. M. Smith, and S. M. Guenther, "Comparison of Gynecological Health Care Problems Between Lesbian and Bisexual Women," *Journal of Reproductive Medicine* 32 (1987), 805–811.

14. See, for example, Stanton L. Jones, "The Loving Opposition," *Christianity Today* 37 no. 8 (July 19, 1993).

15. See Danya Glaser and Stephen Frosh, *Child Sexual Abuse*, 2nd ed. (Houndmills, England: Macmillan, 1993), 13–17; and Kathleen Coulbourn Faller, *Understanding Child Sexual Maltreatment* (Newbury Park, CA: Sage, 1990), 16–20.

16. See Frank G. Bolton Jr., Larry A. Morris, and Ann E. MacEachron, *Males at Risk: The Other Side of Child Abuse* (Newbury Park, CA: Sage, 1989), 61.

17. Part of the problem here arises from the grossly simplistic categorization of people into two (or, at best, three) sexual orientations; heterosexual, homosexual, and bisexual. Clearly, there is great variety within (and beyond) these

categories. See Frederick Suppe, "Explaining Homosexuality: Philosophical Issues, and Who Cares Anyhow?" in Timothy F. Murphy, ed., *Gay Ethics: Controversies in Outing, Civil Rights, and Sexual Science* (New York: Harrington Park Press, 1994), esp. 223–268, published simultaneously in the *Journal of Homosexuality* 27, nos. 3–4: 223–268.

18. "An Essay on 'Paederasty,'" in Robert Baker and Frederick Elliston, eds., *The Philosophy of Sex* (Buffalo, NY: Prometheus, 1984), 360–361. Bentham uses the word "paederast" where we would use the term "homosexual"; the latter term was not coined until 1869, and the term "heterosexual" was coined a few years after that. Today, "pederasty" refers to sex between men and boys—a different phenomenon from the one Bentham was addressing.

19. The Ramsey Colloquium, "Homosexual Movement," 17–18.

20. The argument is a classic example of the fallacy of denying the antecedent: if X promotes procreation, then X is good; X does not promote procreation, therefore X is not good. Compare: if X is president, then X lives in the White House; Chelsea Clinton is not president, therefore Chelsea Clinton does not live in the White House.

21. Actually, Williams makes the point with regard to celibacy, while making an analogy between celibacy and homosexuality. See Chapter 6 of this volume.

22. All biblical quotations are from the New Revised Standard Version.

23. See also Deut. 23:19, Lev. 25:35–37, Neh. 5:7–10, Jer. 15:10. Ezek. 22:12, and Luke 6:35. For a fuller explication of the analogy between homosexuality and usury, see John Corvino, "The Bible Condemned Usurers, Too," *Harvard Gay and Lesbian Review* 3, no. 4 (Fall 1996): 11–12.

24. See Richard P. McBrien, *Catholicism*, study ed. (San Francisco: Harper & Row, 1981). 1020.

25. *Loving v. Virginia*, 388 U.S. 1967.

26. One might object here that I am equivocating on the term "relationship," since throughout the paper I have been discussing acts, not relationships. But I maintain that Tommy and Jim's sexual act is *relational* in a way that Tommy and Fido's simply could not be. Even apart from their love for each other, Tommy and Jim have capacities for mutual communication and respect that Tommy and Fido simply do not have. Thus, one can approve of Tommy and Jim's sexual act without implying anything about Tommy and Fido's (possible) sexual acts: the two are fundamentally different.

1. Write a three-page rebuttal to this essay, using real evidence and information you have researched. Be sure to address any plausible objections that could be directed at your argument.

2. Write a three-page assessment of the essay's argument. Consider each premise and the strength or validity of the reasoning. Take into account possible objections to your view.

3. Select a premise from Corvino's essay and evaluate it for plausibility. Do online research if you need to. Write a one-page summary of your evaluation.

Essay 5

More Innocents Die When We Don't Have Capital Punishment

Dennis Prager

A couple of weeks ago, three New Hampshire prisoners, one a convicted murderer, escaped from prison. What if the murderer had murdered again? On whose hands would the victim's blood have been?

One of the most common, and surely the most persuasive, arguments against capital punishment is that the state may execute an innocent person. One reason for its effectiveness is that proponents of capital punishment often do not know how to respond to it.

That's a shame. For while the argument is emotionally compelling, it is morally and intellectually shallow.

First of all, there is almost no major social good that does not lead to the death of innocent individuals. Over a million innocent people have been killed and maimed in car accidents. Would this argue for the banning of automobiles? To those whose criterion for acceptable social policy is that not one innocent die, it should.

If it were proven that a strictly enforced 40-mile-per-hour speed limit on our nation's highways would save innocent lives, should we reduce highway limits to 40 miles per hour? Should all roller coasters be shut down because some innocents get killed riding on them?

Anyone whose criterion for abolishing capital punishment is saving innocent lives should be for a 40-mile-per-hour speed limit and for abolishing roller coasters.

But death-penalty abolitionists aren't. And that is why they cannot logically build their case against capital punishment on the argument that an innocent may die. They accept a large number of social policies that kill innocents. Therefore, if abolitionists were intellectually honest, they would have to argue that capital punishment achieves no social good or that it is immoral to kill any murderers, not that it must be abandoned because an innocent may die.

But they do not make those arguments because they know that most Americans do not share their view that killing a murderer is immoral and that all murderers deserve to live. So they make the emotional but intellectually dishonest argument that, sure, some murderers ought be put to death, but we just can't do that because an innocent person may one day die.

The abolitionist argument that an innocent might be killed is false for a second reason. Far more innocent people have already died because we did not execute their murderers. The abolitionist has convinced himself, and a sincere but gullible public, that only a policy of capital punishment threatens innocent lives, while abolition of capital punishment threatens no innocent lives. That is entirely untrue.

Murderers who are not executed have murdered innocent people—usually fellow prisoners. And the very real possibility of escape from prison means that murderers threaten far more innocent lives than capital punishment does.

So here is the bottom line: If the escaped New Hampshire murderer had murdered someone, would opponents of capital punishment have acknowledged that the blood of that victim was on their hands? I doubt it. They believe that only advocates of capital punishment can have blood on their hands, when and if the state executes an innocent person. But they, the abolitionists, somehow have no blood on their hands when a convicted murderer murders an innocent.

As a proponent of capital punishment, I fully acknowledge my moral responsibility for any innocent person executed by the state. It is time that the abolitionists confronted their responsibility for every innocent already murdered and yet to be murdered by murderers who should have been executed. Or at least let them drop this false argument and state the truth: They believe murderers should never be killed.

1. Outline the argument in this essay, indicating the premises and the conclusion. Determine whether the argument is deductive or inductive. Address the question of whether the argument is sound or cogent.

2. Write a two-page rebuttal to Essay 5. Spend at least a half hour online researching the topic.

3. Write a one-page essay defending Prager's argument. Then write another one-page essay arguing against his conclusion.

Essay 6

What's Wrong with Adultery?

Bonnie Steinbock

According to a 1980 survey in *Cosmopolitan*, 54 percent of American wives have had extramarital affairs; a study of 100,000 married women by the considerably tamer *Redbook* magazine found that 40 percent of the wives over 40 had been unfaithful. While such surveys are, to some extent, self-selecting—those who do it are more likely to fill out questionnaires about it—sexual mores have clearly changed in recent years. Linda Wolfe, who reported the results of the *Cosmopolitan* survey, suggests that "this increase in infidelity among married women represents not so much a deviation from traditional standards of fidelity as a break with the old double standard." Studies show that men have always strayed in significant numbers.

Yet 80 percent of "COSMO girls" did not approve of infidelity and wished their own husbands and lovers would be faithful. Eighty-eight percent of respondents to a poll taken in Iowa in 1983 viewed "coveting your neighbor's spouse" as a "major sin." It seems that while almost nobody approves of adultery, men have always done it, and women are catching up.

The increase in female adultery doubtless has to do with recent and radical changes in our attitudes toward sex and sexuality. We no longer feel guilty about enjoying sex; indeed, the capacity for sexual enjoyment is often regarded as a criterion of mental health. When sex itself is no longer intrinsically shameful, restraints on sexual behavior are loosened. In fact, we might question whether the abiding disapproval of infidelity merely gives lip service to an ancient taboo. Is there a rational justification for disapproving of adultery which will carry force with everyone, religious and nonreligious alike?

Trust and Deception

Note first that adultery, unlike murder, theft, and lying, is not universally forbidden. Traditional Eskimo culture, for example, regarded sharing one's wife with a visitor as a matter of courtesy. The difference can be explained by looking at the effects of these practices on social cohesiveness. Without rules protecting the lives, persons, and property of its members, no group could long endure. Indeed, rules against killing, assault, lying, and stealing seem fundamental to having a morality at all.

Not so with adultery. For adultery is a *private* matter, essentially concerning only the relationship between husband and wife. It is not essential to morality like these other prohibitions: there are stable societies with genuine moral codes which tolerate extra-marital sex. Although adultery remains a criminal offense in some jurisdictions, it is rarely prosecuted. Surely this is because it is widely regarded as a private matter: in the words of Billie Holiday, "Ain't nobody's business if I do."

However, even if adultery is a private matter, with which the state should not interfere, it is not a morally neutral issue. Our view of adultery is connected to our thoughts and feelings about love and marriage, sex and the family, the value of fidelity, sexual jealousy, and exclusivity. How we think about adultery will affect the quality of our relationships, the way we raise our children, the kind of society we have and want to have. So it is important to consider whether our attitudes toward adultery are justifiable.

Several practical considerations militate against adultery: pregnancy and genital herpes immediately spring to mind. However, unwanted pregnancies are a risk of all sexual intercourse, within or without marriage; venereal disease is a risk of all non-exclusive sex, not just adulterous sex. So these risks do not provide a reason for objecting specifically to adultery. In any event, they offer merely pragmatic, as opposed to moral, objections. If adultery is wrong, it does not become less so because one has been sterilized or inoculated against venereal disease.

Two main reasons support regarding adultery as seriously immoral. One is that adultery is an instance of promise-breaking, on the view that marriage involves, explicitly or implicitly, a promise of sexual fidelity: to forsake all others. That there is this attitude in our culture is clear. Mick Jagger, not noted for sexual puritanism, allegedly refused to marry Jerry Hall, the mother of his baby, because he had no intension of accepting an exclusive sexual relationship. While Jagger's willingness to become an unwed father is hardly mainstream morality, his refusal to marry, knowing that he did not wish to be faithful, respects the idea that *marriage* requires such a commitment. Moreover, the promise of sexual fidelity is regarded as a very serious and important one. To cheat on one's spouse indicates a lack of concern, a willingness to cause pain, and so a lack of love. Finally, one who breaks promises cannot be trusted. And trust is essential to the intimate partnership of marriage, which may be irreparably weakened by its betrayal.

The second reason for regarding adultery as immoral is that it involves deception, for example, lying about one's whereabouts and relations with others. Perhaps a marriage can withstand the occasional lie, but a pattern of lying will have irrevocable consequences for a marriage, if discovered, and probably even if not. Like breaking promises, lying is regarded as a fundamental kind of wrong-doing, a failure to take the one lied to seriously as a moral person entitled to respect.

Open Marriage

These two arguments suffice to make most cases of adultery wrong, given the attitudes and expectations of most people. But what if marriage did not involve any promise of sexual fidelity? What if there were no need for deception, because neither partner expected or wanted such fidelity? Objections to "open marriage" cannot focus on promise-breaking and deception, for the expectation of exclusivity is absent. If an open marriage has been freely chosen by both spouses, and not imposed by a dominant on a dependent partner, would such an arrangement be morally acceptable, even desirable?

The attractiveness of extramarital affairs, without dishonesty, disloyalty, or guilt, should not be downplayed. However satisfying sex between married people may be, it cannot have the excitement of a new relationship. ("Not *better*, a friend once said defensively to his wife, attempting to explain his infidelity, "just *different*.") Might we not be better off, our lives fuller and richer, if we allowed ourselves the thrill of new and different sexual encounters?

Perhaps the expectation of sexual exclusivity in marriage stems from emotions which are not admirable: jealousy and possessiveness. That most people experience these feelings is no reason for applauding or institutionalizing them. Independence in marriage is now generally regarded as a good thing: too much "togetherness" is boring and stifling. In a good marriage, the partners can enjoy different activities, travel apart, and have separate friends. Why draw the line at sexual activity?

The natural response to this question invokes a certain conception of love and sex: sex is an expression of affection and intimacy and so should be reserved for people who love each other. Further, it is assumed that one can and should have such feelings for only one other person at any time. To make love with someone else is to express feelings of affection and intimacy that should be reserved for one's spouse alone.

This rejection of adultery assumes the validity of a particular conception of love and sex, which can be attacked in two ways. We might divorce sex from love and regard sex as a pleasurable activity in its own right, comparable to the enjoyment of a good meal. In his article "Is Adultery Immoral?"[1] Richard Wasserstrom suggests that the linkage of sex with love reflects a belief that unless it is purified by a higher emotion, such as love, sex is intrinsically bad or dirty.

But this is an overly simplistic view of the connection between sex and love. Feelings of love occur between people enjoying sexual intercourse, not out of a sense that sexual pleasure must be purified, but precisely because of the mutual pleasure they give one another. People naturally have feelings of affection for those who make them happy, and sex is a very good way of making someone extraordinarily happy. At the same time, sex is by its nature intimate, involving both physical and psychological exposure. This both requires and creates trust, which is closely allied to feelings of affection and love. This is not to say that sex necessarily requires or leads to love; but a conception of the relation between love and sex that ignores these factors is inadequate and superficial.

Alternatively, one might acknowledge the connection between sex and love, but attack the assumption of exclusivity. If parents can love all their children equally and if adults can have numerous close friends, why should it be impossible to love more than one sexual partner at a time? Perhaps we could learn to love more than one sexual partner at a time? Perhaps we could learn to love more widely and to accept that a spouse's sexual involvement with another is not a sign of rejection or lack of love.

The logistics of multiple involvement are certainly daunting. Having an affair (as opposed to a roll in the hay) requires time and concentration; it will almost inevitably mean neglecting one's spouse, one's children, one's work. More important, however, exclusivity seems to be an intrinsic part of "true love." Imagine Romeo pouring out his heart to both Juliet *and* Rosalind! In our ideal of romantic love, one chooses to forgo pleasure with other partners in order to have a unique relationship with one's beloved. Such "renunciation" is natural in the first throes of romantic love; it is precisely because this stage does *not* last that we must promise to be faithful through the notoriously unromantic realities of married life.

Fidelity as an Ideal

On the view I have been defending, genuinely open marriages are not *immoral*, although they deviate from a valued ideal of what marriage should be. While this is not the only ideal, or incumbent on all rational agents, it is a moral view in that it embodies a claim about a good way for people to live. The prohibition of adultery, then, is neither arbitrary nor irrational. However, even if we are justified in accepting the ideal of fidelity, we know that people do not always live up to the ideals they accept and we recognize that some failures to do so are worse than others. We regard a brief affair, occasioned by a prolonged separation, as morally different from installing a mistress.

Further, sexual activity is not necessary for deviation from the ideal of marriage which lies behind the demand for fidelity. As John Heckler observed during his bitter and public divorce from former Health and Human Services Secretary Margaret Heckler, "In marriage, there are two partners. When one person starts contributing far less than the other person to the marriage, that's the original infidelity. You don't need any third party." While this statement was probably a justification of his own infidelities, the point is valid. To abandon one's spouse, whether to a career or to another person, is also a kind of betrayal.

If a man becomes deeply involved emotionally with another woman, it may be little comfort that he is able to assure his wife that "Nothing happened." Sexual infidelity has significance as a sign of a deeper betrayal—falling in love with someone else. It may be objected that we cannot control the way we feel, only the way we behave; that we should not be blamed for falling in love, but only for acting on the feeling. While we may not have direct control over our feelings, however, we are responsible for getting ourselves into situations in which certain feelings naturally arise. "It just happened," is rarely an accurate portrayal of an extramarital love affair.

If there can be betrayal without sex, can there be sex without betrayal? In the novel *Forfeit*, by Dick Francis, the hero is deeply in love with his wife, who was paralyzed by polio in the early days of their marriage. Her great unspoken fear is that he will leave her; instead, he tends to her devotedly. For several years, he forgoes sex, but eventually succumbs to an affair. While his adultery is hardly praiseworthy, it is understandable. He could divorce his wife and marry again, but it is precisely his refusal to abandon her, his continuing love and tender care, that makes us admire him.

People do fall in love with others and out of love with their spouses. Ought they refrain from making love while still legally tied? I cannot see much, if any, moral value in remaining physically faithful, on principle, to a spouse one no longer loves. This will displease those who regard the wrongness of adultery as a moral absolute, but my account has nothing to do with absolutes and everything to do with what it means to love someone deeply and completely. It is the value of that sort of relationship that makes sexual fidelity an ideal worth the sacrifice.

Neither a mere religiously based taboo, nor a relic of a repressive view of sexuality, the prohibition against adultery expresses a particular conception of married love. It is one we can honor in our own lives and bequeath to our children with confidence in its value as a coherent and rational ideal.

Note

1. In Wasserstrom's *Today's Moral Problems* (New York: Macmillan, 1975), 288–300. Reprinted in R. Baker and F. Elliston, eds., *Philosophy and Sex*, 1st ed. (Buffalo, NY: Prometheus, 1975), 207–21; 2nd ed. (1984), 93–106.

1. Write a one-page summary of Steinbock's essay, noting what you consider its weakest premise and why you think that.
2. Write a three-page essay assessing Steinbock's argument, noting the truth or falsity of the premises and the strength or validity of the reasoning. Spend at least a half hour online researching the issue.
3. Write a three-page rebuttal to Steinbock. Consider possible objections to your view.

Essay 7

A Pat-Down Is Better Than a Blow-Up

Caroline Baum

Imagine my horror when I read that two male Transportation Security Administration agents had singled out Orlando passenger Eliana Sutherland for further airport screening because of the size of her breasts.

As a woman, I was offended, outraged, disgusted—not to mention jealous. What does Eliana have that I don't have? No TSA agent has ever singled me out because of the size and shape of my breasts or any other body part.

All the outrage about full body scans and pat-downs seems off the point. What's the alternative? Yes, we could do it smarter (TSA, please contact Israel's Shin Bet immediately). Absent that, the latest techniques beat getting blown up in an airplane at 30,000 feet.

The objection to a full body scan from a vocal 15 percent of the populace, according to a CBS Poll, seems lame. It's hard to imagine the grainy images—about as racy as an X-ray—arousing anyone when far more graphic material is available at newsstands in most airports.

The TSA employs 56,000 people and has a budget of $8.2 billion, with $5.5 billion going toward airport security and screening. Airlines take security precautions as well. How many potential terrorists have been snagged by asking travelers, "Did you pack your own bags?" If you answered zero, you would be correct. What about, "Has anyone asked you to carry anything aboard this aircraft?" (Yes, and that ticking sound is driving me nuts!) One wonders what these employees would do if the passenger answered "no" in the first instance and "yes" in the second. Probably ask a supervisor.

In the same way the United States enacts new regulations to make sure the last financial crisis doesn't happen again, it excels at preventing a recurrence of the last terrorist attack. We haven't had another shoe bomber since Richard Reid attempted to blow up a plane in 2002 because we dutifully remove our shoes before going through security. But the TSA couldn't quite bring itself to institute strip searches after Umar Farouk Abdulmutallab tried to light up the skies last Christmas with a pair of explosive-packed Jockey shorts.

Could we do smarter security? Of course. We could learn a few things from the Israelis, maybe even outsource airport security to the Shin Bet, Israel's domestic security agency, which is charged with protecting El Al, the national airline. Ben-Gurion International Airport outside Tel Aviv has been recognized as the safest in the world. By the time passengers arrive at the airport, Israeli security agents know who they're looking for. The screening process begins when a ticket is booked.

Israel employs ethnic profiling, spending more time interviewing a young Arab male with a one-way ticket paid for in cash than an elderly Jewish grandmother or Hebrew University students off on a summer holiday. Muslim Arabs may be singled out unfairly, but they're the ones committed to the destruction of the Jewish state. It's this same group—albeit a small minority—that's targeting the United States.

Another thing: Israeli security agents are highly trained military veterans. They aren't looking for box cutters, toe nail scissors or liquid explosives. Israel's strategy is to "find the bomber, not the bomb," as the saying goes. Practical necessity trumps political correctness. El Al has at least one plainclothes armed marshal on all its flights. In 30 years it can boast a perfect record of no hijackings or hijacking attempts.

Israel has clearly figured out what works in a small nation surrounded by enemies. With two airports and 50 flights a day, it's easier to manage than our 450 airports and thousands of daily flights. Still I'm sure we would benefit from our Middle East ally's experience under fire.

1. Write both an outline and a summary of this essay. Include the premises as well as the evidence or reasoning that supports them.

2. In a two-page essay, write an assessment of Baum's argument. Be explicit about whether you think the argument is good or bad and why.

3. Write a two-page rebuttal to Baum. That is, argue that pat-downs and other security measures are morally impermissible or impractical. Be sure to address any plausible objections that could be directed at your argument.

Essay 8

The Cohabitation Epidemic

Neil Clark Warren

A few summers ago, tennis stars Andre Agassi and Steffi Graf announced that their first child would be born. "This is a very exciting time for us," Agassi said. "We are so happy to be blessed with this gift." No one seemed to notice—or care—that the couple wasn't married. Only a generation ago, this revelation would have raised eyebrows.

Yes, things have changed dramatically over the past few decades. According to the U.S. Census Bureau, 1 million people were in "unmarried-partner households" in 1970. The number rose to 3.2 million in 1990. And in 2000, the figure soared to 11 million. Now, half of all Americans ages 35 to 39 have lived with someone outside of marriage, according to researcher Larry Bumpass. Make no mistake: We are witnessing a major societal shift before our very eyes.

When an epidemic reaches this level of societal acceptance, many well-meaning people begin to ask, "Should we accept cohabitation as another social trend akin to fast food, cell phones and casual Fridays?" You may be wondering whether all this hubbub about living together is much ado about nothing. As a psychologist who has worked with singles and married couples for 35 years, I think our alarm over this issue is much ado about a lot.

Who Cohabits and Why

Typically, people who cohabit fall into two categories. First, there are those who have little or no intention of getting married. They simply want to enjoy the benefits of living together—the availability of sex, combined financial resources, shared household responsibilities and so on. This arrangement allows for a "quick exit" if things turn sour. The second group are those who see living together as a trial marriage—a half-step toward the altar. These people say, "We'll live together first and see how it goes." They consider it prudent to take a test drive before signing on the dotted line.

Though I don't want to oversimplify a complex issue, I believe there are three primary reasons why these couples forgo or delay marriage:

1. Marriage has lost a lot of its luster in our society. The truth is, many people have never seen a successful, thriving marriage, mainly because great marriages are becoming scarce. Several years ago, I conducted a survey in which I asked 500 individuals to tell me about the marriage they most admired. To my dismay, nearly half said they couldn't recommend even one healthy, exemplary marriage! With such a dearth of model marriages, it's understandable why so many young people hesitate to take the plunge.

2. Beyond the lack of model marriages, millions of people have suffered significant pain from broken marriages. One researcher estimates that 70 percent of all Americans have been impacted by divorce—either their parents' or their own. When a broken marriage devastates someone's life, she or he may figure that getting married is just too risky.

3. The majority of singles have lost confidence in their ability to correctly judge a highly compatible and thus long-lasting match. Yet their needs for companionship, sexual satisfaction and economic sufficiency motivate them to search for a person with whom they can have at least a temporary partnership.

So Why Bother with Marriage?

We can certainly argue against cohabiting from a biblical standpoint, because numerous Scriptures admonish us to avoid sexual immorality and to keep marriage sacred (Hebrews 13:4, 1 Corinthians 6:18, 1 Thessalonians 4:3). But let's be realistic: Many couples who live together don't care about biblical principles, and even faith-oriented people often ignore what the Bible says. This is why psychological and other social science research becomes so critical. The findings of this research overwhelmingly support marriage over cohabitation. Consider:

Marriage vows serve as glue that holds people together. Numerous empirical studies destroy the myth that living together is good preparation for marriage, thus reducing the risk of divorce. In fact, one study involving 3,300 cases found that people who cohabited prior to marriage had a 46 percent higher marital failure rate than noncohabiters.

Think about it. The fundamental agreement upon which live-in relationships are based is conditional commitment. This attitude says, "I'll stick with you as long as things go well. But if we run into problems, all bets are off." Relationships that begin with a quasi-commitment carry the same mind-set into marriage. When things become trying, as inevitably they will from time to time, the spouses say goodbye.

As David Popenoe and Barbara Dafoe Whitehead wrote in their extensive review of recent literature, "Virtually all research on the subject has determined that the chances of divorce ending a marriage preceded by cohabitation are significantly greater than for a marriage not preceded by cohabitation."

Marriage provides the most stability for children. Few live-in couples intend to have children, but it often happens. More than a quarter of unmarried mothers are cohabiting at the time of their children's birth. Further, two-thirds of children who end up in stepfamilies have parents who are cohabiting rather than married.

This means that each year thousands of children are born or moved into families where Mom and Dad's commitment to each other is tenuous or, at least, informal. These children, during their most vulnerable developmental stages, are deprived of the security that comes from knowing their parents have pledged themselves to each other for a lifetime. To make matters worse, 75 percent of all children born to cohabiting parents will experience their parents' separation before they reach age 16. Only about one-third of children born to married parents face a similar fate.

Marriage offers promised permanence. Most wedding vows still include the promise to "love, honor and cherish in sickness and in health, in plenty or in want, till death do us part." One reason this is so important: The best relationships require partners who are genuine and authentic—who can be their real selves. The promised permanence of marriage allows just that: "I'll stick with you even when I come to know the real you, with all your imperfections and shortcomings."

But how can two individuals be authentic and genuine if they think their partner may bolt at the first sign of trouble? With the conditional commitment of live-in relationships, partners are left wondering, If I'm not who my partner wants me to be—if he sees my faults—will he pack his bags and leave?

Marriage creates healthier individuals. Scores of studies have shown that married people are better off emotionally, physically, financially and vocationally than unmarried partners. For example, annual rates of depression among cohabiting couples are more than three times what they are among married couples. And women in cohabiting relationships are significantly more likely than married women to suffer physical and sexual abuse.

Marriage partners are more likely to be faithful. Four times as much infidelity is reported among cohabiting men than among married men. Moreover, one married woman in a hundred reports having had an affair in the past year, compared to 8 percent of cohabiting women.

Amid the alarming statistics about cohabitation, we can confidently tell singles that a "trial marriage" is unnecessary. In addition to the research showing the detriments of living together, several studies have discovered—with 80 percent to 94 percent accuracy—the variables that predict which marriages will thrive and which will not. This means unmarried couples can know in advance if they have a better-than-average chance of succeeding in marriage. With this available information, hopefully the cohabitation trend will begin to cycle downward.

1. Study this essay and identify the rhetorical use of any euphemisms or dysphemisms and write a one-page paper about it.
2. Write a two-page rebuttal to Essay 8, assessing its argument and pointing out as many fallacies as possible.
3. Make a list of the support (studies, expert testimony, authority, statistics, etc.) that Warren uses to support his argument. Then write a two-page essay examining how strong or weak this evidence is and how it could be stronger.

Essay 9

Not Being Vaccinated Is Not Acceptable
David Ropeik

What does society do when one person's behavior puts the greater community at risk? We make them stop. We pass laws, or impose economic rules or find some other way to discourage individual behaviors that threaten the greater common good. You don't get to drive drunk. You don't get to smoke in public places. You don't even get to leave your house if you catch some particularly infectious disease.

Then what should we do about people who decline vaccination for themselves or their children and put the public at risk by fueling the resurgence of nearly eradicated diseases? Isn't this the same thing: one person's perception of risk producing behaviors that put others at risk? Of course it is. Isn't it time for society to say we need to regulate the risk created by the fear of vaccines? Yes, it is.

The evidence is overwhelming that declining vaccination rates are contributing to outbreaks of disease.

Take just one example, measles. The World Health Organization reports outbreaks in countries where vaccination rates have gone down, including France (7,000 cases so far this year, more than in all of 2010), Belgium, Germany, Romania, Serbia, Spain, Macedonia and Turkey. There have already been 334 measles cases in England and Wales this year, compared with 33 all of last year. The U. S. has seen 118 cases as of mid-May, compared with 56 cases a year from 2001 to 2008.

Small numbers, you say? True, but consider their cost (beyond the suffering of the patients), as illustrated in this case published this year by the Oxford Journals. When a woman from Switzerland who had not been vaccinated for measles visited Tucson in 2008 and became symptomatic, she went to a local hospital for medical attention.

This initiated a chain of events that over the next three months led to at least 14 people, including seven kids, getting measles. Seven of the victims caught the disease while visiting health care facilities. Four people had to be hospitalized. The outbreak cost two local hospitals a total of nearly $800,000, and the state and local health departments tens of thousands more, to track down the cases, quarantine and treat the sick and notify the thousands of people who might have been exposed.

Fueling that outbreak? None of the victims had been vaccinated or had "unknown vaccination status," and remarkably, 25 percent of the workers in the health care facilities where the patients were treated had no immunity to measles (either they had not been vaccinated or the antibodies from an earlier vaccination could no longer be detected). One health care worker got the disease and gave it to two other people.

That's just one example of the growing threat to public health caused by people worried that vaccines will cause autism and other harms, despite overwhelming evidence to the contrary. In many places, particularly in affluent, liberal, educated communities (San Diego, Marin County, Boulder, Colo.), unvaccinated people are catching diseases that vaccines can prevent, like measles, whooping cough and meningitis.

In 2010, as California suffered its worst whooping cough outbreak in more than 60 years (more than 9,000 cases, 10 infant deaths), Marin County had one of the lowest rates of vaccination statewide and the second-highest rate of whooping cough. A 2008 study in Michigan found that areas with "exemption clusters" of parents who didn't vaccinate their kids were three times more likely to have outbreaks of whooping cough than areas where vaccination rates matched the state average.

And this is a risk to far more people than just those who have opted out of vaccination. People are getting sick who have been vaccinated but the vaccine either doesn't work or has weakened. Infants too young to be vaccinated are getting sick, and some of them are dying horrible deaths from whooping cough after exposure in communities where "herd immunity" has fallen too low to keep the spread of the disease in check.

Unvaccinated people who get sick and visit doctor's offices or hospitals increase the danger for anyone else who uses those facilities.

Outbreaks are costing the health care system millions of dollars, and local and state government (that's taxpayer money, yours and mine) millions more as they try to chase down each outbreak and bring it under control to protect the public's health. Your health, and mine.

No one doubts the honest passion of those who fear vaccines. And for some people, no amount of communication or dialogue or reasoning will stop them from worrying. But risk perception is ultimately subjective, a combination of the facts and how those facts feel, and sometimes our fears don't match the evidence. The dangers that sometimes arise because of the way we perceive risk must be managed too. But we must act in the face of this threat to public health.

There are many potential solutions, each fraught with pros and cons and details that require careful thought and open democratic discussion.

- Perhaps it should be harder to opt out of vaccination. (Twenty-one states allow parents to decline vaccination of their children simply for "philosophical" reasons; 48 allow a religious exemption, but few demand documentation from parents to support claims that their faith precludes vaccination.)
- Perhaps there should be higher health care and insurance costs for unvaccinated people, or "healthy behavior" discounts for people who do get vaccinated, paid for from what society saves by avoiding the spread of disease.
- There could be restrictions on the community and social activities in which unvaccinated people can participate, like lengthy school trips for kids, etc.

This is not about creating more government to intrude further into our lives. This is about calling on government to do what it's there for in the first place: to protect us from the actions of others when as individuals we can't protect ourselves. It is appropriate, and urgent, that we act to protect public health from those whose choices about vaccines are putting the rest of us at risk: We make them stop.

1. Write a three-page assessment of this essay's argument. Consider each premise and the strength or validity of the reasoning.
2. Write both an outline and a summary of this essay. Include the premises as well as the evidence or reasoning that supports them.
3. Go online to research the controversy over whether there is a strong link between autism and vaccinations. Then write a three-page essay arguing either for or against the theory. Be sure to address any plausible objections that could be directed at your argument.

Essay 10
Women and the Afghanistan Peace Process
Ann Jones

Looking for a way out of Afghanistan? Maybe it's time to try something totally different, like putting into action, for the first time in history, the most enlightened edict ever passed by the U. N. Security Council: Resolution 1325.

Passed on Oct. 31, 2000, the resolution was hailed worldwide as a great victory for both women and international peace. In a nutshell, it calls for women to participate equally in all processes of conflict resolution, peacemaking and reconstruction.

The resolution grew out of a recognition that while men at the negotiating table still jockey for power and wealth, women who are included commonly advocate for interests that coincide perfectly with those of civil society. They are concerned about their children and consequently about shelter, clean water, sanitation, jobs, health care, education—the things that make life livable for peaceable people.

It's been nine years since I started doing aid work in Afghanistan, and I am frustrated by the lack of progress toward a peaceful and livable society.

Yet whenever I present my modest proposal for the implementation of 1325 to American big men who lay claim to expertise on Afghanistan, most of them strongly object. They know the theory, they say, but they are precluded from throwing their weight behind the resolution by delicate considerations of "cultural relativism." Afghanistan, they remind me, is a "traditional" culture when it comes to women. Westerners, they say, must respect that.

Yet the eagerness of Western men to defer to this "tradition" seems excessive, especially since few of the Afghan men who actually governed Afghanistan between 1919 and 1989 would have shared their sentiments.

Modern ideas, including the idea of equality between the sexes, have been at the heart of Afghan cultural struggles for at least a century. In the 1920s, King Amanullah founded the first high school for girls and the first family court to adjudicate women's complaints about their husbands; he proclaimed the equality of men and women, banned polygamy and the burka and banished ultraconservative mullahs who undermined the moderate Sufi ideals of Afghanistan. His modern ideas cost him his crown, but Amanullah and his modern, unveiled queen, Soraya, are remembered for their brave endeavor to drag the country into the modern world.

Thousands of Afghan citizens have shared Amanullah's modern views, expressed later by successive leaders, kings and communists alike. But in 2001 the United States—and by extension the entire international community—cast its lot with Hamid Karzai.

We put him in power after a power-sharing conference in Bonn, to which only two Afghan women were invited. We paid millions to stage two presidential elections, in 2004 and 2009, and looked the other way while Karzai's men stuffed the ballot boxes. Now, it seems, we're stuck with him and his ultraconservative, misogynist "traditions," even though an ever-growing number of Afghanistan watchers now identify the Karzai government as the single greatest problem the United States faces in its never-ending war.

And what has Karzai done for the women of Afghanistan? Not a thing.

That's the conclusion of a recent report issued by the Human Rights Research and Advocacy Consortium, an association of prominent aid and independent research groups in Afghanistan. Afghan researchers conducted extensive interviews with prominent male religious scholars, male political leaders and female leaders at the local, provincial and national levels.

The report notes that Karzai has supported increasingly repressive laws against women, most notoriously the "Taliban-style" Shia Personal Status

Law, which not only legitimizes marital rape but prevents women from stepping out of their homes without their husbands' consent. The report points out that this law denies women even the basic freedoms guaranteed all citizens in Afghanistan's 2004 constitution.

In fact, Karzai's record on human rights, as the report documents, is chiefly remarkable for what he has not done. He holds extraordinary power to make political appointments, yet today, after nearly 10 years in office, only one Cabinet ministry is led by a woman: the Ministry for Women's Affairs, which has only advisory powers.

Karzai has appointed only one female provincial governor, Dr. Habiba Sarabi, among 33 men. (Is it by chance that her province, Bamiyan, is generally viewed as the most peaceful in the country?) Among Afghanistan's city governments, he has named only one female mayor. And to the Supreme Court High Council, he has appointed no women at all.

It should come as no surprise, then, that when Karzai named a High Peace Council to negotiate with the Taliban, its members initially consisted of 60 men and no women. They were the usual suspects: warlords, Wahhabis, mujahedin, all fighting for power to the bitter end. Under international pressure, Karzai belatedly added 10 women to the group. The United States has signed off on this lopsided "peace" council.

I suppose this means my modest proposal doesn't stand a chance, and that's a shame. We know from experience that power-sharing agreements among combatants tend to fray, often unraveling into open warfare within a few years. We also know that just because the big men in power stop shooting at each other doesn't mean they stop the war against civilians—especially women and girls. Rape, torture, mutilation and murder continue unabated or increase.

Thus, from the standpoint of civilians, a war is not always over when it's "over," and the "peace" is not necessarily a real peace at all. Think of the Democratic Republic of Congo, the notorious rape capital of the world, where thousands upon thousands of women have been gang-raped even though the country has been officially at peace since 2003.

I don't expect men in power to take seriously the Security Council's proposition that the involvement of women in negotiations makes for a better and more lasting peace.

Progressive, peaceable men would prefer to live in a peace created by women and men together. But too many big men, in both Afghanistan and the United States, are doing very nicely, thank you, with the traditional arrangements in their country and ours.

1. Write an outline and a one-half page summary of this essay.
2. In a two-page essay state whether you agree with Jones and give reasons for your view. Consider possible objections to your view.
3. Go online to research women's rights in Afghanistan or Saudi Arabia. Then write a three-page essay explaining how women's rights are restricted and why women should have the same rights as men.

Essay 11
A Deviance from God's Norm
Richard Land

Recently, Senator Rick Santorum was attacked by the liberal media, politicians, and pro-homosexual groups for comments he made about a case being argued currently before the U.S. Supreme Court.

The plaintiff in this case, who was arrested by Houston sheriff's deputies and fined for engaging in homosexual behavior outlawed in Texas, is attempting to have Texas' anti-sodomy law ruled unconstitutional. When asked by an Associated Press reporter to state his opinion about homosexual behavior, Mr. Santorum referred to the Supreme Court case and commented that activities like sodomy "undermine the basic tenets of our society and the family."

In return for stating his honest opinion Mr. Santorum has been subjected to an endless, venomous diatribe. Liberals and pro-homosexual groups have decided that Mr. Santorum is bigoted and intolerant and no longer worthy material for Senate leadership. The treatment Mr. Santorum has endured for stating his opinion—which by the way, is the opinion of the vast majority of Americans— serves as a vivid reminder of the tactics of his attackers.

Because the homosexual-rights groups have been unable to persuade the majority of Americans that homosexuality is good for us, they have resorted to attacking anyone who speaks the majority opinion. In so doing the gay thought police have revealed themselves for what they really are—bullies who threaten and intimidate those who dare to speak out against them.

We must ask who the real bigots are here. In America, speaking one's mind is a Constitutionally-protected right. The real bigots are those who label anyone who disagrees with them as bigoted and intolerant and attack them for sharing their beliefs. Mr. Santorum has not called for anyone's resignation or dismissal. His detractors have. Once again, the homosexual-rights groups have revealed that they are the real bigots.

Our society has the responsibility and the right to discourage the practice of homosexuality. The Judeo-Christian teaching on this is clear. Homosexuality is a deviance from God's norm. It is neither normal nor healthy behavior. Lest anyone think that this theological position is merely sectarian, it is important to note that even the renowned theologian Wolfhart Pannenberg concluded that when the church has "ceased to treat homosexual activity as a departure from the biblical norm" it "would no longer stand on biblical ground but against the unequivocal witness of Scripture" and "would thereby have ceased to be one, holy, catholic, and apostolic."

Furthermore, any attempt to equate homosexuality with race or ethnicity should offend all of us. There is no evidence that homosexuality is an inborn trait, in spite of numerous efforts to prove the contrary. Homosexuality has many contributing causes, but it is obviously not to be equated with race or ethnicity. A person's ethnicity is what one is, whereas homosexual behavior is what one does.

As Christians, we will continue to support politicians who speak out against homosexuality and to oppose those who support special rights for homosexuals and who seek to support societal approval of homosexual behavior. I applaud Mr. Santorum for courageously sharing his beliefs. We hope other politicians will be emboldened by his stand to hold firm to their convictions about the immorality of homosexual behavior and resist the bullying and intimidation tactics of radical homosexual-rights groups.

1. Write both an outline and a summary of this essay. Include the premises as well as the evidence or reasoning that support them.

2. In a three-page paper, compare Land's argument with that in Essay 4. Decide which essay makes the stronger case and explain your reasons for thinking so.

3. Identify the premises and conclusions of any arguments in this essay and write a two-page rebuttal. As part of your critique, identify any fallacies used by the author.

Essay 12

Marriage Still Evolving, as Ever

BUFFALO NEWS
April 2, 2006

The refrain echoes from pulpit to parishioner, from megaphone to protester, from blogger to reader: Marriage is a bond between a man and a woman, and *only* that.

In most cases, perhaps 90 percent, it is. But as New York prepares for a Court of Appeals decision this summer that could legalize or pave the way for gay marriage, people might want to try getting their heads around the idea that marriage is and has been many things. But it never was engraved in romantic, heterosexual—even monogamous—marble. Marriage is an evolving, dynamic, living arrangement.

Marriage only recently, say in the last 150 years, focused on two people in love. Before that, it was more often than not—at all income levels—a forced or coerced arrangement about status, property or power. You could be a prince or a pauper, but your father was often trying to enhance his kingdom, or diet, by hooking you up with someone who could help him do that.

There was a time when women entering marriage lost all their rights to their husbands, something most women today would find laughable. Even more extreme, women at one time, as part of marriage, became a man's property. There were laws in this country that said marriage protected men against accusations of spousal rape. If you were a woman, your husband could rape you with impunity. Marriage, by law or custom, was restricted along racial or religious lines. "Intermarriage" was viewed as hurting or weakening a race, religion or group.

Finally, marriage used to be unviolable, something impossible to split. Today divorce is routine, with half ending before death do us part. That may or may not be good for society, children and spouses, but it shows how marriage is still evolving.

So when supporters talk about gays and lesbians marrying—and thereby gaining an estimated 1,500 rights that accrue to married people but are routinely denied to gays—it's more evolution. You may not agree; you may believe that *only* men and women should marry. But as more states approve, it might help to understand marriage's history and its dynamic place in our lives by examining its fluid reality.

1. Write an outline and a one-half page summary of this essay.
2. Identify the conclusion and premises of the argument, and write a one-page rebuttal to it.
3. In a two-page paper compare this essay with Essay 8 ("The Cohabitation Epidemic") and determine which one makes the stronger argument and why.

Essay 13
Slouching Toward Chimeras
Jeremy Rifkin

What happens when you cross a human and a mouse? Sounds like the beginning of a bad joke but, in fact, it's a serious high tech experiment recently carried out by a research team headed by a distinguished molecular biologist, Irving Weissman, at Stanford University's Institute of Cancer/Stem Cell Biology and Medicine. Scientists injected human brain cells into mouse fetuses, creating a strain of mice that were approximately 1 percent human. Dr. Weissman is actively considering a follow-up experiment that would produce mice whose brains are 100 percent human.

What if the mice escaped the laboratory and began to proliferate in the outside environment? What might be the ecological consequences of mice who think like human beings, let loose in nature? Dr. Weissman says he would keep a tight rein on the mice and if they showed any signs of humanness he would kill them. Hardly reassuring.

In a world where the bizarre has become all too commonplace, few things any longer shock the human psyche. But, experiments like the one that produced a partially humanized mouse at Stanford University stretch the limits of human tinkering with nature to the realm of the pathological.

The new research field at the cutting edge of the biotech revolution is called chimeric experimentation. Researchers around the world are combining human and animal cells and creating chimeric creatures that are part human and part animal, reminiscent of the ancient Greek chimeric myths of human-animal hybrids.

The first such chimeric experiment occurred many years ago when scientists in Edinburgh, Scotland, fused together a sheep and goat embryo—two completely unrelated animal species that are incapable of mating and producing a hybrid offspring in nature. The resulting creature, called a Geep, was born with the head of a goat and the body of a sheep.

Now, scientists have their sights trained on breaking the final taboo in the natural world—crossing humans and animals to create new human-animal hybrids of every kind and description. Already, aside from the humanized mouse, scientists have created pigs with human blood running through their veins and sheep with livers and hearts that are mostly human.

The experiments are designed to advance medical research. Indeed, a growing number of genetic engineers argue that human-animal hybrids will usher in a golden era of medicine. Researchers say that the more humanized they can make research animals, the better able they will be to model the progression of human diseases, test new drugs, and harvest tissues and organs for transplantation into human bodies. What they fail to mention is that there are other equally promising and less invasive alternatives to these kinds of bizarre experiments including sophisticated computer modeling to study diseases and test the effectiveness and toxicity of drugs as well as in vitro tissue culture, nanotechnology, and artificial prostheses to substitute for human tissue and organs. When it comes to chimeric experimentation, then, the question is, at what price?

Some researchers are speculating about human-chimpanzee chimeras—creating a humanzee. A humanzee would be the ideal laboratory research animal because chimpanzees are so closely related to human beings. Chimps share 98 percent of the human genome and a fully mature chimp has the equivalent mental abilities and consciousness of a four-year-old human child. Fusing a human and chimpanzee embryo—a feat researchers say is quite feasible—could produce a creature so human that questions regarding its moral and legal status would throw 4,000 years of human ethics into utter chaos.

Would such a creature enjoy human rights and protections under the law? For example, it's possible that such a creature could cross the species barrier and mate with a human. Would society allow inter-species conjugation? Would a humanzee have to pass some kind of "humanness" test to win its freedom? Would it be forced into doing menial labor or be used to perform dangerous activities?

The horrific possibilities are mind-boggling. For example, what if human stem cells—the primordial cells that turn into the body's 200 or so cell types—were to be injected into an animal embryo and spread throughout the animal's body into every organ? Some human cells could migrate to the testes and ovaries where they could grow into human sperm and eggs. If two of the chimeric mice were to mate, they could potentially conceive a human embryo. If the human embryo were to be removed and implanted in a human womb, the resulting human baby's biological parents would have been chimeric mice.

Please understand that none of this is science fiction. The American National Academy of Sciences, the country's most august scientific body, issued guidelines for chimeric research on April 25, anticipating a flurry of new experiments in the burgeoning field of human-animal chimeric experimentation. What would be the ramifications of creating hundreds, even thousands, of new life forms that are part human and part other creature? Creatures that could mate, reproduce, and repopulate the Earth?

Bio-ethicists are already clearing the moral path for human-animal chimeric experiments, arguing that once society gets past the revulsion factor, the prospect of new, partially human creatures has much to offer the human race. And, of course, this is exactly the kind of reasoning that has been put forth time and again to justify what is fast becoming a macabre journey into a monstrous Brave New World in which all of nature can be ruthlessly manipulated and reengineered to suit the momentary needs and even whims and caprices of just one species, the Homo sapiens. But now, with human-animal chimeric experiments, we risk even undermining our own species' biological integrity in the name of human progress.

With chimeric technology, scientists now have the power to rewrite the evolutionary saga—to sprinkle parts of the Homo sapiens species into the rest of the animal kingdom as well as fuse parts of other species into our own genome and even to create new human subspecies and superspecies. Are we on the cusp of a biological renaissance, as some believe, or sowing the seeds of our own destruction? Perhaps it is time to ask what we mean by progress.

1. Study this essay, identify its conclusion and premises, and write a two-page rebuttal to it. Consider possible objections to your view.

2. Write a two-page assessment of this essay's argument. Consider each premise and the strength or validity of the reasoning.

3. In a half page, identify this essay's weakest premise and explain how you would strengthen the argument.

Essay 14

Fighting Islamic Extremists Who Stifle Free Speech
Ayaan Hirsi Ali and Daniel Huff

Earlier this year, after Comedy Central altered an episode of *South Park* that had prompted threats because of the way it depicted Islam's prophet Muhammad, Seattle cartoonist Molly Norris proposed an "Everybody Draw Muhammad Day." The idea was, as she put it, to stand up for the First Amendment and "water down the pool of targets" for extremists.

The proposal got Norris targeted for assassination by radical Yemeni American cleric Anwar Awlaki, who has been linked to the attempted Christmas Day bombing of a Northwest Airlines flight and also to several of the 9/11 hijackers. This month, after warnings from the FBI, Norris went into hiding. The *Seattle Weekly* said that Norris was "moving, changing her name and essentially wiping away her identity."

It's time for free-speech advocates to take a page from the abortion rights movement's playbook. In the 1990s, abortion providers faced the same sort of intimidation tactics and did not succumb. Instead, they lobbied for a federal law making it a crime to threaten people exercising reproductive rights and permitting victims to sue for damages. The Freedom of Access to Clinic Entrances Act, or FACE, passed in 1994 by solid bipartisan margins. A similar act is needed to cover threats against free-speech rights.

A federal law would do two things. First, it would deter violent tactics, by focusing national attention on the problem and invoking the formidable enforcement apparatus of the federal government. Second, its civil damages provision would empower victims of intimidation to act as private attorneys general to defend their rights.

Such an act is overdue. Across media and geographies, Islamic extremists are increasingly using intimidation to stifle free expression.

In 2004, Theo van Gogh was murdered on an Amsterdam street in broad daylight for his film criticizing Islam's treatment of women. By 2006, it was reported that "dozens of people" across Europe were "in hiding or under police protection because of threats from Muslim extremists."

Some targets, including the co-author of this commentary, fled to the United States, where it seemed safer—and so it is, for now. However, the stark truth is that the United States was never immune and the situation is deteriorating.

In 1989, two American bookstores carrying Salman Rushdie's *The Satanic Verses* were firebombed. Spooked major chains took it off display. And there have been many more threats that received less publicity. Few have heard, for example, about Oklahoma atheist Sabri Husibi, who received death threats after writing a 2009 article critical of his former faith. His aged mother in Syria was warned she would never see him again. "Clearly shaken," he requested the paper that published his article clarify that he is critical of all faiths.

These kinds of threats have had a formidable chilling effect. Mindful of the retaliation others faced, Yale University Press, the Met, the director of the disaster epic *2012* and countless others have decided to pre-emptively censor themselves.

The kind of legislation we propose is essential if we are to win the war of ideas against extremists, who use threats to drive the moderate message out of public discourse.

Existing state laws prohibiting intimidation are inadequate. On the criminal side, the heightened standard of proof deters prosecutors from investing scarce resources. Explicit grounds for a civil action do not always exist, and damages can be difficult to quantify. By contrast, the FACE Act, which provides the model for the proposed legislation, lets victims opt for preset damages.

The *South Park* incident neatly illustrates the benefits. On April 15, following the first of a two-part episode mocking Jesus, Buddha and Muhammad, RevolutionMuslim.com announced that "(w)e have to warn Matt and Trey that what they are doing is stupid and they will probably wind up like Theo van Gogh." The "warning" included the names, photos and work address of the *South Park* creators, a graphic image of van Gogh's mutilated body and pictures of other targets of Muslim extremists. Overlaying this was audio of Awlaki preaching about assassinating anyone who defamed the prophet. Panicked, Comedy Central heavily censored the episode.

This rather obvious threat could not be prosecuted. New York Police Department officials explained it did not rise to a crime. Were the FACE Act applicable here, a civil suit would have been available, and precedent suggests it would have been successful.

In 2002, on very similar facts, the U.S. 9th Circuit Court of Appeals upheld a civil award to doctors who sued using the FACE Act. A fringe pro-life group, the American Coalition of Life Activists, had in various public venues displayed "Wanted"-style posters bearing the names, photos and addresses of doctors who performed abortions. Their names were also posted on the Internet alongside a list of wounded and murdered doctors whose names were struck through. The court held that the ACLA's activities constituted true threats unprotected by the First Amendment.

If we leave our artists, activists and thinkers alone to weather the assault, they will succumb and we will all suffer the consequences.

1. Write a one-page summary of this essay, noting what you consider to be its weakest premise and why you think so.

2. Write a two-page essay assessing the argument, noting the truth or falsity of its premises, the strength or validity of the reasoning, and possible objections to the essay's thesis.

3. In a two-page paper, discuss one of the examples of extremist attacks on free speech given by Hirsi Ali and Huff, explain how such incidents affect free speech, and argue that they should not be tolerated by democratic governments.

Essay 15
Is Sluttishness a Feminist Statement?
Wendy Kaminer

Fifty years after the onset of the modern feminist movement, sexual violence remains a primary issue, especially for young women asserting their right to dress or undress as they choose. The "slut walk" is the latest protest gimmick, inspired by the stupidity of a Toronto police officer who advised women (rather unoriginally) to "avoid dressing like sluts in order not to be victimized." So, to make their point about victim blaming, women are proclaiming their sluttishness, trying to reframe it as a healthy, confident sexual choice; they're "reappropriating" the word *slut*, along with its dress code, while simultaneously protesting their sexual objectification.

Good luck with that. A more dissonant strategy is hard to imagine. You don't have to share the dim-witted belief that rape is caused even partly by provocatively dressed females to suspect that tottering around half-naked in stilettos may not be the most effective way for women to discourage their objectification.

I'm not making moral judgments about women's sartorial or sexual preferences; I sympathize with the desire to demoralize discussions of female sexuality. I'm simply questioning the utility of sluttishness in a fight against sexual violence. My concerns are practical, not moral; as a practical matter, we can control the way we present ourselves but not the ways in which we are perceived. Young women who proudly dress like sluts intending only to assert their sexual confidence should not be surprised if some onlookers believe that they're advertising their availability as sexual toys. They should expect at least occasionally to be evaluated by their forms and not their intellectual or characterological contents.

Indeed, celebrating sluttishness probably encourages girls to rely on appearances; it tends to reduce sexuality, and self-regard, to a matter of appearance.

A recent study from Kenyon College considering the influence of girl's clothing styles on their "self-objectification" determined that about 25 percent of the clothes found in popular stores for girls was "sexualized." Of course, sexualized dress is a fairly subjective concept: the Kenyon researchers defined it as "clothing that revealed or emphasized a sexualized body part, had characteristics associated with sexiness, and/or had sexually suggestive writing." But talk to the mothers with young daughters, and you can accumulate a lot of anecdotal evidence and concern about the naïve idealization of sluttishness and the "power" it gives girls over boys. It's a perverse version of feminism that encourages sexually vulnerable girls to feel protected by highly sexualized femininity.

Slut walks seem about as likely to advance a feminist agenda as Disney princesses or the viewing parties organized around the wedding of Will and Kate. Princesses or sluts? Virgins or whores? The choices are familiar, like the belief that girls and women are empowered by aggressively asserting their sexuality, in the most conventional ways. Power sluttishness was the theme of *Cosmo* girls decades ago and was reinvented by lipstick feminism (and Madonna) in the 1990s. It has always held obvious, understandable appeal to young women eager to disassociate from the stereotypical image of feminists as unattractive, desexualized, and (at least aspirationally) emasculating.

But lipstick feminism, under various rubrics, has contributed to feminism's incoherence, effectively embracing or "appropriating" sexual objectification in the vain hope of defeating it and positing sexual allure as a political act. It is, however, a *personal* act, and the personal is often apolitical. Celebrating depoliticized female empowerment, lipstick feminism helped confer popular feminist credibility on such antifeminist celebrities as Sarah Palin. The feminist movement has never been monolithic; women's rights advocates have been divided historically by differing visions of equality or protectionism for women, individualism or collectivism, as well as by class and racial conflicts. But these days feminism is so splintered and so ideologically confused that it barely exists as a movement at all.

That's too bad for women, because they're regularly losing fundamental rights, most notably their rights to privacy and reproductive choice. At the state and federal levels, lawmakers have proposed or enacted a long list of prohibitive limitations on access to abortion; intrusive conditions on women seeking abortions (like mandatory sonograms); and financial burdens or punishments for women who obtain abortions and for organizations that provide them (notably Planned Parenthood, which is primarily devoted to women's health care). Meanwhile, not surprisingly, the right to dress like a slut remains secure.

1. Write both an outline and a summary of this essay. Include the premises as well as the evidence or reasoning that supports them.

2. In a two-page paper, evaluate this essay's argument and explain whether you agree with its conclusion and why.

3. Write your own three-page essay on this topic, laying out your argument, supporting the premises, and defending your view against at least one objection.

Essay 16

Torture: Time for Congress to End the Debate

USA TODAY
November 13, 2007

Does "waterboarding"—an interrogation technique that simulates drowning—constitute torture?

Yes, says Malcolm Wrightson Nance, a former Navy survival instructor who was waterboarded as part of a training exercise. "It is an overwhelming experience that induces horror and triggers frantic survival instincts," Nance told a congressional panel.

Not sure, says Michael Mukasey, who was confirmed as attorney general last week after the question boiled over at his confirmation hearings.

Now that Mukasey has been sworn in, the issue shouldn't be allowed to fester. Congress, which is considering several measures to prohibit waterboarding, should move promptly to eliminate any lingering doubt about where America stands.

The debate, of course, is about more than just one technique. At base is the smoldering question of whether the United States can devise a system to extract valuable information from suspected terrorists without abandoning its basic values.

Since 9/11, the Bush White House has planted itself on one side of that debate, pushing no-holds-barred, "enhanced" interrogation methods, including waterboarding, against prime terror suspects.

Congress has been on the other side, sort of. It has deplored torture but never explicitly outlawed waterboarding. Many lawmakers wanted to have it both ways: To be on record against torture, but to avoid blame if there's a terror attack that conceivably might have been averted.

In 2005, Congress passed a law banning "cruel, inhuman or degrading treatment" of detainees. It was sponsored by Sen. John McCain, R-Ariz., a Vietnam prisoner of war who was tortured. But that measure, and a 2006 law that was supposed to set interrogation limits, left the boundaries murky. The 2006 law allowed the White House to preserve its CIA interrogation program and the ability to define what methods are used. The Bush Justice Department did the rest: Two secret memos in 2005, revealed last month by the *New York Times*, fudged whatever rules Congress had set.

Those who would preserve methods such as waterboarding say they are sometimes necessary to get information from terrorism suspects. The White House claims its practices have yielded useful information. But details are classified, so it's impossible to judge.

On a practical level, torture is rarely effective. Suspects will say just about anything to escape pain. The British, French and Israelis have tried torture at various points and found that over time, the means compromised the ends. All abandoned it.

Further, torture encourages similar abuse of captured Americans.

Defenders of torture counter by raising the "ticking bomb" scenario. If Osama bin Laden were captured, they ask, wouldn't you favor doing anything to disrupt attacks he had planned? Well, yes. But that is an extraordinarily rare circumstance that the public might accept as an aberration. Barring torture in other circumstances is the only way to prevent it from becoming routine.

What the country needs most is a clear, consistent policy against waterboarding and its ilk. The new attorney general could provide that in a legal opinion. Even better, Congress could lay it down as the law of the land.

1. Study this essay and Essay 17 ("Torture: Severe Interrogations Work"). Decide which essay presents the stronger arguments, and write a two-page paper defending your view.
2. In three pages, write your own original essay on the morality of using torture to thwart terrorist attacks. Back up your conclusions with well-supported premises. Go online to get the facts.
3. In a half page, explain how you would make Essay 16's argument stronger.

Essay 17
Torture: Severe Interrogations Work
Trent Franks

America's distinguishing hallmark, its bedrock foundation, is that we hold to the self-evident truth that all men are created by God, which imparts to each of them equal, inestimable and eternal value.

The first and foremost purpose of our government is to defend the lives and constitutional rights of all Americans.

Tragically, at times in our history, we have crossed paths with those who do not value innocent life or freedom. We now face a merciless jihadist ideology that threatens the peace and security of the entire human family. The tactic of this insidious enemy is to secretly plot and carry out horrifying acts of violence upon our innocent civilians. Our greatest challenge in defeating them is knowing what their next evil act might be.

This has placed America in the crushingly painful position of having to resort to severe interrogations with certain terrorists during those times when no other alternative exists and hundreds or thousands of innocent lives may be at stake.

In the case of Khalid Sheikh Mohammed, the suspected 9/11 mastermind, severe interrogation was successfully used to glean critical intelligence that saved countless innocent lives. Mohammed stayed quiet for months, often answering questions with Koranic chants. According to an article in the Aug. 13 issue of *The New Yorker*, interrogators eventually waterboarded him—for just 90 seconds. Mohammed "didn't resist," said one CIA veteran. "He cracked real quick."

Mohammed's revelations helped authorities arrest at least six major terrorists, including some who may have been plotting attacks that could have taken the lives of thousands of innocent Americans, according to the *National Review Online*.

My definition of severe interrogation has never included—nor would I ever condone—torture. Torture of prisoners in American custody is a felony, and if a prisoner dies in that process, the perpetrator is subject to the death penalty. This is as it should be.

However, we should not tie the hands of those who are given charge to defend us all when, in rare circumstances, they are forced to choose between waterboarding a known terrorist or allowing him to proceed to inflict massive, torturous and hideous brutality upon thousands of innocent U.S. civilians.

1. Write a two-page paper to rebut the argument in this essay. Use an argument that is not used in Essay 16 ("Torture: Time for Congress to End the Debate").

2. Imagine that you are the person who must decide whether to torture an alleged terrorist to extract life-saving information from him. In two pages explain your reasoning about why you would or would not torture him.

3. In a half page explain how you would make Essay 17's argument stronger.

Essay 18

Freedom of Expression: Protect Student Speech—Even "Unwise" Bong Banner

USA TODAY
March 21, 2007

The 18-year-old high school student in Juneau, Alaska, who unfurled a "BONG HiTS 4 JESUS" banner on a sidewalk across from his school when the Olympic torch passed by in 2002 says he was merely trying to provoke his school's strict principal and get himself on TV.

If that was the goal, he certainly succeeded. The principal did get angry. Concluding that "bong hits" clearly meant pot smoking, she crumpled up the banner, suspended the student for 10 days and touched off a free-speech dispute that's pending before the U.S. Supreme Court. The case sounds like something out of *Ferris Bueller's Day Off*, the 1986 film featuring a wisecracking senior who bedevils the dean of students. But the court's decision, likely to come by the end of June, is expected to be an important marker of the limits of student expression—one that should be settled in the student's favor.

As any principal knows, kids often say and do things adults find dumb and offensive; when that happens at school, it's reasonable to restrict disruptive speech that interferes with education. But the bong-banner incident neither took place on school property nor disrupted classroom activity.

Teachers and principals have to make tough calls like these every day, and their authority extends off campus to school-connected events such as field trips or football games. Yet the courts have appropriately set a high bar for limiting student speech: Their standard is a landmark 1969 Supreme Court ruling that allowed students to wear black arm bands to protest the Vietnam

War, because students didn't give up their free speech rights "at the schoolhouse gate" unless their actions significantly disrupted or interfered with school activities.

In the Juneau case, the school board, joined by the Bush administration, is asking the court to lower that bar by redefining "disruption" to mean not just interfering with the educational environment, but also interfering with the school's "educational mission." They make a superficially appealing case. The principal found the bong banner obnoxious and embarrassing, particularly in light of the school's anti-drug policy, and she saw no reason not to discipline students for flouting that policy, even off school grounds.

But where to draw the line? How can the court best balance the principal's need to control her school against students' right to express their opinions, particularly political or religious opinions? Several religious groups filed briefs on the student's behalf.

When the case was argued Monday before the Supreme Court, the justices bantered about what other banners would or wouldn't be permissible: "Vote Republican"? "Smoke Pot, It's Fun"? "Rape is Fun"? "Extortion is Profitable"?

They reached no obvious conclusions, and there was no claim that "BONG HiTS 4 JESUS" was articulate, reasoned or much more than the nonsensical statement the student intended when he took a slogan he saw on a snowboard and turned it into a banner meant to anger an authority figure.

But the line around protected speech is appropriately wide, even when it's subversive or sophomoric. The student's attorney was on target when he told the justices that this sort of expression is "the kind of speech we must tolerate, no matter how unwise it is."

If students don't shed their free-speech rights at the schoolhouse gate, they surely don't on the public sidewalk across the street from the school.

1. Write a three-page paper arguing against the claim defended in this essay. Be sure to address any plausible objections that could be directed at your argument.

2. Write a three-page essay in which you argue that student speech should *not* be protected.

3. Study this essay and Essay 19 ("Freedom of Expression: Policy Reflects Common Sense"). Decide which essay presents the stronger argument, and write a paper defending your view.

Essay 19

Freedom of Expression: Policy Reflects Common Sense
Kenneth W. Starr

One year ago, the U.S. Court of Appeals for the 9th Circuit issued a decision that confounded school boards and administrators nationwide. A conscientious public high school principal enforced a longstanding student conduct policy against a student entrusted to her care. For that entirely appropriate action, the 9th Circuit subjected her to the prospect of punitive damages.

Principal Deborah Morse was in charge of a school event celebrating the Olympic Torch Relay as it arrived in Alaska for the first time ever. The event occurred during school hours. The assembled student body (accompanied by teachers and administrators) lined both sides of the street in front of the school. Cheerleaders were in uniform. The pep band played. And four students acted as torchbearers. At the very moment that the torch (and television cameras) arrived in front of the school, then-senior high school student Joseph Frederick unfurled his now-famous banner festooned with the slang marijuana reference, "BONG HiTS 4 JESUS."

Principal Morse reasonably determined on the spot that Frederick's obtrusive sign violated school policy prohibiting students from advocating the use of substances that are illegal to minors. This policy expressly applied to on- and off-campus activities. School rules such as this are commonplace throughout the country.

For decades, local school officials, acting *in loco parentis*, have relied on these policies to convey that illegal substances are wrong and harmful. In view of the staggering drug problem in America—half of high school students use drugs illegally by graduation, often on school property—policies that keep pro-drug messages out of the school environment reflect common sense.

Frederick certainly may have a First Amendment right to display his banner on his own time, out of school. But in stealing the focus of a school event for his own drug-promoting publicity stunt, he ran afoul of a reasonable regulation. It would be unwise for the Supreme Court to follow the 9th Circuit in rendering such rules unenforceable. The Court should not compound further the problem by allowing a lifelong educator like Deborah Morse to be saddled with the specter of a draconian civil damages lawsuit.

1. Write a paper in rebuttal to this essay. Use an argument that is *not* put forward in Essay 18 ("Freedom of Expression: Protect Student Speech—Even 'Unwise' Bong Banner").

2. In a two-page paper, defend the proposition that free speech can be curtailed by the government only if the speech incites violence.

3. In a two-page paper, argue that free speech can never be curtailed just because it offends someone.

Essay 20

It's Irresponsible to Spread Fear of Vaccine

USA TODAY
September 18, 2011

One of the most alarming public health developments in recent years has been the emergence of a strident chorus of vaccine fear-mongers who have scared too many parents away from getting their children immunized.

The result has been a comeback of deadly diseases such as whooping cough, mumps and measles. Measles alone killed 3,000 to 5,000 people a year before vaccines emerged to virtually eliminate it in this country. But parents' refusal to vaccinate their kids—spurred largely by unfounded, discredited links between autism and the MMR (measles, mumps and rubella) vaccine—has let measles creep back. There have been 193 cases so far this year, the largest U.S. outbreak in 15 years.

So it has been deeply disturbing to hear Rep. Michele Bachmann, R-Minn., speaking from the fear-mongers' playbook. During last week's debate in Tampa among the Republican presidential hopefuls, Bachmann described the vaccine against the human papillomavirus (HPV) in sinister terms, calling it "flat out wrong" to have "innocent little 12-year-old girls be forced to have a government injection." Making matters worse, Bachmann told TV interviewers after the debate that a mother had come up to her to say her daughter had become mentally retarded after receiving the HPV vaccination.

Presidential candidates get big megaphones and an outsized opportunity to steer the national debate. But there's an implicit requirement to be careful, and even by the low standards of political speech, Bachmann's nationally broadcast suggestion that a vaccine can cause mental retardation was appallingly irresponsible.

If Bachmann had bothered to check before repeating the story, she would have found that there has been no link between the HPV vaccine and mental retardation after 35 million doses. Though every vaccine can have side effects, those have to be measured against the greater good. HPV causes almost all of the more than 12,000 cases of cervical cancer that occur every year, killing about 4,200 women, and the best time to administer the vaccine is before girls become sexually active.

The HPV vaccine came up during the GOP debate when Bachmann and others criticized Texas Gov. Rick Perry for his 2007 executive order that all girls in the state be vaccinated, while allowing parents to opt out for religious and other reasons. Perry's attempt to mandate vaccination was widely criticized at the time, including by this page, in part because the vaccine was then fairly new and it was unclear whether widespread use would reveal unforeseen side effects. So far, that has not been the case. But another concern—that moving too quickly toward a mandate could promote a backlash—has proved to have more merit.

The Texas Legislature blocked Perry's order, and the issue has resurfaced during the presidential campaign because many conservatives see Perry's action as the sort of big government mandate they detest. Bachmann also suggested that Perry had crossed an ethical line because his former chief of staff had become a lobbyist for Merck, maker of one of the two HPV vaccines, and Merck had donated to Perry's gubernatorial campaign.

Attacking Perry for mandating vaccination and for his ties to the vaccine maker is fair game. But Bachmann's decision to spread scare talk about the vaccine is out of bounds.

The standards for any public figure are higher than, "I'm just passing along something I heard from someone." And they're even higher for someone who wants to be president.

1. Write a two-page paper arguing against the claim defended in this essay.
2. In a two-page paper, evaluate the argument in this essay. Address whether there are any plausible counterarguments.
3. Write a two-page paper arguing for the same view defended in this essay—but use premises not mentioned by the author.

Essay 21

Flag Amendment: Flag Needs Protection

Dianne Feinstein

On the morning of February 24, 1945, when I was a 12-year-old girl, I picked up a copy of the *San Francisco Chronicle*. On its cover, there was a full-page picture of the now iconic Joe Rosenthal photograph of American marines raising the United States flag at Iwo Jima.

For me and for the nation, the photograph was a jolt of electricity boosting our morale during the terrible island-to-island Pacific battles of World War II. The sight of those troops hoisting Old Glory forever cemented my view of our flag.

Today, our flag remains a vibrant symbol of our democracy, our shared values, our commitment to justice, and our eternal memory of those who have sacrificed to defend these principles. It is because of all that our flag embodies that I have co-sponsored the Flag Protection Amendment. . . .

Throughout our nation's history, the flag has been protected by law. In 1989, 48 of our 50 states had statutes restricting flag desecration. In 1974, Supreme Court Justice Byron White wrote that: "(T)here would seem to be little question about the power of Congress to forbid the mutilation of the Lincoln Memorial or to prevent overlaying it with words or other objects. The flag is itself a monument, subject to similar protection."

I agree with Justice White; the American flag is our monument in cloth.

But its protection ended in 1989, when the U.S. Supreme Court struck down a Texas law prohibiting flag desecration. Congress responded by passing the Flag Protection Act of 1989, but the Supreme Court struck down that law as well. The only way to restore protection to the flag is to amend the Constitution. Otherwise, any legislation passed by Congress would be struck down.

The Flag Protection Amendment would not prohibit flag burning. Rather, the Amendment would simply return to Congress the ability to protect the flag as it has been protected throughout most of this nation's history.

Some opponents of the Flag Protection Amendment argue that we must choose between trampling on the flag and trampling on the First Amendment. I strongly disagree.

There is no idea or thought expressed by the burning of the American flag that cannot be expressed equally well in another manner. This Amendment would leave both the flag and free speech safe.

1. In a two-page paper, evaluate the argument in this essay. Provide at least two reasons for accepting your view.
2. Write a two-page paper arguing against the claim defended in this essay. Be sure to address possible objections to your argument.
3. Write a two-page essay arguing that criminalizing the desecration of the flag would unnecessarily restrict a right of free expression and conflict with the nation's values.

Chapter 1

Exercise 1.1

1. Critical thinking is the systematic evaluation or formulation of beliefs, or statements, by rational standards.

4. Critical thinking operates according to rational standards in that beliefs are judged by how well they are supported by reasons.

6. The *critical* in critical thinking refers to the exercising of careful judgment and judicious evaluation.

8. A statement is an assertion that something is or is not the case.

11. An argument is a group of statements in which some of them (the premises) are intended to support another of them (the conclusion).

14. In an argument, a conclusion is a statement that premises are intended to support.

17. No.

19. Indicator words are words that frequently accompany arguments and signal that a premise or conclusion is present.

23. Look for the conclusion first.

Exercise 1.2

1. No statement.
4. No statement.
7. Statement.
10. No statement.

Exercise 1.3

1. Argument.
   Conclusion: He should avoid her.
4. No argument.
7. No argument.
11. Argument.
    Conclusion: Don't outlaw guns.
15. Argument.
    Conclusion: Noisy car alarms should be banned.

Exercise 1.4

1. Argument.
   Conclusion: Faster-than-light travel is not possible.
   Premise: Faster-than-light travel would violate a law of nature.
4. Argument.
   Conclusion: The flu epidemic on the East Coast is real.
   Premise: Government health officials say so.

Premise: I personally have read at least a dozen news stories that characterize the situation as a "flu epidemic."

7. No argument.

10. No argument.

Exercise 1.5

3. Premise: Freedom of choice in all things is a basic moral right.
Premise: Abortion is no different than scraping off a few cells from one's skin, and a woman certainly has the right to do that.

6. Premise: Vaughn has admitted that he knows nothing about animals.
Premise: The Society for the Prevention of Cruelty to Animals has declared Vaughn a dummy when it comes to animals.

9. Premise: The Internet has led to the capture of more terrorists than anything else.
Premise: The U.S. attorney general has asserted that the Internet is the best friend that antiterrorist teams have.

12. Premise: All the top TV critics agree that *The Sopranos* is the greatest series in TV history.
Premise: I have compared *The Sopranos* to all other TV series and found that the show outshines them all.

Exercise 1.6

2. Conclusion: School vouchers have decreased the quality of education in thirteen states and the District of Columbia.

4. Conclusion: As a married person, you are happier than people who aren't married.

8. Conclusion: The government does not do anything about pornography on the Internet, even though kids have access to all kinds of porn.

Exercise 1.7

1. Argument.
Conclusion: The Religious Right is not pro-family.
Premise: Concerned parents realize that children are curious about how their body works and need accurate, age-appropriate information about the human reproductive system.
Premise: Thanks to Religious Right pressure, many public schools have replaced sex education with fear-based "abstinence-only" programs that insult young people's intelligence and give them virtually no useful information.

3. Argument.
Conclusion: There is no archeological evidence for the [biblical] Flood.
Premise: If a universal Flood occurred between five and six thousand years ago, killing all humans except the eight on board the Ark, it would be abundantly clear in the archaeological record.
Premise: The destruction of all but eight of the world's people left no mark on the archaeology of human cultural evolution.

Chapter 2

Exercise 2.1

1. For critical thinking to be realized, the process must be systematic, it must be a true evaluation or formulation of claims, and it must be based on rational standards.

5. We take things too far when we accept claims for no reason.

7. You are most likely to let your self-interest get in the way of clear thinking when you have a significant personal stake in the conclusions you reach.

11. Group pressure can affect your attempts to think critically by allowing your need to be part of a group or your identification with a group undermine critical thinking.

14. A worldview is a set of fundamental ideas that help us make sense of a wide range of issues in life.

17. Critical thinking is concerned with objective truth claims.

21. Reasonable doubt, not certainty, is central to the acquisition of knowledge.

Exercise 2.2

1. Self-interest.
4. Group pressure (in this case, the we-are-better-than-them type).
7. Group pressure.
10. Self-interest.

Exercise 2.3

1. a. The charges are false.
   c. Important evidence that would exonerate Father Miller was not mentioned in the newspaper account.
3. a. A study from Harvard shows that women are less violent and less emotional than men.
6. No good reasons listed.

Exercise 2.4

1. Better-than-others group pressure; Possible negative consequence: failure to consider other points of view; discrimination against people who disagree with Ortega.
3. It's not entirely clear what the group's motivations are. This passage could easily be an example of better-than-others group pressure.
7. Appeal to popularity. Possible negative consequence: overlooking other factors that might be a lot more important than popularity.

Exercise 2.5

1. Face-saving; Possible negative consequences: poor academic performance due to overconfidence; embarrassment of failure after being so cocky; alienation of friends.
2. Self-interest; Possible negative consequences: wasting the taxpayer's money; being thrown out of office for misconduct.

Chapter 3

Exercise 3.1

4. Deductive.
8. Sound.
12. No.

Exercise 3.2

2. Step 1: Conclusion: She has a superior intellect.
   Premises: Ethel graduated from Yale. If she graduated from Yale, she probably has a superior intellect.
   Step 2: Not deductively valid.
   Step 3: Inductively strong.
   Step 4: Does not apply.
6. Step 1: Conclusion: Thus, every musician has a college degree.
   Premises: Every musician has had special training, and everyone with special training has a college degree.
   Step 2: Deductively valid.
   Step 3: Does not apply.
   Step 4: Does not apply.
9. Step 1: Conclusion: So some actors who sing also play a musical instrument.
   Premises: Some actors sing, and some play a musical instrument.
   Step 2: Not deductively valid.
   Step 3: Not inductively strong.
   Step 4: Intended to be deductive.
15. Step 1: Conclusion: So it's impossible for androids to have minds.
   Premises: If minds are identical to brains—that is, if one's mind is nothing but a brain—androids could never have minds because they wouldn't have brains. Clearly, a mind is nothing but a brain.
   Step 2: Deductively valid.
   Step 3: Does not apply.
   Step 4: Does not apply.

Exercise 3.3

3. Valid.
8. Valid.
14. Invalid.
18. Valid.
23. Invalid.

Exercise 3.4

I.

1. Senator Greed was caught misusing campaign funds.
5. She's not incompetent.
9. The engine started right away.

II.

3. Sixty percent of the teenagers in several scientific surveys love rap music.
6. Assad's fingerprints are on the vase.
9. The murder rates in almost all large cities in the South are very high.

Exercise 3.5

1. Valid; *modus tollens.*
6. Valid; *modus tollens.*
9. Valid; *modus ponens.*

Exercise 3.6

2. If Lino is telling the truth, he will admit to all charges.
   Lino is telling the truth.
   So he will admit to all charges.
   If Lino is telling the truth, he will admit to all charges.
   He will not admit to all charges.
   So he is not telling the truth.

5. If religious conflict in Nigeria continues, thousands more will die.
   The religious conflict in Nigeria will continue.
   Therefore, thousands more will die.
   If religious conflict in Nigeria continues, thousands more will die.
   Thousands more will not die.
   Therefore, religious conflict in Nigeria will not continue.

9. If solar power can supply six megawatts of power in San Francisco (which is certainly not the sunniest place in the world), then solar power can transform the energy systems in places like Texas and Arizona.
   Solar power can supply six megawatts of power in San Francisco.
   So solar power can transform the energy systems in places like Texas and Arizona.

   If solar power can supply six megawatts of power in San Francisco (which is certainly not the sunniest place in the world), then solar power can transform the energy systems in places like Texas and Arizona.
   But solar power cannot transform the energy systems in places like Texas and Arizona.
   So solar power cannot supply six megawatts of power in San Francisco.

Exercise 3.7

4. If the Queen of England were a man, she would be mortal.
   She is mortal.
   Therefore, the Queen of England is a man.
   If *a*, then *b*.
   b.
   Therefore, *a*.

5. If Bill Clinton was the president of the U.S. in 1970, then he would be an American.
   Bill Clinton was not president of the U.S. in 1970.
   Therefore, he is not an American.
   If *a*, then *b*.
   Not *a*.
   Therefore, not *b*.

7. If Vaughn is a dog, he is a mammal.
   He is a mammal.
   Therefore, he is a dog.
   If *a*, then *b*.
   b.
   Therefore, *a*.

8. If ducks are sea turtles, then they are at home in the water.
   Ducks are not sea turtles.
   Therefore, ducks are not at home in the water.
   If *a*, then *b*.
   Not *a*.
   Therefore, not *b*.

11. If Chicago is the capital of Illinois, then Chicago is in Illinois.

Chicago is in Illinois.
Therefore, Chicago is the capital of
Illinois.
If *a*, then *b*.
b.
Therefore, *a*.

Exercise 3.8

1. (1) The stores are closed. (2) We have
no money. (3) And we have no way
of traveling to any place of business.
(4) Therefore, we are just not going to
be able to go shopping right now.

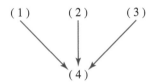

4. (1) If the pipes are busted, there will
be no running water. (2) The pipes are
busted. (3) And if all the water is rusty,
we won't be able to use it anyway,
(4) and all the water is rusty. (5) So we
have no usable water at this point.

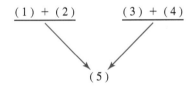

Exercise 3.9

6. (1) If Marla buys the house in the suburbs, she will be happier and healthier.
(2) She is buying the house in the suburbs. (3) So she will be happier and
healthier.

10. (1) The existence of planets outside
our solar system is a myth. (2) There
is no reliable empirical evidence at all

showing that planets exist outside our
solar system.

17. (1) There are at least two main views regarding the morality of war. (2) Pacifism
is the view that no war is ever justified
because it involves the taking of human
life. (3) Just-war theory is the view that
some wars are justified for various
reasons—mostly because they help
prevent great evils (such as massacres,
"ethnic cleansing," or world domination
by a madman like Hitler) or because
they are a means of self defense.
(4) I think that our own moral sense
tells us that sometimes (in the case of
World War II, for example) violence
is occasionally morally justified. (5) It
would be hard for anyone to deny that
a war to prevent something like the
Holocaust is morally right. [Implied con-
clusion] (6) Just-war theory is correct.

20. (1) The picnic will probably be spoiled
because (2) there is a 90 percent probability of rain.

Exercise 3.10

1. Conclusion: The idea that God is
required to be the enforcer of the
moral law is not plausible.
Premises: (4) In the first place, as an empirical hypothesis about the psychology

of human beings, it is questionable. (5) There is no unambiguous evidence that theists are more moral than nontheists. (6) Not only have psychological studies failed to find a significant correlation between frequency of religious worship and moral conduct, but convicted criminals are much more likely to be theists than atheists. (7) Second, the threat of divine punishment cannot impose a moral obligation. (8) Might does not make right.

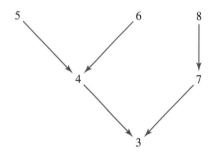

Chapter 4

Exercise 4.1

4. We should proportion our belief to the evidence.
10. Two additional indicators are reputation among peers and professional accomplishments.
17. By making a conscious effort to consider not only information that supports what we believe, but also the information that conflicts with it.

Exercise 4.2

4. Proportion belief to the evidence; the claim is not dubious enough to dismiss out of hand, and not worthy of complete acceptance. Low plausibility.
6. Reject it; it conflicts with a great deal of background information.
10. Proportion belief to the evidence; the claim is not dubious enough to dismiss out of hand, and not worthy of complete acceptance. Moderate plausibility.
14. Reject it; it conflicts with a great deal of background information.
17. Reject it; it conflicts with a great deal of background information.

Exercise 4.3

3. Do not agree. Persuasive evidence would include the body of an alien or the alien craft itself, both scientifically documented as being of extraterrestrial origin.
8. Do not agree. Persuasive evidence would include several double-blind, controlled trials demonstrating that meditation and controlled breathing shrink tumors.

Chapter 5

Exercise 5.1

4. The fallacy of composition is arguing that what is true of the parts must be true of the whole.
10. They are fallacious because they assume that a proposition is true merely because a great number of people believe it; however, as far as the truth of a claim is concerned, what many people believe is irrelevant.
15. Yes.
19. People are often taken in by false dilemmas because they don't think beyond the alternatives laid before them.

Exercise 5.2

1. Composition.
5. Genetic fallacy.
10. Appeal to the person.
14. Equivocation.
19. Appeal to the person.
24. Stereotyping.
26. Euphemism.

Exercise 5.3

4. False dilemma.
6. Hasty generalization.
10. False dilemma.

Exercise 5.4

3. Jones says that Mrs. Anan deserves the Nobel Prize. But he's a friend of hers.

Clearly then Mrs. Anan does not deserve the Nobel Prize.

6. In light of ethical considerations, the Boy Scouts of America should allow gay kids to be members. The reason is that banning gay kids from the organization would be in conflict with basic moral principles.

11. There are too many guns on the streets because our politicians are controlled by the National Rifle Association and other gun nuts. We don't want the NRA telling us what to do.

Chapter 6

Exercise 6.1

1. Conjunction; Components: The Democrats raised taxes, The Republicans cut programs; &

5. Conditional; Components: Taslima can read your mind, You're in trouble; →

7. Conditional; Components: God is all-powerful, He can prevent evil in the world; →

Exercise 6.2

1. $p \vee q$
4. $e \,\&\, f$
8. $\sim g \,\&\, \sim h$
14. $\sim\sim p$

Exercise 6.3

2. False.
6. True.
8. False.

Exercise 6.4

2. True.
5. True.
10. True.

Exercise 6.5

2. Either John is home or Mary is home.
5. If the sun is not shining, then we will not go outside.
10. If the day goes well, then we will not regret our efforts.

Exercise 6.6

2. $p \vee q$
5. $\sim a \rightarrow \sim b$
9. $p \rightarrow q$

Exercise 6.7

2. Alligators are reptiles and dogs are reptiles.

a	d	$a \,\&\, d$
T	T	T
T	F	F
F	T	F
F	F	F

6. Either dogs are not mammals, or snakes are reptiles. [*Hint*: To avoid confusion, you can *add* columns after the guide columns, such as the one for $\sim d$ in this truth table. This extra column reminds you that the truth values for $\sim d$ are the flip side of those for d.]

d	s	$\sim d$	$\sim d \vee s$
T	T	F	T
T	F	F	F
F	T	T	T
F	F	T	T

8. Alligators can bark, and dogs are not reptiles.

a	*d*	*~d*	*a & ~d*
T	T	F	F
T	F	T	T
F	T	F	F
F	F	T	F

Exercise 6.8

2. Valid.

$p \rightarrow q$
p
$\therefore q$

p	*q*	*p → q*	*p*	*q*
T	T	T	T	T
T	F	F	T	F
F	T	T	F	T
F	F	T	F	F

7. Valid.

$p \rightarrow q$
$~q \& r$
$\therefore r$

	p	*q*	*r*	*~q*	*p → q*	*~q & r*	*r*
1	T	T	T	F	T	F	T
2	T	T	F	F	T	F	F
3	T	F	T	T	F	T	T
4	T	F	F	T	F	F	F
5	F	T	T	F	T	F	T
6	F	T	F	F	T	F	F
7	F	F	T	T	T	T	T
8	F	F	F	T	T	F	F

14. Valid.

$p \rightarrow q$
$~(q \lor r)$
$\therefore ~p$

	p	q	r	~p	p → q	~(q v r)	~p
1	T	T	T	F	T	F	F
2	T	T	F	F	T	F	F
3	T	F	T	F	F	F	F
4	T	F	F	F	F	T	F
5	F	T	T	T	T	F	T
6	F	T	F	T	T	F	T
7	F	F	T	T	T	F	T
8	F	F	F	T	T	T	T

Exercise 6.9

3. Jake is the plumber or Jake is the carpenter. Jake is not the carpenter. Therefore, Jake is the plumber.

$p \lor c$
$\sim c$
$\therefore p$

p	c	p v c	~c	p
T	T	T	F	T
T	F	T	T	T
F	T	T	F	F
F	F	F	T	F

Valid.

11. Unless both Mary goes and Henry goes, the party will be a disaster. The party will be a disaster. Therefore, both Mary and Henry will not go.

$\sim(m \& h) \to p$
p
$\therefore \sim(m \& h)$

	m	h	p	~(m & h)	~(m & h) → p	p	~(m & h)
1	T	T	T	F	T	T	F
2	T	T	F	F	T	F	F
3	T	F	T	T	T	T	T
4	T	F	F	T	F	F	T
5	F	T	T	T	T	T	T
6	F	T	F	T	F	F	T
7	F	F	T	T	T	T	T
8	F	F	F	T	F	F	T

Invalid.

Exercise 6.10

3. $p \lor q$
   p
   $\therefore \sim q$

	T				T		F
p	$\lor$	q			p		$\sim q$
T		T			T		T

   Invalid.

10. $p \rightarrow q$
    $\therefore p \rightarrow (p \And q)$

		F					F		
p	$\rightarrow$	q			p	$\rightarrow$	$(p$	$\And$	$q)$
T		F			T		T		F

    Valid.

15. $(d \lor e) \rightarrow (d \And e)$
    $\sim(d \lor e)$
    $\therefore \sim(d \And e)$

			T						F					F		
$(d$	$\lor$	$e)$	$\rightarrow$	$(d$	$\And$	$e)$			$\sim(d$	$\lor$	$e)$			$\sim(d$	$\And$	$e)$
T	T	T	T						T		T			T		T

    Valid.

Exercise 6.11

2.

1. $P \rightarrow Q$	Premise
2. $\sim Q \lor R$	Premise
3. $P \,/\, R$	Premise/Conclusion
4. Q	1, 3, MP
5. $\sim \sim Q$	4, DN
6. R	2, 5, DS

9.

1. $E \lor F$	Premise
2. $\sim G \lor H$	Premise
3. $\sim (E \lor H) \,/\, F \And \sim G$	Premise/Conclusion
4. $\sim E \And \sim H$	3, DM
5. $\sim E$	4, SIMP
6. F	1, 5, DS
7. $\sim H$	4, SIMP
8. $\sim G$	2, 7, DS
9. $F \And \sim G$	6, 8, CONJ

Chapter 7

Exercise 7.1

1. S = scientists, P = Baptists; universal negative; E.
5. S = theologians who have studied arguments for the existence of God, P = scholars with serious misgivings about the traditional notion of omnipotence; universal affirmative; A.
8. S = people who play the stock market, P = millionaires; particular negative; O.
12. S = terrorists, P = Saudi citizens; particular affirmative; I.
16. S = death row inmates, P = death penalty supporters; universal negative; E.

Exercise 7.2

1. All Giants fans are fanatics [or, are people who are fanatical]. A.
5. All good investments are cell phone companies that keep up with the latest technology. A.
9. All intelligent thoughts are thoughts that have already happened. A.
13. Some things are memories meant to be forgotten. I.

Exercise 7.3

1. All guardians of the soul are poets. A.
4. All androids like Commander Data are nonhumans. A.
5. No things that satisfy the heart are material things. E.
8. Some treatments said to be part of "alternative medicine" are treatments that are unproven. I.
12. All days that give her any joy are Fridays. A.
15. All pictures identical with the one hanging on the wall are things that are crooked. A.
20. All nations without a conscience are nations without souls. A.

Exercise 7.4

1. No persons are persons exempt from the draft in times of war.
   S = persons; P = persons exempt from the draft in times of war.

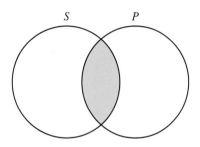

5. No things are things more pitiable than the reasons of an unreasonable man. S = things; P = things more pitiable than the reasons of an unreasonable man.

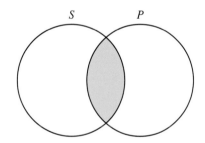

8. Some good talkers are good listeners. S = good talkers; P = good listeners.

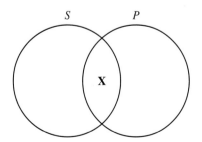

12. All commanders are persons who are alone.
    S = commanders; P = persons who are alone.

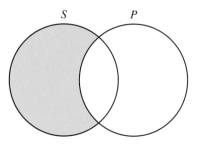

Exercise 7.5

1. No P are S; No S are P.

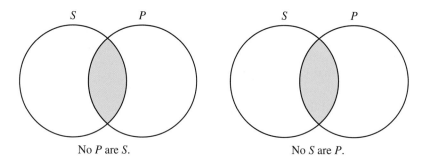

No P are S.   No S are P.

Equivalent.

3. All S are P; All P are S.

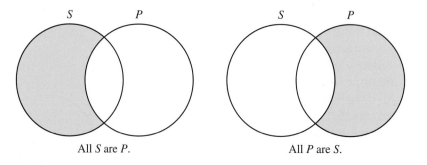

All S are P.   All P are S.

Not equivalent.

6. All *P* are non-*S*; All *S* are non-*P*.

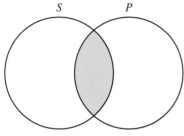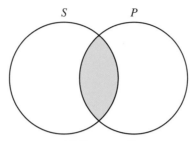

All *P* are non-*S*.   All *S* are non-*P*.

Equivalent.

9. Some *S* are not *P*; Some *P* are not *S*.

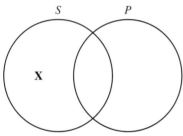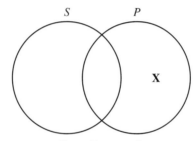

Some *S* are not *P*.   Some *P* are not *S*.

Not equivalent.

Exercise 7.6

2. All horses are mammals, and no mam-
   mals are lizards. Therefore, no
   lizards are horses.
   Minor = lizards (*S*)
   Major = horses (*P*)
   Middle = mammals (*M*)

   > All *P* are *M*.
   > No *M* are *S*.
   > Therefore, no *S* are *P*.

6. Some videotapes are not film classics,
   but all black-and-white movies
   are film classics. Therefore, some black-
   and-white movies are not videotapes.
   Minor = black-and-white movies (*S*)

Major = videotapes (*P*)
Middle = film classics (*M*)

> Some *P* are not *M*.
> All *S* are *M*.
> Therefore, some *S* are not *P*.

9. No elm trees are cacti. Some tall plants
   are elm trees. So some tall plants are not
   cacti.
   Minor = tall plants (*S*)
   Major = cacti (*P*)
   Middle = elm trees (*M*)

   > No *M* are *P*.
   > Some *S* are *M*.
   > Therefore, some *S* are not *P*.

2. All *P* are *M*.
   No *M* are *S*.
   Therefore, no *S* are *P*.

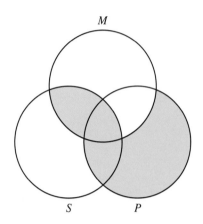

Valid.

6. Some *P* are not *M*.
   All *S* are *M*.
   Therefore, some *S* are not *P*.

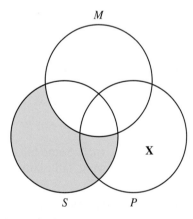

Invalid.

9. No *M* are *P*.
   Some *S* are *M*.
   Therefore, some *S* are not *P*.

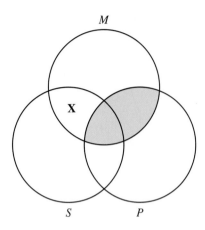

Valid.

1. Some architectural structures are nontraditional designs, for all houses are architectural structures, and some houses are
   nontraditional designs.

   Some houses are nontraditional designs.
   All houses are architectural structures.
   Therefore, some architectural struc-
   tures are nontraditional designs.

   Some *M* are *P*.
   All *M* are *S*.
   Therefore, some *S* are *P*.

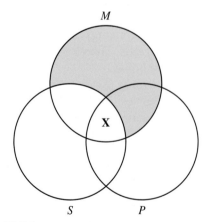

Valid.

3. All worshippers of God are spiritual giants because all worshippers of God are

redeemed souls, and all redeemed souls are spiritual giants.

> *All redeemed souls are spiritual giants.*
> *All worshippers of God are redeemed souls.*
> *Therefore, all worshippers of God are spiritual giants.*

All *M* are *P*.
All *S* are *M*.
Therefore, all *S* are *P*.

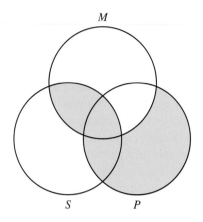

Valid.

Exercise 7.9

4. Some *S* are *P*. No *S* are *P*. (False)
8. All *S* are *P*. Some *S* are not *P*. (False)

Exercise 7.10

I.
3. No Buddhists are voters. Converse: No voters are Buddhists. Equivalent.
8. Some legislators are not brilliant persons. Converse: Some brilliant persons are not legislators. Not equivalent.

II.
2. No runners are acrobats.
8. No humans are non-mammals.

III.
4. All *P* are non-*S*. Not equivalent.
8. All *S* are *P*. Equivalent.
12. All non-*P* are non-*S*. Equivalent.

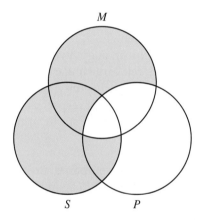

Valid.

8. No wimps are social activists because no wimps are people of honest and strong conviction. And all social activists are people of honest and strong conviction.

> *All social activists are people of honest and strong conviction.*
> *No wimps are people of honest and strong conviction.*
> *Therefore, no wimps are social activists.*

All *P* are *M*.
No *S* are *M*.
Therefore, no *S* are *P*.

Chapter 8

Exercise 8.1

1. Target group: people in the country; sample: adults in New York and San Francisco; relevant property: being "pro-choice" in the abortion debate. The argument is weak because the sample is not representative.

4. Target group: students at this university; sample: first-year students at this university; relevant property: being against such a militant policy. The argument is weak because the sample is both too small and not representative.

8. Target group: dentists; sample: dentists who suggest that their patients chew gum; relevant property: recommending Brand X gum. The argument is weak because the sample is not representative.

12. Target group: Americans; sample: adults with an annual income of $48,000–$60,000; relevant property: being happy and satisfied with one's job. The argument is weak because the sample is not representative. (Middle-income workers are likely to have attitudes toward job satisfaction that are different from those of workers in other income brackets, especially lower ones.)

Exercise 8.2

1. Weak. To ensure a strong argument, randomly draw the sample from the entire U.S. population, not just from a couple of bicoastal cities.

4. Weak. To ensure a strong argument, randomly draw a sample of several hundred students from the whole university population, not just the first-year students.

8. Weak. To ensure a strong argument, randomly draw the sample from the set of all dentists, not just the dentists who recommend gum.

12. Weak. To ensure a strong argument, randomly draw the sample from the set of all American workers, including respondents representative of all income groups.

Exercise 8.3

1. Does not offer strong support for the conclusion. The problem is nonrandom—and therefore nonrepresentative—sampling.

Exercise 8.4

1. a, c.

Exercise 8.5

1. Not more likely to be true.

Exercise 8.6

2. Literary analogy.

6. Argument by analogy. Two things being compared; relevant similarity: working with numbers; conclusion: "he'll be a whiz at algebra"; weak argument.

8. Argument by analogy; four things being compared; relevant similarity: being pork; conclusion: "I will like chitlins"; weak argument.

12. Argument by analogy; two things being compared; relevant similarity: being foundations; conclusions: "no lasting reputation worthy of respect can be built on a weak character"; strong argument.

Exercise 8.7

1. Instances being compared: the personality traits of Ronald Reagan and George W. Bush; relevant similarities: staunch conservatism, strong Christian values, almost dogmatic adherence to conservative principles; diversity among cases not a significant factor; conclusion: "President Bush will likely be involved in a similar foreign policy mess for similar reasons"; weak argument (because of several unmentioned dissimilarities).

5. Instances being compared: Having terminal cancer and being threatened by an assailant; relevant similarities: being threatened with death or great pain; diversity among cases not a significant factor; conclusion: "suicide must sometimes be morally justified when it is an act of self-defense against a terminal disease that threatens death or great pain." This is a strong argument—*if* all the relevant similarities and dissimilarities have indeed been taken into account. A critic could argue, though,

that killing oneself in self-defense is just not relevantly similar to killing another human in self-defense. The critic, then, would have to specify what the significant difference is.

Exercise 8.8

2. Conclusion: "Research suggests that eating lots of fruits and vegetables may provide some protection against several types of cancer." Correlation. The argument is strong. The conclusion is a limited claim ("*may* provide some protection . . . "), which the stated correlation could easily support.

7. Conclusion: "Education increases people's earning power." Correlation. The argument is strong.

13. Conclusion: "Tune-ups can improve the performance of lawnmowers." Method of difference. The argument is strong.

16. Conclusion: [Implied] "Having a major war somewhere in the world causes the price of oil to hit $40 a barrel." Method of Agreement. The argument is strong if all relevant factors have been taken into account, which may not be the case.

19. Conclusion: [Implied] "Only five students got A's on the midterm exam because they studied the night before the exam and reviewed their notes just before walking into class to take the test." Method of Agreement. The argument is strong.

Exercise 8.9

2. a, d.
7. a.
13. a.
16. a, b, d.
19. a, b.

Exercise 8.10

1. a.
4. b.
9. a.

Chapter 9

Exercise 9.1

4. A theoretical explanation is an explanation that serves as a theory, or hypothesis, used to explain why something is the way it is, why something is the case, or why something happened.

8. A causal explanation is a kind of theoretical explanation. Like all theoretical explanations, causal explanations are used in inference to the best explanation.

Exercise 9.2

2. The state of affairs being explained is the endangered status of the spotted owl. The explanation is the powerful influence of the logging industry.

5. The state of affairs being explained is the incidence of robberies. The explanation is that there aren't enough gun owners.

8. The state of affairs being explained is the many times that psychics have seemed to predict the future. The explanation is that psychics really can predict the future.

Exercise 9.3

3. Interpretive.
7. Theoretical.
12. Interpretive.

Exercise 9.4

2. Theory 1: Jack's house was burglarized.
   Theory 2: Jack's dog went on a rampage.

6. Theory 1: Alice was not exposed to any germs.
   Theory 2: Vitamin C supercharged Alice's immune system.

Exercise 9.6

2. The minimum requirement of consistency is the criterion that any theory worth considering must have both internal and external consistency—that is, be free of contradictions and be consistent with the data the theory is supposed to explain.

6. A theory that does not have much scope is one that explains very little—perhaps only the phenomenon it was introduced to explain and not much else.

Exercise 9.7

2. The second theory is both simpler and more conservative.
4. The first theory is both simpler and more conservative.
7. The first theory is both simpler and more conservative.

Exercise 9.8

3. Theory 3.

Chapter 10

Exercise 10.1

6. (1) Identify the problem or pose a question, (2) devise a hypothesis to explain the event or phenomenon, (3) derive a test implication or prediction, (4) perform the test, (5) accept or reject the hypothesis.
9. If H, then C. Not-C. Therefore, not-H.
12. No. Hypotheses are tested together with other hypotheses. A hypothesis can always be saved from refutation by making changes in one of the accompanying hypotheses.

Exercise 10.2

2. Hypothesis: Two guys are perpetrating a Bigfoot hoax. Test implication: If the two guys are perpetrating a hoax, then monitoring their behavior day and night should yield evidence of hoaxing activity.
6. Hypothesis: Creatine dramatically increases the performance of weight trainers. Test implication: If creatine increases performance, then giving creatine to weight trainers in a controlled way (in a double-blind controlled trial) should increase various measures of performance in the trainers compared to weight trainers who get a placebo (inactive substance).

Exercise 10.3

3. Theory: Local climate changes. Competing theory: Heat from volcanic activity around the planet is melting the glaciers. Both theories are about equal in terms of testability, fruitfulness, and scope. The volcanic theory, however, is neither simple nor conservative. It's not simple because it assumes an unknown process. It's not conservative because it is not consistent with what is known about the effects of heat from volcanoes.
7. Theory: Religion fosters terrorism. Competing theory: Terrorists commit terrorist acts because they are insane. Both theories are about equal in terms of testability, fruitfulness, scope, and simplicity. The insanity theory, though, is not conservative. It conflicts with what we know about those who commit terrorist acts. In general, terrorists may be fanatical, but they do not seem to be clinically insane.

Exercise 10.4

2. Test implication: If brighter street lights decrease the crime rate, then reducing the brightness of the lights (while keeping constant all other factors, such as police patrols) should increase the crime rate. The test would likely confirm the theory.
6. Test implication: If eating foods high in fat contributes more to overweight than eating foods high in carbohydrates, then over time people should gain more body weight when they are eating X number of grams of fat per day than when they are eating the same number of grams of carbohydrates per day.

Exercise 10.7

4. The appeal to ignorance.
6. Something is logically impossible if it violates a principle of logic; something is logically possible if it does not violate a principle of logic.

Exercise 10.8

2. Theory 1: The aging of the building materials in the house caused creaking.
   Theory 2: The wind blowing against the house caused the creaking.
   Theory 3: A ghost caused the creaking.
7. Theory 1: A coincidental matching between the dream and real events made the dream seem prophetic.
   Theory 2: Leroy had the same dream every night because he was concerned about his uncle, so there was a good chance that the dream would match something in reality.
   Theory 3: The dream was a genuine prophetic dream.

Exercise 10.9

3. Alternative theory: As a prank, the girls cut drawings of fairies out of a book, posed them in the garden, and took photos of themselves with the cutouts. Then they claimed that the photos showed actual fairies. Both theories seem to be about equal in testability and fruitfulness. The prank theory has more scope because faked photos can explain many other phenomena, including many different kinds of paranormal hoaxes. The fairy theory is neither simple nor conservative. Fairies are unknown to science, and claims about their existence conflict with many things that we know.

Chapter 11

Exercise 11.1

5. We cannot infer what should be or ought to be from what is.
9. Moral theories try to explain what makes an action right or what makes a person good.
13. Internal consistency—the requirement that the theories composing our worldview do not conflict.

Exercise 11.2

1. Nonmoral.
6. Moral.
9. Moral.

Exercise 11.3

4. The Indian government posed an imminent threat to Pakistan and the world. When a foreign government poses an imminent threat to Pakistan and the world, Pakistanis are justified in attacking that government. So the Pakistanis were justified in attacking Indian troops.
9. Hacking into a database containing personal information on thousands of people and invading their privacy is immoral. You hacked into a database containing personal information on thousands of people and invaded their privacy. Therefore, what you did was immoral.

Exercise 11.4

3. Killing another human being in self-defense is morally permissible. So it is not the case that in all circumstances the killing of a human being is wrong.
7. If helping someone to commit suicide would somehow save the lives of millions of people, the act would seem to be morally permissible. So it is not the case that assisted suicide is never morally justified.

Chapter 1

1. A group of statements in which some of them (the premises) are intended to support another of them (the conclusion).
2. Premise indicators: *because, due to the fact that, inasmuch as*. Conclusion indicators: *therefore, it follows that, it must be that*.
3. b. Read the story and write a complete review of it.
4. c. Campus speakers should be allowed to speak freely without being shouted down.
5. No argument.
6. Argument. Conclusion: War can solve problems.
7. Argument: President Bush is not slashing domestic spending.
8. Conclusion.
9. Premise.
10. Conclusion.
11. Premise.
12. Conclusion.
13. Premise: DNA evidence is unreliable. Premise: Unreliable evidence should not be used in cases of capital murder.
14. Premise: No computer has yet been able to converse with a human being well enough to be indistinguishable from humans. Premise: Such a feat requires consciousness, and machines cannot even in principle produce consciousness.
15. Premise: All of Nostradamus's predictions have come true. Premise: The prediction about September 11 was unambiguous and specific.
16. 10.
17. 6, 7, 9.
18. 1, 2, 3, 5.
19. 8.
20. 4, 11.

Chapter 2

1. Systematic process, involving genuine evaluation or formulation of beliefs, gauged according to rational standards.
2. A surge of strong emotions.
3. We may ignore facts that contradict our beliefs and search out facts that support them.
4. The we-are-better pressure.
5. A philosophy of life, a set of fundamental ideas that helps us make sense of a wide range of important issues in life.
6. Reasonable doubt.
7. Failure to look for opposing evidence increases the chance of error.
8. Face-saving.
9. Face-saving.

10. Self-interested thinking.
11. Group pressure.
12. Group pressure.
13. Group pressure.
14. Self-serving.
15. Group pressure.
16. Face-saving.
17. Group pressure.
18. Subjectivist fallacy.
19. Subjectivist fallacy.
20. Social relativism.

Chapter 3

1. Deductive argument: intended to provide logically conclusive support for its conclusion. Inductive argument: intended to provide probable, not conclusive, support for its conclusion.
2. Valid argument: a deductive argument that succeeds in providing conclusive support for its conclusion. Invalid argument: a deductive argument that fails to provide conclusive support for its conclusion. Strong inductive argument: an inductive argument that succeeds in providing probable, but not conclusive, logical support for its conclusion.
3. Sound argument: a deductively valid argument that has true premises.
4. Deductive.
5. Inductive.
6. Inductive.
7. Deductive.
8. Anyone who doesn't openly criticize any military action against any Middle Eastern nation is a warmonger.
9. The most likely reason for Maria's failing her driving test three times is that she's not paying attention.
10. People who believe in astrology or tarot cards do not do well in college science courses.
11. If the job is worth doing, then it's worth doing well. The job is worth doing. Therefore, it's worth doing well.

12. If Austin is happy, then Barb is happy. Barb is not happy. Therefore, Austin is not happy.
13. If Einstein invented the steam engine, then he's a great scientist. Einstein did not invent the steam engine. Therefore, he is not a great scientist.
14. If Buffalo is the capital of New York, then Buffalo is in New York. Buffalo is in New York. Therefore, Buffalo is the capital of New York.
15. Cole is up to no good. He's been acting suspiciously for days, and he told Rachel that he was going to steal something valuable.

16. The sitcom *Friends* is becoming really lame. The writing is predictable and plodding. The acting is worse than ever.

17. If dolphins have minds comparable to ours, then these creatures are self-conscious, intelligent, and creative. If they are self-conscious, then they should react appropriately when they see their reflections in a mirror. They do react appropriately. If they're intelligent, they should be able to solve complex problems. They can solve such problems. If they're creative, they should be able to create some form of art. In a rudimentary way, they do create art. They are definitely self-conscious, intelligent, and creative.

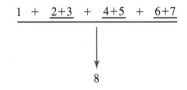

18. If the dictum to always tell the truth in all circumstances is a valid moral principle, then it should fit well with our considered moral judgments. But it does not fit well with our considered moral judgments because there are times when lying is actually the right thing to do, as when we lie to save a life. So the dictum to always tell the truth is not a valid moral principle.

19. I don't think that I should vote for any independent candidate in the next election. Independents never win, and I want the person I vote for to win. Also, independents have a tendency to be a little wacky. And we definitely don't need any more wacky politicians in power.

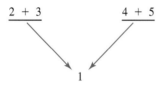

20. Creationism is an inadequate theory about the origins of life. It conflicts with science, and it is incapable of predicting any new facts.

Chapter 4

1. If a claim conflicts with her background information, she has good reason to doubt it.

2. It is not desirable to believe a statement when there is no good reason for doing so.

3. (1) Education and training from reputable institutions or programs in the relevant field; (2) experience in making reliable judgments in the field; (3) reputation among peers (as reflected in the opinions of others in the same field, relevant prestigious awards, and positions of authority); and (4) professional accomplishments.

4. The expert is guilty of blatant violations of the critical thinking principles or of simple factual or formal errors; the expert's claims conflict with what you have good reason to believe; the expert does not adequately support his or her assertions; the expert's writing contains logical contradictions or inconsistent statements; the expert does not treat opposing views fairly; the expert is strongly biased, emotional, or dismissive; the expert relies on information you know is out of date.

5. Impairment due to environmental factors, fatigue, and stress.

6. Reasons for doubt due to low visibility.

7. Reasons for doubt due to vague stimuli.

8. There may or may not be reasons for doubt; the main factor is the reliability of memory.

9. Almost certainly false.

10. Probably true.

11. Almost certainly false.

12. Almost certainly false.

13. Almost certainly false.

14. Almost certainly false.

15. Almost certainly false.

16. Probably false.

17. Yes. Slanted in favor of U.S. policy in Iraq.

18. Yes. Loaded or biased language includes "Ba'ath Party murderers," "Iraqi goon squads," and "regime diehards."

19. The Pentagon.

20. The story lacks the perspective of non-administration sources and less biased reporters. Some aspects not mentioned: details about specific criticisms of U.S. policy, casualties among Iraqis, evidence for Rumsfeld's claims.

Chapter 5

1. Straw man.
2. Appeal to ignorance.
3. Appeal to the person.
4. Appeal to the person.
5. Red herring.
6. Appeal to the person.
7. Appeal to emotion.
8. Appeal to popularity.
9. Begging the question.
10. Composition.
11. False dilemma.
12. Appeal to ignorance.
13. Appeal to the person.
14. Slippery slope.
15. False dilemma.
16. Hasty generalization.
17. Dysphemism.
18. Straw man.
19. Red herring.
20. Rhetorical definition.

Chapter 6

1. Conjunction, &; disjunction, v; negation, ~; conditional, →.

2.

Conjunction:

p	q	p & q
T	T	T
T	F	F
F	T	F
F	F	F

Disjunction:

p	q	p v q
T	T	T
T	F	T
F	T	T
F	F	F

Negation:

p	$\sim p$
T	F
F	T

Conditional:

p	q	$p \rightarrow q$
T	T	T
T	F	F
F	T	T
F	F	T

3. When just one statement in the conjunction is false.

4. When the antecedent is true and the consequent is false.

5. $c \rightarrow q$ false
   a & $\sim q$ false
   a v $\sim c$ true

6. $p \rightarrow q$

7. p v q

8.

Invalid:
$p \rightarrow q$
$q \rightarrow r$
$\therefore q$

p	*q*	*r*	*p* → *q*	*q* → *r*	*q*
T	T	T	T	T	T
T	T	F	T	F	T
T	F	T	F	T	F
T	F	F	F	T	F
F	T	T	T	T	T
F	T	F	T	F	T
F	F	T	T	T	F
F	F	F	T	T	F

Valid:

p v (*q* & *r*)
~(*q* & *r*)
∴ *p*

p	*q*	*r*	(*q* & *r*)	*p* v (*q* & *r*)	~(*q* & *r*)	*p*
T	T	T	T	T	F	T
T	T	F	F	T	T	T
T	F	T	F	T	T	T
T	F	F	F	T	T	T
F	T	T	T	T	F	F
F	T	F	F	F	T	F
F	F	T	F	F	T	F
F	F	F	F	F	T	F

9. If the temperature rises, then the water will rise. If the water rises, the dam will break. Either the water rises, or it doesn't rise. The water will not rise. Therefore, the dam will not break.

Invalid
p → *q*
q → *r*
q v ~*q*
~*q*
∴ ~*r*

p	*q*	*r*	*p* → *q*	*q* → *r*	*q* v ~*q*	~*q*	~*r*
T	T	T	T	T	T	F	F
T	T	F	T	F	T	F	T
T	F	T	F	T	T	T	F
T	F	F	F	T	T	T	T
F	T	T	T	T	T	F	F
F	T	F	T	F	T	F	T
F	F	T	T	T	T	T	F
F	F	F	T	T	T	T	T

10. Either Joe goes to the movie, or Julia goes to the movie. If the movie is *Gone with the Wind*, then Julia goes to the movie. So if Joe goes to the movie, the movie is not *Gone with the Wind*.

Invalid

$p \lor q$
$r \to q$
$\therefore p \to \sim r$

p	q	r	$p \lor q$	$r \to q$	$p \to \sim r$
T	T	T	T	T	F
T	T	F	T	T	T
T	F	T	T	F	F
T	F	F	T	T	T
F	T	T	T	T	T
F	T	F	T	T	T
F	F	T	F	F	T
F	F	F	F	T	T

11. $x \to y$
$y \to z$
$\therefore x \to z$
If it rains, the roof will leak. If the roof leaks, the carpet will be ruined. Therefore, if it rains, the carpet will be ruined.

12. $a \to b$
$\therefore a \to (a \,\&\, b)$
If I am late, she will be late. Therefore, if I am late, then both of us will be late.

13. $a \,\&\, b$
$\sim b$
$\therefore a$
John is in the boat, and Maria is in the boat. Maria is not in the boat. Therefore, I am in the boat.

14. $(p \lor q) \to (p \,\&\, q)$
$p \,\&\, q$
$\therefore p \lor q$

If either the profits fall or the sales go down, then both the profits will fall and the sales will go down. Both the profits will fall and the sales will go down. Therefore, either the profits will fall or the sales go down.

15. $p \to q$
$\sim p$
$\therefore q$

If the sky clears, the game proceeds. The sky does not clear. Therefore, the game proceeds.

16. $p \to q$
$\sim q$
$\therefore \sim p$

$p \to q$		$\sim q$	$\sim p$
T	F	F	T

Invalid

17. $p \,\&\, q$
$q \to r$
$\sim q$
$\therefore r$

$p \,\&\, q$		$q \to r$		$\sim q$	r
T	T	T	F	T	F

Valid

18. $p \to q$
$q \to r$

$\therefore q \rightarrow r$

$p \rightarrow q$	$q \rightarrow r$	$q \rightarrow r$
T	T　F	T　F

Valid

19. p v $(q \& r)$
    $\sim p$
    $\sim q$
    $\therefore r$

p **v** $(q \& r)$	$\sim p$	$\sim q$	r
T　F　F	T	F	F

Valid

20. $a \rightarrow b$
    $b \rightarrow c$
    $\therefore (b \& c)$ v $(a \& b)$

$a \rightarrow b$	$b \rightarrow c$	$(b \& c)$ **v** $(a \& b)$
F　F	F	F　　F　F

Invalid

21.

1. $P \rightarrow Q$	Premise
2. $R \rightarrow S$	Premise
3. P v R / Q v S	Premise/ Conclusion
4. $(P \rightarrow Q) \& (R \rightarrow S)$	1, 2, CONJ
5. Q v R	3, 4, CS

22.

1. P v Q	Premise
2. $R \rightarrow S$	Premise
3. $\sim P \& \sim S$ / $Q \& \sim R$	Premise/ Conclusion
4. $\sim P$	3, SIMP
5. Q	1, 4, DS
6. $\sim S$	3, SIMP
7. $\sim R$	2, 6, MT
8. $Q \& \sim R$	5, 7, CONJ

Chapter 7

1. A word that expresses the quantity, or number, of a categorical statement. Universal and particular.
2. Affirmative and negative.
3. A: All S are P. (universal affirmative)
   E: No S are P. (universal negative)
   I: Some S are P. (particular affirmative)
   O: Some S are not P. (particular negative)
4. Some tax cuts are economic mistakes. Subject term: tax cuts; predicate term: economic mistakes; quality: affirmative; quantity: particular; name: particular affirmative.
5. No philosophers are five-year-old kids. Subject term: philosophers; predicate term: five-year-old kids; quality: negative; quantity: universal; name: universal negative.
6. All patients treated with herbal medicine are Chinese. Subject term: patients treated with herbal medicine; predicate term: Chinese people; quality: affirmative; quantity: universal; name: universal affirmative.
7. Some ghost stories are not fabrications devised by true believers. Subject term: ghost stories; predicate term: fabrications devised by true believers; quality: negative; quantity: particular; name: particular negative.
8. Only if something is a watercraft is it a canoe. All canoes are watercraft. A
9. "Baseball is pastoral." [George Carlin] All things identical with baseball are things that are pastoral. A
10. Sheila is the finest scholar in the department. All persons identical with Sheila are the finest scholars in the department. A
11. No one with any sense would drive a car without headlights on a rainy night. No persons with sense are persons who would drive a car without headlights on a rainy night. E
12. "Slow and steady wins the race." [Aesop] All races won are races run slowly and steadily. A
13. A politician is someone who firmly believes that getting elected makes one smart. All politicians are persons who firmly believe that getting elected makes them smart. A

14. "A fanatic is someone who can't change his mind and won't change the subject." [Winston Churchill]
All fanatics are persons who can't change their mind and won't change the subject. A

15. All *M* are *P*. Some *S* are *M*. Therefore, some *S* are *P*.
Valid.

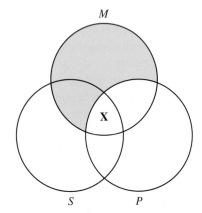

16. No *M* are *P*. No *S* are *M*. Therefore, all *S* are *P*.
Invalid.

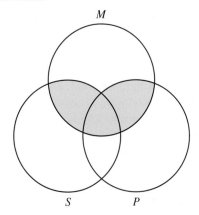

17. All *P* are *M*. No *S* are *M*. Therefore, no *S* are *P*.
Valid.

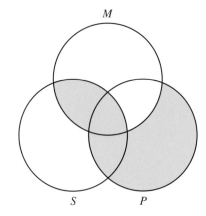

18. Some *S* are not *P*. All *S* are *P*. *False*
19. No *S* are *P*. All *S* are *P*. *False*
20. All *S* are *P*. Some *S* are *P*. *True*

Chapter 8

1. X percent of the observed members of group A have property P.
Therefore, X percent of all members of group A probably have property P.

2. Target group: The class of individuals about which an inductive generalization is made.
Sample: The observed members of a target group.
Relevant property: The property under study in a target group.

3. Its sample can be (1) too small or (2) not representative.

4. Thing A has properties P_1, P_2, P_3 plus the property P_4.
Thing B has properties P_1, P_2, and P_3.
Therefore, thing B probably has property P_4.

5. All the women in my yoga class are against the war. Ninety percent of the members of a national women's group (twelve thousand members) are against the war. And all my women friends are against the war. The fact is, almost all American women oppose this war.
Weak. Not representative.

6. Recently there was a racially motivated murder in Texas. Two white men killed a black man. Then another murder of a black man by some racist whites occurred in Louisiana. And in Mississippi an admitted racist finally was convicted of the murder of a black man that occurred years ago. The South has more racist killers than any other part of the country. Weak. Small sample; not representative.

7. Most professors at this college are not grading as strictly as they used to. They now give B's for work to which they used to assign C's. The grading standards in American colleges are dropping. Weak. Not representative; probably small sample.

8. The first time Ariana encountered trigonometry, she couldn't understand it. And the first time she read Shakespeare, she didn't get it. She will never understand anything.
   Weak. Small sample; not representative.

9. Americans are quite satisfied with the administration's recent foreign policy decisions. An "instant poll" conducted yesterday on the CNN website got fifteen thousand responses from site visitors—and 95 percent of them said that American foreign policy was on the right track.Weak. Not representative.

10. Judging from what I've seen, anti-war demonstrators are just a bunch of peaceniks left over from the Vietnam War era. Weak (if "what I've seen" means personally witnessed). Small sample; not representative.

11. "Suppose that someone tells me that he has had a tooth extracted without an anaesthetic, and I express my sympathy, and suppose that I am then asked, 'How do you know that it hurt him?' I might reasonably reply, 'Well, I know that it would hurt me. I have been to the dentist and know how painful it is to have a tooth stopped without an anaesthetic, let alone taken out. And he has the same sort of nervous system as I have. I infer, therefore, that in these conditions he felt considerable pain, just as I should myself.'" [Alfred J. Ayer]
    Two things compared: experiences of tooth extraction; conclusion: that the other person was in considerable pain; strong.

12. "As for one who is choosy about what he learns . . . we shall not call him a lover of learning or a philosopher, just as we shall not say that a man who is difficult about his food is hungry or has an appetite for food. We shall not call him a lover of food but a poor eater. . . . But we shall call a philosopher the man who is easily willing to learn every kind of knowledge, gladly turns to learning things, and is insatiable in this respect." [Socrates]
    Two things compared: philosopher and eater; conclusion: that a philosopher is someone easily willing to learn every kind of knowledge; strong.

13. "Let us begin with a parable [showing that statements about God have no meaning]. . . . Once upon a time two explorers came upon a clearing in the jungle. In the clearing were growing many flowers and many weeds. One explorer says, 'Some gardener must tend this plot.' The other disagrees, 'There is no gardener.' So they pitch their tents and set a watch. No gardener is ever seen. 'But perhaps he is an invisible gardener.' So they set up a barbed-wire fence. They electrify it. . . . But no shrieks ever suggest that some intruder has received a shock. No movements of the wire ever betray an invisible climber. . . .Yet still the Believer is not convinced. 'But there is a gardener, invisible, intangible,

insensible.'. . . At last the Sceptic despairs, 'But what remains of your original assertion? Just how does what you call an invisible, intangible, eternally elusive gardener differ from an imaginary gardener or even from no gardener at all?'" [Antony Flew]

Two things compared: belief in an elusive gardener and belief in God; conclusion: that talk of an undetectable being such as God is meaningless. Weak.

14. School violence is caused mainly by teens playing violent video games. Incidents of violence in schools have increased as more and more teens are playing violent video games, as the video games themselves have become more graphically and realistically violent, and as the number and variety of video games have expanded dramatically.

    Conclusion: School violence is caused mainly by teens playing violent video games. Weak. Overlooking relevant factors, failing to rule out coincidence.

15. Smoking and exposure to secondhand smoke among pregnant women pose a significant risk to both infants and the unborn. According to numerous studies, each year the use of tobacco causes thousands of spontaneous births, infant deaths, and deaths from SIDS. Death rates for fetuses are 35 percent higher among pregnant women who smoke than among pregnant women who don't smoke.

    Conclusion: Smoking and exposure to secondhand smoke among pregnant women pose a significant risk to both infants and the unborn. Strong.

16. Why are crime rates so high, the economy so bad, and our children so prone to violence, promiscuity, and vulgarity? These social ills have arisen—as they always have—from the "moral vacuum" created when Americans turn away from religion. Our current slide into chaos started when prayer was banned from public schools and secular humanism swooped in to replace it. And as God has slowly faded from public life, we have got deeper in the hole.

    Conclusion: Serious social ills occur because Americans turn away from religion. Weak. Overlooking relevant factors, failing to rule out coincidence.

17. The twelve of us went on a hike through the mountains. We all drank bottled water except Lisa, who drank from a stream. Later she got really sick. Some intestinal thing. But the rest of us were fine. We've repeated this adventure many times on other hikes, with all but one of us drinking bottled water and one drinking from a stream. Everything else was the same. Each time, the person who drank from the stream got really ill. Drinking from streams on these hikes causes intestinal illness. Don't do it.

    Conclusion: Drinking from streams on these hikes causes intestinal illness. Strong.

18. Ever since I started drinking herbal tea in the morning, my energy level has improved and I'm a lot calmer during the day. That stuff works.

    Conclusion: Herbal tea boosts energy and calms the nerves. Weak. Overlooking relevant factors, failing to rule out coincidence, possibly confusing cause and effect.

19. Yesterday my astrological chart— prepared by a top astrologer—said that I would meet an attractive person today, and I did. Last week, it said I'd come into some money, and I did. (Jack paid me that hundred dollars he owed me.) Now I'm a believer. The stars really do rule.

    Conclusion: The stars rule. Weak. Failing to rule out coincidence.

20. Most of the terminal cancer patients in this ward who had positive attitudes about their disease lived longer than expected. Most of the negative-attitude patients didn't live as long as expected. A positive attitude can increase the life

expectancy of people with terminal cancer. Conclusion: A positive attitude can increase the life expectancy of people with terminal cancer. Weak. Failing to rule out other relevant factors, failing to rule out coincidence, possibly confusing cause and effect.

Chapter 9

1. Inference to the best explanation:

    Phenomenon Q.
    E provides the best explanation for Q.
    Therefore, it is probable that E is true.

    Enumerative induction:

    X percent of the observed members of group A have property P.
    Therefore, X percent of all members of group A probably have property P.

    Analogical induction:

    Thing A has properties P_1, P_2, P_3 plus the property P_4.
    Thing B has properties P_1, P_2, and P_3.
    Therefore, thing B probably has property P_4.

2. A standard of internal and external consistency that a theory must meet to be eligible for further consideration.

3. Testability: Whether there is some way to determine if a theory is true.
    Fruitfulness: The number of novel predictions made.
    Scope: The amount of diverse phenomena explained.
    Simplicity: The number of assumptions made.
    Conservatism: How well a theory fits with existing knowledge.

4. With testable theories there is a way to determine whether they are true or false; untestable theories cannot be checked.

5. Four steps to finding the best explanation:

    Step 1. State the theory and check for consistency.
    Step 2. Assess the evidence for the theory.
    Step 3. Scrutinize alternative theories.

    Step 4. Test the theories with the criteria of adequacy.

6. The best theory is the eligible theory that meets the criteria of adequacy better than any of its competitors.

7. d

8. a, b

9. a, b

10. a

11. Phenomenon: The rise in popularity of a newly elected president.
    (1) The so-called honeymoon effect in which a new president enjoys popularity until he or she is involved in serious or controversial decisions.

12. Phenomenon: Your friend has been skipping class, and you haven't seen her in days.
    (1) She's in bed with the flu.

13. Phenomenon: Ships, boats, and planes have been disappearing off the coast of Florida for years.
    (1) Considering the meteorological and atmospheric conditions of the area, it's normal for some craft to be lost from time to time.

14. Phenomenon: The rapid spread of an unknown, dangerous, viral disease throughout North America.
    (1) The lack of awareness and defenses against a new mutated virus.

15. (1) People buy high-ticket merchandise because of subliminal advertising—their minds are being influenced by imperceptible stimuli designed by ad execs. (2) The purchase of high-ticket merchandise. (3) Normal advertising and sales ploys influence people to purchase high-ticket merchandise. (4) The alternative theory is more plausible.

16. (1) In cold fusion research, skepticism skews scientists' observations. (2) The lack of evidence for cold fusion. (3) Cold fusion does not exist. (4) The alternative theory is more plausible.

17. (1) Eleanor must have a system that enables her to pick winning numbers.

(2) Eleanor's winning the state lottery twice in nine months. (3) Coincidence. (4) The coincidence theory is more plausible.

18. (1) The embezzlement was caused by the divorce of his parents when he was very young. (2) The embezzlement. (3) He embezzled because he needed the money to pay debts. (4) The alternative theory is more plausible.

19. (1) Schoolchildren do poorly in school because of the low or negative expectations of their teachers. (2) Poor performance of schoolchildren. (3) Students do poorly because teachers want them to fail. (4) The expectations theory is more plausible.

20. (1) The woman is possessed. (2) The woman's bizarre behavior, including stigmata (bleeding from the palms). (3) The woman suffers from some form of psychosis, which can manifest itself in many strange symptoms, including bleeding from the skin. (4) The alternative theory is more plausible.

Chapter 10

1. An observational consequence implied or predicted by a hypothesis.
2. No. Hypotheses often contain concepts that aren't in the data.
3. If *H*, then *C*.
   not-*C*.
   Therefore, not-*H*.
4. If *H*, then *C*.
   C.
   Therefore, *H*.
5. It's always possible that we will some-day find evidence that undermines or conflicts with the evidence we have now.
6. A hypothesis can always be saved from refutation by making changes in the background claims.
7. Hypothesis: Lack of sufficient lighting on Blind Man's Curve is contributing to an increase in automobile accidents. Test

implication: If the hypothesis is true, ensuring sufficient lighting on Blind Man's Curve should cause a decrease in accidents.

8. Hypothesis: Juan did the fatal stabbing. Test implication: If the hypothesis is true, at least some of the blood on his shirt is likely to belong to the victim, which a DNA test can confirm.

9. Hypothesis: The lights were coming from a meteor fireball breaking up in the atmosphere, and the claim of alien spacecraft was the result of misinterpretation caused by viewer expectation and poor viewing conditions. Test implication: If the hypothesis is true, scientists should be able to confirm that a meteor fireball did enter the atmosphere at the time the mysterious lights were said to appear.

10. (1) Maria drank contaminated water from the creek. (2) Maria ate poisonous berries. (3) The water from the creek contained toxins that can cause gastrointestinal illness, and Maria drank some; Maria ate berries that were poisonous and known to cause gastrointestinal illness. (4) Evidence that Maria drank the water and that it contained the suspected toxins would confirm the hypothesis; failure to detect the toxins would disconfirm the hypothesis.

11. (1) Students pay more attention with two teachers in the class. (2) Students get more individual attention from the teachers. (3) Students concentrate more on their studies when two teachers are in the class; when there are two teachers, they spend more time with each student. (4) Evidence that students were paying more attention would confirm the hypothesis; evidence that students did not pay more attention would disconfirm the hypothesis.

12. (1) Higher levels of air pollution cause more stress. (2) An increase in crime causes more stress. (3) Air pollution levels have increased, and they contribute

to stress; crime has increased, and the amount of crime correlates with stress. (4) Evidence of pollution causing stress and of a significant increase in pollution would confirm the hypothesis; evidence showing no change in air pollution levels would disconfirm it.

13. (1) Super Cold-Stopper With Beta-Carotene prevents colds. (2) The Vaughns have been exposed less often to people with colds. (3) Taking Super Cold-Stopper With Beta-Carotene decreases the incidence of colds; the Vaughns have come in contact with fewer people with colds. (4) Evidence that the product does in fact decrease the incidence of colds would confirm the hypothesis; a failure to demonstrate this effect in well-controlled studies would disconfirm the hypothesis.

14. Esther stole the book from the library. Test implication: Esther should be seen on security cameras stealing the book. Evidence: Video from the security camera clearly showing Esther stealing the book.

15. Most people—both white and black—are economically better off now than their parents were thirty years ago. Test implication: Economic data from the past thirty years should show significant increases in several indicators of economic well-being. Evidence: Data from several trustworthy sources showing the relevant changes in the indicators.

16. The health care system in this country is worse now than it was when Bill Clinton was president. Test implication: There should be significant declines in several standard measures of the quality of a health care system, including the number of people who have access to health care, the effectiveness of medical treatments, and infant mortality rates. Evidence: Reliable data from nonpartisan sources that show the relevant declines.

17. d

18. a, b

19. a, b, c

20. Theory: Joseph is possessed. Phenomenon: Joseph's strange behavior. Alternative theory: Joseph is an epileptic. The evidence for the possession theory is almost nonexistent. Strange behavior, common among humans, is not evidence for possession, and science has demonstrated that seizures are an indication not of possession but of epilepsy and other neurological disorders. The epilepsy theory is testable; the possession theory is not. The possession theory is a failure in fruitfulness, scope, simplicity, and conservatism; the epilepsy theory does well by these criteria. The latter is the better theory.

Chapter 11

1. A moral statement is a statement asserting that an action is right or wrong (moral or immoral) or that something (such as a person or motive) is good or bad.

2. At least one premise is a moral statement that asserts a general moral principle or moral standard. At least one premise makes a nonmoral claim. And the conclusion is a moral statement, or judgment, about a particular case (usually a particular kind of action).

3. Consistency with our considered moral judgments; consistency with our experience of the moral life; workability in real-life situations.

4. By trying to think of counterexamples to it.

5. No.

6. Of course we should have offered protection to the Kurds. They were in grave danger and they asked for our help. *And it is our duty to offer protection to people if they are in grave danger and they request our help.*

7. The supplement manufacturers knew that the herb ephedra was dangerous. *If a company is aware that its product is*

dangerous, it is obligated to remove it from the market. So they should have removed it from the market.

8. The Democrats insulted the president. *Insults to the president should never be allowed.* They should have never been allowed to do that.

9. The Smiths were consenting adults who were having sex in the privacy of their own home. *Sex between consenting adults in the privacy of their own home is morally permissible.* These actions by the Smiths are morally permissible.

10. Randi killed his neighbor, and the killing was not in self-defense. *Killing someone except in self-defense is morally wrong.* He should not have committed such an act.

11. Lying is wrong under all circumstances. *Counterexample: Lying to save the lives of a thousand people.*

12. People who commit crimes should not be punished—they should be retrained to act legally. *Counterexample: Adolf Hitler committed massive crimes against humanity. Wasn't he deserving of punishment?*

13. All humans, whatever their circumstances, have full moral rights. *Counterexample: Do insane individuals have full moral rights? murderers? people in comas?*

14. All creatures that are alive and sensitive to stimulation are equally valuable and should be accorded equal respect. *Counterexample: Is it just as wrong to kill a goldfish as it is a horse? Should we give turtles the same respect we give to children?*

15. The morally right action is the one that produces the most happiness, everyone considered. *Counterexample: Is it morally right to arbitrarily imprison and torture an innocent person if doing so will produce the most happiness for the most people?*

16. Right actions are those that are in one's own self-interest. *Counterexample: Murdering a friend could conceivably be in your own best interest—would it therefore be morally permissible?*

17. Medical experimentation on a patient without her consent. *Defense: If the experimentation could save hundreds of lives and would have no major negative consequences for the patient or for society, it would be justified.*

18. Taking food, shelter, and other resources from rich people and distributing them equally among poor people. *Defense: A more equal distribution of resources would result in greater happiness for a greater number.*

19. Any form of expression or speech that offends people of faith should not be tolerated. *Penthouse* magazine definitely offends people of faith. Ban it! *Evaluation: The first premise is dubious, for it would have us violate the autonomy of persons—by, for example, dramatically curtailing freedom of speech.*

20. Anyone who disagrees with the basic moral dictums of the prevailing culture should be censored. Dr. Tilden's graduation speech clearly was inconsistent with the prevailing moral opinions on campus. She should be reprimanded. *Evaluation: The first premise runs counter to several plausible moral principles, including respect for autonomy, freedom of speech and conscience, and tolerance.*

Arguments and Argumentative Essays

As we note in Chapter 1, an argument is a group of statements in which some of them (the premises) are intended to support another of them (the conclusion). This configuration of statements-supporting-another-statement is not only the basic structure of an argument—it's the general design of an argumentative essay. An argumentative essay tries to support a particular conclusion or position on an issue by offering reasons to support that conclusion. Arguments (in the critical thinking sense) are not passionate exchanges of unsupported views, pointless contests of the is-too-is-not variety. And neither are argumentative essays. A mere sequence of statements expressing your views is not an argument, just as several pages of such statements do not constitute an argumentative essay.

So in an argumentative essay, your main task is to provide rational support for a claim. If you are successful, you will have shown that there are good reasons to accept your view of things. Readers who think critically may well be persuaded by your arguments. If you write well, you may be able to make your essay even more persuasive through rhetorical or stylistic devices that add emphasis, depth, and vividness to your prose. No one wants to read a boring essay. What you should not do, however, is rely entirely on non-argumentative elements to persuade your audience. Strong emotional appeals, for example, can indeed persuade some people, but they prove nothing. In truly effective argumentative essays, the primary persuasive device is critical reasoning.

Basic Essay Structure

Good argumentative essays generally contain the following elements, though not necessarily in the order shown here:

- Introduction (or opening)
- Statement of thesis (the claim to be supported)

- Argument supporting the thesis
- Assessment of objections
- Conclusion

In the *introduction*, you want to do at least two things: (1) grab the reader's attention and (2) provide background information for the thesis. Effective attention-grabbers include startling statistics, compelling quotations, interesting anecdotes, opinions of experts, shocking or unexpected claims, and vivid imagery. Whatever attention-grabbers you use, *they must relate to the topic of the essay*. No use telling a good story if it has nothing to do with your thesis. Providing background for your thesis often means explaining why your topic is important, telling how you became concerned, or showing that there is a problem to be solved or a question to be answered. Very often the introduction is laid out in the first paragraph of the essay, sometimes consisting of no more than a sentence or two. In general, the briefer the introduction, the better.

The *thesis statement* also usually appears in the first paragraph. It's the statement that you hope to support or prove in your essay, the conclusion of the argument that you intend to present. You want to state the thesis in a single sentence and do so as early as possible in the essay. Your thesis statement is like a compass to your readers, guiding them through your essay from premise to premise, showing them a clear path. It also helps you stay on course, reminding you to keep every part of the essay related to your single unifying idea. Your thesis statement should be restricted to a claim that can be defended in the space allowed (often only 750 to 1000 words). Not restricted enough: "Tuition is too high." Better: "Tuition increases at Podunk College are unacceptable." Better still: "The recent tuition increase at Podunk College is unnecessary for financial reasons." (More on how to devise a properly restricted thesis statement in a moment.)

The main body of the essay is the fully developed argument supporting the thesis. This means that the basic essay structure consists of the thesis statement followed by each premise or reason that supports the thesis. Each premise in turn is clearly stated, sufficiently explained and illustrated, and supported by examples, statistics, expert opinion, and other evidence. Sometimes you can develop the essay very simply by devoting a single paragraph to each premise. At other times, each premise may demand several paragraphs. In any case, you should develop just one point per paragraph, with every paragraph clearly relating to the thesis statement.

A sketch of the argument for the Podunk College essay, then, might look like this:

Premise: If the college has a budget surplus, then a tuition increase is unnecessary.
Premise: The college has had a budget surplus for the last five years.
Premise: If the college president says that the school is financially in good shape and therefore doesn't need a tuition increase, then it's probably true that the school doesn't need a tuition increase.

Premise: In an unguarded moment, the president admitted that the school is financially in good shape and therefore doesn't need a tuition increase.

Thesis statement: Therefore, the recent tuition increase at Podunk College is probably unnecessary for financial reasons.

Good argumentative essays include an *assessment of objections*—an honest effort to take into account any objections that readers are likely to raise about the thesis statement or its premises. When you deal with such objections in your essay, you lend credibility to it because you're making an attempt to be fair and thorough. In addition, when you carefully examine objections, you can often see ways to make your argument or thesis statement stronger. It isn't necessary to consider every possible objection, just the strongest or the most common ones. Sometimes it's best to deal with objections when you discuss premises that relate to them. At other times it may be better to handle objections near the end of the essay after defending the premises.

Finally, your essay—unless it's very short—must have a *conclusion*. The conclusion usually appears in the last paragraph of the essay. Typically it reiterates the thesis statement (though usually not in exactly the same words). If the argument is complex or the essay is long, the conclusion may contain a summary of the argument. Good conclusions may reassert the importance of the thesis statement, challenge readers to do something about a problem, tell a story that emphasizes the relevance of the main argument, or bring out a disturbing or unexpected implication of a claim defended in the body of the essay.

Guidelines for Writing the Essay

1. *Determine your thesis statement.* Do not write on the first thesis idea that pops into your head. Select a topic you're interested in and narrow its scope until you have a properly restricted thesis statement. Research the topic to find out what issues are being debated. When you think you have an idea for a thesis statement, stop. Dig deeper into the idea by examining the arguments associated with that claim. Choose a thesis statement that you think you can defend. If you come to a dead end, start the process over.

2. *Create an outline.* Establish the basic framework of your outline by writing out your thesis statement and all the premises that support it. Then fill in the framework by jotting down what points you will need to make in defense of each premise. Decide on what objections to your argument you will consider and how you will respond to them.

3. *Write a first draft.* As you write, don't be afraid to revise your outline or even your thesis statement. Writing will force you to think carefully about the strengths and weaknesses of your argument. If need be, write a second draft and a third. Good writers aren't afraid of revisions; they depend on them.

4. *Stay on track.* Make sure that each sentence of your essay relates somehow to your thesis statement and argument.

5. *Zero in on your audience.* Determine for what audience your essay is intended, and write to them. Is it readers of the local paper? fellow students? people who are likely to disagree with you?

6. *Support your premises.* Back up the premises of your argument with examples, expert opinion, statistics, analogies, and other kinds of evidence.

7. *Let your final draft sit.* If possible, when you've finished writing your paper, set it aside and read it the next day. You may be surprised how many mistakes this fresh look can reveal. If you can't set the essay aside, ask a friend to read it and give you some constructive criticism.

From Issue to Thesis

For many students, the biggest challenge in writing an argumentative essay is deciding on an appropriate thesis—the claim, or conclusion, that the essay is designed to support or prove. Very often, when an essay runs off the track and crashes, the derailment can be traced to a thesis that was bad from the beginning.

Picking a thesis out of the air and beginning to write is usually a mistake. Any thesis statement that you craft without knowing anything about the subject is likely to be ill-formed or indefensible. It's better to begin by selecting an issue—a question that's controversial or in dispute—then researching it to determine what arguments or viewpoints are involved. To research it, you can survey the views of people or organizations involved in the controversy. Read articles and books, talk to people, go online. This process should not only inform you about various viewpoints but also tell you what arguments are used to support them. It should also help you narrow the issue to one that you can easily address in the space you have.

Suppose you begin with this issue: whether the United States has serious industrial pollution problems. After investigating this issue, you would probably see that it is much too broad to be addressed in a short paper. You should then restrict the issue to something more manageable—for example: whether recent legislation to allow coal-burning power plants to emit more sulfur dioxide will harm people's health. With the scope of the issue narrowed, you can explore arguments on both sides. You cannot examine every single argument, but you should assess the strongest ones, including those that you devise yourself. You can then use what you've already learned about arguments to select one that you think provides good support for its conclusion. The premises and conclusion of this argument can then serve as the bare-bones outline of your essay. Your argument might look like this:

[Premise 1] Excessive amounts of sulfur dioxide in the air have been linked to increases in the incidence of asthma and other respiratory illnesses.
[Premise 2] Many areas of the country already have excessive amounts of sulfur dioxide in the air.

[Premise 3] Most sulfur dioxide in the air comes from coal-burning power plants. [Conclusion] Therefore, allowing coal-burning power plants to emit more sulfur dioxide will most likely increase the incidence of respiratory illnesses.

For the sake of example, the premises of this argument are made up. But your essay's argument must be for real, with each premise that could be called into question supported by an additional argument. After all, your readers are not likely to accept your argument's conclusion if they doubt your premises.

In some cases, your paper may contain more than one argument supporting a single conclusion, or it may offer a critique of someone else's argument. In either case, investigating an issue and the arguments involved will follow the pattern just suggested. In a critique of an argument (or arguments), you offer reasons why the argument fails and thus support the thesis that the conclusion is false.

This process of devising a thesis statement and crafting an argument to back it up is not linear. You will probably have to experiment with several arguments before you find one that's suitable. Even after you decide on an argument, you may later discover that its premises are dubious or that they cannot be adequately supported. Then you will have to backtrack to investigate a better argument. Backtracking in this preliminary stage is relatively easy. If you postpone this rethinking process until you are almost finished with your first draft, it will be harder—and more painful.

From Thesis to Outline

We have just seen that the second step in writing an argumentative essay (after determining your thesis statement, or conclusion) is creating an outline. Outlines are useful because, among other things, they help avert disaster in the essay-writing phase. Imagine writing two-thirds of your essay, then discovering that the second premise of your argument cannot be supported and is in fact false. You might have to throw out the whole argument and start over.

At the head of your outline, insert your thesis statement, articulating it as clearly and as precisely as possible. At every stage of outlining, you can then refer to the statement for guidance. The premises and conclusion of your argument (or arguments) will constitute the major points of your outline. The following, for example, is the preliminary outline for the essay discussed earlier:

THESIS: Allowing coal-burning power plants to emit more sulfur dioxide will most likely increase the incidence of respiratory illnesses.

    I. Excessive amounts of sulfur dioxide in the air have been linked to increases in the incidence of asthma and other respiratory illnesses.

    II. Many areas of the country already have excessive amounts of sulfur dioxide in the air.

III. Most sulfur dioxide in the air comes from coal-burning power plants.

IV. Therefore, allowing coal-burning power plants to emit more sulfur dioxide will most likely increase the incidence of respiratory illnesses.

After you clearly state the premises, you need to ask yourself whether any of them need to be defended. As discussed earlier, any premise likely to be questioned by your readers will need support. That is, the premise itself will need arguments to back it up, and the supporting arguments should be indicated in your outline. (Some premises, though, may not need support because they are obvious or generally accepted.) As discussed in Chapter 3, you can support a premise (claim) through deductive or inductive arguments with premises made up of examples, analogies, empirical evidence (such as scientific research or trustworthy observations), and authoritative judgments (such as those from reliable experts). Here's how the preceding outline might look with (fictional) supporting arguments clearly shown:

THESIS: Allowing coal-burning power plants to emit more sulfur dioxide will most likely increase the incidence of respiratory illnesses.

I. Excessive amounts of sulfur dioxide in the air have been linked to increases in the incidence of asthma and other respiratory illnesses.
   A. EPA data show an association between high amounts of sulfur dioxide and increased respiratory illnesses.
   B. Cities that monitor air pollution have noted increases in hospital admissions for asthma and other respiratory ills when sulfur dioxide emissions are high.
II. Many areas of the country already have excessive amounts of sulfur dioxide in the air.
   A. Scientists have reported high levels of sulfur dioxide in the air in fifteen major cities.
III. Most sulfur dioxide in the air comes from coal-burning power plants.
   A. Many environmental scientists assert that coal-burning power plants are the source of most sulfur dioxide.
   B. A few owners of coal-burning power plants admit that their plants emit most of the sulfur dioxide in their region.
IV. Therefore, allowing coal-burning power plants to emit more sulfur dioxide will most likely increase the incidence of respiratory illnesses.

You should expand your outline until you've indicated how you intend to provide support for each claim that requires it. This level of detail helps ensure that you will not encounter any nasty surprises in the writing phase.

Your essay should somehow address objections or criticisms that your readers are likely to raise, and your outline should indicate how you intend to do this. Answering objections can make your case stronger and lend credibility to you as the writer. Sometimes it's best to address objections where they are likely to arise—in connection with specific premises or arguments. At other times, your essay may be more effective if you deal with objections at the end of it, near the conclusion.

As you work through your outline, don't be afraid to rework your thesis statement or to make changes in arguments. Satisfy yourself that the outline is complete and that it reflects a logical progression of points.

From Outline to First Draft

If you have developed a detailed outline, then you have a path to follow as you write. And while you're writing an argumentative essay, having a path is much better than searching for one. Your outline should make the writing much easier.

No outline is a finished work, however. As you write, you may discover that your arguments are not as strong as you thought, or that other arguments would be better, or that changing a point here and there would make an argument more effective. If so, you should amend your outline and then continue writing. The act of writing is often an act of discovery, and good writers are not afraid of revisions or multiple drafts.

Start your draft with a solid opening that draws your readers into your essay and prepares the way for your arguments. Good openings are interesting, informative, and short. Grab the attention of your readers with a bold statement of your thesis, a provocative quote, a compelling story, or interesting facts. Prepare the way for your arguments by explaining why the question you're addressing is important, why you're concerned about it, or why it involves a pressing problem. Don't assume that your readers will see immediately that the issue you're dealing with is worth their time.

Include a clear statement of your thesis in your opening (in the first paragraph or very close by). In many cases, you will want to tell the reader how you plan to develop your argument or how the rest of the essay will unfold (without going into lengthy detail). In any case, by the time your audience reads through your opening, they should know exactly what you intend to prove and why.

Consider this opening for our imaginary essay on air pollution:

Respiratory experts at the National Institutes of Health say that sulfur dioxide in the air is a poison that we should avoid. Yet the current administration wants to loosen environmental rules to allow coal-burning power plants to emit more sulfur dioxide than they already do. That's a bad idea. The latest evidence shows that letting the plants emit more of this poison will most likely increase the incidence of respiratory illnesses in hundreds of communities.

This opening gets the reader's attention by sounding the alarm about a serious health hazard. It provides enough background information to help us understand the seriousness of the problem. And the thesis statement in the last sentence announces what the essay will try to prove.

The body of your essay should fully develop the arguments for your thesis statement, or conclusion. You should devote at least one paragraph to each premise, though several paragraphs may be necessary. You may opt to deal with objections to your argument as you go along, perhaps as you put forth each premise, or at the end of the essay just before the conclusion. Each paragraph should develop and explain just one idea, which is usually expressed in a topic sentence. Each sentence in each paragraph should relate to the paragraph's main idea. Any sentence that has no clear connection to the main idea should be deleted or revised. Link paragraphs together in a logical sequence using transitional words and phrases or direct references to material in preceding paragraphs.

Here are two paragraphs that might follow the air pollution opening:

Scientists used to wonder whether there is a connection between airborne sulfur dioxide and respiratory illness—but no more. Research has repeatedly shown a strong link between high levels of sulfur dioxide in the air and diseases that affect the lungs. For example, data from studies conducted by the Environmental Protection Agency (EPA) show that when levels of airborne sulfur dioxide in urban areas reach what the EPA calls the "high normal" range, the incidence of respiratory illnesses increases dramatically. According to several EPA surveys of air quality, many major cities (not just Los Angeles) often have high normal levels of sulfur dioxide in the air. In addition, data from health departments in large cities show that when levels of airborne sulfur dioxide are at their highest, hospital admissions for asthma and other respiratory ills also increase.

These findings, however, tell only half the story. Many parts of the country have more than just occasional surges in levels of airborne sulfur dioxide. They must endure unsafe levels continuously. New studies from the National Institutes of Health demonstrate that in at least ten major cities, the amount of sulfur dioxide in the air is excessive all the time.

In this passage, a single paragraph is devoted to each premise. Each paragraph develops a single idea, which is stated in a topic sentence. (The topic sentence for the first paragraph: "Research has repeatedly shown a strong link between high levels of sulfur dioxide in the air and diseases that affect the lungs." The second paragraph: "[Many parts of the country] must endure unsafe levels continuously.") Each sentence in each paragraph relates to the topic sentence, and the relationships among the sentences are clear. Likewise the connection between the discussion in the first paragraph and that of the second is apparent. The transitional sentence in the second paragraph ("These findings, however, tell only half the story") helps bridge the gap between the paragraphs. Both of them help support the thesis statement.

How you end your essay is often as important as how you start it. In short or simple essays, there may be no need for a conclusion. The thesis may be clear and emphatic without a conclusion. In many cases, however, an essay is strengthened by a conclusion, and sometimes a conclusion is absolutely essential. Often without an effective conclusion, an essay may seem to end pointlessly or to be incomplete. The typical conclusion reiterates or reaffirms the thesis statement without being repetitious. Or the conclusion of the essay's argument serves as the conclusion for the whole essay. In long or complex essays, the conclusion often includes a summary of the main points discussed.

Sometimes a conclusion is a call to action, an invitation to the reader to do something about a problem. Sometimes it relates a story that underscores the importance of the essay's argument. Sometimes it highlights a provocative aspect of a claim defended earlier. In all cases it serves to increase the impact of the essay.

The conclusion, however, is not the place to launch into a completely different issue, make entirely unsubstantiated claims, malign those who disagree with you, or pretend that your argument is stronger than it really is. These tacks will not strengthen your essay but weaken it.

Matters of Style and Content

1. *Write to your audience.* Almost everything you write—from college papers to love notes—is intended for a particular audience. Knowing who your audience is can make all the difference in what you say and how you say it. Unless things have gone terribly awry, you would not ordinarily address members of the town council the same way you would your one true love; nor your one true love as you would readers of the *New England Journal of Medicine*. You may wonder, then, who is the intended audience of your paper?

Your instructor, of course, may specify your audience and thus settle the issue for you. Otherwise, you should assume that your audience consists of intelligent, curious readers who are capable of understanding and appreciating clearly written, well-made papers on many subjects. Writing to your proper audience means that you will have to define unfamiliar terms, explain any points that may be misunderstood, and lay out your argument so that its structure and significance would be clear to any intelligent reader. This approach will both force you to attempt a better understanding of your subject and help you demonstrate this understanding through your writing.

2. *Do not overstate premises or conclusions.* Overstatement is the problem of exaggerating claims, of making an assertion sound stronger or more inclusive than it deserves. We are all guilty of overstatement, most often in everyday speech.

We may say, "Everyone dislikes Professor Jones" or "Americans think the French are snobbish" when in fact only *some* students dislike Professor Jones and only *a few* of our American friends think that *some* French people are snobbish. In everyday conversation, such exaggerations are often understood as such and are used innocuously for emphasis. But too often the overstatements are simply distortions, assertions that claim too much and lead us into error or prejudice. To a disconcerting degree, assertions regarding opposing views in religion, politics, and morality are overstatements.

Overstatement can arise in at least two ways. First, particular statements—including premises—can be exaggerated. You may be tempted to assert that whatever issue you are addressing in your essay is "the most important issue of our time." You might declare that a premise is certainly or undoubtedly true (when in fact it is merely probable) or forgo important qualifiers such as "some," "perhaps," and "many." You may get carried away and say, for example, that killing another human being is *always* morally wrong, even though you would admit that killing in self-defense is morally permissible.

Second, the conclusions of arguments can be overstated: They can go beyond what logical inference would permit. Because of your commitment to your conclusion, you may overstate it. The result is an invalid or weak argument.

3. *Treat opponents and opposing views fairly.* Sometimes it seems that most of what people know about arguing a position they have learned from the worst possible teachers—political debate-type television programs. In these forums, the standard procedure is to attack the character and motivations of opponents, distort or misrepresent opposing views, and dismiss opponents' evidence and concerns out of hand. But in good writing, abusive or unfair tactics are out of order. They are also ineffective. When readers encounter such heavy-handedness, they are likely to be suspicious of the writer's motives, to wonder if the writer is close-minded, to question whether his or her assertions can be trusted, or to doubt the worth of arguments defended with such gratuitous zeal.

4. *Write clearly.* Being clear is a matter of ensuring that your meaning is understood by the reader. In most kinds of writing, clarity is almost always a supreme virtue.

Lack of clarity in your writing can occur in several ways. Inexperienced writers often produce some very murky papers because too often they assume that because they know what they mean, others will know too. Typically, others do *not* know. The problem is that new writers have not yet developed the knack of viewing their own writing as others might. In other words, they fail to adopt an objective stance toward their own words. Good writers are their own best critics.

Trying to view your writing as others might takes practice. A trick that often helps is to not look at your writing for a day or two then go back to it and read it cold. You may discover after you take this little break that some passages that seemed clear to you earlier are mostly gibberish. Another technique is to use peer review. Ask a friend to read your paper and pinpoint any passages that seem unclear.

5. *Be careful what you assume.* Behind every argument there are presuppositions that need not be made explicit because they are taken for granted by all parties. They may be too obvious to mention or in no need of justification. (They are distinct from implicit premises, which are essential to an argument and should be brought out into the open.) In arguments about the rights of hospital patients, for example, there would typically be no need to explain that a hospital is not a Chevrolet truck, or that patient rights have something to do with ethics, or that such rights may be important to patients. You should, however, be careful not to presuppose a claim that may be controversial among your readers. If you wish to establish that abortion is morally permissible, you should not assume your readers will agree that women have a right to choose abortion or that a fetus is not a person.

PURSUING CLARITY: DEFINITIONS, AMBIGUITY, AND VAGUENESS

Writing with clarity involves careful attention to language and how it's used. Most often this means properly defining terms, sorting out ambiguities, and eliminating excessive vagueness.

Definitions. As noted earlier, sometimes a dispute can hang on the meaning of a single term. Clarify the meaning, and the disagreement dissolves. In an argumentative essay, clarifying terms often comes down to offering precise definitions of words that are crucial to your argument.

In general, any definition you offer should decrease vagueness or ambiguity and thereby increase the effectiveness of your writing. Your definitions should also be consistent. If you provide a definition for a term in your essay, then you should stick to that definition throughout. Altering the meaning of a term in mid-essay, or using more than one term to refer to the same thing, can be confusing to the reader—and might even subvert your essay's argument.

As we saw in Chapter 5, good writers are also very much aware of another kind of meaning—the meaning that comes from a word's connotations. Connotations can be put to work as both euphemisms and dysphemisms. Consider these words: "soldier," "warrior," and "grunt." These terms have nearly the same literal meaning, but they differ in the emotions or attitudes they convey. Or what about these terms: "tavern," "saloon," "bar," "watering hole," and "dive." They refer to the same kind of establishment, but the images or emotions conveyed are diverse, ranging from the respectable and pleasant (tavern) to the lowly and odious (dive).

Ambiguity. *Ambiguity* can also make writing less clear. A term or statement is ambiguous if it has more than one meaning (and the context doesn't help clear things up). Some ambiguities are *semantic*; they are the result of multiple meanings of a word or phrase. Consider the sentence, "Kids make nutritious snacks." The word *make* could mean *prepare* or *constitute*. If the former, the sentence says that kids can prepare food. If the latter, the sentence means that kids are food.

Some ambiguities are *syntactic*; they are the result of the way words are combined. Read this sentence straight through without stopping: "Maria watched a bird with binoculars." Who had the binoculars, Maria or the bird? We don't know because the sentence is poorly written; words are misplaced. If we want the sentence to say that Maria was the one holding the binoculars, we might rewrite it like this: "Looking through her binoculars, Maria watched the bird."

Vagueness. Often a lack of clarity comes not from ambiguous terms but from *vague* terms—words that fail to convey one definite meaning. This failure can be the result of many kinds of sloppiness, but at the head of the list is the tendency to use words that are too *general*. General words refer to whole groups or classes of things, such as *soldiers, artists,* and *books. Specific* words, on the other hand, refer to more particular items, such as *Sgt. Morris, van Gogh,* and *The Sun Also Rises*. There is nothing inherently wrong with using general words; in fact, we must employ them in many circumstances. Used to excess, however, they can easily muddy a paper.

An Annotated Sample Paper

Let's see how all this might be applied in an actual student essay.[1] The following incorporates the main elements of good argumentative papers and, as even the best essays do, exhibits both strengths and weaknesses—many of which are noted in the margins. Read the paper carefully, taking in the annotations as you go, making sure you understand each point before moving on to the next.

Free Speech on Campus

Seem to be three arguments to discuss but this summary does not make that as clear as it should.

In order to meet the goals and purposes of higher education, free speech must remain intact. Thus, the University of Missouri should not adopt a campus hate speech code. ① The First Amendment protects all speech outside the university setting, and what happens outside of the university setting also should be allowed inside. ② Without an open forum for thought, though it may include hate speech, the university fails in its mission to provide a realistic experience for its students. By abolishing hate speech on university campuses, that open forum for discovery and knowledge is eliminated. As a result, learning and knowledge are stunted. ③ Without the exchange of controversial ideas and opinions, there can be no real change in our society. Experiencing and debating is almost always better than suppressing, because censoring speech can never invoke real change.

Thesis statement

Summarizes the arguments to be made.

Provides background for first argument.

The First Amendment protects the right for every person to express opinions about the government and about each other. It actually "protects speech no matter how offensive the content" (Hate Speech on Campus, 1996). Just because something is offensive to one person does not mean it is offensive to another. Justice John M. Harlan wrote in Cohen v. California (1971), "One man's vulgarity is another's lyric" (Free Speech, 1996). In other words, just because something is offensive to one person does not mean that it is offensive by definition.

Needs a more explicit transition to first argument.

Sources cited

Speech that is protected outside of the university setting also should be protected inside. Some would argue that hate speech hinders the abilities of minority students to learn, but part of the goal of higher education is to put students out of their comfort zone and to challenge their ways of thinking. In response to a sexual harassment policy being implemented

Responds to an objection to thesis.

at the University of Massachusetts, lawyer Harvey A. Silverglate (1995) wrote a memo to university administrators opposing the proposal.

> One of the primary purposes of a college education and experience is to challenge students, to make them question their comfortable lives and assumptions in short, to discomfort them in one way or another. (Silverglate, 1995)

In the same memo, Silverglate also wrote:

> If I am allowed to say something on the street corner, in a letter to the editor of a newspaper, or on a radio talk show, surely I should be allowed to say it on the campus of the University of Massachusetts.

Not clear how these quotations—which refer to sexual harassment—relate to hate speech.

First argument for thesis

This is equally true for the University of Missouri. What can possibly be gained by excluding an element of real life such as offensive speech from the campus experience? The university would only serve to deceive its students by shielding them from realistic situations while they are in school. This, in turn, only serves to place them into the real world with false expectations.

Alternatively, exploring and debating is almost always better than suppressing. The organization Justice on Campus (1995) contends that:

Introduces quotation

> When we hear speech or see images that offend us, nothing is more human than our urge to suppress or to destroy them. But as deeply human is our need to think and to share our thoughts with others. Censorship is the greatest evil because the censor's goal is to imprison the human spirit.

Second argument for thesis

In addition to providing a realistic picture of nonacademic life, allowing all types of speech on campus encourages an open forum for the discussion of all types of ideas. Discussion of controversial issues and different points of view are the fuel for a useful education. That is why higher education has a responsibility to ensure that all forms of speech are protected, analyzed, and addressed. "The right of free speech is indivisible. When one of us is denied this right, all of us are denied" (Hate Speech on Campus, 1996). By denying one point of view, we eliminate the open forum. A speech code on any university campus only hinders the ability of students and faculty to fully explore the market of ideas available to them. The University of Missouri is no exception to the idea that academic freedom is the bedrock of a free society.

Third argument for thesis

If we do not allow open expression, however hateful it is, then there can be no change, no growth. Racism, sexism, ageism, etc. are not going to diminish without being addressed in higher education. As noted by the ACLU (Hate Speech on Campus, 1995), "Verbal purity is not social change." Barring certain types of speech would be a seeming quick fix for issues such as racism, sexism, ageism, and homophobia, which often comprise hate speech. But racist statements are not the real problem between the races; racism is. If we bar all racially biased comments on campus, all we have done is fuel the racism. We have then given hatred the power to lurk and grow within us instead of communicating and debating about it in the open.

If hate speech is not allowed to occur openly, the problem of racism is never addressed. Like racism, hate speech itself is not the problem; hate is. As members of a society, we must communicate in order to solve problems and grow as individuals. This includes addressing hateful ideas and opinions. We can make no progress if we do not allow offensive kinds of speech to exist on campus. By barring them, we run the risk of being silenced ourselves.

Conclusion summarizes main arguments.

A hate speech code at the University of Missouri would be detrimental to everyone, from students to faculty. The First Amendment protects all kinds of speech, including the offensive. It does this in order to

Restatement of thesis

ensure that all voices are heard and that all issues can be addressed. To go through college with the idea that offensive speech does not happen is detrimental to students and to the society in which they live. The educational system is based on the idea that communication leads to learning and that learning leads to personal growth. Without the open forum for thought and the freedom to express controversial ideas, a higher education is worthless. Moreover, no one ever solved a controversial gender issue or a racial conflict in silence. There must be communication so that debate can transpire. In order for any change in our society to transpire, offensive speech must be allowed to continue. It can only be addressed and learned from if it is equally protected by the Constitution. Mike Godwin, of the Electronic Frontier Foundation, says, "when it comes to the Bill of Rights, what you don't use, you lose. The First Amendment is a terrible thing to waste" (Comments and quotes, 1995). If anyone has a responsibility to use the freedom granted by the First Amendment, higher education is at the top of the list.

References

American Civil Liberties Union. (1996). Hate speech on campus. [Online]. Available: http://www.aclu.org/library/pbp16.html

American Civil Liberties Union. (1996). Free speech. [Online]. Available: www.aclu.org/issues/freespeech/isfs.html

Justice on Campus. (1996). Comments and quotes on sexual harassment and free speech. [Student paper]

Justice on Campus. (1995). Speech codes and disciplinary charges. [Student paper]

Silverglate, H. A. (1995, November 23). Memo from Harvey Silverglate. [Student paper]

Chapter 2

1. Francis Bacon, "Idols of the Mind," in *Novum Organum, The Works*, 3 vols., ed. and trans. Basil Montague (Philadelphia: Parry & MacMillan, 1854).

2. *Ibid.*

3. Bertrand Russell, *Let the People Think* (London: William Clowes, 1941), 2.

4. W. K. Clifford, "The Ethics of Belief," in *The Rationality of Belief in God*, ed. George I. Mavrodes (Englewood Cliffs, NJ: Prentice-Hall, 1970), 159–60.

5. For a thorough review of various forms of relativism, see Theodore Schick and Lewis Vaughn, *How to Think About Weird Things*, 3d ed. (Mountain View, CA: Mayfield Publishing, 1999), 68–92.

Chapter 3

1. This step-by-step procedure is inspired, in part, by Greg Bassham et al., *Critical Thinking: A Student's Introduction* (San Francisco: McGraw-Hill, 2002), 56–62.

2. Elias E. Savellos, *Reasoning and the Law: The Elements* (Belmont, CA: Wadsworth, 2001), 59–60.

3. This procedure is inspired, in part, by Brooke Noel Moore and Richard Parker, *Critical Thinking*, 6th ed. (Mountain View, CA: Mayfield Publishing, 2001), 274–75.

Chapter 4

1. Bertrand Russell, *Let the People Think* (London: William Clowes, 1941), 1.

2. Elizabeth Loftus and Hunter G. Hoffman, "Misinformation and Memory, The Creation of New Memories," *Journal of Experimental Psychology: General* 118(1) (March 1989):100–104.

3. Terence Hines, *Pseudoscience and the Paranormal* (Buffalo, NY: Prometheus Books, 1988), 170.

4. Adam Liptak, "Study of Wrongful Convictions Raises Questions Beyond DNA," *New York Times*, 23 July 2007.

5. This example inspired by L. W. Alvarez, letter to the editors, *Science* (June 18, 1965):1541.

6. Hines, *Pseudoscience and the Paranormal*, 4–5.

7. Thomas Gilovich, *How We Know What Isn't So* (New York: The Free Press, 1991), 54.

8. J. Cocker, "Biased Questions in Judgment of Covariation Studies," *Personality and Social Psychology Bulletin* 8 (June 1982):214–20.

9. Stephen Law, *Believing Bullshit: How Not to Get Sucked into an Intellectual Black Hole* (Amherst, NY: Prometheus Books, 2011).

10. National Safety Council, "What Are the Odds of Dying?" <www.nsc.org> (June 12, 2004).

11. John Ruscio, "Risky Business," *Skeptical Inquirer* (March 2000).

12. Eugene Kiely and Lori Robertson, "How to Spot Fake News," *FactCheck.org*, November 18, 2016.

13. "Work Farce," *New York Post*, June 26, 2003.

14. "Soldiers Sweep Up Saddam's Hit Goons," *New York Post*, July 1, 2003.

Chapter 5

1. The inspiration for this unconventional categorization comes primarily from Ludwig F. Schlecht, "Classifying Fallacies Logically," *Teaching Philosophy*

14(1) (1991):53–64 and Greg Bassham et al., *Critical Thinking: A Student's Introduction* (San Francisco: McGraw-Hill, 2002).

2. Tara Parker-Pope, "Prominent Cancer Doctor Warns About Cellphones," *New York Times*, 24 July 2008, <http://well.blogs.nytimes.com/2008/07/24/prominent-cancer-doctor-warns-about-cellphones/?scp=2&sq=herberman%20&st=cse>, September 11, 2008.

3. Robert T. Carroll, "The Paralyzing Precautionary Principle," *The Skeptic's Dictionary*, 26 July 2008, <http://www.skepdic.com/skeptimedia/skeptimedia20.html>, September 11, 2008.

4. W. Ross Winterowd and Geoffrey R. Winterowd, *The Critical Reader, Thinker, and Writer* (Mountain View, CA: Mayfield Publishing, 1992), 447–48.

5. Reported in Richard Whately, *Elements of Logic* (London: Longman, Greens, and Co., 1826).

6. Theodore Schick and Lewis Vaughn, *How to Think About Weird Things*, 3d ed. (Mountain View, CA: Mayfield Publishing, 1999), 192.

Chapter 8

1. Jeneen Interlandi, "Obama Is Not the Antichrist—And Nobody Really Thinks He Is," *Daily Beast/Newsweek*, 26 March 2010, <http://www.thedailybeast.com/newsweek/blogs/the-gaggle/2010/03/26/obama-is-not-the-antichrist-and-nobody-really-thinks-he-is.html> (10 October 2011).

2. Susan Blackmore, "Psychic Experiences: Psychic Illusions," *Skeptical Inquirer* 16:367–76.

3. David G. Myers, "The Power of Coincidence," *Skeptic Magazine* 9(4) (September 2002).

4. Francis Collins, "No Link Between MMR Vaccine and Autism, Even in High-Risk Kids," National Institutes of Health, NIH Director's Blog, April 28, 2015.

Chapter 9

1. Charles Darwin, *The Origin of Species* (New York: Collier, 1962), 476.

2. Arthur Conan Doyle, *A Study in Scarlet* (New York: P. F. Collier and Son, 1906), 29–30.

3. Arthur Conan Doyle, "The 'Gloria Scott,'" *Memoirs of Sherlock Holmes* (London: George Newnes, 1894).

4. "Shark Attacks Are Down for Third Year in a Row," <CNN.com> (January 29, 2004).

5. "Study Examines Cancer Risk from Hair Dye," <CNN.com> (January 28, 2004).

6. John Hagee, interview on *National Public Radio*, 18 September 2006, <http://www.npr.org/templates/story/story.php?storyId=6097362>, September 15, 2008.

7. Mathew Schmalz, "Did God's Wrath Smite Houston and Florida? It's Not That Simple," *Courier-Journal*, September 12, 2017.

8. NASA, "The Great Moon Hoax," Science@NASA website, <http://science.nasa .gov>.

9. W. V. Quine and J. S. Ullman, *The Web of Belief* (New York: Random House, 1970), 43–44.

10. For the latest research and discussion on the placebo effect, see A. Hrobjartsson and P. C. Gotzsche, *New England Journal of Medicine* 344 (2001):1594–1602; J. C. Bailar, "The Powerful Placebo and the Wizard of Oz," *New England Journal of Medicine*, 344 2001:1630–32, and Keith Bauer, "Clinical Use of Placebo," <www .ama-assn.org> (July 2001), journal discussion.

11. See C. Hill and F. Doyan, "Review of Randomized Trials of Homeopathy," *Review of Epidemiology* 38 (1990):139–42; Report, Homeopathic Medicine Group, Commission of the European Communities, December 1996; J. Wise, "Health Authority Stops Buying Homeopathy," *British Medical Journal* 314 (1997):1574; K. Linde et al., "Are the Clinical Effects of Homeopathy Placebo Effects?" *Lancet* 350(9081) (Sept. 20, 1997):824.

12. Fred L. Whipple, *Earth, Moon and Planets* (Boston: Harvard University Press, 1968).

13. Robert A. Baker, "Can We Tell When Someone Is Staring at Us?" *Skeptical Inquirer*, March/April 2000.

Chapter 10

1. I owe the inspiration and general outline for this section to Theodore Schick, Jr., in Theodore Schick, Jr., and Lewis Vaughn, *How to Think About Weird Things*, 4th ed., 2005.

2. Excerpted from Robert L. Park, "The Seven Warning Signs of Bogus Science," *Chronicle of Higher Education*, 31 January 2003, <http://chronicle.com/free/v49/i21/21b02001.htm>, September 15, 2008.

3. See Stephen Barrett et al., *Consumer Health*, 6th ed. (New York: WCB/McGraw-Hill, 1993), 239–40.

4. Thomas S. Kuhn, *The Copernican Revolution: Planetary Astronomy in the Development of Western Thought* (Cambridge, MA: Harvard University Press, 1957), 179.

5. Section 4a of Act 590 of the Acts of Arkansas of 1981, "Balanced Treatment for Creation-Science and Evolution-Science Act."

6. National Academy of Sciences, *Science and Creationism* (Washington, DC: National Academy Press, 1998).

7. *Ibid.*

8. George S. Bakken, "Creation or Evolution?" National Center for Science Education website, <www.ncseweb.org>.

9. Theodosius Dobzhansky, quoted in National Academy of Sciences, *Science and Creationism*, www.nap.edu/openbook.php?record_id=6024

10. National Academy of Sciences, "Preface," in *Science and Creationism*.

11. Kenneth Chang, "In Explaining Life's Complexity, Darwinists and Doubters Clash," *New York Times*, August 22, 2005.

12. Tom Byrne and Matthew Normand, "The Demon-Haunted Sentence," *Skeptical Inquirer*, March/April 2000.

13. Theodore Schick and Lewis Vaughn, *How to Think About Weird Things*, 3d ed. (San Francisco: McGraw-Hill, 2002), 190–91.

14. Stephen Barrett, "High Doses of Vitamin C Are Not Effective as a Cancer Treatment," <Quackwatch.com> (July 6, 2003).

15. Theodore Schick, Jr., in Theodore Schick, Jr., and Lewis Vaughn, *Doing Philosophy: An Introduction Through Thought Experiments* (New York: McGraw-Hill, 2010), 490, 492.

16. Hillary Mayell, "Crop Circles: Artworks or Alien Signs?" *National Geographic News*, August 2, 2002.

17. Matt Ridley, "Crop Circle Confession," *Scientific American*, August 2002.

18. Richard Wiseman, Matthew Smith, and Jeff Wiseman, "Eyewitness Testimony and the Paranormal," *Skeptical Inquirer*, November/December 1995.

19. Ray Hyman, "How Not to Test Mediums," *Skeptical Inquirer*, January/February 2003.

20. Robert T. Carroll, "Ouija Board," The Skeptic's Dictionary, <http://skepdic.com> (October 27, 2003).

21. Robert T. Carroll, "Bigfoot," The Skeptic's Dictionary, <http://skepdic.com> (October 27, 2003).

22. Joe Nickell, "Psychic Pets and Pet Psychics," *Skeptical Inquirer*, November/December 2002.

23. NOVA Online, "Hot Science, Alien Evidence?" <www.pbs.org/wgbh/alienactivity> (October 27, 2003).

24. Henry Roberts, *The Complete Prophesies of Nostradamus* (Great Neck, NY: Nostradamus, 1969), 18, as cited in Andrew Neher, *The Psychology of Transcendence* (Englewood Cliffs, NJ: Prentice-Hall, 1980), 188.

Chapter 11

1. "Ethics," Internet Encyclopedia of Philosophy, <www.utm.edu/research/iep>.

2. Katherine Zoepf, "A Dishonorable Affair," *New York Times*, 23 September 2007, <http://www.nytimes.com/2007/09/23/magazine/23wwln-syria-t.html?scp=15>, September 16, 2008.

3. Lawrence Blum, *"I'm Not a Racist But . . ." The Moral Quandary of Race* (Ithaca, NY: Cornell University Press, 2002), 1–2.

4. Blum, 8.

5. Blum, 9.

6. Immanuel Kant, *Groundwork of the Metaphysic of Morals*, trans. H. J. Paton (New York: Harper & Row, 1964), 88.

7. David Hopkins, "10 More Moral Dilemmas," *Listverse*, April 18, 2011, http://listverse.com/2011/04/18/10-more-moral-dilemmas/.

Appendix A

1. Federal Reserve Bank of New York, "The Labor Market for Recent College Graduates," January 11, 2017, https://www.newyorkfed.org/research/college-labor-market/college-labor-market_compare-majors.html.

2. T. Rees Shapiro, "For Philosophy Majors, the Question after Graduation Is: What Next?" *Washington Post*, June 20, 2017.

3. Carolyn Gregoire, "The Unexpected Way Philosophy Majors Are Changing the World of Business," *Huffpost*, March 5, 2014, https://www.huffingtonpost.com/2014/03/05/why-philosophy-majors-rule_n_4891404.html.

4. David Silbersweig, "A Harvard Medical School Professor Makes a Case for the Liberal Arts and Philosophy," *Washington Post*, December 24, 2015.

5. Shapiro, "For Philosophy Majors."

6. Shapiro.

7. American Philosophical Association, "Who Studies Philosophy?" (accessed November 14, 2017), http://www.apaonline.org/?whostudiesphilosophy.

8. PayScale, "Highest Paying Bachelor Degrees by Salary Potential," *2017–2018 College Salary Report*, https://www.payscale.com/college-salary-report/majors-that-pay-you-back/bachelors.

9. PayScale; reported by Rachel Gillett and Jacquelyn Smith, "People with These College Majors Get the Biggest Raises," *Business Insider*, January 6, 2016, http://www.businessinsider.com/college-majors-that-lead-to-the-biggest-pay-raises-2016-1/#20-physics-1.

Appendix E

1. Student paper reproduced by permission of Mitchell S. McKinney, University of Missouri, <http://www.missouri.edu/~commpjb/comm104/Sample_Papers/Free_ Speech/free_speech.html>.

ad hoc hypothesis: A hypothesis, or theory, that cannot be verified independently of the phenomenon it's supposed to explain. Ad hoc hypotheses always make a theory less simple—and therefore less credible.

ad hominem **(appeal to the person):** The fallacy of rejecting a claim by criticizing the person who makes it rather than the claim itself. *Ad hominem* means "to the man."

affirming the antecedent: *See modus ponens.*

affirming the consequent: An invalid argument form:

> If *p*, then *q*.
> *q*.
> Therefore, *p*.

analogical induction: *See* **argument by analogy.**

analogy: A comparison of two or more things alike in specific respects.

antecedent: The first part of a conditional statement (If *p*, then *q*.), the component that begins with the word *if*. *See* **conditional statement.**

appeal to authority: The fallacy of relying on the opinion of someone deemed to be an expert who in fact is *not* an expert.

appeal to common practice: The fallacy of accepting or rejecting a claim based solely on what groups of people generally do or how they behave (when the action or behavior is irrelevant to the truth of the claim).

appeal to emotion: The fallacy of using emotions in place of relevant reasons as premises in an argument.

appeal to ignorance: The fallacy of arguing that a lack of evidence proves something. In one type of this fallacy, the problem arises by thinking that a claim must be true because it hasn't been shown to be false. In another type, the breakdown in logic comes when you argue that a claim must be false because it hasn't been proved to be true.

appeal to pity: The attempt to persuade people to accept a conclusion by evoking their pity, compassion, or empathy.

appeal to popularity (or to the masses): The fallacy of arguing that a claim must be true merely because a substantial number of people believe it.

appeal to the person: *See ad hominem.*

appeal to tradition: The fallacy of arguing that a claim must be true just because it's part of a tradition.

apple polishing: The attempt to persuade people to accept a conclusion by flattering them.

argument: A group of statements in which some of them (the premises) are intended to support another of them (the conclusion).

argument by analogy (analogical induction): An argument making use of analogy, reasoning that because two or more things are similar in several respects, they must be similar in some further respect.

background information: The large collection of very well supported beliefs that we all rely on to inform our actions and choices. It consists of basic facts about everyday things, beliefs based on very good evidence (including our own personal observations and excellent authority), and justified claims that we would regard as "common sense" or "common knowledge."

begging the question: The fallacy of attempting to establish the conclusion of an argument by using that conclusion as a premise. Also called arguing in a circle.

biased sample: A sample that does not properly represent the target group. *See* **representative sample.**

burden of proof: The weight of evidence or argument required by one side in a debate or disagreement.

categorical logic: A form of logic whose focus is categorical statements, which make assertions about categories, or classes, of things.

categorical statement: A statement, or claim, that makes a simple assertion about categories, or classes, of things.

causal argument: An inductive argument whose conclusion contains a causal claim.

causal claim: A statement about the causes of things.

claim: A statement; an assertion that something is or is not the case.

cogent argument: A strong inductive argument with all true premises.

composition: The fallacy of arguing that what is true of the parts must be true of the whole. The error is thinking that the characteristics of the parts are somehow transferred to the whole, something that is not always the case.

compound statement: A statement composed of at least two constituent, or simple, statements.

conclusion: In an argument, the statement that the premises are intended to support.

conditional statement: An "if-then" statement; it consists of the antecedent (the part introduced by the word *if*) and the consequent (the part introduced by the word *then*).

confidence level: In statistical theory, the probability that the sample will accurately represent the target group within the margin of error.

conjunct: One of two simple statements joined by a connective to form a compound statement.

conjunction: Two simple statements joined by a connective to form a compound statement.

consequent: The part of a conditional statement (If p, then q) introduced by the word *then*.

conservatism: A criterion of adequacy for judging the worth of theories. A conservative theory is one that fits with our established beliefs.

copula: One of four components of a standard-form categorical statement; a linking verb—either "are" or "are not"—that joins the subject term and the predicate term.

criteria of adequacy: The standards used to judge the worth of explanatory theories. They include *testability, fruitfulness, scope, simplicity,* and *conservatism.*

critical thinking: The systematic evaluation or formulation of beliefs, or statements, by rational standards.

decision-point fallacy: Arguing that because a line or distinction cannot be draw at any point in a process, there are no differences or gradations in that process.

deductive argument: An argument intended to provide logically conclusive support for its conclusion.

denying the antecedent: An invalid argument form:

> If p, then q.
> Not p.
> Therefore, not q.

denying the consequent: *See* **modus tollens.**

dependent premise: A premise that depends on at least one other premise to provide joint support to a conclusion. If a dependent premise is removed, the support that its linked dependent premises supply to the conclusion is undermined or completely canceled out.

disjunct: A simple statement that is a component of a disjunction.

disjunction: A compound statement of the form "Either p or q." A disjunction is true even if only one disjunct is true, and false only if both disjuncts are false.

disjunctive syllogism: A valid argument form:

> Either p or q.
> Not p.
> Therefore, q.

In the syllogism's second premise, either disjunct can be denied.

division: The fallacy of arguing that what is true of the whole must be true of the parts. The error is thinking that characteristics of the whole must transfer to the parts or that traits of the group must be the same as traits of individuals in the group.

dysphemism: Words used to convey negative attitudes or emotions in place of neutral or positive ones.

enumerative induction: An inductive argument pattern in which we reason from premises about individual members of a group to conclusions about the group as a whole.

equivocation: The fallacy of using a word in two different senses in an argument.

euphemism: Words used to convey positive or neutral attitudes or emotions in place of more negative ones.

expert: Someone who is more knowledgeable in a particular subject area or field than most others are.

explanation: A statement or statements intended to tell why or how something is the case.

fallacy: An argument form that is both common and defective; a recurring mistake in reasoning.

false dilemma: The fallacy of asserting that there are only two alternatives to consider when there are actually more than two.

faulty analogy: A defective argument by analogy.

fruitfulness: A criterion of adequacy for judging the worth of theories. A fruitful theory is one that makes novel predictions.

gambler's fallacy: The error of thinking that previous events can affect the probabilities in the random event at hand.

genetic fallacy: The fallacy of arguing that a claim is true or false solely because of its abstract or nonhuman origins.

hasty generalization: The fallacy of drawing a conclusion about a target group based on an inadequate sample size.

hypothetical syllogism: A valid argument made up of three hypothetical, or conditional, statements:

If p then q.
If q, then r.
Therefore, if p, then r.

independent premise: A premise that does not depend on other premises to provide support to a conclusion. If an independent premise is removed, the support that other premises supply to the conclusion is not affected.

indicator words: Words that frequently accompany arguments and signal that a premise or conclusion is present.

inductive argument: An argument in which the premises are intended to provide probable, not conclusive, support for its conclusion.

inference: The process of reasoning from a premise or premises to a conclusion based on those premises.

inference to the best explanation: A form of inductive reasoning in which we reason from premises about a state of affairs to an explanation for that state of affairs:

Phenomenon Q.

E *provides the best explanation for* Q.

Therefore, it is probable that E *is true.*

innuendo: Suggesting something denigrating about a person without explicitly stating it.

invalid argument: A deductive argument that fails to provide conclusive support for its conclusion.

logic: The study of good reasoning, or inference, and the rules that govern it.

margin of error: The variation between the values derived from a sample and the true values of the whole target group.

modus ponens (affirming the antecedent): A valid argument form:

If p, then q.
p.
Therefore, q.

modus tollens (denying the consequent): A valid argument form:

If p, then q.
Not q.
Therefore, not p.

moral statement: A statement asserting that an action is right or wrong (moral or immoral) or that something (such as a person or motive) is good or bad.

necessary condition: A condition for the occurrence of an event without which the event cannot occur.

peer pressure: Group pressure to accept or reject a claim based solely on what one's peers think or do.

philosophical skepticism: The view that we know much less than we think we do or nothing at all.

philosophical skeptics: Those who embrace philosophical skepticism.

post hoc, ergo propter hoc (**"after that, therefore because of that"**): The fallacy of reasoning that just because B followed A, A must have caused B.

predicate term: The second class, or group, named in a standard-form categorical statement.

premise: In an argument, a statement, or reason, given in support of the conclusion.

property in question: *See* **relevant property.**

propositional logic: The branch of deductive reasoning that deals with the logical relationships among statements.

quality: A characteristic of a categorical statement, based on whether the statement affirms or denies that a class is entirely or partly included in another class. A categorical statement that affirms is said to be affirmative in quality; one that denies is said to be negative in quality.

quantifier: In categorical statements, a word used to indicate the number of things with specified characteristics. The acceptable quantifiers are "all," "no," or "some." The quantifiers "all" and "no" in front of a categorical statement tell us that it's *universal*—it applies to every member of a class. The quantifier "some" at the beginning of a categorical statement says that the statement is *particular*—it applies to some but not all members of a class.

quantity: In categorical statements, the attribute of number, specified by the words "all," "no," or "some."

random sample: A sample that is selected randomly from a target group in such a way as to ensure that the sample is representative. In a simple random selection, every member of the target group has an equal chance of being selected for the sample.

red herring: The fallacy of deliberately raising an irrelevant issue during an argument. The basic pattern is to put forth a claim and then couple it with additional claims that may seem to support it but in fact are mere distractions.

relevant property (property in question): In enumerative induction, a property, or characteristic, that is of interest in the target group.

representative sample: In enumerative induction, a sample that resembles the target group in all relevant ways. *See* **biased sample**.

rhetoric: The use of non-argumentative, emotive words and phrases to persuade or influence an audience.

rhetorical definitions: Influencing someone through an emotion-charged skewed definition.

ridicule: The use of derision, sarcasm, laughter, or mockery to disparage a person or idea

sample (sample member): In enumerative induction, the observed members of the target group.

scare tactics: The attempt to persuade people to accept a conclusion by engendering in them an unwarranted fear.

scope: A criterion of adequacy for judging the worth of theories. A theory with scope is one that explains or predicts phenomena other than that which it was introduced to explain.

simple statement: A statement that doesn't contain any other statements as constituents. *See* **compound statement.**

simplicity: A criterion of adequacy for judging the worth of theories. A simple theory is one that makes minimal assumptions.

singular statements: In categorical logic, statements that assert something about a single person or thing, including objects, places, and times.

slippery slope: The fallacy of arguing, without good reasons, that taking a particular step will inevitably lead to further, undesirable steps.

social relativism: The view that truth is relative to societies.

sound argument: A deductively valid argument that has true premises.

square of opposition: Standard-form statements with the same subject and predicate but different quantity or quality have truth values that are predictably correlated. This relationship is formalized and illustrated in the square of opposition.

standard-form categorical statement: In categorical logic, a categorical statement that takes one of these four forms:

1. All *S* are *P*. (All cats are carnivores.)
2. No *S* are *P*. (No cats are carnivores.)
3. Some *S* are *P*. (Some cats are carnivores.)
4. Some *S* are not *P*. (Some cats are not carnivores.)

statement (claim): An assertion that something is or is not the case.

stereotyping: Drawing an unwarranted conclusion or generalization about an entire group of people.

straw man: The fallacy of distorting, weakening, or oversimplifying someone's position so it can be more easily attacked or refuted.

strong argument: An inductive argument that succeeds in providing probable—but not conclusive—support for its conclusion.

subjective relativism: The idea that truth depends on what someone believes.

subjectivist fallacy: Accepting the notion of subjective relativism or using it to try to support a claim.

subject term: The first class, or group, named in a standard-form categorical statement.

sufficient condition: A condition for the occurrence of an event that guarantees that the event occurs.

syllogism: A deductive argument made up of three statements—two premises and a conclusion. *See modus ponens* and *modus tollens.*

symbolic logic: Modern deductive logic that uses symbolic language to do its work.

target group (target population): In enumerative induction, the whole collection of individuals under study.

testability: A criterion of adequacy for judging the worth of theories. A testable theory is one in which there is some way to determine whether the theory is true or false—that is, it predicts something other than what it was introduced to explain.

TEST formula: A four-step procedure for evaluating the worth of a theory:

> Step 1. State the **T**heory and check for consistency.

Step 2. Assess the **E**vidence for the theory.
Step 3. **S**crutinize alternative theories.
Step 4. **T**est the theories with the criteria of adequacy.

theoretical explanation: A theory, or hypothesis, that tries to explain why something is the way it is, why something is the case, or why something happened.

truth-preserving: A characteristic of a valid deductive argument in which the logical structure guarantees the truth of the conclusion if the premises are true.

truth table: A table that specifies the truth values for claim variables and combinations of claim variables in symbolized statements or arguments.

tu quoque **("you're another"):** A type of *ad hominem* fallacy that argues that a claim must be true (or false) just because the claimant is hypocritical.

two wrongs make a right: Arguing that your doing something morally wrong is justified because someone else has done the same (or similar) thing.

valid argument: A deductive argument that succeeds in providing conclusive support for its conclusion.

variables: In modern logic, the symbols, or letters, used to express a statement.

Venn diagrams: Diagrams consisting of overlapping circles that graphically represent the relationships between subject and predicate terms in categorical statements.

weak argument: An inductive argument that fails to provide strong support for its conclusion.

worldview: A philosophy of life; a set of beliefs and theories that helps us make sense of a wide range of issues in life.

CREDITS

Photos

Essays

1. "Death Penalty Discriminates Against Black Crime Victims," from *USA Today*, a division of Gannett Co., Inc. Reprinted with Permission.
2. "Marine Parks," from ESL Planet by Bill Daly. Copyright © 2003 by Bill Daly. Reprinted by permission of the author.
3. "A Feminist Defense of Pornography." Wendy McElroy, from *Free Inquiry*, Fall 1997, 14–17.
4. "Why Shouldn't Tommy and Jim Have Sex?" John Corvino, originally *in Same Sex: Debating the Ethics, Science, and Culture of Homosexuality*, ed. John Corvino (Lanham, MD: Rowman & Littlefield, 1999), 3–16.
5. "More Innocents Die When We Don't Have Capital Punishment." By permission of Dennis Prager and Creators Syndicate, Inc.
6. "What's Wrong with Adultery?" *QQ: Report from the Center for Philosophy and Public Policy, 6:1* (Winter, 1986). Used by permission of Bonnie Steinbock.
7. "A Pat Down is Better Than a Blow-Up" by Caroline Baum, *Buffalo News*, December 5, 2010.
8. "The Cohabitation Epidemic," from *Focus on the Family*, © 2003, Neil Clark Warren. Reprinted with permission of the author.
9. "Not Being Vaccinated Is Not Acceptable" by David Ropeik, from *Buffalo News*, July 24, 2011.
10. "In Afghanistan, a Woman's Place Is at the Peace Table," LA Times, January 13, 2011, adapted from a longer essay "Can Women Make Peace?" by Ann Jones, TomDispatch.com, January 13, 2011.
11. "A Deviance from God's Norm." This article appeared originally on www.beliefnet.com, the leading website for faith, spirituality, inspiration & more. Used with permission. All rights reserved.
12. "Marriage Still Evolving as Ever." Reprinted with permission of the Buffalo News.
13. "Slouching Toward Chimeras." This article appeared originally on www.beliefnet.com, the leading website for faith, spirituality, inspiration & more. Used with permission. All rights reserved.
14. "It's Time to Fight Islamic Extremists Who Use Threats to Stifle Free Speech" by Ayaan Hirsi Ali and Daniel Huff, Los Angeles Times, September 27, 2010.
15. "Is Sluttishness a Feminist Statement?" *Free Inquiry*, August/September 2011, 13, 41. © Wendy Kaminer
16. "Torture: Time for Congress to End the Debate," from *USA Today*, March 27, 2011 © 2011 Gannett. All rights reserved. Used by permission and protected by the Copyright Laws of the United States. The printing, copying, redistribution, or retransmission of this Content without express written permission is prohibited.
17. "Torture: Severe Interrogations Work" from *USA Today*, March 27, 2011 © 2011 Gannett. All rights reserved. Used by permission and protected by the Copyright Laws of the United States. The printing, copying, redistribution, or retransmission of this Content without express written permission is prohibited.
18. "Freedom of Expression: Protect Student Speech—Even 'Unwise' Bong Banner" from *USA Today*, March 20, 2007 © 2007 Gannett. All rights reserved. Used by permission and protected by the Copyright Laws of the United States. The printing, copying, redistribution, or retransmission of this Content without express written permission is prohibited.
19. "Freedom of Expression: Policy Reflects Common Sense" from USA Today, March 20, 2007 © 2007 Gannett. All rights reserved. Used by permission and protected by the Copyright Laws of the United States. The printing, copying, redistribution, or retransmission of this Content without express written permission is prohibited.
20. "Bachman Irresponsible to Spread Fear of Vaccine" from USA Today, September 18, 2011 © 2011 Gannett. All rights reserved. Used by permission and protected by the Copyright Laws of the United States. The printing, copying, redistribution, or retransmission of this Content without express written permission is prohibited.
21. "Flag Amendment: Flag Needs Protection" from USA Today, a division of Gannett Co, Inc. Reprinted with permission.

INDEX

A

Adams, Douglas, 439
Adams, Evelyn Marie, 294
ad hoc hypothesis, 339
ad hominem (to the man). *See* appeal to
    the person
adultery, 480–84
advertising
    appeals to emotion in, 139
    appeal to authority in, 139
    appeal to popularity in, 139
    fallacies in, 139
    faulty analogy in, 139
    hasty generalizations in, 139
    identification in, 140
    misleading comparisons in, 140–41
    persuasion and, 138–41, 143
    purpose of, 138–39
    slogans in, 140
    weasel words in, 141
affirming the antecedent (*modus ponens*)
    defined, 79–80, 102
    proof and, 216
    symbolized, 80–82, 202
affirming the consequent
    defined, 81
    hypothesis testing and, 369
    symbolized, 82, 202
Afghanistan, peace process of, 490–92
Aguilera, Christina, 120
air travel, danger of, 348–50
aliens
    crop circles and, 393–95
    possibility of, *392*
almighty self. *See* self-interested
    thinking
alternative explanations, 346–47

alternative medicine, 351–52
alternative news sources, 135
alternative scientific theories, 346–47
ambiguity, 553–54
analogical induction
    causal arguments and, 286
    criteria for judging, 75, 282
    defined, 277–78
    degrees of probability and, 278–79
    in law, 75
    in moral reasoning, 279
    number of instances compared in,
      281
    patterns, 282, 318
    relevant dissimilarities in, 281
    relevant similarities in, 280–81
    summary of, 305
analogy
    arguments by, 277–80
    defined, 173, 277
    faulty, 139, 171, 173–74
    reasoning by, 75, 439, 442
Anaximander, 376
annotations, for proof, 216
antecedent
    affirming, 79–82, 102, 202, 216
    of conditional, 79, 197
    defined, 79
    denying, 81–82, 202
appeal to authority, 116, 165
    in advertising, 139
    by public figures, 117, 119–20
appeal to common practice, 39
appeal to emotion
    in advertising, 139
    irrelevant premises and, 161–63, 165
    in persuasion, 60, 161–63

appeal to ignorance, 122, 158–61, 165
appeal to pity, 163
appeal to popularity (or to the
    masses), 39, 139, 157, 165
appeal to the person (*ad hominem*),
    152–53, 155–56, 165
appeal to tradition, 158, 165
apple polishing, 163
argumentative essays
    ambiguity in, 553–54
    arguments in, 544–45
    assessment of objections in, 545
    audience identification for, 546
    clarity in, 552–54
    conclusion of, 543–47, 551–52
    content of, 551–53
    definitions in, 553–54
    final draft of, 546
    first draft of, 545, 549–51
    introduction of, 543–44
    issues in, 546
    outline of, 545, 549–51
    sample, 554–58
    structure of, 543–45
    style of, 551–53
    thesis statement of, 543–45
    vague terms in, 553–54
    writing guidelines for, 545–46
arguments. *See also* conclusions;
    premises; tricky arguments;
    specific arguments
    appeal to emotion in, 161–63
    in argumentative essays, 544–45
    conclusions in, 13, 15, 19
    in critical thinking, 10–15
    defined, 10, 316
    diagramming, 86–91, 95, 102

domino theory, 171
evaluation of, 59, 65, 70, 73, 75, 82–83, 95, 101
for existence of God, 166–67
explanations confused with, 13, 17–18
goals of, 151
identification of, 11, 16–17, 19
indicator words in, 13, 15, 19
inductive inferences and, 438–39
invalid, 59–61
lack of development of, 12
legal, 438–39
long, assessing, 95–98
missing parts of, 73–79, 101
moral, 418–23, 441–42
about necessary conditions, 63, 298–300
non-arguments distinguished from, 11, 17
patterns of, 79–83, 102
persuasion and, 60
persuasive writing and, 96
premises in, 13, 15
purpose of, 151
in real world, 16–18
as reasons, 10–15
simple, 201–5
sound, 62
statements in, 19
statistical, 154
straw man, 14–15, 163–65, 175
structure of, 10–11, 59
about sufficient conditions, 63, 298–300
truth-preserving, 59–61
arguments by analogy, 277–80. See also analogical induction
Aristotle, 190, 214, 227, 228, 374
Asimov, Isaac, 372
A-statement, 235, 239, 241, 246, 250–53
audience, writing to, 546, 551
authors, assessment of, 134
autism, 488–90, 505–6
autonomy, principle of, 421
availability error, 132–34
awareness, in critical thinking, 31
Ayer, A. J., 13

B

background information, claims conflicting with, 113–14
Bacon, Francis, 32, 32
Bair, Sheila, 452, 452–53
begging the question, 166–67, 171

Behe, Michael J., 381–83
belief
    without evidence, 36–37
    evidence for, 120
    fooling ourselves and, 128–34, 142
    good reasons for, 4
    morality and, 36
    personal experience and, 5, 121, 127
    as statement, 9, 19
    truth of, 43, 110
    in weird theories, 333–34
    as worth believing, 4
beneficence, principle of, 424
benevolence, principle of, 421
Bentham, Jeremy, 430, 432
Bergamín, José, 115
Beveridge, William Henry, 16
bias
    checking, 136
    confirmation, 130–32, 136
    of experts, 118, 122
    group pressure leading to, 40–42
    left-wing, 41–42
    media, 41–42, 67
    in news, 41–42
    of public figures, 67–68
    right-wing, 41–42
biased sample, 265–66, 272
biconditional, 217
Biden, Joe, 131
Bierce, Ambrose, 69
Bigfoot, 364
Blackmore, Susan, 290, 290–91
bloggers, assessment of, 134
bogus science, 364–65
Bohr, Niels, 117
Boston Tribune, 136
Bower, Doug, 396–98
Brecht, Bertolt, 363
Breyer, Stephen, 453
Brezhnev, Leonid Ilich, 317
Bronowski, Jacob, 366
The Buddha, 39
burden of proof, 160–61
Bush, George W., 120, 131
Butterfield, Stewart, 452, 452

C

Camus, Albert, 167
capital punishment, 130, 479–80
careers, for philosophy majors, 451–54
Carlson, Tucker, 172
Carroll, Robert T., 159–60
categorical equivalence, 252–53, 256
categorical logic
    categorical statements in, 227

categorical syllogisms, 231–32, 243–48, 255
    defined, 227
    diagrammed, 231–32, 238–48, 250, 255
    equivalence, 252–53, 256
    evaluation of, 243–48
    propositional logic and, 227
    websites, 231–32
categorical statements. See also standard-form categorical statements
    in categorical logic, 227
    classes of, 227–29, 255
    defined, 227
    diagrammed, 231–32, 238–48, 250, 255
    square of opposition, 250–52, 250f, 255
    summary of, 255
categorical syllogisms, 231–32, 243–48, 255
category 1 obstacles. See psychological obstacles
category 2 obstacles. See philosophical obstacles
causal arguments
    analogical induction and, 286
    both agreement and difference, 288–89
    correlation and, 289–90
    defined, 285–86
    ESP and, 290–91
    necessary conditions in, 298–300
    sufficient conditions in, 298–300
    summary of, 306
    testing for causes and, 287
causal claim, 285
causal confusions, 292–98
causal explanations, 317
cause
    effect confused with, 296–98
    temporal order confused with, 295–96
cereologists, 395–96
Chapman, Mark David, 112
chimeras, 495–97
Chinese Proverb, 66
Chorley, Dave, 396–98
Christmas, Levinia, 293–94
Christmas, Lorraine, 293–94
church-state debates, 164–65
Circlemakers, 394
claims. See also statements
    background information
        conflicting with, 113–14

claims (*continued*)
  causal, 285
  credibility of, 134
  critical thinking and, 9–10
  evaluating, 132
  evidence conflicting with, 115, 120
  inconsistency of, 155
  of media sources, 137
  negative, 161
  in news, 112, 134–37, 143
  other claims conflicting with,
    110–15, 120, 142
  unsupported, 110–13, 115–16,
    118–19
clarity, in argumentative essays,
  552–54
Clifford, W. K., 36
Clinton, Hillary, 14, *14*
cogent inductive arguments, 64
cohabitation, 486–88
coherent worldview
  internal consistency for, 440
  morality and, 418, 439–42
coincidence
  Lincoln–Kennedy, 293–94
  misjudged, 126
  misled by, 292–95
Colbert, Stephen, *453*
cold reading, 402–4
commands, 9
common practice, appeal to, 39
common sense, 388, 504–5
comparisons, misleading, 140–41
composition, 153–54, 165
compound statement, 79, 192, 217
conclusions
  in argumentative essays, 543–47,
    551–52
  in arguments, 13, 15, 19
  defined, 10, 16, 316
  diagramming, 246
  false, 83
  identifying, 16
  indicator words in, 13, 19
  overstated, 551–52
  as questions, 15
conditional
  antecedent of, 79, 197
  consequent of, 197–98
  premises, 79
  in propositional logic, 191*t*, 197–99
  symbolized, 197
  in truth table, 197
  words used in, 198
confidence level, 271–72
confirmation bias, 130–32, 136

confirming evidence, 130–32
conflicting claims, 110–15, 120, 142
conformism, 31, 38–39
conjunct, 192
conjunction
  defined, 192, 220
  in propositional logic, 191*t*, 192–94
  in simple argument, 201–2
  in simple statement, 192
  symbolized, 192
  in truth table, 193
connectives
  propositional logic and, 191–99
  statements and, 192, 198
  summary of, 220
  in symbolic logic, 191–92
  truth values and, 191–99
consequent
  affirming, 81–82, 202, 369
  of conditional, 197–98
  defined, 79
  denying, 80–82, 102, 202
conservatism
  criteria of adequacy and, 343
  in evaluation of scientific theories,
    374
  in evaluation of weird theories,
    339–40
  inference to the best explanation
    and, 339–44
  of theories, 331, 339–44
considered moral judgments, 424, 428
consistency
  external, 328
  internal, 328, 440
  theories and, 327–28, 345–46, 356
conspiracy theories, 338, 341–42
constructive memories, 122–23, 127
constructive perception, 122–24, 127,
  335–36
content, of argumentative essays,
  551–53
contradictions, 251, 328
contraposition, as type of equivalence,
  253, 256
contraries, 250
contrary evidence, resisting, 128–30
conversion, as type of equivalence,
  252, 256
Cooley, Mason, 242
Copernicus, Nicolaus, *373*, 373–75
copula, 228
correlation, causal arguments and,
  289–90
counterexample method, 82–83, 102
crazy theories. *See* weird theories

creationism, 168, 375–83
creativity, critical thinking and, 7–8, 19
credible premises, 76–77
Crisp, Quentin, 158
criteria of adequacy. *See also*
    conservatism; fruitfulness;
    scope; simplicity; testability
  alternative explanations and, 347
  application of, 330
  conservatism and, 343
  defined, 329–30
  inference to the best explanation
    and, 330
  for moral theories, 426–30, 442
  scientific theories and, 372–73, 411
  theories and, 329–30, 356
  weird theories and, 333–34
critical, as negative term, 7
critical thinking
  arguments in, 10–15
  awareness in, 31
  Bacon on, 32
  claims and, 9–10
  creativity and, 7–8, 19
  defined, 4
  environment, 46
  evaluation in, 4–6, 18–19
  exploring skills through, 5, 8
  formulation in, 4, 18–19
  freedom as result of, 5, 19
  importance of, 5–8, 19
  as independent thinking, 43
  lack of, 8, 19
  law and, 74–75
  learning skills through, 5, 8
  logic and, 4
  motivation for, 31
  objectivity and, 31, 47
  philosophical obstacles to, 43–47
  practice of, 31
  processes of, 8–19
  psychological obstacles to, 31–43, 47
  rational standards in, 4, 18
  reasons in, 9–15
  role of, 4, 8
  systematic, 4, 8, 18–19
  as thinking outside of the box, 7–8
crop circles, 392–401, *393*, *394*
crop-circle vortex theory, 395

D

The Daily Show, 67, *67*
Darrow, Clarence, 88
Darwin, Charles, 322, *322*, 376, 380
Davis, Angela, *453*
Dawkins, Richard, 374

death, survival after, 401–5, 441
death penalty, 130, 458–59, 479–80
decision-point fallacy, 169–71
deductive arguments. *See also*
    categorical logic; propositional
    logic
    defined, 59, 64–65, 101, 316
    indicator words, 66, 68
    inductive arguments and, 64
    invalid, 59–61
    in law, 75, 438
    manipulated, 64
    valid, 59–63, 101, 190–91
deductive logic, 261
definitions
    in argumentative essays, 553–54
    in critical thinking, 4–6, 18–19
    lexical, 176
    precising, 176
    rhetorical, 176
    stipulative, 176
Del Ray, Lana, *453*
Democritus, 285
denying the antecedent, 81–82, 202
denying the consequent (*modus tollens*)
    defined, 80, 102
    symbolized, 80–82, 202
dependent premises, 87–88, 99
Descartes, René, 71
descriptive statements, 419–21
diagramming. *See also* Venn diagrams
    arguments, 86–91, 95, 102
    categorical logic, 231–32, 238–48,
        250, 255
    conclusions, 246
    premises, 246
Diaz, Cameron, 120
Dingwall, Eric, 399
Diogenes, 162
discrimination
    death penalty and, 458–59
    by racial profiling, 97
disjunct, 194
disjunction
    defined, 194, 220
    in propositional logic, 191*t*,
        194–96, 198
    symbolized, 194
    in truth table, 194–95
disjunctive syllogism
    basics of, 82–83
    defined, 82
    symbolized, 83, 202
    truth tables and, 195–96
Disraeli, Benjamin, 34
diversity among cases, 281–82

divine command theory, 426, 428
division, fallacy of, 154–55, 165
Dobzhansky, Theodosius, 380
doctors, as experts, 116
domino theory argument, 171
Doolittle, Russell F., 382
dose-response relationship, 289
double-blind experiment, 372
doubt
    toward experts, 118–19
    of personal experience, 121
    reasonable, 46–47
dowsing, 343, *343*
Doyle, Arthur Conan (Sir), 129
dysphemisms, 174–75

E
Eddington, Arthur, 334, 370
Edward, John, 401, *401*
effect, cause confused with, 296–98
egalitarianism, 45
egocentrism, 34, 47
Einstein, Albert, 329, 334–35, 367, 370,
    394
Emerson, Ralph Waldo, 298
emotions
    appeal to, as persuasive tactic, 60,
        161–63, 165
    strong, 35–36
emotivism, 419
enumerative induction
    defined, 261–62
    hasty generalizations and, 262,
        264, 272
    in opinion polls, 266–73
    pattern, 262, 318
    property in question in, 262
    relevant property in, 262–63, 272
    representativeness, 265–66
    sample in, 262–63, 272
    summary of, 272, 305
    target population in, 262, 272
Epicurus, 93
equivocation fallacy, 156–57, 165
error
    availability, 132–34
    Bacon on, 32
    defense against, 6
    hasty generalization, 133–34
    margin of, 271–72
    in weird theories, 347, 390
Erwin, Douglas H., 381
ESP. *See* extrasensory perception
essays. *See* argumentative essays
E-statement, 235, 239, 241, 246, 250–53
ethical egoism, 427–28

ethics. *See* Kantian ethics
ethnocentrism, 40, 42
euphemisms, 174–75
evaluation
    of arguments, 59, 65, 70, 73, 75,
        82–83, 95, 101
    of categorical logic, 243–48
    of claims, 132
    in critical thinking definition, 4–6,
        18–19
    of moral theories, 426–30
    of scientific theories, 374, 411
    short method for, 208–10, 220
    of sources, 134–35, 143
    streamlined, 208–11
    of theories, 330, 344, 348
    of validity, 208–11
    of weird theories, 339–40, 350,
        390–405
evidence
    available, preference for, 132–34
    for belief, 120
    belief without, 36–37
    claims conflicting with, 115, 120
    confirming, looking for, 130–32
    contrary, resisting, 128–30
    denial of, 129–30
    experts and, 115–20, 142
    fooling ourselves with, 128–34, 142
    lack of, 36, 158
    Russell on, 115
    in scientific research, 130
    self-interested thinking and, 34
evolution, 168, 375–83
expectation, personal experience
        influenced by, 124–27
experience. *See* personal experience
experts. *See also* nonexperts
    biased, 118, 122
    defined, 115
    disagreement among, 115–16
    doctors as, 116
    evidence and, 115–20, 142
    knowledge of, 157
    prerequisites for, 117
    reasons to doubt, 118–19
    unsupported claims supported by,
        116, 118–19
expert testimony, 438–39
explanandum, 320
explanans, 320
explanations
    alternative, 346–47
    arguments confused with, 13, 17–18
    causal, 317
    defined, 13, 16

explanations (*continued*)
  for Hurricanes Katrina and
      Harvey, 336–37
  inference to the best explanation
      and, 317–19, 321, 323, 330, 356
  interpretive, 320
  lore of, 320
  procedural, 320
  in science, 321
  teleological, 320
  theoretical, 317, 319, 363
explicit premises, 97
exploring skills, 5, 8
external consistency, 328
external world, 330
extraneous statements, 86–90
extraordinary theories. *See* weird
      theories
extrasensory perception (ESP), 37,
      129, 290–91
"eye for an eye" principle, 166
eyewitnesses
  to paranormal phenomena, 399–400
  unreliable, 125

F

FactCheck.org, 135–36
facts. *See also* PolitiFact.com
  fabricated by selves, 35
  opinions distinguished from, 113
  statements and, 113
Fairy Tale: A True Story, 129, *129*
fake news, 135–38, 143
fallacy. *See also* irrelevant premises,
      fallacies with; unacceptable
      premises, fallacies with
  in advertising, 139
  appeal to authority, 116–17, 119–20,
      139, 165
  appeal to emotion, 60, 161–63, 165
  appeal to ignorance, 122, 158–61, 165
  appeal to pity, 163
  appeal to popularity, 39, 157, 165
  appeal to the person, 152–53,
      155–56, 165
  appeal to tradition, 158, 165
  apple polishing, 163
  begging the question, 166–67, 171
  of composition, 153–54, 165
  cost of, 153
  decision-point, 169–71
  defined, 151–52
  of division, 154–55, 165
  equivocation, 156–57, 165
  false dilemma, 167–69, 171
  faulty analogies, 139, 171, 173–74

gambler's, 126–27
genetic, 152–53, 165
hasty generalizations, 133–34,
      171, 173
post hoc, ergo propter hoc, 295–97
red herring, 163, 165
rhetoric and, 152
with scare tactics, 163
slippery slope, 170–71, 173
of straw man, 14–15, 163–65, 175
subjectivist, 44
two wrongs make a right, 165–66
false conclusions, 83
false dilemma, 167–69, 171
famous people, 117, 119–20, 453–54
faulty analogy, 139, 171, 173–74
feminism, 461–66, 499–500
Feynman, Richard, 127, 397
final draft, writing guidelines for, 546
Fiorina, Carly, 452, *452*
first draft, of argumentative essay,
      545, 549–51
flag amendment, 507
fooling ourselves, 128–34, 142
formulation, in critical thinking, 4, 18–19
fossil record, *379*, 379–80
Fox, Megan, 120
Fox News, 41
freedom, 5, 19, 440
free speech, 497–99, 503–5
fruitfulness, 331–35

G

Galbraith, John Kenneth, 213
Galileo, 375
gambler's fallacy, 126–27
Garrett, Brandon L., 125
genetic fallacy, 152–53, 165
geocentric theory of planetary
      motion, 373
Gilovich, Thomas, 130
Giuliani, Rudy, 14, *14*, 172
Gladstone, William E., 234
goals, of arguments, 151
God
  arguments, for existence of, 166–67
  theories about, 131, 339, 428,
      440–41, 493–94
Goldman, Emma, 71
Goleman, Daniel, 268
Gould, Stephen Jay, 375
Greer, Germaine, 93
greetings, 9
group pressure
  avoiding, 41
  bias and, 40–42

prejudice and, 40, 42
  as psychological obstacle, 38–43, 47
  racism and, 40
group thinking, 42
gut feeling, 131

H

Hagee, John, 336–37, *337*
Hahnemann, Samuel, 351
Hannity, Sean, *41*
harm, principle of, 421
hasty generalizations
  in advertising, 139
  enumerative induction and, 262,
      264, 272
  errors and, 133–34
  sample and, 133, 264
  unacceptable premises and,
      133–34, 171, 173
Hayes, Chris, *454*
Hayes, Judith, 378
headlines, reading beyond, 136
Heisenberg, Werner, 117
heliocentric theory of planetary
      motion, 375
Herberman, Ronald B., 159–60
Hines, Terence, 124
Hitler, Adolf, *60*, 155
Holmes, Sherlock, 129
homeopathy, theories of, 351–52
homosexuality, 466–76, 493–94
honesty, principle of, 421
honor killings, *430*, 430–31, *431*
Horowitz, Damon, *453*
Hubbard, Elbert, 4
human freedom. *See* freedom
Hume, David, 11, 283, 285
Hurricane Harvey, 336–37
Hurricane Katrina, 336–37
Huxley, Aldous, 267
Huxley, Thomas H., 36, 243, 351
Hyman, Ray, 402–3
hypnagogic imagery, 35
hypotheses
  ad hoc, 339
  in scientific method, 366–70
  testing of, 367–69
hypothetical syllogism, 80–81, 202

I

ID. *See* intelligent design
identification, in advertising, 140
ideology, science contrasted with, 363,
      365, 411
Idols of the Cave, 32

Idols of the Marketplace, 32
idols of the mind, 32
Idols of the Theater, 32
Idols of the Tribe, 32
ignorance, appeals to, 122, 158–61, 165
Iles, George, 321
impairment, 121–24
implicit premises
    finding, 76–77
    moral, 422
    in weak inductive arguments,
        75–76
impossibility, 391–92
independence, of critical thinking, 43
independent premises, 87–88
indicator words
    in arguments, 13, 15
    in conclusion, 13, 19
    of deductive arguments, 66, 68
    defined, 13, 16, 19, 316
    in extraneous statements, 88–89
    of inductive arguments, 66, 68
    in premises, 13, 19
inductive arguments. See also
    analogical induction; causal
    arguments; enumerative
    induction; inference to the best
    explanation; strong inductive
    argument; weak inductive
    argument
    cogent, 64
    deductive arguments and, 64
    defined, 59, 64–65, 101, 316
    indicator words, 66, 68
    inferences and, 438–39
    inference to the best explanation
        as, 286–87, 317
    in law, 75
    manipulated, 64
    in science, 160
    summary of, 316
    truth not preserved by, 61–62
    valid, 59–63, 101
inference, 11
    in law, 438–39
    rules of, 215–17, 221
inference to the best explanation
    conservatism and, 339–44
    criteria of adequacy and, 330
    defined, 317–18
    explanations and, 317–19, 321, 323,
        330, 356
    external world and, 330
    fruitfulness and, 331–35
    as inductive reasoning, 286–87, 317
    pattern of, 318–19

    in science, 321
    scope and, 335–37
    Sherlock Holmes and, 323
    simplicity and, 331, 338–39, 374–75
    theories and, 322–23, 330
    weird theories and, 411
Information Age, 111
injustice, 125
innuendo, 174
innumeracy, 126–28
insults, 155
intelligent design (ID), 380–83
internal consistency, 328, 440
Internet
    evaluating sources on, 134–35, 143
    unsupported claims on, 111–12
interpretive explanations, 320
intervention studies, 371
introduction, of argumentative essay,
        543–44
intuition, 131
invalid arguments, 59–61
irrelevant premises, fallacies with
    appeal to emotion, 161–63, 165
    appeal to ignorance, 122, 158–61,
        165
    appeal to pity, 163
    appeal to popularity, 157, 165
    appeal to the person, 152–53,
        155–56, 165
    appeal to tradition, 158, 165
    composition, 153–54, 165
    defined, 152
    division, 154–55, 165
    equivocation, 156–57, 165
    genetic fallacy, 152–53, 165
    red herring, 163, 165
    straw man, 163–65
    summary of, 177
    two wrongs make a right, 165–66
Islamic extremists, 497–99
issues, in argumentative issues, 546
I-statement, 235, 238, 241, 251–53

J

James, William, 40
Jamieson, Dale, 426
Jefferson, Thomas, 197, 440
Jesus Nebula, 33
Joint Method of Agreement and
        Difference, 288–89
Jones, Rashida, 454
judicial rulings, reasoning and, 75,
        439, 442
justice, principle of, 421

K

Kafka, Franz, 73
Kant, Immanuel, 430, 434–36
Kantian ethics, 430, 434–36
Kardashian, Kim, 120
Kennedy, John F., 293, 293–94
King, Jr., Martin Luther, 454

L

La Bruyere, Jean de, 157
Langer, Gary, 270
language, fuzziness of, 234
law
    analogical induction in, 75
    arguments in, 438–39
    critical thinking and, 74–75
    deductive arguments in, 75, 438
    inductive arguments in, 75
    inference in, 438–39
    philosophy majors and, 452
    reasoning by analogy and, 75, 439,
        442
    summary of, 442
Law, Stephen, 131
lawfulness, principle of, 421
learning, skills for, 5, 8
left-wing bias, 41–42
legal proceedings, reasoning and,
        74–75
legal reasoning. See law
legislation, reasoning and, 74
legitimate reasons, for distrusting
        mainstream media, 137
Leibniz, Gottfried, 190
Lennon, John, 112
Leno, Jay, 106
Lenski, Richard E., 382–83
letters, statements represented by,
        235, 250–53
Lewis, C. I., 190
Lewis, John, 454
lexical definition, 176
life after death, 401–5, 441
Limbaugh, Rush, 172
Lincoln, Abraham, 293, 293–94
Lind, James, 302
literacy, scientific, 368
logic. See also categorical logic;
        propositional logic; symbolic
        logic
    Aristotle, as father of, 190, 227, 228
    critical thinking and, 4
    deductive, 261
    defined, 4
    negative critiques of, 7

logic (*continued*)
    Russell on, 190, 261
    truth-functional, 190, 227, 243
    turned tables test, 68
logical equivalence, 217
logical impossibility, 391–92
logical possibility, 391, 412
logical structure
    assessed, 70
    defined, 59
long arguments, assessing, 95–98
lore, 320
Lorenz, Konrad, 376
Lowell, Percival, 124
lunacy, 132
Lundberg, John, 394

M

Maimonides, 152
mainstream media, 137
major premise, 243–44
major term, 243–45, 255
Malick, Terrence, *454*
manipulation, 6
    of deductive arguments, 64
    of inductive arguments, 64
margin of error, 271–72
marine parks, 459–60
marriage, 494–95
Martel, Yann, *454*
Martian canals, 124, *124*
Maurois, André, 76
Mayhew, Henry, 263
McCabe, George, 294
McCain, John, 174, 336–37
McKay, David, 342
mean, 269
media. *See also* news
    bias, 41–42, 67
    mainstream, 137
median, 269
medicine
    alternative, 351–52
    philosophy majors and, 452
mediums. *See* psychics
Mehta, Deepa, *454*
memories
    constructive, 122–23, 127
    inaccurate, 35
    unreliability of, 123
Method of Agreement, 287
Method of Concomitant Variation, 289
Method of Difference, 288
middle term, 243–44, 255
Mill, John Stuart, 12, 287–88, 430, 432
Miller, Jerry, 125, *125*

Miller, Sienna, 119
minor premise, 243–44
minor term, 243–45, 255
Mitchell, Maria, 122
Mizner, Wilson, 16
mode, 269
modus ponens. See affirming the
    antecedent
modus tollens. See denying the
    consequent
Montague, Phillip, 100
moon landing, conspiracy theories
    about, 341–42
Moore, Roy, 172
moral arguments, 418–23, 441–42
morality
    as absolute, 435–36
    analogical induction and, 279
    beliefs and, 36
    coherent worldview and, 418,
        439–42
    emotivism and, 419
    moral arguments and, 418–23
    moral premises and, 421, 423–25
    moral statements and, 418
    theories of, 425–26
moral judgments, 424–27, 428
moral premises, 442
    implicit, 422
    morality and, 421, 423–25
moral principles. *See* moral premises
moral relativism, 427
moral statements, 418–25
moral theories
    criteria of adequacy for, 426–30, 442
    critique of, 427–28
    evaluation of, 426–30
    human freedom in conflict with, 440
    Kantian ethics, 430, 434–36
    scientific theories and, 331, 428–29
    summary of, 442
    traditional utilitarianism, 424–26,
        430, 432, 434
Morgan, Ted, 283
motivation, for critical thinking, 31
multiple factors, mishandled, 292
Myers, David G., 293
Myers, Laura, 293

N

NASA, 341–42
national polling, 268, 271
natural selection, 377
necessary conditions
    in causal arguments, 298–300
    defined, 63

negation
    defined, 196, 220
    in propositional logic, 191*t*, 196, 198
    symbolized, 196
    in truth table, 196
negative claims, proving, 161
news. *See also* mainstream media
    alternative sources, 135
    American, 138
    bias in, 41–42
    claims in, 112, 134–37, 143
    critical approach to, 137
    fake, 135–38, 143
    Fox, 41
    newspapers, 138
    sources, 134–37
newspapers, 138
Newton, Isaac, 335
New York Times, 41, *42*, 137
Nietzsche, Friedrich, 61
Noah, Trevor, 67, *67*
non-arguments, arguments
    distinguished from, 11, 17
non-attitudes, 272
nonexperts, 115–17, 122
nonintervention studies, 371
nonmoral statements, 419–23
Norman, Marc, 342
Noyes, Alfred, 283
number of instances compared, in
    analogical induction, 281

O

Obama, Barack, 14, *14*, 270
objections, assessing, 545
objectivity
    critical thinking and, 31, 47
    of truth, 44
observational studies, 371
obstacles. *See* philosophical obstacles;
    psychological obstacles
obversion, as type of equivalence,
    252, 256
odds, 126–27
opinion polls
    confidence level, 271–72
    enumerative induction in, 266–73
    margin of error, 271–72
    mean, median, mode in, 269
    survey questions, 267–68
opinions
    facts distinguished from, 113
    passionate, 36
    unsupported, 96
O'Reilly, Bill, 172
Orwell, George, 139

O-statement, 235, 250–53
outline, for argumentative essay, 545, 549–51
overstatement, 551–52

P

palm reading, 403, *403*
parallax, 375
paranormal phenomena, 123, 129, 343
    eyewitnesses to, 399–400
    UF0s, 392
    weird theories for, 389–90
pareidolia, *33*, 125–26
passionate opinions, 36
pat-downs, 484–85
Paulos, John Allen, 292, 294
peer pressure, 39
Peirce, Charles Sanders, 227
perception. *See also* extrasensory perception
    constructive, 122–24, 127, 335–36
    expectation and, 124–27
Perry, Rick, 172
personal benefit, 421
personal experience, 142
    belief and, 5, 121, 127
    doubt of, 121
    expectation influencing, 124–27
    impairment of, 121–24
    innumeracy and, 126–28
    probability and, 126–28
    self-fabricated, 35
    weird theories and, 390–91
personal freedom, 5, 19, 440
persuasion. *See also* rhetorical devices
    advertising and, 138–41, 143
    appeal to emotion and, 60, 161–63
    arguments and, 60
persuasive writing, arguments and, 96
philosophical obstacles
    to critical thinking, 43–47
    skepticism, 45–46
    social relativism, *44*, 45, 47
    subjective relativism, 43–45, 47
philosophical skepticism, 45–47, 330
philosophical skeptics, 46
philosophy majors
    careers for, 451–54
    of famous people, 453–54
    law, medicine and, 452
    meaning for, 456
    salaries of, 454–56
philosophy of life, 6
physical impossibility, 391–92
physical possibility, 391–92, 412
pity, appeal to, 163

placebo effect, 296, 370, 372
plane crash, theories of, 348–50
planetary motion, theories of, 373–75
poisoning the well, 156
political discourse
    post hoc reasoning in, 295–97
    stereotypes in, 175
    straw man fallacy in, 175
PolitiFact.com, 172
polls. *See* opinion polls
Popper, Karl, 322
popularity. *See* appeal to ignorance
population studies, 371
pornography, feminist defense of, 461–66
possibility, 391–92, 412
post hoc, ergo propter hoc ("after that, therefore because of that"), 295–97
Powell, Michael, 242
practice, of critical thinking, 31
precautionary principle, 160
precising definition, 176
predicate term, 227–28, 232–34
prejudice. *See also* bias
    defense against, 6
    group pressure leading to, 40, 42
premises. *See also* irrelevant premises, fallacies with; unacceptable premises, fallacies with
    in arguments, 13, 15
    basics of, 16–17
    conditional, 79
    credible, 76–77
    defined, 16, 316
    dependent, 87–88, 99
    diagramming, 246
    explicit, 97
    identifying, 16–17
    implicit, 76–77
    independent, 87–88
    indicator words in, 13, 19
    major, 243–44
    minor, 243–44
    moral, 423–25, 442
    overstated, 551–52
    reasons and, 10
    statements and, 10, 19
    true, 62–64, 82–83
presuppositions, 553
Priestley, J. B., 266
probability
    analogical induction and, 278–79
    personal experience and, 126–28
probable support, 64
procedural explanations, 320

proof
    burden of, 160–61
    method of, 214, 221
    modus ponens and, 216
    rules of inference and, 215–17, 221
    rules of replacement and, 217–18, 221
    of validity, 214–18, 221
property in question, 262
propositional logic
    categorical logic and, 227
    conditional in, 191*t*, 197–99
    conjunction in, 191*t*, 192–94
    connectives and, 191–99
    defined, 190
    disjunction in, 191*t*, 194–96, 198
    negation in, 191*t*, 196, 198
    reductio ad absurdum and, 204
    symbolic logic and, 191
    of tricky arguments, 205–8
    truth values and, 191–99
    validity and, 201–11, 220
psychics, 290–91, 401–5
psychological obstacles
    to critical thinking, 31–43, 47
    group pressure, 38–43, 47
    self-interested thinking, 32–38
Ptolemy, 339, 373–75
public figures
    appeals to authority of, 117, 119–20
    as biased, 67–68
publishers, assessment of, 134

Q

quality, 229
quantifiers, 228–29, 232, 236–37
quantity, 228
questions
    begging, 166–67, 171
    conclusions disguised as, 15
    survey, 267–68

R

Rachels, James, 423
racial profiling, discrimination by, 97
racism, group pressure leading to, 40
random sample, 268–70, 272
rational standards, in critical thinking, 4, 18
reading critically, 134
reasonable doubt, 46–47
reasoning
    by analogy, 75, 439, 442
    judicial rulings and, 75
    legal proceedings and, 74–75
    legislation and, 74

reasons
    arguments as, 10–15
    for belief, 4
    in critical thinking, 9–15
    for doubt, 46–47
    legitimate, for distrusting
        mainstream media, 137
    premises and, 10
red herrings, 163, 165
reductio ad absurdum (reduction to
    absurdity), 204
Reid, Harry, 172
relativism
    honor killings and, 430–31
    social, *44*, 45, 47
    subjective, 43–45, 47, 427
relevant dissimilarities, 281
relevant factors, misidentifying, 292
relevant property, 262–63, 272
relevant similarities, 280–81
replacement, rules of, 217–18, 221
replication, of studies, 372
representative sample, 265–66
requests, 9
rhetoric, 152
rhetorical definition, 176
rhetorical devices
    dysphemisms, 174–75
    euphemisms, 174–75
    innuendo, 174
    rhetorical definitions, 176
    ridicule, 176
    stereotyping, 175
    summary of, 178
ridicule, 176
rights, 421, 424
right-wing bias, 41–42
Ritchie, Guy, 120
Robertson, Pat, 172
Rowling, J. K., 172
rules of inference, 215–17, 221
rules of replacement, 217–18, 221
Ruscio, John, 133
rush to judgment, 75
Russell, Bertrand, 36–37, 44–45,
    94, 110
    on evidence, 115
    on fuzziness of language, 234
    on logic, 190, 261

S

Sagan, Carl, 124, 328, 388
salaries, of philosophy majors, 454–56
sample
    argumentative essay, 554–58
    biased, 265–66, 272

in enumerative induction, 262–63,
    272
hasty generalization and, 133, 264
margin of error, 271–72
random, 268–70, 272
representative, 265–66
self-selecting, 269–70
size, 264–65
sample members. *See* sample
Samsel, R. C., 284
Samuels, Stephen, 294
sanctity-of-life, principle of, 424
Sanger, Larry, *453*
Santorum, Rick, 15, *15*
scare tactics, 163
Schiaparelli, 124
Schick, Béla, 327
Schick, Theodore, Jr., 392
Schwarzenegger, Arnold, 120
science
    bogus, 364–65
    confirmation bias and, 130–32
    evidence in, 130
    function of, 363
    ideology contrasted with, 363, 365,
        411
    inductive reasoning in, 160
    inference to the best explanation
        in, 321
    literacy in, 368
    scientism contrasted with, 365–66,
        411
    technology contrasted with, 363
    theories, explanations in, 321
    weird theories and, 333–34, 388–89,
        411–12
scientific method, 38, 366–70, 411
scientific theories. *See also* weird
    theories; *specific theories*
    alternative, 346–47
    credibility of, 429–30
    criteria of adequacy and, 372–73, 411
    evaluation of, 374, 411
    evolution versus creationism,
        375–83
    judging of, 372–83
    moral theories and, 331, 428–29
    scientific method and, 38
    simplicity in, 339, 374–75
    testing, 331–32, 356–57, 370–72,
        377–78, 411
    theories about God and, 339
scientism, 365–66, 411
scope
    in evaluation of weird theories,
        334–35

inference to the best explanation
    and, 335–37
    of theories, 331, 335–39
Searle, John, 94
selective attention, 37, 266
self-determination, right of, 424
self-discovery, tools for, 6
self-interested thinking, 52
    avoiding, 37
    evidence and, 34
    as psychological obstacle, 32–38
    selective attention and, 37
    strong emotions and, 35–36
self-selecting sample, 269–70
Shaw, George Bernard, 272, 332
Sherlock Holmes, 323
Shermer, Michael, 402
short method, for evaluation, 208–10,
    220
Silbersweig, David, 452
simple arguments, 201–5
simple statement, 192
simplicity
    in evaluation of scientific theories,
        339, 374–75
    in evaluation of weird theories, 339
    inference to the best explanation
        and, 331, 338–39, 374–75
    of theories, 331, 338–39, 374–75
singular statements, 234
skepticism, philosophical, 45–47, 330
Skeptic's Dictionary (Carroll), 159–60
slippery slope, 170–71, 173
slogans, 140
sluttishness, 499–500
social moral relativism, 427
social relativism, *44*, 45, 47
Socrates, 5, 8, 419
Sontag, Susan, *454*
sound arguments, 62
sources
    comparing, 135
    considering, 135–36
    Internet, 134–35, 143
    of media, claims of, 137
    news, 134–37
    news, alternative, 135
    purposes of, discerning, 135
Spencer, Herbert, 284–85
square of opposition, 250–52,
    250*f*, 255
standard-form categorical statements,
    228–37
    defined, 228
    diagrammed, 238–42
    fuzziness *versus*, 234

nonstandard equivalents of, 235–37
summary of, 255
translation of, 230–37, 255
Star Trek: The Next Generation, 38
statements. *See also* categorical
    statements; overstatement
in arguments, 19
A-statement, 235, 239, 241, 246,
    250–53
beliefs as, 9, 19
compound, 79, 192, 217
conclusions and, 10
connectives and, 192, 198
defined, 9, 16, 19, 316
descriptive, 419–21
E-statement, 235, 239, 241, 246,
    250–53
extraneous, 86–90
facts and, 113
I-statement, 235, 238, 241, 251–53
letters representing, 235, 250–53
moral, 418–25
nonmoral, 419–23
O-statement, 235, 250–53
premises and, 10, 19
simple, 192
singular, 234
thesis, 543–45
truth values of, 192
statistical arguments, 154
statistical syllogism, 261
stereotype
group thinking leading to, 42
as rhetorical device, 175
stipulative definition, 176
straw man arguments, 14–15,
    163–65, 175
streamlined evaluation, 208–11
strong emotions, 35–36
strong inductive argument
basics of, 61–62
defined, 61, 101
structure, of argumentative essays,
    543–45
style, of argumentative essays, 551–53
subcontraries, 251
subjective relativism, 43–45, 47, 427
subjectivist fallacy, 44
subject term, 227–28, 232–34
sufficient conditions
in causal arguments, 298–300
defined, 63
survey questions, 267–68
Suzuki, Daisetz Teitaro, 71
syllogism. *See also* disjunctive
    syllogism

categorical, 231–32, 243–48, 255
defined, 80, 261
disjunctive, 82–83, 195–96, 202
hypothetical, 80–81, 202
statistical, 261
symbolic logic
connectives in, 191–92
defined, 191
propositional logic and, 191

T

target group, 262, 272
taxpayers, 154
technology, science contrasted
    with, 363
teleological explanations, 320
temporal order, cause confused with,
    295–96
terms
major, 243–45, 255
middle, 243–44, 255
minor, 243–45, 255
predicate, 227–28, 232–34
subject, 227–28, 232–34
in translation, 232
vague, 553–54
testability
in evaluation of scientific theories,
    331–32, 356–57, 370–72, 377–78,
    411
in evaluation of weird theories,
    350, 390–405
of theories, 331–32, 356–57,
    377–78, 411
TEST formula, 346–48
defined, 345, 357
in evaluation of weird theories,
    350, 388, 412
testimony, expert, 438–39
testing for causes, 287–90
theoretical explanations, 317, 319, 363
theories. *See also* moral theories;
    scientific theories; *specific
    theories*
conservatism of, 331, 339–44
consistency and, 327–28, 345–46,
    356
conspiracy, 338, 341–42
contradictions in, 328
criteria of adequacy for, 329–30,
    356
evaluation of, 330, 344, 348
evolution versus creationism, 168,
    375–83
explanations from, 317, 319
fruitfulness of, 331–35

about God, 131, 339, 428, 440–41,
    493–94
of homeopathy, 351–52
inference to the best explanation
    and, 322–23, 330
lack of formula in, 343–44
moral, 425–26
phenomena explained by, 322*t*
scope of, 331, 335–39
simplicity of, 331, 338–39, 374–75
telling good from bad, 345–52
testability of, 331–32, 356–57,
    377–78, 411
thesis statement, of argumentative
    essay, 543–45
thinking outside the box, 7–8
Thomas Aquinas, 81, 100, 206
Thoreau, Henry David, 97, 277, 285
tilde, 196, 204
Tocqueville, Alexis De, 337
torture, 501–3
tradition, appeal to, 158, 165
traditional utilitarianism, 424–26, 430,
    432, 434
translation
quantifiers in, 228–29
of standard-form categorical
    statements, 230–37, 255
terms in, 232
tricky arguments
propositional logic of, 205–8
truth table for, 205, 207–8
valid, 205–8
true premises, 62–64, 82–83
Trump, Donald, 14, *14*, 120
truth
appeal to popularity and, 157
of belief, 43, 110
not preserved, by inductive
    arguments, 61–62
objectivity of, 44
subjective relativism and, 44
truth-functional logic, 190, 227,
    243. *See also* propositional
    logic
truth-preserving arguments, 59–61
truth table
conditional in, 197
conjunction in, 193
defined, 193
disjunction in, 194–95
disjunctive syllogism in, 195–96
negation in, 196
for simple arguments, 202–3, 205
test of validity, 202–3, 205, 220
for tricky arguments, 205, 207–8

truth values
    connectives and, 191–99
    defined, 192
    propositional logic and, 191–99
    of statements, 192
    summary of, 220
tu quoque (you're another), 156
Tur, Katy, 453, *453*
turned tables test, 68
TWA flight 800, 348–50
Twelve Angry Men, 33–34
two wrongs make a right, 165–66

U

UFOs, *392*
unacceptable premises, fallacies with
    begging the question, 166–67, 171
    decision-point, 169–71
    defined, 152
    false dilemma, 167–69, 171
    faulty analogies, 139, 171, 173–74
    hasty generalizations, 133–34, 171,
        173
    slippery slope, 170–71, 173
    summary of, 178
unreliable eyewitness, 125
unsupported claims, 110, 113, 115
    expert support for, 116, 118–19
    on Internet, 111–12
unsupported opinions, 96
utilitarianism, traditional, 424–26, 430,
    432, 434

V

vaccination, 488–90, 505–6
vague terms, 553–54

valid arguments
    credible premise making, 76
    deductive, 59–63, 101, 190–91
    defined, 59
    inductive, 59–63, 101
    simple, 201–5
    tricky, 205–8
    as truth-preserving, 59
validity
    of deductive arguments, 190–91
    evaluation of, 208–11
    proof of, 214–18, 221
    propositional logic and, 201–11,
        220
    rules of inference and, 215–17
    rules of replacement and, 217–18
    of simple arguments, 201–5
    truth table test of, 202–3, 205, 220
    with Venn diagrams, 247
Van Fraassen, Bas, 345
Van Praagh, James, 401
variables, 191
Venn diagrams
    of categorical logic, 231–32, 238–48,
        250, 255
    defined, 238
    validity with, 247
    website tutorial for, 231
Vogt, Karl, 284

W

weak inductive argument
    basics of, 61
    implicit premises and, 75–76
weasel words, 141
Weaver, Warren, 365

websites, about categorical logic,
    231–32
web sources, evaluation of, 143.
    See also Internet
weird theories. *See also specific theories*
    belief in, 333–34
    criteria of adequacy and, 333–34
    errors in, 347, 390
    evaluation of, 339–40, 350,
        390–405
    inference to the best explanation
        and, 411
    for paranormal phenomena,
        389–90
    personal experience and, 390–91
    science and, 333–34, 388–89,
        411–12
    scope of, 334–35
    simplicity, in evaluation of, 339
    TEST formula for, 350, 388, 412
White, E. B., 269, 284
Wilson, Woodrow, 173
Wittgenstein, Ludwig, 194, 203
worldview
    coherent, 418, 439–42
    defined, 6, 43, 418
    science, ideology and, 411
Wright, Steven, 380
writing
    to audience, 546, 551
    guidelines, for argumentative
        essays, 545–46
    persuasive, 96

Z

Zwanzig, Carl, 283